MANY AND ONE:
A SOCIAL HISTORY
OF
THE UNITED STATES

Robert Cruden
Lewis and Clark College

MANY AND ONE

a social history of the united states

PRENTICE-HALL, INC., Englewood Cliffs, New Jersey 07632

Library of Congress Cataloging in Publication Data

CRUDEN, ROBERT
Many and one.

Bibliography: p.
Includes index.
1. United States—Social conditions. I. Title.
HN57.C78 309.1'73 79-14811
ISBN 0-13-555714-3

Cover photos *(clockwise from top left)* courtesy of Oregon Historical Society; *Asher and Adams' New Columbian Railroad Atlas and Pictorial Album of American History,* 1876 (Copyright 1976 by Rutledge Books, a division of Arcata Consumer Products Corporation); Smithsonian Institution, National Anthropological Archives; Historical Society of Pennsylvania; Wide World Photos; and Michigan Department of State, Lansing.

Printed in the United States of America
10 9 8 7 6 5 4 3 2 1

Editorial production/supervision
and interior design by Lynda Heideman
Cover design by Allyson Everngam
Manufacturing buyer: Ed Leone

Prentice-Hall International, Inc., *London*
Prentice-Hall of Australia Pty. Limited, *Sydney*
Prentice-Hall of Canada, Ltd., *Toronto*
Prentice-Hall of India Private Limited, *New Delhi*
Prentice-Hall of Japan, Inc., *Tokyo*
Prentice-Hall of Southeast Asia Pte. Ltd., *Singapore*
Whitehall Books Limited, *Wellington, New Zealand*

contents

preface

In 1893, Frederick Jackson Turner, one of the great interpreters of the American experience, delivered to the American Historical Association an epoch-making paper on "The Significance of the Frontier in American History." He concluded with this observation: "Since the days when the fleet of Columbus sailed into the waters of the New World, America has been another name for opportunity. . . ." Sixty years earlier another influential historian, George Bancroft, asserted that "a favoring Providence" had "conducted the country to its present happiness and glory."

The view of American history as a success story has a long and distinguished lineage. This view has an undeniable psychological appeal, and there is even considerable truth to it. Americans won their national independence in a long war against the mightiest empire of the day. The Declaration of Independence committed the new nation to lofty moral principles. The structure of government Americans created withstood the crucial test of a civil war that further advanced the nation's reputation by bringing an end to slavery in the United States. The society that Americans evolved welcomed refugees from religious and political persecution in Europe. It had an even wider appeal to those Europeans, Asians, and Latin Americans who thought of America symbolically as a "mountain of gold." Indeed, the American standard of living became the envy of the rest of the world, and "moving up" was easier in America than in other societies. In addition, Americans enjoyed a wide range of civil and religious liberties. Thus, for many Americans their national experience was indeed a success story.

It was not the whole story, however. White Americans often attained their success at the expense of other peoples. The original Americans, the Indian peoples, were nearly destroyed during the invasion and occupation of their homelands. For two hundred years the success of many whites depended on black slavery. When slaves won their freedom, they experienced a brief period of equality during Reconstruction—and then faced repression and degradation for generations. Such was also the fate of Asian and Mexican Americans in the West. Today, many of our cities are thronged with blacks, Puerto Ricans, Asians, and Chicanos to whom America is something other than another name for opportunity.

For many whites, too, America was no success story. Poor people who had to be supported by private charity or public funds appeared in colonial times and have been present ever since. The "rejects" of society—prostitutes, prison inmates, the mentally ill—have generally fared ill at the hands of society. Much more numerous were those of the "working poor" who tried to "move up" and never made it. Not until after World War II did large numbers of blue-collar workers gain an uncertain foothold in the lower reaches of the middle class.

Despite their commitment to democracy, Americans often proved intolerant of those whose ideas did not meet with majority approval. At one time or another, Quakers, Jews, Catholics, and Mormons felt the sting—and often the violence—of prejudice. Labor unions long met with hostility and repression. Exponents of radical social change—anarchists, socialists, communists—found their freedom restricted by law and public opinion.

This book is concerned largely with the history of those Americans who never "made it." It tells their story by setting it against the record of the successful. Since business was and is the principal American road to success, special attention has been given to the evolution of business institutions.

Chronological tables are supplied so that readers may relate developments discussed here to other major events with which they may be more familiar. The short bibliographical essays are designed to stimulate further reading in works that are readily available. My apologies to the authors of many excellent books that for reasons of space could not be included.

ACKNOWLEDGMENTS

Many people contributed to the completion of this book. President John Howard and Vice-President John Brown of Lewis and Clark College provided positive support for my work. Likewise, I appreciate the cooperation of my colleagues in the department of history: Henry Bair, Nosratollah Rassekh, Allan Kittell, and Stephen Beckham. I am particularly grateful to Irene Hecht and Jeffrey Barlow who read portions of the manuscript. My thanks also to G. J. Barker-Benfield for insights provided while he was on the faculty of Lewis and Clark College.

Staff members of Prentice-Hall, Inc., have labored long and productively with me. I am grateful to Brian Walker and John Busch, editors; Lynda Heideman, production editor; and Robert McNally, copy editor. My special thanks go to the anonymous academic reviewers who corrected errors and otherwise contributed to improving the quality of the work. I regret that limitations of space made impossible incorporation of some excellent suggestions they made.

The staff of the Oregon Historical Society, particularly Janice Worden, were extremely helpful in obtaining pictures.

My thanks also to Virginia Diegel, who typed the manuscript.

MANY AND ONE:
A SOCIAL HISTORY
OF
THE UNITED STATES

The Age of Anne Hutchinson, Pontiac, Crispus Attucks, Sam Adams, and Eliza Pinckney

phase one COLONIAL AMERICA

10,000 B.C. to A.D. 1783

	North American cultures of early Asian immigrants already well established by 10,000 B.C.
(A.D.) **1492**	Columbus's discovery opens way for conquest of original Americans.
1565	Spanish settle Fort Augustine, Florida.
1607	First permanent English settlement at Jamestown, Virginia.
1620	Pilgrims establish Plymouth colony.
1630	Puritans colonize Massachusetts Bay.
1638	Anne Hutchinson banished from Massachusetts Bay.
1662	Slavery formally established in Virginia.
1675	King Philip's War; destruction of Indian power in New England.
1676	Bacon's Rebellion in Virginia.
1680	Pueblo Indian revolt against Spain temporarily successful.
1689	King William's War ushers in series of Anglo-French wars that shape the destinies of all peoples in North America.
1712	Major slave insurrection in New York City.
1739	Stono uprising of slaves (Cato conspiracy) in South Carolina.
1763	Anglo-French wars end with expulsion of France from North America.
1765	Stamp Act crisis symbolizes growing conflict between colonists and Britain.
1770	Crispus Attucks, black worker, killed in Boston Massacre.
1771	Regulator movement of small farmers crushed in North Carolina.
1773	Boston Tea Party typifies growing "mob" action in colonies.
1776	Declaration of Independence.
1777	Abigail Adams urges equal rights for women.
1781	Articles of Confederation formalize new government.
1783	Britain recognizes American independence.

America's first settlers arrived from Asia at a time still unknown, but scholars agree that they were well established in North America by 10,000 B.C. These earliest Americans were relatively undisturbed by European influences until A.D. 1492, when Columbus "discovered" the New World and mistakenly identified its inhabitants as "Indians." Thereafter, Spanish, French, Dutch, and English invaders steadily encroached upon the homelands of the first Americans and brought with them another people—enslaved Africans. The original Americans resisted, but they were too divided and too primitive in their technology and political organization to cope with white power.

The white invaders came with beliefs, customs, and institutions from the Old World, including a sense of community, respect for class distinctions, religious conformity, belief in private property in land, harshness toward the poor, and the patriarchal family. Africans could not reproduce their institutions in slavery, but they did preserve some basic elements of African cultures. From such adaptation came a new culture that was neither African nor white—a culture that later would be called Afro-American.

The necessities of New World existence forced changes in white traditions and institutions. The sense of community gave way before a rising tide of individualism. Women in England's American colonies won more rights than their English sisters enjoyed. Rhode Island and Pennsylvania provided a larger measure of religious freedom than was common at the time. While poverty was a problem in all the colonies, it proved easier for colonial people of the "baser sort" to move up the social scale than it did for their European counterparts. Class distinctions remained strong, but farmers and working people fought for admission to public life.

English power eventually dominated colonial North America, except for the Spanish holdings in Florida and west of the Mississippi. The Dutch gave up New Amsterdam (New York) in 1664, and France surrendered its North American territories in 1763. But England did not long enjoy the fruits of its latest conquest. Within a generation it had to recognize the independence of the new republic of the United States, a nation dedicated to the principles that all men were created equal; that they were entitled to life, liberty, and the pursuit of happiness; and that they had a right to revolution to secure such goals. But the architects of American independence meant "men" in a restricted sense of the word. They did not extend the rights of the new nation to blacks, Indian peoples, and women.

1 red, white, and black

Millions of years ago the earth took form in violent upheavals and foldings. The land was scrubbed, scoured, and finally molded by the comings and goings of four great ice sheets, which at widely different times covered all of North America as far south as the Ohio River and beyond. When these ice sheets advanced, they carried with them masses of uprooted trees, boulders, and gravel gouged out of virgin earth. Their retreat left the debris behind, furnishing the basis for a rich soil in which the seeds of new growth lay. Those regions that escaped the ice sheets were nevertheless shaped by them as advances and recessions changed climates and thus altered the flora and fauna of these areas, just as they changed the flora and fauna of lands to the north.

When the land emerged from the last ice age about 11,000 years ago, it was a scene of incredible variety: awesome mountain ranges, mighty rivers, great inland seas, forbidding deserts, vast interior plains, a stern and rock-bound coast on the Pacific with few natural harbors, and an Atlantic coast with many—a fact of major importance when European invaders later cast their eyes on a land for which they yet had no name. The waters, grasslands, and forests nurtured a diverse population of fishes, insects, birds, and mammals. Today it is hard to believe that in what is now the United States there roamed such animals as elephants, mastodons, camels, ground sloths, and bison much bigger than the later buffalo. Under the soil, and unsuspected for centuries, waited other riches: coal, iron, copper, gold, lead, silver and oil.

THE FIRST AMERICANS

The first Americans came from Asia over what is usually called a "land bridge," across the Bering Sea between Siberia and Alaska. The term is somewhat misleading, since it gives the impression of a narrow funnel. In fact, during the ice ages, ocean levels dropped so much that immense land areas were uncovered, linking Asia to America, and over these areas moved land animals, birds, and peoples.

No one knows why they came. Presumably food became scarce in Asia, and animals and people migrated to survive. Those who traveled east found a source of food. The forests, grasslands, swamps, and streams of America abounded in food supplies. As to when the migrants came, the evidence is inconclusive. All that can be said with certainty is that they were here at least 10,000 years ago. We also know that they survived by hunting and fishing and by gathering berries, nuts, and roots.

Over the centuries these peoples spread southward until they reached the tip of South America. During the long wanderings some groups settled in specific areas and developed advanced civilizations, such as those of the Incas in Peru and the Mayans and Aztecs in Central America. No longer nomadic, these peoples made their living from the land, producing such crops as corn, potatoes, beans, and tobacco. Others, who settled in the Pacific Northwest, lived well on what they gathered from rivers and the sea. Still other peoples, such as the Pueblos of the Southwest, evolved a highly structured town life based on agriculture. Yet other peoples, such as those living along the Atlantic Coast, combined farming with hunting and fishing.

Thus, there emerged many diverse cultures among these native Americans, which white invaders later, following the error of Columbus, lumped together as "Indians." There was no one Indian culture, no one Indian language, no one Indian people, no one Indian social and political structure, no one code of moral and religious behavior. Instead, there was diversity among the native peoples, and there were sometimes rivalries—a circumstance that whites exploited to their advantage.

Despite their differences, however, the native peoples did share common attributes. They all lived in organized societies and were thus subject to social discipline. All had moral codes. All were deeply religious in the sense that religion was not simply a body of formal belief but the means through which mortal beings survived here and in the hereafter. Mother Earth was venerated as the source of sustenance, but her bounty depended on the gods, whose favor must be earned. As a result, the daily living and the great ceremonies of these peoples bore religious significance.

Further, since most native peoples believed that Mother Earth provided sustenance for all, it followed that no one person could own a piece of the Mother. Thanks to the bounty of the gods, a people in a given area enjoyed the land they occupied: it was the land of the people, not the property of individuals. To be sure, individual families in the agricultural societies used land, but the allocation of lands was determined by public authority, however chosen. The concept of perpetual private ownership of the land was alien to most native societies—a belief that proved a source of discord and bloodshed when white invaders, convinced of the sanctity of private property in land, confronted the first Americans.

Such were the native American societies, with a population estimated at 2.5 million in what is now the continental United States, when their indigenous evolution was changed utterly by the arrival of fair-skinned invaders from Europe, beginning in 1492.

WHITE INVASIONS AND SETTLEMENT

First came the Spanish, then the French, followed by the English, Dutch, Scots, Germans, and Irish. There were others, too. Swedes settled along the Delaware River, and to the English settlement at Jamestown, Virginia, came Polish, German, French, and Italian artisans recruited to stimulate the economic growth of the colony. The newcomers came from every stratum of society, from aristocrats to unskilled laborers. Their religious beliefs were as diverse as their backgrounds: Catholics, Anglicans, Lutherans, Calvinists, Quakers, Moravians, Mennonites, and Jews—the last a small community engulfed in a Christian society.

In those days the whites' religion indicated not only their relationship to God but also their relationship to government. And here again the invaders varied widely, ranging from those who accepted political absolutism as God's form of government to Quakers and Mennonites who saw in no earthly government the expression of God's will.

Given the hazards of trans-Atlantic travel at the time—shipwreck, scanty and poorly prepared food, polluted water, crowded and unsanitary quarters, disease (often of epidemic proportions), and high mortality—the incentives for voluntary migration to the New World had to be compelling. One was the lure of easy wealth, which had a special attraction for younger sons of the English gentry. Since the practice of primogeniture (that is, inheritance of all property by the eldest son) made it unlikely they would inherit paternal lands, they had to resign themselves to church or professional careers or naval or military service—prospects that did not appeal to all such young men. America offered a tempting alternative. It was generally believed in England that gold and silver were plentiful in Virginia and that Indian slave labor could be had to provide the work. Indian slaves would also till the fields and staff the households to provide the necessities and amenities of life. In short, the newcomers would lead the lives of gentlemen while amassing the wealth that would notably improve their social standing for the inevitable return to England.

But when the gentlemen came to Virginia, they found themselves pining for England much sooner than they had expected. Gold and silver were nowhere to be found, and Indian peoples provided few slaves. Hunger and disease cut the colonists down in fearful numbers. To survive, the gentlemen, who despised manual labor, had to work side by side with the "baser sort" of men in chopping wood and growing food. As early as 1614 Governor Thomas Dale of Jamestown noted there was "a general desire in the best sort to return for England." Indeed, at no later time did America offer much incentive for aristocrats to settle. Those who came were mostly exiles who returned home as soon as the political situation turned favorable—such as the royalists who fled to America to escape the wrath of Oliver Cromwell and who hurried back to England as soon as Charles II was restored in 1660. The nobles who acquired vast estates in the colonies rarely visited them. They preferred to be absentee landlords, profiting from the sale and renting of land.

More significant to the long-range development of the American people was another economic incentive: the desire of sturdy, self-respecting common folk to escape what appeared to be inevitable impoverishment. The transformation of the English economy from a medieval order to modern capitalism, symbolized in the rise of the woolen trade and the shift in agriculture from production of foodstuffs to the raising of sheep, undermined the foundations of the independent yeoman farmer. Great landowners took over the traditional common lands, stripping small farmers of their fuel and of pasturage for their cattle and hogs. By fair means and foul the wealthy acquired the farms of the less affluent and turned them into sheepruns, which required little labor. Thousands of small farmers and their families were turned off the land, to eke out a living as best they could.

Such a living was hard to come by, for with the change in the economy came a sharp rise in the English population: from fewer than 3 million in 1500 to about 4.5 million in 1640. Employment opportunities increased far more slowly than the number of people seeking work. To make matters worse, the inflow of gold and silver to Europe from the New World helped produce rampant inflation everywhere. Prices in England rose to record highs during the sixteenth century. Wages rose too, but they lagged far behind living costs. All these factors led to chronic large-scale unemployment and underemployment, widespread undernourishment as well as sheer hunger, and increasing numbers of English folk doomed to hereditary poverty.

But poverty in itself does not explain the compulsion to emigrate. Poverty, as we know, is a condition that feeds upon itself. An inadequate diet, cultural deprivation, overcrowded housing, the contempt visited upon the poor by the rest of society, and the consequent internalization among the poor of that contempt in forms of self-hatred—all these dulled the intelligence, sapped the will, and stripped their victims of the energy required to bring about change. The results were not rebellion, but apathy; not resistance, but resignation.

This was the hell, embodied in the slums of London and other towns, from which the "new poor"—the declassed yeoman farmers and skilled craftsmen losing ground as inflation eroded their status—recoiled even as they were being forced relentlessly into it. Peasants rebelled, but the Tudor monarchs ruthlessly crushed the uprisings. Artisans tried to organize to protect themselves, but the common law and new statutes put an end to that. For the self-respecting folk who were determined to save themselves and their children from the vice and crime in which the slums abounded, there now appeared a way out: emigration to the colonies.

The authorities were glad to see the emigrants go. Until well into the seventeenth century, England's social ills were largely thought the result of overpopulation, and settlement in the colonies was seen as a prime method of easing social tensions at home. In addition, emigrants increased the wealth and strength of the homeland. The products of colonial labor were exported to England, while supplying the needs of the colonists stimulated English trade and manufacturing. Further, since England had been late in entering the New World, it must stake out its claims before France in Canada and Spain in Florida seized the rest of the continent. Thus, English policy-makers thought emigration a positive good and acted accordingly. Even in the eighteenth century, when official opinion was questioning the wisdom of encouraging emigration, no attempt was made to halt the mass migration of Ulster Scots (usually called Scotch Irish) to the colonies.

Religious motives also spurred emigration. At the time religious and political beliefs were so woven together that a threat to one was a menace to the other. The prevailing doctrine of the day was that the safety of the state required uniformity in religion. Religious dissent was viewed as political subversion. In England the relatively tolerant reign of Elizabeth I gave way to the increasingly repressive policies of the Stuarts. The new monarch, James I, summed up both his commitment to the Anglican establishment and the accepted wisdom of his time in his famous epigram: "No bishop, no king."

Among those who felt the heavy hand of the authorities was a small sect known as Brownists, who were Calvinists in theology and democrats in church government. In 1609 the Brownists sought refuge among Dutch Calvinists, but in less than a generation some of them were bound for the New World in the *Mayflower*. They fled for many reasons, including the usual frictions between refugees and their hosts, the dangers of war between the Netherlands and Spain, and English pressure on the Dutch to curb Brownist activity. The most important reason, according to William Bradford, governor and historian of the Plymouth Colony, was that parents felt they were losing control of their children. In Bradford's view, "the great licentiousness of youth" in the Netherlands made parents feel their "posterity would be in danger to degenerate and be corrupted."

The Pilgrims of Plymouth were a mere handful compared to the Puritans who sailed into Massachusetts Bay in 1630. The Puritans were not poor zealots, like the Pilgrims, but people of substance. Some, such as Sir Richard Saltonstall, came from the gentry. Others were moderately successful farmers, merchants, professional men, skilled workers, and of course, ministers, the leading spirits of the migration. Under the Stuarts the Puritans' hopes of reforming, or "purifying," the Church of England from within had been continually frustrated. By 1629 the monarchy felt secure enough to disband Parliament and to initiate a policy of exterminating religious dissent. Puritans were faced with three alternatives: submission—and many submitted; resistance—and many more resisted, even to the point of civil war, which broke out in 1642; and emigration to the New World, where they would be free to create their own model of God's church and society.

Emigration occasioned a bitter controversy among the Puritans who did not submit. Resisters claimed that every hand and mind was needed to battle the hosts of Satan on English soil and that little good could come from a settlement thousands of miles distant from the scene of struggle. Emigrationists responded that the prospects in England were bad and that it was God's will that His people should build in the New World a city to serve as a model of His governance for the rest of mankind. The brethren thus divided on distinctly unfriendly terms, and the emigrationists, having wangled a royal charter for a Massachusetts Bay Company, set sail for the New World. They took much of their property with them. They also took the company charter, which established its headquarters in the colony, not in London as was the practice, thus putting it beyond the immediate reach of the Crown. Their success lured thousands more in succeeding years. The Pilgrim colony at Plymouth grew slowly, but the Massachusetts Bay colony developed rapidly in both numbers and wealth.

Other persecuted religious groups followed the Puritan lead. When Louis XIV in 1685 ended toleration of French Protestants, the refugees fled all over Europe and to America. Two years earlier the harassed Mennonites of the Rhineland had established their first settlement at Germantown, near Philadelphia. In the eighteenth century Moravians founded a colony at Bethlehem, Pennsylvania. Presbyterian Ulster Scots, suffering from religious discrimination as well as economic distress, began to people the frontier about the same time.

INDENTURED SERVANTS

No matter how compelling the reasons for emigration, however, great numbers of people could not have made the journey without assistance. They were too poor to pay for passage and for setting themselves up in a new land. To be sure, the Puritans financed themselves, and as the various colonies prospered, increasing numbers of individuals paid their own way, but there were many emigrants who lacked the cash to go to America. In the early years, businessmen footed the bill, hoping that profit would flow from settlement. ''Merchant adventurers'' in London and Plymouth made possible the voyage of the *Mayflower,* and the Virginia Company subsidized the settlement of Jamestown.

As the colonies took root and labor shortages developed, particularly in the South, a new method emerged to spur emigration of poor people. This was an adaptation of the old English system of indentures, whereby apprentices bound themselves to masters for specified terms of years in return for learning a trade. Prospective emigrants were induced to sign for service in America, often with a fraudulent promise that they would receive fifty acres of land at the end of their service. The indentures were then sold to shipmasters, who transported the emigrants and resold the indentures to colonists at whatever price the market would bring, which, given the labor shortage, was usually well above the cost of transportation. Profits ranging from 50 to 300 percent on each servant who survived the crossing seemed to be customary.

Southern colonies had a special appeal to profit-minded merchants and their sea captains. These colonies granted fifty acres of land to each ''settler'' who brought in ''settlers'' at his own expense. The shipmasters got their land warrants, sometimes amounting to thousands of acres for a single voyage, and then sold these to colonial land speculators. The captains and the merchants who employed them made a triple profit in the servant trade: the profit from the simple sale of indentures; the return-voyage profit of taking back low-priced raw products for sale in the high-profit European markets; and the profit from selling land for which they had paid nothing.

With such lucrative incentives, shipmasters were loath to sail without a full complement of suitable human cargo. Suitable meant single young people in good health, preferably with some marketable skills, such as carpenters and coopers, who fetched premium prices in the colonial servant markets. Suitable also meant Scots, who were highly regarded in the colonies. Less acceptable were English, and least wanted were Irish, who had a reputation for being lawless and violent. When the number of voluntary emigrants proved insufficient, shipmasters were not too choosy.

They prowled the coasts of the British Isles, sending gangs of sailors ashore to round up young men, women, and children, usually with the connivance of local agents who made sure that the dragnet caught up none of the young of the gentry. So many victims of such kidnapping were sold without legal indentures that colonial legislatures were compelled to regulate the practice. Indentures were required and had to be recorded. Kidnapped children were generally required to serve until they were twenty-one years old. The kidnappers, however, plied their trade with impunity.

Public authorities also took a hand in forcing the poor to America. In 1619, London officials dispatched a hundred poor children to Virginia to serve until they were twenty-one. A year later rebellion broke out among others who had been rounded up, and the Privy Council intervened to force the youngsters to board ship. Thereafter, at irregular intervals, officials sought to trim relief costs by shipping off children whose families were on welfare.

Adults fared no better. The wandering unemployed were arrested and given their choice of flogging or service in the colonies. Wardens of overcrowded prisons "sold" inmates to merchants who resold them as servants in America. Until 1718 a convicted felon could escape punishment by opting for a term as a colonial servant. Political and religious opponents of the Stuarts and of the Puritan Commonwealth and Protectorate, including at various times Irish Catholics, Presbyterian Scots, and English Quakers, were deported to the colonies when they escaped more drastic punishment.

SLAVE CARGOES

If some whites came against their will, all blacks did. The white myth had it that the enslaved Africans were savages living in jungles, as devoid of morals as of clothes. In fact, the peoples of coastal West Africa, the center of slaving activity, were the products of a long civilization. Well before the advent of the whites they had developed stable societies, which were based on agriculture but also included growing handicraft industries and a commerce that linked them, through overland Arab traders, with the Middle East and Europe.

Such societies were characterized by extended family relationships, organized governments, social and religious institutions, and moral codes. They produced works of art that are now valued throughout the world. Indeed, this very background attracted slavers to West Africa: the people were familiar with the techniques of farming and crafts, they were accustomed to the discipline of field labor and to social control, and there were large numbers of young people in good health. The slavers, like the shipmasters in the white-servant trade, were not interested in the sick, the aged, or the very young.

The Africans, like the indentured whites, were victims of the rapidly expanding business that had found a bonanza in supplying the insatiable labor needs of New World plantations. Merchants of every maritime nation flocked to share in the profits from marketing black gold: Portugal, Spain, France, England, the Netherlands, Denmark, and Sweden. Later, New England Puritans and Quakers joined in the holy work of reclaiming lost savage souls for God and civilization.

Africans also kept slaves, a fact that made the work of white slavers easier.

African slavery, however, was unlike that of the New World. As Basil Davidson has pointed out, the status of African slaves was more akin to that of serfs in feudal Europe, "often with valued human rights," than to chattel slavery, in which slaves were simply movable properly. In many African societies, slaves could marry, own property, and testify in court—rights that no black slave in America enjoyed. Through adoption slaves often became members of their owner's family and their children were free. African slaves were not fixed in status; they could work to improve their lot and attain eventual freedom.

When European traders showed an interest in human merchandise, African rulers and merchants saw nothing unusual in trading off slaves for rum, horses, and firearms. The wealth that arose from the traffic made it alluring to African dealers. So great was the demand that the supply on the traditional "slave coast" virtually dried up. Slaving expeditions then raided inland as far as 300 miles. Egged on by white traders, African rulers warred on each other to take prisoners for sale as slaves. The white traders themselves expanded operations into new areas on the west African coast.

Once in the hands of European and American traders, blacks were systematically degraded. They were crowded in compounds until slave ships arrived, then herded out for inspection. Men and women were stripped naked in public, a violation of African taboos. White men checked them for physical flaws. The unfit were cast aside. The fit were branded with hot irons to identify their ownership. They were chained together to prevent escape.

The worst was yet to come. Slave-ship captains wanted maximum cargoes, so chained blacks were packed below decks. Sanitary conditions in all vessels of the period were poor, but in slave ships they were frightful. Disease flourished. The seriously ill and dead were casually tossed overboard. Although the blacks had been selected for prime physical fitness, the death rate was high. French records examined by Professor Curtin show an average death rate of 15 percent per voyage, and numerous English captains reported losses of a third of their original shipment. White merchants were little disturbed, for it was a rare slaver indeed who made a less than handsome profit.

Bad as were the physical conditions, the psychological strains on the new slaves were worse. Torn away from their homelands and loved ones and chained among strangers, the blacks dreaded the future, for many believed that the white people intended to kill and eat them. They were terrorized by the whites, men "with horrible looks, red faces, and loose hair," whose brutality appalled blacks. A former slave, Olaudah Equiano, telling of his experiences on a slave ship, commented, "I had never seen among my people such instances of brutal cruelty, and this not only shown towards us blacks but also to some of the whites themselves."

Not all Africans submitted meekly. Some went on hunger strikes, preferring death to New World slavery. Captains flogged such resisters until they ate—a treatment only occasionally successful. Other blacks leaped overboard when opportunity offered and drowned themselves. Still others organized rebellions, which the slavers put down ferociously. One such revolt counted a woman among its leaders. According to the ship's surgeon, she was hoisted up by her thumbs, whipped, and slashed with knives, "before the other slaves, till she died." So great became the problem of slave-ship rebellions that some businessmen offered insurrection insurance to slave traders.

Before the Atlantic slave trade ended in the early nineteenth century, at least 8 million Africans were delivered to the New World, according to Philip D. Curtin, who has made an exhaustive study of the subject. Of these, nearly 500,000 arrived in what is now the United States. More than 70 percent of them came between 1740 and 1808, when the importation of slaves was outlawed. How many were brought in illegally thereafter remains uncertain.

THE COLORING OF AMERICA

Thus strangers overran the land of the original Americans. English-speaking peoples dominated the Atlantic seaboard. French settlers occupied the Mississippi Valley. The Spanish colonized Florida, the Southwest, and California. Africans were brought in to work as slaves on southern farms and plantations. By 1790, when the new republic of the United States held its first census, there were more than 3 million white people within its boundaries. In addition, there were more than 750,000 blacks. It is not known how many native Americans there were, for the census did not count them.

FOR FURTHER READING

The first settlers in North America are discussed in C. W. Ceram, *The First American* (1971). Indian cultures are described in Alvin M. Josephy, Jr., *The Indian Heritage of America* (1968), and Harold E. Driver, *Indians of North America* (1969).

Recent works dealing with the English background include Peter Laslett, *The World We Have Lost* (1965); Wallace Notestein, *The English People on the Eve of Colonization* (1954); and Carl Bridenbaugh, *Vexed and Troubled Englishmen* (1968).

Influences that prompted English Puritan migration, among other things, are dealt with in two works by Christopher Hill: *Puritanism and Revolution* (1958) and *Society and Puritanism in Pre-Revolutionary England* (1964). See also Alan Simpson, *Puritanism in Old and New England* (1955), and Edmund S. Morgan, *The Puritan Dilemma* (1958).

The legal and illegal trades in indentured servants are described in Abbott E. Smith, *Colonists in Bondage* (1971).

The African background is portrayed in Basil Davidson, *The African Genius* (1970), and in Lewis H. Gann and Peter Duignan, *Africa and the World* (1972). On the New World slave trade see Basil Davidson, *The African Slave Trade* (1961), and Philip D. Curtin, *The Atlantic Slave Trade* (1969).

2 the early white invaders

As we have seen, the white newcomers were transplanted Europeans who crossed the ocean for many reasons. Whatever their ends, they sought to reach them through familiar, Old World means. They came from agricultural societies, and the adjustment to a similar, but more primitive, society in the New World did not entail the "culture shock" that traumatized nineteenth-century peasants thrust into the inferno of Pittsburgh steel mills. Besides, the climate and soil of Virginia and New England were not so markedly different from those of Western Europe as to pose major problems in farming techniques. The problems that did arise were solved with the aid of Indian peoples, who were at first willing to share their knowledge with the whites. Adjustment was also easier because the newcomers were able to manage things their own way; that is, they made their own social order dominant over that of the native Americans.

These early settlers were people of a particular place and time, Western Europeans of the seventeenth century. On the one hand, they were men, women, and children of the emerging modern world, affected by the Renaissance, the Protestant Reformation, and the Commercial Revolution. On the other hand, they were still deeply influenced by the traditions of the Middle Ages. Both inheritances played a part in the newcomers' adaptation to America, especially as filtered through the English experience. New World conditions did not duplicate those of the Old. Habits, attitudes, and institutions had to be modified to enable white society to survive and develop. But they were only modified, not abandoned.

A SOCIETY OF STATUS

The cultural baggage brought by the whites contained a medieval model of society, in which everyone had a proper place ordained by God. The concept was being modified in England, but the basic idea of a class hierarchy still imbued English thinking and feeling. No matter how individuals might rise or fall in what was a relatively fluid society, there were still classes. The "lower orders" owed deference and obedience to those above them, while the ranks at the top exercised their God-given responsibility to rule.

Such concepts shaped the early English settlement of America. Control of Virginia was first vested in a handful of English businessmen and exercised by them through their appointed agents in the colony. Later such power was used by agents of the Crown. The Mayflower Compact provided legitimacy for the rule of a minority of true believers in Plymouth. Massachusetts Bay was subject to the control of the sponsoring company's stockholders. This was a small group, but the colony was actually dominated at first by the even smaller number of stockholders who emigrated.

Attempts to impose such rule soon provoked dissent, which in turn occasioned frank defense of minority control. John Winthrop, the first governor of Massachusetts Bay, regarded a petition to repeal a law of the colony as a transgression against God. Said he, "When the people have chosen men to be their rulers, now to combine together . . . in a public petition . . . savors of resisting an ordinance of God. For the people, having deputed others, have no right to make or alter laws themselves, but are to be subject." John Cotton, the most learned and humane of the early Puritans, could not stomach the suggestion of democracy. "Democracy," he wrote, "I do not conceive that ever God did ordain as a fit government for church or commonwealth. If the people be governors, who shall be governed?"

In economic and social terms these ideas entailed acceptance of a class society based on property, particularly landed property. As in Europe, those with much land enjoyed high status, those with less land a lower status, and so on down the social ladder to those who owned no land and had the lowest social standing. Political power was naturally exercised by the elite of the rich, the well-born, and the educated. John Winthrop summed up such thinking in his observation, "In all times, some must be rich, some poor; some high and eminent in power and dignity; others mean and in subjection." Such thinking was not confined to New England. It also permeated New Amsterdam, Pennsylvania, and the southern colonies.

These attitudes found expression not only in personal relationships but also in institutional arrangements. Church members may have been equal in the eyes of God, but church officials saw to it that members were seated according to social status. Educational institutions also followed the pattern. Harvard, for example, carefully ranked its students according to social station. Social distance was reflected in terms of public address. A "gentleman" was as clearly distinguished from a "master" or "mister," as the "mister" differed from a "yeoman," who was altogether distinct from a humble "goodman." So intent were the upper classes on preserving social distance that some colonial governments prescribed "dress codes" to make sure that humble folk did not wear clothing and ornaments above their "station."

The successful resistance to these laws indicated that in America the application of such thinking had to be tempered. English social structure and social attitudes derived from scarcity of land, but in America land was obtained with relative ease. Besides, the scarcity of skilled workers in the New World made it difficult to keep those workers in their supposedly rightful place. As a result, there developed a growing number of small landowners, and craftsmen strove to acquire sufficient capital to become property-owners. That men could rise in the relatively egalitarian conditions of early colonial life raised expectations. Frustrating those expectations produced the rebellious temper of which Winthrop complained. Significantly, Winthrop's strictures did not win compliance. Far from submitting, the settlers who were excluded from government kept protesting until they gained concessions that made them dominant in the lower house of the Massachusetts legislature. In Virginia, small farmers expressed their grievances in the House of Burgesses, established in 1619. Such concessions were also dictated, in part, by the colonies' need for more settlers. Rigid insistence on a system of privilege was no way to attract newcomers.

The protesters were not revolutionists. They accepted the class system, but in the New World they expected to rise within it. When various local elites put obstacles in their way, they grew angry. New England farmers and artisans, for example, resented the practice by which, in the periodic distribution of township land, local officials allotted to themselves and their friends more and better lands. One of the most bitter clashes between Governor Winthrop and the people of Boston arose from just such a situation. In Virginia, small tobacco farmers were aroused by the growing influence of the as yet small group of great planters and fur traders in such fields as taxation and Indian affairs. Taxes bore most heavily on small farmers, and to frontier planters, the Indian policy of the colony smacked of appeasement of the native Americans at the expense of the whites.

Whatever the elites might concede to popular sentiment, they retained the substance of power. The original ruling group of New England—preachers, magistrates, and big landholders—grew to include great merchants and later men from poor ancestry who had nevertheless accumulated wealth. In the southern tobacco colonies the violent fluctuations in tobacco prices forced planters of slender means to depend more on great planters who could furnish credit and supplies. Similar developments took place in other colonies.

Political power continued to rest in a relatively small group of rulers. The lower houses of colonial legislatures might represent the mass of voters—and remember that universal male suffrage was not the rule in colonial times—but their actions were subject to veto, both by the appointed upper houses and by the governors. Governors and councils controlled judicial and administrative appointments. The major check on the political power of the elites was the authority of the legislatures to grant funds for the operation of government, the "power of the purse." Legislatures occasionally used this power, and prudent executives sought to avoid confrontations whenever possible.

How is one to explain the persistence of a class society in the New World? The first and most obvious answer is that the colonists had no other model of society. A class society was simply part of the natural order of things in that day and age. The habits of deference to one's superiors died hard, and such habits were constantly reinforced with the arrival of newcomers from England. Second, challenges to authority came largely from other property-owners—smaller, to be sure, but still devoted to the principle of private property and the authority that went with it. When they were challenged by rebellious servants, they were all too happy to resort to higher authority for enforcement of their own power. Third, conflicts with Indian peoples opposing white encroachment on their lands called for a united front, regardless of class or opinion, which further strengthened dominant groups. Thus, the exiled Roger Williams aided his Bay Colony persecutors during King Philip's War. Yet, when small farmers felt that the ruling elite was pro-Indian, they were willing to use arms against the established government, as during Bacon's Rebellion in Virginia in 1676. Fourth, and perhaps most important, there was room at the top—and on the way up. The expansion of the colonial economy provided many opportunities for shrewd, industrious people to improve their lot. Even formerly indentured servants shared in the good fortune. Such successful people naturally had no quarrel with a system through which they benefited. The unsuccessful blamed either themselves or bad luck, not the system, for their failure.

Apart from such considerations, the elites, whether at the local or provincial level, profited from the conflicting interests of their potential opponents. The baker who complained about the high cost of building his shop was assailed by carpenters and masons for adulterating his bread. The subsistence farmer who eked out a living by selling his small surplus to nearby towns resented the intrusion of new commercial farmers who undersold him in the markets. With the under classes divided, the ruling class easily held sway.

In no place was the ability of an elite to manipulate rival interests better demonstrated than in the New England town meeting, long regarded as a sacred symbol of direct democracy. The records indicate that small groups of officials, usually men of wealth and prestige, were elected again and again over periods of many years. Contributing to an elite's success, of course, was the fact that the elites provided the men who had enough learning, experience, and leisure to devote themselves to public affairs. Poorer people simply could not afford to hold public office.

SOCIETY, PROFITS, AND WAGES

Just as the colonists brought with them fixed notions about a class society, so also did they bring concepts about the economic order that were designed to assure social stability. Since the great danger in the economic world was the tendency of individuals to profit at the expense of others, especially in times of shortages, both prices and wages had to be curbed. From medieval times it had been held that merchants must charge only a "just price"; that is, they must price their goods, not according to the market, but according to what they needed to sustain their families in decency and comfort. The "fair wage" required workers to refrain from demanding wage increases when labor was in short supply and to accept such wages as suited their station in life. That such teachings derived from medieval Catholic doctrine disturbed the New World Protestants not a whit, for John Calvin himself had upheld them. Nor did it bother colonists that such concepts were already outmoded in the capitalistic order emerging in Europe.

In America, faced with chronic shortages of manufactured goods and skilled labor and sometimes with actual food shortages, such concepts proved unworkable. Massachusetts Bay tried to fix prices in 1630, but after five years of failure it gave the task over to local communities. Virginia's effort to set prices for tobacco failed. When towns tried to control prices, merchants and shopkeepers cheated on weights and measures and adulterated their products. This caused public authorities to institute controls of quantity and quality. Such efforts were only partially successful, for few offenders received severe punishments. Although many small offenders came before the courts, few great merchants were called to account. One such, a notorious Boston profiteer named Robert Keayne, was fined £200 in 1639 while pulpit and public denounced him. His fine was later canceled, while the court tried to mollify public opinion by censuring his behavior.

Attempts to fix wages, at least for skilled labor, likewise failed. It was relatively easy to control the unskilled, but the demand for carpenters, coopers, blacksmiths, and other artisans was too strong to make wage regulation effective. There are numerous records of fines imposed on artisans for demanding wages above the legal limits, but such decisions were self-defeating. The fined workers simply moved to towns where laws were less strict, a migration that aggravated the labor shortage in the communities they left. Often, too, employers connived with their skilled help to evade wage regulations. Employers themselves tried to hold down wages by importing craftsmen as indentured servants, but the demand for such workers was so great that they fetched premium prices.

RELIGIOUS UNIFORMITY AND DISSENT

Colonists also brought with them the belief that social stability required uniformity in religion, a uniformity thought all the more necessary in America where for so long there was a question whether the initial settlements would even survive. The Puritans held to the conviction that since they were executing God's will, dissent not only subverted society but also defied the Almighty. Thus, in all good conscience, dissidents such as Anne Hutchinson and Roger Williams were banished from Massachusetts Bay. They were more fortunate than the later Quakers and Baptists who tried to work in the Bay Colony; they were flogged, sometimes sold into slavery in the West Indies, and sometimes executed.

Such intolerance was not confined to New England. When Protestants got the upper hand in Maryland in 1654, they ended the religious freedom enjoyed by Catholics, who were persecuted for five years until the Calvert family, the colony's proprietor, was able to reestablish its authority. Jews, barely tolerated in New Amsterdam, were unwelcome everywhere else, except in Rhode Island, where the exile Baptist colony of Roger Williams set a unique example of religious freedom. Except for Rhode Island and Pennsylvania, the colonies supported specific churches from public funds: Congregational in New England, Anglican in Virginia and later in Maryland, and Dutch Reformed in New Amsterdam.

But the New World proved uncongenial to uniformity. Heretics banished from Massachusetts found refuge in Indian lands not too far distant and communicated secretly with friends left behind. When the exasperated Massachusetts Puritans plotted the destruction of Rhode Island, Roger Williams forestalled them by obtaining an English charter for the colony. Maryland furnished a haven for Catholics, although it is notable that fewer English Catholics than Protestants went there. Pennsylvania was a Quaker stronghold, but it also welcomed all kinds of Protestants. The very diversity of colonies made religious conformity impossible. Crown colonies, such as Virginia, were ruled from London and reflected the royal preference for the Church of England, often called the Anglican church. Proprietary colonies, such as Pennsylvania, were literally owned by the men to whom they had been granted and reflected the religious views of the owners. Charter colonies, such as Massachusetts, enjoyed considerable autonomy and reflected the views of the settlers. In addition, as each colony developed, it sought settlers or they came in of their own accord. In either case public authorities found it increasingly impolitic to impose religious beliefs. This trend was accentuated by the growth of the merchant class, whose values became increasingly secular as the seventeenth century went on. Even in New England, the stern orthodoxy of the Puritan founders declined, symbolized in 1657 by the adoption of the "Half Way Covenant," which permitted children of godly parents to be baptized even if the children had not undergone the required religious "experience." And, as the influence of orthodoxy waned, the prestige of the clergy, the principal proponents of religious uniformity, likewise declined.

Significantly, however, one set of religious values did become accepted by Puritan, Quaker, Catholic, Baptist, and Anglican alike. Indeed, they became so imbedded in American life that they have conditioned our thinking and attitudes ever since. These were the values we associate with the "Protestant ethic," which was based on the belief that God and humanity were best served by hard work, frugality, thrift, and sobriety. Such an imperative was admirably adapted to the needs of a society trying to survive in what it viewed as a wilderness, surrounded by Indian peoples who were steadily becoming more hostile.

MARRIAGE AND FAMILY

The family structure the newcomers brought from Europe was patriarchal. The father's authority over wife, children, and servants was in theory almost absolute. In practice, the father often shared authority with the mother, and in America paternal absolutism was eroded even more by law and by custom.

The colonial family served many functions. Most obviously, it controlled the sexual life of the people; marital sex was the only legitimate form of sexual expression, morally sanctioned by the production of children. The family was also the basic institution through which the young were conditioned to accept the standards of their society, the process social psychologists call the "internalization of social control." Thus, long before adulthood, children were accustomed to the niceties of a society of status and to the different roles expected of boys and girls, men and women. These roles were basically the same as in our society, but with significant differences. The colonial family, unlike ours, was the basic economic unit of society, the group in which all members must cooperate if they were to survive and prosper. Even the very young had simple chores. While fathers and sons cleared the woods, worked in the fields, and did the heavy farm work, mothers and daughters baked the family's bread, brewed the beer (as essential then as coffee is now), fashioned the clothing, made the soap and candles, cooked the meals, and washed and repaired the clothes.

The colonial family provided its members with basic psychological fulfillment: each member felt needed, each knew his or her importance in the family's scheme of things. Also, as John Demos suggests, the involvement of youngsters in meaningful family activities may have eased the painful transition from childhood to adulthood.

The family also served larger social needs. It provided a haven for aged parents too feeble to work and for unmarried women relatives with nothing other than domestic skills. Indeed, in the early days, the sick or disabled poor with no relatives to care for them were sent to live with private families at public expense. If the parents were literate, the family was for long almost the only place where children could learn to read and write. The New England school laws about which we read so much were rarely effective until late in the seventeenth century. Other colonies were even more laggard, and what schooling there was, was schooling at home.

In all the colonies marriage was a civil contract rather than a religious rite. This was true as much in Anglican Virginia, where civil marriage developed from expediency, as in Puritan New England, where it was such a matter of principle that for a long time only civil magistrates were permitted to perform marriages. Social controls on the institution, however, were as binding as those of England. Once a couple showed interest in marriage, they were formally betrothed in a contract that bound them to marry after a given period of time.

At this point the authority of fathers proved decisive, for their power in the law, which required parental consent for marriages of children, was enhanced by their control of family property. Since it was the custom of the day that few young men married without their own land and dwelling, the power of the father to grant or withhold such assets gave him a veto over marriages. Fathers were sometimes reluctant to grant approval, not because they objected to the woman or her family, but because in a day of intense labor shortage they disliked giving up experienced help. Similarly, the father of a prospective bride was likely to look with a jaundiced eye on a future son-in-law with no visible means of supporting a wife and family. He, too, could forbid a marriage and back his prohibition by refusing to assign the usual dowry of a betrothed woman.

Our usual reading of the colonial past tells us of marriages between teenagers, the deaths of young mothers worn out by endless childbirths, and frequent remarriages by surviving husbands. That picture seems flawed in the light of recent research, at least as far as colonial New England was concerned. There, the average age for first marriage for men ranged between twenty-five and twenty-seven, and for women between twenty and twenty-three. Further, since young adults of either sex who had outlived childhood diseases had every prospect of a ripe old age, fewer marriages were broken up by death than we used to believe. In addition, most survivors of such marriages remarried only once.

The great hazard for married women was, of course, childbirth, but it appears to have taken less of a toll than once thought. In Plymouth colony, which embraced several towns, only about 20 percent of women's deaths were ascribed to birth and its complications. This is high by our standards, but explainable in terms of the then primitive level of medical knowledge and practice. Nor were families as large as we once supposed. The average number of living children in a family seems to have been eight, spaced at intervals of about two years. Compared to our time, the death rate of children was high, but John Demos estimates that at least 75 percent of Plymouth children survived to adulthood.

Whether these findings from settled New England communities apply to southern colonies is not yet established. We may speculate, however, that since considerations of family and property were as powerful in the south as in New England, they produced a similar outlook on marriage. It is noteworthy that where such considerations were lacking, as in frontier settlements, the traditional picture of early marriage appears to have been more accurate.

Divorce, for women as well as men, was easier in the New World than in the Old. It was also easier to get a divorce in New England than in Virginia; there, the dominance of the Anglican church and the authority of the Crown helped maintain the strictness of England, where women could not sue for divorce. In Calvinist New Amsterdam and Puritan New England, marriage was looked upon as purely a civil affair, and annulment and divorce were permitted for marriages that violated accepted moral standards or failed to serve useful social functions.

When the Crown took control of New York and Massachusetts in the latter part of the seventeenth century, such liberal policies were ended. By 1773 even divorces granted by colonial legislatures were held invalid. One wonders how much English abridgment of such personal rights contributed to mounting colonial discontent.

SEX AND SIN

Marriage helped control the sexual energies of the early colonists, but marriage then could no more contain sexual expression than marriage in other societies at other times.

Cases of adultery, regarded as a most heinous offense, appear on early court records. In 1642 Governor Bradford deplored adultery in Plymouth. Massachusetts Bay and Connecticut made it a capital offense, but few convicted offenders were executed. Usually they were heavily fined, whipped, and publicly humiliated, like Hester Prynne in Hawthorne's *Scarlet Letter*. Women offenders were likely to be punished more drastically than men, on the assumption that their temptations had seduced the men.

More common than adultery was fornication—sexual relations between single men and women. The punishments were severe—fines, whippings, public disgrace—but again the man was more likely to receive mercy than the woman. Usually, the affairs that came to public notice were those revealed by a woman's pregnancy. If the man responsible was willing to marry the woman or care for the child, his punishment was apt to be light. The reason for mercy was that taxpayers would not have to support fatherless children. The same close-fistedness helps explain those occasions when women were freed from punishment—providing they betook themselves and their children out of town. It likewise shows why, in those cases where the woman had not named the father, the agonies of childbirth were used to extort from her the name of the father, so that he could be charged for supporting the child. Thus, moral and economic considerations entered into application of the law. In fact, as time went on, the economic interests tended to prevail, with consequent tempering of the law's rigors.

With the increase in trade and the emergence of bustling seaports there emerged an evil that Puritans and Quakers thought they had left behind in unregenerate

Europe: prostitution. Sailors and landlubbers alike patronized the bawdy houses that flourished in the seaboard towns. Ironically, the "whores of Boston" gave that Puritan town an unwanted ill-fame. The houses recruited from what seemed an ample supply of young women, drawn mainly from the poor: widows of sailors, fishermen, and laborers, often with youngsters to support; deserted mothers of families; and single women with no better way to earn a livelihood. In 1672 Massachusetts Bay banned bawdy houses, and other colonies likewise tried to end prostitution. The drastic punishments meted out were confined to the women. Their male patrons, at most, might be charged with being "drunk and disorderly."

At the time, magistrates and other upper-class spokesmen attributed most sexual offenses to the poor—laborers, sailors, fishermen, and indentured servants. Servants, of course, could not marry without their master's permission, and since permission was rarely given, they had little opportunity for sexual expression other than fornication or, in the case of males, resort to prostitutes. Sailors and fishermen, degraded by brutal conditions of work, took their pleasures where they found them. Free laborers, who could not afford marriage, were in similar plight. But it is difficult to believe the poor had a monopoly on sin. Obviously, upper class males found it to their advantage—and had the means—to keep their transgressions out of court. Even so, a sufficient number of cases involving the prestigious and wealthy show that violations of the moral code were not confined to the poor. Indeed, indentured women servants were almost as much the sexual victims of their masters as were slave women.

THE NATURAL INFERIORITY OF WOMEN

A basic assumption underlying family structure, and the whole social order, was the inferiority of women. This belief has so long been a part of Western culture that its origins are still a subject of speculation. In the seventeenth century it was universally held that God himself decreed the subjugation of women. Eve, by tempting Adam, brought evil into the world and God's wrath upon the human race. Henceforth, man must earn his bread by the sweat of his brow; as for woman, she must bear children "in sorrow" and her husband "shall rule over" her.

Such views were imbedded in law as well as in custom. English common law held that a woman lost her legal identity when she married. Her property became her husband's; control over the children was exclusively his; he could beat her in moderation; she could not sue for divorce, but he could, if the charge were adultery. The wife's personal rights received little legal recognition. Her task in life was to please and obey her husband. The harshness of the law was mitigated to some degree by the rise of courts of equity, which protected the property rights of married women who had entered into premarital contracts.

The English inheritance had another side. The Quakers, for example, brought with them a belief in sexual equality. In contrast to other denominations, women actively participated in church affairs and were admitted to the sect's ministry.

In the New World other religious groups adhered to the basic doctrine of women's subjection, but in modified form. John Robinson, the Pilgrim pastor in Holland, reminded his charges that while Eve was a great transgressor, it was likewise true that God created both man and woman and that since creation she was no more "degenerated than he from the primitive goodness." John Cotton, the Puritan divine so eminent in Massachusetts that many of the pious thought that "God would not permit Mr. Cotton to err," went even further. He expressly repudiated the doctrine that women were "a necessary evil." Women, said he, were "a necessary good; such as it was not good that men should be without."

The English businessmen promoting the Virginia colony came to the same conclusion for pragmatic reasons. They shipped off young women to Virginia, offering them in marriage to planters for the costs of transportation. Such a step, they argued, would at once help quiet the unruly men and through the establishment of families give them an incentive to develop the colony.

Such considerations help explain the relatively high status of women in colonial times. The ideas of Robinson and Cotton, as well as the Quaker belief in sexual equality, had their influence, but behind them, and reinforcing them, was the fact that attitudes derived from feudal Europe had limited value in meeting the problems of the New World. In Europe, women were plentiful, there was a surplus of laborers, and war was the business of professional male soldiers. In the United States, women were scarce, laborers were hard to come by, and wars between the native Americans and the white invaders necessitated that women as well as men carry their load. Women, then, had relatively high status, as active and needed participants in the growth of white society.

This status was reflected in laws and judicial decisions, which represented a mixture of English common law and Biblical teachings adapted to American conditions. Thus, while the doctrine survived that married women were legal nonpersons, its application was softened. Wives kept control of their property if their husbands had so agreed before marriage. A husband's right to dispose of his own property was limited by the claims of wife and children. If exercise of his property rights might make the family public charges, then sale of his property was forbidden in Rhode Island and Plymouth. It was customary for a widow to receive a third of her husband's estate, but if that was deemed inadequate, courts in some colonies awarded her more, even if the husband's will specified otherwise. In America, unlike England, wives could obtain divorces and be awarded damages from the husband's estate. Even the husband's right of movement was limited. Many colonies forbade husbands to leave their wives alone for extended periods of time when that might expose the women to the hazards of Indian warfare.

In some colonies husbands were forbidden to exercise their English privilege of beating their wives. If a wife's behavior warranted punishment, the husband must bring the matter to court. In one such case in Plymouth, the husband charged that his wife not only beat and reviled him, but also egged on their children to help her, "bidding them knock him on the head, and wishing his victuals might choke him." Such wifely outbursts must not have been too rare, for various colonies enacted laws to protect husbands from shrewish and violent wives. And, despite the laws, wife-beating continued: travelers in remote areas reported instances where husbands continued to whip their wives with impunity.

The laws usually vested control of children in the father; in practice, management was often the actual responsibility of the mother. The mother's approval was legally required in some places before children were bound out to service. In some colonies both parents had to approve the marriage of a child. The steady erosion of the law of primogeniture—under which all property of a father passed to his eldest son—eventually made it possible for daughters to share equally with sons when fathers died intestate, except in New York and the southern colonies, where primogeniture in modified form continued until the Revolution. Massachusetts law limited the shares of daughters by a provision that eldest sons were to receive a double portion.

Opportunities for formal education were rare in the early colonies, and rarer for girls than for boys. There were few schools, and those few were designed for teaching boys. Most youngsters received the informal education afforded by home, church, and community, which stressed the different roles assigned the sexes. Since the proper role of woman was in the home, girls were trained to be good wives and mothers. If they learned to read and write, so much the better, but these skills were not regarded as essential. Illiteracy was the more readily accepted because so many boys and men were also unlettered.

Any role for women larger than that of housewife was ruled out by the universal belief that woman was mentally inferior to man. As Pastor John Robinson said, God endowed woman with lesser intelligence so that man could lead her to righteousness. Also, intellectual activity was likely to disturb woman's delicate mental balance. John Winthrop wrote that a mentally ill woman had brought on her condition "by giving herself wholly to reading and writing." If she had not "gone out of her way and calling to meddle in such things as are proper for men, whose minds are stronger . . . she had kept her wits and might have improved them usefully and honorably in the place God had set her."

But if women were barred from the "higher" callings, a variety of occupations was open to the growing number who lived in towns. Women owned and ran inns and taverns; operated retail stores, especially groceries; and did sewing, embroidering, and weaving. Others, either trained through apprenticeship or by their husbands, were skilled artisans, even in such lucrative crafts as coopering, the art of making barrels. Since barrels provided the prime packaging of goods in the growing colonial trade, the workers who made them were held in high esteem and paid accordingly.

There were even women merchants on the grand scale, especially in New Amsterdam. The most notable woman merchant was Margaret DeVries Phillipse. When her first husband died, she sold off their lands on Staten Island, invested in shipping, and established a regular carrying service between Europe and America. She herself often went along on voyages to supervise the buying and selling. When she remarried, she kept up the business, and she and her husband (who was no poor man himself) became the wealthiest couple in New Amsterdam.

Probably the most prestigious calling for women was that of midwife. In those days, before the advent of obstetrics, the midwife was the only person available for assisting in childbirth. She was qualified by her own experience, oral tradition, and sometimes by training in European midwifery schools. For long her testimony was decisive about whether a couple had engaged in fornication prior to marriage. Since her services were vitally needed, she was held in great repute. Indeed, in some colonies her responsibilities were held to be so great that she had to be licensed to practice.

No matter how hostile society was to the intellectual claims of its women, it could not entirely repress their talents. Anne Bradstreet (c. 1612–72), wife of a Massachusetts Bay official and mother of eight children, was America's first woman poet. In one of her poems she referred wryly to men's attitudes toward a woman's writing. If her work was poor, she said, it would be attributed to her being a woman, but "if what I do proves well, . . . They'll say it's stolen, or else it was by chance."

Margaret Brent was a Maryland plantation owner who managed her business affairs so ably that Governor Leonard Calvert appointed her to administer his estate after his death. She, in turn, demanded the right to sit and vote in the Maryland Assembly, the first woman to raise the issue of political rights (1647). The Assembly denied her a seat but gave her the right to vote as representative of the Calvert estate.

The most outstanding woman of the period, however, was Anne Hutchinson (1591–1643), one of the first exponents of religious freedom and of women's rights. An expert midwife and herself the mother of fourteen children, she still found time to expound to her neighbors the doctrine that individual persons, men and women alike, could know God directly through intuition. Such teaching, like that of the Quakers, obviated the clergy and implied that all truly religious experiences were equally valid. Such teachings presented an obvious threat to the Puritan elite, especially so since Hutchinson won a wide following, including for a time even the eminent John Cotton. She was tried for heresy. One of the counts was that she taught men and in so doing had subverted the natural order of things, acting as "a Husband [rather] than a Wife, and a Preacher than a Hearer; and a Magistrate than a Subject." In her defense Hutchinson cited Biblical authority for her teachings and expounded her right as a person to teach God's word as she understood it. For her temerity, she was banished. She and her family found refuge first in Rhode Island, then in New Netherlands, where she and most of her household were slain by Indians who mistakenly associated the Hutchinsons with some Dutch settlers who had swindled them.

Fear of women was enhanced by the popular belief in witchcraft. In the latter half of the seventeenth century New England courts tried numerous women on witchcraft charges. The hysteria reached a climax in 1692 in the notorious Salem trials. Of the twenty people executed, fourteen were women.

CHILDREN WITHOUT CHILDHOOD

Children were the victims of adult ambivalence. On the one hand, they were regarded as blessings of God. On the other, they were seen as sharers in original sin, easy prey for the snares of Satan unless parents took all necessary precautions. Once past infancy, a hazardous time in which babies received much maternal solicitude, children were put to work as early as possible. Every hand, however small, was badly needed, and work would save youngsters from the sins of laziness and idleness. Further, children were subject to unceasing discipline to make sure they grew up to be God-fearing, law-abiding adults. Childhood, as a phase of life important in itself, was as unknown in the New World as in the Old.

Pastor John Robinson summed up the outlook of the day on child training. Parents, said he, had to assure that children did not develop wills of their own. Children must be "restrained and repressed" at a very early age, lest they soon nourish their own "natural pride" against the will of their parents. Such pride must "be broken and beaten down," he said.

Puritan authorities held that obedience to parents was not the only end of child training: children must also be taught to obey magistrates, masters, preachers—indeed, all adults with authority. Since such thinking formed the pattern of the parents' own experience, the discipline of children was apt to be rigorous, not only in New England but also in other colonies.

Parents who did not behave according to the pattern had their children taken from them by magistrates and bound out for service with other families. This seems to have taken place mostly among poor families whose children might become public charges. Youngsters themselves were subject to punishment if they did not behave appropriately. In the 1670s Massachusetts Bay created a new set of public officials whose duty it was to check on family situations in their neighborhoods, including reports of "stubborn and disorderly children and servants." The miscreants were to be whipped, "not exceeding ten stripes" for each offense.

Young people were blamed for many of the troubles of Puritan society. In 1661 the legislature of Massachusetts Bay ascribed the plight of the colony in part to the "inclination of the rising generation to vanity, profaneness, and disobedience." Less than a generation later the legislators were growling at "the younger sort" again, denouncing young men who wore "long hair, like women's hair," and young women for "cutting, curling, and immodest playing out their hair."

Obviously, most parents and children got along without recourse to law. All questions of family affection aside, the labor of children was too valuable for parents to be unduly tyrannical. Parents were too powerful, especially in terms of property and marriage, for children to be too rebellious. And children for the most part internalized the behavior expected of them—and when they married, they expected the same kind of behavior from their children.

Not all boys and girls spent their childhood at home. A considerable number were bound out to service in other homes, sometimes as early as six years old. Most such children came from families too poor to support them any longer or from families broken up by the death of a parent. Some relatively well-off parents, however, also bound out their children, apparently believing that the discipline of another household would benefit the youngsters. The children were classified legally as servants, and as such were under the complete control of their masters. Such training as the youngsters received was often casual, for their major task was to help with the unskilled labor of household, farm, and shop. The length of their service was set forth in the indentures their parents signed for them.

A greater number of children served as apprentices, the one way to learn a skilled trade, with its eventual higher wages and promise of economic independence. Boys, and girls too, began as apprentices between the ages of ten and fourteen; boys served until they were twenty-one, girls until they were eighteen. During their apprenticeship, boys and girls, like servants, were completely subject to their masters, in whose homes they lived. The law prescribed whipping and extension of service for unruly and disobedient apprentices. The law did require the masters of apprentices to teach their trades to the children, however. Courts awarded damages against masters who shirked that obligation. Because of the shortage of skilled labor, apprentices went off on their own long before their prescribed period of service was completed, sometimes finding jobs after only four years of training. Laws were passed to enforce the apprenticeship standard of at least seven years, but they appear to have been little enforced and few masters found it expedient to sue their apprentices for early departure.

These apprentices and servants had little enough voice in choosing their masters—their parents took care of that—but there was another class of laboring children that had no voice at all: the orphans, neglected children, and others who might become dependent on the community. These youngsters, some of them still infants, were assigned by public authorities to masters until they reached twenty-one years of age. Supposedly they were apprentices, but all too often they were treated as servants, performing menial labor and learning few skills. Like other apprentices, they were subject to the masters' authority, but unlike the others, they had little protection against cruel and unscrupulous masters. Others could, and did, invoke parental intervention against such men—court records bear ample testimony to such actions by angry parents—but these friendless waifs could avail themselves little of the laws protecting servants and apprentices. Perhaps even more unfortunate were the youngsters kidnapped from the British Isles or shipped off to the colonies by the authorities. Friendless and alone in a strange country, they were at the mercy of any master who bought them. So great became the abuses that laws were passed to protect them, but they were rarely invoked.

SERVANTS AND MASTERS

The great need of the developing colonies was cheap labor. In the tobacco colonies such labor was needed for the backbreaking work of clearing the land of trees and underbrush and for working the new fields. There were two major sources of labor: the free laborer, who often worked on yearly contracts and who was relatively expensive and hard to find, and the indentured servant, who was bound for long periods of time and subject to rigorous servant codes. Most indentured servants were imported from the British Isles, although as the colonies developed, many children born in America found themselves serving out long indentures. Indentured servants were to be found in all colonies, but they were most common in Virginia and Maryland.

Colonial law categorized "servants and children" as one, and once formally in service, the servant was a legal child, no matter what his or her age. In the seventeenth century the servant codes became increasingly harsh, and the servant's condition worsened. Servants could be whipped for disrespect or disobedience to their masters. Although permitted to own a little property, they could neither buy nor sell goods, on the presumption that such goods must have been stolen. They could not stay out at night or absent themselves from their master's place without his permission. Taverns were expressly forbidden to entertain servants.

Perhaps the most galling badge of servitude was denial of a servant's right to marry without the master's permission, which was rarely forthcoming. Masters did not want to lose a woman's labor when she bore legitimate children, and they wanted no family life that might interfere with servants' complete obedience to them. In 1682 Pennsylvania went even further. All servant marriages were declared unlawful, the children illegitimate, and the married couple subject to penalties for fornication.

Servants, denied legal sexual expression, met anyhow. Women servants, of course, did become pregnant, a situation the master could turn legally to his profit. By assuming the cost of maintaining the child, the master could get extra service from the father to repay his supposed expenses. In addition, since the master lost the woman's labor during childbirth, he got two years' extra service from her even though, at the most, a mother lost only six weeks' labor. This was such a boon to masters that some masters impregnated servant woman themselves. The abuse grew so commonplace in Virginia that in cases where it could be proved, the woman was taken from the master. She was punished nonetheless; the authorities sold her for her unexpired term plus two years in addition, the proceeds going to maintain the child. White women servants who bore children of blacks were subjected to flogging and extension of their service up to seven years. Here was a situation made to order for unprincipled masters!

But servants, however degraded their position, were not slaves. They were subjects of the king and as such had certain rights, limited though those might be. They brought law suits charging masters with providing poor food, inadequate clothing, and little medical care. They accused masters of excessive punishment and of forced sexual relations. Sometimes they won, but in all cases they dealt with magistrates who were themselves masters and shared the masters' view that most servants were a worthless lot, given to laziness, shirking, drunkenness, and fornication. Convict servants were rated even lower; as convicted felons they had demonstrated their depravity. At the bottom of the servant heap were convict women. Universally despised, they had no one to speak out for them against exploitive masters.

There was no lack of such masters, a fact attested to by the court actions brought against them by servants and by the British instructions to colonial governors to help shield servants from cruelty. Servants unable to obtain redress of grievances through the law had two alternatives: rebellion or running away. There were a few instances of collective resistance. Some servants in Maryland went on strike—unsuccessfully—in the 1660s because they had to live on bread and beans. A servant uprising was planned in Virginia in 1661, again on the issue of poor food, but failed to get a following. Two years later a more general rebellion demanding servants' freedom was aborted when an informer tipped off the authorities.

Running away was a far more common expression of dissatisfaction. A fugitive reaching New Amsterdam or Connecticut was fairly safe, for these colonies showed little interest in returning runaways. Authorities in other colonies, however, were zealous in hunting down fleeing servants. A captured fugitive faced longer service as well as such punishment as the master meted out. Most colonies prescribed two days' additional service for each day of absence. In addition, the servant had to pay all the costs of reclaiming him, which meant still more additional service. In some cases servants were also compelled to compensate masters, by putting in still more extra time, for any losses the latter might have suffered because of the servant's absence. In determining extension of service, the courts accepted masters' testimony without question.

Rebels and runaways were a small minority. Most servants served out their time, however unsatisfactory conditions might have been. The "freedom dues" awarded at the expiration of the servant's indentures were an inducement to steady service. These generally included a suit of clothes, an ax, a hoe or two, and several bushels of corn or wheat. The Carolinas, Maryland, and Pennsylvania also granted land to freed servants, although the two latter colonies abandoned the practice late in the seventeenth century.

The "freedom dues" were obviously hardly sufficient to enable the mass of free servants to become independent farmers or artisans. At best they provided servants a start as free laborers. The poverty of most freed servants also prevented them from making use of land grants. Without capital to hire labor, clear the land, and erect buildings, they had little choice except to sell their grants. This situation was made worse by the lack of good land, most of which was already occupied by people with capital. Servants were likely to get poor land or land in frontier areas. Thus, in Maryland during the 1670s, of 1,243 freed servants who got fifty acres of land each, 869 sold their grants immediately.

It should be noted, however, that among the purchasers were other freed servants, men and women who had managed to acquire some capital during their servitude or shortly thereafter. While such former servants were exceptional, they were by no means unknown, and some even rose to prominence. There were seven such men in the Virginia House of Burgesses in 1629, and fifteen in the Maryland Assembly of 1637. But, as the colonies filled up and class lines hardened, opportunities for enterprising servants became more limited. The former servants who had acquired their own farms in the tobacco colonies were particularly hard hit by the drastic fall in tobacco prices in the 1660s. Many lost their land; in 1676 an official report to London said that a fourth of Virginia's freemen were landless. Faced with loss of their hard-won independence, the former servants joined with other small planters in riots, in crop burning, and eventually in Bacon's Rebellion.

Yet, by the end of the century, the status of servants was rising, largely because there were increasing numbers of people whose status was even lower and whose color marked them off as apart from and inferior to whites. The long-held fear of the masters that white servants might make common cause with blacks and Indians, and even with foreign invaders, was largely forgotten, replaced with a community of blood that bound white masters and servants together against the other races. Manifesting the change, servant codes were liberalized while slave codes were intensified. Further, the gradual replacement of white servants by black slaves meant that those servants who remained received better treatment. The Carolinas expressed the new relationship between white masters and servants in the requirement that a certain proportion of white servants be maintained in relation to blacks, in order to guard against the dangers posed by a preponderance of blacks. Finally, the pressures on the white elites in the tobacco colonies, arising from the presence of so many poor freed servants and angry freemen who had lost their land, were eased by the opening of the back country for settlement. The industrious poor went west, where their conflicts with Indian peoples added to the sense of white community.

FOR FURTHER READING

There is probably no better introduction to the realities of early colonial life than William Bradford, *History of Plymouth Plantation,* especially the version edited by Samuel E. Morison (1952). Wesley F. Craven, *The Southern Colonies in the Seventeenth Century* (1949), is an excellent survey. For fresh insights into colonial life see Stanley N. Katz, ed., *Colonial America* (1971).

Colonial family life was first explored by Arthur W. Calhoun, *Social History of the American Family,* Vol. 1 (1917). Renewed interest in the family is indicated in two more recent works: Edmund S. Morgan, *The Puritan Family* (1966), and John Demos, *A Little Commonwealth* (1970), which discusses family life in Plymouth.

Recent studies of Massachusetts towns provide fresh interpretations of social structure and change. See Kenneth Lockridge, *A New England Town* (1970), which deals with Dedham, and P. J. Greven, Jr., *Four Generations* (1970), which deals with Andover.

For other aspects of New England life see Perry Miller, *The New England Mind: The Seventeenth Century* (1939), and Kai T. Erikson, *Wayward Puritans* (1966).

3 white expansion

By 1700 the white invaders had firmly planted their society in American soil. The ''starving times'' that had brought death and disaster to the early settlers were long since over. The independent Indian peoples had been driven to the mountains. More than 200,000 whites now dominated the seaboard plains and the hilly back country to the Appalachians. Their various churches, governments, and business institutions were well established, as were the moral and social codes that governed behavior among whites. Perhaps even more authoritative were the formal and informal codes designed to maintain social distance between whites on the one hand and blacks and Indians on the other.

During the eighteenth century white society was dynamic, steadily expansive, and increasingly prosperous, despite periodic economic setbacks. It showed signs of repeating European experiences: population pressures, urbanization, rule of an elite increasingly dominated by merchants, emergence of extremes of wealth and poverty, and decline in the status of upper-class women. It was also developing features of its own: African slavery, now entrenched in the Southern colonies; a frontier culture, with its own outlook and values; and a growing feeling of white egalitarianism, which eventually found expression in the Declaration of Independence.

POPULATION GROWTH

Population pressures arose from a veritable population explosion that appeared to outrun available good land, farmed yet by primitive methods that prevented any increase in yield per acre. It is estimated that by 1760 the white population had reached 1.3 million—more than a sixfold increase over the number in 1700—because of natural increase, a death rate far below that of Europe, and mass migrations from

Northern Ireland and Germany. In the same period the black slave population increased more than ten times, reaching at least 300,000 in 1760.

The pressure of people was accentuated by other factors. Most individuals and families preferred to remain in developed areas, where life was relatively secure, comfortable, and prosperous. To be sure, there was land available in the West, but few prudent people wanted to go there. Not only was it remote and dangerous, but also frontier farming entailed the most arduous, backbreaking toil and life under wretched, "uncivilized" conditions. Besides, frontier folk were regarded widely among seaboard people as the misfits and outcasts of civilized society—and few sober easterners wanted to incur that stigma. Thus, only the strong and the desperate tried their luck in the wilderness. This left a vacuum, filled by the Ulster Scots, who poured southward through the back country as far as the Carolinas.

But the wilderness was not to be had simply for the taking. Vast tracts of it were owned by land speculators, who received grants from colonial governments for services rendered or as tokens of political friendship. This was as true of New England as of other regions, for the attempt of the early Puritans to make new settlement an orderly, community affair had long since given way to the individualistic occupation characteristic of Virginia—a process that left the way open for land speculation. In the eighteenth century millions of acres were held speculatively. Some speculators tried to induce settlement by asking low prices. Others leased land to tenants, and when a lease expired, they expropriated all the tenant's improvements. Others simply held their land, hoping to profit from the expected rise in land prices.

Land prices did rise sharply in the towns and cities along the Atlantic seaboard, growing rapidly as a result of expanding domestic and foreign trade. Philadelphia set the pace, becoming in the eighteenth century the third largest city in the British Empire, exceeded only by London and Bristol. Thanks to the Navigation Acts, which restricted English trade to English ships, the colonies developed a shipbuilding industry that by 1775 accounted for one-third of all British registered shipping, and that furthered the economic boom of the seaboard.

The influx of people to cities brought consequences we know in our day. Land prices and rents shot up. In some towns the well-to-do moved from older areas to more tranquil outskirts. The old core areas became overcrowded slums, in which poverty, disease, alcoholism, crime, and prostitution flourished—while the rents went to the affluent. The "middling sort," the small shopkeepers and the skilled workers, maintained their own "respectable" communities and kept their social distance from the "undeserving poor" in the slums. Public authorities faced all kinds of problems: the building of roads and bridges; controlling private privies to protect public health from periodic epidemics; regulating buildings to reduce disastrous fires: and reducing crime, which seems to have been as common then as now.

THE ELITES

The early white invaders, as we have seen, brought with them a model of English status society. By the eighteenth century a stratified society, dominated by elites made up of British officialdom, great merchants, and great planters, had developed. This was as true of Puritan New England as elsewhere. There, the secular spirit displaced the initial sense of religious mission, and with that displacement came a decline in status of the clergy. Much the same thing happened in Pennsylvania, where the original evangelical zeal of the Quakers gave way to quiet pietism.

At the apex of the eighteenth century elites were the royal officials, headed by governors. Some of the governors were native-born, some of them Englishmen. They set the social tone for upper-class colonial life, imparting to it a flavor of aristocratic sophistication otherwise lacking, a flavor especially valued by social climbers eager for all the trappings of status. But merchants, planters, lawyers, and doctors had other reasons for cultivating deputies of the Crown. Such men, as officers of government, had power. Through them could be obtained land grants, sinecures in public office, government contracts, favorable interpretation of rules and regulations, and a blind eye to smuggling. It paid to collaborate. By the same token, shrewd officials saw advantages in collaborating with merchants and planters who so obviously dominated the colonial scene.

If the royal officials relied on political power, the merchants' source of authority was wealth, wealth that multiplied again and again as trade developed. By 1771, for example, the top 10 percent of Boston taxpayers, most of whom were merchants, held 63 percent of the town's wealth. One of the richest was John Hancock, who in 1764 inherited his uncle's merchant business and a legacy of £70,000, both of which he shrewdly expanded.

The merchants' wealth came from their strategic economic position: they controlled both exports and imports, and thus were in a position to charge whatever the market would bear both ways. The slave trade was especially lucrative, not simply because unfortunate Africans could be bought cheap and sold dear, but also because it was part of the chain of "triangular trade" in which every link paid a profit. Ships carried colonial products to England for sale there. Then the vessels bore English cargoes to Africa to exchange for slaves, who were sold in the West Indies. From there sugar and molasses were brought home for sale in the mainland colonies.

Merchants added to their wealth from other sources. They profited tremendously from supplying British armed forces during the wars that involved operations in North America. Such wars were frequent: King William's War (1689–97); Queen Anne's War (1702–13); King George's War (1740–48); and the French and Indian War (1754–63). Merchants speculated in land, both in town and country. They became moneylenders; John Hancock, for instance, had £11,000 out at interest in 1771. While the merchants benefited from the Navigation Acts, they also added to their incomes by wholesale smuggling, usually with the connivance of their friends in the customs service. Such wealth meant political power, and while lesser men might fill necessary but politically innocuous offices, key positions were occupied by merchants and their retainers, of whom a growing number were lawyers.

Similarly, a class of landed magnates came to dominate southern society. For much of the seventeenth century the tobacco colonies were made up of relatively small holdings, but when the tobacco boom ended toward the end of the century, small farmers tended to lose their land to more prosperous neighbors. Not only were they less well prepared to deal with hard times economically, but also they were less able to cope with plant diseases, soil exhaustion, and other ills of agriculture than were neighbors who had cash or credit. Even in good times the small planter was at a disadvantage. Tobacco was labor-intensive—that is, it required a high investment in labor. The man who worked his own farm with the aid of his family and a few slaves or servants could not hope to get a return proportionate to that of a plantation with many slaves. In South Carolina, with its emphasis on rice and indigo, crops that also required heavy investment of labor, the small farmer never had much opportunity.

From these developments emerged what is often called the southern aristocracy, a misleading term if it leads one to imagine a class that had little in common with Yankee merchants. As Aubrey Land suggests, the two groups in fact had much in common. They were both concerned with profits, and both had sources of revenue outside their major business interests. The great planter was often a land speculator. He also tended to be the neighborhood merchant, taking advantage of his monopolistic position to inflate prices. Like wealthy Yankees, the southern magnates turned moneylender, opening the way for them to acquire the assets of unfortunate borrowers.

The growing wealth of the magnates was enhanced by the eighteenth century boom in tobacco, rice, and indigo. It is not surprising, then, that the southern colonies produced some of the richest men of the period. Among them were Charles Carroll of Maryland and Robert Carter of Virginia, each of whom accumulated estates worth £100,000.

Associated with the great merchants and planters were practitioners of two old professions that became firmly established in the eighteenth century: law and medicine. Professional lawyers were held in ill repute in the early colonies, an attitude reflected as late as 1733 in Benjamin Franklin's *Poor Richard's Almanac:*

> God works wonders now and then;
> Behold! a lawyer, an honest man.

But the early colonial practice of arguing one's own case in court or employing a more learned friend or neighbor to do so proved impracticable in face of the accumulating decisions of colonial courts, the expanding body of colonial legislation, the increasing significance of parliamentary legislation relating to the colonies, and the mounting flow of orders and decrees from London, not all of them consistent. To protect his interests, the man of property needed professional skill. Thus, there slowly emerged a class of men devoted entirely to the practice of law, symbolized by Connecticut's authorization of the profession in 1708.

Some lawyers rose to fame as defenders of constitutional liberties, such as Andrew Hamilton, who established a basic precedent for freedom of the press, and James Otis and John Adams, who resisted the Crown's encroachments on colonial rights.

Most lawyers, however, were little concerned with issues of great constitutional import. They were preoccupied with such matters of property as wills, contracts, and collecting debts. Because of the inside knowledge of business lawyers acquired, they were able to take advantage of any opportunities that presented themselves, giving them a source of income besides legal fees. Lawyers engaged in land speculation, commercial and industrial investment, and money-lending. Many of them became wealthy: Roger Wolcott in Connecticut, William Fitzhugh in Virginia, and Thomas

Bordley in Maryland, who by his death in 1726 had accumulated the largest single fortune in the colony. Lawyers as a profession did not then dominate public life as they later came to do, but the tendency was there: lawyers eagerly sought out offices from royal officials and offered themselves for election to colonial legislatures. Political influence was one way to affluence.

As with lawyers, the growing complexity of colonial life called for professional medical practitioners. The primitiveness of early colonial days offered few inducements for doctors to migrate to the New World, and colonists had to make do with the folk medicine of housewives and clergymen. But as towns developed, congestion prompted the spread of epidemic diseases like smallpox. Seepage from slaughter houses and countless privies polluted water supplies, causing outbreaks of dysentery and deadly fevers. Seamen and traders brought diseases from abroad. Folk medicine could not cope with these afflictions, and the growing wealth of the colonies lured doctors from abroad. They came principally from Britain and France, and usually practiced their medicine (and dentistry, for in those days doctors acted as dentists, too) in the larger towns where they achieved both high status and considerable wealth.

Doctors also served a vital function as medical educators, training native-born American apprentices according to the standards of such prestigious medical schools as Edinburgh and Paris. Many physicians also contributed to colonial growth because of their interest in the larger scientific aspects of their profession. Doctor Cadwallader Colden, who got his medical degree at London and is best known to history as the Loyalist lieutenant-governor of New York in the stormy days before the Revolution, noted medicinal uses of many native plants. He also theorized that yellow-fever outbreaks might be traced to swamps and marshes, a provocative suggestion whose accuracy was not recognized for generations.

Even before the influx of British and French doctors, however, there was a small group of American doctors trained abroad or by doctors already here. Among them was Zabdiel Boylston of Massachusetts, who received his medical education from his father and another physician. Although he never earned a medical degree, young Boylston became the most famous of colonial doctors because of his successful demonstration of the value of inoculation in combating smallpox during an epidemic in Boston in 1721.

The Puritan and Anglican clergy continued to be part of the elites, although their status had declined since the early days. Both clerical and secular elites had little use for Baptists and Methodists, and they detested the emotional extravagances of the Great Awakening, a series of religious revivals that swept the colonies for a generation after 1726. Their disgust arose in part from the fact that the revivals appealed largely to poor people. More welcome to upper-class folk were the professors who taught in the nine colleges founded before the Revolution. The professors themselves were members of the educated elite, and many shared the elites' contempt for the masses and otherwise identified themselves with the outlook of merchants and planters.

The colonial elites did not constitute a closed class; there was movement in and out. Most newcomers came from the ranks immediately below the mercantile and planting aristocracies, but some poor men, such as Thomas Hancock, uncle of the

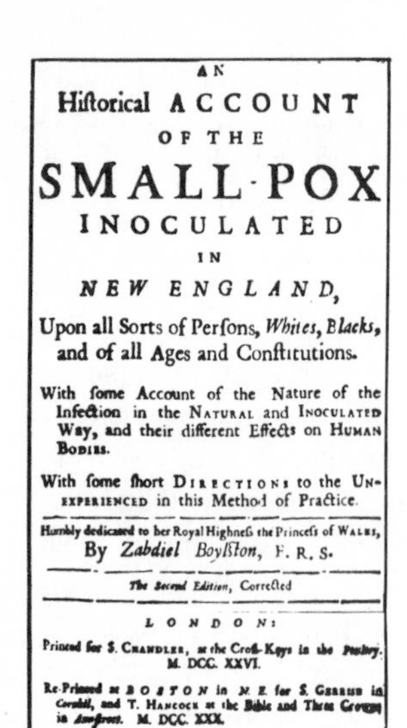
AN
Hiſtorical ACCOUNT
OF THE
SMALL-POX
INOCULATED
IN
NEW ENGLAND,
Upon all Sorts of Perſons, *Whites*, *Blacks*, and of all Ages and Conſtitutions.

With ſome Account of the Nature of the Infection in the NATURAL and INOCULATED Way, and their different Effects on HUMAN BODIES.

With ſome ſhort DIRECTIONS to the UNEXPERIENCED in this Method of Practice.

Humbly dedicated to her Royal Highneſs the Princeſs of WALES,
By *Zabdiel Boylston*, F. R. S.

The Second Edition, Corrected

LONDON:
Printed for S. CHANDLER, at the Croſs-Keys in the *Poultry*. M. DCC. XXVI.

Re-Printed at *BOSTON* in *N. E.* for S. GERRISH in *Cornhil*, and T. HANCOCK at the Bible and Three Crowns in *Annſtreet*. M. DCC. XXX.

Zabdiel Boylston of Boston reports on his campaign for inoculation against smallpox. He and others were attacked by mobs fearful that the doctors were spreading the dread disease.

famous John Hancock, made it to the top within their own lifetimes. Nor did members of the elites see eye to eye on all things. They were divided in opinions and interests, and when occasion demanded, dominant groups were prepared to use the powers of government to discipline other members who were endangering their interests. Thus, when West Indian importers barred entry of inferior flour and meat and complained of short weight, Pennsylvania and Rhode Island regulated their own merchants lest they lose the lucrative island trade. New York, where fraudulent suppliers apparently had more power, failed to act—and lost its West Indian markets.

The elites might very well have devoted their wealth and power to purely private interests, but they construed these interests in terms that included the public good. It was they who initiated measures for road, bridge, and harbor building; for fire prevention; for public sanitation; for rudimentary police controls; for enforcement of standard weights and measures. In so doing they served their own interests, but they served the larger public interest as well. As Carl Bridenbaugh has pointed out, the sense of civic responsibility in colonial towns far exceeded that of English cities.

Whatever their differences, elites were bound together by a feeling that they were better than the mass of the people. They sought to maintain their social distance from inferiors and to protect their wealth through intermarriage among themselves.

THE "MIDDLING SORT"

These inferiors were largely what was called the "middling sort," neither the very rich nor the very poor. In the towns they ranged from wholesale merchants who depended on the great merchants for credit and supplies to skilled workers who depended on wages for their sustenance. In the country, the middling sort included all farmers, exclusive of great landowners, who made a respectable living from owning and working their own land, usually with the aid of servants or slaves. In an economy literally dependent on horse power, the blacksmith occupied a key position both in town and country—a status enhanced by his expertise in folk veterinary medicine. Coopers were of great importance in seaports.

Two other categories—one old, one new—came within the middling sort. The old category included men and women in the "licensed trades"—skills with a direct public interest, such as butchers, bakers, teamsters, and porters. These were subject to strict municipal regulation, but in return the towns restricted competition in the trades, especially by excluding "interlopers" from other towns. The new category marked the beginnings of America's white-collar class. It was made up of literate young men who knew some shorthand and the latest bookkeeping methods, often learned at primitive "business schools" that sprang up in the towns. They were employed in the great merchant houses as clerks and bookkeepers and, when found trustworthy, as agents in other colonial ports or abroad. They were in demand because the expansion of commerce made it impossible for merchants to continue to handle all their business through family connections.

Within the ranks of the middling sort, however, divisions of interest appeared. Bitter quarrels between masters and skilled workers often erupted, as when employers hired black craftsmen, slave or free, over whites because the blacks were cheaper. Whites got authorities in many places to ban such black employment, but the practice continued. The laws often had loopholes, and public officials found it more politic to go along with masters than with workers.

Such disputes were most acute when jobs were scarce, as they often were in the eighteenth century. The loose apprenticeship system plus an influx of skilled immigrants produced a surplus of journeymen—men and women who had completed apprenticeship—during the depressions that followed the wars. Journeymen found it increasingly difficult to become masters, and small masters often found themselves back in the ranks of wage earners during the slumps. It was legal for masters to combine to fix wages, but unlawful for workers to combine to protect wages in bad times or raise them in good. Rebellious workers were also curbed by agreements among employers not to hire employees who lacked recommendations from their latest employer—an early example of the later practice of blacklisting active union members.

No permanent union organizations developed in this period, but some artisans did organize "friendly societies" designed to provide aid for sick members and death benefits for families. On occasion such societies served as informal labor organizations to enforce wage and other standards. Other types of concerted action were evident. In 1741 Boston ship caulkers agreed not to accept employers' scrip for wages. New York tailors went on strike in 1768, as did carpenters in a New Jersey iron works six years later. Peter Hasenclever, whose iron works in northern New Jersey became the single largest industrial undertaking in the colonial period, was confronted with slow-down strikes by his immigrant workers until he agreed to raise their wages.

Such forms of protest were not open to an important section of the colonial working class: the seamen. Although they were indispensable to growing marine trade, they were held in general disrepute. Good folk deplored their behavior on shore and ignored the brutalizing conditions of their work. Engaged in a highly skilled and hazardous calling, sailors nevertheless were paid miserable wages, fed poorly, crowded into literally lousy accommodations, and subjected to the absolute authority of the ship's master. Organized protest was mutiny—a capital crime—and individual protestors were whipped, sometimes to death. Canny Yankee merchants saw to it that ships were never overmanned; indeed, it was a rare ship that sailed with a full complement of seamen. In addition, seamen faced a hazard few landsmen experienced: impressment, a form of legal kidnapping we shall discuss later.

LESS THAN "MIDDLING"

Socially, there was a gap between the skilled workers and the growing number of unskilled laborers, their ranks swollen by a renewed emigration of indentured servants from England and a new kind of servant from Germany, called "redemptioners." Unlike the English, who came as single persons, the Germans migrated as families. By and large they were people of sufficient means to pay for all or part of their passage, but often before they sailed they were swindled or robbed of their money and their possessions.

Sea captains transported redemptioners on credit, packed them into overcrowded ships, and charged them exorbitant fares to justify extended terms of service when the newcomers were auctioned off at the American ports. Costs of passengers who died en route were charged against surviving relatives, a practice that meant additional service. Captains callously separated families when it brought them better returns. On occasion parents willingly gave up their youngsters, planning to use the proceeds to reduce their own terms and hoping the children would make good use of any training they received. Such children, whether bound out with parental permission or by captains, served until they were twenty-one. The redemptioners had little protection against abuses. They were strangers, ignorant of the English language and equally ignorant of their rights under the law. They were easy picking for sea captains and mainland masters alike, and the latter valued the immigrants all the more because of their docility and industry. Eventually, in 1764, prosperous Germans in Philadelphia founded a society that brought the plight of the newcomers to public attention, obtained legislation to curb some abuses, and provided aid to incoming families.

Indentured servants in the eighteenth century seemed more content with their lot than in the seventeenth, when rebellions flared sporadically. There appears to have been renewed opportunity for English-speaking servants to move up in society. Such were the origins of Daniel Dulany, a wealthy Maryland lawyer; Matthew Thornton, signer of the Declaration of Independence; and Charles Thomson, secretary of the Continental Congress. Yet what Richard B. Morris calls "the most serious insurrection of white workers" in the British mainland colonies broke out in 1768, although no English-speaking servants were involved. Italian and Greek servants, recruited to establish a colony at New Smyrna, Florida (then under British rule), armed themselves, shot an English overseer, and seized a ship in the hope of escaping to Cuba. The rebels were quickly overpowered, their leaders executed, and the rank and file pardoned.

Almost at the bottom of the social scale were the ''paupers,'' as the chronically poor were known. These included the ''deserving poor''—widows, the old, the blind, the physically and mentally ill—who, lacking relatives to care for them, were supported grudgingly by public funds or private charity. The ''undeserving poor,'' the able-bodied people who for one reason or another could not get steady work, were put to hard labor in the workhouses, grim and bleak places designed to keep welfare recipients to a minimum. Since authorities wanted to keep taxes at a minimum, they also used the workhouses as jails for criminals. This did little for the morale of honest poor folk, but it did symbolize the attitude of the affluent: poverty was a crime for which the poor, not society, were responsible.

Perhaps in even worse plight were the itinerant poor, people wandering from town to town in search of jobs. Since they had no claims against any community, they were ''warned out'' of towns where they sought to stay. That is, they were told they would not be allowed to become public charges and sent on their way, sometimes after being given a meal or two. Recent Irish immigrants were the most common victims, for they often had no resources at all and were in no demand as servants. They had to go on relief, much to the anger of Protestant taxpayers. Mobs rioted to keep the Catholic Irish from landing, and authorities harassed them from one town to another.

Another group of ''new poor'' were refugees fleeing the destruction of their farms in the back country, where the British and French and their Indian allies fought their wars. At first they were given warm welcome and support in the towns they fled to, but when they became a long-term burden, the welcome cooled. Soon they were accused of idling, drinking, and neglecting their children, and the attitude of authorities hardened. Even so, when the wars ended, many refugees either could not or would not return to their frontier homes. They stayed in the towns, swelling the numbers of the poor.

Doubtless, some drifted into the lowest stratum of society, the criminal class that gave signs of becoming a permanent feature of American life. These were not men and women who occasionally broke the law out of necessity, as when fathers stole food for their families, but people to whom crime was an acceptable way of making a living. The growing numbers of pickpockets, thieves, pimps, and burglars indicated that in some ways the New World was not so different from the Old.

Many of the poor came from the middling sort, a group that eroded at both ends of the scale as some moved up and others slipped down. The constant subdivision of family farms among sons and daughters eventually made for plots too small to support a family. Many made extra money by growing produce for sale in towns, but this source of income was drastically reduced when commercial farms located near towns began to dominate urban markets. The frequent wars, which encouraged farmers to go into debt when prices were high, ruined many when peace brought a collapse in prices and farmers could not pay their debts—a situation made worse by the chronic shortage of hard currency, in which debts had to be paid. Some colonies issued paper money or organized land banks to aid farmers, but while such steps slowed dispossession of yeoman farmers, they could not halt the process completely. Then the British government, to the joy of American creditors and the sorrow of the farmers, outlawed such devices. Farmers who no longer could make a living from their land went to work for others as part-time laborers, migrated to towns to find work, or tried their luck in the West. Within the towns, skilled workers were in danger of slipping into the ranks of the working poor during depressions.

Such developments, combined with the rapidly growing wealth of merchants, in the eighteenth century led to a concentration of wealth on the one hand and the emergence of what Jackson T. Main calls a ''permanent proletariat'' on the other. He estimates that on the eve of the Revolution propertyless workers made up 20 percent of the white population. At the other extreme, the richest 10 percent owned 45 percent of the wealth in the North and 50 percent in the South. Allan Kulikoff's figures for Boston reveal even more the general trend of erosion of the middling sort. In 1687 the top 10 percent of Boston's taxpayers owned nearly 47 percent of taxable property; in 1771 they owned over 63 percent. The middle group, making up six-tenths of the taxpayers, suffered a drop in their share of the wealth from 51 percent to 36 percent in the same period. The share of the bottom 30 percent fell from nearly 2.5 percent to 0.1 percent. As Henry George was to observe a century later, progress and poverty went hand in hand.

PEOPLE ON THE FRONTIER

Extremes of wealth and poverty were not so apparent in the West—the back country between long-established settlements and the forbidding Appalachians. Some farmers had large holdings, but most were poorer folk on small farms. Families labored from sunup to sundown, making a bare living, much as the early settlers had done. Individualists all, they nevertheless had to aid one another to survive. Neighbors helped each other erect cabins and barns; shared tools, implements, and any available oxen; contributed to each other's lore of wilderness farming; and joined together first against Indian peoples and later against more insidious foes among seaboard merchants and planters.

The result was a strong sense of frontier community, enhanced by remoteness from centers of civilization. Under the pressures of poverty, incessant hard labor, and isolation, frontier people shucked off the graces and amenities of seaboard living. They cultivated only those attributes that had survival value: sheer physical strength and courage, a crude pragmatic way of thinking, an assertive egalitarianism, and an obsession with purely material things coupled with the highly emotional religious outlook that found an outlet in the Great Awakening. Symbolically, but for purely functional reasons, frontier folk abandoned European dress for Indian. They clothed themselves in deerskins, and in hot weather the men wore as little as Indians.

For westerners, respectable eastern folk had a contemptuous term: ''buckskins.'' The term had many implications: that frontier people were wild and uncouth; that they were whites who had reverted to savagery; that they were weaklings and incompetents who could not survive in civilized society; that they were the outcasts of colonial society, living in drunkenness and immorality. The usually perceptive Crevecoeur in 1782 wrote off frontier folk as ''no better than carnivorous animals of a superior rank.''

In fact, frontier people were simply evolving their own way of life while adhering to the values, if not the forms, of their upbringing. Hard work, thrift, and private property were as much respected in the West as in the East. The charge of immorality paradoxically grew from the frontier's adherence to monogamous marriage. Since magistrates and clergymen were scarce in the back country, men and women married themselves in public ceremonies that carried community sanction. In their own eyes and in those of the community, such marriages were as binding as any performed according to the forms of law. Indeed, when magistrates and clergymen did appear later, couples were formally married and their children duly baptized.

Nevertheless, the stereotype of the westerners persisted. Among other things, it proved politically useful when back-country people were sufficiently numerous to challenge the rule of the seaboard elites. So exploitive was such rule and so indifferent were ruling groups to western grievances that frontiersmen, like poorer farmers elsewhere, were driven to armed revolt. Bacon's Rebellion of 1676 was not purely a protest of the West or the poor, but the participation of both westerners and poor folk gave the movement its popular strength. Although the rebellion was savagely repressed, armed bands of Virginia farmers systematically destroyed tobacco crops six years later in a futile attempt to raise prices. Two of their leaders were hanged.

In 1764, 600 armed Pennsylvania frontiersmen, the "Paxton boys," aroused by attempted arrest of their leaders for murdering Indians, marched on Philadelphia. Only the suave diplomacy of Benjamin Franklin averted open warfare, and westerners gained added representation in the Pennsylvania legislature. There was no Franklin to mediate in the Carolinas. In 1769 "Regulators" and militia battled at the Saluda River in South Carolina. The government abandoned its coercive policy against the organized frontiersmen and agreed to establish courts in the back country, where no courts had yet been set up. North Carolina "Regulators" were not so fortunate. A bloody clash with militia at the Alamance River in 1771 broke the back of their resistance. Nine of their men were killed, as were nine of the militia. Seven captured "Regulator" leaders were put to death. Other activists fled from the colony.

WHAT WERE THE "MOBS"?

Such uprisings testify to some of the tensions in white colonial society. So also do the activities of "mobs," which played so significant a role in urban life. Today we associate the term with gangsterism, lynchings, and other mass violence we disapprove of. In the eighteenth century *mob* had a different connotation. Despite riot acts passed in England and the colonies to curb mass action, the mob was nevertheless accepted as a fact of political life. When public authorities failed in their duties, when major grievances were not redressed, when government acted arbitrarily and capriciously, then even respectable citizens felt they had a right to take direct action. The right had its limits. Action could not be taken against the Crown as such, for that would have been revolution. Also it could not be so well organized and prolonged as to constitute rebellion. Colonial Americans observed these limits and even imposed some of their own. Boston mobs, for example, never acted on Sundays.

Usually the mob had specific objectives. When these were attained, the mob

Rhode Island Historical Society

Colonial mob action was not confined to land. Here a mob in 1772 sets fire to the *Gaspee*, a British ship enforcing antismuggling laws.

dissolved. People took to the streets to protest food shortages. They tried to keep Irish immigrants from landing. They closed down brothels. They rioted against inoculation, fearing it would spread rather than protect against smallpox. Dr. Zabdiel Boylston and his clerical supporter, Cotton Mather, were early victims of such anti-inoculation mobs, but Boston was not the only town where violent attempts were made to halt the new practice. On many occasions mobs were led by prominent members of the community.

Nor was mob action confined to towns. In New Jersey and New York farmers rioted to protest injustices in such matters as land titles and conditions of tenancy.

During the eighteenth century, however, mob action took on a political color as colonists resorted to it in protest against British policies, especially after 1763. In that year Britain attempted to pay off debts incurred in the French and Indian War by levying new import taxes on the colonies. Further, the Royal Navy was empowered to collect the taxes. Both moves threatened the lucrative mainland trade with the West Indies, which had flourished with the connivance of a corrupt customs service. Two years later, in another move to assert British authority, Parliament passed the hated Stamp Act.

Both actions resulted in a series of mob uprisings along the Eastern seaboard that rapidly became outright challenges to British authority. Parliament repealed the

Stamp Act, while asserting its authority over the colonies. The mobs helped divide colonial society. On the one hand were British officialdom and its American allies. On the other were those elements of the colonial elites whose interests were menaced by new British policies and their allies among "the baser sort" of people.

Impressment was another tie that bound these latter groups together. Impressment was a polite term for kidnapping men and boys for involuntary service in the Royal Navy. Impressment was necessary because conditions in the navy were so miserable that there were never enough volunteers to meet the navy's requirements. Impressment took two forms: kidnapping merchant seamen and fishermen at sea, and forcibly rounding up poor able-bodied males in seaports, regardless of whether they were seamen.

Impressment soon led the well-to-do to discover that they could not get along without the services of those whom they branded, as at a Boston town meeting in 1747, as "persons of mean and vile condition." Impressment stripped ships of needed crewmen, and seamen on shore swiftly deserted ports where press gangs were active, thus giving a competitive advantage to those ports where the navy was not so zealous. Boston suffered especially from the raids by press gangs. Further, fishermen and inland farmers stopped supplying markets where they might be impressed. Faced with shortages of food and firewood and menaced in their prospects of trade, merchants tried to end the practice legally. When such appeals failed, antiimpressment riots broke out in every port, led by seamen but supported by upper-class public opinion. The sailors looked upon their struggle as one of human rights against the intolerable power structure of the time, embodied in the Royal Navy. As the struggle against Britain intensified, the seamen's fight for their own independence merged with the larger war of national liberation.

If sailors had allies among the affluent, they also had friends among the working poor: longshoremen, sail makers, rope makers, and other workers whose labor made possible the sailing of ships. The closely knit fraternity of maritime workers, already aroused over impressment, was angered even more by British army actions. Having established garrisons in major towns after 1765, the army permitted off-duty soldiers to engage in civilian occupations. The soldiers, who were fed, clothed, and housed at public expense, were able to work for lower pay than men and women who supported themselves and their families. Since much of the work on the docks was unskilled, soldiers gravitated there. Displaced civilians found allies among the seamen, and mobs soon took action to drive soldiers from the docks. Actual fighting flared up in New York in 1770, when British soldiers and American workers fought the bloody battle of Golden Hill, with many casualties on both sides. That year another confrontation culminated in the Boston Massacre, in which five Americans were killed. First to fall was Crispus Attucks, a black seaman.

THE SPIRIT OF EQUALITY

The participation of sailors, longshoremen, and others of what aristocrats called "the rabble" in anti-British activities points up the growing egalitarian sentiment of the eighteenth century. This feeling was expressed by such men as John Wise and Sam

Adams. Wise, son of an indentured servant and a clergyman in Massachusetts, wrote in 1717 that "every man must be conceived to be perfectly in his own power and disposal, and not to be controlled by the authority of any other. . . . every man must be acknowledged equal to every other man." Sam Adams, idolized by the workers of Boston because he espoused their causes, wrote in 1771 that governments were organized by all the people to promote equality. That government "which admits equality in the most extensive degree . . . is the best," he said.

Such formulations, vague though they may seem today, spoke to the countless workers and farmers who could find no redress for their grievances in existing institutions. Freedom from British rule, followed by a popular government dedicated to equality, held out prospect of a better life.

WOMEN ASSERT THEMSELVES

The egalitarian spirit was also manifest among women, although those of the elite found the freedoms they had earlier enjoyed increasingly restricted. Women continued to be employed in a wide variety of occupations, and many, attracted by the profits of trade, set themselves up as merchants. Such enterprises were usually small, but some women became substantial wholesale merchants. At least one, Mary Alexander of New York, won a contract to supply British troops during the French and Indian war. Legislation and court decisions enhanced the property rights of widows. That girls should attend public schools became accepted as a matter of course in New England. In some colonies there, women who owned the requisite amount of property were allowed to vote. Colonial women also enjoyed a freedom of movement unknown to their sisters in England, where it was dangerous for an unescorted woman to travel. Sarah Knight went from Boston to New York in 1704 with no hazards except those offered by floods, poor roads, and bad accommodations. Her experience was typical rather than exceptional. Women servants shared in the general rise of servant status, even to the extent of trying to choose their own employers. In 1734 a New York newspaper advertised servants who were available only to ladies who would guarantee that their husbands would not "do tender women mischief."

But in other ways women's freedom became more limited than before. A basic protection of married women was lost when the British government outlawed colonial divorces. Wives who could not afford, and later could not get, divorces simply ran away. They were advertised for in newspapers in the same way as fugitive servants and slaves, but some spirited runaways retorted with ads that were not at all flattering to their husbands!

Perhaps the most significant shift was in the status of upper-class women. In the early decades women of all strata were economically functional. They shared the labor of men, although they alone bore the burden of childbearing, and they shared the sweat and calloused hands of men as well as the men's tobacco and rum. In the eighteenth century the typical upper-class woman avoided sweat as if it were smallpox. She cultivated soft and dainty hands, wrinkled her nose at the lower-class women who still puffed at their pipes, and looked upon public drunkenness as a disgrace. One economic function remained to her, managing her husband's household, which involved no manual labor since the work was done by servants. Her basic function apart from bearing children was social. The wife was an item of conspicuous consumption, demonstrating to the world her husband's wealth and prestige, much like his elegant house, his landscaped estate, and his liveried servants. Girls were trained for that role, which meant that their education was limited. Abigail Adams noted, "It was fashionable to ridicule female learning. . . . Female education in the best families went no further than writing and arithmetic; in some few and rare instances, music and dancing."

With property considerations so important among the elites and those just below them, arranged marriages, with appropriate prenuptial contracts, became an accepted custom. Forced marriages were hardly necessary, since young women had internalized the values of their society and since the circle of friends and acquaintances was limited to their own kind. There were, of course, rebels who eloped with their lovers, but such behavior was looked at askance by those who shared Benjamin Franklin's view that marriage was a matter of prudence, not romance.

Many young women played out their roles as giddy, frivolous playthings—until they were married, at least—but there were still among the elites women of strong religious background who looked upon marriage and subjection to one's husband as God's will. One such woman was eulogized by her husband when she died at age twenty-four after bearing six children, four of whom died: "She would sometime say to me that bearing, tending and burying children was hard work, and that she had done a great deal of it for one of her age, . . . yet would say it was the work she was made for, and what God in His providence had called her to, and she could freely do it all for Him."

Such religious devotion was uncommon among literate people of the eighteenth century, strongly influenced as they were by the rationalism of the Enlightenment. Yet among the poor, traditional religious impulses ran deep, as exemplified in the Great Awakening. They found unique expression in Ann Lee (1736–84), who became leader of the Shakers. Under her influence the sect took on a strong feminist cast. She herself was regarded as the Second Coming of Christ, thus revealing that both men and women were necessary for the revelation of God, who was both Father and Mother.

Far removed from her were three other notable colonial women: Jane Colden, Eliza Lucas Pinckney, and Phyllis Wheatley. Jane Colden, daughter of the famous Doctor Cadwallader Colden, was America's first woman botanist. She discovered nearly 400 new plants, made detailed drawings of many of them, and classified them according to the then new Linnaean system. Eliza Pinckney was interested in plants for strictly economic reasons. She experimented with various crops to increase the income of her father's South Carolina plantations, which she managed whenever he was away. She eventually produced a superior strain of indigo, much in demand as a dye, which soon became a major source of the colony's prosperity. Phyllis Wheatley was America's first recognized black poet, a woman who won acclaim in both England and the colonies for her talent.

FOR FURTHER READING

A good general introduction is Arthur M. Schlesinger, Sr., *The Birth of the Nation* (1969). Carl M. Bridenbaugh describes urban life in *Cities in the Wilderness* (1964) and *Cities in Revolt* (1964). See also his *Colonial Craftsman* (1950). Class distinctions are explored in Gary B. Nash, ed., *Class and Society in Early America* (1970). The book contains a reprint of Aubrey Land's significant article, "Economic Base and Social Structure: The Northern Chesapeake in the Eighteenth Century." For a discussion of the role of colonial mobs see Pauline Maier, *From Resistance to Revolution* (1972).

Aspects of Southern life are discussed in Richard M. Brown, *The South Carolina Regulators* (1963); Richard L. Morton, *Colonial Virginia* (1960); and Julia C. Spruill, *Women's Life and Work in the Southern Colonies* (1938).

For discussion of specific aspects of colonial life see Richard B. Morris, *Government and Labor in Early America* (1946); Lawrence Cremin, *American Education: The Colonial Experience* (1970); Richard Shryock, *Medicine and Society in America* (1960); and S. E. Ahlstrom, *Religious History of the American People*, Vol. 1 (1972).

4 beginnings of the black community

The year 1619 is often referred to as marking the beginning of black slavery in America. This is a misunderstanding of what happened when the famous (but unidentified) Dutch warship disposed of twenty blacks at Jamestown. English law made no provision for slavery, but it did for indentured servants; thus, the early blacks were treated as servants. They served for a period of years, then were released from further service and paid the customary "freedom dues" of clothing, tools, and food. Some of these freed blacks eventually operated their own farms, established families, and participated in public affairs.

Gradually black servants lost the indentured status and became "servants for life"—a status first formalized in 1641 in, ironically, the Massachusetts Body of Liberties. Even this did not establish slavery as an institution, for children of "perpetual servants" were presumed free. Beginning in the 1660s laws were passed in various colonies, both northern and southern, providing that children would assume the status of the mother, a tacit admission that in interracial sexual relations the male was likely to be white.

In these early days, the black population grew slowly. Most planters were really small farmers, greedy for cheap labor but unable to put up the capital to buy slaves. Besides, there were problems of communication between Africans and Englishmen, and differences in color disturbed the yeoman farmer. Also, blacks as well as whites proved susceptible to epidemics and suffered with whites when Indian peoples struck back against encroachment on their lands. There were only 300 blacks in Virginia in 1650 and so few in Maryland that they escaped legislative attention until 1663.

But by the end of the century the situation had changed drastically. Fluctuations in the tobacco market coupled with restrictive trade regulations imposed by England forced out many of the yeoman planters. The result was the rise of the plantations, great spreads of land devoted to producing tobacco, rice, indigo, and later cotton and worked by servile labor.

The labor supply was a major problem for the plantations. White indentured servants proved increasingly unsatisfactory. They served only as long as required, and just as the master was about to maximize his profit on them, they quit. When they ran away—as they did frequently—it was difficult to reclaim them, no matter how strict the laws were, for runaways found it easy to melt into the white population. Those who had been the victims of swindlers and kidnappers and were indentured against their will had little incentive to work hard. Further, the growing number of turbulent former servants, who had neither property nor masters, stirred fears in Virginia about the internal stability of the colony.

The shortcomings of white labor pointed up the advantages of black slaves. For little more than the price of a white servant's contract the planters could buy a servant for life, and after the laws of the 1660s and 1670s, they could also acquire all that servant's children for the cost of the servant alone. Here was a labor supply that expanded itself, no mean addition to a master's assets. The female black servant also could be worked in the fields, which custom forbade for white women. The slave was more subject to discipline than a white, for he or she no longer enjoyed even the few rights English law assigned to white servants. Above all, black people could not run away as safely as whites—their color betrayed them.

Such considerations help explain the black population explosion of the eighteenth century. Planters preferred black to white labor; the aggressive English slave trade, backed by a friendly government, was only too willing to supply the colonies' needs; and the planters, for reasons of self-interest, followed policies that fostered natural increase.

Thus, in the mainland British colonies, while white population increased rapidly, the black population increased even faster. Indeed, says Winthrop Jordan, the total population of what is now the United States "contained a higher proportion of Negroes in the period 1730–65 than at any other time in the nation's history." By 1765 blacks outnumbered whites in South Carolina by more than two to one. Virginia, which in 1670 counted only 2,000 blacks in a total population of 40,000, had 120,000 blacks compared to 173,000 whites in 1756.

Nor was the growth confined to the South. Large-scale farming employing black slave labor developed in Rhode Island and eastern Connecticut, reproducing on a minor scale the plantation system of the South. Blacks outnumbered whites in such areas. Rhode Island was also the center of the Yankee slave trade, which helps explain why its black population in relation to total population was second in the North only to that of New York colony, which was 14 percent black. New York's primacy was due to the large number of blacks who worked in New York City as sailors, longshoremen, teamsters, and servants. Growing black populations also lived in other major seaport towns.

The rapid growth of the black population bred tensions among whites. In those areas where blacks were the majority, whites grew fearful. These fears were intensified by the periodic wars with France, which brought both economic dislocation (especially in the postwar depressions) and anxiety that the French and their Spanish allies would use blacks and Indians against the English colonists. Whites reacted with ever more stringent slave codes, both in the North and South. Lightly applied in times of comparative calm, the codes were severely enforced in times of crisis, particularly in cases of real or imagined slave rebellion.

Two assumptions underlay the codes. One was the absolute authority of the master over the slave, set forth succinctly by none other than John Locke, the great exponent of the liberal tradition in Anglo-American political theory. When he drafted the Fundamental Constitutions of Carolina in 1669, he provided that "every freeman . . . shall have absolute power and authority over his Negro slaves." The other assumption was typified in the slave code adopted by Carolina, which held that blacks were "of barbarous, wild, savage natures, . . . wholly unqualified to be governed by the laws, customs, and practices" that applied to white society. These beliefs held sway throughout the colonies, no matter whether the codes were harsh, as in Carolina, or mild, as in New England. In fact, relative mildness or harshness depended on whether the black population was large or small in relation to the number of whites. This was as true in the North as in the South. New York, with its high proportion of blacks, had a tough code, and repressive local ordinances were adopted in those areas of Rhode Island and Connecticut where the black population was significant. Massachusetts, with its relatively few blacks, had a mild code.

The codes varied from colony to colony, but they possessed some common elements. Slaves were forbidden to be absent from their work places without the master's permission or to be on the streets after dark. They could not carry firearms, clubs, or sticks. They could not visit taverns or associate with free blacks. They could not own property. They were barred from testifying in court against whites in most colonies. Intermarriage with whites was prohibited, although in New England only Massachusetts specifically forbade it. Illegal sexual relations between whites and blacks were more heavily punished than relations between whites. Slaves could not legally marry in the plantation colonies, although some masters tried as best they could to maintain stable family relationships. In New England, slave marriages were legally valid, but their duration depended on the master's fortunes or the decisions of his executors when he died. After all, slaves were property. As property they were subject to such discipline as a master chose to impose, including "moderate" corporal punishment. If a slave died in the course of such "moderate" whipping, the master was usually absolved of guilt—surely, the stock defense ran, no one would destroy his own property!

Maintaining the slave system, however, required more than upholding the authority of the master. Public authority also had to be invoked. The interests of the slaveholding community required that individual masters and whites generally be held to their responsibilities in keeping blacks in their place. So, whites were required to apprehend suspected fugitives and to man the patrols that operated nightly in those areas of great black population. Whites could not entertain slaves or buy goods from them, and they had to report instantly to authorities any black behavior they found suspicious. For reasons of personal interest individual masters might wink at infractions of the law by their slaves, but public authority insisted these be punished.

Accused slaves were usually tried in special slave courts made up of white officials, with the blacks barred from testifying against whites (except in some northern colonies). Those found guilty of murder or rape of white women were hanged, and the master compensated for the loss of his property. For such crimes as robbery Southern slaves had their ears cut off and were suitably flogged. For other offenses slaves were castrated, flogged, and branded.

AFRO-AMERICAN CULTURE

Given the nature of slavery and its eventual entrenchment in law and custom, slaves, if they wished to survive, had few alternatives except to adapt. Adaptation, though, was not passive acceptance. Rather it was a complex and pragmatic psychological process in which generations of slaves worked out ways of getting along with white people while at the same time maintaining their own sense of dignity and self-respect. This process resulted in two levels of black behavior. For whites, blacks displayed the responses whites expected of them. Whites wanted "Sambo," and blacks gave them Sambo: forever chuckling, not too bright, always deferential, aping the ways of white folks. Doubtless many blacks learned this mode of behavior all too well and did indeed become Sambos, but to assume that all slaves were Sambos is to ignore the second level of slave behavior—that of maintaining their self-respect within a hostile white culture. In this process slaves developed a subculture of their own, with its own subtle means of communication, its own folklore, its own system of values, and later its own interpretations of Christianity.

Black, or Afro-American, culture may be broadly defined as the way of life blacks evolved to adapt to slavery while keeping alive their sense of humanity. It was a product of a unique historical situation, arising out of the transplanting of Africans to the New World. As slaves, they could neither transplant African institutions nor continue entirely African patterns of behavior. Coming from diverse peoples with different traditions and languages and, until the rise of the great plantations, widely dispersed and often isolated, Africans had to adapt to white ways. Black culture was the product of interaction between blacks and whites in a given historical context.

To adapt to slavery blacks had to be very flexible. This was true not only for those suddenly wrenched from freedom to bondage, but also for those born in bondage, since slavery itself was a constantly changing institution. It spread throughout the Atlantic seaboard, from Massachusetts to the newest colony of Georgia, which early abandoned its founder's dream of a free society. Black experience and responses that worked in New England did not prepare a slave for life in South Carolina. And as the plantation system grew in the eighteenth century slaves found themselves increasingly isolated from the master. On the great plantations they might rarely see their owner, for such plantations were usually managed by overseers, a new class of white men who made their living by acting for absentee owners.

Slavery became increasingly differentiated at the same time that it became concentrated. That is, slaves were wanted not simply as field hands but also as house servants, skilled artisans, seamen, longshoremen, and miners. The emergence of a class of skilled black workers indicates still another aspect of slavery: it gradually became an urban as well as a rural institution, reaching its highest point in the nineteenth century. Some such blacks worked directly for their masters, working in small foundries or in construction work, for example. Other blacks were rented out by their owners for specific periods of time, the owners receiving the slaves' earnings. Still other slaves "hired their own time." That is, they agreed with their owners to find employment on their own and to divide the income on some mutually acceptable basis. Such arrangements made it possible for some urban slaves to buy freedom for themselves and sometimes for their wives and children too.

White businessmen were eager to get black labor. Black artisans were as good as white and their presence served to check what employers thought the "outrageous" wage demands of white workers. The very conditions of city life weakened white control of blacks, however, especially of those rented out or hiring their own time. Blacks got together, as did whites, in taverns—and once the fear of insurrection gripped the white psyche, whites looked on any gathering of blacks with suspicion. Blacks walked the streets after dark, sometimes in boisterous groups. It was easy to attribute the mounting urban crime and vice to them. Public authority then undertook to replace the authority of the master. Every major town took steps to curb the freedom of "turbulent" blacks. Tavern keepers were forbidden to sell liquor to blacks, and those parading after dark were to be whipped. Connecticut provided not only that every black disturber of the peace should receive up to thirty lashes but also that any "defamation" of a white person by a black would earn the black forty lashes!

Most slaves, of course, lived in the rural South on plantations. Many lived on small plantations, but more and more of them lived on the great plantations that were driving out the smaller farmer. There they planted, cultivated, and harvested crops of tobacco, rice, and indigo, working long hours the year round. It is significant that the South Carolina legislature, after the slave uprisings of the 1730s, tried to limit the working day to fifteen hours in the busy season and to fourteen in the "slack" season. In his spare time the slave was expected to grow much of his own food. The slave quarters usually were wooden huts, where slaves cooked their food over open fires set in the middle of the earthen floor and got what rest they could on primitive bedding laid on the ground. While at work, the slaves were under the constant surveillance of the black driver who used the whip to keep his charges from dawdling, regardless of whether they were men, women, or children.

Whether working or resting, slaves were always at the mercy of the overseer or master, subject to punishment for real or imagined infraction of rules. But even if slaves were faithful and obedient, they had no security. A good master might get into financial trouble or might die, problems often solved by selling the slaves. Ironically, the most hard-working were often the first to go because they fetched the highest prices. Slaves might well have to adjust to a succession of new masters in the course of a lifetime.

The trauma of enslavement was great, but not sufficient to strip slaves of their sense of identity. They had neither property nor institutions. They worked without wages from sunup to sundown, but from sundown to sunup, as George Rawick has pointed out, the slave was as much a human being as a slave could be. The slaves could indulge their own memories, tell of their people's past as it came to them through oral tradition, and reveal the workings of their deities. And these were passed on from generation to generation, until the Ibo and the Mandingo faded away to be replaced by the American black to whom the traditions were bequeathed, now melded into a common Afro-American heritage.

All these became fused in a black religion embodying various aspects of African belief, which persisted because many masters resisted the conversion of slaves to Christianity. Some clergymen tried to persuade masters that Christianity would make slaves more docile and industrious, but many masters were not persuaded. They believed Christianity might make slaves too discontented with their lot. The basic Christian belief that all people were equal in the sight of God was a bit too egalitarian for their taste. Thus, slaves were left largely to their own traditions until the nineteenth century, when masters concluded that conversion provided an additional means of control.

Just as no line could be drawn between spiritual and material affairs in medieval Europe, so no line could be drawn in black religion. Religious belief was an integral part of living, explaining not only the eternal but also the earthly problems of humanity. And since black living was community living, black religion was a community affair, involving ritual dancing, chanting, invocations by the leading religious figure of the community (sometimes a native African priest fallen victim to the slavers), and "messages." In contrast to the church services of Europe, the members of the black "churches" actively participated in theirs, singing, shouting, finding release from tensions in whole-hearted emotional expression. It was this community expression that so vexed whites. Masters cared little about their slaves' beliefs, but they cared a great deal about their getting together without white supervision. When such meetings were forbidden—as they often were—slaves met secretly in some hidden, isolated spot to express their joys and sorrows and to invoke the aid of sympathetic black deities.

If religion played a basic role in developing the black community, so also did the slave family. Much has been written arguing that since no stable family life was possible under slavery a tradition of sexual irresponsibility became established, and that tradition in turn contributes to the problems of today's urban ghettos. Such a view fails to take into account that blacks carried with them from Africa their own family pattern and shaped it to the needs of slavery. The African pattern was not the nuclear family of the whites, but the extended family characteristic of peasant societies. Such a family consisted not only of parents and children but also grandparents, aunts, uncles, cousins, and other relatives, no matter how remote the kinship. Children were thus rarely without a home. Their parents might die or be sold, but there were usually relatives to care for them and nurture the sense of family.

Parents could not be legally married in the eyes of white law, but they were so regarded in the eyes of the black community, which enforced its own sanctions of mutual pledges and public rituals before a couple could live together with the community's approval. On some plantations that were prosperous and remained within one family for generations, such couples might have lifelong unions. Even so, families were broken up. The only solace for those taken away from their immediate families was that they might well find relatives in their new "homes" and perhaps a new partner with whom to share a slave's life. This was not enough for many slaves; the number of runaways who sought husbands or wives from whom they had been forcibly separated was large. This evidence of strong family affection is all the more impressive when one recalls the dire punishments meted out to captured runaways.

Whatever refuge the extended family afforded blacks, it could not protect them from slavery's corrosive effects on family life. The slave husband and father was powerless to resist sexual demands by whites on his wife and daughters, just as the women and girls had little choice but to yield in what was the most humiliating symbol of white supremacy. Children learned early that authority rested not with their fathers, but with their masters, who could punish their fathers with impunity or sell them off as casually as they sold horses. The corrosion worked in another way, too. Some slave women enjoyed the privileges which came with being a master's mistress—gifts of jewelry and clothing, a subtle but well-understood (among blacks) sharing of the master's authority, and expectation that their children would be given special consideration, perhaps even freedom. Such women took risks for their privileges. Many white wives closed their eyes to their husbands' infidelities with blacks—until they saw the black women as dangerous. Then they used their authority to have the black women sold or barbarously punished.

From such sexual exploitation of black women came an addition to the black community: a growing number of those of mixed descent. In some Caribbean societies such folk were granted privileges and status denied to pure blacks, but this was not the case in mainland America. Here they were regarded as "niggers," still slaves, often sold by their own fathers. Some white fathers, however, saw to it that their black children were freed and educated. These blacks and their children became the free black elites of Charleston, Mobile, and New Orleans.

The role of the slave mother was crucial and difficult. If she was sold, some of her children likely went with her. If the father was sold, she had all the family responsibilities. Thus, in addition to the work expected of her in the field or in the master's house, she had to bring up her own children. In cases of long-lived unions she might share authority with the father, but in most cases it was on the mother that responsibility fell for training children in the dual role of playing Sambo for whites while behaving as acceptable members of the black community.

Binding the growing slave community together was an informal but effective communications network that tied even the remotest plantation to the cities, and linked blacks of New England to those of Georgia. The grapevine carried news of special significance to blacks as well as gossip that helped relatives keep in touch with each other. The sources that contributed to the grapevine included house servants, who learned more at the "big house" than whites ever dreamed of; urban slaves, who usually had information to pass on when they ran into plantation slaves; black seaman who sailed into seaports all along the Atlantic coast; and free blacks, who despite all the laws to the contrary, kept up contact with their brethren in bondage. Lacking the written word, blacks developed their own means of communication: a spoken language that combined English and African, with its own syntax, its own idioms, its own inflections, and its own nuances of meaning. These nuances provided excellent cover for black communication, even in the presence of whites.

BLACK RESISTANCE

Black adaptation to slavery was not mere passive accommodation; it involved some degree of resistance. Indeed, unless slaves were always to be Sambos, they had to assert themselves. And such assertion was common, ranging all the way from such devices as feigned stupidity through sabotage of tools and implements to arson and murder, depending on the relationship between master and slave. Runaways were frequent. But many fugitives never left home, so to speak. Disgusted with conditions where they worked, but unable or unwilling to undertake a long journey, they simply resorted to nearby swamps, woods, or thickets, remaining hidden while supplied by sympathetic slaves. From their hiding places they bargained with their masters on the conditions of their return—a primitive form of the strike that was especially effective at the height of the planting or harvesting seasons. The fugitives took risks, of course, but taking risks was part of the slave culture.

Resistance sometimes flared into open rebellion. This might take the form of individual black response to white violence, as when a slave tried to protect himself by hitting back at a master or overseer. This was an offense punishable with death in the plantation colonies. If the slave did not make good his escape, he was turned over to the public authorities to be made an example of. More often, the master, with an eye to his property's value, did the job himself, gathering other slaves around to witness the rebel whipped into submission. On occasion, particularly on small farms where slaves were few and rigorous sanctions were felt less necessary than on great plantations, individual rebels were left alone as long as they continued to do their work.

Much more ominous to whites were the collective rebellions that flared up in the mainland colonies from time to time. While never as great or as bloody as the slave rebellions in the West Indies and in Latin America, they nevertheless struck panic among whites. The record is unclear on the precise number of slave revolts. Many revolts did occur. Others were planned but betrayed. Some "conspiracies," for which the alleged participants were duly punished, took place only in the minds of informers eager to win cash and freedom from grateful authorities or in the imaginations of whites increasingly fearful of the blacks around them. "Proof," of course, was nearly always forthcoming. After a few sessions in the torture chamber, most victims were ready to confess anything.

Of the rebellions in colonial times, two of the most important took place in New York in 1712 and 1741. The uprising of 1712 was led by slaves recently imported from Africa, involved at least twenty-four blacks, and was carefully planned. Before the fighting ended, nine whites were killed; the slave leaders committed suicide rather than surrender. The aroused whites rounded up all blacks even remotely suspected of having shared in the conspiracy. Most were later released. Twenty-seven slaves were finally tried before a special court, and twenty-one were convicted. These suffered what Governor Hunter called "the most exemplary punishments that could possibly be thought of." Four of the prisoners were burned alive; the body of another was broken on the wheel; and the rest were hanged. The other New York uprising, in 1741, was significant in that white people were charged with providing the slaves with the necessary arms. The whites, including a Catholic priest, were hanged, as were eighteen blacks; an additional thirteen blacks were burned alive.

Rebellions and conspiracies were frequent in the South. As early as 1663 a planned rebellion of black slaves and white indentured servants was betrayed in Gloucester County, Virginia. Purely black plots and uprisings followed at intervals, climaxing with the Stono uprising of 1739. In that year about twenty rebellious slaves rose up near Charleston, South Carolina, armed themselves, and set out for Spanish Florida, adding recruits as they went, burning houses, and killing any whites that tried to stop them. Eventually they were overwhelmed by superior force, but not before thirty whites and forty-four blacks lost their lives.

FREE BLACKS

Not all blacks were slaves. There was a small but growing number of free blacks scattered throughout the colonies who made their living as farmers, fishermen, laborers, and artisans. Some were descendants of those early blacks who had served as indentured servants. Some were slaves legally freed by their masters. A few were former slaves given freedom by a grateful legislature for some meritorious service, such as informing on a conspiracy. A considerable number were slaves who had freed themselves, fugitives who had eluded capture. And there were some who could little enjoy their freedom—the sick, injured, or aged slaves "freed" by their masters to become public charges.

For years free blacks enjoyed a status superior to that of slaves but not quite that of whites. As slavery spread, whites sought to widen the social distance between themselves and blacks, and the status of free blacks declined. There was no uniformity in the decline—it varied from colony to colony—but the trend was decisive.

Political freedom was drastically curtailed in the eighteenth century, as various colonies, such as Virginia, Georgia, and the Carolinas, stripped free blacks of their rights to vote and hold office. In the colonies without such laws, white opposition effectively checked black participation in governmental affairs. New England continued to allow blacks to testify in court against whites, but the Southern colonies did not—although slaves were permitted to testify against free blacks. Southern colonies required blacks to serve in the militia, while New England did not permit such service. Free blacks, instead, were compelled to labor on public works. When war came—as it did frequently—blacks were expected to serve, law or no law. They did indeed serve in every colonial war.

An important reason for the decline in black status was the intensification of white racism with the spread of slavery. So long as blacks were a small and manageable part of the population, whites felt they could accord rights to them without endangering themselves. But the expansion of slavery increased the number of blacks to be dealt with—in some places, there were more blacks than whites—and whites felt endangered. The stereotype of the black as savage and immoral took on new life as whites sought to protect themselves from imagined dangers. The stereotype extended beyond slaves to free blacks. Indeed, it fixed on free blacks as the real source of danger.

Free blacks were considered dangerous because, despite the laws, they sheltered fugitive slaves. Again in defiance of laws, they entertained slaves in their homes and workplaces. On occasion they intermarried with whites, thus violating the taboo against "spurious extraction," as Governor Gooch of Virginia put it in 1736. He also pointed out another source of white displeasure. Free blacks acted as if they were equals of "the best of [their] neighbors." Thus, their very presence was a source of unrest among slaves. Given such a premise, it was easy for whites to see in slave conspiracies and rebellions the directing hand of free blacks. In fact, free blacks were rarely involved in such happenings, but whites believed they were, and historians must take into account not only what the facts were but also what people of the time thought the facts were.

Racial feelings were also intensified by the tensions of the long period of cold and hot wars between England on one side and France and Spain on the other. Whites found it easy to believe that French and Spanish agents were inciting black and Indian uprisings. American whites, feeling themselves endangered by blacks within and enemies abroad, responded with ever more stringent controls over both slave and free blacks, especially after slave insurrections. Then, as later, the fate of blacks was shaped by whites.

FOR FURTHER READING

No matter what your specific interest in black history may be, a good place to start for reference is James M. McPherson and others, *Blacks in America: Bibliographical Essays* (1971). It is the most comprehensive work of its kind. Valuable documentary material is available in Herbert Aptheker, ed., *A Documentary History of the Negro People in the United States,* Vol. 1 (1951), and Leslie Fishel, Jr., and Benjamin Quarles, eds., *The Black American* (1970).

A good survey is provided in J. H. Franklin, *From Slavery to Freedom* (1974). More detailed is Lorenzo J. Greene, *The Negro in Colonial New England* (1942). Much new material is examined in Herbert G. Gutman, *The Black Family in Slavery and Freedom* (1976). Another good recent study is John W. Blassingame, *The Slave Community* (1972). See also George P. Rawick, *From Sundown to Sunup* (1972).

On slave resistance see Herbert Aptheker, *American Negro Slave Revolts* (1943), and Gerald W. Mullin, *Flight and Rebellion* (1972).

White attitudes are discussed in Thomas F. Gossett, *Race: The History of an Idea in America* (1963), and Winthrop Jordan, *White Over Black* (1968).

A basic comprehensive study is David B. Davis, *The Problem of Slavery in Western Culture* (1966).

5 indians defend their homelands

Blacks learned to adapt to American slavery. The original Americans had to adapt to the white invaders in other ways. White men did try to enslave Indians. The Indians of the Southeast and Southwest early developed implacable hostility toward the Spanish because of Spanish slave raids among them. English settlers were no less willing than Spanish to make slaves of Indians, as indicated by the Massachusetts Body of Liberties of 1641, which provided for Indian enslavement. The English plans miscarried, though. For long the reason for the failure was said to be that the Indians, unlike the Africans, were not by nature adapted to slavery. But the vast numbers of Indians enslaved in Spanish colonies indicate that nothing in Indian "nature" made them immune to slavery, any more than Africans were slaves by "nature." We must seek for the reasons why Indians were not generally enslaved in North America in the conditions of the time and the place.

First, the Indians had a relative advantage over the whites for a long while. They were more numerous, they knew the country, and they had long since learned how to survive in it. Thus, it was in the interest of the whites to get along with the Indians. This interest was seen in London as well as on this side of the Atlantic. The commercial companies did not want to endanger their investments by provoking Indian hostility. As the colonies prospered, the British government sought to make alliances with Indian peoples, planning to use them against France and Spain and their Indian allies. Further, a thriving fur trade developed in the colonies. Since the white traders depended on Indian suppliers, the whites brought their considerable pressure to bear on colonial governments to maintain friendly relations with Indians—even at the cost of white settlers, who were eager to get cheap labor regardless of color and to help themselves to Indian lands. In sum, Indian peoples were not the object of a concerted drive to enslave them.

Second, the Indians never suffered the culture shock experienced by Africans. Africans were torn violently from their own cultures, subjected to inhuman treatment and degradation, and then compelled to adopt the ways of their captors. They knew that for them there was no return to Africa, no one to whom they could turn for aid and comfort. This was not true of Indians. Except for those sold off to the West Indies, no enslaved Indians were far away from friendly peoples who would aid them if they escaped. Nor could the Indians be easily stripped of identity when strong Indian cultures remained within reach. This in turn made whites look upon Indians as a less prudent slavery investment than Africans.

Third, white fear also worked against enslaving Indians. Once the Indians had shown that they could inflict severe losses on white invaders, whites wanted no Indian enemies within their gates, unless they were enslaved women and children or Christianized Indians confined to their own settlements.

Finally, conditions in the English colonies were not conducive to slavery. The Spanish enslavement policy was most successful in Mexico and Peru, centers of advanced Indian civilizations. These regions had extensive populations accustomed to a social discipline enforced by a privileged ruling class and accepted by the masses in much the same way that Europeans accepted the class distinctions of their society. It was relatively easy for the Spanish to substitute their rule for those of the Aztecs and Incas. No such center of Indian civilization existed in British North America. Instead of one source of authority, there were many, exercised by each people in its own way. Instead of a complex economic system based on agriculture and mining, there was a primitive economy of farming, fishing, and hunting. Instead of a mass of docile serfs there were warriors able and willing to protect their land. Slavery was ill-suited to the circumstances, but even so, many North American Indians were enslaved.

CONFLICT OF CULTURES

The history of white-Indian relations was one of mounting suspicion and hostility. At first, both sides were generally friendly. Whites were glad to get Indian aid in order to survive. William Bradford, for example, thought the Indians around Plymouth were "a special instrument of God." Indians expected that the small settlements would supply them with superior tools, implements, and weapons to use against their enemies and would, in fact, be nothing more than trading posts. When it became apparent that the white villages were becoming centers of expansion into Indian territory, Indian attitudes changed. So did those of whites when they no longer depended on Indian help. There were enough sources of friction to inflame feelings on both sides.

One such source was the prevalent English feeling that Indians were both inferior and evil. That feeling was symbolized by a sermon preached to Virginia-bound settlers before they sailed, warning them against "mixing their seed" with that of the heathen. Cotton Mather, the famous Massachusetts Puritan, opined that Indians were "miserable savages" under "the absolute empire of Satan" whose only salvation lay in Christianization. When Indians in Virginia began fighting white encroachment in the 1620s, the colonial council declared them so treacherous that only "perpetual enmity" with them would promote the cause of Christian civilization.

To Indians, white behavior left much to be desired. Whites broke promises, disregarded treaties, and violated their own laws with impunity when Indian rights were involved. White men lived with Indian women, but few whites married Indians. Indeed, white opinion censored such unions. Some colonies forbade whites to live among Indians, but Christianized Indians were encouraged to live in segregated villages in white-occupied areas.

Christianization itself was suspect among most Indian people. They might be willing to add a Christian god to their pantheon, but they refused to accept the Christian dictum that their own gods were false. Denying their gods meant denying themselves, their ancestors, and all the spiritual world that gave meaning to life. Since religion was so deeply imbedded in their daily lives, they could not sacrifice their gods without sacrificing their own identity. Most Indians rejected this prospect.

There were other sources of trouble. Whites enslaved some Indians and impressed Indian children as "servants," promising authorities to bring them up as Christians—thus, in Indian eyes, compounding the original crime of stealing the children by training them to turn against their parents, their people, and their gods. Indian parents, no less than Pilgrim, did not want "their posterity . . . to degenerate and be corrupted."

Also, white laws increasingly regulated Indian behavior in white settlements, eventually including Indians in the codes directed against blacks—a derogation of status that did not escape Indian notice. For example, Indians and blacks were forbidden, on penalty of flogging, to strike whites, no matter what the provocation.

As time went on, Indians found themselves increasingly dependent on whites for blankets, kettles, pots, knives, firearms, ammunition, and rum. They paid with furs and skins. In this trade they were so defrauded and swindled that colonial authorities tried to regulate commerce with the Indians, which attracted the most avaricious and unscrupulous white businessmen. Not only did the traders adulterate the rum they sold, but they also frequently filled the rum kegs with water. Despite the rules, licensed traders took advantage of Indians, while the illegal traders continued to thrive.

The basic conflict, however, was over land. This issue allowed no compromise, for it was a matter of survival to both cultures. Whites needed Indian land for their livelihood. Indians could afford to, and did, yield some land to the newcomers, but the white appetite was never satisfied. Indians, who needed their traditional planting, hunting, and fishing grounds for survival, were then faced with three alternatives. They could yield, becoming laborers for white masters and giving up their way of life for white civilization, which meant spiritual death. They could resist white encroachment, which meant war. Or they could retreat into the interior and intrude on the lands of other Indian peoples, which would also mean war unless some accommodation could be reached.

Colonists did not see the takeover of Indian lands as encroachment, of course. In their own view, they were instruments of divine purpose. At first, they said they wished not to dispossess the Indians, but to share with them the rich resources of the

New World. In the sharing the Indians would benefit, both in a better standard of living and in the spiritual and moral gains of Christianity. As attitudes changed when white dependence on Indians declined, the rationale changed too. Then it was held that God intended land in the New World for believers, for those who could make best use of it. He certainly did not intend His gifts to be squandered on savages when Christian Englishmen needed food.

At a more mundane level, Englishmen claimed they were doing Indians a favor by occupying their land: if the English did not take over, the French and Spanish would. And while the French would debauch the Indians, the Spanish would exterminate them—a staple of English anti-Spanish propaganda of the time. Thus, Englishmen felt an exalted moral purpose behind their expansion. Legally, too, the English felt they were justified. Had not the English king granted these lands to Englishmen? To which the Indians answered: How could a distant and unknown king give away what he did not possess?

The friction was intensified by the way in which the acquisition of Indian lands was institutionalized, that is, as private property. Whites felt that God himself ordained private property and that His will was expressed in both law and custom. As private property, land could be bought and sold. To Indian peoples private property in land made no sense, and as white expansion went on, they perceived it as a dangerous idea. Their basic belief was that the Great Spirit gave Mother Earth to his peoples and that her fruits were to be enjoyed communally. Thus, no Indian could own land as an individual; land belonged to the whole people. As such, land could not be sold or bought, not even by chiefs.

Given the utterly different cultural contexts of whites and Indians, it is not surprising that the contracts and treaties aimed at settling disputes simply provided fresh grounds for new suspicion and hostility, even when intentions were good. Puritans, for example, reduced their agreements with Indians to written contracts—in English, of course—in which the terms were carefully spelled out and the signatures of both parties required. Interpreters explained the terms to Indians. To further insure that whites "of a covetous disposition" did not swindle Indians, several colonies required official approval of land "sales" to individuals. But approved contracts were legally binding and enforced by the white authorities.

Contracts were, and still are, a fertile source of litigation between whites who speak the same language. What are we to say about Indians involved in them? Given the complexities of legal phraseology, how could an interpreter explain to Indians the full extent of the obligations they were taking upon themselves? Nor did Indians live in a contract society. They had not the faintest notion of written contracts and the concept of private property that lay behind them. The situation was one in which misunderstanding and conflict were inevitable.

Besides, the lands the New England peoples first transferred to whites were surplus in Indian eyes. Recent epidemics had depopulated many of the coastal areas, and survivors could dispose of land without endangering their own livelihoods and security. The process was made easy by English recognition in the early years of Indian hunting and fishing rights on the lands Englishmen had "bought." Only when English expansion threatened Indian livelihood and security did serious trouble arise, but that expansion was not long in coming.

In Virginia the story was essentially the same as in New England, except that the critical struggles came sooner and the colonists flagrantly violated their own laws when it suited them and then changed the laws to the Indians' disadvantage. Thus, in 1646, Indians who had risen in revolt in 1644 agreed to a peace treaty in which, in return for a land cession, they were guaranteed legal title to their remaining lands. Whites were prohibited from entering Indian territory. Within three years the ban on white instrusion was lifted. The ensuing troubles led the Assembly in 1656 to affirm Indian land titles—unless the Assembly decided otherwise. Two years later the Assembly did decide otherwise, restricting Indian title to such "seats of land" as they then held. By 1662 the issue had become so dangerous that Virginia adopted a new comprehensive Indian code, which frankly conceded that trouble arose from "the violent intrusions of diverse Englishmen made into their [Indian] lands, forcing the Indians by way of revenge to kill the cattle and hogs of the English." The new code forbade further transfer or sale of Indian land, provided Indians the same legal protection as Englishmen, and barred Indian enslavement—a public confession that previous laws against such enslavement had been largely ignored. As for the ban on the sale of Indian land, wily whites soon found a way to get around it. They no longer "bought" land; they "leased" it for long terms.

ARMED CONFLICT

The various English and Indian wars that erupted under such conditions naturally had different immediate causes, but basic to them all was one element: the expansion of white power and the threat it posed to the Indian way of life. That way of life was also menaced indirectly by the willingness of many Indian peoples, for reasons of their own, to ally themselves with the invaders against rival Indian powers, as we shall see later.

In the conflict between white and red peoples, the Indians were doomed. Even after they obtained firearms, they were usually outgunned by the whites. Perhaps more deadly than white guns were white diseases, such as measles, tuberculosis, and smallpox. Europeans had built up some immunity to these, but to the Indians the infections, which were new to them, were disastrous. One reason why Englishmen found so few Indians around Massachusetts Bay was a recent plague that had decimated the residents. When diseases did not appear naturally, whites introduced them deliberately in an early form of biological warfare: blankets that had been used to cover people suffering from smallpox were distributed among unsuspecting Indians.

At the same time, whites undermined Indian morals and morale by fostering addiction to alcohol. Laws passed to curb the practice were simply disregarded. The practice expanded rapidly when New England began large-scale production of cheap rum, thus affording whites an inexpensive way of trading for lands and furs and at the same time corrupting Indian society.

The white invaders had other advantages. They had superior economic and political organization, an advantage that became more and more pronounced as settlements grew into towns and white authority moved to the frontier with farmers and planters. Whites also were race-conscious to a degree unknown to Indians. While occasionally an individual colony might refuse to cooperate with another colony planning war against Indian peoples, as did Massachusetts in 1642 when Connecticut solicited its support for such a project, no colony took up arms against another to defend Indians.

This was not true of Indian peoples. Their statesmanship was primitive and pragmatic. They had alliances with their friends and made war against their enemies when occasion demanded, although such wars were relatively bloodless until white traders put guns into Indian hands. Since the whites had so much to offer by way of trade, diverse Indian peoples made allies of diverse white peoples—Dutch, French, and English. The Europeans, in turn, found it useful to stimulate Indian feuds, both for reasons of trade and of strategy. Indians warring among themselves depended on European arms and were unlikely to present a common front against white expansion.

The English were the masters of the strategy of dividing and conquering by alliance. In Virginia, the powerful Powhatan Confederacy was crushed with the help of other Indian peoples. Narragansetts and Mohegans aided Puritans in their war of extermination against the Pequots in 1637. Forty years later King Philip failed in his war of liberation in New England partly because some Indian peoples fought for the whites.

The English enjoyed one other advantage, for which the Indians had no counterpart. Christianized Indians served not only as warriors against their own peoples but also as informers and scouts. The Indians never benefited from such inside, firsthand knowledge of white ways and white tactics.

The first major war broke out in Virginia, where planters eager to cash in on the booming tobacco market pushed into Indian lands. The Powhatans tried to negotiate a white retreat. When that failed, they went to war in 1622, cutting off exposed farms and settlements and killing 350 of the invaders. But the Indians, unaccustomed to the strategy of prolonged warfare and inadequately supplied to wage such a fight, did not follow up their advantage. Jamestown survived, and when new settlers and supplies arrived, whites took the offensive. Employing the strategies of both cold and hot war and making good use of Indian allies, the English wore down Indian resistance. When the Indians fought back, the whites resorted not only to combat but also to a deliberate policy of destroying the sources of Indian strength. Crops and villages were ruthlessly destroyed, and captives enslaved. Even when the Indians won an engagement, they lost, for in proportion to population their losses far exceeded white casualties and could not be replaced. Whites, on the contrary, made good their losses. A last convulsive struggle of the Powhatans in 1644 ended in crushing defeat. Two years later the Powhatans signed a treaty marking the end of major organized Indian resistance in Virginia.

That not all Indian spirit had been broken by the defeat of the Powhatans was demonstrated in 1675. The Maryland Susquehannocks, until then relatively immune to white pressure, now confronted the white invaders. At the same time, Maryland, long their ally, deserted them for an alliance with Senecas, long their foes. Susquehannocks and their allies went to war, spreading the conflict into Virginia. They inflicted such losses on whites that planters big and small rallied to the banner of Nathaniel Bacon, who wreaked bloody vengeance on the Indians before attempting to overthrow the regime of Governor Berkeley. The governor, in Bacon's view, was ''soft'' on Indians. By 1705, Robert Beverly, one of the few whites who sympathized with native Americans, noted sadly that the Indians of Virginia were ''wasted.''

''Wasted'' indeed were many once-proud native peoples, but other southern Indian peoples continued to fight white aggression. In North Carolina the Tuscaroras finally revolted in 1711 against repeated slave raids on their villages. Defeated, they fled north to sanctuary among the Iroquois of New York. In South Carolina, the powerful Yamasee rose in 1715. In wars lasting thirteen years they were all but exterminated. Refugees from these and less noted conflicts found their way to Florida. In wild areas remote from Spanish authority they helped form in time the Seminole nation—a blending of Indians escaping white violence, dissident members of the Creek nation, and escaped black slaves.

Not all Indian peoples suffered so. Some, awed by demonstrations of white power, accommodated themselves to whites as best they could. Some became active allies of whites in wars against other Indian peoples. Some were so powerful that both English and French courted them. Thus, the Cherokees, Chickasaws, Creeks, and Choctaws thrived in the eighteenth century, thanks to the rivalry of English and French in seeking their cooperation. So prosperous did they become, and so admiring of white ways of life, that they—particularly the Cherokees—took on the shape of European civilization.

Even so, the tide of white expansion caught up with them. The Cherokees, first to be threatened, yielded some land in 1755. Further white invasion led to war in 1759. Finally, after years of sporadic fighting, the Cherokees made peace in 1770 by yielding up yet more of their land. But that was still not enough. ''Civilized'' though the Cherokees and the other peoples might be, they could not be allowed to block white expansion—as they learned in the 1830s.

English policies toward Indians in the South were shaped by more than considerations of trade, land, and international politics. The growing number of black slaves together with increasing Indian hostility prompted white fears that the two aggrieved peoples might ally to challenge white rule. To avert this, whites resorted to the age-old stratagem of ''divide and rule.'' As a South Carolinian of the time remarked, whites used wile ''to make Indians and Negroes a check upon each other lest by their vastly superior numbers we should be crushed by one or the other.''

Every effort was made to discourage peaceful contacts between blacks and Indians, both to keep fugitive slaves from escaping into Indian territory and to avoid such breaches in white security as occurred when black fugitives revealed white designs on Indian peoples. To arouse animosity blacks were used as soldiers in the campaigns against Indians, despite the white aversion to arming slaves. The repeated use of black soldiers was also intended to impress on the Indians the lesson that they could not count on slave aid should they attempt another large-scale revolt, such as that of the Yamasees. Indian animosity was intensified when whites encouraged them to believe that disastrous outbreaks of smallpox among them originated in blacks recently arrived from Africa.

Whites fanned the fires of black resentment against Indians by using friendly Indians as fugitive-slave catchers. Not only were they astute in tracking down fleeing slaves in country unknown to whites, but also they had the resources to attack the fugitive slave settlements that developed in remote swamps and mountain areas. To encourage the Indians, whites offered munificent rewards for the return of live fugitives. The return of one such black won an Indian the equivalent of several months of hunting and trapping. Later, South Carolina authorities provided rewards for scalps of dead fugitives. From experience, blacks also knew that when Indians rose against white encroachment they distinguished little between whites and blacks and killed slaves as quickly as masters. And whites lost no opportunity to impress on blacks the white version of the brutal treatment of prisoners by Indians. The whites, though, were not altogether successful. Fleeing slaves often did find refuge among Indian peoples, especially among the Seminoles, and blacks did pass on information to Indians.

WARS OF EXTERMINATION

If Indians fared ill in the South, they did little better in the North. There, as in the South, whites tried to expand peacefully, but when that failed, they crushed Indian resistance remorselessly, aided by Indian enemies of the victims. This was the pattern of the Pequot War of 1637.

That unhappy people, expelled from its ancestral holdings by the Mohawks, had settled in the lush Connecticut River valley and dominated the other Indian peoples there—a rule that did not endear them to the original inhabitants. Into the valley came Puritan settlers from Massachusetts Bay. The Pequots tried to drive them out in bloody raids, and the whites responded with savage reprisals. As all-out war became imminent, the Pequots tried to win over the Narragansetts in Rhode Island. Massachusetts Puritans, who had just expelled Roger Williams as an undesirable character—not least because he questioned the validity of their Indian land titles—now successfully appealed to him to use his influence with the Narragansetts to keep them neutral. With the Pequots isolated and with the support of the Pequots' enemies, Massachusetts and Connecticut embarked on a war of extermination.

At dawn on May 26, 1637, the English and their Indian allies surrounded a major Pequot encampment on the Mystic River, set it on fire, and shot down those who tried to escape from the flames. In little more than half an hour, the village was destroyed and at least 400 Pequots were dead. English losses amounted to a mere two dead and twenty wounded. The massacre was the will of God, said Captain John Mason, leader of the campaign. God, said Mason, had punished the enemies of "His people" by "making them as a fiery oven . . . filling the place with dead bodies." But this slaughter was not enough for the whites. They relentlessly pursued the fleeing remnants of Pequots, who were making for the New Netherlands border, until they cornered the Indians in a swamp near New Haven. Old men, women, and children were allowed to come out. Then the English rushed in and slaughtered the unresisting Indians who remained. The Pequots who survived had little cause to rejoice. The men were sold off as slaves in the West Indies. The women and children were distributed among Puritans and their Indian allies to serve as slaves. The war served two purposes: it got rid of a people militantly defending their land and culture, and it served notice on all other Indian peoples that resistance to whites meant extermination. As Alden Vaughan remarks, "The other New England Indians trembled at the thoroughness of the English victory".

For nearly forty years New England Indians continued to "tremble," powerless to halt the erosion of their societies. Whites took over more and more Indian land. They undermined traditional culture through vigorous Christianizing campaigns carried on by such men as John Eliot, "the apostle to the Indians." Perhaps as many as 2,500 Indians of 15,000 in the region were converted and segregated in five villages of "praying Indians," where they were completely subject to white religion and white law.

A steady flow of cheap rum from Puritan distilleries helped debauch the non-Christian Indians. Whites grew increasingly confident that they had put the Indians "in their place." This confidence grew into arrogance, as when Plymouth Colony arrested Wamsutta, the new chief of the Wampanoags, on suspicion that he was planning renewed Indian resistance. Indian anger mounted when Wamsutta died in Plymouth a few days after his release. His successor was his brother, Metacom, who became much better known to the English as King Philip.

Philip, seeing how Indian disunity played into the hands of whites aiming at expansion, sought to develop a common Indian front to stem the white tide. He had some success with minor peoples, and eventually he won over the reluctant but powerful Narragansetts. Indian informers, including Philip's own secretary, betrayed his plans. Philip was ordered to give up his arms—a demand he evaded, evidently feeling the time not yet ripe for open warfare. Whites, too, were not ready for armed conflict. As tensions mounted, the secretary was slain. Two Indians were hanged for his murder on dubious evidence, one of whom was a trusted aide to Philip. This assertion of white power brought no immediate overt response. Philip continued his preparations. Then in 1675 a white settler shot and wounded an Indian near Philip's headquarters, and the war was on.

Forces from Plymouth and Massachusetts converged on the Indians encamped in Rhode Island, but Philip and his warriors escaped to carry the war into the Bay Colony. Philip's initial successes prompted other Indian peoples to join his ranks, even including 200 Christian converts. For a time the Indian patriots carried all before them: they totally destroyed more than a dozen towns and inflicted severe damage on many more, costing in property damage what was then an astronomical £100,000. In human terms the cost was even higher. According to Alden Vaughan, "A higher percentage of the [white] population suffered death or wounds in King Philip's War than in any subsequent American conflict".

But the odds were against the Indian patriots. They lacked both an overall command and a long-range strategy, relying on the tactic of the hit-and-run raid. In addition, they were dangerously short of reserve manpower, food, and ammunition. Their white enemies had ample supplies of all three and developed strategy and tactics to make full use of them. They shrewdly recruited Philip's Indian foes to their cause. Their armies relentlessly ground down Philip's hungry forces, depleted by widespread desertion during the winter of 1675. The Narragansetts, on whom Philip had counted so heavily, were wiped out before they could enter the war. Finally, in the summer of 1676 Philip himself was betrayed and killed. His body was butchered, the hands sent to Boston and his head to Plymouth, where it remained on display for twenty years for the edification of whites and as a deterrent to Indians who might think of challenging white power.

White power asserted itself in other ways, including treachery. Two of Philip's lieutenants, who surrendered with their followers on the promise that they would be treated as prisoners of war, were summarily executed. Indians—men, women, and children—captured during the war were delivered into slavery to Indian allies, to white families, and to West Indian plantations. The lands of the "rebels" were confiscated and sold to private white owners "to promote the public worship of God, and our own public good."

"Praying Indians," for all their help to the white cause, fared little better. During the initial phase of the war, enraged whites, aroused by the desertion of Christian Indians to Philip and fearing treachery, vented their fury on the converts, beating and killing them. Public authority finally bowed to public opinion and deported the hapless Indian Christians to an island where many perished from hunger and disease. In the meantime, white Christians made off with the property of the Indian Christians.

Indian power in New England was broken, as it had been in Virginia. But white fears were not now allayed. The ideas of Christianizing and "civilizing" the native peoples withered away. In their place came the white belief that "the only good Indian is a dead Indian."

Elsewhere, the erosion of Indian power went on apace. Only in Delaware and Pennsylvania, where Quaker influence provided some check on white rapacity, were Indian rights respected, although some Indian lands were still occupied by whites. But even in Pennsylvania, Indians suffered. As Quaker influence waned in the eighteenth century and Ulster Scots, lusting for land, occupied the back country, Indians fell back westward under what was for them unprecedented white violence. Christianized Indians found they were no better off than their "savage" brethren. Ulstermen massacred the converts with as much good conscience as they killed off the unbelievers. In fact, the task was easier, for the pious Moravians who worked with the Indians had gathered them in villages and taught them the virtue of nonviolent resistance to evil.

THE TOLL OF THE FUR TRADE

By the end of the seventeenth century, Indian societies as far west as the Missouri and as far south as the Gulf of Mexico were affected by French, Dutch, and English businessmen struggling to dominate the fur trade. Government agents sought to enlist Indian allies against rival powers, and Christian missionaries, mainly French, worked to convert people quite happy with their own religious beliefs. The French, like the English, disregarded the right of Indians to their own land. They claimed the entire Mississippi Valley from the Great Lakes to the Gulf of Mexico and named it Louisiana in tribute to Louis XIV. Like the English, the French ruthlessly crushed Indian resistance whenever it appeared. In 1729, for example, the powerful Natchez people attacked a French post. The whites, with Indian allies, responded with a war so ferocious that few Natchez survived.

It was the fur trade, however, that proved most disruptive of Indian life. Native Americans, who at first looked on European goods as luxuries, speedily found them necessities. Guns, for example, became essential in warfare, and perhaps more important, they became necessary for hunting, not only for furs but also for food. As Indian dependence on white trade increased, the traders extorted more and more furs for their goods. The ecological balance was upset as Indians strove to meet the traders' demands; whole regions were stripped of beaver and other prized animals. Eastern peoples thus deprived of their source of trade began raiding the lands of Indians around the Great Lakes, a fertile source of furs. These raids developed into wars, made all the more bloody because the Indians now had firearms and because the conflicts involved rival European powers. The aggressors were usually allied with the English, and the defenders with the French. Among the most ferocious of the aggressors were the Iroquois. Their depredations in French-occupied territory sent their Indian victims fleeing westward. They in turn drove out other Indian peoples, a process made easier by the lack of firearms among many western Indian peoples. Even the distant Sioux in Minnesota felt the effects of the displacement of Indian peoples by the fur trade.

The Iroquois, actually a five-nation confederation of Mohawks, Senecas, Cayugas, Oneidas, and Onondagas, emerged from these seventeenth-century conflicts as the strongest Indian power in North America. They dominated western and northern New York, straddling the vital trade routes from the Great Lakes and the St. Lawrence Valley. During thirty years of war to gain control of the Great Lakes fur areas for their Dutch patrons, they wiped out such Indian peoples as the Eries and Hurons, wreaked havoc with the French trade, and suffered severe losses themselves. The losses were more than compensated by displaced Indians, such as the Tuscaroras, seeking refuge from white power east of the Appalachians and ready to support an Indian power willing to extend them protection. When the Dutch surrendered to the English in 1664, the Iroquois transferred their allegiance to the victors. Continued Iroquois depredations against French fur sources led to a series of wars in the 1680s and 1690s in which the French, through their Indian allies, tried to destroy the Iroquois.

The five nations emerged triumphant, partly because they reshaped their political organization. Formerly a loose association in which each people did much as it pleased, the League of the Iroquois became a unified confederation that, while permitting tribal autonomy on purely tribal concerns, directed all affairs concerning the peoples as a whole. The Iroquois were thus able to mobilize the resources of all their peoples when dealing with whites. So impressed was Benjamin Franklin with the Indian accomplishment that he urged it as a model for quarreling white colonies at the abortive Albany Congress in 1754.

Although the defeat of the French campaigns was due in part to English arms, the Iroquois used their new-found power to strengthen their independence. Instead of becoming English pawns, they pursued their own policies, playing off French and English rivalries against each other. During the frequent Anglo-French wars of the eigthteenth century they observed "benevolent neutrality" toward the English, although in the French and Indian war they finally sided with the English. Such policies were based on shrewd appraisals of which white power would eventually win.

RESISTANCE IN THE SOUTHWEST

Other peoples also felt the effects of white expansion. In the sixteenth century Spanish slaving raids terrorized Indian villages in Florida and other parts of the Southeast. Exploring expeditions, frustrated in their search for gold and harassed by Indians aroused by slave raids, looted and burned villages and massacred their inhabitants. Captured Indians were enslaved. Spanish settlements spread north from Florida to Virginia, but Indian resistance was so fierce that by 1600 the Spanish had withdrawn to Florida. Despite some uprisings, many Indian peoples there were brought under Spanish control.

Spanish power also invaded the Southwest. In 1598 white soldiers and settlers moved up from Mexico and took over the country of the Pueblos along the Rio Grande. They occupied the Indian towns, established farms, wiped out or enslaved the Indians who resisted, and lived well off the forced labor of the native inhabitants. Such forced labor was known as the *encomienda* system. The Pueblos gradually organized themselves, and under the leadership of Popé, they finally revolted in 1680. The bloody fighting drove the Spanish out, but twelve years later, when Popé had died, the invaders returned. Many Pueblos, however, lacking a taste for Spanish civilization, fled to seek sanctuary among neighboring peoples, such as the Navahos, Hopis, and Apaches. There the Spanish did not bother them, wishing to avoid clashes with these warlike folk. And, thought the Spanish, such peoples could be used to check French expansion.

PONTIAC'S WAR OF LIBERATION

The fur trade and involvement of Indian peoples in European power politics disrupted Indian societies, but more ominous for the Indian future was the steady enlargement of white settlement, a process facilitated by the willingness of some peoples to cede lands to oncoming whites. The Iroquois, for example, having assumed protection of the Delawares and Shawnees, sold off some of their Pennsylvania lands to whites. But whether whites acquired Indian lands peacefully or through war, they left little place on those lands for the native Americans.

For a time landless Indians found some sanctuary in the West beyond the Appalachians, but in the 1750s the advance guards of English invaders began to trickle through the mountains. Native peoples, such as the Delawares and Shawnees, who had so recently experienced the consequences of white expansion, turned on the new wave of invaders and their cause was taken up by France. That government saw in English expansion beyond the mountains a threat to its control of the Great Lakes and of the Mississippi—meaning control of the fur trade—and it backed the Indian resistance. Fighting began in 1754. On July 4 of that year a force of Virginia troops headed by George Washington, which had hoped to capture the French fort (Duquesne) at what is now Pittsburgh, Pennsylvania, was forced to surrender to the French and Indians. The following year a combined army of British and Virginia troops was ambushed near the fort, and settlers hastily retreated eastward.

This war soon merged into the greater French and Indian war, which lasted until 1763. Indian peoples were used by both sides. The prolonged combat weakened them all, but the allies of the French suffered worse. After the fall of Quebec in 1759, control of France's Indian allies was vested in the British military commander Sir Jeffrey Amherst. He detested Indians and thought that "the only method of treating these savages is to keep them in proper subjection."

It is in this context that the great Indian uprising led by Pontiac in 1763 is to be understood. Once Canada had fallen, white settlers came over the mountains again. British traders, now enjoying a monopoly of the Indian trade, raised prices and reduced quality. Amherst, in a display of arrogance, ended the French practice of providing Indians with guns, ammunition, tools, and emergency rations. To Indians, this spelled disaster, for they were short both of food and of guns and ammunition for hunting. Angry young men, including the Ottawa warrior Pontiac, urged war against the British. Their appeals were encouraged by French settlers, who themselves looked forward to a rumored French and Spanish expedition that would come north from New Orleans to reclaim the Ohio Valley and the Great Lakes. These beliefs bolstered Indian hopes that the English invaders could be crushed.

The optimism helped Pontiac rally a great number of otherwise dissident peoples together for a united campaign. His message was all the more telling because a religious prophet of the Delaware people had received a divine message that whites must be forced to give up this land, which God had intended for Indian peoples, and retire to the lands beyond the sea, which God had set aside for them. Indeed, God was offended that his Indian people had yielded to white men's ways. Thus, the impending struggle was not simply a fight over immediate grievances, but a war of Indian liberation, to protect Indian culture as well as Indian land.

The Indians rose in large-scale revolt in May 1763, soon captured such strategic forts as Mackinac, St. Joseph, and Presque Isle (now Erie, Pennsylvania), and eventually reduced English power to the two forts at Detroit and Pittsburgh. Both forts were under siege, a new development in Indian tactics. Also new was an Indian unity that embraced Ottawas, Senecas, Hurons, Shawnees, Chippewas, Sauks, and other tribes.

With English military power all but destroyed, the Indian patriots drove back across the mountains the settlers who had come into the West. Bloody warfare ensued as frontiersmen, militia, and British troops made common cause against the Indians, vowing to avenge the white blood shed when Indians expelled the settlers. Amherst called for a policy of genocide. Indians, said he, were "the vilest race of beings that ever infested the earth, and whose riddance from it must be esteemed a meritorious act, for the good of mankind." He recommended that smallpox be deliberately spread among the Indians.

But even as the battles raged in the western wilderness, forces over which Pontiac had no control undermined his position. Early in 1763 Britain and France made peace, but word of the pact did not reach the West until June, a month after the Indian uprising began. Pontiac refused to believe the reports, but French settlers, who had been aiding the Indians, now began cultivating the English. Their changed attitudes influenced some chiefs. If the French would no longer support them, what chance did they have against the English?

In August, the British demonstrated their strength: a relief force, crushing Indian resistance on the way, reached Fort Pitt and resumed control of the Ohio Valley.

Only Detroit remained under siege. Pontiac's hope that the garrison would surrender proved illusory. As the weeks passed without perceptible change, the besieging Indian peoples turned restless and discontented, their unity undermined by French and British propaganda. The Indians themselves wanted a quick end to the affair, so they could go hunting and resume trading with the whites, on whom they now depended so heavily. As it became evident that no quick end was in sight, one people after another submitted to the whites and went home. Finally, in October, after receiving affirmation from a French officer that the Anglo-French war had indeed ended, Pontiac yielded. But rankling in the minds of many Indians was a feeling of white betrayal. In the peace treaty France had given up land it did not possess—the land of the Indians. And France's surrender of its allies to their enemies was white perfidy at its worst!

Thus ended the last great Indian war of the colonial period. In vain, Pontiac tried to revive Indian resistance farther west and in the South. Later, when Indian unrest did stir again, the disillusioned chief counseled peace—a plea that to warriors confirmed rumors that Pontiac had "sold out" to the British. These rumors had been fostered by the British themselves, who all along had sought to undermine Pontiac's moral authority among the Indians. With Pontiac discredited, the British felt safe. Not only was the immediate danger contained—no other Indian leader approached Pontiac in talent and shrewdness—but also they had planted seeds of doubt and distrust that would hinder Indian movements for unity.

There was an outcome of the war that neither Amherst nor his victims foresaw. In the Proclamation of 1763 an alarmed British government set up a boundary along the Appalachian mountains, west of which white settlement was banned without official permission. In effect, the proclamation reserved the vast new British territory between the Appalachians and the Mississippi for the Indians and, of course, the fur trade. Thus, for reasons of self-interest, the British conceded a major Indian war aim. But London's decisions found little support among white colonists and colonial governments. Land speculators, with the aid of colonial governments, found ways of circumventing the ban, and settlers simply ignored it. The mounting friction between British and colonial interests in relation to the Indian West produced one of the basic grievances that eventually led, in less than a generation, to war between Britain and its colonies.

FOR FURTHER READING

A good general introduction is Alvin M. Josephy, Jr., *The Indian Heritage of America* (1968). For brief biographies of Indian leaders see his *Patriot Chiefs* (1961). More recent and detailed studies are Gary B. Nash, *Red, White and Black* (1974); Wilcomb E. Washburn, *Red Man's Land—White Man's Law* (1971); and Wilbur R. Jacobs, *Dispossessing the American Indian* (1972).

A pioneer study in its field is Alfred W. Crosby, Jr., *The Columbian Exchange: Biological and Cultural Consequences of 1492* (1972).

Puritan policy toward Indian peoples is described in Alden T. Vaughan, *New England Frontier* (1965). The problems of other peoples are discussed in David H. Corkran, *The Cherokee Frontier* (1962) and *The Creek Frontier* (1967). The Iroquois are the subject of study by Georgiana C. Nammack, *Fraud, Politics, and the Dispossession of the Indians* (1969).

C. A. Westlager, *The Delaware Indians* (1972), argues that Indian and white peoples could coexist peacefully, at least in Pennsylvania.

For some other aspects see Grace Woodward's biography, *Pocahontas* (1969); Howard H. Peckham, *Pontiac and the Indian Uprising* (1947); and Douglas E. Leach, *Flintlock and Tomahawk* (1959).

6 war of national liberation

The American Revolutionary War, like more recent wars of national liberation in China, Algeria, and Vietnam, divided colonial society. Opposing the war were the Loyalists, or Tories as the Patriots contemptuously called them, representing perhaps as much as one-third of the population. The Loyalists included the colonial bureaucracy, those who served it, and their allies among the business and professional elites. The Loyalists also included some, like Joseph Galloway, a wealthy Philadelphia lawyer, who had opposed British policies but refused to break with the mother country. They were sustained both by belief in the righteousness of their cause and by their confidence in British victory.

Not all Loyalists were rich and well-born. In New York, many tenant famers who had rioted in the 1760s against oppressive landlords took up arms against their landlords again, this time because they were "rebels." Likewise, in the back country of the Carolinas poor folk still embittered by the crushing of the Regulators and resentful yet of the seaboard aristocracy went to war for the king when the aristocrats chose independence. Thousands of such men joined the British army or enlisted with Tory militias like the Tory Rangers, St. Leger's Loyal Greens, or Tarleton's Legion.

Many Loyalists chose or were forced into exile. The more affluent of the 75,000 who went abroad sought refuge in England, where they subsisted on meager government pensions. Poorer Loyalists fled to Canada, where they led hard lives on land given them by Britain.

Still others remained in America, working in subtle ways to subvert the Patriot cause without calling undue attention to themselves. A number, indeed, survived the war with property and person intact. There were some who posed as ardent Patriots while acting as spies. Perhaps the most notorious spy was Doctor Benjamin Church, who was closely associated with General Washington as chief of the Continental army's medical service. He provided valuable information to the British before he was unmasked early in the war. And there were a few, typified by Benedict Arnold, who had been sincere Patriots but went over to the enemy when their ambitions were disappointed.

If Loyalists represented a minority of the population, so also did the Patriots, or "rebels" as the British tagged them. Like the Loyalists, they had followers in all classes, ranging from wealthy men like John Hancock and George Washington to poor seamen like William Widger. The Patriot cause also included a great diversity of social and political philosophy, stretching from the conservatism of John Adams and Alexander Hamilton to the radicalism of Tom Paine. However they differed, they were united on the goal of independence and in the faith that it could be attained.

Between Loyalists and Patriots was a large mass of people committed to neither cause. They were people who sought to turn a profit by selling supplies to whichever side paid best or who simply tried to survive in turbulent times by obeying the government that dominated the area they lived in. Their numbers diminished as the war went on, largely because the behavior of British troops drove them into Patriot ranks.

ROOTING OUT THE LOYALISTS

Patriots regarded Loyalists with that loathing reserved for traitors. The British and their German mercenaries were bad enough, but they did only what was expected of them. The Loyalists, however, were seen as Americans betraying their own people. On one occasion George Washington suggested hanging several of the most ardent Loyalists as a deterrent.

The most drastic punishment meted out was confiscation of Loyalist property by state governments. The biggest losers were the great absentee landlords and those who had chosen exile. These included the Calverts in Maryland, the Granvilles in North Carolina, Sir William Pepperell in Massachusetts, and the Penn family in Pennsylvania. The confiscations were sweeping, entailing thousands of square miles of land, and they broke the back of British landlord power in America.

Tom Paine, the great pamphleteer of the Revolution, and other radicals advocated confiscation as a step toward social democracy. They wanted the land distributed among a host of poor farmers, thus assuring a government that would be responsive to the needs of the common people. This outlook was not shared by state governments, which were hard pressed for money and often dominated by conservative revolutionaries. The confiscated lands were sold to the highest bidders—indeed, such sales of valuable land provided an added incentive for some of the wealthy to support the Patriot cause.

In addition to confiscation, Loyalists faced other penalties. Some were banished. Suspected Loyalists were compelled to take loyalty oaths to the new government. They were also mobbed, beaten, and smeared with tar and feathers. Such mob actions were usually directed against Loyalists who publicly derided the Patriot cause, ''damning'' the ''rebels'' and toasting the king.

BLACK LOYALISTS

Not all Loyalists were white. Great numbers of blacks joined the British, because they loved not King George but freedom. And the British, perceiving the weakness in America's spiritual armor, offered slaves freedom if they came over to the British lines. This brought cries of outrage from southern planters, and it helped bind the southern states more closely to their northern sisters. How many slaves escaped into British lines may never be known. It is suggestive, however, that when the British left New York they took with them 4,000 blacks. Another 6,000 went along when the British evacuated Charleston, South Carolina, and 4,000 blacks left in the evacuation of Savannah, Georgia. While some of these undoubtedly were slaves of departing Loyalists, many appear to have been blacks who were fugitives from their masters. Indeed, so many tried to escape after Yorktown that Washington ordered his soldiers to head them off before they reached the haven of British naval vessels.

British motives were hardly humanitarian. The policy made good propaganda against the rebels, contrasting the freedom offered by Britain with the defense of slavery waged by ''liberty-loving'' Americans. More important, draining off the South's labor force weakened the southern economy.

The British were not content only to welcome young black fugitives who could serve in the army. They also raided plantations, carrying off as many as a total of 5,000 able-bodied slaves. They left behind the old, the very young, and the sick. Planters complained bitterly that they could not work their properties because their best slaves had been taken.

Slaves captured by the English were not freed. They became ''public slaves,'' used mostly as laborers to dig trenches, build defense works, and otherwise do the dirty, hard labor white soldiers resented. Some slaves, both young men and young women, were sold as servants to officers and groups of enlisted men. Whether captured or fugitive, blacks demonstrated their talents. They served not only as laborers but also as combat troops, spies, guides, pilots, and sailors in the Royal Navy. The slaves were told, however, that if they labored faithfully and well they would be freed when the war ended.

It should be noted that the British did not accept all fugitives. The promise of freedom applied only to the slaves of rebels. Fugitive slaves of Loyalists were returned to their masters. Even so, the ardor of many southern Loyalists was dampened by the British arming of fugitives from rebels.

When the British evacuated American seaports, they took with them slaves of Loyalists and thousands of blacks who considered themselves free. Many were taken to the British West Indies, where the free blacks were often kidnapped and reenslaved. Several thousand freed blacks were taken to Nova Scotia in Canada where they lived in destitution. Eventually, after many protests from the blacks and their white spokesmen in London, the British agreed to ship the blacks from Canada to Sierra Leone in Africa, where a British company was having difficulty developing a colony. In 1782 one thousand American blacks arrived, only to find that no preparations had been made to receive them. The blacks literally had to start from scratch in order to survive.

A WHITE MAN'S WAR?

If the British welcomed some black participation in the war, American patriots opposed it strongly. Northern and southern whites alike dreaded the prospect of black men with guns in their hands. Thus, early in the war neither the Continental army nor the state militias enlisted blacks. The Continental Congress also made it plain that the fight for American freedom had little to do with black freedom. Fugitive slaves from Patriot masters were returned to their owners. Slaves seeking escape from Loyalist masters or captured in Patriot raids on Loyalist plantations were regarded as spoils of war. Many became public slaves, performing hard labor in lead and iron mines and in iron works as well as serving in the military and navy. Others were distributed among officers and soldiers as personal servants or sold for the benefit of their captors.

But as the first glow of patriotic enthusiasm faded, white enlistment fell off, and members of the state militias went home when their short-term enlistments were up. By 1777 Washington and other leaders realized they must have more manpower, and the major source was black. Free blacks were encouraged to enlist in the Continental army with promises of bounties and land grants. To stimulate such enlistment, states such as Massachusetts and Maryland made free blacks subject to the draft that had been ordered by the Continental Congress. Some state militias were opened to free blacks, but the number of blacks in militias was far below the number in the army. Blacks also served in the Continental navy, the various state navies, and the privateers that raided British seagoing commerce.

So great was the need for manpower that eventually even slaves were accepted. Masters who sent slaves to the army were themselves exempted from the draft and awarded compensation in cash, as in Rhode Island, or in land grants, as in New York. The drafted slaves were to be freed at the war's end, a policy that met with marked hostility in the South. Virginia refused to sanction the arming of slaves. In 1779, when the British were penetrating the South, a proposal that South Carolina furnish 3,000 slaves (with compensation) to the Continental army was angrily rejected. Some legislators even talked about a separate peace with the British if the plan were pursued. A similar response came from Georgia. Slaveholders were disturbed not only by the threat of possible slave insurrections but also by the fear that large numbers of blacks in the army would undermine slavery itself. Slavery, after all, was justified on the ground that blacks were so inferior that they could not take care of themselves. But blacks were already proving competent in combat. Further, if slaves fought for American freedom, they would demand their own freedom after the war. Such a demand would be supported by growing antislavery movements in both the North and South.

The South tried to meet army needs and preserve slavery at the same time. Virginia, South Carolina, and Georgia offered slaves as bounties to white men who enlisted. Many slaves, however, in the South as well as in the North, served in the army. Some were sent as substitutes by white masters facing a draft. Others passed themselves off as free blacks, and hard-pressed recruiting officers did not question them too closely. Altogether, it is estimated that at least 5,000 blacks, slave and free, served in the Continental army and in the militias.

While southern states objected strongly to armed black men on the land, they objected little to using them on the sea, perhaps because black men on ships were seen as less dangerous than soldiers. The navies of both Virginia and South Carolina shipped black seamen, free and slave. Virginia actually purchased slaves from planters to fill out the ranks of its navy. When the war ended, the slaves' war service counted for little. They were sold off to private masters.

In the meantime, black soldiers distinguished themselves in combat. They participated in nearly every major battle from Lexington to Yorktown, earning the praise of a German mercenary as "able-bodied, strong and brave." While the soldiers were fighting, other blacks were pointing out the contradiction inherent in the American cause: how could white Americans claim they were fighting for freedom while they defended slavery at home?

Petitions from blacks asking an end to slavery were regularly presented to New England legislatures. One such request, submitted to the Massachusetts House of Representatives in 1777, bluntly expressed "astonishment that it had never been considered that every principle from which America has acted . . . pleads stronger than a thousand arguments in favor of your [abolitionist] petitioners." Urging that all slaves be freed at age twenty-one, the petition added that such action would free white Americans from the charge of "inconsistency of acting themselves the part which they condemn and oppose in others."

In fact, many whites were well aware of the inconsistency. Manumission societies, devoted to voluntary freeing of slaves, spread through the North and South. Curiously, many of the members of these societies could not envision a nation in which whites and free blacks lived amicably together; they looked toward deporting freed blacks to Africa. Thomas Jefferson, like Lincoln later, detested slavery but thought peaceful coexistence between the races impossible. Another outlook was represented by Patrick Henry. He admitted to inconsistency in holding slaves on the one hand while avowing the rights of man on the other. But, said he, "I am drawn along by the inconvenience of living here without them [slaves]. I will not, I cannot justify it [slavery]."

The growing antislavery sentiment, however, did find expression. The Continental Congress banned the importation of slaves. Gradual emancipation followed in all northern states, except New York. In Massachusetts the legislature's failure to act left the way open for the courts. The famous Quork Walker case (1781–83) held that slavery was unconstitutional in light of the Massachusetts Constitution of 1780.

When the war ended, most slaves who served with the American forces were freed. Masters who had offered slaves as substitutes received little sympathy from the courts when they tried to reenslave the blacks. In the North, slaves of Loyalists were freed—but not in the South, where they were sold. Perhaps the most incisive comment on the black experience in America to that time came from St. George Tucker, a white Virginian. America, he said, had been a "land of promise" for Europeans and their descendants, but "it hath been a vale of tears to millions of the wretched sons of Africa."

ARE BLACKS PEOPLE?

The very presence of the sons and daughters of Africa threatened the national unity the Patriots needed. Thomas Jefferson was forced to delete from his draft of the Declaration of Independence a condemnation of the trans-Atlantic slave trade as "cruel war against human nature itself, violating its most sacred rights of life and liberty."

When the Continental Congress began considering the Articles of Confederation as a framework of national government, the issue rose again in the form: Were slaves people or property? The problem centered on how the new government was to be financed. All were agreed on denying the new government the power to tax; all agreed that the individual states should contribute required funds to the national treasury. But on what basis? On the basis of population, including slaves, said New England, anxious to avoid contributions based on improved real estate. The South agreed on population as long as slaves were not counted. After all, the representatives of the South argued, slaves were property, like cattle. After bitter debate, the South lost in a vote along sectional lines—but not before Thomas Lynch of South Carolina made the ominous threat that unless slaves were treated as property, there would be no United States!

The threat had substance. Samuel Chase of Maryland vowed that his state would never ratify the articles until the offending measure was amended. Similar sentiment was expressed elsewhere. Confronted with such a crisis in the midst of the war, many northerners yielded to the southern position. New England was outvoted, and state levies were based on land and improvements. But the issue would not go away. It plagued the Constitutional Convention of 1787, resulting in the famous three-fifths compromise, which held in effect that a slave was three-fifths of a man, to use James Madison's description.

PATRIOT DISCORD

If white Americans argued over the status of blacks, they quarreled even more bitterly over who should rule among whites. At one extreme were the radicals, such as Tom Paine and Sam Adams, who believed in power to the people. In their view, society should be governed in the interest of the mass of farmers, shopkeepers, artisans, seamen, and urban workers, all those whom the aristocratic revolutionary Gouverneur Morris classified as "The mob . . . Poor reptiles!" although he warned, "They will bite."

At the other extreme were the conservatives, men of property and standing, typified by Robert Morris, the great Philadelphia merchant; George Washington, the Virginia planter now general of the army; and Alexander Hamilton, an up-and-coming New York lawyer. The conservatives held the masses unfit for self-government and looked to carrying on the rule of colonial elites. Between these two groups was another, symbolized by Thomas Jefferson, that both opposed elitist government and distrusted unchecked expression of the popular will. The struggle of the contending parties for control of national and state governments was embittered by a galloping monetary inflation that enriched some while it impoverished many.

The inflation began when the Continental Congress decided to finance the war by issuing bills of credit, which in effect became paper money. Lacking the power to tax, the Congress expected that the currency would be supported by state tax levies, which would be paid into the national treasury. The states proved as dilatory in meeting their financial obligations as they did in supplying troops for the army, and they even made the situation worse by issuing paper money of their own.

Through 1776, Americans were happy. The demands of the war and incipient inflation raised wages and prices, jobs were plentiful, and prosperity smiled on all. By 1777 the euphoria had passed. Driven by the exigencies of what was going to be a long war and realizing that the states could not be relied on, Congress went on turning out paper money. The British contributed to the inflation by printing large issues of counterfeit Continental bills. By 1779 the American government was over $200 million in debt, and prices had risen astronomically. A week's board and lodging in Philadelphia, the nation's capital, cost $4 in 1776. In 1779 it cost $100.

In desperation, Congress practically repudiated its own money in 1780. But there was little confidence in the new money the Congress authorized. The inflation continued. In 1781 shoes sold for $100 a pair, tea was $90 a pound, and a barrel of flour cost $1,575. Only the infusion of French and Dutch loans kept the infant government financially alive.

There was money to be made in this financial chaos, providing one had sufficient capital, credit, inside information, and shrewdness. Farmers did well for a time, especially those so situated as to sell food for gold and silver to the British and later to the French. Merchants did much better, particularly those who, like Robert Morris of Philadelphia, were members of key committees of the Congress and thus able to obtain secret information. While Morris labored in the cause of revolution, his partner, Thomas Willing, conducted business as usual with the British during their occupation of the city. As a result of his operations, Morris became the richest man in America. As he himself observed, "There has never been so fair an opportunity of making a large fortune since I have been conversant in the World."

Merchants added to their fortunes in a variety of ways. They cornered supplies of such vital necessities as iron, cloth, shoes, and flour and held them off the market until prices were right. Of course, the withholding of the goods sent prices skyrocketing. The Continental army suffered so dreadfully from shortages and high prices that an angered Washington proposed hanging some profiteers as examples. The canny merchants disposed of the depreciating currency they received as quickly as possible, investing it in more goods, urban real estate, land speculation in the West—anything of substance whose value was held bound to go up.

The merchants also did well by investing in long-term government bonds. As long as only the faith and credit of the national government supported such obligations, wealthy men were little interested. When French loans made it possible for the government to pay interest in gold, such men changed their minds. With paper money worth less than $8 million in gold they bought $63 million worth of securities, collected interest in gold, and looked forward to the day when they would collect the $63 million in hard cash.

Not all were able to wait long enough. In 1782 the government was forced to suspend interest payments in gold, and the price of government bonds fell sharply. Many bondholders sold out, and wealthier men bought, confident now after Yorktown that the United States was a going concern. The same spirit infused those who were busy buying up Continental currency for a few cents on the dollar and investing in state securities, which were also selling at much depreciated rates. Their faith was rewarded when the new federal government in 1790 pledged redemption in gold not only of all national obligations but also of state debts.

Privateering was another source of relatively easy wealth. Private individuals received authority from the states or Congress to raid British merchant ships. The captured ships and their cargoes were then sold at auction, the proceeds distributed among privateer owners, captains, and crews. The government involved, state or national, was also supposed to share in the booty, but all too often its interests were neglected. So profitable was privateering that more than 2,000 ships were ultimately involved. Their crews were said to number more men than were in the Continental army. The chief beneficiaries of this legalized piracy were the owners of the ships. For example, the Cabot brothers of Beverly, Massachusetts, who owned forty privateers, piled up a fortune by selling their prizes abroad for cash and depositing the proceeds with Spanish merchant-bankers.

MOBS AGAINST INFLATION

Popular discontent over inflation began early in the war, as soon as price-gouging made itself felt. The discontent was first expressed in the work of local revolutionary committees, which imposed price ceilings and forced open the warehouses of merchants unwilling to sell at the ceiling prices. Then, as the crisis mounted, some states took action, fixing wages and allowing price rises to provide 25 percent profit. But farmers and merchants were no more satisfied than they had been with the committee ceilings. They held goods off the market, sold them on the developing black market, or shipped them to states with no price controls.

Wholesale evasion of state laws led the New England states to form a regional compact to regulate prices and wages in 1776. The beginning was promising, and Congress urged other regions to follow suit. None did, and the New England experiment was abandoned within a year. Some states continued to try to enforce price regulations, but their efforts were ineffectual. Lacking a uniform national policy, the states were unable to cope with widespread evasion, which brought high rates of return, sometimes as high as 1,000 percent, to farmers and merchants.

The failure of price control greatly distressed urban working-class families and those with fixed incomes. Price regulations were easily evaded, but workers found it more difficult to escape wage-fixing in the states that attempted it. The reason largely was that employers had an obvious interest in keeping wages down, while farmers and merchants had a vested interest in driving prices up. Even so, the labor shortage was so acute that wages went up sharply, but they still lagged behind the prices of food and clothing.

The impoverishment of growing numbers of industrious men and women was all the more bitter because every day the newly poor could contrast their plight with the wealth flaunted by the newly rich. These well-fed men paraded the streets in elaborate carriages, attended by liveried servants. Their wives and daughters appeared in public in luxurious imported finery, decked out with expensive jewelry, while the men affected satin breeches and silk shirts. They gave lavish dinners, banquets, and balls. At one such dinner in Philadelphia in 1779 a guest noted he was served no less than 169 different dishes.

Urban workers then resorted to direct action in two forms: strikes and mobs. Gunsmiths, ship carpenters, teamsters, sailors, and others struck on various occasions, but the wage increases they won were of comparatively little value as prices continued upward. When strikes threatened direct war production, Congress used enlisted men from the army and Hessian prisoners of war as strikebreakers—a sharp contrast to the Congress's tolerance of profiteering merchants.

Mob action, in which women were often prominent, took place in a number of towns and cities. Warehouses were attacked and merchants forced to sell goods at reduced prices. On occasion, recalcitrant merchants were roughly handled and their goods seized. The most dramatic action, in Philadelphia in 1779, had political as well as economic objectives. Workers and their families, angered by high prices and the opulence displayed by the city's gentry, were also stirred to wrath by the gentle treatment accorded Loyalist merchants who remained after the British army evacuated the city. An armed mob attacked the house of James Wilson, a wealthy Patriot lawyer who had defended accused Tories. Several of the mob were shot before they were driven off by a cavalry outfit drawn from the city's elite. Plans to punish arrested rioters were abandoned when nearby militia units threatened action to free the prisoners. The rioters were released, but conservatives were alarmed.

Conservatives entrenched themselves in the new governments. The constitutions of such key states as Massachusetts, New York, Virginia, and South Carolina were written to preserve the rule of local elites. Four states provided for greater popular participation in government: North Carolina, Delaware, Georgia, and Pennsylvania. Of these, Pennsylvania went furthest, setting up a one-house legislature to be elected annually by taxpayers in each district, an arrangement that meant much greater political power for small farmers in the West. This legislature exercised supreme authority in the state until conservatives eventually won a government more to their liking.

"RABBLE IN ARMS"

Civilians suffered much from shortages and high prices, but the men of the Continental army fared even worse. At first the army was no more than a makeshift amalgamation of state troops besieging Boston in 1775. Many quit when their terms of enlistment were up, and late in 1776 Congress voted to raise an army of 75,000. Recruits were promised 100 acres of land when the war ended and a bounty of $20. Some states added their own bounties. Even so, only several hundred veteran soldiers reenlisted, and new recruits were slow to come in. Eventually an army of 34,000 was raised, but at any given time the number of effective troops was only a fraction of the number on the rolls. The others were out of service because of wounds, sickness, lack of clothing, and sheer fatigue resulting from hard work and starvation rations. And some simply deserted. Lafayette commented that, "No European army would suffer the tenth part of what the Americans suffer. It takes citizens to support hunger, nakedness, toil and total want of pay, which constitutes the condition of our soldiers, the hardiest and most patient that are to be found in the world."

A basic grievance of the soldiers was pay—or rather, the lack of it. Often they went unpaid for months. When they were paid, the money was Continental currency, whose value fell almost daily. Officers were in a sense worse off than enlisted men. They were paid more generously, but they were supposed to feed and clothe themselves. It is not surprising that when officers found themselves sinking into debt, while civilians were enriching themselves, many resigned their commissions, sometimes hundreds of officers at a time. Enlisted men also got into debt, but they could not resign. They had to serve out the term of their enlistment. If they decided to quit, it was accounted desertion—a capital crime.

Food and clothing for enlisted men came in sporadically and scantily. The states were slow to respond to requisitions for supplies. The transportation system was poorly organized, so that troops went hungry while fifty miles away food intended for them lay rotting. In some cases, government wagons were diverted to private use, leaving the army without transport. Merchants and farmers withheld goods from the army until they got the prices they wanted. Even when supplies reached the army, there was no certainty they would actually get to the troops. For a long time corruption was rife in the quartermaster corps, with officers selling food and other supplies on the black market.

In consequence, until 1780 when conditions improved, soldiers went hungry, ill-clad, and ill-shod. In winter their plight was desperate. During the record cold winter of 1779–80 many a soldier was reported on duty clad only in a blanket and shirt. At Valley Forge (1777–78) the winter was mild, but soldiers, lacking tents, had to improvise their own shelters from logs and mud. Food was so scanty that breakfast all too often was simply a drink of cold water and dinner a mouthful of food. General Anthony Wayne found a brigade in which not one man possessed a whole shirt. "Give us linen," he implored. The officers and men, he said, were "covered with rags and crawling with vermin." Such appeals including many from Washington himself, went largely unheeded. Not only was Congress chronically short of funds, but also many members felt that a big army might threaten the new republic. Better, they thought, to keep the soldiers on short rations and to control the army's size.

Medical care in the army was abysmal. A medical service was organized for northern troops, but it was rent by dissension among its top officers and it suffered from insufficient funding. There were never enough doctors, and many of them were amateurs and frauds. Hospitals were likewise too few, and they were chronically understaffed, lacking enough doctors, nurses, and other necessary help. Often they lacked bedding, food, and medicines too. Where hospitals were unavailable, sick and wounded were cared for in barns, outbuildings, private homes, or tents. The southern theater of war had no organized medical service at all until the war was almost over, even though the South was the scene of many of the bloodiest battles of the war. Care of the wounded and sick did improve in the later years of the war, thanks largely to the influence of French military physicians.

The wounded fell victim to the crude surgery of the day, which carried off many a trooper suffering from a relatively minor wound. The sick far outnumbered the wounded, however, and their care was so poor that Doctor Benjamin Rush, a leading physician and director-general of the medical service for a time, remarked bitterly that hospitals "robbed the United States of more citizens" than did British Redcoats.

Congress was partly responsible for this situation. Miserly in dealing with medical service, it appropriated so little money that Washington wondered how any self-respecting doctor would serve at the salaries offered. (That many of the prominent physicians of the day did serve with the army indicates that they, like the soldiers they served, were willing to put country above self-interest.)

Eventually, of course, even patriotic soldiers could no longer endure their condition. Minor mutinies, including one at Valley Forge, were easily suppressed, but a major revolt broke out in 1779. Connecticut troops, unpaid for six months and suffering from a 75 percent cut in their meat ration, mutinied. They were put down by Pennsylvania troops. Lesser outbreaks occurred the following year. Then on January 1, 1781, about 1,500 Pennsylvania troops—a substantial portion of the Continental army—rose in another major rebellion. Their specific grievance, besides the usual complaints of lack of pay and inadequate food, related to their length of service. The troops claimed that they had enlisted for only three years and their terms were completed. The state authorities insisted that the soldiers had signed up for the duration of the war. When officers attempted to restore order, three of them were killed and many others injured.

The British seized the opportunity to disrupt the American army. Agents were sent in with promises of payment of all wages due the soldiers and amnesty for all past offenses. The mutineers, who maintained their own excellent discipline in camp, promptly turned over the agents to American authorities, who hanged them.

The mutiny got results. Congress sent in a committee to discuss the soldiers' grievances, and Pennsylvania officials stopped insisting on the "duration of war" clause. Half of the troops won immediate discharge, and the remainder were furloughed.

Encouraged by the success of the Pennsylvanians, New Jersey troops staged their own uprising. They, however, were only 200 strong, and Washington, who had stayed out of the Pennsylvania crisis, intervened with New England troops. The mutiny was put down and two of its leaders executed. Another mutiny broke out in June 1783, when troops disgruntled by Congress's failure to pay them seized the arsenals in Philadelphia and beseiged the Congress, forcing its members to leave town. The uprising collapsed when Washington ordered loyal units into the city.

The mutinies won gains for many soldiers not involved in them at all. Congress and the states began to pay more attention to the soldiers' plight. And some states, principally in New England, suddenly found cash to pay troops whose wages were long in arrears.

More potentially dangerous than mutiny was the spread of disaffection among officers. Many were in debt. Promises that they would receive special benefits were not honored. There was a mounting bitterness toward Congress, together with a feeling that soldiers had been called upon to make undue sacrifices while civilians enjoyed life. Indeed, the indifference, and sometimes hostility, of "the better sort" toward soldiers at the end of the war convinced many that they were looked on as the rejects of society. After Yorktown the army was inactive for a long while. Rebelliousness flared up when the states and Congress failed to provide for paying off the troops when the Army was disbanded.

The discontent among the officers first surfaced in 1782, when Colonel Lewis Nicola suggested to Washington that the republic be ended and be replaced with a constitutional monarchy headed by Washington himself—a proposal the general quickly squelched. A year later Washington was confronted with the threat of a military coup headed by his own officers. The threat was made in the anonymously written Newburgh Addresses, which set forth the army's grievances and urged use of the army against Congress to compel action. Washington forestalled the rebellious officers, warning of civil war and bloodshed if the plan were carried through. He suggested a petition to Congress instead.

This time Congress acted, an action hastened by the Philadelphia mutiny. Officers were assured five years' full pay, and enlisted men were paid three months of their back pay. The cash was so long reaching the troops, however, that many went home without any pay at all. All pay arrears of soldiers were eventually met with Continental notes. Unfortunately for the soldiers, these fell steadily in value, and many hard-pressed veterans sold them for what they could get. The speculators who bought them made phenomenal profits when the federal government a few years later redeemed the notes at full face value.

TRAITORS OR P.O.W.'S?

It is difficult to conceive of men in worse condition than the Continental soldiers, but some were—the soldiers and sailors captured by the British. In the eyes of Britain they were not prisoners of war but traitors, and as such subject to death. Some British officials did indeed look forward to hanging American rebels as a deterrent to revolution, and some American prisoners were taken to England with public execution in mind. One of them was Ethan Allen, hero of the Patriot capture of Fort Ticonderoga on Lake Champlain, who was later captured by the British. Herman Melville's novel *Israel Potter* vividly describes how Allen was put in chains and on public display in England. Perhaps the American threat to take reprisals against captured Britons argued against implementing such a policy. In any case, the British government held back from treason trials and executions.

In the meantime, many patriots died while held as prisoners. They were jammed into "prison hulks" in New York harbor and elsewhere, with barely enough air to breathe, given putrid drinking water, fed poorly and inadequately, and exposed to such fatal diseases as smallpox and dysentery, which spread rapidly in the crowded quarters. The situation was not altogether happenstance. In the early part of the war, severe confinement was deliberate policy, designed to break the morale of the prisoners and persuade them to desert to the British. The refusal of most prisoners to defect simply hardened the resolve of the British—and American Loyalists upbraided the

British because they were too ''soft'' on rebels. (In contrast, American sailors held prisoners in England found their scanty rations supplemented with food donated by English sympathizers.) How many men died in the hulks is not known, but it appears that in the prison fleet in New York harbor alone nearly 12,000 soldiers and sailors perished.

GUERRILLAS AND THE PEOPLE

Soldiers and sailors were not the only Patriots who fought. Important to American success were the state militias and irregular partisan bands. Indeed, says John C. Miller, ''Washington could not have taken the field without militia.'' Organized for military service within state boundaries, the militia units were very much on their own. Only when collaborating with the Continental army were they required to follow army orders. Usually they fought only when their own state was endangered. They were nearly all poor farmers, mechanics, and laborers, for the well-to-do bought their way out of service by hiring substitutes. Although the states paid high bounties for service, the militiamen usually had to provide their own supplies. The irregular bands were made up of farmers and frontiersmen not formally called into service. They took to the field largely to avenge British and Loyalist depredations.

The militia played a major role in several major American victories. Saratoga, which helped bring France into the war, was largely the work of militiamen. The battles of Cowpens and King's Mountain, which ended British hopes of occupying the interior of the Carolinas, were even more purely militia victories. The British strategy of winning the war by ''pacifying'' the South and then crushing Washington's army in the North was disrupted by the guerrilla warfare waged by such partisan leaders as Francis Marion of South Carolina, appropriately named ''The Swamp Fox.''

The guerrillas, operating mostly in the South, posed problems with which the British, accustomed to the standard warfare of Europe, could not cope. The rebels staged hit-and-run raids, wiping out foraging parties and cutting off stragglers. They cut lines of communication and supply, making off with as much booty as possible. They harassed British troops constantly, allowing them neither rest nor a sense of security. They supplied vital intelligence to the Continental army. They were the nemesis of Loyalist auxiliaries to the British army, wreaking vengeance on men they thought of as traitors. They carried total war into the camps of Indians allied with the British. Damage to the enemy done, they resumed their roles as peaceful farmers and mechanics, even taking the oaths of allegiance required by the British when they dominated an area.

Obviously, the guerrillas could not function without the support of the people. Since the guerrillas could not be reached directly, the British decided to make life so unpleasant for people that they either would refuse to shelter the guerrillas or would betray them to the British. British soldiers were turned loose on the countryside. Looting, destruction, beating, and rape all fit into a policy calculated to destroy the American will to resist. British terror in the countryside had the reverse effect; it unified the people behind the guerrillas and contributed to mounting hatred of the Redcoats. Perhaps nothing infuriated Americans more than the rape of girls and women by British soldiers. Protests against the outrage were met with the disdainful cynicism toward women typical of the British aristocracy. Lord Cawdon, a British commander, was amused by the charges brought by victims of uniformed rapists. "Girls of New York," he wrote, "are in wonderful tribulation, as the fresh meat our men have got here has made them riotous as satyrs. A girl cannot step into the bushes to pluck a rose without . . . being ravished, and they are so little accustomed to these vigorous methods that they don't bear them with proper resignation, and of consequence we have most entertaining courts-martial every day."

Such attitudes help explain the failure of British "pacification" policy. Previously neutral Americans turned hostile to the British, and the guerrillas found new recruits.

WOMEN AT WAR

As part of the people in arms, women took a much more active part in the war than is generally recognized. Some actually disguised themselves as men and fought in the army. A great many more accompanied their husbands and boyfriends, and their presence resulted in much cleaner and more wholesome camps. The soldiers thought that washing clothes and cleaning their quarters was beneath their dignity. Women took over the camp chores, washing and mending clothes, cooking food, and keeping living quarters clean. Washington, who was displeased by women and children in camp, eventually was persuaded that they were so essential they should be issued rations. One army wife, Margaret Corbin, was honored by Congress. When her husband was killed, she took his place in battle until she herself was wounded.

Women were especially active on the home front. They worked in gun and munitions shops and in the production of other war supplies. Working-class women were in the forefront in enforcing price controls, and they led many of the riots and demonstrations against profiteering merchants and Loyalists. Upper-class women organized relief societies to provide aid for soldiers and their families, showing more

WILLIAM JACKSON,
an *IMPORTER*; at the
BRAZEN HEAD,
North Side of the TOWN-HOUSE,
and *Oppoſite the Town-Pump, in*
Corn-hill, BOSTON.

It is deſired that the Sons and Daughters of *LIBERTY*, would not buy any one thing of him, for in ſo doing they will bring Diſgrace upon *themſelves*, and their *Poſterity*, for *ever* and *ever*, AMEN.

The active role of women in the Patriot cause is suggested in this appeal for a boycott of a pro-British importer in 1770.

concern for the wounded and sick than did the politicians at Philadelphia. Two of the most notable women of the period, Mercy Otis Warren and Abigail Smith Adams, served as effective intelligence agents for their husbands and other leaders of the Patriot cause.

Warren and Adams are significant for more than their reporting, however. Both of them possessed first-rate minds, and both believed that the Revolution must liberate women as well as men. Their political outlooks differed. Warren, like her husband, James, was a thorough democrat, while Adams, like her husband, John, was conservative. Even so, both sought to use their influence to promote women's rights. Warren decried restrictions on women, asserting their right to participate in public affairs. She pointed out that the alleged intellectual inferiority of women was due not so much to "inferior contexture of female intellects as in the different education bestowed on the sexes." Adams was even more pointed. In a letter to John in 1777 she took a position that has become a classic in American feminist literature:

> In the new code of laws which I suppose it will be necessary for you to make, I desire you would remember the ladies and be more generous and favorable to them than your ancestors. Do not put such unlimited power into the hands of husbands. Remember, all men would be tyrants if they could. If particular care is not paid to the ladies, we are determined to foment a rebellion, and will not hold ourselves bound by any laws in which we have no voice or representation.

PAWNS IN THE WAR

For Indian peoples, the war was clearly a white man's affair. Involvement posed grave dangers for them, no matter which side they took. Their initial response was to stay out of the conflict, avowing friendship for both sides. Whites would not have it so. The Patriots, fearful of British influence over the Indians, were willing to accept neutrality if necessary, but they preferred actual assistance. The British, confronted with a manpower shortage in their army, began to recruit Indian allies actively. Some peoples joined the rebels, more tried to remain neutral, and many went over to the British. Some neutrals abandoned their policy when Americans invaded Indian territory.

Apart from American invasion of Indian lands, there were good reasons why so many Indians opted for the Empire. The British could supply them with tools, blankets, firearms, and other necessities, while the rebels could not. Perhaps even more important, the British had shown, through the Quebec Act and the Proclamation of 1763, that they meant to halt American expansion into Indian lands. On the other hand, it was clear that white Americans were determined to take the Indian lands for themselves. Finally, it was as obvious to many Indians as to the statesmen of England and Loyalist America that Britain was bound to win.

Both sides used Indians when they could, and both deplored, for the record, the "savagery" of Indian warfare. The British blamed some bloody incidents on their Indian allies, but went on paying the Indians for American scalps. The Americans denounced Indian atrocities, but a British army officer reported in 1782 that Americans had "butchered in cold blood or burnt alive" Cherokee women and children. That same year, a party of Pennsylvanians seeking land in Ohio enjoyed three days of rest and hospitality at Gnaddenhutten, a settlement of Delawares living under the guidance of pacifist Moravian missionaries. Then the Pennsylvanians fell upon their hosts, killing ninety men, women, and children gathered together in church for a Christian service. That atrocity helped to bring Ohio's neutral Indians into the British camp.

Indian peoples paid dearly for siding with the British. In the South, Virginians and Carolinians, long covetous of Cherokee lands, used the Indians' alliance with the British to carry the war into Indian territory in late 1776. Killing as they went, the whites burned villages and destroyed crops, in a policy calculated to deprive the Cherokee people of both food and shelter in the approaching winter. The policy of terror worked. In 1777 the Cherokees yielded vast tracts in the western Carolinas to the white invaders. But whites were not yet satisfied, and Indians sought revenge. White power again crushed the Cherokees. In 1781 they gave up yet more of their land.

Such land cessions brought a fresh influx of whites into what are now Kentucky and Tennessee, adding to the thousands already encroaching on Indian planting and hunting grounds. Indian peoples, confident of British aid, fought back. Kentucky came to be known as "the dark and bloody ground."

In New York and the Ohio country, Americans cut wide swaths through Indian territory. The Iroquois, who backed the British, were temporarily subdued, and George Rogers Clark made himself a hero in 1778 by leading a victorious expedition that captured British outposts on the Mississippi and brought the Illinois Indians under subjection. But the Americans could not maintain their hold. Indian warriors soon undid Clark's "conquest" in the Northwest, and in New York the Iroquois wreaked so much destruction in 1780 that the citizens of Albany feared for the safety of their city.

But Indian resistance proved futile. Just as the Indians had been betrayed by the French in 1763, they were betrayed by the British in 1783. In making peace, the British sacrificed their Indian allies, giving up all their western lands to the United States. There was no longer a Proclamation of 1763 or a Quebec Act to shield Indian peoples from the designs of white Americans. Those Indians who occupied or had claims on the country north of the Ohio River were cajoled, coerced, and bribed into giving up the land. Then a liberally bribed Congress sold 6.5 million acres of Indian territory to land speculators at ridiculously low prices.

WHAT DIFFERENCE DID IT MAKE?

The Revolution affected the lives of all American peoples, just as all major wars do. The nature of the changes and their consequences depended on skin color and, in the case of the whites, on social class.

Indian peoples, of course, were worse off than before. They had lost the protecting arm of Britain. To be sure, Britain held on to its forts in the Northwest, even though the peace treaty called for them to be abandoned, and the British continued to trade and conspire with Indians. But revival of British power in Indian country was remote. A veritable white tide of American settlers engulfed the Ohio Valley and poured through the Cumberland Gap to the south, authorized and protected by the new government of the United States.

For black people, the situation was not so clear. Slavery was being phased out in the North, although few northern whites believed that they now had to deal with blacks as equals. In the South, while antislavery sentiment was strong in Virginia and North Carolina, proslavery feeling was even stronger in South Carolina and Georgia. And there was no longer even the faint possibility that Parliament or the Crown would intervene to curb the absolute power of slaveholders. Black slaves, more than ever, were at the mercy of their owners.

The life of small farmers and urban workers went on much as before: a constant round of hard work accompanied by penny-pinching to make ends meet. Many, especially the farmers, were perhaps worse off after the war than before, since they stood to lose their property unless they could pay off high wartime debts in hard money at a time when prices were falling.

Continental army men could well take pride in their accomplishments, but there was little sign that their compatriots felt grateful. For many, the end of the war meant returning to their farms, which, despite the hard labor of wives and children, were in poor condition and burdened with debt. Such soldiers had little alternative save to sell to speculators, for a few cents on the dollar, the land warrants and Continental certificates with which they had been paid off.

There were soldiers and militiamen, however, who were not so hard pressed. Many of them used their land warrants to take up land in the West, hoping to make a fresh start in life. Along with them went small farmers with sufficient capital to move and to pay the prices charged by land speculators. Since the speculators wished to promote rapid settlement, prices were relatively low, even though they did bring the speculators a substantial profit. Even poor folk who could not afford the low prices went west. They simply "squatted" on available land, building crude dwellings and barns and working the land as if it were their own. They, of course, settled on the far frontier, hoping to escape the notice of landowners and authorities.

For some Americans, the war proved a boon. Loyalist elites were driven from power, opening room at the top for "new men" who had made fame or fortune from the struggle. Merchants, generals, planters, lawyers, and politicians swarmed in. Their rise left room below for lesser but equally ambitious men to move up a rung or two on the social ladder. The most obvious gainers were the great merchants, living lavishly on war profits. With victory they turned to investment in western lands. Some, such as William Duer of New York and his associates, had no thought of developing the West. They held the land they got from Congress to sell to other speculators at home and abroad.

If merchants looked inward, they also looked outward. Peace freed them from the restrictions of the British mercantile system, and now the world was their oyster—except for Britain and its colonies, which restricted American trade. Americans made up the lost markets by expanding trade with Europe and competing with the British for the markets of China. The first American vessel designed for the China trade, the *Empress of China,* sailed from New York in 1784. When it returned fifteen months later, its owners reported 25 percent profit on the voyage. The China trade thereafter grew rapidly.

The native white elites emerged from the war stronger than before, for now they were freed from the restrictions of British control. Symbolically, the single most powerful person in the country at the end of the war, apart from George Washington, was Robert Morris, the Philadelphia merchant. As superintendent of finance he was granted sweeping power, including control of all French aid, by Congress in 1781 to bring order out of the country's financial chaos. He also used his personal credit to pay and supply the troops for the victorious Yorktown campaign—an example that few of his fellow merchants cared to follow.

Such men looked forward to guiding and controlling the expansion of the new nation, just as they had controlled the Revolution. Their experiences with urban mobs during the war intensified their already profound distrust of the masses. The ways in which some states had interfered with property rights, as in making debts payable in paper money, made them suspicious of both state power and government too responsive to the people. In their view, the interests of the country—which they, like all ruling groups, identified with their own—demanded a strong central government dedicated to protecting and promoting the rights of property. As John Jay, the conservative New York lawyer who helped draft his state's constitution, put it, "Those who own the country ought to govern it." As it turned out, Jay's dictum proved to be the rule rather than the exception. Indeed, it was embodied in the new federal Constitution adopted in 1789.

No matter what its limitations, the Revolution marked a road taken. White Americans were now free to pursue their own destiny, untrammeled by imperial policy. The vast West, which the British had threatened to close to Americans, was now open. American society was more open and more fluid, at once making it easier than before to move up and increasing psychological tensions as people competed more and more to clamber up the ladder—tensions that were more obvious in the nineteenth than in the late eighteenth century. Politically, also, the new nation was less exclusive than before. Servants, farm laborers, and many urban workers were still denied the ballot, but more white men than ever could vote and hold office. Few people even considered that women had political rights.

Private citizens were more secure in their personal rights than before, at least insofar as the written state constitutions were concerned. Freedom of speech and of the press was generally guaranteed. Accused persons had the rights of jury trial and habeas corpus. Private property could not be taken by government without due process of law. The citizen's privacy was protected against unreasonable search and seizure. These, of course, had been traditional rights of Englishmen in common law, but British courts and officials had demonstrated that such rights could be interpreted to serve imperial interests. Americans secured themselves against such tyranny by spelling the rights out as part of a body of supreme law.

The Revolution also brought a greater measure of religious freedom to Americans. Individuals were free to worship as they pleased. In Maryland and Virginia the Anglican church lost its tax support, setting a precedent for the later disestablishment of the Congregational church in the New England states. Americans also obtained control over churches that had previously been directed from England. Episcopalians and Methodists set up their own governing bodies in the United States. Father John Carroll, later Bishop of Baltimore, replaced the Roman Catholic vicar apostolic in England as the representative of the Papacy in the United States.

But religious freedom was far from complete. Jews were barred from public office by tests requiring officeholders to be Christians. Three states thought this requirement inadequate: New Jersey and North and South Carolina allowed only Protestants to hold office. Delaware held that only those who believed in the Holy Trinity were to be trusted, thus excluding Quakers. Gradually such religious limits on political freedom were removed.

Perhaps more important in the long run than these immediate consequences of the Revolution is the document that, in a sense, transcends the Revolution that gave it birth. The Declaration of Independence was much more than its title indicates: it was an assertion of universal moral principles to which the new nation committed itself. In so doing it justified not only the American effort to overthrow the established government by force and violence but also held out hope for oppressed people everywhere. The principles of the Declaration are set forth with stark simplicity: all men are created equal, and all enjoy certain inalienable rights—life, liberty, and the pursuit of happiness. (The last, vague though it may be, is surely a more lofty concept of humanity than that contained in John Locke's triad of human rights—life, liberty, and property.) When government fails to assure these rights, says the Declaration, the people have the right to alter or abolish it and to set up a new government that will promote their safety and happiness.

From Jefferson's day to ours, the Declaration has injected a moral tension into American society—a tension resulting from the discrepancy between principle and practice, ideal and reality. With few exceptions, such as slaveholders before the Civil War, Americans have accepted the principles of the Declaration, but they have been slow and grudging in putting them into practice.

It is significant, however, that aggrieved Americans historically have appealed to the nation's conscience as part of the struggle for their rights. Black people, women, labor unionists, advocates of Indian rights—all have stressed their moral claims in light of the Declaration. Dr. Benjamin Rush was perceptive when he commented in 1783, "The American War is over, but this is far from being the case with the American Revolution."

FOR FURTHER READING

A good survey of the Revolution is John C. Miller, *Triumph of Freedom* (1948). Stimulating reinterpretations of some aspects of the Revolution are provided in Richard B. Morris, ed., *The American Revolution Reconsidered* (1967), and J. H. Hutson and S. G. Kurtz, eds., *Essays on the American Revolution* (1973). Issues of class are discussed in Jackson Turner Main, *The Social Structure of Revolutionary America* (1965).

The black role is discussed in Benjamin Quarles, *The Negro in the American Revolution* (1961). Arthur Zilversmit, *The First Emancipation* (1967), deals with the abolition of slavery in the North. For the problems raised by slavery to Revolutionary thought, see Winthrop Jordan, *White over Black* (1968).

Special aspects of the Revolution are covered in Jack Sosin, *The Revolutionary Frontier*

(1967), and R. Calhoon, *The Loyalists in Revolutionary America* (1973).

The Revolution is seen as part of a pattern of European change in R. R. Palmer, *The Age of the Democratic Revolution* (1959).

For differing interpretations of the Revolution see Merrill Jensen, *The Articles of Confederation* (1940) and *The Founding of a Nation* (1968); Gordon S. Wood, *The Creation of the American Republic* (1969); and Forrest McDonald, *E Pluribus Unum* (1965).

The Age of Tecumseh, Francis Lowell, Sarah Bagley, Nat Turner, and Elizabeth Cady Stanton

phase two

PRE-INDUSTRIAL AMERICA

1783 to 1865

1786	Shays' Rebellion in Massachusetts stimulates movement for powerful central government.
1789	Federal government established under new Constitution.
1793	Samuel Slater's cotton factory marks beginning of Industrial Revolution in the United States.
1793	Eli Whitney's cotton gin gives new lease on life to southern slavery.
1794	Labor unions take hold among skilled workers.
1800	Gabriel slave uprising in Virginia.
1803	Louisiana Purchase extends power of United States over Indians.
1811	Tecumseh's plan for Indian power frustrated by battle at Tippecanoe.
1815	End of War of 1812. Indian peoples lose British support.
1820	Missouri Compromise bans slavery in northern area of Louisiana Purchase.
1829	David Walker's *Appeal* marks new era of militant abolitionism.
1831	Nat Turner slave insurrection in Virginia.
1832	Nullification crisis in South Carolina.
1836	"Trail of tears" of Cherokees climaxes Indian-removal policy.
1842	Labor unions gain limited legality in Massachusetts.
1846	United States gains Pacific Northwest in settlement with Britain.
1848	United States gains Southwest and California from Mexico.
1848	Seneca Falls convention inaugurates women's movement.
1848	Massive Irish and German immigration in progress.
1850	Compromise of 1850 includes harsh fugitive-slave law.
1854	Kansas-Nebraska bill repeals Missouri Compromise.
1857	Dred Scott decision says blacks are not citizens.
1859	John Brown's raid symbolizes growing hostility to slavery.
1860	South Carolina secedes after election of Lincoln.
1861–65	Civil War.

Preindustrial America, roughly the period from 1783 to 1865, refers to the phase of the nation's development in which the economy, except in the South, was in transition from the farming-trading complex of colonial times to the industrialism that characterized the North after 1865. It was the era of the first Industrial Revolution, which vastly increased the productive capacity of the country by harnessing water and steam power to run the new machines in the ever-growing factory system. The economy, then, both changed and expanded.

Economic expansion was further stimulated by territorial growth. By 1850 the United States ranged between the "natural" boundaries of the Atlantic and Pacific oceans and between the political boundaries of the Rio Grande in the south and the forty-ninth parallel in the north. The lands acquired peacefully from France through the Louisiana Purchase in 1803 were supplemented in 1848 with the territory wrested from Mexico after its defeat in war. In 1846 Britain ceded to the United States what is now the Pacific Northwest.

The acquired lands made available to Americans great mineral deposits, including gold and silver; vast open ranges, which supported cattle-raising on a large scale; and fertile soil, which attracted cotton planters in the South and wheat farmers in the

North. The new lands provided raw materials for industry in the North and for export and furnished foodstuffs for a growing national population. In turn, settlement of the new lands swelled the national market for the expanding industry of the North.

Industrialization had major social consequences. Towns and cities grew apace, with new inhabitants streaming in from abroad and from the American countryside. This trend toward urbanization has continued to this day. Two cultures emerged—rural and urban—to live together uneasily.

Two new social classes appeared, also. One was that of the industrial capitalists whose wealth was invested in factories, mines, and railroads. The other class was the industrial proletariat, the mass of wage-earners who owned little or no property and depended entirely on their wages for survival. These were the "working poor."

There was still another significant class, partly old, partly new. It was a middle class, made up of two distinct elements. One, as in earlier times, included doctors, lawyers, clergymen, minor merchants, and well-to-do farmers. The other embraced such "new" elements as accountants, engineers, master mechanics, managers, and supervisors. The rapid expansion of the economy opened up opportunities for many of this class to move upward on the social scale.

Preindustrial America was more than expansive; it was turbulent. The economy was highly unstable. Periods of prosperity, marked by wild speculation and "paper fortunes" made overnight, alternated with depressions, in which countless people lost wealth and status and many were reduced to poverty.

Few Americans, apart from those elites who were secure in their positions, were spared the anxieties that arose from an unstable society. If, in an age of economic expansion and its concomitant fluid society, it was relatively easy to make one's way up the social ladder, it was even easier to slip down. In fact, an individual's destiny was not of one's own making, but that was no excuse among a people who believed in the gospel of success, which held each individual responsible for his or her own success or failure. Thus, aspiring Americans were plagued with anxieties about security and status.

Turbulence and anxiety did not indicate internal disintegration. Rather, they may be interpreted as the growing pains of a developing nation. Society may have been fluid, with all the uncertainities that entailed, but at the top, elites remained stable and secure, bound together in a network of ties of family, tradition, association, and economic interest. Their rule remained unshaken, despite the "democratic revolution," symbolized by Andrew Jackson, thus affording a basis of order in an unstable society. Their position remained secure as long as countless Americans shared their value systems. Such Americans were obsessed with "bettering" themselves, and many aspired to enter the ranks of the elites. Given the prevalence of those feelings, elites had little to fear. As it happened, the greatest threat to order came not from discontented masses, but from southern planter elites who sought to establish a society in which they would dominate.

Another, and perhaps more powerful, factor binding white people together was patriotism. It was, of course, natural that successful folk should sing the praises of America, but even among "losers" the sentiment was so strong that foreign observers, such as Charles Dickens, found it abrasive. The Declaration of Independence was the secular bible of Americans. The successful prized its commitment to liberty as a natural right, by which they usually meant the freedom of all individuals to seek their own economic advancement. The unsuccessful emphasized the commitment to equality, and they recalled the contributions of poor farmers and artisans to the revolutionary cause. They might be alienated from existing American society, but not from the principles on which the nation was founded.

Contributing to this spirit was the feeling that the grievances of white people could be and often were redressed under the American system. As Americans looked at England and Europe, where common folk were ruthlessly exploited and treated with contempt, even "losers" were convinced that America, for all its imperfections, was better than anywhere else. America, in their eyes, was the hope of the oppressed of human kind. But white Americans simply assumed that blacks, Indian peoples, and Mexican-Americans were not included in that hope.

7 expropriating the native americans

The white settlers who poured into Indian country west of the Appalachians after the Revolutionary War came with fixed notions about Indian people. These notions, which had little relation to reality, were held all the more tenaciously because they served to justify white behavior toward Indians. The Indians, according to white mythology, were inferior, savage, lazy, immoral, and treacherous.

A minority of whites, typified by Thomas Jefferson, did not share all these views. They found much to admire in Indian society, but they believed it inferior to white society and doomed to extinction unless it was insulated from whites. They proposed two solutions. One was for the Indian to take up the white man's ways, acquire private property, and abide by white man's law. This accomplished, "You will unite yourselves with us," President Jefferson told an Indian delegation, "and we shall all be Americans."

The other white solution was to remove Indian peoples far beyond the reach of whites. This was thought to be a more realistic plan because the Indian population was being decimated by white man's diseases, such as smallpox, which in the eighteenth century had carried off as many as half the Cherokees and ravaged many other Indian peoples. Further, the Indians, because of their declining population, could not stand their losses in warfare with whites, who were increasing in numbers daily. Finally, avaricious whites were debauching Indian societies with alcohol. If Indians were to survive, they must be removed far from white settlements.

The basic drive for Indian removal, however, came from the whites' desire for Indian land. Here again white beliefs justified white ambitions. Although the Indians east of the Mississippi were largely settled agricultural peoples who supplemented their food supply by hunting and fishing, whites held that all Indians were wandering nomads who could not legitimately claim their lands as their own. Andrew Jackson referred to them as "wandering savages" and rejected their claims to land "on which they have neither dwelt nor made improvements, merely because they have seen them from the mountains or passed them in the chase." Whites could legitimately take Indian land because, in their own view, they were a civilized people who would put the land to good use. They quoted the Bible to prove that God intended land for those who made best use of it. The whites also invoked patriotism. For the American people to fulfill their "manifest destiny" by demonstrating the virtues of democracy, whites must have the land.

Not all whites shared such attitudes, however. There was a mounting, if still ineffective, body of white opinion that Americans had a duty to treat Indians with justice. That justice entailed faithful observance of the various treaties signed with Indian peoples to guarantee them their lands. These white "friends of the Indian" had little regard for Indian culture as such. They believed it inferior to white culture—but whites had an obligation to Christianize and civilize Indians and to avoid taking advantage of them. Indians responded favorably to such an attitude, they said, pointing to the progress made by the Cherokee nation in northern Georgia and Alabama.

When Congress in 1830 passed a law aimed at moving the Cherokees west of the Mississippi, such whites were outraged. Senator Theodore Frelinghuysen of New Jersey asked rhetorically: "Do the obligations of justice change with the color of the skin? Is it one of the prerogatives of the white man, that he may disregard the dictates of moral principle, when an Indian shall be concerned?"

WHITE POLICY: IMAGE AND REALITY

The image projected by official statements of federal Indian policy is that of a benevolent government treating Indian peoples with honesty and justice and with special concern for Indian welfare. The reality was quite different. The federal government became an instrument through which rapacious whites took over Indian lands and deported Indians from their homelands. Laws and treaties were so interpreted as to provide legal cover for such actions. White officials also resorted to a more basic justification: dispossession of the Indians was in the best interest of the Indians. Alexis de Tocqueville had such rationalization in mind when he noted in the 1830s that it was impossible "to destroy men with more respect for the laws of humanity" than did white Americans in their relations with Indians.

The official policy was first set forth in the famous Northwest Ordinance of 1787, providing a framework of government for the new territories north of the Ohio River and for their eventual organization as full-fledged states within the Union. In relation to Indian peoples within the territories, said the ordinance,

> The utmost good faith shall always be observed towards the Indians; their land and property shall never be taken from them without their consent; and in their property, rights, and liberty, they shall never be invaded or disturbed, unless in just and lawful wars authorized by Congress; but laws founded in justice and humanity shall from time to time be made, for preventing wrongs being done to them, and for preserving peace and friendship with them.

Such principles were applied nationally in policy formulated for the new federal government by Secretary of War Henry Knox and Secretary of State Thomas Jefferson. This policy provided that Indian peoples were to be treated as "foreign nations," not subject to state laws. Only the federal government could make treaties with such nations. The Indian peoples, said Knox, "possess the right of the soil of all lands within their limits . . . and they are not to be divested thereof, but in consequence of fair and bona fide purchases" approved by the United States. At first glance this policy appears to protect Indian land claims, but in fact it carefully avoided recognizing Indian title to land. It simply recognized Indian "right of the soil," which was a very different matter.

United States Attorney General William Wirt held in 1819 that the Indians' right of the soil referred to "use of the lands . . . as intended for their [Indians'] subsistence." Indians could sell surplus food they grew themselves, but they could not dispose of such other assets as timber. "They have no more right to sell the standing timber . . . than they have to sell the soil itself," said Wirt. By implication, Indians also enjoyed no subsoil mineral rights, leaving Indian lands wide open for white prospectors.

By 1830 even Wirt's limited recognition of Indian rights was denied. The Committee on Indian Affairs of the House of Representatives submitted a report that year asserting as a "fundamental principle, that the Indians had no right, by virtue of their ancient possession, either of soil or sovereignty." The committee put in plain words what John Marshall, Chief Justice of the United States Supreme Court, had said in 1823 in the case of *Johnson and Graham's Lessee* v. *McIntosh*. Marshall held that white discovery and settlement destroyed Indian sovereignty over the lands.

From Marshall's opinion and the report of the House committee it was a short step to an outright assertion of white sovereignty over Indian lands. Georgia first raised the issue in 1823, when it applied unsuccessfully for federal aid in expelling Indians. All lands within its borders, said Georgia, were subject to its sovereignty. The state could not permit the existence of rival powers, such as the Indians. President James Monroe replied that under existing law and treaties Indians could be removed only if they consented. When the succeeding president, John Quincy Adams, proved equally unsympathetic, Georgia took action on its own. In defiance of presidential directives, Indian lands were first surveyed, then occupied by whites. This assertion of states' rights proved successful. When Adams consulted Congressional leaders on possible federal action, he was advised to drop the issue. He did.

The next president, Andrew Jackson, was all that white expansionists could ask for. No great lover of Indian peoples, he supported Georgia's moves and himself engineered passage of the Indian-removal bill of 1830, which authorized him to move eastern Indian peoples west of the Mississippi. Removal was to be made in accord with treaties, a provision that was at once a gesture to reduce white hostility to the measure and a powerful incentive to whites to wring new and more favorable treaties from Indians. And, in still another provision designed to disarm opposition, the deported Indians were to enjoy in perpetuity the land to which they were assigned. To compensate Indians for losses, Congress appropriated $500,000.

The trend in national policy reflected the pressures from westerners, land speculators, and miners who were determined to have Indian territory. Federal laws regulating trade with Indians and white behavior were disregarded with impunity. Boundaries set by treaty were routinely flouted by whites seeking gold or land. The federal government itself behaved little better. It used the flare-ups of Indian resistance to extort from defeated peoples vast tracts of land, as in the Treaty of Greenville (1795). There, Northwest Indians who had been routed at the battle of Fallen Timbers were compelled to give up and leave nearly two-thirds of Ohio.

THE USES OF SUBVERSION

While willing to use force if necessary, the federal government preferred peaceful means to appease white land hunger. The result was a cold war against Indian peoples, in which subversion rather than force became a prime instrument of policy. A veritable network of American agents, including Christian missionaries, traders, and officials, provided intelligence and worked to disrupt attempts at Indian unity and resistance. Long-standing feuds between the Creeks and the Cherokees in the Southeast, and between the Iroquois and other Indian peoples in the North, were fanned to prevent the development of an Indian national front.

Indian society is no more immune than white to personal rivalry for leadership, and white Americans took full advantage of ambition as a means to their ends. Thus, in the 1830s they helped build up Keokuk, the collaborator among the Foxes and the Sauks along the upper Mississippi River, to challenge the leadership of Black Hawk, who advocated resistance. In like manner, they labored among the Cherokees to foster a clique against John Ross, the leader who adamantly opposed giving up Cherokee land.

Everywhere American agents spread the spirit of defeatism, emphasizing the long history of Indian failures in contests with whites. The missionaries, for their part, undermined Indian culture by insisting that Indian gods were false and that salvation could come only from adopting the white man's religion. The missionaries were especially successful in the Southeast, where the Indian ruling elites gave them free rein to carry on religious and educational activities.

Chiefs who collaborated with Americans were richly rewarded with gifts. Most important, such chiefs were supported by the United States as the legitimate representatives of their people, thus strengthening their internal rule. Also, of course, the federal government clothed the chiefs with authority to sign treaties giving up their lands. Objections from other Indians that chiefs had no such rights were brushed aside by the United States. Dissidents who could not be won over by flattery and whiskey were, as far as possible, isolated and their influence undermined.

One of the most effective means of breaking down Indian unity and providing additional stimulus for "voluntary" emigration was the system of land allotment. In this policy the federal government conceded that at least some Indians, especially in the Southeast, occupied and tilled their land like white farmers. Therefore, such Indians would be allotted lands, which they would own totally after five years of occupancy. Treaties to this effect were signed with the Creek, Chickasaw, and Choctaw nations.

The size of allotments was such, however, that after land had been assigned to Indians, millions of acres were surplus. White speculators speedily grabbed the excess. In the case of Creek lands, for example, 2 million acres were assigned to the Indians—and 5 million acres went to white "developers."

Indian ownership was not expected to last long, and it did not. A few of the wealthy elites who knew how to bargain fared well in the transaction. But the small farmers, unfamiliar with the intricacies of Anglo-American law, strapped for the credit needed to carry on under the new system, and often under the influence of alcohol, were induced to sign over their land rights to traders, who sold them goods on credit at highly inflated prices. The traders, in turn, sold off the land rights to speculators at a profit. When the Indians defaulted on their obligations, the white speculators took over. Soon there was a body of propertyless Indians living from hand to mouth and willing to emigrate.

Those who opted for allotments were a minority, but their defection opened up Indian lands to white occupation. On a much larger scale, the government sales of Indian lands to whites had the same effect. The white influx made the majority of Indians, who clung to their ancestral lands, vulnerable to mounting white pressures. The misfortunes of the poor Indians who had taken up allotments were used to point up to these Indians the benefits of emigration. Governor Gayle of Alabama told Creek chiefs in 1834:

> You know nothing of the skill of the white man in trading and making bargains, and cannot be guarded against the artful contrivances which dishonest men will resort to, to obtain your property under forms of contracts. In all these respects you are unequal to the white men, and if your people remain where they are, you will soon behold them in a miserable, degraded and destitute condition.

Federal agents in the meantime emphasized to Indians that they were now subject to laws of the states they lived in. The agents emphasized the disadvantages of that status. Indians could be jailed for trespassing if they went on to land acquired by whites. They were subject to service in the militia and to work on public roads, and they had to pay taxes. Above all, if they persisted in following Indian customs and laws, they could be heavily punished. Surely it was better for them to accept the generous offers of the United States and move west, where they would have their own land and could live freely according to their own laws and customs.

Indian peoples desperately clung to the lands of their ancestors, but their very desperation indicated mounting white pressure from without and subversion from within. Indian collaborators were able to take advantage of the consequent demoralization of their peoples and carry through treaties by which their peoples gave up their lands and moved beyond the Mississippi. The only hope of the Indian peoples now was the pledged word of the United States that the new land was theirs "as long as trees grow and the waters run."

Thus, the once-great nations of Choctaws, Chickasaws, and Creeks took the long trek west. Even the militant Seminoles in Florida were eventually forced into line. Collaborators had induced many Seminoles to move west in the 1830s, but others, led by Osceola, remained to fight. They were finally crushed in 1842. Some survivors escaped into the Everglades. The others were deported to the new Indian Territory.

INDIAN PATRIOTIC RESISTANCE

A major element in the success of collaborators was widespread Indian defeatism. Since the tragic days of the Pequots and the Powhatan Confederacy, the white tide had rolled on remorselessly. Indians either fell back, were overwhelmed, or learned to swim with the tide. This reading of Indian history was not acceptable to Indian patriots who loved their country and their ways of life. In the early nineteenth century local leaders such as Osceola among the Seminoles and Black Hawk among the Foxes and Sauks rallied their peoples for resistance. In the end, both were defeated. There was a certain symbolism in the fate of Osceola. Captured and degraded, he died—and the white doctor, whose services the Seminole had rejected, worked the final indignity. He cut off Osceola's head to keep as a souvenir!

The most significant of these Indian patriots, however, was Tecumseh, a Shawnee born in 1768 near what is now Dayton, Ohio. A warrior legendary among both whites and Indians in his own time, his fame rests on his attempt to forge an Indian nationalism to stem the white tide. The Indian problem, as Tecumseh perceived it, was that local or regional resistance was powerless to cope with a national, united, white government. The situation required a unified Indian power, embracing peoples of both the North and South. Ancient suspicions and animosities had to be submerged in the common cause. Chiefs who cooperated with whites from a genuine desire to save their people from harm would be won over. Collaborators who were corrupt would be driven from power. Until they attained unity, Indian peoples would refrain from local wars against whites. When unity was achieved, then it would be possible to confront white power with a prospect of success. In short, Tecumseh was trying to organize what today we would call a national liberation front.

Tecumseh's political appeal was enhanced by the religious message of his brother, Laulewasika, whom whites called the Prophet. Like Christian mystics, Laulewasika communed with God. God's message to Indian peoples was clear. They must abstain from liquor—Laulewasika was himself a reformed alcoholic—for whiskey was the white man's way of destroying Indian self-respect. They must shun Christianity, another white device to undermine Indian respect for themselves. They must prepare for that day when God's children would reclaim the land God had set aside for them. Let the white men depart for that country God had allotted to them on the other side of the Atlantic. Thus, the political message of Tecumseh was imbued with deep religious and moral feeling.

Tecumseh's work was difficult. He traveled through the North and South, trying to arouse a spirit of militancy and appealing to the Indian peoples to forget the past and unify themselves against the white power that now menaced them all. He made some converts, but such powerful Indian nations as the Iroquois in the North and the Cherokees in the South turned him down. Feuds between some peoples, such as those between the Creeks and Cherokees, were so bitter that they could not be put aside. Other peoples were unwilling to provoke whites. Chiefs who collaborated with whites were enraged at Tecumseh's call to replace them with Indian patriots. American agents used every menas at their disposal to frustrate the development of Indian unity.

Tecumseh's grand strategy was never put to the test. In 1811, while the Shawnee leader was in the South trying to arouse support, Governor Harrison of the Indiana Territory marched against Prophet's Town, a settlement on Tippecanoe Creek presided over by Laulewasika. Despite Tecumseh's explicit directions to give no battle until the day of war arrived, Laulewasika sanctioned an Indian attack. It failed, and the defeated Indians melted into the woods. Harrison burned the settlement and informed the War Department that he had inflicted a defeat on Indians more severe than any "since their acquaintance with white people." This exaggeration, eagerly accepted by whites, helped elect Harrison president in 1840.

There was, however, a core of truth to Harrison's bombast. His attack on Prophet's Town had ruined Tecumseh's strategy of keeping the peace until Indians could be united for war. Localized uprisings took place, and Americans subdued them. Then in 1812 came renewed hope. America went to war with Britain, and the British promised to establish an Indian country in the Great Lakes region in return for Indian aid. Tecumseh and his followers accepted the bargain, and they played a leading role in such British successes as the taking of Detroit. But once again Indian hopes were dashed when Tecumseh fell in battle in southern Ontario. With him perished the vision of a united Indian nation.

But Tecumseh's message had won over some peoples, the most important of which were the Red Stick Creeks in the Southeast—so called because they represented the patriot party in the nation, as against the collaborators, called appropriately White Sticks. Aroused by continued encroachment on their lands by whites and promised aid by British agents, the Red Sticks went to war in 1813, massacring the white population of Fort Mims, on the Alabama River north of the Spanish Florida border. White retribution came swiftly. Under the command of Andrew Jackson an army of 5,000 militiamen plus allies from such friendly Indian peoples as the Cherokees embarked on a campaign of "search and destroy." Creek villages were burned and their peoples exterminated. At the battle of Horseshoe Bend in 1814, the last stronghold of the Creeks was taken in a savage struggle in which some 800 Creek warriors were slain. The victorious Jackson dictated peace terms to the whole Creek nation: they must give up half of their lands. The chiefs protested, but they signed.

The outcome of the War of 1812 ended all hope of further aid from Britain. The British abandoned their idea of an Indian buffer zone in the Northwest to protect Canada. With British aid withdrawn and rebellious peoples crushed, the stage was now set for the next stage of American policy toward Indians: removing eastern peoples beyond the Mississippi.

THE FAILURE OF ACCOMMODATION

Indians could fall back before the white tide, or they could try to halt it and be destroyed. There was, many Indians thought, a third way. They would swim with the tide—and save themselves, their lands, and their self-respect. Such opinion was strong in southeastern peoples, and the Cherokees carried the experiment out most completely.

That experiment basically meant accommodation to white men's ways. Cherokee society would be reorganized to prove to whites that Indians were not savages, but hard-working, thrifty, law-abiding folk who would prove to be good neighbors. Cherokees had a strong basis for this policy. Although the nation had lost half of its ancestral lands, the Cherokees still occupied 10 million acres of land in northern Georgia and Alabama. There they had developed a stable, prosperous society of small farmers who produced corn and vegetables for the market as well as their own subsistence. The society was dominated by an elite of wealthy merchants and planters, most of whom were of white-Indian descent.

The policy of the elite had already alienated many of the poorer and more traditional Cherokees. The program of the leaders in the 1820s to reorganize their society antagonized them even more, and opened a rift in Cherokee society of which American agents took full advantage. In the meantime, the leadership went ahead with its plans.

A program to end illiteracy was initiated. This campaign was made easier by the development, in 1821, of a Cherokee alphabet by the famous Sequoyah, known in English as George Gist. With the aid of Christian missionaries, eighteen schools were operating by 1826, where children were taught religious doctrine, reading, writing, and arithmetic. The strong tradition of sexual equality among the Cherokees required that girls as well as boys be educated. But while both sexes were taught to read and write, boys were trained in vocational skills but girls learned only household skills. Literacy had advanced enough by 1828 to warrant the publication of a newspaper, the *Phoenix,* which appeared in both Cherokee and English. The newspaper served as a means to influence white opinion in the mounting struggle to keep Cherokee land for the Cherokees.

In still another effort to impress white opinion, the Cherokee government was reorganized in 1828. A written constitution, based on that of the United States, was adopted. All member peoples of the Cherokee nation were represented on a national council or legislature, while a national committee of thirteen members was to act for the nation as a whole. One member of the committee would serve as chief of state in dealing with outsiders. An independent judiciary was established, with eight district courts throughout the nation and a national superior court, similar to the United States Supreme Court, empowered to hear cases on review.

The new government acted energetically. No land was to be ceded without the consent of the national council. Chiefs, whether acting independently or jointly, were forbidden to interfere with either council or judicial decisions, a prohibition designed to halt the white practice of winning land cessions from individual chiefs. In addition, the new government declared that title to all gold or other valuable minerals in Cherokee territory was vested in the nation, not in individuals. Discoverers of such deposits were to be rewarded with one-fourth of the net income derived from their development. To be sure, the immediate aim was to frustrate white prospectors and Indian chiefs who could be persuaded to sell off rich lands—but the principle of public ownership of subsoil minerals invoked is significant.

Such a demonstration of Indian unity and power was exactly what land-hungry whites did not want. They needed to believe that Indians were nomadic savages—a need intensified by the discovery of gold in Cherokee territory in 1829. Whites by then also had a new rationale for getting rid of southeastern Indians: the Indian peoples really were willing to move, but they were prevented from leaving by rich elites who were not really Indians at all but people of predominantly white extraction. These leaders, it was said, ruthlessly exploited the poor Indians and used their power to mislead them into believing that removal was evil. Whites also believed that the leaders' motives were entirely selfish; they wanted to stay to maintain their power and their privileges at the expense of genuine Indians. Thus, in white eyes, the Indian-removal policy assumed the aspects of a moral crusade to liberate poor Indians from tyrannical chiefs.

So, holding the torch of liberty in the one hand and the sword of state sovereignty in the other, the Georgia legislature acted in 1829. All Cherokee lands were incorporated into the state and the inhabitants made subject to the laws of Georgia. The laws of the Cherokee nation were nullified and its government held to be only a "pretended" government. Heavy penalties were meted out to persons who tried to persuade Indians not to emigrate or who tried to interfere with chiefs who wanted to give up land. Then, in a catch-all provision designed to wipe out the Cherokee leadership, the law held that if the offenses against Georgia law were justified under the laws of the Cherokee nation, the penalties would also apply to the "pretended executive, ministerial or judicial officers," even if they were not involved individually.

The law, of course, flatly violated existing treaties between the United States and the Cherokees, but Georgia was not fearful. With Jackson as president, Georgia felt confident it would win. That confidence was well founded. Jackson in his first annual message came out strongly for Indian removal, denying the Cherokees' right to set up their independent government and upholding the rights of states to complete authority within their boundaries. Georgians could also appreciate Jackson's pious plea that this was all for the good of the Indians themselves. So long as Indians were in close contact with whites, they were doomed to extinction. "Humanity and national honor demand that every effort should be made to avert so great a calamity," said the president.

For their part, the Cherokees felt they could protect themselves by resisting Jackson in the white man's way. The growing feeling among whites that Indians were a sadly mistreated people gave them a way of appealing to the white conscience. Jackson was opposed by many of the most powerful men of the United States, and the Indian-removal issue provided his foes with new ammunition. Chief Justice John Marshall was well known as a foe of Jackson, and other justices might well be persuaded of the justice of the Cherokee cause. The Cherokees took their case as a sovereign nation directly to the Supreme Court, asking for an injunction against Georgia.

Their faith in the courts was rudely shaken. In *The Cherokee Nation* v. *the State of Georgia* (1831), Marshall held that Indian peoples could not be considered "foreign nations." They were rather "domestic dependent nations," in "a state of pupilage.'' In substance, ''Their relation to the United States resembles that of a ward to his guardian.'' As such, Indian nations could not ''maintain an action in the courts of the United States,'' and the court could not interfere with the Georgia laws. Marshall went on to emphasize that Indians could expect no redress from the Supreme Court for their grievances:

> If it be true that the Cherokee nation have rights, this is not the tribunal in which those rights are to be asserted. If it be true that wrongs have been inflicted, and that still greater are to be apprehended, this is not the tribunal which can redress the past or prevent the future.

For the moment it appeared that the Cherokees had lost all, but soon the issue arose in another form. Significantly, the new issue involved the rights of white men: missionaries working in the Cherokee country. When Georgia moved against the Cherokees, one of the state's prime aims was to rid the country of the Christian missionaries who were commonly regarded as the inspiration behind the Indian opposition. State licenses were required of all missionaries. Some missionaries complied with the law, but the Indian-rights activists refused. They were arrested, then freed by a local court that said the missionaries were agents of the United States. President Jackson then declared that missionaries were not federal agents. To emphasize his point, Jackson stripped Samuel A. Worcester, a leading missionary activist, of his United States postmastership. Georgia advised the recalcitrant missionaries to leave the state, on pain of imprisonment. Worcester and others ignored the advice. They were arrested, beaten and chained, and sentenced to four years at hard labor—with promise of a pardon if they agreed to leave. Worcester and another missionary, Elizur Butler, appealed to the United States Supreme Court.

In *The Cherokee Nation* v. *the State of Georgia* case Marshall had evaded the issue of validity of Georgia laws by denying the court's jurisdiction. Now he met the issue head-on, although that meant modifying the principles set forth in the earlier case. In *Worcester* v. *Georgia* (1832) Marshall, with the backing of the court's majority, held that only the United States could regulate relations with Indian peoples. It followed then that the Georgia laws against the Cherokees were invalid. Said Marshall:

> The Cherokee nation . . . is a distinct community, occupying its own territory, with boundaries accurately described, in which the laws of Georgia can have no force, and which the citizens of Georgia have no right to enter, but with the assent of the Cherokees themselves, or in conformity with treaties, and with the acts of Congress.

The Supreme Court reversed the convictions of Worcester and Butler.

Georgia paid no attention. Worcester and Butler were kept in prison. Surveys of Cherokee country went on, and in 1834 the state permitted white occupation of the lands. Citizens of the Cherokee nation were given two years to leave. This nullification of federal law brought no such ringing declaration of federal supremacy as

Jackson made when South Carolina nullified a tariff law in 1832. In the Cherokee case, the president made no effort to enforce the Supreme Court decision. On the contrary, he committed the federal government to helping Georgia get the Cherokees out of the state.

The means was subversion: exploitation of the grievances of poorer Cherokees against the elite, and development within the elite of a faction that would challenge the authority of John Ross, the most powerful leader and an unyielding opponent of removal. The end, of course, was to obtain a new treaty that would legalize Cherokee removal. In 1834 American agents made such a treaty with a group of collaborators among Cherokee chiefs. Ross alerted his friends among whites, and the Senate rejected the treaty. The following year, another treaty, modified to meet objections to the earlier measure, passed the Senate. When it was submitted for ratification by the Cherokee nation, the people rejected it.

By now the federal government was impatient. Still another treaty with collaborating chiefs was drawn up at New Echola in 1835, providing payment of $5 million to the Cherokees in return for yielding their lands and moving west. Despite the protests of the Ross government, the Senate ratified the treaty even though the document was so patently fraudulent that such diverse men as Daniel Webster of Massachusetts, Henry Clay of Kentucky, and John C. Calhoun of South Carolina denounced it.

Some Cherokees, influenced by collaborators, departed, but the majority held on to their lands, despite the treaty of New Echola. United States troops then invaded Cherokee territory and forcibly expelled its inhabitants along the "trail of tears" to what is now Oklahoma. Young and old, sick and well—all were compelled to take the 1,200-mile trek. As they went, whites looted the Cherokees of their possessions while the troops looked the other way. The death toll was high: more than one-fourth of the 14,000 Cherokees who set out died on the way. President Martin Van Buren, however, informed Congress in December 1838, that removal of the Indians had "had the happiest effects . . . The Cherokees have emigrated without any apparent reluctance." In fact, several hundred had fled the deportation and settled in the mountains of North Carolina.

Sooner or later the fate of the Cherokees was the fate of other Indian peoples. One by one they were either "persuaded" to move beyond the Mississippi or were forcibly deported. By 1850 the United States east of the river was white man's country. The peoples that remained were too weak and demoralized to threaten white expansion, or, like the Menominees in northern Wisconsin, were too isolated to be dangerous.

For all Indian peoples west of the Mississippi, whether of recent arrival or ancient origin, there were soon new dangers. In 1846 the United States acquired more than 285,000 square miles of land in the Pacific Northwest when it settled the Oregon boundary dispute with Britain. Two years later it wrested from Mexico nearly 530,000 square miles of the Southwest, including California. Now white American power stretched from ocean to ocean, and all Indian peoples in that great expanse were subject to its rule.

FOR FURTHER READING

The fate of Southeastern Indian peoples is discussed in a number of works: Grant Foreman, *Indian Removal* (1953); Robert S. Cotterill, *The Southern Indians* (1954); Marion Starkey, *The Cherokee Nation* (1946); Edwin C. McReynolds, *The Seminoles* (1957); and Thurman Wilkins, *Cherokee Tragedy* (1970).

Alvin Josephy, Jr., *The Indian Heritage of America* (1968), and Ruth M. Underhill, *Red Man's America* (1953), are good surveys. See also Harold E. Fey and D'Arcy McNickle, *Indians and Other Americans* (1959).

For American policy toward Indian peoples, see Wilcomb E. Washburn, *Red Man's Land—White Man's Law* (1971), and F. P. Prucha, *American Indian Policy in the Formative Years* (1962).

White attitudes and beliefs about Indians are examined in Roy H. Pearce, *The Savages of America* (1965).

Alvin M. Josephy, Jr., presents biographical sketches in *The Patriot Chiefs* (1961). See also Glenn Tucker, *Tecumseh* (1956).

M. P. Rogin probes psychological factors in Andrew Jackson's attitudes toward Indians in *Fathers and Children* (1975).

Valuable documentary material is available in Wayne Moquin and Charles Van Doren, eds., *Great Documents in American Indian History* (1973).

8 black freedom—limited

While the number of Indians was declining, the population of blacks increased many times over. In 1790, when the first census of the United States was taken, there were 757,000 blacks in the country; by 1860, the number grew to nearly 4.5 million. The overwhelming mass—4 million in 1860—were slaves, concentrated in the South. Counted among the blacks were those of mixed descent, the "mulattoes." There were at least half a million such people among the slaves, and considerable numbers among free blacks. The white community made little distinction on grounds of color. Light-skinned or dark-skinned—all were black, and all assigned the inferior status regarded as "natural" for blacks in a white society.

Free blacks, who numbered about 488,000 in 1860, were almost equally divided between the North and South, with slightly more living in the South. Some free blacks were descendants of colonial slaves who had been freed, many of them because of service in the Revolution or because of emancipation laws passed in northern states. Others were former slaves who had bought their freedom or whose masters had freed them voluntarily. Among the last were some light-skinned blacks whose white fathers had freed them, provided them with extensive education—often abroad—and seen to it that they lived well above the level of most free blacks.

Free blacks tended to congregate in towns and cities, where employment opportunities were greater than in the countryside. The pressures of urban life resulting from poverty and overcrowding, sharp race and class contrasts, ease of communication, and opportunities for black people of talent to rise to leadership helped bring about a mounting militancy among free blacks in the North. The white South, afraid of such a development because of the way it could affect slavery, took steps to reduce the danger by progressively limiting the liberties of free blacks.

FREE BLACKS IN WHITE SOCIETY

In both sections of the country, free blacks were barely tolerated by white society. As with Indians, whites held a whole body of necessary, self-serving beliefs to justify their attitudes and behavior toward free blacks. As members of a slave race, blacks were considered inferior to whites. Whites might disagree on the reason for that inferiority; some held it to be a punishment by God for past sins, others believed it a product of nature. The point was that, whatever justification they claimed, nearly all whites believed blacks inferior.

Such inferiority, whites believed, was most marked in intelligence. Black brain capacity was limited, whites solemnly agreed. Up to a certain age blacks could be educated, but at puberty black intellect faltered and the senses took over. Free blacks, then, were held to be idle and vicious, feeding their sensual habits through recourse to crime and vice. For proof, whites pointed to the disproportionate number of blacks in prison. Blacks, it was said, could not stand the pressures of a competitive society. They cracked mentally under the strain and furnished an undue number of the inmates of insane asylums. This point was made dramatically by the census of 1840, and whites continued to believe it long after it had been proved that the census was riddled with inaccuracies.

The most pervasive belief of all was the strong white conviction that any close association of the races would cause white deterioration. Association, said whites, did not bring blacks up to white levels; rather, it pulled whites down to the blacks. Association was especially dangerous to white children and adolescents, who were easily led into wickedness by blacks who lacked a moral sense. Eventually, such association would lead to that most dreadful evil of all, racial "amalgamation," which would mean the end of Anglo-Saxon civilization and its surest safeguard, pure white womanhood. In the South, such views were intensified by the belief that free blacks were instigators of slave plots and insurrections. Such blacks, said Thomas R. Dew, a leading defender of slavery, were "worthless and indolent" but "admirably calculated to excite plots, murders and insurrections." Blacks had to be kept at a distance—a great distance.

Some whites thought the distance should be as great as the Atlantic Ocean is wide. The American Colonization Society, founded in 1816, proposed a free-black removal program, similar to Andrew Jackson's Indian-removal policy. It is not surprising that Jackson was one of the society's many illustrious patrons, among whom were also Francis Scott Key, author of *The Star-Spangled Banner,* Chief Justice John Marshall, and former president James Madison. The society's program was "voluntary" emigration to Africa by free blacks. The society had no intention of interfering with slavery. The society had a rationale for its stand. Free blacks, said the society, could not function sucessfully in a white society. For their own good they should be sent back among their own people, where they could be leaders in winning for Christian civilization the savages supposedly roaming the African jungles. Such removal would also free white society from "an intolerable burden" of black depravity, incompetence, and poverty. By 1830 the society had settled about 1,400 blacks in Liberia, but its large-scale removal program proved a failure.

A major reason for the society's failure was white opposition. Whites wanted distance between themselves and free blacks, but not as much distance as the society did. After all, free blacks performed the hard and dirty work of white society. With free blacks on hand, white men were "spared for higher purposes," as one New England journal put it. Leon Litwack has pointed out that the labor of free blacks was as necessary for the North as slave labor was for the South and that both systems were justified in part on the ground that they freed white men to pursue the higher callings of civilization.

Free blacks, then, were regarded as a necessary evil—although white southerners increasingly questioned the necessity. The problem, as the white North saw it, was to keep the evil in its place. One way was overt violence. Sporadically, whites invaded black ghettos in northern towns, assaulted the inhabitants, and put churches and houses to the torch. An especially flagrant outbreak in Cincinnati in 1829 forced more than half the town's black population to flee the city for refuge in Canada. Police harassment and police brutality were also employed. In 1813, for example, a prominent black businessman, James Forten, protested police persecution of blacks in Philadelphia. Arrested blacks faced white judges and juries, who were rarely sympathetic. Blacks, for their part, knew little of their rights and few could afford counsel. As a consequence, blacks went to prison far out of proportion to their number in the general population.

Also indicative of white attitudes were laws designed to stop black migration between states. This policy of exclusion sprang from a general fear that blacks, both free and fugitive slaves, would come north in large numbers. Allied with this idea was a belief that if a state provided favorable opportunities for them, blacks would congregate there, including many old and sick people who would become public charges. The western states, which boasted of their pioneering democracy, pioneered also in reducing black rights. Illinois, Indiana, and Oregon explicitly barred black settlement through constitutional provisions. Missouri, which had been admitted as a

James Forten, successful black businessman in Philadelphia in the early nineteenth century, was also an outspoken advocate of racial equality.

Historical Society of Pennsylvania

state on the condition that it abandon such a provision, attained the same end by legislative action. Ohio admitted no blacks who could not produce certificates of freedom and post $500 bond to guarantee good behavior—an amount so high that few blacks could afford it.

It is significant, however, that the laws against black migration were only sporadically enforced. Apparently white society felt that the risk of a black presence was outweighed by the advantages of cheap labor: men to work in the mines and on the docks, and women to do white folks' laundry and housework. Besides, there were other ways to maintain distance between the races.

Intermarriage, for example, was prohibited in many states, and where no laws existed, custom was strong enough to prevent it. Interracial sex went on, of course, but it was tolerated as long as it was discreet and no attempt was made to legitimatize it through marriage.

Another method of keeping blacks at proper distance was excluding them from political life. As of 1860 they could vote only in five New England states, where their numbers were insignificant. Six states—Pennsylvania, New Jersey, Connecticut, Maryland, North Carolina, and Tennessee—which had previously allowed blacks to vote stripped them of the right. When New York extended the suffrage to all white adult males in 1821, it imposed on blacks property requirements so high that few could qualify. Indeed, the assault on black political rights was an integral part of the "democratic revolution" of the early nineteenth century. Proponents of wider white suffrage said it was unjust to permit inferior blacks to vote while many white men were barred. Further, to the conservative argument that the ballot should be confined to those fit to use it, white democrats retorted that the most obviously unfit were blacks and they demanded black exclusion. Thus, the triumph of the "democratic revolution," so far as blacks were concerned, reinforced white supremacy.

Exclusion from political life mirrored exclusion in other areas. No blacks could legally own land or enter into contracts in Oregon. Universally, blacks were barred from juries. In many states they could not testify in court cases involving whites. Blacks were thus vulnerable to white criminals, with little hope of redress unless white persons were willing to testify on their behalf.

Black exclusion from political life received its ultimate sanction from the United States Supreme Court. The Dred Scott decision of 1857 stripped blacks of their citizenship. Chief Justice Roger Taney, an appointee of Andrew Jackson, held that the Constitution was never intended to include blacks as citizens. Indeed, when it was adopted, blacks were "regarded as being of an inferior order, and altogether unfit to associate with the white race, . . . and so far inferior, that they had no rights which a white man was bound to respect." Nor could states grant citizenship to blacks, since blacks "were not intended to be embraced" as citizens within the Union.

Shut out from political life, free blacks were also denied unrestricted rights to education. Although blacks were taxed to support public schools, their children were long denied entrance. Whites argued that since black intelligence was limited, it was wasteful to spend money trying to develop it. Besides, association of black and white children would lead to "amalgamation." When public education was finally opened to black children in the North, the schools were segregated. The buildings were ramshackle, the curriculum limited, and the instruction poor. Such conditions led blacks to fight for integrated schools, and in some cases they won. But then they faced new problems: black children were beaten, insulted, and treated like pariahs by children and teachers alike. In the South, the few school systems that existed were restricted to whites.

White hostility to black education was not confined to public schools. Private institutions that attempted to teach blacks were subjected to legal harassment, legislative restriction, and mob action. Thus, Prudence Crandall, a young Quaker, was forced in 1834 to close down her school for black girls at Canterbury, Connecticut. An abolitionist plan to set up a black college in New Haven devoted to vocational training was thwarted by the local town meeting. Noyes Academy in Canaan, New Hampshire, which admitted blacks as well as whites, was destroyed by a mob in 1835. Black schools in Ohio were burned down.

As with schools, so with churches. White Christians were reluctant to accept blacks as church members, and when blacks were accepted, they were not treated as equals. Black worship was tolerated, provided that blacks were willing to sit in segregated sections. Even the Quakers, the most outspoken group on the evils of slavery, fell victim to what an English Quaker called "the influences of a corrupt public sentiment." Only the Roman Catholic church appears to have raised no racial barriers, but at the time there were few black Catholics.

Free blacks were kept in their place most effectively, perhaps, by limited opportunities to earn a living. There was a black elite of preachers, doctors, lawyers, hotelkeepers, and undertakers. There was also what might be called a middle class, made up of barbers, hotel waiters, and others who depended on white patronage. But most blacks lived by manual labor in the lowest-paid, most arduous, and in some cases, most dangerous occupations. They were in demand for such hazardous callings as miners, seamen, and longshoremen. They could also find jobs as day laborers, teamsters, and domestic servants. Because they were paid poorly, workers and their families lived in fetid slums in the black ghettos—and whites said blacks lived in such squalor because they liked it.

Two major barriers blocked black economic progress. One was the belief of white employers that blacks were too stupid to be entrusted with responsibility. They held to this opinion despite the evidence around them that black business managers, such as James Forten who ran a prosperous sail-making establishment in Philadelphia, were just as shrewd as white mangagers. The other barrier was the conviction of white artisans that skilled blacks were too competent to be accepted as competitors. The whites feared for their jobs; and as a result, skilled blacks often had to earn their bread as laborers.

Such economic security as free blacks had was endangered in the 1840s. The great influx of impoverished Irish immigrants provided a mass of workers who would work for even less than blacks—a situation that occasioned the saying that the immigrants were "white niggers." Blacks soon lost jobs as teamsters, laborers, longshoremen, and domestic servants to the Irish. Black bitterness was enhanced when the new arrivals, egged on by Democratic politicians, demanded that the "Naygurs" be deported to Africa.

Defenders of slavery pointed to the plight of the northern black poor as proof both of black inferiority and of the benign character of slavery, which sheltered blacks who were by nature incapable of making their way in a competitive society. But there was a vast difference between freedom and slavery, a fact appreciated by blacks if not by apologists for slavery. And free blacks began to use that freedom both to end slavery and to win recognition of the civil and political rights of blacks who were already free.

BLACK ACCOMMODATION

For blacks, as for Indian peoples, there were three major responses to white pressure: outright accommodation to white ways; temporary acceptance of conditions while striving to change them; and resistance, including violence if necessary.

For the most part, blacks supporting accommodation were "making it" in American society. They were business and professional people who enjoyed some measure of success, however small. Some of them, such as barbers and hotel waiters, relied entirely on white patronage. Proud of their superior status, they still felt insecure. On the one hand, their status depended in large measure on white recognition—and that might be withdrawn at any moment. On the other, they felt endangered by poor blacks whose behavior might arouse open expression of white hostility. When that hostility broke out in mob attacks, the homes and buildings of prosperous blacks as well as the hovels of the poor were destroyed.

Faced with the realities of white power, lacking faith in their own people, and concerned primarily with their own status, such blacks counseled accommodation to white ways. Such accommodation, they said, would eventually improve the black condition, for whites were bound to respect industry, thrift, sobriety, and strict observance of family responsibility. In the meantime, blacks were to do nothing to provoke whites. Such an attitude was reflected in the stance of some black churches, in which people favoring accommodation were influential. These institutions not only refused to participate in the mounting struggle for black rights but also avoided condemning slavery. One Ohio church, for example, advised blacks to seek "continuation of the smiles of the white people as we have hitherto enjoyed them."

More extreme than the blacks supporting accommodation were the "emigrationists." These were blacks so overwhelmed by a sense of the futility of black struggle that they surrendered to the white racist claim that the United States was a country for whites. Black salvation, they said, could only come through emigration to Haiti, Canada, or preferably Africa, the black homeland. Some also urged colonization in some remote part of American territory, an idea proposed as well by whites eager to get free blacks out of the settled areas of the country. Among the emigrationists were such figures as Edward Blyden, a clergyman who became a propagandist for Liberia, and Dr. Martin R. Delany and Henry Highland Garnet, militants who, in times of despair, advocated a black exodus.

Most blacks agreed with the denunciations of American society made by emigrationists, but they rejected the message. They steadfastly opposed the emigration schemes of the American Colonization Society, and they were equally hostile to similar counsel from blacks. After all, they said, black blood and labor had built

America as much as white blood and labor, and blacks had as much claim to the country as whites. "This is our home and this is our country," declared a meeting of New York blacks in 1831. A convention of Ohio blacks in 1849 told white and black emigrationists their "appeals to us are in vain; our minds are made up to remain in the United States, and contend for our rights at all hazards."

THE STRUGGLE FOR CIVIL RIGHTS

Blacks seeking their rights found inspiration and leadership in an educated black elite made up of intellectuals, ministers, lawyers, doctors, and business managers. Among them were James Forten, the Philadelphia sail maker; Richard Allen, founder of the African Methodist Episopal Church; Doctor Martin R. Delany, recently described as the "founding father of black nationalism"; Doctor James McCune Smith, graduate of the University of Glasgow and author of a work challenging the assumptions of white racism; and William C. Nell, pioneer historian of the black role in the Revolution and the War of 1812. A young black poet, Frances Ellen Watkins, threw herself actively into the struggle. William Wells Brown and Frederick Douglass, two articulate former slaves, rapidly won influence in the black community. Brown used his talents as lecturer, novelist, and dramatist to promote abolition. Douglass, famous as orator, editor, and leading spokesman, became, in the words of August Meier, "the most distinguished Negro in 19th century America."

Such active militants had a broad base within the black community from which to operate: the independent black church. The very existence of the institution indicated the mounting resentment of black people against white supremacy. When white Methodist churches in Philadelphia tried to restrict their black worshipers, the blacks separated and under the leadership of Richard Allen formed their own congregations. By 1816 there were sufficient separatist churches to form a national body, the African Methodist Episcopal Church. Six years later other black Methodists organized another national body, the African Methodist Episcopal Church Zion. Black Baptists also set up their own local churches and regional conferences. Black congregations of predominantly white churches, such as Episcopalian, Congregational, and Presbyterian, also played an active role in the black community, although white control limited their independence.

In addition to purely religious functions, black churches served important social purposes. They were, like the parish churches of the Middle Ages, convenient community centers in which black people could meet, talk, sing, and carry on community activities without white intrusion. As W.E.B. DuBois noted, the black church was "the first social institution fully controlled by black men in America." The church afforded black people an opportunity to manage their own affairs in their own way, and it provided men and women of talent a chance to rise to leadership.

Some local churches remained aloof from the black rights campaign, and national bodies, such as that of the African Methodist Episcopal church, were chary of condemning slavery too harshly lest their southern members be exposed to white reprisals. But most local churches in the North were sympathetic to the black cause. Abolitionist meetings could be held there when white churches and halls were hostile.

They provided quarters for the vigilance committees that aided escaping slaves. Moral and practical support were given to a wide range of black activities, from militant abolitionism to such self-help programs as temperance, mutual aid, and libraries. Because of their role as community centers, the churches, while not in the vanguard of struggle themselves, provided a base from which the struggle could be waged by other organizations.

Such civil rights organizations sponsored legal challenges to discriminatory laws. They submitted petitions time and again to state legislatures and the Congress, demanding an end to both slavery and discrimination. Through meetings, discussions, and public appeals they strove to unify the black people and to raise its level of consciousness. Beginning in 1830 national black conventions met irregularly to give voice to the grievances and aspirations of black people as a whole. Such groups were able to broaden their appeal when a black press emerged, beginning with publication of *Freedom's Journal* in 1827. Probably the most significant black newspaper was *The North Star,* edited by Frederick Douglass, which first appeared in 1845. Blacks also found an outlet for their views in the organ of white abolitionists, *The Liberator,* edited by William Lloyd Garrison. So impressed were they by Garrison's work that blacks, through their subscriptions, helped keep the publication alive in its troubled early years.

Despite overall white hostility, blacks made gains in the North. In collaboration with sympathetic whites they were eventually able to win public funds for black education, although the schools were segregated. In some places, such as Rochester, New York, and Hartford, Connecticut, they won school integration, but black children were so persecuted that parents reluctantly asked for separate schools. In 1849 black pressure helped bring about repeal of Ohio's notorious Black Laws, which severely restricted black freedom. Six years later blacks played a significant role in ending school segregation and in gaining the admission of blacks to juries in Massachusetts. Earlier, that state had repealed its law prohibiting racial intermarriage.

Militant free blacks were not content to fight only for their own rights. Perceiving that slavery set limits on all black progress, they were abolitionists from the beginning. They joined in the new, militant abolitionism symbolized by David Walker and Garrison. When some white societies discouraged their participation, blacks set up their own. The whole movement was stimulated by the work of William Wells Brown and Frederick Douglass. In addition, the lectures given in Britain by such former slaves helped bring significant British support to the antislavery cause in America.

Some blacks went beyond words to action. Sojourner Truth and Harriet Tubman were the most famous of a number of men and women who penetrated the South and brought out slaves seeking freedom. Many Underground Railroad operations were carried on by blacks, who were better able to establish rapport with fugitives than were whites. Black communities maintained their own vigilance committees to aid escaping slaves and protect them from seizure. Black informers who betrayed fugitives received community punishment in the form of flogging and ostracism.

Mass action became the way of freeing captured fugitives. Detroit blacks in

1833 battled the police and liberated arrested slaves. Later, blacks forcibly freed seized fugitives in Boston, Chicago, and Pittsburgh. As Benjamin Quarles notes, "Up to 1850 the rescuing of fugitive slaves had been a business conducted almost exclusively by Negroes."

To put an end to such activities, Congress in 1850 passed a new and drastic Fugitive Slave Law. The law, an attempt to appease southern white opinion aroused over the admission of California as a free state, extended federal authority to help slaveholders recover runaways. Any black could be accused of being a fugitive. No proof was called for, except for a statement of the claimant or his agent that the black was indeed a fugitive. State officials were enjoined to help enforce the law, and state courts forbidden to interfere. Individuals who aided runaways were subject to heavy penalties. Federal commissioners who passed on cases of fugitives were paid $10 if they upheld the white claimant, $5 if they upheld the black.

Blacks were frightened, appalled, and angered by the measure. Thousands fled to Canada as slave catchers began to roam the North. Most blacks remained, many of them ready to resist what Frederick Douglass called "that horrible and hell-black enactment." Some vowed they would die fighting rather than be taken. A fugitive slave who had become an abolitionist clergyman, J. W. Loguen, told an audience, "I will not live a slave, and if force is employed to reenslave me, I shall make preparations to meet the crisis as becomes a man." Samuel R. Ward, an editor, pointed out that since the law stripped them of their legal rights, blacks were thrown back upon the "natural and inalienable right of self-defense." He cautioned slave catchers that they courted "inevitable death."

Such words were not idle, as demonstrated in 1851. That year a Maryland planter led an armed band to seize his runaways living with other blacks in Christiana, Pennsylvania. The blacks fought back, and during the battle the planter was killed and his son wounded. The federal government sent in United States Marines to restore order. Of the thirty-eight suspects arrested, three were white. Two trials failed to bring convictions, and charges were dropped. That same year blacks in Boston invaded the courthouse, seized a fugitive, and dispatched him to Canada. Arrests were made, but no convictions were obtained. Similarly, abolitionists in Syracuse, New York, forcibly liberated an alleged fugitive and sent him across the border. Indictments followed, but no convictions.

The pattern—forcible resistance, arrest, and failure to convict—indicated a growing unity of blacks and whites opposed to slavery or at least to the expansion of slavery into the territories. These people now found allies among businessmen and farmers who felt that southern domination of the federal government endangered their interests. As they saw it, enforcement of the Fugitive Slave Law imposed slave-owning power on the free states. The response to the law went beyond freeing the accused liberators of captured fugitives. Legislatures strengthened their personal-liberty laws by making slave catching a form of kidnapping, subject to drastic penalties. Massachusetts barred from public life "forever" any state official who helped enforce the Fugitive Slave Law. The Wisconsin Supreme Court held the federal law unconstitutional—and was itself reversed by the same United States Supreme Court that handed down the Dred Scott decision.

ABOLITIONISTS—BLACK AND WHITE

The struggle over the Fugitive Slave Law gave new impetus to black thinking about political action and about black relationships with white abolitionists. The white movement took national form in 1831 with the organization of the American Anti-Slavery Society. Within ten years the society had split.

One wing, led by Garrison, advocated full rights for women, rejected the use of force, and opposed political action. Indeed, said Garrison, the political process was tainted in its origins, for the Constitution was "a most bloody and Heaven-daring arrangement." He relied instead on moral suasion.

The opponents of Garrison, organized in the American and Foreign Anti-Slavery Society, tended to be the more "respectable" abolitionists. They wanted nothing to do with women's rights, condemned Garrison's attacks on churches and the Constitution, and were willing to use all practical methods to bring an end to slavery, including forcible resistance to the Fugitive Slave Law and any and all political means available.

Since neither national society was strong enough to impose discipline on its affiliates, the local and regional antislavery societies really exercised power. Among them the demand mounted for political action to back up moral suasion. This sentiment found expression in the organization of the Liberty Party in 1844 and of the Free Soil Party four years later. Neither party attracted a mass following. They tipped the balance in New York, however, and that state's electoral vote proved decisive in electing James K. Polk in 1844 and Zachary Taylor in 1848. Such actions antagonized abolitionists who were building antislavery strength in the Whig and Democratic parties.

The black community was dismayed by the feuding between white abolitionists. Most blacks revered Garrison. He was the most militant abolitionist, willing to endure abuse and physical attack for the sake of the cause. He was not only against slavery; he also fought for black equality in the North, a cause for which many abolitionists were lukewarm. And, rare among abolitionists, Garrison treated blacks as social equals. Some blacks, most notably Frederick Douglass, also admired Garrison's stand for women's rights.

Yet, despite all these claims on their loyalty, blacks came to feel that Garrison's policy led to a dead end. Unless the political process were used, "immediate emancipation" turned out to be questionable emancipation in the indefinite future. The Garrison slogan, "No Union with Slave-holders," was not militant at all, but reactionary. It implied disunion, with a South left to maintain slavery and a white North cleansed of the moral stain of slavery. In fact, on the eve of the Civil War, Garrison counseled letting the seceding states depart in peace.

As some blacks perceived, many white abolitionists, deeply troubled by slavery as a social sin, were more concerned with their own moral redemption than with waging a general struggle for black rights. Blacks, bearing no guilt for slavery, were able to engage single-mindedly in the struggle for both abolition and equal rights. Symbolic of the shift in black opinion was Frederick Douglass, long one of Garrison's disciples. In 1853 he broke openly with his mentor on the issue of political action. The bitter personal quarrel that ensued dismayed abolitionist groups and brought discord into the ranks of black abolitionists, many of whom remained faithful to Garrison.

One reason why blacks continued to support Garrison was his all-out belief in racial equality, a belief not shared by many white abolitionists who typically believed blacks inferior. Some said blacks were inferior by inheritance; others, that slavery had made blacks backward. Believing in inferiority, the abolitionists tried to keep blacks out of policy-making positions in antislavery societies, and some even questioned whether blacks should be admitted to membership. Martin R. Delany reported that blacks in antislavery societies found themselves in "the very same position . . . as we do in relation to the pro-slavery part of the community—a mere secondary, underlying position."

Since blacks had no significant voting power, they had to work through white politicians sympathetic to the black cause. As the antislavery movement spread in the North, many such politicians emerged, later to become famous in American history. Among them were Charles Sumner of Massachusetts, who helped end school segregation in Boston; Benjamin Wade and Joshua Giddings of Ohio, leaders in the antislavery struggle in Congress; and Thaddeus Stevens of Pennsylvania, who as early as 1837 blocked an attempt to write exclusion of blacks into the new Pennsylvania constitution.

Most antislavery politicians, however, held blacks at arm's length, afraid of offending white opinion by espousing the black cause. Thus, when the new Republican party held its first national convention in 1856, it chose Francis P. Blair, Sr., of Maryland, a slaveowner, to preside over its opening session. The party emphasized that it was not opposed to slavery where it existed, but only to its expansion into the territories. The convention also endorsed a constitution for the "free" state of Kansas that prohibited black entry into the state. Blacks complained during the campaign that the Republican party discouraged black participation. But blacks had nowhere else to go, in view of the proslavery stand of the Democrats.

For blacks, the election of 1860 was even more dismal than the Republican convention of 1856. Knowing that antislavery sentiment in the North was already solidly behind them, Republican leaders appealed to pragmatic white interests by calling for free land for farmers in the West, a transcontinental railroad, a protective tariff, and unlimited immigration. Only the commitment to halt the expansion of slavery remained to call attention to the basic issue that had given rise to the party. Some blacks, such as H. Ford Douglass of Illinois, recoiled from the party and its nominee, Abraham Lincoln. Frederick Douglass conceded the weaknesses of the new party, but he concluded, "as between the hosts of Slavery . . . and the Republican party—incomplete as is its platform . . . our preferences cannot hesitate."

The satisfaction blacks derived from Republican victory was soon dispelled. Powerful party figures, such as Henry Ward Beecher, the most prominent Protestant preacher of the day, and Horace Greeley, editor of the New York *Tribune,* urged that seceding states be allowed to depart in peace. Thus, slavery would remain entrenched in the South, and slaves cut off from their allies in the North. Republicans in Congress helped pass a measure asking northern states to repeal laws directed against slave catchers, and some states complied. Republican votes made possible the organization of the new territories of Colorado, New Mexico, and Dakota—with no prohibition of slavery. With Republican backing, Congress passed the Thirteenth Amendment, which guaranteed slavery where it existed and forbade any future constitutional amendment giving Congress the power to abolish slavery. Three states actually ratified the amendment before the fall of Fort Sumter. Thus, the party to which so many blacks had looked for salvation turned out to be willing to fasten black slavery on the United States forever. Unhappy blacks felt a keen sense of betrayal. Frederick Douglass upbraided Republicans for "an utter abandonment of their principles."

Black hopes were once again buoyed with the attack on Fort Sumter in April 1861. Douglass was exultant. Fort Sumter, he said, put an end to "cowardly, base, and unprincipled truckling" to the slaveholders. Now northerners had "to elect between patriotic fidelity and pro-slavery treason." And he went on, "for this consummation we have watched and wished with fear and trembling. God be praised! that it has come at last." But Douglass and other militants exulted too soon. The Lincoln administration had no intention of waging a war of abolition.

BLACK PRIDE

A major problem confronting black militants was lack of unity among their own people. Blacks supporting accommodation were one indication of the disunity in the black community. There were others, perhaps even more pervasive and deep-rooted. Northern blacks looked down upon recent arrivals from the South. Light-skinned folk, usually to be found among the more affluent, kept aloof from the poor and darker-skinned. Even members of different religious denominations held themselves apart from each other. In 1841 David Ruggles, a leading black abolitionist, denounced "the sin of sectarian, geographical and complexional proscription."

Such divisions were harder to combat because they had their origins in white racism, as Ruggles himself noted. He was all too well aware of the psychological strains imposed on the black community by such racism. The process had been delineated clearly a few years earlier by that perceptive observer of American democracy, Alexis de Tocqueville. The American black, he noted,

> makes a thousand fruitless efforts to insinuate himself among men who repulse him; he conforms to the taste of his oppressors, adopts their opinions, and hopes by imitating them to form a part of their community. Having been told from infancy that his race is naturally inferior to that of the whites, he assents to the proposition, and is ashamed of his own nature.

Such self-hatred poisoned black social relationships and thwarted the emergence of black pride and racial consciousness. To accomplish their aims of liberation, black militants had to break down the psychological enslavement of the free black community.

The first major expression of black pride came, not from a member of the educated elite, but from David Walker, a self-taught free black who made a living as a used-clothes dealer in Boston. In 1829 he published *Walker's Appeal . . . to the Coloured Citizens of the World,* in which he expressed satisfaction in being black: "We are as thankful to our God, for having made us as it pleased Himself, as [whites] are for having made them white." Whites, he said, think "we wish to be white, . . . but they are dreadfully deceived—we wish to be just as it pleased our Creator to have made us.'' Why? Because God had a special destiny for blacks. They were his new ''chosen people,'' and when the time came for open struggle against white oppressors, ''Jesus Christ, the King of Heaven and of Earth, . . . will surely go before you.'' Walker's invoking of black pride, however, contributed to a larger message: outright resistance to white supremacy. The status of a chosen people was not to be achieved easily. Blacks must turn away from acceptance of their lot to militant struggle against oppression. If necessary, force must be used against the legalized violence of slavery, and blacks must be prepared to die. Better to die fighting, said Walker, ''than to be a slave to a tyrant, who takes the life of your mother, wife and . . . children.'' In dealing with such tyrants, ''it is no more harm for you to kill a man . . . than it is for you to take a drink of water when thirsty.'' For whites, too, Walker had a message: let them abandon oppression or face black retribution:

> Remember, Americans, that we must and shall be free and enlightened as you are. Will you wait until we shall, under God, obtain our liberty by the crushing arm of power? . . . Woe, woe, will be to you if we have to obtain our freedom by fighting.

Walker's blunt language shocked abolitionists, both black and white, and brought outraged demands from white southerners for suppression of the pamphlet. Many abolitionists were committed to non-violence, and others were afraid of the *Appeal*'s effect on northern white opinion. The cause of abolition had hard enough going without injecting the idea of black insurrection. Many felt that southern blacks, free and slave, would suffer as fearful whites took precautions against possible uprisings. Nevertheless, even blacks who disagreed with Walker felt a new sense of pride in a black man who had boldly defied white power. They questioned his judgment, but admired his courage.

Walker made few converts, but among them was Henry Highland Garnet, a young clergyman who served white congregations. In 1843 he startled a national black convention at Buffalo, New York, with a call for slave rebellion. God, he said, would not absolve slaves of their moral obligations simply because they were slaves. Since slavery made it impossible to lead moral lives, it was the slaves' God-given duty to destroy it, peacefully if possible, forcibly if necessary. Garnet was not optimistic about gaining freedom without a struggle: ''However much you and all of us may desire it, there is not much hope of redemption without the shedding of blood. If you must bleed, let it all come at once—rather die freemen, than live to be slaves.'' The convention, by one vote, denied endorsement to Garnet's message. Six years later, however, a state convention in Ohio voted to distribute 500 copies of *Walker's Appeal* and Garnet's Buffalo speech. Black militancy was spreading.

But the militancy found expression in freeing captured fugitive slaves and in the legal and political struggle for equal rights, not in inciting insurrection. It is significant that no black leader accompanied John Brown on his famous raid in 1859. Only Frederick Douglass was involved in Brown's project, and he backed out when he learned that Brown planned to take over the United States arsenal at Harper's Ferry. Such a move, Douglass told Brown on the eve of the raid, would doom the whole project of liberation. It would bring about armed federal intervention and turn "the whole country against us." Five obscure blacks did go with Brown. One of them, Dangerfield Newby, was the first to die when United States Marines stormed the arsenal, which Brown's band had occupied. Another was killed, two were executed, and one—Jeremiah Anderson—escaped. In a later report of the fighting in and around the arsenal, Anderson emphasized the active role of slaves in the neighborhood who had responded to Brown's call for aid.

Brown's courageous bearing during his trial and execution won him the affection and admiration of countless blacks. To their pantheon of black heroes—Gabriel, Denmark Vesey, and Nat Turner—was now added a white hero: John Brown. On Martyr Day, when Brown was hanged, black communities halted all activities. Thousands thronged to churches and meeting places to pay their respects to a fallen leader. Mindful of the immediate problems facing Brown's widow, they raised funds to help her and other widows whose husbands had perished in John Brown's cause.

SOUTHERN FREE BLACKS

Despite continuing problems, northern free blacks could feel they were making some progress. Southern free blacks felt no such confidence. On the contrary, their situation became ever more precarious.

The southern free black community was more highly stratified than the northern. At one extreme were the relatively wealthy, well-educated, light-skinned elites of such cities as Charleston and New Orleans, linked by illegitimate family ties with the white planter aristocracy. They shared that class's social and political outlook, and they behaved accordingly. They lived in elegant houses, promoted intermarriage between their families, kept slaves as domestic servants, and maintained a wide social distance between themselves and poorer blacks. Some were planters, using slave labor. The extent of their wealth is shown by the $15 million worth of property owned by New Orleans blacks in 1860. Unlike the northern black elite, the southern provided little leadership to discontented blacks.

At the other end of the scale were the welfare cases—often sick or worn-out slaves freed by their masters to avoid the expense of caring for them. Such action was eventually forbidden by law, but masters continued to dump unwanted slaves in cities, where they became public charges.

Between these extremes was most of the free black population. Some, such as doctors, hotel keepers, undertakers, and other business proprietors, were relatively well-off. There was a larger group of artisans: river and harbor pilots, carpenters, bricklayers, coopers, tailors, blacksmiths. Much more numerous, and more poorly paid, were the blacks who toiled as longshoremen, field hands, day laborers, laundresses, and maids. Another group lived marginally as fishermen, gatherers of shellfish, and small farmers. Business people and workers naturally tended to live in urban centers, where opportunities were greater than in the countryside. By 1860 nearly one-third of the South's free blacks lived in towns and cities, despite persistent attempts to reduce their presence.

Urban workers, skilled and unskilled, felt mounting white pressures most keenly. In effect, the wages of both white and free black workers were set by the

Harper's Weekly, *1861*

In the pre-Civil War South some poor free blacks supplemented their meager incomes by processing freshly caught fish. The women here are "heading herring." Pipe smoking by women was common among poor blacks and poor whites.

wages paid for slaves hired out to employers by their owners. Both free groups suffered as a consequence. Whites, however, wanted no black competition at all, and they were able to obtain laws designed to exclude blacks from a host of skilled occupations. Thanks to the resistance of white employers, who wanted labor as cheaply as possible, the laws were enforced only sporadically. White workers sometimes resorted to violence against black workers. Many black artisans managed to survive, but others sank into the ranks of the unskilled or went north in search of better opportunities. Young blacks, moreover, found it increasingly difficult to become apprentices in the skilled trades.

The economic position of blacks was further undercut by European immigration. While most immigrants went to the North, a sufficient number came to the South to endanger the traditional black domination of certain occupations. Compelled by their poverty to work for any wage, Irish and German men and women replaced many blacks.

The policy of reducing the numbers of free blacks was directed not at the elites, but at the business proprietors and working people of the cities. They were, in white eyes, becoming much too independent and at the same time subverting slavery. The spirit of independence was dramatically shown in 1816 when black Methodists in Charleston, South Carolina, seceded from the white church and established their own. Further, the black church affiliated with a northern black church, the African Methodist.

This was bad enough in itself, for whites suspected any black organization not under white control. But, as in the North, the church was a community center that attracted free blacks and slaves. There slaves not only learned to read and write—although this learning was prohibited by law—but also listened to black travelers from the North and other parts of the South, picked up the black-grapevine news from all over, and discussed the grievances of both free people and slaves. Black churches also produced "exhorters," eloquent preachers who could transport their listeners to emotional heights. All too often for the taste of whites, the exhorters failed to understand that Christian liberty was to be realized in the hereafter, not in the here and now. It was easy for whites to believe that such close association between free blacks and slaves boded no good for the "peculiar institution." Such beliefs were vindicated by the alleged Denmark Vesey "conspiracy" of 1822 to stage a slave uprising in Charleston, South Carolina; Vesey was a free, church-going carpenter and his lieutenants were active churchmen. The black church thus became a target for white repression.

The church was not the only target, though. Equally detested by whites were the taverns that catered to black trade. These were gathering places for urban blacks—and also for some poor whites who ignored the color line. Not only did blacks and whites eat and drink together, and exchange news and opinions, but also white women who patronized the taverns violated the taboos associated with "pure white womanhood." In effect, the taverns were the symbol of the inarticulate rebellion against the most cherished values of the white South. Further, the white owners of such establishments, together with white "grocers" who operated grog shops in the ghettos, constituted a core of political power opposed to any policy that would deprive them of customers. Such opposition from within their own race intensified the determination of white authorities to thin out the number of free blacks and slaves in cities.

White authorities began making life unpleasant for free blacks even before the Denmark Vesey conspiracy, and the hysteria that attended that event made conditions even worse. Many states forbade the entry of free blacks and banned the reentry of those who had left. Owners who wished to free slaves were required to take them outside the state, and eventually manumission itself was prohibited almost entirely throughout the South. Free blacks were taxed to support public schools in the few places they existed, but black children could not attend. Schools set up by blacks were so harassed that many ceased to exist openly. "Underground" schools continued, however, to afford some black youngsters the rudiments of education.

There were other ways of letting free blacks know they were not wanted. The three states that had admitted them to the suffrage—Maryland, Tennessee, and North Carolina—took away their right to vote. Universally, free blacks could not testify against whites, but slaves were permitted to testify against free blacks. To break down association between free and slave blacks, free blacks were forbidden to entertain slaves. Eventually black freedom itself was endangered. By 1860 five states—Tennessee, Texas, Louisiana, Maryland, and Arkansas—provided for the "voluntary" enslavement of free blacks. But urban free blacks had lived long with this hazard: one of the penalties for breaking local law was enslavement.

FOR FURTHER READING

A good introduction to the problems of free blacks is Leon Litwack, *North of Slavery* (1961). Northern white racism is explored in Eugene H. Berwanger, *The Frontier Against Slavery* (1967), and Eric Foner, *Free Soil, Free Labor, Free Men* (1970). See also James A. Rawley, *Race and Politics* (1969), for an analysis of racism in Kansas, and Edmund Fuller, *Prudence Crandall* (1971), for an example of racism in Connecticut.

Studies of free blacks include John H. Franklin, *The Free Negro in North Carolina* (1943); Emma L. Thornbrough, *The Negro in Indiana* (1957); and Letitia W. Brown, *The Free Negro in the District of Columbia* (1972).

For other aspects of the free black experience see Martin E. Dann, ed., *The Black Press* (1971); E. Franklin Frazier, *The Negro Church in America* (1964); and Joseph R. Washington, *Black Religion* (1964). W.E.B. DuBois, *Black Reconstruction* (1935), has an incisive discussion of the black church's historic role.

The basic work on black abolitionism is Benjamin Quarles, *Black Abolitionists* (1969). Larry Gara, *The Liberty Line* (1961), emphasizes the black role on the Underground Railroad. One black protest movement is discussed in Howard H. Bell, *A Survey of the Negro Convention Movement* (1969).

Benjamin Quarles presents the biography of a leading black abolitionist in *Frederick Douglass* (1948). See also his collection of documents and interpretations, *Frederick Douglass* (1968), which includes an appraisal of the abolitionist by August Meier. A more comprehensive collection of speeches and writings, together with biographical material, is Philip S. Foner, ed., *The Life and Writings of Frederick Douglass,* Vols. 1–4, (1950–55).

9 survival under slavery

The slave society of the nineteenth century differed in many ways from that of the eighteenth. It had both expanded and matured. In sheer numbers it had increased from fewer than 700,000 in 1790 to almost 4 million in 1860. This population was about evenly distributed between the sexes, a fact that significantly influenced the development of family relationships within the slave community. Further, despite the continued import of Africans in the now illegal slave trade, few nineteenth century slaves experienced the profound culture shock of their ancestors. Rather, most slaves now were born into American slavery, and from infancy conditioned to it. Africanisms in speech, customs, and religion did not disappear, but they tended to decline as slaves became increasingly Americanized.

Slave society no longer existed nationwide. It was now concentrated in one section, the South. But this was no longer the old South of the Atlantic seaboard. By 1860 the slave South extended from Florida westward through Texas. As formerly, most slaves lived on farms and plantations, but here again there was an important change. Slave ownership tended to be concentrated in fewer and fewer families. By 1860 more than 50 percent of the slave population was owned by only 12 percent of slave-owning families. This concentration of slaves on a relatively small number of large plantations fostered the growth and development of the slave community, allowing that community to develop and maintain its own standards and sanctions quite apart from those called for by outward submission to white society.

But slavery itself was also changing. While most slaves were in rural areas, increasing numbers lived in towns and cities. These slaves were in demand. Many of them were artisans, while others served as unskilled laborers.

There also emerged in the nineteenth century, as Robert S. Starobin has pointed out, a new form of the ''peculiar institution'': industrial slavery. The Industrial Revolution had affected the South as well as the North, with some whites seeking to diversify the southern economy to eliminate its dependence on Britain and the North for manufactured goods. By 1860 the South accounted for about 15 percent of national industrial output. To supply its factories and mines, the white South relied considerably on black slave labor. Such workers made up about 5 percent of the total slave population. Slaves were to be found in a wide range of industrial enterprises: cotton textiles; iron foundries; tobacco manufacture; lead, coal, iron and gold mining; and lumbering. In short, slavery proved to be quite compatible with industry.

THE HUMAN FACTOR

Slavery was not only a labor system but also a complex of relationships between white and black humans. By the nineteenth century these relationships had become so formalized and ritualized that blacks could conform to white expectations without damaging their own inner lives, which were tuned to slave society. Since slaves had to be deferent, humble, submissive, and obedient, they provided the outward and visible signs of such slave grace, while retaining their own inward and spiritual grace. Indeed, so ritualized had white-slave relationships become that shrewd slaves were able to manipulate the symbols of the relationships to avoid punishment or to win concessions from masters. Properly humble blacks, using flattery to enhance the master's self-esteem, were able to obtain better working conditions, a little more food, perhaps even the dismissal of an especially detested overseer.

But no matter how much slaves gained through such means, they still remained

An invoice of ten negroes sent this day to John B Williamson by Geo Kremer named & cost as follows

To wit .. Betsey Kackley . . . . . $ 410.00
Nancy Aulick 515.00
Harry & Helen Miller . . . 1200.00
Mary Kootz 600.00
Betsey Ott 560.00
Isaac & Fanny Brent . . 992.00
Lucinda Luckett 467.50
George Smith 510.00
Amount of my traveling expences & boarding 5254.50
of lot No 9 not included in the other bills . . 39.50
Kremers expences Transporting lot No 9 to Richd 51.00
Carryall hire . . 6.00
$ 5351.00

I have this day delivered the above named negroes costing including my expences and other expences five thousand three hundred & fifty dollars this May 26th 1835

John W. Pittman

I did intend to leave Nancy child but she made such a damned fuss I had to let her take it I could of got fifty Dollars for so you must add forty Dollars to the above

A slave dealer's invoice for slaves sold in 1835. Note the last paragraph, which tells of a slave mother's successful resistance to the sale of her child.

Library of Congress

slaves. And no matter what an individual slave's status might be—and there was social stratification in slave society—he or she was still excluded from and oppressed by white society. Thus, slaves identified with each other, and this identity gave meaning and authority to the slave community.

Over the years the slave community had evolved its own codes of morality and behavior, to which all members were held accountable. Rape of slave women was a crime. Taking food from the master's pantry was permissible, but theft of food from other slaves was a serious offense. One had to bow and scrape to get along with "ole massa," but it was the community's obligation to aid runaways. Men and women who stood up against "ole massa" were honored. Informers who betrayed their fellows were despised. Since slaves had no place to go except in the slave community, ostracism from their own kind was a penalty few slaves were willing to incur. Those few accepted exile from their fellows as the small price they had to pay for freedom and cash.

Since the slave community presented a center of power to rival the master, why did masters let it function? In the first place, they could not get along without it. The masters were interested in profit. To obtain maximum profit, masters required a willing, cooperative work force. This meant coming to terms with the slave community, providing *de facto* recognition of its existence in such basic considerations as realistic work loads. Second, masters hoped to control the slave community by using the stratification of that society. At the top of the slave heap were the black overseers, men who actually managed entire plantations. As Fogel and Engerman point out, this group was somewhat larger than formerly supposed. Indeed, in states where employment of black overseers was forbidden by law, planters sometimes employed whites as nominal overseers while vesting real authority in slave managers—a source of no little dissatisfaction among such white "overseers."

The masters had good reason for using black overseers. The blacks were slaves whose long-term interest lay in promoting the masters' interests. The whites, hired on contract, were concerned with short-term interests of their own. Their incomes depended on making exceptionally good crops, regardless of long-range costs in land, tools, and slave morale. Their hard usage of slaves often led to runaways, sabotage, and sullen discontent. Masters on occasion found themselves obliged to dismiss white overseers who proved especially obnoxious to slaves. Black overseers drastically reduced such problems. These men could manage things so as to promote high productivity without incurring the hidden costs of massive slave discontent. In addition, black overseers were able to furnish masters with firsthand intelligence on the slave community, which enabled masters to maintain control.

Perhaps even more important in helping masters were the domestic servants, who occupied the second rank in slave society. The servants were children, who often innocently betrayed matters that their elders were keeping secret, and older folk whose fidelity had long been proved. John W. Blassingame has called them "the plantation's secret police." They were better clothed and better fed than field hands. Because of their intimate ties with masters' families, servants earned a reputation of betraying slave conspiracies and otherwise informing on their fellows. But some domestic servants found twenty-four-hour contact with whites intolerable. While field hands had the nights to themselves, many servants were under white surveillance day and night. Those who resented such control ran away. During the Civil War, house servants were among the first to leave plantations when Union armies approached.

Third rank in slave society was assigned to foremen, or "drivers," as they were called. They occupied a somewhat ambivalent position. During the day, they were representatives of the master. Their job was to supervise the work gangs in the fields. At night they returned to the slave quarters, together with the men and women whom they bossed during the day. Their responsibilities toward the master had to be balanced by sensitivity to their own position in the slave community. It was in their interest, then, to argue for realistic work loads and to apply the lash sparingly and lightly. Those who conformed to slave community standards were accepted as arbiters of disputes and family quarrels—a role in which the driver helped maintain the "peace in the quarters" so ardently desired by masters, while enforcing the sanctions of the slave community itself. Those drivers who did not meet community standards met with social disapproval, including retribution for daytime cruelty.

Occupying a special niche in slave society were the craftsmen. These men had proved themselves as field hands and had also demonstrated qualities that prompted masters to have them trained as masons, carpenters, and blacksmiths, and in other skilled occupations essential to the functioning of a plantation. Also, such men provided another benefit to masters. When their services were not required at home, they could be rented out or allowed to "hire their own time" in towns and cities. The craftsmen's mobility made them an invaluable link in the slave "grapevine" that helped knit the far-flung units of the slave community together. Craftsmen often used their skills and mobility to escape.

At the bottom of slave society was the mass of field hands. These were engaged not only in producing cotton, tobacco, sugar, or rice, but also in raising food for humans and animals, caring for livestock, improving land and buildings, and making clothing. In short, slaves worked the year round in a variety of occupations that called for considerable skill. During the cotton season they worked in organized gangs, each assigned enough tasks to keep the slaves working long and hard throughout the day—an early form of what twentieth-century factory workers were to call the "speed-up." Field hands fared less well in terms of food, clothing, and housing than did slaves in other categories. Of all the slaves, field hands ate the worst, dressed the poorest, and slept the coldest.

Masters hoped to control the slave community by dominating its upper ranks. The social structure also made possible another means of control: incentives. Field hands could aspire to become drivers or craftsmen, and good drivers could hope to become overseers. Such promotion from the lower ranks depended, of course, on gaining the master's favor—an important means of control. On many plantations other incentives were provided, both to increase productivity and to keep slaves reasonably happy. Outstanding workers were rewarded with bonuses: cash, food, clothing. Prolific slave women also received such awards for making new slaves. Slaves were often encouraged to grow their own food, with the right to sell any surplus. The community as a whole had an incentive to be faithful and industrious in the bounties the master dispensed at Christmas.

Slavery, then, within its limits, was a flexible institution that allowed some scope for the expression of black competence. More than that, slavery as a system was porous. Despite the efforts of the slave South to develop a closed society, slaves were well aware of the changed situation of the "peculiar institution." In the eighteenth century slavery was universally accepted. In the nineteenth, it was well on the way to being universally rejected. Slavery was abolished in the Caribbean islands. It was outlawed in Mexico. Former slaves established an independent black republic in Haiti. Slavery persisted in Brazil, but the only great remaining slave power was the United States—and even there it was under attack. Such developments were known in the slave community, affording hope that sooner or later American slaves, too, would win their freedom.

SLAVE RESPONSES

Despite their efforts, then, masters could not control the slave community as a whole, however much they might tie individual slaves to white interests. How did slaves other than these favored few respond to their bondage? Some accommodated themselves completely, becoming indeed Sambo, the embodiment of the white myth that slaves were by nature irresponsible, lazy, docile, superstitious, content with their lot, and loyal to their masters.

All slaves had to play Sambo on occasion. It was the role prescribed for them by the ritual of master-slave relationships. Through such role-playing slaves gained favors, escaped punishment, and otherwise eased their lot. Some succumbed to the role, but for most it was a conscious sham. Their inner life was reserved for the slave quarters, where it found free expression. Nevertheless, the contradictory roles imposed on slaves set up tensions, for the temptation to live Sambo instead of playing Sambo was ever present. As George P. Rawick has observed: "Unless the slave has had a tendency to be Sambo he can never become Nat Turner. One who has never feared becoming Sambo never need rebel to maintain his humanity."

Overwhelmed by white power, slaves who were neither Sambos nor Nat Turners—and that was the great majority—sought to improve their lot in subtle ways that would gain their objectives without bringing down the wrath of the master or overseer. One was a form of the "slow-down strike." That is, workers seemed to be working as hard as ever, but when the day was over, output was below standard. Floggings of suspected leaders brought work back to normal in some places, but in others it resulted in sullen noncooperation. Many planters found it expedient to set realistic work quotas, while others went even further and offered cash and other inducements to prompt maximum output.

There were many other methods of resistance to unduly oppressive conditions. Slaves feigned stupidity when asked to try new techniques or implements. They mimicked the symptoms of illness with marked success. They played on the conflict of interest between masters and white overseers to get rid of harsh overseers. They sabotaged tools and equipment and maimed livestock. At night, they stretched ropes across the roads to foil the mounted white patrols whose job it was to keep slaves at home.

Other responses were not subtle at all. Slaves sometimes fought back directly, as when Frederick Douglass beat a slave breaker to a standstill. (A slave breaker was a white man who earned his living by beating and torturing rebellious slaves into

Frederick Douglass, former slave and black abolitionist who became a confidant of Abraham Lincoln.

submission.) "He never again laid the weight of his finger against me in anger," wrote Douglass later. "I was a changed being after that fight. I was nothing before—I was a man now." In like manner Solomon Northup so worsted his master that he was sold off quickly. In extreme cases slaves resorted to arson and to murder.

Discontent took an even more significant form in running away. Some fugitives had no intention of leaving permanently. They simply took refuge in nearby woods or swamps while awaiting promises of better treatment. Some ran away to return to wives and children from whom they had been forcibly separated. But other runaways wanted nothing less than freedom. These tended to be the young, the sturdy, and often the highly skilled—the very people whom masters could least afford to lose. But the long journey to freedom was arduous and hazardous, taxing the psychic and physical endurance of the fugitives, and they faced the prospect that recapture meant exemplary punishment. Only the young and the brave dared undertake such missions, but youth and bravery alone were not enough. Success depended on support from slave communities. Only there could the runaways find rest, refreshment, and intelligence about the next stage of their journey.

Most permanent runaways went as individuals, but some went in groups. Harriet Tubman, for example, always led small parties out of the South. Other blacks banded together in attempts to escape, although they rarely succeeded. At different times armed bands of fugitives in Maryland, Kentucky, and Missouri engaged in bloody—and unsuccessful—battles with white pursuers. But in 1826 slaves being shipped to the Deep South revolted on a Mississippi steamboat and escaped to Indiana, and in 1841 rebellious slaves took over the slave ship *Creole* en route from Virginia to New Orleans. After killing one white officer they "persuaded" the others to take the ship to the British Bahamas, where the slaves were eventually freed, except for those held responsible for killing the officer. They were hanged. An outraged American government protested—not the hangings, but the freeing of the slaves. Many years later the British government paid $110,000 to the United States in compensation.

In a class by themselves were the runaways who made good their escape while remaining in the South. A considerable number found refuge among Indian peoples—a fact that helps explain the determination of planters to get rid of the southern Indians. Although the Indians themselves might keep the fugitives as slaves, Indian slavery was such that it was easy for blacks to become members of Indian society and intermarry. A significant number joined the Seminoles in Florida, where some rose to positions of influence and shared in leading the fight against Indian removal.

Still other runaways escaped into swamps and mountains, where they eventually established communities that lasted for long periods of time. These "maroons," as they were called, became an object of special white anger, because they provided a haven more easily accessible to fleeing slaves than the North. Many of the "maroon" communities were wiped out in bloody battles as white expansion made it feasible to use force against them. Survivors retreated farther into the swamps and mountains to form new communities.

SLAVE REBELLIONS

Some slaves went beyond resistance to armed rebellion. Compared to the great uprisings of slaves in the Caribbean and in Latin America, those in the United States were small, infrequent, and less bloody; yet they were put down with a savage ferocity that belied their size. Sporadic, isolated uprisings occurred from time to time and were easily suppressed, but two major revolts are worth noting. One, in 1811, involved several hundred slaves in Louisiana, who marched on New Orleans after crushing initial planter resistance. They were intercepted by federal troops, who killed sixty-six blacks in the battle that followed. Of those captured, sixteen were executed and their heads displayed on roadside poles to discourage notions of future rebellion.

The other, and more famous, rebellion occurred twenty years later, in Southampton County, Virginia, under the leadership of Nat Turner. Although only about seventy slaves participated, they wreaked havoc, killing fifty-five whites before they were crushed. Thirteen slaves and three free blacks were executed, while scores of slaves were deported—some of them for merely expressing sympathy with the rebels. Outside the courts, panic-stricken whites took private vengeance, flogging and killing blacks indiscriminately. Turner himself escaped for more than two months, until he was betrayed by two slaves. He went to his death stoically, leaving behind him his famous *Confessions,* a statement he made to his lawyer, Thomas R. Gray.

More numerous than actual rebellions were conspiracies to rebel—plots revealed before they could be carried out. Unfortunately, we cannot tell how many were actual conspiracies and how many were the products of white hysteria. If whites had to believe in Sambo, they also had to reckon with the reality of Nat Turner, the rebel. The consequence was an almost constant state of psychological tension, in which whites saw black menace in the most innocent gathering. All it took was a rumor or an accusation, and the hunt was on. A certain type of slave found it expedient to cooperate with the whites; informers were rewarded with freedom and liberal cash rewards. Thousands of slaves were flogged, deported, or executed for participation in plots that existed only in inflamed white imaginations. On occasion, slaveholders, concerned with the loss of property, brought some sanity to the situation, but all too often they, too, fell prey to their fears.

But there were genuine conspiracies. One of the most notable was the plot of Gabriel in 1800. This Virginia slave showed a talent for guerrilla organization, including political shrewdness in dealing with sympathetic whites. He raised an army of several thousand slaves in the vicinity of Richmond, the state capital. Under his leadership they made their own swords and bullets, while they planned to seize guns stored by whites. Gabriel's plan was to march on Richmond, destroying white opposition on the way. Significantly, whites who had shown sympathy to blacks were to be spared, such as Quakers, Methodists, and French people. Gabriel also hoped to enlist the active aid of poor whites, who resented the planting aristocracy. Once Richmond had been captured, the city would be fortified and held until whites agreed to freedom for the slaves. On the day Gabriel's uprising was to begin, it was betrayed, and his operations halted by a violent storm that flooded the area. Whites rounded up Gabriel and his followers. He and thirty-five of his most active associates were put to death.

Another major "conspiracy" was uncovered in 1822 in Charleston, South Carolina. It involved urban slaves rather than plantation slaves, and among its leadership were some of the most skilled artisans of the city. The organizer of the planned rebellion was Denmark Vesey, a free carpenter who was active in the black church, as were many of the other leaders. Their aim was to capture Charleston and hold it hostage for black freedom. Among the rebels were slaves taken in Africa, who were more bitter about enslavement than blacks born into American slavery. The plot was betrayed. Vesey and thirty-four others were hanged, another thirty were deported, and many others flogged. Governor Thomas Bennett justified the severe punishments because they served to "produce a salutary terror" among blacks, both slave and free. The details and extent of the conspiracy remain unclear because, with few exceptions, the leaders, despite torture and offers of reward, said nothing. Vesey himself steadfastly denied the charges against him, and he went to his death without revealing anything. This, together with other elements involved in the Vesey plot, has led to belief that the whole plot was the product of white hysteria, exploited to serve the ends of ambitious white politicians. Other historians believe the conspiracy was genuine, although blown out of proportion.

The "insurrection panic" of 1856 arose out of some imagined plots and some that were genuine. The emergence that year of the new Republican party on a national scale stimulated white fears, played on by Democratic politicians, that a Republican triumph would signal a general slave uprising. From Texas to Virginia "plots" were discovered and their alleged participants put to death. In many cases the only evidence was "confessions" wrung from accused slaves under torture, but in others there were more substantial grounds for conspiracy charges. Iron workers and miners in Montgomery County, Tennessee, cached supplies of arms and ammunition preliminary to an uprising aimed at mass flight to the North. In northeastern Kentucky forty armed slaves were captured at a black festival. They had planned to arouse slaves in the area for escape to Ohio. Cooperation between blacks and Mexicans characterized a conspiracy in Colorado County, Texas. The rebels accumulated a store of weapons, planning to fight their way to Mexico and freedom. Five blacks were put to death, and all Mexicans ordered out of the county. They were forbidden to return on penalty of death.

There is sufficient evidence of actual rebellion and genuine plots to show that slave unrest was widespread. It appeared among workers in industrial enterprises as well as among plantation hands and among those living in the relatively benign atmosphere of Virginia as well as among those toiling under the rigorous conditions of the Deep South.

SLAVES AND SLAVE CODES

As slavery expanded into the rich soil of Alabama, Mississippi, and Arkansas, its apparent profitability ensured it new life. Whites came to feel that slavery was not a necessary evil but a positive good, both for whites and blacks. Since slavery was to be a permanent institution, it was essential that slaves be reminded of their subjection and that all sources and signs of unrest be suppressed. Thus, beginning in the 1820s the slave community found itself increasingly hemmed in by revised slave codes designed to break black spirit. That spirit survived the repression, thanks in part to the resourcefulness of blacks in evading the laws. Their success was also due to the extremely rigorous codes themselves, which slaveholders found convenient to ignore except when conspiracies and rebellions made it expedient to enforce the law.

The first major step in revising the codes was to deprive slaves of any hope of freedom. Some slaves, especially skilled workers who hired their own time, scrimped and saved to buy their own freedom and, when possible, the freedom of wives and children. Others were freed by their masters, often through the master's will. Southern states tried to halt such practices. In the Upper South, slaves freed by masters were required to leave the state within a specified time limit. In the Deep South, any kind of manumission was eventually prohibited.

The codes also sought to regulate the slave community. Slaves had to be respectful and obedient always, not only to their masters but to all whites. Any behavior, even "a look, the pointing of a finger," that whites deemed insulting was punishable. Any violence toward whites, including self-defense, brought drastic penalties. Of course, slaves were not permitted to testify against whites, denying the blacks even legal protection against the white hoodlums whom they were forbidden to strike in retaliation. Slaves were not permitted to beat drums or blow horns, since these were seen as means of clandestine communication. Slaves could not preach except to other slaves on the same plantation, and then only with a white person present. Slaves were forbidden by the codes to attend black meetings away from home, and travel in general required a pass from the master. Slaves could not legally possess whiskey, guns, or animals, including dogs. They could not practice medicine, a provision designed to undermine the leadership of "conjure men" who carried on the African tradition of combining religion and folk medicine and thus possessed great influence in the slave community. Teaching slaves to read and write was forbidden. Runaways and those who sheltered them were subject to heavy penalties.

Slaves showed ingenuity in evading the codes. They forged passes so they could travel, sometimes to visit relatives or friends, sometimes to reach the North or

Mexico. Ellen Craft, a slave who looked nearly white, dressed as a man and escaped with her husband, William, by posing as his master. Slaves learned to read and write, sometimes with the connivance of whites. Others, like Frederick Douglass, tricked white playmates into teaching them the alphabet. Forbidden to beat drums, slaves devised other means of communication. They could not avoid white supervision of their religious gatherings. But when they sang "Steal Away to Jesus," how was the white to distinguish between a purely spiritual meaning and the message that Harriet Tubman or some other black Underground Railroad agent was in the neighborhood? Slaves who wished to visit friends and relatives nearby slipped off plantations at night, employing ruses of all kinds to evade the white patrols on the roads. Runaways sprinkled pepper in their tracks to confuse the dogs sent to pursue them. In short, in life as in black folklore, the weak Br'er Rabbit used his wits to overcome more powerful enemies.

Violators of the slave codes, when caught, were subject to harsh penalties. Some offenses, such as theft or fighting with whites, brought punishment designed to terrify violators without impairing their ability to work: ear cropping, branding in the hand, flogging, and castration. Other crimes called for death: rebellion, conspiracy, robbery, arson, rape or attempted rape of white women, and murder or attempted murder. In such cases owners were compensated for loss of their property. The codes, however, were not fully enforced except in times of white hysteria over conspiracies, real or imagined. And slaveholders, fearful for their property, often intervened to help their slaves escape the full rigors of the law.

Despite the slave codes and the various devices used privately by masters to keep slaves in fear, slaves emerged from bondage in the 1860s eager to learn, to work for themselves, to legalize their marriages, and to take part in the life of the nation, including combat service in the Union army. These were hardly the signs of a people whose spirit had been broken.

FOR FURTHER READING

An excellent collection of source materials is Willie Lee Rose, *A Documentary History of Slavery in the United States* (1976). Two works focus on the slave community: John W. Blassingame, *The Slave Community* (1972), and George P. Rawick, *From Sundown to Sunup* (1972). The role of the slave family is discussed in Herbert Gutman, *The Black Family in Slavery and Freedom* (1976).

Conflicting interpretations of slavery are found in Eugene Genovese, *Roll, Jordan, Roll* (1974); Kenneth M. Stampp, *The Peculiar Institution* (1956); Stanley Elkins, *Slavery* (1968); and R. W. Fogel and S. L. Engerman, *Time On the Cross* (1974).

Little known aspects of slavery are discussed in Richard C. Wade, *Slavery in the Cities* (1964), and Robert S. Starobin, *Industrial Slavery in the Old South* (1970).

Slave rebellions—real and imaginary—are discussed in Nicholas Halasz, *The Rattling Chains* (1966); Robert S. Starobin, ed., *Denmark Vesey* (1970); John B. Duff and Peter M. Mitchell, eds., *The Nat Turner Rebellion* (1971). Mary Cable, *Black Odyssey* (1971), tells the story of the uprising on the slave ship *Amistad*.

Very little work has been done on the domestic slave trade. Frederic Bancroft, *Slave Trading in the Old South* (1931), is still the best account available.

10 white women in white america

In 1857 the Presbyterian minister F. A. Ross of Huntsville, Alabama, published a defense of black slavery. One of his arguments was that the condition of the slave was akin to that of the white married woman. ''Do you say, the slave is held to involuntary servitude?'' he asked. And he answered, ''So is the wife.''

There is irony in using the subjection of white women to defend slavery, but such ironies abound in the history of women in the early nineteenth century. Well-to-do women enjoyed more comfort and wealth than ever before, but they had less freedom than in colonial times. They were told that their duties lay in home, hearth, and church, while women of the poor were told that their proper place was in mill and factory. Respectable women were not supposed to speak in public, but the South Carolina aristocrat Sarah Grimké took to the platform to promote abolition. Middle-class men agreed that women's minds were too fragile to cope with serious problems, but they sent their daughters to the women's colleges that were just making their appearance.

THE SUBJECTION OF WOMEN

Except for the South, young American women were brought up in an atmosphere of freedom and independence unknown to European women. With marriage, however, they were reduced to a condition of servitude. Alexis de Toqueville, the perceptive French observer of American society in the 1830s, concluded that ''in America the independence of woman is irrecoverably lost in the bonds of matrimony; if an unmarried woman is less constrained there than elsewhere, a wife is subjected to stricter obligations.''

The subjection of married women was written into the law. The conservative spirit of Sir William Blackstone, the famous expounder of the English common law, triumphed in free America, even after the Revolution, classifying married women as legal nonpersons of the same sort as convicted felons, children, and the mentally ill. What little legal standing a wife possessed was exercised through her husband.

The husband was the head of family, with full control over children and property, unless the wife's property was protected through premarital contract. A working woman had no legal claim on her earnings, since they belonged to her husband. A husband had absolute right over his wife's "person," meaning her body. She could not avoid his presence, for he had a right to her company. If she ran away, the husband could bring her back, by force if necessary. If a wife behaved improperly, her husband had the right to beat her, although the courts drew the line at excessive brutality and murder. Divorced women lost all claims to their children and family property.

Obviously, the law gives us little insight into real family relationships, for most families managed their affairs without recourse to the law. Nevertheless, a married woman had to adjust, happily or otherwise, to her husband's dominance. And such dominance, as John Stuart Mill observed of the comparable English situation in his famous essay *The Subjection of Women,* was as available to the depraved as to the honorable. The law was with the husband, be he good man or bad.

The law, however, was less effective in keeping women subject than women themselves, who so internalized the values of a male-oriented society that these values became their own. This was true of women in all classes, but it was especially notable among those of the upper-middle class and those who aspired to such status. From infancy onward, girls of such families were conditioned to see marriage with men of their own class as their great aim in life. The independence of unmarried American girls that so impressed foreigners was expressed within that framework. The formal education of women, which was limited and superficial, was directed toward that end. The various schools and academies that catered to girls of the well-to-do taught them reading, dancing, singing, needlework, and music. In some schools girls were exposed to French and a little "science." In short, education was designed to make them suitable candidates for marriage rather than to stimulate their minds.

THE "CULT OF THE LADY"

As part of their education, young women were inculcated with the precepts of two related cults: that of "the lady" and that of "purity," or prudery. The "cult of the lady" was a rationale for economic uselessness. Since middle-class women were no longer producers, they were taught to glory in the role of consumers. Husbands and fathers encouraged such consumption, for their own social prestige was measured by the opulence of their houses and by the wealth displayed by wives and daughters in the form of dress, jewelry, and other finery.

The lady's proper sphere was in the home, and her principal duty, besides bearing children, was to make it a haven of refuge for a husband worn out by the toils of business. She herself was always to be cheerful, complaisant, and available. Since many of the well-to-do women were "new money"—that is, they were related to men who had only recently become wealthy—they were often at a loss on the fine points of etiquette, deportment, and behavior that were second nature to families of "old money." For the newcomers, *Godey's Lady's Book* and its imitators supplied the answers and introduced them to the world of high fashion. The lady did not work, of course, not even in the home. There her role was to supervise the work of servants, who were cheap and plentiful after the mass arrival of immigrants in the 1840s. Thus, in a fluid society, the "cult of the lady" helped to set the class line between those who did not work and those who had to work.

Outside the home, the lady's sphere was restricted. She was supposed to be an active church member. She was permitted to aid charitable societies. If she were serious-minded, she might take part in movements to curb alcoholism or promote "moral purity." Abolitionism, however, smacked too much of radicalism to be acceptable. She was expected to engage in such social activities as dinners, balls, the theater, and the opera. A lady, of course, never spoke at public meetings, nor did she take part in controversial causes.

There were women of breeding and background who possessed all the qualifications of ladies except one—money. The opportunities for such women to earn a living were limited. They were accepted as dressmakers. They could teach, but education was still a field jealously dominated by men. They could operate shops, as did Elizabeth Peabody in her famous bookstore, which served as an intellectual center for early feminists in Boston. Or they could serve as companions to elderly women. Louisa May Alcott, later the noted author of *Little Women,* found the conditions of such employment so degrading and humiliating that she vowed never to do it again. Until the 1840s it was also possible for genteel women to work in the textile mills of New England without losing caste, but when immigrants came to dominate the working force, such jobs lost their respectability.

THE "CULT OF PURITY"

The "cult of purity" reinforced the teachings of the "cult of the lady." Women were regarded as the transmitters of moral standards from generation to generation. As such they themselves had to be morally beyond reproach. Thus they were to repress their feelings, making no outward show of affection to lovers or husbands. They must be pious, passive, chaste, and cold. Young women were enjoined not to read novels lest their purity be corrupted. The highest function of woman was motherhood, but discussion of sex was taboo. Mention of anything even remotely connected with sex was banned. The word *leg,* for example, was not mentioned in polite conversation. In the South, some editions of the Bible were expurgated to remove such offensive terms as "womb." The behavior of women reflected the code of purity. No "lady" appeared in public while pregnant, and some even confined themselves to their rooms during the period. A young woman of Cincinnati approved the suggestion of Frances Trollope, a visiting English woman, for a picnic, but she thought it would not succeed. "It is considered very indelicate," she said, "for ladies and gentlemen to sit down together on the grass."

American men observed the code. Europeans noted with astonishment that it was completely safe for an upper-class woman to travel unaccompanied and that in inns and hotels she was treated with deference. The seamy side of the code, though, showed itself in brothels found in every town and city. Servants and factory girls were regarded as fair game by "honorable gentlemen" as well as by other men. Amateur and professional prostitution was widespread, not simply because of the great number of unattached males, such as sailors and immigrants. The very life style of the middle class encouraged it. Young men postponed marriage until they were able to support a wife in proper fashion, and in the long time between manhood and marriage the brothel was a regular stopping place. Married men practiced sexual abstinence and turned to prostitutes instead of their wives.

Such behavior had a number of causes. The aspirations of the middle class did not permit large families. Too many children were a drain on the father's wealth. Further, large families argued a man's lack of self-control in his private life, and men who lacked self-control were looked at askance in the business world. The opinion was commonplace that the basic difference between the rich and the poor was the capacity of the rich for abstinence, as against the incapacity of the poor. Indeed, that incapacity was the very reason why the poor were poor. Thus, small families implied the superior moral character of the well-to-do and justified their privilege. The cult of prudery played its part, too. Since sex was looked on as at best a necessary evil, yielding to it too frequently argued moral weakness. Besides, out of consideration for his wife's feelings, a good husband could not require her to submit more than necessary to what both considered human frailty.

That women, too, had sexual needs was an idea whose time had not yet come. It was generally presumed that no good woman had any physical desire. When ladies of indisputable character showed signs of sexual tension, doctors wrote them off as abnormal. The consequent spread of what was called "nervous disease" and various forms of psychosomatic illness were attributed by male doctors of the day to the special "hysterical" constitution of women. (Female *hysteria* meant a mental condition arising from the womb.)

But moral codes, however great their authority, have never been able to contain sexual energy. Some young women did become pregnant outside marriage. For lower-class women this meant either forced marriage or involuntary prostitution. Upper-class women, single or married, could get rid of unwanted pregnancies with the aid of abortionists, who advertised their services in the newspapers. In 1845 Dr. Edward D. Mansfield reported that in New York abortion was "quite common" among those who could afford it.

In the pre-Civil War years, upper-class women came to occupy another role besides moral guardian. They became the promoters of cultural values, a role they continue to play today. Unless he were a man of great wealth, the middle-class man devoted so much time and energy to his business that he had little time for the finer aspects of life. Nevertheless, he felt socially obligated not only to show an interest in cultural affairs but also to promote them. This he could do by allowing his wife to serve as substitute. The boards of the various societies that cultivated interest in literature, painting, music, the theater, and the opera were dominated by men, but women played an ever-increasing role in the actual work of such organizations. In

1855, Nathaniel P. Willis, editor of an influential women's magazine, noted that women "patronize and influence the Arts, and pronounce upon Operas and other foreign novelties."

LIBERATING THE MIND

Woman's role as promoter of culture was due in part to the growing number of educated women. Most middle-class girls never got beyond the academies, which taught them to be ladies, but an increasing number of young women attended colleges, which called on them to use their minds and opened up vistas few women had envisioned before.

The first major breakthrough came in 1821, when Emma Hart Willard opened the Troy Female Seminary. She won a charter, but no funds, from the state of New York. The town of Troy provided a building, and operating funds were raised through donations. Public support was won by emphasizing the seminary's program of producing properly prepared schoolteachers. But Willard's educational aim had another emphasis as well. She wanted to demonstrate that women's intellects were as capable as men's of rigorous work. To this end, her students studied mathematics, history, philosophy, and the sciences. They even studied human physiology, although the prudishness of the day required that the textbook illustrations of the human body be covered up! The seminary proved amazingly successful, and its graduates carried with them the gospel of higher education for women throughout the country.

Willard's success doubtless influenced Mary Lyon, a Massachusetts teacher dissatisfied with the education of women. Largely through her own efforts, she was able to open Mount Holyoke Seminary in 1837—an inauspicious year, in view of the Panic and ensuing depression. Nevertheless, the school thrived, although entrance requirements were high and the full course lasted three years, instead of the two years usual in other female seminaries. Lyon was not interested in training teachers or housekeepers. She was concerned with educating women as human beings. Of housework, she said, "However important this part of a woman's education, a literary institution is not the place to secure it." The curriculum, patterned after that of nearby Amherst College, provided for study in mathematics, English, Latin, science, and philosophy.

But while Lyon was devoted to the development of individual talent, she had a larger moral end in view: namely, that such talent must be used productively to serve society. This view was expressed in the statement in the seminary catalog that education at Mount Holyoke would be "a handmaid to the Gospel and an efficient auxiliary to the great task of renovating the world." Higher education for women in New England was a vital part of the great upsurge of moral reform in New England that found expression in such causes as abolition, temperance, and women's rights.

Troy and Mount Holyoke confined admission to women, but in 1833 Oberlin College, a center of abolitionist activism in Ohio, initiated coeducation by admitting women. At the same time it opened its doors to blacks, causing misgivings among many whites, including some abolitionists, who opposed coeducation of black men and white women. But even Oberlin was not prepared to concede educational equality to women. They were excluded from the full college program, on the ground that

In 1861 *Harper's Weekly* featured Matthew Vassar's endowment of a new college for women.

higher education for women was designed to make them better wives and mothers. Education that might encourage them to enter professional or public life would endanger family life and was thus unacceptable. Eventually, under pressure from students, including Lucy Stone and Antoinette Brown, who later were noted feminists, the college yielded. In 1841 the first women who had taken the same program as men were graduated.

Oberlin might well have argued that there was little sense in training young women for the professions when the professions were closed to them. Neither clergymen nor doctors nor lawyers nor professors welcomed women into their ranks. Elizabeth Blackwell broke the medical barrier in 1849 when she received a degree from Geneva Medical College in New York State after having been denied admission to the leading medical schools of the day. Antoinette Brown (who later married Elizabeth's brother) pioneered in winning a degree in theology from Oberlin College in 1850. But both encountered discrimination when they sought to follow their careers.

Higher education contributed to the discontent of women who chafed at the restrictions imposed upon them. Such education, after all, posed a basic contradiction: it stimulated intellectual development, but once out in the world educated women found themselves barred from using their talents except in such fields as teaching and writing. And even there society looked upon such employment as temporary until women found their proper place as wives and mothers. No matter what Willard and Lyon might think about woman's intellectual potential, many parents sent their daughters to the seminaries and colleges to prepare them to marry suitably. But here again the educated woman found the restrictions of marriage more galling than did her less literate sisters.

Higher education simply added to the discontent; it did not create it. The feeling was there, awaiting expression. That expression came sharply in the early nineteenth century. We have noted already Abigail Smith Adams's stricture against the tyranny of men and Mercy Otis Warren's demand for equal education. In 1790, two years before publication of Mary Wollstonecraft's classic of women's liberation, *A Vindication of the Rights of Woman,* Judith Sargent Murray, daughter of a successful merchant of Gloucester, Massachusetts, published an essay anticipating many of Wollstonecraft's arguments. Was a woman, she asked, "to be allowed no other ideas, than those which are suggested by the mechanism of a pudding?" The dissatisfaction of women in the nineteenth century was articulated by three notable women: Frances Wright, Sarah Grimké, and Margaret Fuller.

Frances Wright was a well-to-do, well educated, and rebellious young Scot who became so enthusiastic about the United States on her first visit in 1818 that she returned to stay in 1824. While other militant women avoided mention of sex, Wright discussed it boldly. She advocated birth control. She urged free and equal unions between men and women rather than conventional marriage, which, she insisted, would be based on moral instead of legal obligations. She attacked organized religion, in part because it taught the subjection of women. Children, she thought, should be placed in public boarding schools at an early age, where both boys and girls would receive the same education, training them for human rather than for sexual roles. The schools would emphasize intellectual development; religious teaching would be banned. From such schools, Wright believed, would come liberated generations who would usher in a more humane society.

Sarah Grimké was a South Carolina aristocrat who, together with her sister, Angelina, turned against slavery, became Quakers, and in the 1830s began public advocacy of abolition in the North. The outcry against their speaking in public was led by the Congregational clergy of Massachusetts, and some male white abolitionists shared the clerics' indignation. To defend her right to speak, Sarah had to challenge the assumptions that underlay male supremacy. Since Sarah Grimké was a deeply religious person, she put the challenge in Christian terms. The Bible had been misinterpreted by men, she insisted: "Men and women were CREATED EQUAL; they are both moral and accountable beings, and whatever is *right* for man to do, is *right* for woman." But men, she wrote bitterly, had denied women their divine birthright:

> Man has subjected woman to his will, used her as a means to promote his selfish gratification, to minister to his sensual pleasures, to be instrumental in promoting his comfort; but never has he desired to elevate her to that rank she was created to fill. He has done all he could to debase and enslave her mind; and now he looks triumphantly on the ruin he has wrought, and says, the being he has thus deeply injured is his inferior.

More moderate in her approach than Wright or Grimké was Margaret Fuller. The most learned woman of her time, Fuller enjoyed the company of such distinguished men as Ralph Waldo Emerson, Horace Greeley, and William Ellery Channing. She edited *The Dial,* the organ of the New England transcendentalists, and served as literary critic for Greeley's *New York Tribune,* one of the most influential newspapers of the day. From her famous "conversations" with a select circle of "well educated and thinking women" in Boston she drew inspiration for her book, *Woman in the Nineteenth Century,* which appeared in 1845. The book, laden with erudition, was an eloquent plea for equality, but it was directed at too restricted a public to make an immediate impression. Fuller avoided Wright's frank approach to sex. To her, true marriage was a union of minds in which sex played no part. Only celibacy, she wrote, could "save a thinking mind." She went on to assert woman's spiritual independence:

I would have Woman lay aside all thought, such as she habitually cherishes, of being taught and led by men. I would have her, like the Indian girl, dedicate herself to the Sun, the Sun of Truth, . . . I would have her free from compromise, from complaisance, from helplessness, because I would have her good enough and strong enough to love one and all beings, from the fulness, not the poverty of being.

A MOVEMENT IS BORN

The cries of Wright, Grimké, and Fuller were symbolic but still individual expressions of women's discontent. Women lacked yet a movement that would bring them together, break down their isolation, and provide a means of struggle for legal and political equality. That movement originated in a bitter struggle within the abolitionist movement over the issue of women's rights.

Abolition attracted a large number of educated middle-class women. Among them were such outstanding persons as Lucretia Mott, Lydia Maria Child, Elizabeth Cady Stanton, Susan B. Anthony, Harriet Beecher Stowe, and Sarah and Angelina Grimké. But many men interested in freeing slaves were not concerned with freeing women. Women were assigned to sexually segregated societies. Men monopolized the public platform and made the decisions. In short, abolitionism, like other reform movements, was male-dominated.

Many women accepted such subordination as inevitable, but the Grimké sisters unwittingly served as a focal point for rebellion. The rebels were supported by William Lloyd Garrison. In 1840 he refused to participate in the World Anti-Slavery Convention in London because it declined to seat women delegates from the United States. Women's rights was one of the issues that contributed to the split in the abolitionist movement the following year.

The struggles within abolitionism had important consequences for women. The virulent attacks upon the Grimké sisters forced many women to conclude that they could not function effectively as abolitionists until they had first established their right to speak. Thus, the struggles to free blacks from slavery and to free women from male supremacy merged.

Another consequence of the abolitionist quarrel was the first women's rights convention, held in Seneca Falls, New York, in 1848. The London convention, with its frustrations, brought together two young women who shared convictions on the subjection of their sex: Lucretia Mott and Elizabeth Cady Stanton. Their plans eventually resulted in the Seneca Falls meeting, where for the first time American women as a group stated their grievances and aired their demands. Of the 300 people present, about 40 were men, including Frederick Douglass, the black abolitionist.

The convention adopted a Declaration of Sentiments modeled after the Declaration of Independence—a shrewd move to state the feminist case to the public in terms of the very principles that public accepted as basic. Thus, "all men and women are created equal," the convention asserted, adding that man, in his relations with woman, had sought "an absolute tyranny over her." For proof, the convention cited the history of the subjection of women in America, example by example.

What was to be done to overcome such subjection? Women were to have free entry into all "trades and professions." They had to be assured the right of higher education and the right to speak in public and to teach in "religious assemblies." Laws that held women in subjection were declared invalid because they were contrary "to the great precept of nature." Men, as well as women, should be held to a single standard of sexual morality. Women should not degrade themselves by "declaring themselves satisfied with their present position." As to the right of women to vote, the delegates to the convention disagreed sharply. By a margin of one vote the convention called for "the sacred right of the elective franchise." Significantly, no mention was made of the right of working women to organize unions and go on strike, although women had in fact been striking off and on for nearly twenty years.

The Seneca Falls convention set a precedent. Successive meetings at local, state, and national levels helped to break down the isolation of middle-class women who sought to improve their status. The ground was prepared for the great national movements for women's rights in post-Civil War America.

From its inception the movement met with intense hostility. Faced with the challenge to male supremacy, editors, preachers, doctors, professors, and politicians elaborated a defensive ideology. In the first place, the ideology held, women were not equal to men. Their bodies were weaker. Their minds were not as strong. They were emotionally unstable, subject to "nervous diseases" peculiar to their sex. Their inferiority was further demonstrated by the lack of great woman philosophers, scientists, or artists. Finally, God Himself had ordained woman's lot when he punished Adam and Eve for their transgression in the Garden. The New Testament did not alter woman's condition. As St. Paul said, "Neither was the man created for the woman; but the woman for the man."

The ideology's second main tenet was that although women were inferior, they exercised great power—not publicly, but privately, through their influence on husbands and sons. As the anti-Grimké clergymen put it in 1837, women's duties "are unobtrusive and private, but the sources of mighty power. When the mild, dependent, softening influence of woman upon the sternness of man's opinions is fully exercised, society feels its effect in a thousand ways."

Third, the woman's movement was held to be dangerous to society. The very claim of equality flew in the face of God's command and demonstrated that the idea of women's rights was rooted in "infidelity"—meaning atheism. Participation in professional and public life would involve women in all the sordid affairs of practicality, degrade them personally, and reduce their moral influence. Such reduction would undermine woman's role as the guardian of morality and society would suffer accordingly. Society would also suffer if weak-minded and emotionally unstable women were allowed to vote, much less allowed to hold office.

Above all, according to the male ideology, the movement's criticism of the role of women in marriage indicated that it was hostile to the family. Since the family was the basic unit of Anglo-Saxon civilization—obviously the best the world had known—the feminists were clearly dangerous to all that society had come to value. Indeed, it was often suggested, the critics of marriage wanted to replace it with "free love," the community of women, and indulgence in lust. This in turn was linked to socialism, a specter that had already frightened the European bourgeoisie and was beginning to haunt the American middle class.

Such arguments were accepted easily by the mass of men, and also by many women. The advocates of women's rights spent many dreary decades trying to persuade women as well as men of the moral and social values of their cause.

Paradoxically, the legal status of women improved during the years when women were openly expressing their grievances. Partly, the improvement was due to pressure from women, but mostly it sprang from other causes. Taxpayers were aroused over supporting families impoverished by irresponsible fathers or desertion. Among the well-to-do, fathers and brothers were concerned with protecting daughters and sisters from loss of property after marriage.

Thus, in 1839 Mississippi gave married women the right to control their own property, and several other states followed suit, including New York, California, and Texas. In 1848, New York not only assured married women of their property rights but also made it possible for them to enter into business on their own responsibility, that is, without having a man take responsibility for their debts. Ohio barred husbands from selling personal property without the consent of their wives. It also held that deserted or neglected wives were entitled to the wages of their husbands and of minor children. In 1860 New York guaranteed working women the right to their own wages.

In the meantime, large numbers of unhappily married women journeyed to Ohio and Indiana, where divorce was relatively easy. The women who sought such divorces must have been desperate indeed, for divorced women were looked down upon by ''decent'' society.

WOMEN WHO WORKED

While middle-class women were told that their place was in the home, other women were told their proper place was in the factories and mills appearing throughout the Northeast in the early years of the nineteenth century. As early as 1792, Alexander Hamilton had given as one of the advantages of industrial development: ''women and children are rendered more useful than they otherwise would be.'' Nearly thirty years later, the economist Mathew Carey said that through factory work, women and children would become ''a source of wealth, rather than an incumbrance.'' Advocates of the factory system also promoted it as a boon to the women of the working poor. Factory work, it was said, trained the working poor in the habits of punctuality, honesty, and hard work. Women who would otherwise be idle and perhaps misled into ''vicious habits'' were given an opportunity to earn an honest living. Through their earnings, women would contribute to higher living standards among the poor.

The factory system spread rapidly after the War of 1812. New England especially became the center of booming woolen and cotton textile industries. So great was the demand for labor that entire families were hired, including children as young as ten. Employers, however, relied mainly on recruiting young women from rural New England, where worn-out farms allowed only bare subsistence. The women were attracted to the mills by the prospects of high wages, personal freedom, and

Rhode Island Historical Society

This bucolic portrayal of Samuel Slater's textile mill at Pawtucket, Rhode Island, in the 1790s gives little hint of its significance. Its use of water to power machinery ushered in the Industrial Revolution. Its use of women and children to tend the machines foreshadowed things to come.

economic independence. Their parents were assured that the girls' morals would be protected by the pious women who ran the boardinghouses where the girls stayed. Women were also recruited from the urban working class. And, in the early years, girls and widows from genteel but impoverished backgrounds found it possible to work in the mills without losing caste. By 1831 there were 39,000 girls and women at work in the cotton mills alone, earning an average of $2 a week, accounted a good wage at the time.

Single women at first enjoyed the completely new way of life. They were earning their own living. They were free from constant family surveillance. They were in daily contact with more men and women than they had ever dreamed possible on their isolated farms. At the paternalistic Lowell mills they were encouraged to develop their interests and talents through classes, lectures, and writing in the *Lowell Offering,* a magazine devoted entirely to the productions of mill girls.

Gradually, however, it dawned on the women that they had merely changed one form of drudgery for another. The working day was long. Even in the model mills of Lowell, so much extolled by Charles Dickens during his visit in 1842, women worked thirteen hours a day, six days a week, except in winter, when they worked from sunup to sundown.

To be sure, the hours of labor differed little in number from those on the farm, but the work differed in kind. On the farm, men, women, and children worked at their own pace. In the factory, they worked at the pace set by the machines. This called for constant, unremitting attention to the job. Adults who could not keep up the pace were summarily dismissed, while in some mills foremen used whips on children, boys and girls alike, who faltered in their duties. Since the working of cotton called for moisture in the air, workers labored in hot, humid rooms with the windows shut tight, breathing fetid air filled with particles of lint and dirt. It is not surprising that respiratory diseases were common, often debilitating, and sometimes fatal.

The swiftly moving machinery was not equipped with protective devices—indeed, the very idea of factory safety was still to come—so that accidents were frequent. The woman who lost a finger, a hand, or an arm had no legal claim against her employer unless she could prove he had been negligent. Indeed, she could not sue in her own name; she had to act through husband or father. In any case, few workers could afford lawyers. Some factory buildings themselves were ramshackle affairs, hastily slapped together with no thought of safety. One such building collapsed in Lawrence, Massachusetts, in 1860, killing about 200 workers, most of them women and girls.

Women found that factory life fell short of the utopia pictured by labor recruiters in other ways as well. Each woman worked on an individual contract giving complete authority to the employer. Tardiness at work or work deemed not up to standard was punished by fines. Workers were forbidden to leave without notice, on penalty of losing two weeks' pay. Employers, however, were free to dismiss workers at any time without penalty. Workers had to agree not to join unions on pain of forfeiting all wages due them—a stiff penalty at a time when many mills paid workers only twice a year.

In their off-duty hours women found little freedom. They were required to attend church on Sundays. They were to be in bed by specified hours. Always they were under the scrutiny of boardinghouse keepers who reported their behavior to employers, especially any overt signs of discontent. Nor could women make much use of the cultural outlets afforded by the Lowell mills. Sarah Bagley, who later emerged as a militant labor leader, had to give up her attempts to hold classes for Lowell girls because they were too exhausted to read or study. And the *Lowell Offering* eventually became a house organ run by William Schouler, a politician identified with the mill interests.

Once the euphoria over factory life had passed, women proved much less docile than employers had expected. As early as 1828 about 400 women went on strike at cotton mills in Dover, New Hampshire. In the next decade thousands of women were involved in strikes among shoe workers, garment workers, tailors, and mill workers. The strikes, generally sparked by wage reductions or attempts to increase work loads, were usually unsuccessful, but they did testify to a rebellious spirit among women and girls. For example, when women and girls at the Lowell mills rebelled against a wage cut in 1836, they organized a Factory Girls Association and refused to talk with management except through their elected representatives. In an appeal for public support they invoked the memories of the Revolution: "As our fathers resisted unto blood the lordly avarice of the British ministry, so we, their daughters, never will wear the yoke which has been prepared for us."

The women's rebellion, however, did not fare as well as that of 1776. The strikers were evicted from their boardinghouses. Lacking shelter, food, and funds, the women either had to make their way home—often scores of miles away—or "wear the yoke" that Lowell had prepared for them. The women had little prospect of getting jobs elsewhere, for other employers would not hire "troublemakers."

The Panic of 1837 ushered in the "Hungry Forties," a long era of mass unemployment and widespread misery among workers, men and women alike. The great number of people desperate for work of any kind naturally checked expression of discontent, but conditions in the factories were such that occasionally women rebelled anyway. In 1845, under the leadership of Sarah Bagley, the Lowell women protested a sharp increase in the workload as well as a wage reduction. On this occasion, they won. Strikes took place in New England and New York and as far west as Pittsburgh, where in 1845, 5,000 cotton mill workers went on strike demanding a reduction in the workweek from seventy-two to sixty hours, with no reduction in pay. Although the women held out for longer than a month, they were defeated.

Bagley perceived that more was needed to improve the lot of working women than sporadic job action. She took the lead in forming what she hoped would be a permanent organization, the Lowell Female Reform Association. The idea spread to other towns throughout New England, New York, and Pennsylvania. Such associations not only tried to improve wages and job conditions but also supported the mounting campaign of men's unions for the ten-hour day. The aim was to obtain state legislation limiting the workday, and striving for that goal brought working women into active politics.

Women could not vote, of course, but they could speak, write, and appeal to an older middle-class opinion that looked with disfavor on the new industrialism. In Massachusetts women helped collect the thousands of signatures on petitions that poured in on the legislature asking for the ten-hour day. The drive failed, however, thanks largely to the work of William Schouler, by then the owner of the *Lowell Offering*. The Lowell Association joined his opposition at the next election and helped defeat him. In retaliation Schouler smeared Bagley for her association with a male labor leader of dubious moral reputation. Given the prudery of the time and place, the charges helped to blast the promising career of an able, young working-class woman.

Coincidentally, the labor-reform associations faded away, not because of Bagley's misfortunes, but because employers got rid of their independent Yankee workers. In the late 1840s hundreds of thousands of destitute Irish arrived in the United States, many in New England. Desperate, willing to work for any wages under any conditions, the Irish were ideal human grist for the mills. The Yankee women were weeded out, replaced by immigrants. The Irish had never been popular in America, and the old resentments were intensified when American workers lost their jobs to the newcomers. The feelings aroused help explain the virulence of the anti-Irish, anti-Catholic campaigns of the 1840s—campaigns in which native-born women took an active part.

Unions of any kind were few and weak in the pre-Civil War period, and confined to skilled workers. They did not welcome women members. Artisans tried to make their crafts male monopolies just as professional men did their professions. Women were feared because they worked for lower wages, and they were regarded as potential strikebreakers. They were also identified with the hated new technology, which undermined the traditional pay and status of craftsmen. As machines intruded more and more upon the artisan's domain, more and more women were employed to run them—and artisans blamed the women for their misfortune. And like middle-class men, many workingmen felt strongly that woman's place was in the home. Some labor leaders, such as Seth Luther in New England, pointed out that working men could never attain their ends without accepting women workers as partners in the struggle. Few men responded to such appeals.

SOUTHERN WOMEN

Little of the turbulence of the North was to be seen in the South. No school comparable to Mount Holyoke appeared. No counterpart of the Seneca Falls convention met to formulate the grievances of southern women. Among the women who toiled in the mills of Georgia and South Carolina there were no Sarah Bagleys. Such apologists for slavery as George Fitzhugh noted happily that in the South there was no women's rights movement, and "no trades unions, no strikes for higher wages." In the South, said he, "all is peace, quiet, plenty and contentment."

If southern women were less publicly rebellious than their northern sisters, the reason was largely that they were subject to a double conditioning. Like their northern sisters, they were taught to be ladies, to prepare for appropriate marriages with men of their own class. But southern women were also indoctrinated in the belief that they were the guardians of racial purity and thus the guarantors of Anglo-Saxon civilization. Far more than in the North, the woman of the South was transformed from a human being into a symbol—the symbol of pure white womanhood, to be revered, extolled, and protected. She was to be protected from predatory white males, of course. Even more, she must be protected from black men. And she must be shielded from her own emotional weakness, lest she surrender to importunate suitors, white or black.

The emotional repression of women was severe enough in the North. It was much more stringent in the South, where no upper-class young woman was allowed to be alone with a man. In 1809 the famous ornithologist Alexander Wilson complained of the "cold, melancholy reserve of the females of the best families." A generation later the British traveler James S. Buckingham reported that in relations between the sexes, "all is decorous, orderly, and irreproachable; but everything is also formal, indifferent and cold."

As if to document Buckingham's comment, Mary Boykin Chesnut, the high-spirited wife of former United States Senator James Chesnut, confided to her diary her response to her husband's query of whether he was not "an open, frank, confiding person." She noted, "Truth required me to say that I knew no more what he thought or felt . . . than I did twenty years ago. Sometimes I feel that we understand each other a little, but then up goes the iron wall once more."

Once married, the southern belle had to be at once submissive wife and active mistress of the household. The dependence of married women on their husbands proved galling to some women, such as Mary Chesnut. "Why should I feel like a beggar, utterly humiliated and degraded, when I am forced to say I need money?" she asked. "I cannot tell, but I do." Plantation wives performed vital economic functions. They generally supervised the cooking, the cleaning, and the labor of the household servants. It was their job to see that slave clothing was produced. It was also their job to provide nursing and medicine for ailing slaves. In short, how well a plantation functioned depended to a considerable extent on the management by its mistress.

Married women also found themselves subject to the double standard of sexual morality, the price women in both North and South paid for the homage rendered them as guardians of morality. Men expected their wives to be cold and unresponsive. Some husbands were content with the situation. Others sought sexual pleasures elsewhere. In the towns such men found cover in the vice districts, but no such cover was possible on plantations. There the consequences of illicit black-white unions were obvious: mulatto children.

While some white wives closed their eyes to what was going on, others did not. Since they could not avenge themselves on their husbands, they vented their anger on the black women, punishing them cruelly, as if the slave women were to blame for the men's behavior. Such an attitude was reflected in a book written by a southern white woman long after slavery was abolished. Myrta Lockett Avary concluded in 1906 that "the heaviest part of the white racial burden [in slavery] was the African woman, of strong sex instincts and devoid of a sexual conscience."

Some upper-class white women came to detest slavery, but others spoke out in its defense. Perhaps the most notable of them was Maria J. McIntosh of Georgia, who saw in black enslavement the work of God. Through it, He had transmuted, "with heavenly alchemy the loathsome selfishness and heartlessness of the slave trade into the partial civilization and Christianization of the race enslaved, and into the means of promoting the intellectual culture and social refinement of those who were forced into the position of their masters." In slavery, woman's role was crucial. She interposed "the shield of her charity between the weak and the strong."

Not all southern white women belonged to the aristocracy, of course. There were considerable numbers of small planters and of middle-class people who aspired to enter it, and thus trained their daughters in the ways of gentility. But there were even greater numbers of folk who eked out a living on small farms, perhaps with a slave or two. The women in such families enjoyed little southern male chivalry. They labored—cooking, baking, washing, sewing, spinning, weaving, mending, and occasionally even working in the fields. They married early and bore children in addition to all their other duties. Their opportunities of breaking out of the rut of rural poverty were few. Industrial development in the South lagged behind the North, but some white women did find employment in the cotton mills of South Carolina and Georgia.

WOMEN OF THE WEST

The white occupation of Indian lands entailed heavy burdens for white women. They reenacted the early colonial experience, doing heavy labor alongside the men in order to survive. Since men recognized how important the women were—and, thus, how valuable—western women enjoyed a rough and ready equality denied to their eastern and southern sisters. The women earned their status. When necessity demanded, girls and women worked in the fields, as did the young Anna Howard Shaw, later a leader in the crusade for woman suffrage, in the Michigan wilderness. In the words of a pioneer Iowa farm wife Maria Foster Brown, life was "hard, *hard,* HARD. The only thing that can make it endurable for a woman is love, and plenty of it."

Such a life took its toll. Frances Trollope, as well as other travelers, noted the aged looks of young mothers. It was not only the constant hard work that wore out women. They were also exhausted by poor nutrition, frequent childbearing, and disease. Many westerners settled in low-lying ground infested with malarial mosquitos and were plagued with what was called "the ague," a recurrent fever that left its victims weak and spiritless. Unsurprisingly, many western women died young.

The women who endured the 2,000-mile, five-month trek to the Far West along the Oregon Trail faced even harsher tests. Like the men, they made their way through prairies, forests, mountains, swamps, and rivers; existed on short rations; and defended themselves as best they could against Indian peoples trying to protect their homeland from white aggression. Many women died along the way, especially from cholera or complications of childbirth.

The girls and women who survived were much sought after, because they were vitally needed to work and because they meant wealth in the form of land. To stimulate settlement in the remote Oregon Territory, Congress passed the Donation Land Law in 1850, providing land grants to settlers. Each man, married or single, received half a square mile. Single women received none, but married women received grants equal to those of their husbands. Although allotments were reduced for arrivals after 1851, wives continued to receive land grants equal to those of their husbands. Wives held their grants in their own names, a significant recognition of the property rights of

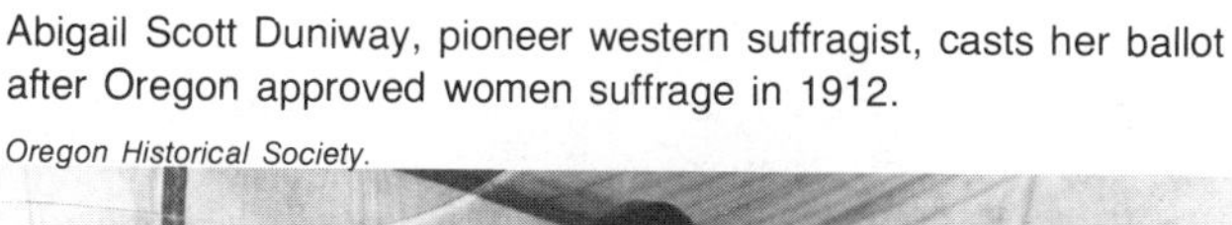
Abigail Scott Duniway, pioneer western suffragist, casts her ballot after Oregon approved women suffrage in 1912.

Oregon Historical Society.

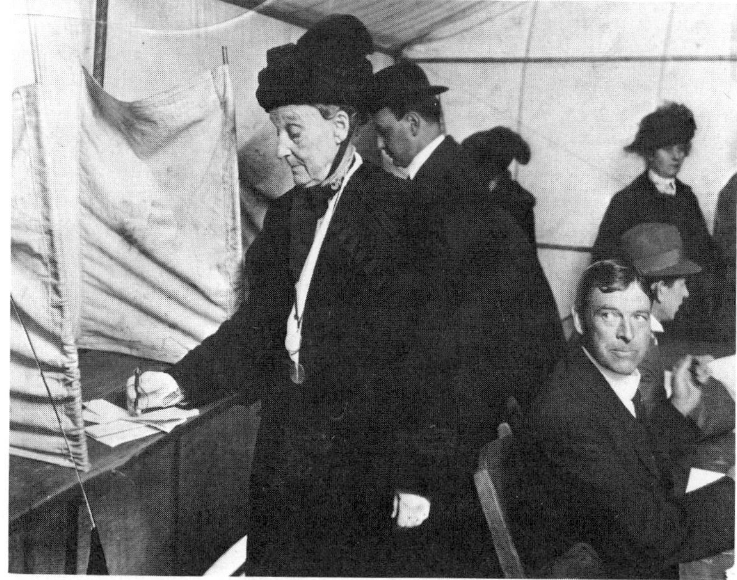

married women. In practice, however, husbands tended to control their wives' property. It is not surprising that single men and widowers sought wives speedily.

However much women might be valued, however much they might enjoy some measure of equality, they were still women. In the Far West as elsewhere, male supremacy prevailed. It was as unacceptable to many of the women who survived the rigors of the trail as it was to their educated sisters back East. Eventually they found an advocate in Abigail Scott Duniway, who made the journey from Illinois to Oregon in 1852 when she was sixteen years old. On the trip her mother and a brother died. Married three years later she became the family breadwinner when her husband was incapacitated in an accident. In a reversal of sex roles that must have dismayed conventional folk, she set up in business while he ran the household. Outraged by examples of male tyranny that she witnessed in the course of her work, she became a leader of the struggle for women's rights in the Far West—a career in which she had the full support of her husband.

It would be a mistake to assume that white women in the decades before the Civil War were swept up in a crusade to end injustice based on sex. Most of them, long accustomed to male supremacy, lived their lives without questioning it. Indeed, for large numbers of women, male supremacy was both acceptable and congenial. But for a growing minority it was not acceptable. A spirit of rebellion was in the air.

FOR FURTHER READING

There is a wide variety of biographies in Edward T. James and others, eds., *Notable American Women,* Vols. 1–3, (1971). Gerda Lerner, ed., *The Female Experience* (1976), is a comprehensive documentary collection. More selective is Wendy Martin, ed., *The American Sisterhood* (1972).

The problems of working-class women are dealt with in John R. Commons and others, *History of Labor in the United States,* Vol. 1 (1918); Philip S. Foner, *History of the Labor Movement in the United States,* Vol. 1 (1947); Caroline Ware, *Early New England Cotton Manufacturing* (1931); and Hannah Josephson, *The Golden Threads* (1949).

On sex and family there is valuable material in Arthur W. Calhoun, *Social History of the American Family,* Vol. 2 (1918). An excellent analysis of sexual stereotypes is G. J. Barker-Benfield, *Horrors of the Half-Known Life* (1976). See also Michael Gordon, ed., *The American Family in Social-Historical Perspective* (1973).

Some other aspects of women's history are discussed in Anne F. Scott, *The Southern Lady* (1970); Eleanor W. Thompson, *Education for Ladies* (1947); Mabel Newcomer, *A Century of Higher Education for American Women* (1959); and Eleanor Flexner, *A Century of Struggle* (1959).

Valuable for its insights into the lives of upper-class Southern women is Mary B. Chesnut, *A Diary from Dixie,* edited by Ben A. Williams (1949). Biographies include Gerda Lerner, *The Grimké Sisters of South Carolina* (1967); Otelia Cromwell, *Lucretia Mott* (1958); Ruth E. Finley, *The Lady of Godey's* (1931), which deals with Sarah J. Hale, the editor of an influential women's magazine; and Alma Lutz, *Susan B. Anthony* (1959) and *Created Equal* (1940), the story of Elizabeth Cady Stanton.

11 the era of the millionaire

The trend toward social stratification that began in colonial times continued in the nineteenth century. The remarkable geographic and economic expansion of the time, however, opened up opportunities for countless Americans, although it also accentuated the concentration of wealth in the hands of a few. The upward mobility of so many Americans, together with extension of the suffrage to most adult white males, persuaded foreign observers like de Tocqueville that for whites America was indeed a land of equality.

THE RICH AND SUPERRICH

Many Americans also believed that their country was a land of opportunity as well as equality. They hailed the emergence of the "self-made man" as an expression of "equality of opportunity." Later, historians came to describe the second quarter of the nineteenth century as the "era of the common man."

Recent research compels us to revise that picture. Evidence from assessment rolls, tax lists, and other sources indicates that between 1825 and 1850 wealth increasingly concentrated in the hands of urban elites, the gap between rich and poor widened, and public life remained dominated by those at the apex of the social pyramid. According to Edward Pessen, by 1850 the top 1 percent of Americans owned about 50 percent of the wealth—double the share held in 1825. Symbolic of the trend was the emergence of a new class of superrich: the millionaires. In New York City alone the millionaires numbered more than one hundred. The most famous was John Jacob Astor, who made his fortune in the fur trade and added to it by speculation in New York real estate. On his death his wealth was reckoned at $20 million.

Astor was exceptional, not only in the extent of his wealth but also in that he was a "self-made man." The overwhelming mass of the rich came, not from poverty, but from already established elites and from those close to the elites in social status. This is not difficult to understand, for they were the people best able to take advantage of the opportunities offered by expansion. The position of the elites was further enhanced by the passing-on of accumulated wealth within families from one generation to the next. Thus, a permanent class of the rich and superrich developed, linked by marriage and united by considerations of class interest.

A major source of strength of this class was its flexibility. Although some "old money" families disdained those with "new money," elites as a whole welcomed newcomers who had the necessary credentials: wealth, prestige, and willingness to abide by the conventions of elite society. Religion was no bar. Among elite members were Protestants, Catholics, and Jews. One of the most prominent members of New York society was August Belmont, a Jewish banker who served as American agent for the powerful Rothschild banking house. He further enhanced his status by marrying a woman of the elite, Caroline Perry, daughter of the famous Commodore Matthew Perry.

Although never more than a small proportion of the population—perhaps about 4 percent— the elites grew in absolute number as the economy developed. Nor were they confined to the East. As white communities developed in the West, so did social stratification. Elites dominated the societies of Cincinnati, St. Louis, Chicago, and Natchez as they did the societies of Boston, New York, and Philadelphia.

Such domination was enhanced by the geographical mobility of so many poorer Americans. Movement from place to place was a marked feature of preindustrial society, involving both the unsuccessful and those who were making their way upward. Elites, enjoying wealth and power, were under no compulsion to move. While the masses came and went, the elites remained. Thus, they were able to exercise control not only from their wealth but also from their continuity.

Initially, trade had been the major source of elite wealth, and indeed, with the expansion of internal and international trade it continued to be a significant source. But that very expansion opened up new ways to make money: transportation, manufacturing, mining, banking, insurance, urban real estate, and western land speculation.

If it ever occurred to pre-Civil War elites that they were living in the "age of the common man," they gave no sign of it. Like all elites, they kept to themselves. As Nicholas Biddle, the wealthy banker of Philadelphia noted, "The most decisive characteristic of American society is its aristocracy; its downright exclusiveness." Social life reflected that exclusiveness. The men dined and dranks at clubs, which charged such high fees that only the wealthy could afford them. They and their families moved in restricted social circles, meeting their peers at lavish dinner parties, balls, soirees, the theater, and the opera. Exclusiveness was in part a way of making sure that children met the "right" kind of people and contracted the "right" kind of marriages.

This was not an aristocracy of the idle rich. On the contrary, the men of great wealth were as diligent in their labors as those who aspired to their rank. They

Asher and Adams' New Columbian Railroad Atlas and Pictorial Album of American Industry, 1876

With industrialism came air pollution, as this print of an iron works in south Boston attests. Note foundry at right built in 1862 to produce cannons for the Union forces during the Civil War.

managed their own businesses and were directors in other enterprises too. Their incessant, utter devotion to work—and their consequent accumulation of wealth—astounded Europeans accustomed to think of wealth as a synonym for leisure. Even the few men whose fortunes were so carefully managed by others that they need not concern themselves personally with business were not likely to live as gentlemen of leisure. For example, Roberts Vaux of Philadelphia, a wealthy Quaker, devoted his life to numerous "good works," ranging from the rehabilitation of prostitutes to the spread of scientific knowledge.

But the men who managed their own business affairs also participated in a wide range of civic and philanthropic activities. They gave money and leadership to societies providing for hospitals, orphanages, and refuges for "fallen women." They were active in such causes as temperance, suppression of vice and crime, prison reform, and relief of poverty. Some went beyond these generally approved causes and supported such controversial movements as abolition. For example, Arthur and Lewis Tappan, great merchants of New York City, gave generously of their time and money to promote emancipation. Further, to an extent that has been largely unappreciated, wealthy folk in Massachusetts, New York, and Pennsylvania used their funds and influence to help bring about free public-school systems in those states.

Nor did the wealthy neglect cultural affairs. They encouraged scientific research and the dissemination of scientific knowledge through natural history societies and such bodies as the Linnaean Society of Philadelphia. While men played a less active role than women in cultivating the fine arts, it was elite patronage that made it possible for American audiences to hear the music of Beethoven and Mozart, to witness the theatrical performances of Edwin Forrest and Fanny Kemble, and to see at first hand the paintings of leading American and European artists in the public arts galleries built in many American cities.

Some causes were promoted on grounds of self-interest. Some wealthy folk argued that free public schools, for example, would stabilize society by providing "equality of opportunity." Another elite argument was that the schools would train children in habits of work, obedience, thrift, and individual responsiblity. Children so trained would make good employees later on. In consequence, fewer adults would become "burdens on society" and thus taxes could be kept low. Still another viewpoint saw in the schools a means of social control. Many wealthy people feared extension of the suffrage as a potential danger to property interests—a fear they thought realized when some Jacksonian politicians appealed to the new voters with radical rhetoric. The schools, such people thought, could be used to condition youngsters against the "excesses" of democracy.

Americans generally attributed elite participation in "good works" to disinterested benevolence. At a time when government recognized few social responsibilities the elites were seen as contributing services that society needed but could not do for itself. Intellectuals, artists, and musicians especially appreciated elite patronage of cultural interests. Whatever the personal motives of elites may have been, their image of benevolence served their class interest. The image enhanced their prestige. It made acceptable elite domination of a myriad voluntary associations devoted to social and cultural advancement. Such domination was accepted because elites furnished time, money, and leadership. Further, elites were viewed not only as strong and wealthy but also as "good." In short, benevolence helped elites to maintain social control.

Such control supplemented the wealthy's domination of political life. At the turn of the century, elite members had participated directly in politics at all levels. They were judges, mayors, governors, legislators, and presidents. From 1789, when George Washington was inaugurated, to 1829, when Andrew Jackson occupied the White House, the presidency was held by patricians, southern and Yankee. But with economic expansion and the increasing complexity of business, men of wealth found it difficult to combine business, philanthropic, and political pursuits. At the same time, the coming of white manhood suffrage in the 1820s seemed to threaten property interests. Thus, while the demands of business required the wealthy to withdraw from direct political participation, the interests of property demanded that they maintain political control.

The solution to the dilemma was found in the professional politician, who now emerged as a distinct social type. Usually lawyers, professional politicians were expert in the ways of government, just as factory managers and accountants were expert in the ways of business—and their services were just as essential. Business leaders not only sought to shape governmental policy to serve their interests; they also wanted such favors from government as financial aid and corporation charters. For all such ends they needed the expertise of politicians. Politicians' services became even more necessary with extension of the suffrage. They knew how to voice the grievances of the masses. Equally important, they knew how to appease them without injuring the interests of property. Jacksonian Democrats showed the way, picturing themselves as the party of the common man, denouncing the "rich and powerful," diverting attention from the fact that party policy was shaped by slaveholders, bankers, speculators, and such elites as Martin Van Buren, a scion of the old New York aristocracy.

Whig politicians were quick to learn. Jacksonian success prompted them to jettison their cherished principle that government, in the words of Alexander Hamilton, belonged to "the rich, the well-born, and the educated." Whigs, too, made their pitch to the common man. The new tactic paid off. In 1840, in the midst of deep economic depression, they won the presidency by portraying President Van Buren, the Democratic candidate, as an aristocrat who was an enemy of the masses. In contrast, their own candidate, William Henry Harrison, was said to have been born in a log cabin, a humble abode symbolic of frontier and poverty. In fact, Harrison had been born to plenty as a member of the Virginia aristocracy.

Many old-line Whigs were outraged at abandoning principle and resorting to demagogy. But more practical elites were favorably impressed. They saw that politicians could contain the feared "excesses of democracy." And they saw that politicians as a group could be counted on to promote the interests of their monied backers on such issues as tariffs, public lands, banking policy, and internal improvements.

The politicians were well rewarded for their services. Their backers saw to it that they had adequate campaign funds—all the more necessary now that larger bodies of voters had to be reached. Businessmen provided inside information that enabled politicians to make handsome returns in stock and commodity speculations. Politicians were cut in on promising business ventures, often at little cost to themselves. Lawyer politicians benefited from the legal business thrown their way by their supporters. Politics was more than a way to wealth; it was also a road to social prestige. The most successful politicians, if they were not already members of the elite, were accepted into exclusive society. If they were single, they might marry daughters of the mighty. Thus, Stephen A. Douglas, the master Democratic politician of Illinois, rose from comparative poverty to wealth. At the age of thirty-four he married a young woman of the southern aristocracy, heiress to plantations in North Carolina and Mississippi. Similar transitions from obscurity to fame and fortune through politics marked the career of Henry Clay of Kentucky and Daniel Webster of Massachusetts, both outstanding Whig politicians.

No conflict of interest was seen in these arrangements. Politicians shared the view of their backers that furthering their private interests was in the public good. Indeed, the prevailing opinion was that what was good for business was good for America. Some, indeed, looked upon political parties as another form of business. William H. Seward, the Whig governor of New York, later Republican secretary of state in the Lincoln administration, said that parties were like business enterprises. The way Seward saw it, those who put the most into the party should get the most out.

The "democratic revolution" did not transform American society. The elites had a more difficult time ruling, but professional politicians took care of the problems. The problems, in fact, were not so great as some politicians made them out to be, for elite fears that white manhood suffrage threatened property were much exaggerated. The new voters were as protective of property rights as were the elites. All they asked for were conditions that would help them acquire property. They were imbued with the same spirit of business as their wealthier compatriots. Since they wanted to move up, and thought they could, they had no basic quarrel with the social system. They might listen to radicals like Frances Wright and Seth Luther, the New England labor spokesman, who talked of class war, but they cast their votes for men who could do something for them. Such attitudes presented little danger to rule of the elites.

THE CULT OF BUSINESS

There was little popular hostility to the acquisition of wealth. As Sigmund Diamond has pointed out, criticism was apt to be directed at the distribution of wealth after death rather than at its accumulation. For most Americans, the pursuit of wealth was laudable. They believed that in America, with its lack of a rigid class system, any white man with the necessary good character, judgment, and habits of work and frugality could "better himself." Even men who failed on occasion could hope to rise again under different circumstances. Since the way to wealth was largely through business, the businessman emerged as a new folk hero, to be venerated and emulated. The cult of business was coming to dominate American life.

For most Americans of the time, as for President Calvin Coolidge a century later, the business of America was business. The idea was not entirely new. As early as 1695, Cotton Mather, the most eminent Puritan divine of his day, said the Bible showed that a man must be "diligent in his business." What was new in the nineteenth century was the widespread obsession for "getting ahead," a prospect made possible by the rich resources of the nation and the relatively fluid nature of society. Since the businessman showed the way to "get ahead," he became almost deified. Orestes A. Brownson, a New England clergyman who was a forerunner of the later Social Gospel, disgustedly wrote in 1840, "The businessman has become the peer of my Lord." Ralph Waldo Emerson, at once an admirer of business leaders and a critic of materialism, noted that those who challenged the "tyranny" of business values were thought of by the public as "mad or morbid, and are treated as such."

THE BUSINESS REVOLUTION

Rapid economic development made older methods of doing business obsolete, leading to what Thomas C. Cochran calls "the Business Revolution." The structure of colonial business, based on family connections and partnerships, could not deal with either the problems or opportunities of a new economic era. Increasingly, great merchants had to depend on "outsiders" as agents, lower-level managers, and accountants. Indeed, the very emergence of accounting as an important aspect of business in the nineteenth century indicated the growing complexity of operations. Thus, the white-collar class, which had appeared in small numbers before the Revolution, expanded.

The magnitude and complexity of operations forced the great merchants to specialize. More and more, they restricted their lines to specific fields: tea and coffee, wines, textiles, hardware. Since the great merchants also served for a time as the prime moneylenders, some became private bankers. Lesser merchants undertook the task of warehousing varieties of goods to serve the domestic market. Within each great mercantile house managerial functions specialized pragmatically: finance, supply, and sales. When industrialism developed after the War of 1812, a management structure already existed that could adapt to the factory system simply by adding a fourth manager in charge of production.

If American business pioneered in the development of managerial functions, it likewise broke ground in the organization of industry. In England, the home of the Industrial Revolution, factories were organized by function. That is, such functions as spinning yarn and weaving cloth were carried out in separate factories, a practice generally followed in the United States. In 1814, however, Francis Cabot Lowell, a wealthy merchant who became interested in manufacturing, wrought a drastic change. At Waltham, Massachusetts, he integrated in one factory all cotton textile operations, from spinning yarn to producing finished cloth. The improved efficiency and profitability of such a system pointed the way for future industrial operations.

Waltham also exemplified another factor in American industrial progress. Paul Moody, who designed the plant's new machinery, typified a generation of inventive mechanics who contributed to major technological advances. Among them were Charles Goodyear, whose vulcanization of rubber made possible the modern rubber industry; Cyrus McCormick and Obed Hussey, whose mechanical reapers revolutionized farming; and Elias Howe, whose sewing machine made cheap clothing possible.

Also significant for the future of American business was the emergence of the

Elias Howe and his first sewing machine, 1845. The invention made possible both cheap clothing and sweatshop conditions in the garment industry.

corporation. States competing with each other for economic advantage became permissive in issuing corporate charters. The old requirement that each charter receive legislative assent gave way to general incorporation laws that made issuance of charters almost routine. Also, the growth of corporations was accelerated by the spread of the legal doctrine of limited liability. Previously, any participant in a business venture was responsible for all its debts if it failed, a responsibility that inhibited investment and so was clearly unsuited to the needs of an expanding economy. The new doctrine limited the liability of investors in proportion to their holdings in the corporation. Such a limitation of risk encouraged investment and contributed substantially to the popularity of the corporate form of business.

From the viewpoint of business the corporation had many advantages. It lived a legal life of its own. Directors and stockholders came and went, but the institution went on forever—or at least as long as it was solvent. Further, the corporation enabled promoters to use other people's money to finance their enterprises through the sale of stock. Since most stockholders rarely attended corporation meetings and in any case were usually ignorant of business details, control rested in a small board of directors. These directors usually owned relatively small blocks of stock, but their holdings were enough to allow them to dominate corporate meetings and to carry out the policies they wanted.

Such control proved attractive to members of the elite. They could diversify their investments in such varied fields as manufacturing, banking, shipping, insurance, and transportation, and thus minimize the risks of fluctuations in any one enterprise. With such investments went more control, for wealthy investors often served as directors of several companies at a time, enhancing their wealth and adding to their economic and political authority.

The corporate form was also useful in masking shady practices. The division between ownership and management made it possible for insiders to line their pockets at the expense of both the stockholders and the public. Directors of canal and railroad companies placed contracts for construction—at highly inflated prices—with companies in which they had an interest. Promoters obtained bank charters, induced businessmen to subscribe more capital, and lured the savings of depositors. When the time was ripe, they decamped with all the assets they could lay their hands on. Insiders manipulated the stocks of companies they dominated, selling when prices were high and buying when prices were low.

Such developments, together with distrust of the new form of business by those accustomed to the old, prompted some hostility to granting corporation charters indiscriminately. But the corporation was too badly needed by the American economy to be shackled, and the spirit of Jacksonian democracy opposed such shackling. In their war against monopolies, Jacksonians espoused the cause of general incorporation. All groups of businessmen were to be treated equally, and private enterprise was to be freed from political interference, which legislative approval for each corporate charter amounted to. Thus, Jacksonians spread over the corporations the mantle of an American ideal: equality of opportunity.

Needless to say, corporations would not have spread had not the investing public found them attractive. Risks were minimized, and the prospects golden. If occasionally evil men swindled investors, that was a risk worth the cost. Indeed, some avaricious investors looked upon crooked promoters, such as Daniel Drew, with favor. They joined in his ventures, figuring that while he was making money for himself, he was also making money for them!

The corporation, together with the factory system, played a major role in the depersonalization of American business. The older system, in which merchants knew their customers and their employees, in which master artisans worked in the same shop with journeymen and apprentices, gave way to the new order in which the cash nexus was dominant. Ownership increasingly was divorced from management. Indeed, few stockholders knew anything about their managers. And, it must be said, few investors cared much so long as stock prices held up and dividends were paid regularly.

For their part, managers knew that their tenure depended on maximizing profit. Such consideration set the context in which they treated labor and consumers. The corporation developed relatively slowly in manufacturing, but as it did, working people found themselves laboring for a faceless aggregate. At some remote and rarefied level decisions were made that set the fate of thousands, but workers could never hope to penetrate to that level except, perhaps, when they went on strike. In any case, they knew that in good times they were hired at the lowest possible wage and in bad times they were summarily laid off, to fend for themselves as best they could. Spokesmen for slavery claimed that their institution at least had a place for humane feelings, sentiments unknown in the northern factories.

This was not how the business managers saw it, of course. Most of them were quite inarticulate about the larger significances of their calling, if indeed they gave much thought to such ideas. But there were some who did. One of the most significant was Edward Atkinson, treasurer of several textile companies and, after the Civil War, head of a major insurance company. In the free market, Atkinson believed, lay the possibility of ending involuntary poverty and war. Through the free play of market forces, labor would become increasingly efficient and living standards would be raised. To accomplish this, all labor must be free; thus, he opposed slavery. On an international scale the operations of free trade would eventually bring peoples together by providing for ever-better living conditions. The improvement would eliminate the need for war. Business, then, had a moral dimension in promoting freedom, eliminating poverty, and abolishing war. The inequities that naturally arose from the functioning of the self-regulating mechanism of the marketplace were a small price to pay for attaining such objectives. It should be added, however, that Atkinson was an unusual businessman. For example, he declined to patent a highly efficient cooking oven he invented, so that all people could benefit from it.

BUSINESS IN THE COUNTRYSIDE

We tend to think of white western settlement as occupation of free land by subsistence farmers. In fact, the land was not free and speculators got there before the farmers. By 1800 millions of acres of land from Georgia to Lake Erie were in the hands of land companies, acquired from federal and state governments for little or nothing with the judicious application of pressure and bribery. Speculators benefited again in 1820 when the federal government ended credit sales of public lands. Thereafter settlers were required to pay in cash a minimum of $1.25 an acre and purchase at least eighty acres. Such terms put the land beyond the reach of many farmers, especially on the frequent occasions when cash was hard to come by. Speculators, however, could well afford to meet the terms and hold the land for higher prices as the West filled up. Business managers also profited from the lavish land grants later given to promoters of canals and railroads by both state and federal governments. Thus, from the beginning, western settlement was dominated by business considerations.

Many settlers, however, ignored both federal law and the titles of land companies. They "squatted" on land that was not legally theirs, making a living until the law caught up with them. Those on private lands either were evicted or made deals with the owners. Those on public lands turned up en masse at the auctions of the lands they occupied. Armed to the teeth and bellicose, they put a damper on rival bidding and usually acquired their holdings at the minimum price. Indeed, a kind of peaceful coexistence emerged between squatters and speculators. The speculators refrained from trying to get squatter land and squatters did not bother the speculators.

Under pressure from western interests, Congress in 1830 passed the first preemption act, permitting those who had cultivated public lands to buy 160 acres at a minimum price. The principle of preemption later became a permanent feature of public-land policy. Still, despite this squatter victory, most migrants to the West acquired their land through speculators, who had taken up the best lands and were in position to afford credit and other benefits to their customers.

Farmers, then, had to think like business managers. They had to plan payment of their debts, make best use of labor and equipment, and hope for a profit. These factors became more important as the West matured from subsistence to market farming, a development spurred when the domestic market was suddenly supplemented by the expansion of the international market, symbolized by repeal of the British Corn Laws in 1846, which threw open the great British market to American wheat farmers. The bonanza opened by such a prospect stimulated farmers even more into business attitudes. To meet the demand, they invested heavily in new plows, mechanical reapers, and other equipment and expanded their holdings. To finance such operations, they borrowed. Much more than formerly, solvency depended upon careful planning and management. Those who failed became farm laborers or tenants, drifted to the towns becoming increasingly characteristic of western growth, or migrated farther west, hoping to do better in new surroundings.

But the farmer was a business manager at a deeper level than such considerations demanded. The mystical attachment to the soil characteristic of European peasant societies had no place in the American farmer's makeup, except in such Old World pockets as those of the Amish in Pennsylvania. Rather, the American farmer looked upon land as wealth, to be exploited to the best advantage as quickly as possible and then sold at a profit. Given such a short-term outlook, it made sense to "mine" the land, extracting from it every possible yield with no thought of replenishing the soil. As newcomers pressed in and land values went up, "old" settlers sold out profitably and moved farther west to repeat the process. Their replacements often held the same view. In short, the farmer tended to be a speculator, too.

The country town played a significant role in making rural America a stronghold of business values. The farmer depended on its artisans, merchants, lawyers, doctors, and bankers and so was meshed in the web of the town's business. The relationship was often marked by suspicion and strife. Farmers felt they were mulcted by high prices, high interest rates, and high professional fees. Townspeople tended to look down on small farmers and believed they were performing essential services for which they had a right to a high return. The farther west one traveled, the more the towns were dominated by young men on the make. Such towns offered ambitious folk an easier way upward than was available in the older towns back east. Townspeople were true believers in the gospel of success, and their influence spread far beyond the town limits.

THE SELF-MADE MAN

Belief in the gospel of success was not confined to country towns. The gospel was, in fact, a kind of civic religion, uniting its devotees in a bond transcending traditional religious divisions. The revelation of the new religion was the "self-made man." Henry Clay, the famous Whig politician from Kentucky, coined the phrase in 1832 in praising factory owners he knew. Even before then, however, the popular mind was enshrining the self-made man in the American pantheon.

The self-made man was the embodiment of material success, making his way from poverty to riches through sheer force of character. The abundance of resources and the expansion of the country had little to do with his success. It was individual character that counted. Even Emerson, who on occasion was a sharp critic of business, joined in the litany: "There are geniuses in trade as well as in war, or the state, or letters; and the reason why this or that man is fortunate is not to be told. It lies in the man; that is all anybody can tell you about it."

As we have seen, few men actually made it from poverty to wealth, but the myth of the self-made man, like all myths, had some basis in reality. Expansion, both economic and geographic, made it possible for many Americans of the "middling sort"—those with marketable skills or some little capital—to profit from the opportunities and move a little upward. Their success was perhaps more impressive to the mass of people than the success of the rare few who made it to the top. Nevertheless, the fabled stories of those who did make it to the top provided a mythology that shaped the way in which Americans looked at themselves and their society.

Andrew Jackson provided a prime example. On Jackson's death in 1845 a eulogist hailed the former president as "the architect of his own fortunes." According to the speaker, Jackson was born of "poor but respectable parents, [and] he became great by no other means than the energy of his own character." Another admirer of Jackson emphasized another element of the myth: namely, that it could happen "only in America." Jackson's life, said the writer, showed that "in this land of equal rights, the humblest youth, with honesty, talents, and perseverance to recommend him, enjoys the same opportunities with the high-born and wealthy."

Together with such luminaries as Jackson, wealthy businessmen were held up as examples to be imitated. *McGuffey's Readers,* the staple of common school education in the 1850s, hammered home to children the lessons that if they were honest, industrious, energetic, frugal, and of strong character, they too could attain the White House or the mansion of a millionaire.

Such teachings rested on a will to believe. Americans wanted desperately to believe that, apart from slavery, theirs was a land of equality. They largely ignored the facts that contradicted their belief. Thus, of the millionaires, only a few such as John Jacob Astor, seem to have been born poor. Andrew Jackson was not quite the penniless orphan his admirers portrayed. His family were substantial landowners, and he was related to one of the wealthiest and most influential men in Tennessee backwoods society, James Crawford.

Americans also ignored the fact that self-made men had emerged elsewhere. In an England still abominated by Americans as "class ridden," the Industrial Revolution had fostered the rise of such men as George Stephenson, Sir Richard Arkwright, Robert Owen, and Robert Peel, grandfather of the famous nineteenth century Tory prime minister Sir Robert Peel. They, too, had risen from obscurity to fame and riches. In France, also, the self-made man appeared, as the novels of Balzac attest.

The pervasiveness of the myth in America had significant consequences. Since individual character was the key to success, and since opportunities were supposedly boundless, it followed that failures had no one to blame but themselves. This in turn led to a harsh, unsympathetic, and moralistic attitude toward the poor, expressed both in private charity and public policy.

Another consequence was popularization of the notion that America was basically a classless society. The growing gap between rich and poor was seen, not in terms of class advantages and privilege, but in terms of individual character. In a society where opportunity was open to all, the rich were rich because they deserved to be. In the process of enriching themselves they contributed to the well-being of society. Society rewarded them accordingly. As one writer put it in 1836, "To the rich of this world are granted privileges which the poor cannot enjoy."

Still another consequence of the self-made man myth was the inhibition of mass movements of social protest, such as socialism. From infancy onward, Americans were taught by preachers, politicians, pundits, and pedagogues that success was within their reach if they would only try. Failure implied some personal flaw. The poor, lacking an alternative social view, internalized these teachings. They developed feelings of inferiority, of guilt, even of self-hatred.

The psychology of success appeared in England and Europe, too, but it was modified by two influences. Socialists made converts with their teaching that poverty was the result of a capitalistic social order, not the consequence of individual weakness. Churches, in contrast, taught that God ordained social classes; both privilege and poverty were part of a divine order. In either case, poor people were absolved of personal responsibility for their condition. Not so in America.

Finally, the cult of business and the myth of the self-made man helped obscure the contributions to national well-being made by black and white working people. To be sure, on appropriate occasions ritualistic homage was paid to labor, but increasingly it was ritual devoid of meaning. The real reverence of aspiring Americans was reserved for successful men.

FOR FURTHER READING

A basic work is Edward Pessen, *Riches, Class and Power Before the Civil War* (1973). Sigmund Diamond, *The Reputation of the American Businessman* (1955), has valuable information on how the media of the day viewed the business elites. Stephan Thernstrom, *Poverty and Progress* (1964), discusses social mobility.

The gospel of success is considered in John G. Cawalti, *Apostles of the Self-Made Man* (1965), and Irvin G. Wyllie, *The Self-Made Man in America* (1966).

Thomas C. Cochran, *Business in American Life* (1972), traces developments in business structure. A somewhat different emphasis is found in Thomas C. Cochran and William Miller, *The Age of Enterprise* (1961). See also William Miller, ed., *Men in Business* (1962).

Contrasting views on the relationship of business to Jacksonian democracy are in Arthur M. Schlesinger, Jr., *The Age of Jackson* (1946), and Bray Hammond, *Banks and Politics in America from the Revolution to the Civil War* (1957).

12 utopias and rebellions

Preindustrial America was becoming the country of the successful. But where there are winners, there must also be losers. The losers were, said the *American Quarterly Review* in 1832, people of "sensual excess, want of intelligence, and moral debasement." In fact, the losers included all kinds of people: the thrifty and the wasteful, the religious and the irreligious, the ascetic and the sensual, the wise and the foolish. They came from a wide range of occupations: merchants, professional people, master craftsmen, journeymen artisans, factory workers, small farmers, day laborers in the cities and on the farms. Most of them were the working poor. But a considerable number were folk who were slipping down the social scale, a drop marked by loss of economic independence, decline in social status, and lowered income.

THE ECONOMICS OF LOSING

The losers were the products of an increasingly complex economy that was also highly competitive and unstable. Between 1800 and 1860 there were seven depressions. The most devastating, that of 1837, lasted for six years. At such times, thousands of business proprietors went bankrupt. The savings of the thrifty were wiped out when banks failed. Masses of workers, skilled and unskilled, were forced out of work and reduced to destitution. Small farmers lost their lands.

Apart from depression, other forces produced losers of personal economic independence. Small independent merchants became increasingly dependent on the great merchants who furnished their supplies. Merchant capitalists invaded the domain of the master artisan. They supplied the necessary raw materials, the credit to work them up, and the market for the finished product, thus undermining the master artisan's independence. It was further undermined when improvements in transportation merged local markets into regional markets. Merchant capitalists then played off artisans in one town against those of another, forcing down prices and in effect transforming independent producers into dependent labor contractors.

The masters tried to save themselves by reducing labor costs. The major victims were the journeymen, the highly skilled craftsmen who hoped one day to become masters and open their own shop. Their day was over. Masters broke down work into phases that could be handled by runaway apprentices—of whom there were plenty—and even by unskilled laborers. Journeymen lost their jobs. The consequent surplus of journeymen enabled masters to reduce wages.

Skilled workers were menaced by yet another development. Independent artisans such as shoemakers who worked out of their own homes were induced to bolster their incomes by involving their families in their work. Merchant capitalists supplied the materials, provided patterns so simple that children could perform some of the tasks, and assured a market for the product. Once locked into the system, the artisans found themselves helpless against reduction in the prices paid them. In some places, like Lynn, Massachusetts, merchant capitalists refused to pay the artisans in cash. Instead, they were paid with "store orders," vouchers that enabled them to purchase goods at stores favored by the merchant capitalist. The prices at such stores were so high that the workers lost one-third of their purchasing power. It is significant that when Lynn shoemakers revolted in 1844, they compared themselves to "slaves in the strictest sense of the word."

Even more important in the displacement of skilled workers were the technological innovations that marked the Industrial Revolution. Machinery made possible increased specialization of labor, rendering many crafts obsolete. To be sure, the new technology produced new classes of skilled workers, such as machinists, toolmakers, and engineers, but that was little comfort to men and women who saw their independence vanishing as factory workers produced goods at prices no artisan could hope to meet.

The power loom put the hand weaver out of business. The sewing machine, invented in 1846, opened the way for a ready-made clothing industry and in the process made custom tailors and dressmakers obsolete. Adapting the sewing machine principle to shoemaking spelled the ultimate end of the cordwainer, the man who could make a boot by himself.

For artisans the factory system had profound psychological consequences. The earlier handicraft system involved close personal relationships, for masters, journeymen, and apprentices worked together in small shops. The atmosphere tended to be relaxed and informal. When work was slack in the shop, the artisans worked the plots of land they owned or went hunting and fishing to supplement their food supply. In short, the artisans were independent.

But the independence began to fade when the merchant capitalist became dominant in the early years of the nineteenth century. It ended with the advent of the factory system after the War of 1812. No master or journeymen—nor even any group of them—could muster the capital necessary to provide plant, machinery, and materials. The artisan had been supplanted by the factory and its workers. Instead of the independent easy-going life style of an earlier day, artisans now faced the prospect of factory life, with its low wages, harsh discipline, and long hours. Factory work also meant complete dependence on the employer, for the long hours left neither time nor energy to farm or to fish. Confronted with an entirely alien way of life, artisans were frightened, angry, and perplexed.

Artisans in the factory system enjoyed none of the independence of earlier skilled workers. Those who built and maintained machines were wage workers, just as much as the men and women who tended the machines. They were better paid than the machine tenders, but they were equally dependent on their employers. They might hope to better themselves through their higher wages and perhaps promotion. They could hope to acquire a small home and plot of land. But never in their wildest dreams could they believe they would own factories themselves.

There was also an entire new class growing out of the factory system in America: the industrial proletariat. These were men, women, and children who depended entirely on their earnings as workers for survival. In 1800 the working class was still miniscule, although the beginnings of a permanent proletariat had emerged in the late colonial period. By 1860 there were more than 1.3 million workers in manufacturing establishments alone. Several hundred thousand more were employed in mining, transportation, and lumbering. These were the majority of the "working poor," folk who made do with what they had so that they rarely became public charges.

There were many working poor in the countryside, too. These were the families who eked out bare livings on sandy, stony, or worn-out land that no one else wanted. When it became impossible to make a living, they moved on to other, equally unpromising land. Socially speaking, they were going nowhere—and they knew it. They found what solace they could in the revivalistic religious sects that flourished among them.

But many farmers with good lands also found themselves in danger of becoming "losers." The change from subsistence to market farming, together with mechanization, meant that independent farmers had to go deeply in debt both to survive and to take advantage of opportunities. A bad harvest or slump in the market might mean foreclosure, while depression spelled disaster. All too often, sober and industrious farmers, lacking the necessary capital or credit to carry them through crises, slipped downward into the ranks of tenants and laborers.

ESCAPE THROUGH RELIGION

Religion in preindustrial America reflected the strains of the society. Resentment of elite rule by many of the poor found religious expression in revolt against the power structures of such establishment churches as the Presbyterian, Methodist, and Baptist. The revolts were aimed not at getting control of existing denominations but at setting up independent churches under direct control by the body of believers. The men who led such movements combined Biblical fundamentalism with vigorous assertion of the worth of the individual, however poor in worldly goods. This appeal to the poor was often accompanied by denouncing the sins of the urban rich and contrasting their evil ways with the superior morality of the converted poor.

There was no criticism of the social order implied in such appeals. Rather, they emphasized that material success was unimportant. The important element in life was spiritual grace, and the test of such grace was adversity. Those who bore adversity with Christian fortitude were assured of salvation. The injustices of this life would be remedied in the next. Such messages conveyed in great urban revivals and rural "camp meetings" by eloquent preachers attracted hundreds of thousands who formed themselves into new churches, such as the Disciples of Christ, made up of former Presbyterians and Baptists.

Even more sweeping in their rejection of current social values were various millenarian doctrines, which taught that the end of the world—the millenium promised in the New Testament—was at hand and exhorted people to forsake the evil ways of this world to attain salvation. The most important such movement was founded by William Miller, a small farmer of upstate New York who had served in the War of 1812. In his view, American society, sinful as all the others, would come before the bar of divine judgment on April 23, 1843—the day of the Second Advent of Christ.

Miller's preaching in the hard times of the early 1840s was phenomenally successful. As the appointed day approached, converts sold or gave away their property. Farmers deserted their plows and artisans their benches. True believers were not discomfited when the appointed day—and successive appointed days—passed without cataclysm. Many converts went on to other sects. With the revival of the economy interest waned, but a sufficient number of believers remained to found a new Protestant church, the Adventists, following the strict moralistic teachings of its founder.

Perhaps most extreme in its expression of alienation was the Church of Jesus Christ of Latter-Day Saints, founded by Joseph Smith in 1830. His teachings, set forth in *The Book of Mormon,* reflected many currents of opinion of the day. The antagonism of the poor to the religious establishment was mirrored in Smith's teaching that no existing church represented God's will. The strong patriotism of Americans was embodied in God's revelation that the center of His true church was to be in the United States. The frustrations of poor folk were reflected in the teaching that poverty had no place among believers. The true church had to help its poor members in practical ways to become independent, self-respecting, productive members of the religious community. The term *community,* then, embraced not simply community of belief. It also called for a separate, self-sufficient, economic and social community united by both religious belief and common social goals. Smith's message won converts by the thousands.

Elites were offended by the "emotionalism" of the new sects, but business managers could appreciate the virtues extolled in their churches: honesty, sobriety, hard work, faithfulness. Further, members of these groups, holding themselves aloof from "sinful" folk, except when they were trying to convert the sinners, rarely joined unions or engaged in strikes. Ironically, the new faiths, growing out of alienation and rebellion, became buttresses of the very social order that had caused their trouble.

ESCAPE TO RELIGIOUS UTOPIAS

More outright than the religious sects in rejecting the gospel of success were the various utopian colonies, which attracted thousands of unsuccessful Americans. These colonies attempted to restore a sense of community based on sharing of labor and wealth. Some reflected daring acceptance of a new role for women by providing for sexual equality. Some were inspired by religious ideals. Others were based on purely secular ideas. The depression of 1837 stimulated interest in such experiments, but communitarian ideas were in the air before and after that collapse. Even in times of prosperity some Americans questioned the moral validity of capitalism. Of the religiously inspired colonies, three are noteworthy: the Shakers, the Oneida Community, and the Mormon settlements.

The Shakers, despite their insistence on both celibacy and sexual equality, attracted 6,000 members by 1850, organized in small groups from New England to Kentucky. Members enjoyed complete economic security through a form of primitive Christian communism, in which all goods were held in common. They sustained themselves by farming and by handicraft work in weaving, knitting, and furniture making. In a day when many manufactured goods were shoddy, Shaker artisans found ready markets for their products.

The Oneida Community in New York was founded by John Humphrey Noyes in 1848 to demonstrate his conviction that "perfection," pure holiness, was possible in this life. Since private property hindered perfection, it was banned and all property was held by the community. The ban on private property applied as well to married women, whom the colonists felt were regarded as nothing but property by the conventional legal forms of marriage. Marriage then was also subject to community control. In marriage, as in all other relationships, women were granted full equality. No marriage could take place, however, until the community had investigated the suitability of the partners for each other and approved the marriage. Thereafter, through insistence on a combination of continence and birth control, the community controlled its population growth and the quality of offspring. Children were cared for in community nurseries and schools. Inappropriate marriages were dissolved, and new partnerships arranged.

This system of "complex marriage" outraged outsiders, to whom it smacked of sexual license and "free love." Eventually they compelled the colony to modify its marital doctrines. Nonetheless, the community prospered. Its production of a superior line of steel traps and superbly crafted silverware won it ever expanding markets. It lasted until the 1880s. Ironically, when it was dissolved, its members became owners of a new corporation that took over the substantial assets of the colony as the private property of the corporation.

The most successful of the communitarian movements was the Mormons. Their leaders, Joseph Smith and Brigham Young, came from families of the wandering poor who settled in the "burnt-over district" of western New York, an area noted for

Mormons were driven out of Nauvoo, Illinois, in 1846.
Library of Congress

both its wretched poverty and religious sectarianism. Neither man had much schooling, a fact that made it easy for them to identify with the masses of semiliterate Americans who shared their hostility to established churches and educated elites. Smith displayed talents as a charismatic leader, and Young proved to be a genius in organization and administration.

Persecution of Mormons, including the killing of the prophet Joseph Smith, finally drove them to the ultimate in alienation—separation. Schisms within the church also contributed to the decision to put the Saints beyond the contaminating influence of gentile society. Beginning in February 1846, nearly 16,000 people trekked across the Great American Desert to found a new Zion. Eventually, in July 1847, "the place" was found by Smith's successor, Brigham Young—the Great Salt Lake Valley. It was arid, wild, remote from the gentiles, and at the time still part of Mexico. Here the Mormons created their own society.

Building a new Zion individualistically in such inhospitable territory was impossible, and in any case individualism ran against the Mormon belief in community. Even in the East believers had subordinated their interests to those of the community, and some had even joined the United Order of Enoch, which practised a limited form of communism under the leadership of Joseph Smith. Now, in the land the Mormons called Deseret, both principle and expediency dictated the primacy of community interests. The settlements had to be defended against possible Indian resistance to occupation of their territory. Farming lands had to be allotted and towns laid out. Destitute arrivals had to be maintained until they were self-supporting. Most important, water had to be brought down from the Wasatch Mountains if the settlements were to survive.

The problems were solved through community effort reminiscent of early Puritan New England. Private property was recognized, but it was subject to the needs of the community. Settlers had a voice in making decisions, but ultimate authority rested with the community leaders, who, as in New England, were also the religious leaders.

Under the leaders' direction, settlers were located in towns rather than on isolated farms. Such planning served two functions: it promoted group cohesiveness, and it made the settlements more defensible. The town lots were assigned by the community leadership, and skilled workers assigned to erect houses and buildings. Farming land was distributed according to family size. Labor was organized to dig the ditches necessary to bring down water from the mountains. An elaborate irrigation system provided water to individual farms, with community officials determining how the supply was to be allocated. Community stores and workshops provided necessary tools and supplies. Destitute newcomers were supported through tithing, under which self-sustaining members contributed one-tenth of their income to the church. Destitution lasted only until the newcomer, with community aid, could be put to work as a farmer or artisan.

In short, the Mormons developed a society in which self-interest was subordinated to the needs of the community. Indeed, from a psychological point of view, Mormons found individual expression and fulfillment in contributing to the well-being of their community. They built a society in which there was neither unemployment nor poverty, in which skilled workers could find full scope for their talents, and in which status came from one's devotion to the cause rather than from mere wealth. It is not surprising, then, that thousands of converts, recruited among the unsuccessful in America and Europe, made the long trek to Deseret.

The Mormons were not left alone long. In 1850, Deseret was incorporated into the American political system as the territory of Utah. Mormons dominated the territorial government, but their independence was limited, as they discovered in their frequent conflicts with the federal government. Gentile settlers entered the territory in increasing numbers, triggering sporadic outbreaks of violence between the Mormons and their foes. The growing prosperity of the Mormons exposed them to the pressures of the American economic system, to which they became more and more vulnerable. The collectivist ideals of the founders withered away as individualism made its inroads. Eventually, the Mormons lost their distinctiveness except in the realm of faith and morals. Even there they had to concede to gentile pressure, later renouncing polygamy as part of their doctrine.

SECULAR UTOPIAS

In addition to the religiously inspired utopias, there were also secular colonies. The most important were those founded on the principles of Robert Owen and Charles Fourier.

Robert Owen was a self-made man, a poor Welsh lad who had become a wealthy British textile manufacturer. Unlike most self-made men, though, he came to view capitalism as evil. Owen's idea was to overcome capitalism by demonstrating on a small scale the virtues of a free, cooperative society in which the profit motive would be eliminated and the techniques of the Industrial Revolution developed for the betterment of all. With this in mind he acquired from a religious sect 30,000 acres at New Harmony, Indiana, complete with houses and buildings. In 1825 he invited believers to join him.

Nearly 1,000 people came, including such enthusiastic intellectuals as William Maclure, geologist; Gerard Troost, chemist; Thomas Say, entomologist; and Frances Wright, the advocate of women's rights. They were attracted not only by the colony's socialistic principles but also by the plans for intellectual and cultural uplift of its members, which included concerts, lectures, adult education, and early schooling of children through a form of kindergarten training.

Despite its great promise, the project failed. Chronic dissension rent the ranks, inhibiting the economic development necessary for the colony's well-being. By 1828 the experiment was over. Owenite communities established elsewhere likewise failed. Perhaps the deeper reason for failure was that for all its socialistic aims, New Harmony was basically an expression of individualism. Robert Owen planned and directed it, not the members. He had little patience with the notion that rank-and-file members could contribute advice. "Until they shall be instructed in better habits, and made rationally intelligent, their advice can be of no value," he said.

More successful for a time were the followers of Charles Fourier, a French utopian who rejected the Industrial Revolution and looked for salvation through small communities based on farming and handicrafts. His colonies, called "phalanxes," were organized as stockholding companies in which each member bought shares. Outsiders could also subscribe to the necessary capital. Workers were guaranteed subsistence, each performing a variety of tasks to ensure that labor would be "joyous." Profits were to be distributed according to a formula that ranked labor first, investors second, and outstanding contributors to the colony's well-being third.

Fourier's message, as interpreted by Albert Brisbane, a wealthy young reformer, reached America in the depression year of 1840 and was received with enthusiasm. Laborers saw in it a means of getting subsistence. Skilled workers viewed it as a way of using their skills and maintaining their status. Intellectuals found in it a solution to the problem of progress and poverty without disturbing the social order. Horace Greeley, editor of the *New York Tribune,* became an influential advocate of the new cause. Thousands joined the more than forty communities that sprang up from New England to the Middle West. The most famous community was Brook Farm in New England—famous not because it succeeded but because it involved in one way or another the leading intellectual figures of the day, including Ralph Waldo Emerson, Nathaniel Hawthorne, Margaret Fuller, and William Ellery Channing.

Few phalanxes lasted more than a decade. For the most part they lacked adequate capital to operate. They were poorly managed. There was conflict with neighbors. Many members knew so little of farming that their labor was almost worthless. Living conditions were hard. There were quarrels over distribution of profits, when there were any profits. In consequence, there was as little harmony in the phalanxes as in New Harmony.

CONFRONTATION AND REBELLION

Although they aimed to reform the social order, the various utopian schemes in effect provided a means for members to escape the tensions of the existing society. They attracted the most alienated, those willing to stake their futures on the success of the group they joined. Most discontented Americans, however, were in no mood for such projects. They preferred to solve their problems pragmatically through economic and political means. If these failed, they were willing to resort to force.

To many Americans of the day forcible resistance to oppression was part of the national heritage. Memories of the colonial mobs were still fresh. The great Declaration of Independence and the Revolution gave hallowed sanction to resistance. In 1786 Daniel Shays, a Revolutionary War veteran, had led an armed rebellion of western Massachusetts farmers protesting their impoverishment. Eight years later farmers in Pennsylvania offered armed opposition to a new federal tax on whiskey that threatened their livelihood. Both rebellions were crushed, but they indicated that the spirit of resistance had not ended with the Revolution.

Resistance was evident again during the depression of 1837. Under pressure from small-business owners, from farmers, and even from some of the well-to-do who were heavily in debt, several states passed "stay laws." Such laws "stayed" the execution of contracts against debtors until certain conditions were met. Obviously, such laws were in conflict with the Constitution, and the United States Supreme Court said so. Debtor influence in some states then obtained long lists of exempted property that could not be seized to pay debts. In some places where feeling ran high, armed mobs halted sales of seized property.

In New York State, the debt issue gave rise to the "antirent wars." Debts were not the only issue involved. When the Dutch had controlled New York, they made vast land grants to favored individuals, hoping to encourage Dutch settlement. When the British took over, they confirmed the grants. The holdings of those landlords who favored the American cause were left intact after the Revolution. The landholding system in New York was feudal. The landlord owned title to the land, but it was worked by tenants on perpetual or long-term leases. No tenant, however industrious and thrifty, could hope to own the land he worked. All improvements made by the tenant belonged to the landlord, and the tenant paid the property taxes, not the landlord. The landlord reserved for himself water, mineral, and timber rights. When a perpetual lease was transferred, the landlord received 25 percent of the price, a hated practice called the "quarter sale." If a long-term lease was sold, the seller had to pay the landlord an extra year's rent. In good times there had been resentment against the system; antirent wars broke out even in the eighteenth century. But the depression of 1837 brought the issue to a head.

The immediate occasion was the death in 1839 of Stephen Van Rensselaer, whose holdings covered more than 1,000 square miles on both sides of the Hudson River. The terms of his will required that all rents in arrears, amounting to $400,000, be collected to pay his debts. The tenants, impoverished by the depression, could not pay. The heirs then obtained writs to seize the property and evict the tenants. The tenants, fearful of losing their land and possessions, petitioned the state to intervene. They recommended that if no agreement could be reached with the landlords, the state should take over the land and sell it to the tenants while offering fair compensation to the former owners. Such a program of land reform held little attraction for legislators, themselves landlords or associated with landlord interests. The tenants' idea died. The tenants then turned to direct action. Guerrilla warfare spread through the vast Van Rensselaer estate. Disguised as Indians, armed tenants prevented sheriffs from serving writs. A deputy sheriff was slain when he tried to seize a tenant's cattle. State troops were sent into the area, and so many tenants were jailed that the revolt collapsed.

Nevertheless, the antirent movement went on. The tenants had many sympathizers outside their own ranks, and this support they turned to account politically. They backed any candidate, regardless of party, who pledged himself to the antirent cause. The election strategy brought results. A new legislature ordered taxation of landlords and abolished seizure of tenants' goods for debt. A court held "quarter sales" illegal. The new constitution of 1846 prohibited new feudal tenures. In 1847 Governor John Young, a Whig, pardoned antirenters still in prison. Under such pressures, and perhaps from a realization that more money was to be made in business than in outdated landholding practices, the landlords gave way.

THE DORR REBELLION

Armed resistance also came to Rhode Island, in this instance over the issue of democratic government. Rhode Island, founded as a colony by Roger Williams to provide a haven for the oppressed and to establish democracy in religion and government, was in 1840 still governed, with some modifications, under the charter granted by Charles II in 1663. The legislature was supreme. It elected the judges, and the governor had only such power as the legislature granted him. The legislature, however, was not democratically elected. Voting and office holding were restricted to "freemen"—that is, men who owned a specified minimum in real estate. The freemen became a minority as the state's population increased from 69,000 in 1800 to nearly 109,000 in 1840. The growing number of workers in the state's textile mills and machine shops had no voice in government at all.The freemen, of course, were not of one mind. Most were Whigs, but a few were Democrats. Thus, Rhode Island was governed by a political majority of a social minority.

Another source of grievance was the gross underrepresentation of industrial centers in the state House of Representatives. The city of Providence, a booming manufacturing town with a population of 23,000, had only four representatives, while sixteen other towns with the same total population had thirty-four representatives among them. The right to vote was seen as all the more important because it was a first step toward gaining other rights enjoyed only by freemen.

Obviously, this political system met neither the demands of the democratic revolution then sweeping other states nor the requirements of an industrial order that called for more flexible and representative government. As early as 1777 attempts had been made to bring Rhode Island into line politically with other states, but real pressure for change did not build up until the nineteenth century. The rapid development of a huge disfranchised class, plus extension of the franchise in neighboring states, provided ground for new movements demanding a written constitution and adult white male suffrage. The legislature rejected all such petitions, claiming that the charter's restriction of political rights "to the sound part of the community, the substantial freeholders of the State" was political wisdom.

The growing tensions within the state, aggravated by the widespread distress occasioned by the depression of 1837, finally erupted during the "Hungry Forties." Led by Thomas W. Dorr, a wealthy young Democrat, the "suffragists" held mass meetings of the disfranchised in 1841 and from them obtained authority to call a People's Convention to write a new constitution. The convention drafted a constitution providing for adult white male suffrage and for more equitable distribution of representation among the towns. In keeping with the democratic principles of the convention, the constitution was first submitted to the people for criticism and suggestions before ratification. The constitution, as amended in the process, was then subject to the will of the new electorate and approved by majority vote. Indeed, it is significant that a majority of the freemen voted for the document.

The convention met again, declared the new constitution in effect, and ordered elections. In 1842 Dorr was swept into office as governor along with his followers, who dominated the new government. Thus, Rhode Island had two governments. The Dorr regime based its legitimacy on the vote of the people. The freemen's government asserted its legitimacy on the grounds of the charter and its long acceptance as the de jure government of the state.

In the meantime, the freemen sought to head off the popular movement by abandoning the charter and offering a new constitution of their own. It liberalized the suffrage and provided more equitable representation for towns, but it fell far short of the reforms provided by the People's Constitution. When the "freemen's" constitution was submitted to those eligible to vote under its liberalized suffrage, it was defeated. Faced with repudiation by its own constituency, the legislature resorted to repression. It passed the Algerine Law, nullifying all elections of the Dorrites. All who were active in such elections were made criminals, and those who took office as a result of such elections were held guilty of treason. The legislature also called upon President Tyler for federal intervention. Tyler responded that such an intervention would be justified only by actual insurrection.

Now the issue came to climax. On May 3, 1842, the new Dorrite government took office, asserted itself as the only legitimate government of the state, and so informed the federal government and the other states. It also repealed the Algerine Law. Next day, Governor Samuel W. King was inaugurated under the old state charter. The charter government hastened to repeat its call for federal intervention, and again President Tyler declined.

Events moved swiftly. After a triumphal visit to New York City, where he said he had been promised 5,000 men to help uphold the new government, Dorr took action. Fearful that the charter government might resort to force, he ordered seizure

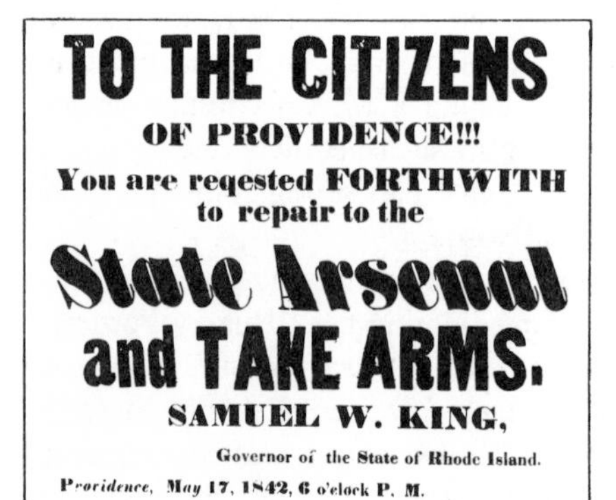
TO THE CITIZENS
OF PROVIDENCE!!!
You are reqested FORTHWITH
to repair to the
State Arsenal
and TAKE ARMS.
SAMUEL W. KING,
Governor of the State of Rhode Island.
Providence, May 17, 1842, 6 o'clock P. M.

This proclamation triggered violent confrontation between friends and foes of a democratic constitution for Rhode Island in 1842.

Rhode Island Historical Society

of two artillery pieces. The charter government responded by mobilizing the militia throughout the state and calling on the citizens of Providence to get arms from the state arsenal. Now convinced that his enemies did plan to use force, Dorr ordered his followers to take the arsenal. When the garrison refused to surrender, Dorr ordered the artillery into action. Both guns misfired. His discomfited followers disappeared into the night. The people's government collapsed, and Dorr fled the state.

The struggle was not over, however. From outside the state, Dorr continued his campaign, sustained by the faith of such followers as Seth Luther, the spokesman for the workers of New England. With their help and with promises of mass support from within the state, he went back to Rhode Island, to find only a handful of men ready to take up arms on his behalf. Dorr, realizing that the mass of his followers were not prepared to use force, wrote that he was disbanding his armed followers.

With the Dorrite movement in disarray, the charter government took its revenge. Claiming that the state was in danger of invasion from out-of-state Dorrites, the government put Rhode Island under martial law. People who had personal scores to settle "informed" on their victims. Homes and business places of suspects were raided and the people in them terrorized. Hundreds of Dorrites, real and suspected, were rounded up on charges of treason. They were packed into overcrowded jails and treated brutally. Seth Luther became so desperate that he set fire to his jail cell in an effort to escape. A reward of $5,000 was offered for delivering Dorr, the "fugitive traitor," to the authorities. On one occasion state troops fired into a crowd at Pawtucket, wounding two and killing one. When Dorr returned openly to Rhode Island in 1843, he was arrested, found guilty of treason, and sentenced to life imprisonment.

The persecution of the Dorrites caused popular revulsion, which found expression in a new convention called by the charter legislature to frame a constitution. Voting rights were extended as the Dorrites demanded. The new voters put the Democrats in control of the state government. Offered his freedom if he would take an oath of allegiance, Dorr refused, on the grounds that he never had been disloyal. In 1845 he was pardoned. Nine years later the charges against him were annulled by the legislature.

THE ALIEN "MENACE"

If some Americans were willing to use a combination of politics and force to liberalize society, others were equally prepared to use the same tools to make society more restrictive. These were traditionally minded folk who found themselves at a loss in a rapidly changing America and so clung all the more intensely to the values inherited from an earlier day. They saw these values—and indeed their country—menaced by alien elements bent on subverting all they held dear. Such anxieties and ideas gave birth to the movement we call *nativism*.

Nativism was the anti-Catholic, antiforeign movement that flourished for a generation between 1830 and 1856. Its major targets were Irish and German immigrants. It was the first nationally organized expression of xenophobia, and it numbered among its leaders such eminent Americans as Samuel F. B. Morse, inventor of the telegraph; Lyman Beecher, a leading Congregational minister; and Millard Fillmore, who served as president of the United States from 1850 to 1852.

Hostility to immigrants, and especially to those from Ireland, was not new in America. But it attained a new virulence in the 1830s, with a mass influx of Irish laborers lured by jobs on canal and railroad construction. That migration was a portent of things to come. In twenty years (1840–60) more than 4.3 million immigrants arrived in the United States, of whom nearly 1.7 million were Irish and 1.4 million German. Newcomers were to be found in all parts of the country, but they tended to settle in urban areas, where jobs were available and where pockets of immigrants already settled in their communities gave new arrivals a sense of being "at home." By 1860 the populations of New York, Chicago, and Pittsburgh were nearly 50 percent foreign born. St. Louis was at the top, with 60 percent foreign born.

So many newcomers in so short a time would have produced strains even in an orderly and stable society, and preindustrial America was anything but orderly and stable. Many Americans, beset with their own frustrations, watched with anxiety as foreigners poured in, speaking strange tongues, following strange customs, and practicing Catholicism, a religion long regarded as dangerous. Their reaction was to reassert the primacy of traditional American values and to look upon the immigrant as the enemy. At a more immediate level, American workers were enraged when employers used immigrants to displace American-born workers, to reduce wage scales, and to break strikes. In their anger they blamed the immigrants. With the spread of such sentiments, Whig politicians took up the cry and fanned the flames of prejudice.

Yet many Americans welcomed the newcomers. The Catholic church opened its arms to its communicants from Ireland and Germany. Employers generally were glad to get cheap and, they hoped, docile labor—although in all cities there were business managers who made it plain that "No Irish Need Apply" for job openings. Middle-class women, even when cherishing nativist opinions, were overjoyed to get servants for low wages. Democratic politicians, quicker than the Whigs to perceive the significance of the immigrant vote, gathered the arrivals into the party's fold.

Immigrant participation in Democratic politics intensified nativist feeling. But the nativist bill of particulars against the Irish was already long. There were too many of them. They were poor. They were clannish. They were drunken, dissolute, and criminal. They took jobs away from Americans. They were Catholic. Middle-class citizens, who were exalting the doctrine of sexual abstinence and restricting family size, saw in large Irish families signs of a lack of moral restraint. Men of learning, pondering the large numbers of Irish in poorhouses and mental hospitals, concluded that there was a peculiar defect in the Irish "constitution" that rendered them subject to poverty and mental illness. Thus, any attempt to ameliorate their condition through social reform was hopeless. In the meantime, they would continue to be an inordinate drain on public funds.

The nativist indictment attributed to the Irish responsibility for conditions of which they were really the victims. The Irish who fled to the United States had been wretchedly poor to begin with. When they arrived, they had to depend on friends or relatives for care—or failing that, they had to seek charity. Since they were unskilled, they had to take the hardest, and lowest-paying, jobs. By Irish standards they were well paid—but America was not Ireland. What had seemed a princely income in Ireland provided only poverty in America, a poverty that was better than the stark poverty of Ireland but poverty nonetheless. All too often they were not paid at all. Time and again, crooked construction contractors, on completion of a project, collected their money and absconded without paying the workers. When the angry men rioted, public authorities blamed the disturbances on "drunken Irishmen."

There were also profound psychological differences between poverty in Ireland and poverty in the United States. In Ireland, most folk were poor, and it was clear that their poverty was due to absentee English landlords. The Irish peasantry derived a sense of community from both their poverty and their hatred of the English oppressors. In short, poverty was no badge of disgrace. In the United States it was, as the Irish could see daily in the attitudes of Americans. The church might counsel acquiescence in existing social relations, but Irish were quick to perceive that in America individuals were expected to "better themselves." If they did not, it was their own fault.

The Irish were blamed for living in slums—but again, they had no choice. Being poor, they had to take the housing offered at the rents they could afford. In eastern cities they were jammed into ramshackle tenements, lacking heat and water, with few windows and little ventilation. Outdoor privies were the rule in the overcrowded slums. Water had to be carried from the nearest well. Garbage littered the unpaved streets, disposed of by the myriad hogs that roamed the cities of the day.

Prolonged overcrowding, as we know now, produces not only high social tensions but also high rates of mental illness. And indeed, many slum dwellers did break down. The slums took other tolls as well. Tuberculosis and pneumonia contributed to a high death rate. Periodically, the immigrants were ravaged by smallpox, cholera, and fevers. Addiction to alcohol became a common means of survival for many. The breakdown of old Irish community standards and sanctions in the slums fostered the rise of a young criminal class, which developed a gang culture with its own socially acceptable patterns of behavior. The gang culture flourished all the more because native-born politicians found the thugs useful in election campaigns and afforded them protection.

Life in the slums, then, was a brutal application of "survival of the fittest." Those with tough physiques and hardy psyches survived, and many eventually escaped the slums altogether. Fathers, mothers, and children all worked, and out of their meager earnings they contrived to save, sometimes to help relatives come to the United States, sometimes to get homes of their own away from the slums. Parents joined with priests to save children from the corruption around them. Many priests, aided by Father Theobald Mathew, the famous Irish advocate of temperance, crusaded against drink.

As time went on, the "lace curtain Irish" drew away from the "shanty Irish," finding ways to move upward in American society and looking down on the poor they left behind. Sometimes success came through sheer hard work, thrift, frugality, and determination. This was especially true when such traits were accompanied by business acumen, as when ditch diggers learned the fundamentals of construction and became contractors themselves. The affinity between the Irish and the Democrats also helped when such contractors sought public works jobs. Irishmen with a flair for politics found a way up through the Democratic machines.

ANTI-CATHOLICISM

The meaning of the intense human struggles going on in the slums escaped the nativists. For them, the Irish, as Irish, were bad enough. But the Irish were also Catholics, which made them dangerous. They were thus dehumanized into the enemy, the symbols of a vast international conspiracy to overthrow American institutions and Protestantism. Said Samuel F. B. Morse, "The question of Popery and Protestantism, or Absolutism and Republicanism, . . . is fast becoming, and will shortly be, the great absorbing question, not only of this country, but of the whole civilized world."

The center of the conspiracy, it was charged, was the Leopold Foundation, inspired by an adviser of Prince Metternich of Austria, architect of the regime of repression and reaction that followed the Napoleonic wars in Europe. Metternich did not hide his hostility to Protestantism, the middle class, republicanism, and democracy. A secret purpose of the foundation, said the nativists, was to stimulate massive Catholic migration to the United States. Given free access to the vote, Catholics, under orders from the pope, would subvert the government, crush religious freedom, and institute an authoritarian regime with Catholicism as the state religion.

So far as nativists were concerned, evidence of the conspiracy was on every hand. Irish hoodlums broke up nativist meetings. The Irish were powerful in the Democratic party, and in cities like New York, they dominated the party, affording them a way to accomplish the grand Catholic design. The church hierarchy put an end to laymen serving as trustees for church property and vested property in the bishops, a move that to the nativists confirmed the antidemocratic nature of the church. In cities where Catholics were strong, such as Baltimore, Philadelphia, and New York, they brought an end to purely Protestant religious exercises in the public schools.

In New York, the aggressive Archbishop John Hughes, himself an Irish immigrant, touched off a major political battle with his demand that public funds be alloted to Catholic parochial schools. He further enraged Protestants by public lectures in which he discussed the "decline" of Protestantism and predicted the eventual triumph of Catholicism. In Massachusetts, where antislavery sentiment was mounting, the hierarchy condemned abolitionism as the work of "infidels and blasphemers, . . . traitors and disorganizers." Thus, the church itself drove many otherwise liberally minded men and women into reluctant alliance with nativists to curb a power that identified with slavery.

Also contributing to the anti-Catholic frenzy was revival of the long-held Protestant belief that monasteries and convents were centers of sexual depravity. Young women, it was said, were held prisoners against their will, forced to yield to the perverted lust of priests on penalty of death. A body of writing appeared, written by real and fake former priests and nuns, catering to the pruriency of Victorian America. The most influential of these books was Maria Monk's *Awful Disclosures* about a convent in Montreal, which appeared in 1836. In detail it described scenes of rape, infanticide, and murder. The book was so successful that *Further Disclosures* was published in 1837. Investigation of Monk's work showed it to be a complete fabrication; No matter; thousands read it and believed it, but few knew of its real nature. It has continued to reappear whenever anti-Catholic feeling runs high.

NATIVISTS AND GERMANS

Nativists resented attempts by the Irish to move into the mainstream of American life. They were also enraged by the Germans, who made it plain that they thought American culture much inferior to German. In every city the German community tried to isolate itself from American contamination. They maintained their own churches, stores, newspapers, clubs, and *Turnvereine,* the societies that combined gymnastic exercises with cultivation of a strong sense of German identity. Indeed, during the 1830s and 1840s refugee intellectuals from a reactionary Germany planned to set up a democratic "New Germany" in Arkansas, Missouri, Wisconsin, and Texas. Despite their democratic ideals, the refugees hoped to make their settlements guardians of German culture, as free from American influence as possible.

The schemes did not materialize, but the ideas behind them found expression in other ways. In cities where Germans were powerful, they won teaching of German as a second language in the public schools. In Pennsylvania they obtained publication of state laws in both English and German. Such success was possible because Germans, like the Irish, joined the Democratic party, their major source of protection against nativist attacks. To nativists, the power of these two immigrant groups in American political life was ominous of disaster.

Nativists found other reasons for loathing the Germans. Like the Irish, there were too many of them, they were often poor, and they took the jobs of Americans. Besides, many were Catholics, and others were Lutherans who kept apart from other Protestant churches. Some were even avowed "infidels," who professed no formal religion at all! Lax German morals were seen in the "desecration of the Lord's Day." On Sundays German families flocked to the beer gardens that flourished in every German community. There they drank, danced, and listened to secular music. To American Protestants this behavior was unforgivable.

There were still other issues that focused nativist antagonism on the Germans. In Texas, where about 35,000 immigrants had settled, the Germans worked their own farms, refusing to use slave labor. They were widely suspected of being secret abolitionists; nativist hostility to them included both Catholics and Protestants. Slaveholders did not allow religious differences to come between them and opposition to abolitionist foreigners. It did not occur to native Texans that the Germans simply did not want blacks around them.

In the urban centers of the East, conservatives were alarmed by the avowed revolutionaries who came to the United States after the collapse of the Revolution of 1848. Among them were Carl Heinzen, a disciple of the French anarchist Proudhon, and Wilhelm Weitling and Joseph C. Weydemeyer, friends of Marx and Engels. Unlike Carl Schurz, another 1848 fugitive who adjusted to American society first as a Democrat and later as a Republican, these men preached revolutionary transformation of the social order. They had little following outside restricted German circles, but nevertheless their teachings aroused anxiety among conservative Americans.

The nativists knew they could not keep these "foreign menaces" out of the country. Their labor was too badly needed. Nativists decided to let them in, except the paupers, but keep them politically powerless once they were here. These aims could be accomplished by making citizenship available only after twenty-one years of residence, restricting public office to native-born citizens, and prohibiting land ownership by aliens.

Such a program was promoted by the Native American Association, formed in 1837, and its branches throughout the country. From these grew several secret societies, which banded together in 1849 as the Order of the Star-Spangled Banner. From such sources evolved the "American" political party—dubbed by its opponents the Know-Nothing party because its members had a standard answer to questions about the party: "I know nothing." In the 1850s the new party came to dominate nine states—the Northeast and Maryland and Kentucky—and elected seventy-five members to Congress. Its triumph was short-lived. Like the Democratic and Whig parties, the Know-Nothings were rent by the mounting issue of slavery expansion. Southerners went over to the Democrats, and northerners to the new Republican party. The Know-Nothing bloc at the Republican convention in 1860 helped prevent the presidential nomination of former New York governor William H. Seward because he had taken up the cause of immigrants. They thus helped Abraham Lincoln be nominated. Their influence, however, made his election difficult. Many midwestern Germans, for example, despite their antislavery sentiments, voted for Stephen A. Douglas, the northern Democrat, because they feared the nativists in the Lincoln camp.

The tensions between nativists and new Americans were too fierce to be contained within the normal political process. Street brawls and minor riots were frequent in the major cities. In Charlestown, Massachusetts, a convent was burned to

American "nativists" and Irish immigrants clash in a bloody riot in Philadelphia in 1844.

Historical Society of Pennsylvania

the ground after its occupants were forced out. Major riots took place in Philadelphia, Cincinnati, and St. Louis. In these disturbances scores of people lost their lives and hundreds were injured. In some places Catholic churches and schools were burned and Irish driven from their homes.

Yet nativism was more of a mood than an ideology. It had many contradictory elements. Among its most militant followers were Ulster Scots, who vented their ancient hatred of Irish Catholics. French Catholics in Louisiana took nativist stands against Irish newcomers in New Orleans. In some places Germans joined forces with nativists against the Irish. In others, Irish went nativist against the "damned Dutch." In short, nativism sometimes was a response to local conditions that transcended religious and ethnic divisions.

A NEW PEOPLE ENTERS

While Protestants were harassing Catholics in the Northeast, the United States government was casually admitting 80,000 Catholics in the Southwest. They were the inhabitants of that half of Mexico's territory taken over by the United States in 1848 as a result of the Mexican War.

Under terms of the Treaty of Guadalupe Hidalgo, Mexicans who did not opt for Mexican citizenship within one year would be considered American citizens, entitled to "all the rights of citizens of the United States according to the principles of the [American] Constitution." Until citizenship was legally bestowed, Mexican people were assured "free enjoyment of their liberty and property, and . . . free exercise of their religion without restriction." A protocol added to the treaty obligated the United States to respect land titles issued by either Spain or Mexico.

The people thus brought into the United States were of diverse racial backgrounds: Spanish, Indian, African, and mixed (mestizo) descent. Class lines were rigid and distinct. Society was dominated by a small elite (the *ricos*), which owned vast domains devoted to farming, mining, and cattle and sheep raising, and prided itself on its Spanish descent. The lands and mines were worked by peons who lived in poverty and were Indian or *mestizo*. It was a simple society, easy-going and traditional. It was as ignorant of the farming techniques of the nineteenth century as it was innocent of the cult of individualism and the gospel of success.

Most, but not all, *ricos* adjusted themselves to the new conditions. Their property was safe—or so they thought. They shared the American contempt for the peons, expressed in the American term *greasers*. They identified themselves with the southwestern American elites, who in turn were proud to link themselves with a "real Spanish" aristocracy. Intermarriage followed. American and Hispanic elites collaborated politically. Of the forty-eight delegates to the California constitutional convention of 1849, eight were *ricos* and they played a significant role. In New Mexico territory, the Hispanics played an even bigger role. Many *ricos* soon found out, however, that American rule could be hard.

Apart from clashes that had occurred earlier when Texas seceded from Mexico, the first outbreak of anti-Mexican feeling took place during the California gold rush. Native Californians of Mexican descent *(californios)* and Mexican immigrants, many of them with mining backgrounds, took up some of the best claims and worked them with a skill unknown to American and other amateurs. Led by enraged Americans, anti-Mexican miners of all nationalities joined in mobs killing "greasers" and burning their settlements.

The gold rush also proved ominous for many *ricos* in California. Unsuccessful prospectors and farmers who saw a market in the booming population looked with envious eyes on Spanish domains. Determined to have the land, they argued that it was immoral for a few men to hold land that would support hundreds of good American farmers. Further, the land was farmed inefficiently, and God intended the land for those who could make the best use of it. In frontier fashion, the Americans simply moved in on the *rico* ranches, occupying the best lands, setting up homesteads, and working them. Also, in frontier tradition, they argued that such occupation and improvement of property gave them legal right to the land. Some were persuaded to pay rent, but others simply "squatted."

The invaders were not content to occupy the land. They wanted title to it. Supported by other Americans who shared their anti-Mexican prejudices, they brought pressure to bear on California congressmen, who in turn persuaded Congress to act in 1851. The law, ostensibly designed to implement the property provisions of the Treaty of Guadalupe Hidalgo, ignored the treaty's assurances that the property of former Mexican citizens was to be respected. Instead, such folk were required to prove the validity of their titles to a special commission set up for that purpose.

Such proof was difficult. Some grants had never been properly registered; others had been destroyed in fires, wars, and revolutions. Even the ones that existed were vague in their terms, for neither Spanish nor Mexican practice called for precise surveys. Yet such precision in setting boundaries was exactly what the commission, in keeping with Anglo-American law and tradition, insisted on. Even so, the commission approved 521 of 813 claims. The successful landowners now confronted another hurdle. Government attorneys appealed more than 400 such approved claims, but their cases were so flimsy that they won only five appeals.

Even when the *ricos* won, they lost. The entire process of validating titles, including commission hearings and appeals, often lasted as long as seventeen years. Costs for legal help and other expenses were high. In the meantime, tenants refused to pay rent and squatters continued to farm their homesteads. Since the original owners claimed title, it was they who paid taxes. Many were compelled to sell much of their property to raise necessary funds, and the buyers were, of course, Anglo-Americans. Some of the *ricos* who held on to their land were terrorized by gangs of Anglos until they sold out at low prices. Thus in California was set a pattern followed throughout the Southwest. Most of the lands held by new Americans of Mexican descent passed into the hands of Anglos.

Poor Mexican-Americans fared no better than the *ricos* under American rule. As rancheros lost their property, many of the peons lost what economic security they had. They became casual laborers, able to get jobs only when they would accept any wage. Anglos derided their culture as backward and superstitious, and in towns segregated them in slums, or *barrios*. Desperados and cutthroats of all nationalities were on the loose in the Southwest, but Anglo opinion blamed all crime and disorder on the "greasers." Mexican-Americans could not enjoy even personal safety. Men were killed and women raped by Anglos, and Anglo authorities showed little concern.

It is not surprising, then, that some Mexican-Americans turned to violence. They figured that if it was right for Anglos to use violence against them, surely it was right for them to retaliate. Moved by poverty, discrimination, and such thinking, young men took to the roads, robbing and killing, often for their own benefit. Others, like the legendary Joaquin Murieta, who operated in the early 1850s in California, looked upon crime as a form of social protest. They robbed the Anglo rich to help the Mexican-American poor. Murieta became a Robin Hood of the peons. Another folk hero was Juan Cortina of Texas, who in 1859 shot a marshal who was beating a peon. Later that same year he and his followers invaded Brownsville, on the Mexican border, and executed three Anglos accused of crimes against Mexican-Americans. His attempt to found a movement among Mexicans in Texas to end their "unhappy condition" failed, but his many exploits on behalf of the oppressed won him such admiration that he still lives on in legend.

FOR FURTHER READING

A good introduction is Alice Felt Tyler, *Freedome's Ferment* (1944). Sydney E. Ahlstrom, *A Religious History of the American People*, Vol. 1 (1972), provides an excellent survey of religious movements. Utopian colonies are discussed in Arthur E. Bestor, *Backwoods Utopias* (1950), and in R. S. Fogarty, ed., *American Utopianism* (1972).

The problems of workers in a changing order are described in Norman Ware, *The Industrial Worker* (1924).

Other aspects of social change are treated in Bernard Wishy, *The Child and the Repbulic* (1968); D. J. Rothman, *The Discovery of the Asylum* (1971); and Gerald Grob, *Mental Institutions in America* (1973).

General works on immigrants include M. A. Jones, *American Immigration* (1960), and Carl Wittke, *We Who Built America* (1964). Anti-Catholic movements are discussed in Ray A. Billington, *The Protestant Crusade* (1938). See also William Shannon, *The American Irish* (1963), and Oscar Handlin, *Boston's Immigrants* (1968).

Two surveys of Mexican-Americans are Carey McWilliams, *North from Mexico* (1968), and Matt S. Meier and Feliciano Rivera, *The Chicanos* (1972).

The neglected history of the Dorr rebellion is told in A. M. Mowry, *The Dorr War* (1901, reprinted 1970).

13 the working poor

Among the people who also suffered from changes in preindustrial America were the white working poor: wage earners entirely dependent on their labor for their livelihood. The responses of the working poor to their situation were many and varied, constituting a kind of trial-and-error method of solving their problems. Some joined the new religious sects or one of the utopian colonies. Some skilled workers organized producer cooperatives, to manufacture and market their own products. Still others formed consumer cooperatives, to try to bring down the cost of necessities by buying as a group. Such enterprises succeeded as little as the utopian colonies.

A great many of the working poor were attracted to the cause of land reform. Land reform appealed to many working people in the 1840s because it promised to solve their problems without requiring a battle against powerful vested interests. George Henry Evans, the English-born prophet of the movement, argued that engrossment of land by a few owners plus the advent of the Industrial Revolution had reduced European workers to wage slavery. American workers could avoid that fate by becoming independent owners of their own land, he said.

Evans's proposal was simple: the federal government should allot public lands in small parcels to all who were willing to work it. To prevent speculators from preying on the small landowners, the land could not be bargained away. The consequent drain of labor to the West would force up wages and reduce rents in the East. The western settlements would give a new lease on life to the artisans. Out in the Republican Rural Townships Evans envisaged, artisans would also be farmers, while turning out the goods needed by their neighbors and trading them for commodities they needed. Evans's proposal had little immediate impact, but some of its principles were embodied in the Homestead Act of 1862.

Evans's movement was significant in yet another way. It typified the belief of most working people, whether they followed Evans or not, that there was nothing wrong with America as such. They were alienated not from the country, but from an economic system they saw as betraying the ideals on which the nation was founded. America, they insisted, was not meant to be a land of rich and poor. It was, rather, a nation dedicated to equality. The principles of the great Declaration of Independence were cited to justify labor resistance to employer oppression. In New England especially, men and women unionists proudly recalled their revolutionary heritage and identified their cause with that of the patriots of 1776.

Seth Luther, the leading spokesman for New England labor, set forth labor's attitude eloquently in a pamphlet, which had wide influence in the 1830s:

> Let us be determined no longer to be deceived by the cry of those who produce nothing and enjoy all, and who insultingly term us—the farmers, the mechanics, and laborers—the lower orders, and exultingly claim our homage for themselves as the *higher orders*—while the Declaration of Independence asserts, ''All men are created equal.''

Neither land reform nor other panaceas offered much help to labor in meeting its immediate problems. Workers, especially skilled workers, turned to unions and to political action to solve their bread-and-butter problems.

EMERGENCE OF UNIONS

Organizing labor was not easy. The prevailing spirit of individualism and the belief that America was a land of opportunity militated against collective action. The workers were divided among themselves. Skilled workers were separated by craft lines, and they had little concern for the unskilled. There were religious and ethnic antagonisms: Catholic against Protestant, native-born against foreign-born, white against black. Sex was another source of division: men did not want women in their unions.

Middle-class opinion was generally hostile to unions, although such leading men of the day as Horace Greeley, editor of the *New York Tribune;* William Cullen Bryant, poet and editor of New York's *Evening Post;* and John Greenleaf Whittier, the poet, were sympathetic. Most middle-class folk shared the view of employers that unions and strikes were un-American, the work of foreign agitators. As a New York judge said in 1836 when he punished strikers, unions were unnecessary ''in this favored land of law and liberty, [where] the road to advancement is open to all. . . . They are of foreign origin . . . and mainly upheld by foreigners.''

Perhaps the greatest obstacle to organization was apathy rooted in a feeling that resistance to employers was hopeless. There was some ground for this belief. Active union men and women were blacklisted and thus forced to move elsewhere to find employment. When strikes hurt them, employers could count on government aid. Police and militia were used to disperse picket lines. Courts punished leaders for criminal conspiracy. The charge was based on English common law, dating back to medieval times, which held that any combination of two or more persons to injure a third person or the general public was a criminal offense.

The legal barriers to organization were modified in 1842, when the Massachusetts Supreme Court decided *Commonwealth* v. *Hunt.* The court held that unions in themselves were not illegal, even if they injured an employer's "gains and profits." The test of legality was the means the unions used. If these were fair and lawful, the union was "innocent." If falsehood or force were used, the union was illegal. This limited decision was, of course, confined to one state, and other states were slow to follow Massachusetts's lead. Even so, the decision set a precedent and made easier the defense of accused union people elsewhere.

Despite the obstacles, unions did appear, although for a long time they were local and short-lived. They were confined to journeymen in a given craft and sometimes included small employers among their membership. Their major aims were to provide sickness and death benefits, maintain craft traditions in workmanship, and restrict the number of apprentices. Such craft organizations had little contact with unions in other crafts in the same town; indeed, they knew little of organizations in their own craft in other towns. The unions arose when some crisis developed, and when it was resolved, the unions disappeared. In 1810 only two crafts, the printers and shoemakers, had long established unions in cities scattered along the eastern seaboard. Many of these were wiped out by the depression of 1819.

Revival of the economy brought renewed labor organization, but Jackson's war on the Bank of the United States in 1832 provided labor with new opportunities. The climate of opinion fostered by the Jacksonians, particularly their appeal to the masses to strike down the forces of privilege, favored the organization of unions. Many unions threw their political support to Jackson. The Jacksonians, needing every kind of support they could muster, rallied to the cause of the unions, with politicians, lawyers, and editors publicly espousing labor's cause. They helped to make unionism more acceptable to hitherto suspicious workers and to large numbers of middle-class folk.

By 1837, it is estimated, union membership had risen to 300,000—nearly 17 percent of the nonfarm working force of the day. No longer confined to the eastern seaboard, unions were to be found in Louisville, St. Louis, and New Orleans. Members worked in a variety of occupations, ranging from house masons to cigarmakers. Women were organized in unions of dressmakers, shoemakers, and umbrella sewers. New England factory women, as we have seen, formed their own associations and went on strike. Indeed, strikes were called on an unprecedented scale—at least 186 in the four years between 1833 and 1837.

From this ferment grew a stronger consciousness of labor's need for unity and a growing emphasis on purely economic issues. Unions now barred employers from membership. Since the fight to restrict the number of apprentices had failed, unions emphasized minimum-wage standards as a means of protecting their members' interests. They also banned mixing political and religious issues with union affairs. Following a pattern established by Philadelphia unions in 1827, labor organizations in thirteen cities formed citywide federations of unions to provide mutual aid and promote more organization. Five craft groups went further and formed national associations: printers, shoemakers, carpenters, combmakers, and hand-loom weavers. In an attempt to unify all labor in a drive for the ten-hour day, the New England Association of Farmers, Mechanics and Other Workingmen (organized in 1832) opened its ranks to all workers, skilled and unskilled. This was the first time a labor organization had made so broad an appeal.

The 1830s also witnessed the first general strike in American history, initiated by Irish coal heavers on the Philadelphia wharves in 1835. Unions throughout the city joined them in strikes for the ten-hour day. As the city's business closed down, the city fathers and private employers conceded the shorter workday.

The triumphs of labor were short-lived. As the panic of 1837 ushered in the "Hungry Forties" and unemployment mounted, unions all but disappeared and union wage scales collapsed. In some cities the unemployed took to the streets, joining in demonstrations to demand jobs and denounce the national policies that had helped bring on the depression. In New York City, a mob of jobless men and women stormed warehouses and took the foodstuffs they so badly needed.

The unions that arose with general economic recovery in the late 1840s followed the pattern set in the 1830s. Craftsmen formed local unions restricted to their own craft—and excluding women. They joined with other craft unions in citywide associations for mutual aid. They joined with others of their own craft in setting up a dozen national unions, of which the most important were those of the printers, iron molders, and machinists and blacksmiths. Profiting from the experience of earlier unions, they built reserve funds and took other steps to protect themselves against another depression. When it came in 1857, a large number of unions collapsed, but an unprecedented number survived, providing a basis for a labor movement during and after the Civil War.

The unions of the 1840s and 1850s concentrated on such job issues as wages and hours. They preferred to gain their objectives through bargaining, but when employers proved uncooperative, they went on strike. These tactics won organized artisans the ten-hour day and substantial gains in pay, although the wage raises in the 1850s lagged behind the rise in living costs caused by the influx of California gold into the economy. Despite their seeming advance, craftsmen were still among the working poor on the eve of the Civil War.

The most spectacular strike of the era arose among the New England shoemakers in 1860. No longer independent artisans, the men, women, and children who worked in the industry were unskilled wage-earners, performing simple, routinized operations. For their work, men in 1859 received $3 a week, women and children much less. The discontent of the workers increased to the point where, in 1860, 20,000 people went on strike. The strike was conducted with a high degree of discipline. Strikers were required to sign pledges to obey rules against rowdyism, drinking, and violence, and marshals were appointed to enforce them. Violators lost their payments from the strike fund. Saloons were advised to sell no liquor to strikers. The evidence of working-class discipline favorably impressed middle-class opinion, already somewhat alienated by the behavior of the employers. Public officials, clergymen, and many local businessmen supported the strike. Despite the nativism that plagued New England, a Catholic priest urged Catholics to unite with Yankee Protestants to assure success. And success came. Employers granted wage increases of at least 10 percent, and some even signed agreements recognizing the unions as bargaining agents for the workers.

The shoe workers' strike dramatized a new trend in responses to the changing economy: namely, organization was taking root among workers dependent on the emerging industrial order. While unions of independent artisans with obsolescent skills died out, new unions arose reflecting labor's dependence on an impersonal relationship with employers. The shift from independence to dependence, beginning in preindustrial America, helps explain the development of a permanent national labor union movement later in the nineteenth century.

THE "WORKEYS"—AND LATER

Skilled workers periodically supplemented economic action with political action, sometimes when organizations and strikes failed to obtain their ends. When unions did not gain the ten-hour day, for example, they turned to the legislatures for relief. When petitions were turned down, they formed their own political organizations to put direct pressure on the politicians. Some issues, such as imprisonment for debt, obviously required changes in the law, and that, too, called for political action. Such action was possible because of the spread of adult white male suffrage.

At first, labor undertook independent political action through local Workingmen's Parties, the first of which was organized in Philadelphia in 1828. By 1834 there were more than sixty such parties, organized in towns and cities ranging from New England to Ohio. Although skilled artisans with some experience in unionism provided a base for the movement, the parties were not confined to workers. Rather, the parties made a broad appeal, addressing themselves to issues that concerned labor but also involved small farmers, small-business owners, and some professional people and intellectuals. When Andrew Jackson opened war on the Bank of the United States, the "workeys," as they were called, rallied to his support, believing the war would end the paper money that plagued workers and shopkeepers. Many joined the Democrats, giving rise to a reform movement within the party.

The broad appeal of the workeys may be seen in their program. Their calls for ending imprisonment for debt, the use of prison labor by private contractors, and compulsory service in the militia struck a responsive chord among many outside the ranks of labor who felt threatened by these practices. The workeys also gained support with their call for mechanics' lien laws, to protect workers against unscrupulous contractors who failed to pay wages.

Commanding even more support was workey advocacy of free public schools, although it should be noted that the proposal was not universally popular at the time. Many of the well-to-do objected to paying taxes to educate the "brats" of the poor. Some of the poor themselves were opposed. Despite their wishes to see their youngsters educated, they could not see how their families could survive without the wages the children brought home. It was hard to persuade them that taking children out of the factories would force up the wages of adults.

Another proposal that won support from small property-owners was tax reform. Under the existing system the wealthy evaded their fair share of taxation through low assessments of real estate—assessments they often made themselves—and the absence of taxes on stocks and bonds, which were becoming a major part of the wealth of elites. Thus, the burden of taxation fell on the smaller property-owners and the working poor. The "workeys" called for either income taxes or fair property taxes, to apply not only to real estate but also to financial securities. Some even suggested taxing church property—a proposal that stirred the wrath of Catholic and Protestant churchmen alike. The wealthy, who had much to lose from tax reform, took the side of the churches and piously portrayed themselves as the defenders of religion and morality! The workeys they denounced as "infidels."

Workeys were also assailed as enemies of "social order" and of "the rights of property" because of their demand that wages be paid in hard money—gold or silver—instead of bank notes. This demand, in turn, was linked to a call for the abolition of bank notes and for an end to monopolies, especially banking monopolies—a position that made "workeys" sympathetic to Andrew Jackson's war upon the Bank of the United States.

Another major element in their program was extension of political democracy. They favored full white male adult suffrage, and one party in Delaware even wanted suffrage extended to women. They also called for opening of all public offices to direct election by the people, thus putting an end to appointive offices and those filled by indirect election, such as the United States Senate. They demanded an end to property qualifications for holding office.

The workeys succeeded in politics. Their candidates were usually Whigs or Democrats who pledged themselves to work for the workey program. In close contests, the workey vote often proved decisive, a fact that did not escape the notice of professional politicians. Factions in both major parties cultivated the workey vote, and as a result a significant number of workey-endorsed candidates won office and helped carry through many of the party proposals.

The very success of the workers' parties contributed to their undoing, however. Utopian reformers, such as George Evans, Robert Dale Owen (son of Robert Owen of New Harmony fame), and Frances Wright swarmed into the organizations, intent upon transforming them into vehicles for their particular crusades. Ambitious politicians, frustrated by existing machines, turned to the workeys to promote their political fortunes. The parties were rent by factionalism as reformers, politicians, and rank-and-file members fought each other.

Hastening the decline in independent political action was Andrew Jackson's war on the Bank of the United States in 1832. Seeing in the struggle a fight for hard money, many workeys joined the Jacksonian Democrats. Jacksonians welcomed the workeys, pledged support for major workey proposals, and indeed helped carry through some of the reforms.

The alliance between workeys and Democratic politicians lasted only long enough for workeys to realize that the victory over the bank was a hollow one so far as ordinary people were concerned. Private banks now flourished, swollen by deposits from the federal government and issuing notes in such profusion as to set off a new wave of inflation. The outraged workeys and their allies then tried to bring the Democratic party in line with their hard-money principles—an attempt that brought them into conflict with party machines. The struggle was most bitter in New York City, where the reform element, dubbed derisively "loco-focos" by its enemies, lost a battle with Tammany Hall for control of the party.

The prospect of further independent political action was dimmed by the depression of 1837, which wiped out unions and turned the attention of many activists to utopian schemes. The depression, however, demonstrated a basic weakness of workeyism. It was a minority movement of labor, restricted to skilled men, usually native-born, articulate, and rebellious, but keeping themselves apart from the growing numbers of unskilled in the mines and factories. They were often hostile to blacks, immigrants, and women.

Besides, many of the workey proposals that enjoyed wide public support were carried out by the regular political parties. Imprisonment for debt and compulsory militia service were abolished. Mechanics' lien laws were passed. Labor unions won limited legality. The ten-hour day was established by law, although with many loopholes. Public school systems were set up, but for long they suffered from inadequate finances, underpaid teachers, short school years, and ramshackle facilities.

The workeys lost their battle to transform the Democratic party partly because most workers, especially foreign-born workers, identified themselves with the regular Democrats. Even after the successful demagogic Whig campaign of 1840, which put William Henry Harrison, the "log cabin candidate," in the White House, the poor perceived the Whigs as the party of the native-born, the rich, and the successful. The Democrats, however, were perceived as the defenders of the poor and unsuccessful. But Democratic power was maintained through more than rhetoric. The party machines delivered the goods that counted most to poor folk. They provided food and fuel for the needy without humiliating questions. They were a source of jobs. They protected those who ran afoul of the law. They defended the immigrants against nativist onslaughts. In addition, the alliance between the Democratic machines and the Catholic hierarchy added to the party's authority among Catholic immigrants.

WHITE WORKERS AND BLACK SLAVERY

The identity of the Democratic party with so many workers helps explain labor indifference—and sometimes hostility—to the antislavery movement. The Whigs, who were also proslavery, had little to say about the plight of the white poor, but southern Democrats, like John C. Calhoun and George Fitzhugh, denounced the cruel and heartless attitudes of northern employers toward their white workers. Indeed, when such men charged that northern white workers were worse off than black slaves, they said what countless white workers felt. In contrast to the condition of white workers, slaves were never unemployed. They never went hungry; they never lacked for housing, clothing, and medical care—so believed many workers. Ironically, they found in the spokesmen for black slavery the spokesmen for freedom of white workers.

The attitudes of many immigrant workers were conditioned by the attitude of the Catholic church. The church, at the time, adhered to a social philosophy that prized order and stability above all else. In the United States, this stand was intensified by the nativist outbreaks against Catholics, which made it necessary for the church to overcome its image as an instrument of alien subversion. In New York City, the church's interest in stability was pragmatic. The hierarchy was linked to Tammany Hall, which was allied with the merchants and bankers who thrived on southern trade. Thus, on grounds of principle and expediency, the church was conservative, which meant accepting slavery as a basic American institution. In 1841, when Daniel O'Connell, the great Irish patriot, called upon Irish-Americans to join the antislavery cause, Archbishop Hughes of New York denounced his action as interference in a purely American issue. Likewise, in Massachusetts the hierarchy aligned itself against abolition.

For the most part, white antislavery people did little to win labor support. With the exception of a few like Wendell Phillips, who became an outspoken advocate of both black and white workers, they were true middle-class believers in the free-enterprise system who were certain that white workers had only themselves to blame for their poverty. As for unions, most antislavery supporters agreed with William Lloyd Garrison that unions were "criminal" in that they inflamed the minds of workers "against the more opulent." In New England, the association of so many antislavery people with nativist causes served to antagonize the masses of Irish workers.

Another element in labor's cool response to abolitionism was the racist nature of American society as a whole. Working people, no less than others, absorbed racism unconsciously in infancy, and their feelings were reinforced by the society in which they matured. Immigrants, who had few racist stereotypes inherited from childhood, soon found that one major way in which to adapt to American society was to assume contempt for blacks. Racism did not necessarily mean acceptance of slavery, for many abolitionists believed in black inferiority while regarding slavery as immoral. But for many Americans, of all classes, slavery was the "natural" condition of blacks.

Moreover, many workers felt themselves threatened by abolition. Proslavery propaganda convinced them that abolition would loose a flood of black labor into the North. White wages would be driven down to the black level. White employers would play off whites and blacks against each other, resulting in even more dire poverty for whites. The prediction seemed borne out by what was already happening on docks, wharves, and other places that employed unskilled labor. Wages went down as black and immigrant workers competed for jobs. Strikes by white workers often collapsed when employers used black strikebreakers. Racial brawls and riots along the waterfronts helped to reinforce white racism. But racism was not confined to the unskilled. The unions of skilled workers routinely excluded blacks from membership and refused to work in the same shops with black employees.

Nevertheless, some labor spokesmen took a favorable attitude toward abolition. George Henry Evans, the apostle of land reform, insisted that chattel slavery was a minor issue compared to white wage slavery, but he also believed that once land was widely distributed among the mass of white workers, the plantation system would wither away and slavery would die out. One of his followers stated the land reform outlook bluntly: "Emancipate the white man first . . . and the day this is done we'll commence the manumission of the much wronged black man."

To others, the contrary was true: black slavery must be abolished before white labor could be freed. Elihu Burritt, the self-taught "learned blacksmith" who worked at his trade until he won a reputation as a pacifist and abolitionist, argued that slave labor set the base wage by which the wages of white labor were determined. Thus, white labor could not improve its lot until black labor was free. Such views had an impact at the 1846 convention of the New England Workingmen's Association. The convention voted that "slavery must be uprooted before the elevation sought by the laboring classes can be effected."

Such sentiment spread slowly, and then found political expression through the Republican party. The occasion was the repeal in 1854 of the Missouri Compromise, thus opening to slavery vast western lands previously reserved for free settlement. Aroused northerners, including former Democrats, Whigs, and Know-Nothings, joined in forming a new Republican party and made a direct appeal for the labor vote. Unless the trend to slavery was reversed, they said, the hope of white workers for free land in the West was doomed. If slavery were allowed to expand, white labor in the North would soon find itself competing with slave labor. They hammered home the theme, popularized by Senator William H. Seward, that there was an "irrepressible conflict" between a system of free labor and one of slave labor. By 1860 the Republicans had won a considerable minority of the workingmen's vote to their cause, including native-born, German, and Swedish. The Republican labor vote, concentrated in key states, helped elect Lincoln.

THE WORST LOSERS

The working poor, bad as their plight was, still fared better than people who had to depend on charity, were mentally ill, or ran afoul of the law. Many of the working poor survived, in one way or another, without having to ask for charity. But there were increasing numbers of people who could not survive without it. These were the destitute aged, the chronically ill, the victims of industrial accidents no longer able to work, and widows and deserted wives with small children. But there were also mounting numbers of able-bodied men who could find no work, and in times of depression their ranks swelled by the thousands.

Given the cult of success in America, the successful were bound to have a harsh opinion toward such people. As successful Americans saw it, the poor had only themselves to blame for their poverty, and they, therefore, should not be taught to live off the industry of others. They had to be helped, of course—that was one's Christian duty—but the help had to be minimal, and it should be directed toward making them sober, hard-working, frugal folk who would pull themselves up out of poverty.

State and local governments, dominated by such an outlook and interested in keeping taxes low, allotted funds for poor relief that were always inadequate—yet still brought charges from the well-to-do that they were pampering the poor. "Outdoor relief," aid given to "respectable" families in their homes, was scanty and given only after investigation. Single people and families deemed "unworthy" were herded into antiquated and overcrowded poorhouses, grim, cheerless places where inmates were subject to neglect, harsh discipline, and poor diet. To make matters worse, in some places poorhouses were operated by private contractors, who aimed to make a profit from their charges.

Since public care was so meager, it was supplemented by private philanthropy. Funds from the wealthy provided orphanages and hospitals. The hospitals were dreaded by the poor as way stations to the grave. Doctors liked the hospitals because they could carry out medical experiments on the poor that they dared not try on private patients. Private philanthropy, however, did not arise simply from a sense of religious duty. The well-to-do were daily vexed by vagrants and beggars, who were as common on the streets as the hogs and sometimes much more dangerous. Societies to relieve the poor—and keep them off the streets—sprang up in every city. In New York City alone there were nearly forty such societies in 1843. The aid the poor received was scanty, and it was granted only after inquisitions and preachments that did little to maintain self-respect among the recipients.

Even more wretched was the plight of men and women confined in jails and prisons, many of them guilty of no worse offense than inability to pay their debts. Since public opinion had turned against the earlier punishments of flogging, ear cropping, and branding, long confinement was the penal fashion. But public funds were not forthcoming for new prisons at the very time when population growth increased the number of offenders. In consequence, existing jails and prisons were overcrowded, filthy, and vermin-ridden. No attempt was made to classify or separate prisoners. Young and old, men and women, first offenders and long-time criminals were herded together at night—a situation made to order for the sexual victimization of women.

Repeated protests by prison-reform societies against such conditions eventually led to change. New prisons were built. Institutions were established for juvenile offenders. Men and women prisoners were separated. Emphasis was placed on rehabilitation rather than on mere punishment. A new "penitentiary" system evolved, designed to foster repentance among prisoners and convert them into Christian, law-abiding citizens.

Two means to accomplish these ends emerged. One, initiated at Auburn Prison in New York in 1824, provided for renting out prisoners during the day, thus saving the taxpayers money, and locking them up in tiny individual cells during the night under a rule of absolute silence. Those who were not rented out did prison labor and were forbidden to communicate with each other. Many states found the money-saving features of the system so attractive that they copied it.

The other model was exemplified in the Eastern State Penitentiary of Pennsylvania in Philadelphia, opened in 1829. It provided for solitary labor, constant solitary confinement, and absolute silence. As one inmate reported, such treatment produced "the most frightful torture one can imagine." Protests finally led to some relaxation of the rules against human contact.

Although some steps were taken to house the mentally ill in special hospitals called "asylums," most were confined to jails and poorhouses. Various prison-reform societies called for change, but little was done until Dorothea Dix, a frail Yankee schoolteacher with a stern Puritan conscience, undertook a crusade for the mentally ill in Massachusetts. After an exhaustive investigation, she submitted a report to the state legislature in 1843.

She told of men and women confined for years in small cages, covered with their own filth. Others she found in dark, damp cellars that lacked heat and light and were never cleaned. Often the inmates were in chains. Most were clad in rags and suffered from malnutrition. At one place a young woman had been locked up naked in a pen in a barn. "There," reported Dix, "without bed and without fire she was left—but not alone. Profligate men and idle boys had access to the den, whenever curiosity or vulgarity prompted." The exhibition ended only after repeated protests by other inmates led by "an insane man." Dix also cited the example of a mentally ill young woman who had just given birth to a child. "Who was the father, none could or would declare," she noted.

The horrified public reaction to Dix's disclosures brought about an intensive program of hospitalization for the mentally ill in the state. She carried her crusade into other states with marked success. She even persuaded Congress to provide land grants for programs to help not only the mentally ill but also other handicapped people. This promising beginning of a federal public health program was, however, vetoed by President Franklin Pierce. And, despite the successes of Dix's crusade, many of the mentally ill continued to suffer in jails and workhouses.

Public opinion might respond positively to the mentally ill, but it had little sympathy with another outcast group—the prostitutes. They were present in every town and city. They ranged all the way from half-starved streetwalkers to the pampered inmates of the luxurious bordellos that catered to wealthy males. The ranks of prostitution were filled by unwed mothers cast off by their families, servants seduced by masters or masters' sons, widows and deserted wives left with small children, working girls who sought something better than the grim life of the factory and the slum, and jobless young women driven to prostitution to survive. Procurers also preyed upon young, unattached immigrant women.

Prostitution was tolerated. Blandly ignoring that brothels drew their customers from all classes, upper-class males and public officials agreed that prostitution was a necessary evil to protect the chastity of "good women" from the lusts of lower-class males. Since the poor obviously lacked the moral restraint that presumably characterized the upper classes, prostitution offered a safe outlet for their incontinence. The irregular sexual behavior of sailors, teamsters, and factory workers was thus understandable, even if it was not approved.

What was neither understandable nor forgivable was that some women were so depraved as to cater to the basest passions of men for money. By the same inversion of logic that made poverty the fault of the poor, prostitution was blamed on the prostitutes, who were by definition women of no morals. Public opinion was so hostile that prostitutes were placed not only beyond the pale of decency but also outside humanity. They were dehumanized. They were not people, but "whores."

Some shift in the attitude toward prostitutes became apparent in the 1830s. The tide of religiously inspired reform, which gave rise to such movements as abolitionism and crusades on behalf of the handicapped and mentally ill, also influenced attitudes toward prostitutes. The reformers, who came from comfortable middle-class backgrounds, agreed that prostitutes were depraved, but they denied that the women were beyond redemption. To save the prostitutes, wealthy folk endowed Magdalen Societies in many cities. These provided "houses of industry," where by a combination of moral preachment, vocational training, and Christian environment, prostitutes were to be transformed into pious Christians and industrious workers.

Even so limited an approach met with distrust among many respectable citizens. Decent folk, they said, should not get involved with such matters. Patrons of the brothels were leery of activities that might expose them. And there was a whole business community that looked upon the reformers with jaundiced eyes. Prostitution was, after all, a profitable business. The labor of the women supported a host of pimps, procurers, and madames, who managed the brothels. Beyond them were the merchants who supplied them, the owners of the brothels, and the respectable businessmen who owned the valuable real estate of the vice districts. For obvious reasons such elements objected to any crusade against prostitution.

Magdalen Societies operated circumspectly so as to offend as few respectable people as possible. Their success was minimal, thanks mainly to their narrow moralistic approach to a complex social problem. The New York City society, however, dramatized some of the issues and hazards involved. In 1832 its agent, a zealous reformer, reported in detail the extent of prostitution in the city and revealed that men from the best families frequented the brothels. This revelation brought the society so much heat that it disbanded.

A more challenging approach to the issue was made, significantly, by the women who organized Female Moral Reform Societies, pioneered in New York City in 1834. The founders also believed in "redeeming fallen women," but they denounced the double moral standard that excused men while condemning the women. Indeed, said the New York society daringly, the man was the more guilty. Their campaigns, then, were directed not only at prostitutes but also at their patrons and at the brothel owners.

Realizing that such policies were inadequate to meet the problems of the double standard, the societies turned to education, attempting to persuade mothers to train young boys so that they would grow up to be "morally pure" adults. They also engaged in politics, pressuring politicians to make seduction a criminal offense. Such a law passed in New York in 1848. Eventually even these approaches were seen to be insufficient. As the societies realized that economic distress was the single largest reason why women became prostitutes, they campaigned for economic reforms.

The societies were of great value in bringing together large numbers of isolated middle-class women and providing them with a sense of identity as women in a male dominated society. Unfortunately, their well-meaning efforts did little to alleviate the lot of the prostitute.

FOR FURTHER READING

Developments in organized labor are told in John R. Commons and others, *History of Labor in the United States,* Vol. 1 (1918); Norman Ware, *The Industrial Worker* (1924); and Philip S. Foner, *History of the Labor Movement in the United States,* Vol. 1 (1947). More detailed studies are W. A. Sullivan, *The Industrial Worker in Pennsylvania* (1955), and Lloyd Ulman, *The Rise of the National Trade Union* (1955).

On labor and land reform see Helen S. Zahler, *Eastern Workingmen and National Land Policy* (1941).

Differing views of the relations between Jacksonian Democracy and workers may be found in Arthur M. Schlesinger, Jr., *The Age of Jackson* (1945); Walter Hugins, *Jacksonian Democracy and the Working Class* (1960); and Edward Pessen, *Jacksonian America* (1969).

14 southern white society

In many ways, white southern society resembled northern society. Both shared a common Anglo-Saxon cultural heritage and the American national inheritance. Both were predominantly Protestant in religion, and both were marked by the intense emotions stirred by the religious revivals of the early nineteenth century. Both were expansive geographically and dynamic economically. Both believed in free enterprise and the gospel of success, and both shared the anxieties that arose from an unstable economic system. Both societies had their rich and poor, and both were dominated by elites. Both experienced the democratic revolution, which opened up the suffrage and public office to white men hitherto denied participation in political life.

Yet, despite similarities, the South was not the North, and it became less like it as the nineteenth century went on. The differences fostered a sense of alienation that eventually led to the attempt at separation.

THE SOUTHERN ECONOMY

The South, for example, remained agrarian while the North became industrialized. This does not mean that the South was static. On the contrary, the southern economy, ranging from the Atlantic seaboard to the western reaches of Texas, expanded and prospered. Cotton production alone jumped from 73,000 bales in 1800 to a record 4.5 million bales in 1859. Less dramatic but significant increases occurred in the output of other cash crops, such as tobacco, rice, sugar, and hemp. The southern economy was invigorated by the introduction of the steamboat on the Mississippi River in 1812 and by the later development of a railroad network of 9,000 miles of track. There were attempts at industrialization in cotton, tobacco, and iron manufacturing, although in 1860 the South still accounted for less than 10 percent by value of the goods manufactured in the United States. Most white southerners lived in the countryside, but urban growth was marked. While the population of some cities, like

Charleston, South Carolina, remained static, Atlanta, Memphis, New Orleans, and Mobile grew phenomenally in the 1850s.

The southern economy was not just agrarian; it was also colonial. That is, it provided raw materials for the industries of New and Old England. Southern export of such raw materials, principally cotton and tobacco, also helped pay for industrialization of the North. Industrialization required large foreign investment and mounting imports of manufactured goods, largely from England. The cost of such foreign aid was beyond the North's ability to pay. Southern cotton helped redress the balance. In 1860 cotton alone accounted for more than half of all the exports of the United States.

The colonial role had a series of important consequences for the South. First, the South was not master of its own destiny. It was locked into a subordinate position in the industrial capitalism of the day, supplying raw materials at the prices the industrialists were willing to pay. The economic fate of the South was decided, not in Charleston or New Orleans, but on the Liverpool Cotton Exchange, where merchants, brokers, manufacturers, and speculators set the price of cotton in view of world conditions and their own self-interest. On a day-to-day basis prices might not vary widely, but in terms of years, prices fluctuated violently. In 1801 cotton sold for 44¢ a pound; ten years later it sold for less than 9¢ a pound. In 1836, it fetched 16½¢ a pound on the market. In 1845, when the effects of the Panic of 1837 were still strong, cotton sold for less than the cost of production—below 6¢ a pound.

Second, since the South lacked adequate industry of its own, it depended on foreign imports and American products for its manufactured goods. Manufacturers set their prices to bring themselves a good profit, and the prices rose as the goods flowed through middlemen to the ultimate consumer. Prices were also raised artificially through tariffs designed to protect American industry by reducing foreign imports, although after 1833 the taxes on imports tended to decline. In short, as both producers and consumers, white southerners were victims of a market over which they had little control.

Third, cotton planters, like farmers everywhere, depended on credit to carry them from crop to crop. The South, with its capital largely tied up in land and slaves and with an inadequate banking system, was in no position to provide such credit. It relied on the services of "factors," agents of British and Yankee mercantile houses who financed the marketing of crops and provided funds for the purchase of goods needed by planters. In this strategic economic position, the factors and their principals did well. For marketing crops, they charged a 2.5 percent commision. For providing goods, they charged commissions ranging as high as 10 percent. In addition, they levied interest on the credit extended. Further, such necessary services as transportation, warehousing, and insurance were largely in the hands of Britons and Yankees. Together, the charges for the various services constituted a significant drain on the southern economy, which southerners bitterly resented.

Southern economic subordination was accentuated by three other factors. Since planters had no means of orderly marketing, they all sold their cotton at the same time. The consequent glut drove prices down. Thus, even in good times, planters were never able to take full advantage of favorable markets. Second, since planters were chronically in debt, they were vulnerable to pressure from creditors to concentrate on cash crops and neglect foodstuffs. Thus, the South had to import from the North great quantities of pork, corn, and flour. Third, the system of slavery made for rigidity in the planter economy, despite fluctuations in cotton prices. When times were bad, northern manufacturers cut costs by laying off workers. Planters had no such alternative. Since slaves represented a capital investment as well as labor power, they had to be maintained in bad times as well as good. Thus, masters went in debt to keep their slaves.

Nevertheless, despite the drawbacks of living in an agrarian, colonial economy, thousands of planters prospered.

THE "NABOBS"

The social structure of the South reflected its economic order, and its functioning reflected the self-image of the planting elites. At the very top of southern society were the "nabobs," great planters who owned one hundred or more slaves and vast plantations. There were nearly 2,300 great planters in 1860. Close to them in status were 44,000 "medium" planters who owned between twenty and one hundred slaves. The two groups, together with members of their families, numbered about 200,000 people. They represented only a tiny proportion of the total southern white population of 7 million. Nevertheless, they received more than half the total annual income of the South and dominated its society.

The southern elites came from three major sources. One was the old eastern-seaboard planting aristocracy, symbolized by Thomas Jefferson and his fellow Virginians, with its traditions of gracious living, tolerance, and an interest in ideas. By the 1830s the economic standing of this traditional aristocracy was slipping, and its intellectual authority had lessened.

Another elite group came from those eastern-seaboard planting families who, faced with exhausted lands at home, went west after the War of 1812 to take advantage of the rich lands, now open for white American occupation after the subjection of Indian peoples. The planters reproduced the life styles they had known in Virginia and South Carolina, and their children grew up in this transplanted culture. Such a man was John Hampden Randolph, son of a migrant Virginia planter, who accumulated a fortune as a sugar planter and was a distinguished member of the Louisiana elite.

Still another group, concentrated in the fertile "black belt" of Alabama and Mississippi and in the lower Mississippi Valley, was made up of the newly rich. These were people originally of modest means and little family distinction. Shrewd men of business, they acquired wealth by speculation during the opening of the "virgin lands" and by gaining land and slaves. Among the more notable were Joseph E. Davis of Mississippi, brother of the more famous Jefferson Davis and eventually a millionaire; and Judah P. Benjamin, a lawyer of New Orleans and later a distinguished confederate official, who acquired a fortune in sugar and was a respected member of the Louisiana elite, even though he was a Jew.

The elites also welcomed into their ranks young men of little wealth but of great talent. These were potential leaders of the great mass of whites who owned no slaves, resented planter domination, and had won the vote. Planters won over such promising young men by many means, including marriage into their families. In this way Joseph E. Brown of Georgia and Albert Gallatin Brown of Mississippi became spokesmen for the aristocracy.

The southern elites, then, were no more closed castes than were those of the North, but entry into their ranks became more difficult after the depression of 1837. Prior to that time thousands of men of small means thought they were becoming rich by acquiring the newly opened lands of the "black belt" and by engaging in the speculation that went with it. The full effects of the depression did not hit the South until 1839, but when it came, the blow was hard. Cotton prices fell precipitously, finally dropping below the cost of production. Men who deemed themselves wealthy were wiped out, their lands and slaves sold at bargain prices to others who had the necessary credit. Thus, the wealthy added to their holdings and would-be members of the elites sank back into obscurity.

Wealth was concentrated in the hands of a few by more than the business cycle, however. Men of wealth enjoyed the advantage of getting credit more easily and at lower interest rates than their less fortunate neighbors. Only the wealthy had the resources and education necessary to apply the new agricultural methods urged by such farm reformers as Edmund Ruffin of Virginia. The new techniques at once conserved the soil and made the land more productive, giving the great planters yet another advantage over others. Further, only the wealthy could afford to maintain levees along the river banks, which gave them a monopoly of rich bottom lands. The great planters also made the most efficient use of slave labor and of management expertise. That is, they benefited from what economists call "economy of scale"—simply, their size reduced costs.

In some agricultural fields there was no room for planters of even moderate means. Rice and sugar required such great capital investment that only the wealthy could plant these crops, but the profits they made were high. It is symbolic that when the rice planter Nathaniel Heyward of South Carolina died in 1851, he owned more than 2,000 slaves—supposedly making him the largest slaveholder in the South. The sugar nabob John Burnside of Louisiana owned more than 1,000 slaves.

Another element tended to narrow entry into the elites. As their wealth increased, the financial threshold for admission into their ranks rose. An amount of wealth that would have admitted a man in 1830 was quite inadequate in 1850. And, of course, as in the North, elite families sought to protect their property by promoting marriage between persons of their own social rank.

THE PLANTER SELF-IMAGE

Southern and northern elites had much in common. Indeed, their value systems were so similar that intermarriage between the two elites was not unusual. Nevertheless, there was a basic difference. Northern elites looked upon the acquisition of wealth as a noble end in itself. Southern elites looked upon this as mere "money grubbing." Certainly, wealth should be acquired, but only as a means to live as "gentlemen," on the pattern of the English landed aristocracy. Thus, the emphasis on land and slaves as status symbols, the lavish hospitality for which the great planters were famous, the maintenance of town houses to which they retired from the countryside in the summers, and the touchy sense of personal honor and its expression in dueling. In short, southern elites thought of themselves, not as businessmen involved in a worldwide market, but as landed aristocrats who disdained the sordid business of making money.

This romantic self-image had significant consequences for the South. Profits that might have been invested in railroads and factories went instead into land and slaves. The attempts of William Gregg and others to establish industry in the South were met with indifference or hostility by planters who saw in the emergence of an industrial capitalist class a threat to their power and way of life. Since "gentlemen" disdained business pursuits, they educated their sons to be planters, lawyers, doctors, and army officers. Thus, the South lacked the managers, bankers, engineers, scientists, and businessmen to carry on its own economy.

And, like their English models, southern "gentlemen" had little real concern with the arts and literature. In addition, they were wary of encouraging intellectual currents that might threaten slavery. Cultural life in the South languished, lacking the patronage of the arts that was a common activity among the northern elites. Since southern publishers were few, southern writers had to place their work with northern publishers, and they wrote largely for a public outside the South. William Gilmore Simms, the outstanding southern novelist of the pre-Civil War era, found few readers in his own section. His literary income came from the North and England.

There was still another reason for the weakness of southern cultural life: it lacked invigoration from below. The potential talents of the common people found little room to develop. Planter hostility helped hold back the emergence of free public school systems. Many of the poorer whites believed that education was for the "better folk," not for "the likes of them." Now and then, determined young men like Simms and Edgar Allan Poe broke through the bonds, but other potential talents died aborning for lack of education.

Again, like the English aristocracy, the southern gentry believed they were born to rule. And rule they did. Until the 1850s, southern elites were politically divided into Whigs and Democrats. They differed among themselves on such national policies as tariffs, with sugar planters seeking tariff protection and cotton planters opposing them. They also divided on state and local issues. Yet, however much they disputed between themselves, they had more in common with each other than they had with the commoners, whom they distrusted. Thus, no matter which party was in power, the interests of the elites were protected. When the national Whig party split in the 1850s, southern Whigs simply moved over into the Democratic party, distasteful though the move was.

The threat to planter rule that seemed implicit in the democratic revolution never developed—and indeed the tide of reform barely touched the established political structures of Virginia and South Carolina. Elsewhere in the South, elites continued to win and hold high public office, as the careers of Whig Robert Toombs in Georgia and Democrat Jefferson Davis in Mississippi attest. The habit of popular deference to "the folks in the big house" was too strong to be easily shaken. Besides, elites relied on professional politicians, who used the subtle arts of political brokerage and manipulation to win popular support for planter leadership.

Many such politicians had emerged as spokesmen for the commoners, and they used that reputation to bargain their way upward. For their part, the elites were able to win over such men with social acceptance, financial aid in times of distress, and marriage into the aristocracy. In the meantime, the commoners were placated through reforms such as abolition of imprisonment for debt and protection of homesteads against seizure for debt, which did nothing to weaken planter rule.

THE MYSTIQUE OF RACE

Above all, planters ruled because they invoked the spirit of the white community against the blacks all around. Anglo-Saxon blood was a prized possession that bound whites together in a common tie transcending class divisions. Commoners, however radical, were reluctant to cause any breach that might endanger white supremacy. The political struggles consequent to the democratic revolution were thus limited by race. Slavery, the one sure means of keeping blacks in their proper place, was immune to attack. Slavery was also the base of planter power. With slavery placed safely beyond challenge, planter rule was secure.

Planter power was so firm, indeed, that the southern defense of slavery that emerged after 1830 was also in part a rationale for elite rule over the white masses. The rationale broke with the traditional principles of the old seaboard aristocracy, rooted in the natural-rights philosophy of the Enlightenment, whose visions of freedom and equality were expressed in the Declaration of Independence.

John C. Calhoun, the leading theoretician of the planter class, denied that "all men are born free and equal." On the contrary, men were unequal in character, talents, and condition. Such inequality was a boon to society, for it spurred individuals to improve themselves and thus contributed to the betterment of society. Society rewarded individuals in proportion to their contributions, and those who contributed the most naturally gained the right to rule.

Thomas R. Dew, professor at William and Mary College, explained that great property-owners had always been and always would be "the virtual rulers of mankind." He went on to say that both nature and God intended that individuals of "superior faculties and knowledge, and therefore of superior power, should control and dispose of those who are inferior. It is as much in the order of nature that men should enslave each other as that other animals should prey upon each other."

George Fitzhugh, the Virginia lawyer whose *Sociology for the South* became a classic defense of slavery, based his case on the assumption that "slavery is the natural and normal condition of the laboring man, whether white or black."

THE PRO-SLAVERY ARGUMENTS

Other arguments justified black slavery more directly. Preachers, who perhaps more than any other class helped mold opinion among the masses, quoted appropriate Biblical passages to demonstrate that slavery enjoyed divine sanction. "Scientists," such as Josiah C. Nott and George R. Gliddon, "proved" that blacks were of a separate origin from whites and were marked by inferiority. This view was shared by Louis Agassiz, the famous geologist who taught at Harvard. These writers argued that although blacks had lived undisturbed for thousands of years in Africa, they had never developed a civilization—a misreading of history that lived on long after the idea of separate origins had been discredited. The reason, it was said, why blacks could not develop a civilization was that they were incapable of intellectual development.

Slavery, so ran the argument, was a boon to such small-minded creatures. It provided the kind of work suitable to their natural characters, gave them guidance in the ways of civilization and Christianity, and brought them to a high point "never before attained by the black race in any age or country." So, argued Calhoun, slavery was a "positive good" for both races, benefitting each and providing "the most safe and stable basis for free institutions in the world."

Senator James H. Hammond of South Carolina also thought that slavery was the basis for a truly great civilization. Slaves, he said, were "happy, content, unaspiring, the mudsills of society," whose labor made possible that class of whites "which leads progress, civilization, and refinement." This structure would create in the South a new and great culture, akin to that of the Golden Age of Periclean Athens, which was also based on slavery.

Other lines of argument for slavery appealed to self-interest and white fears. Dew and Jefferson Davis declared that only through slave labor could the South develop economically. Calhoun asserted that slavery was the only basis on which the races could live together harmoniously. Abolition would mean race war and black domination of whites; blacks "and their Northern allies would be the masters, and we the slaves," said Calhoun.

Some planter spokesmen made direct appeals to the poorer whites. J. D. B. DeBow, editor of the influential *DeBow's Review,* asserted that wages and living conditions in the South were better than in the North and that southern workers were saved from the blight of factory work. Poor men in the South, protected from the competition of cheap immigrant labor, could accumulate wealth and look forward to becoming slaveholders. Most important of all, the poor man in the South "preserves the status of a white man. . . . The poor white laborer at the North is at the bottom of the social ladder, whilst his brother here has ascended several steps and can look down upon those beneath him, at an infinite remove."

Planters were not content simply to defend slavery. They sharply criticized "free" industrial society as a hypocritical order that enslaved white workers. The most significant spokesman of the view was George Fitzhugh, who contrasted the miserable conditions of white workers in Europe and the North with the happy servitude of blacks in the South. Free society was doomed, he said, because white workers, resenting exploitation, would eventually revolt, and society would collapse. From the chaos would arise a new order in which slavery either would be entirely destroyed or reinstituted everywhere. Fitzhugh had little doubt about the outcome.

REPRESSION AND REACTION

However persuasive such arguments may have been, planters felt they were insufficient in themselves to protect planter interests. Partly in response to hostile criticism outside the South and partly in response to the Nat Turner insurrection in 1831, southern elites moved to suppress any ideas that might conceivably endanger the "peculiar institution." Men and women who had doubts about it, or who opposed it, were silenced or driven out of the South. Among the most notable of those who left the South were Sarah and Angelina Grimké and James G. Birney, a successful lawyer in Alabama. All became active in abolitionist movements in the North.

But even silencing antislavery sentiment was not enough. Especially after 1830, elites also felt threatened by the spirit of free inquiry that accompanied the rapid spread of science in the nineteenth century. The spirit was not confined to science. It showed itself in religion, history, economics, and political science. But while their predecessors at the turn of the century had welcomed new ideas, the elites of the prewar generation were hostile, afraid of how these notions would affect slavery and the traditional southern life-style.

The southerners looked at the North, where such new ideas were making inroads, and they did not like what they saw: women claiming "rights," men advocating socialism, workers going on strike and defying their masters, preachers in influential pulpits denying the existence of the Holy Trinity and saying that the Holy Bible was to be understood symbolically, not literally. To white southerners generally, these all evidenced decay and disintegration, a potent example of the corrosive influence of the new ideas.

In their campaign to suppress new ideas planters found powerful allies among the Protestant clergy, especially among Presbyterians, Methodists, and Baptists. Indeed, the southern wings of these churches broke away from the national bodies and set up sectional organizations of their own. Elites also gained support from recently organized religious groups that appealed to poorer whites, such as the Christian Church of Alexander Campbell. The clergy quarreled among themselves on doctrinal points, but they were as one in defending slavery and in hostility to free inquiry. And they exercised vast power over the masses of southern whites.

Thus, there emerged in the South a rigid religious orthodoxy, based on accepting the King James Bible as the literal word of God. Dissident clergymen were silenced or forced to leave the South. Aristocrats who were religiously unorthodox felt it prudent to keep quiet. Unitarian churches, bastions of freedom of thought, went out of existence. Doctor Horace Holley, a religious liberal, was driven from the presidency of Transylvania University in Kentucky. A similar fate overtook Doctor Thomas Cooper, free-thinking president of South Carolina College, the state university. He was succeeded by a rigidly orthodox Presbyterian divine. Thomas Jefferson's vision of a University of Virginia free from sectarian influence faded as students and faculty voted to institute religious exercises.

The sciences continued to be taught, but few scientists challenged the prevailing orthodoxy on slavery or religion. Indeed, Reuben Fontaine Maury, the distinguished pioneer in oceanography, vigorously upheld the validity of the Bible in the sciences. Noting that critics said the Bible was "no authority in matters of science," Maury retorted, "The Bible is authority for everything it touches."

Thus, under the leadership of its master class, the South tried to insulate itself from the fresh intellectual currents flowing in the nineteenth century.

THE OTHERS

In terms of prestige the class closest to the aristocracy was that of the professionals: doctors, lawyers, well-to-do clergymen, and college professors. The formal education required of such persons marked them off as people of substance. Some were born into the aristocracy. Some came from professional families, others from the ranks of small planters and farmers. If they were not of the elite originally, they hoped to enter it by marriage, wealth, or distinction in their fields. Their services were essential, they were suitably rewarded, and they identified their interests with those of the master class.

Much less well regarded by the elites were the businessmen. These were the merchants, bankers, factory owners, mine operators, commission agents, slave traders, and all the others who kept the southern economy functioning. Their services were necessary, but they bore the stigma of being in business for money. Besides, the great planters had a profound distrust of a class that, if allowed to grow, might one day challenge their rule. They kept their social distance from such people. In fact, businessmen had no notions of challenge. They wanted nothing more than to move into the ranks of the aristocracy. They aped the living style of the elites and trained their sons and daughters to be gentlemen and ladies. Whenever possible they branched out from commerce into plantations and slaves, edging their way upward.

Some businessmen, of course, with an eye on their Yankee counterparts, saw fabulous profits to be made in industrializing the South, a process they thought would eventually diversify and strengthen the entire southern economy. But they lacked both the capital and the power of northern businessmen, and they too were enmeshed in slavery. Many industrial and mining operations used slave labor, and businessmen, like other whites, looked on slavery as the only viable system of race relations. Thus they offered no real challenge to planter rule. Both professional people and businessmen were too involved in the system to foster the growth of an independent middle class.

Much lower on the social scale were the millions who made up the great mass of the southern white people. For the most part they were country dwellers, ranging from farmers and small planters who owned a few slaves and were relatively well off to yeoman farmers and mountaineers who eked out a poverty-stricken existence on poor land. They were intensely proud that they owned their own land and were their own masters. Equally proud and independent were the artisans and mechanics of the towns—blacksmiths, coopers, carpenters, and other skilled tradesmen.

These people held ambivalent attitudes toward the elites. On the one hand, common folk looked on the "folks in the great house" with awe, respect, and envy. On the other, they resented planter control and were bitter that the plantations engrossed more and more of the good land. Many of them detested slavery, because it both degraded white labor and meant an unwelcome black presence in their midst, but at the same time they could conceive of no other way to keep blacks in "their place."

The common folk had their grievances. While many held to the traditional position that education was properly reserved for their "betters," increasing numbers of poorer whites resented the absence of public schools, which would give their children a better chance in life. They felt also that in times of economic depression, the law was interpreted in favor of the rich against the poor, with hard-working families losing land and goods to satisfy the demands of wealthy creditors. Since social services were few, care for the chronically ill, the mentally sick, and the aged poor fell upon their families, many of whom were already barely able to make a living. The lack of social services meant low taxes, but common folk noticed that the tax structure favored the wealthy. Skilled workers bitterly objected to competition from slave labor, which kept white wages low.

Thanks to their numbers, the masses of southern whites potentially had the ability to change conditions after men won the right to vote. That potential, though, was not realized. To be sure, some reforms were initiated. Steps were taken toward free public schools, notably in Kentucky and North Carolina, but they were financed inadequately. Penitentiaries were established, but their inmates were leased out to work for private contractors, giving businessmen a supply of cheap, servile labor against which free workers had to compete for jobs. Some states assumed responsibility for care of the mentally ill and the handicapped, but the facilities opened were few. As in the North, the care of most such folk continued to rest with their families.

There were many reasons why votes in the hands of yeomen failed to threaten planter rule. Come election time, aristocrats and politicians unbent with the common folk, showing a proper deference to the voters, providing a sympathetic ear to complaints, promising to redress grievances, and pledging favors in the future for men who might prove useful. The liquor flowed freely, and good fellowship was cemented by appeals to the racial mystique that bound white southerners together, regardless of class, religion, or other divisions.

The racial mystique blocked any concerted move by commoners to weaken slavery, the aristocracy's power base. There was a growing antislavery sentiment among small farmers and working people, symbolized by Hinton R. Helper, but it was too weak to shape the course of events. Helper in 1857 published *The Impending Crisis of the South,* a book that attributed the economic backwardness of the South to slavery. Black Slavery, he said, degraded white labor and so condemned the mass of whites to poverty and ignorance. He urged these whites to work for "the complete annihilation of slavery." Planter response was so hostile that Helper fled to the North. Helper, like the people he spoke for, was no friend of blacks. He wanted blacks removed from the South so that white commoners could shape society in their own interest.

Abolition of slavery, however, meant black freedom—and black freedom was unthinkable to most white southerners. They viewed slavery, however objectionable, as the only means through which blacks could be kept "in their place." Like the planters, most common whites felt that the South must be "a white man's country." This belief frustrated accomplishment of a real democratic revolution in the South.

Among the victims of such frustration were the skilled workers of the South. They suffered in many ways. The plantation tradition of master and servant carried over into business, with the result that any attempt by workers to challenge employers was regarded as a menace to the southern way of life. The association of manual labor with slavery also degraded white labor. Maria J. McIntosh, a southern woman who wrote a defense of slavery in 1859, noted this contempt for labor as a defect in her society. Merchants and mechanics, she said, "however intelligent and even polite,'' are ''completely shut out from the pale of good society.'' At the basic level of livelihood, white mechanics competed with skilled slave workers. The low wages paid the slaves in effect set the wages paid free whites.

White labor responses to slave competition varied. Sometimes they drove out black workers, free or slave, by violence or by simply refusing to work with them. Through political pressure they obtained legislation excluding blacks from many crafts. Such laws were enforced only sporadically, thanks to the influence of planters who found it profitable to rent out skilled slaves.

More important in reducing the numbers of slave craftsmen in some cities was the growing body of white opinion that sympathized with the white workers. This opinion saw in the presence of slave workers in the towns, free from direct rule of the master and behaving as if they were free people, a menace to slavery itself. Such opinion also saw in white competition with blacks a breach of the bond of white brotherhood that was daily becoming more important to the South. Thus, in some places, slave competition with white labor diminished—but it was far from ending.

White artisans who tried to form unions met an even more hostile reception than they did in the North. With no tradition of labor organization, the South was dominated by the master-servant tradition. Still another tradition, strong among both planters and yeomen, who prided themselves on their independence, was individualism. It provided soil for the gospel of success, which was as prevalent in the South as in the North. If a craftsman remained a wage earner instead of becoming a master, it was his own fault. Servants should not try to compel masters, through collective action, to pay more wages than masters thought suitable. If workers did, the courts were at hand to correct them.

There was an even more tangible factor for union-minded workers to contend with. If they went on strike, they were replaced by slaves. The most dramatic instance took place in Richmond, Virginia, in 1847. When white workers went on strike at the big Tredegar Iron Works over the introduction of slave labor, they were all dismissed and their places taken by slaves—except for a few whites retained to teach slaves their jobs. Under such circumstances, it is not surprising that labor unionism, except for a few units of the printers' union, took little root in the South.

"POOR WHITE TRASH"

At the very bottom of the white social scale were the folks contemptuously called ''poor white trash.'' Owning no land of their own, they made up as much as 20 percent of the white population. Some were tenants who eked out a wretched existence on poor land rented by planters. Some were laborers who worked for farmers and planters. Their wages were low, for they competed directly with slaves. Laborers were also employed on docks, railroad construction, and projects in malaria-infested districts where planters refused to rent out slaves for such dangerous work. Contractors favored Irish immigrants on these projects. The poverty-stricken Irish worked for low pay. If they fell ill or died, no compensation had to be paid, as would have been the case had the laborers been slaves.

Most poor whites, however, were a people unto themselves, with their own subculture and a way of life that offended the rest of white society. They squatted on land, often public land, no one else wanted: pine barrens, swampy wastes, remote mountain areas. For the most part the men hunted, fished, and raised a few hogs and cattle that were as poorly fed as their owners. The sparse crops of cotton, corn, and sweet potatoes were usually raised by girls and women. The diet of poor whites was so lacking in proteins and other essentials as to make endemic among them such diet-deficiency diseases as rickets and pellagra. Malaria also took a toll among those who lived in regions where the malaria mosquito was active. Inhabitants of the pine barrens and other areas of sandy soil were also plagued with hookworm, a parasite that entered barefoot infants and thereafter drained their hosts of energy and contributed to a short life span.

Other whites, looking on the gaunt, listless poor whites and their squalid farms, called them lazy and shiftless. And, noting the prevailing alcoholism among the "peckerwoods," upper-class whites attributed their poverty to drink. They failed to note that alcohol was a way of escape for people trying to survive in the midst of grinding poverty, debilitating disease, early death, and the pervasive contempt with which they were treated by the rest of white society. What was even more galling to the intensely racist poor whites was that the slaves looked upon them with the same contempt their masters did. Outcasts of white society, the poor whites preserved their self-respect by separating themselves as much as possible from other whites. They married among themselves, often into closely related families, a practice that added to their difficulties by transmitting genetic disorders. Their churches, fervently emotional, sounded the theme of personal redemption in the hereafter and thus provided release from the frustrations of the here and now. Knowing there was little hope of breaking out of their condition, they rejected the gospel of success and enjoyed life from day to day as best they could. This attitude, so strange in American society, perplexed and vexed both southern and northern white Americans.

Nevertheless, planter society had its uses for poor whites. Given their hatred of blacks, they and their scroungy hounds were invaluable in helping track down fugitive slaves. Some made a little money as professional floggers for local authorities. More added to their meager incomes by serving as substitutes for more prosperous whites on the night patrols required to keep blacks off the roads after dark. In such contacts the poor white could take a measure of pride. He might be poor and degraded, but he was still a member of the white brotherhood, immeasurably superior to all black folk.

A LAST LOOK

The white South, then, developed its own distinctive social order and a body of belief to hold that social order together. Despite the democratic revolution, planter rule remained undisturbed. Challenges were turned back by the racial mystique that bound all whites together in the determination to keep the South "a white man's country." Mounting criticism of the South from without contributed to a growing feeling of alienation from the rest of the country, expressed in an intense sectional self-consciousness that culminated in a southern nationalism. Not all whites were ready to take the drastic next step of separation, but they were swept aside by those who saw in independence, even at the cost of war, the solution to the South's difficulties.

FOR FURTHER READING

Readers will benefit from Clement Eaton, *A History of the Old South* (1975). His *Freedom of Thought Struggle in the Old South* (1964) describes the attempts of the slaveholders to make the South a closed society. For an incisive analysis of white thought see W. J. Cash, *The Mind of the South* (1941).

More detailed treatment of the South is in T. P. Abernethy, *The South in the New Nation* (1961); C. S. Sydnor, *The Development of Southern Sectionalism* (1948); and Avery O. Craven, *The Growth of Southern Nationalism* (1953).

Recent analyses of southern society will be found in Eugene Genovese, *The Political Economy of Slavery* (1965), and *The World the Slaveholders Made* (1970). A good selection of proslavery arguments appears in Eric McKitrick, ed., *Slavery Defended* (1963).

The role of women of the planting aristocracy is portrayed in Anne F. Scott, *The Southern Lady* (1970).

For the tradition of southern violence see John H. Franklin, *The Militant South* (1956).

Valuable insights into southern white upper-class attitudes are to be found in R. M. Meyers, ed., *The Children of Pride* (1972).

For a description of other white southern ways of life, see F. L. Owsley, *Plain Folk of the Old South* (1948).

15 war for the union

The Civil War, like the Revolutionary War, marked a major phase in the history of the American peoples. The earlier war saw the emergence of the United States as an independent nation. The later war determined that the nation would remain united. It also shaped the kind of nation America would be, for the war marked the transition from preindustrial to industrial America.

There was another dimension to the Civil War: race. Four million slaves won freedom, and blacks saw a new day dawning. But white America, though conceding freedom, was not prepared to yield to racial equality. Thus was bequeathed to the future the great unresolved issue of the war: the place of blacks in American society.

SOLDIERS IN BLUE

In war as in peace there were winners and losers. Those who stood to lose most, of course, were the common soldiers. The war, to them and their families, was not an abstract matter of strategy but a personal matter of survival. And survival was not easy. The war records are confused and incomplete, but it appears that about 2.5 million men served in the Union and Confederate armies. Of these, 622,000 perished—a death toll of nearly 25 percent. More died from disease than combat, but that was small comfort to grieving parents, widows, and children. Survival itself was a mixed blessing. Many who lived through the war faced a bleak future; these were the men broken in health and the wounded who lost arms or legs. To be sure, the federal government provided pensions to widows and orphans and to the wounded, but they were niggardly, and for long no provision was made for continued medical care of the ill and wounded. Confederates, of course, got nothing.

For their services, common soldiers were miserably paid. Union soldiers, who fared much better than their Confederate counterparts, received $11 a month in 1861. By 1864 the pay scale had reached $16 a month, but inflation was such that in 1864 the soldier had less purchasing power than in 1861. Soldiers with families were expected to support them. Combat troops were often in dire straits, for during campaigns they were unpaid for months at a time.

The poor pay offered Union soldiers helps explain the drop in enlistments after 1861. To stimulate recruiting, local and state governments offered increasingly generous bounties to volunteers, and for a time the federal government itself offered a $300 grant payable on enlistment. The bounties were supposed to tide poor folk over the early months of service. In practice, much of the bounty money ended up in the pockets of bounty brokers, men who were in the business of furnishing "volunteers." The business attracted unscrupulous characters who all too often swindled the men out of their bounty money.

Many of the "bounty men" enlisted under the spur of the federal conscription law passed in March 1863. They, and soldiers generally, were bitter over the law because it allowed the well-to-do to escape service. Men who could afford to do so hired substitutes at substantial fees or paid a commutation fee of $300 to the federal government.

The soldiers were also poorly supplied. For the first year of the war there was so little government supervision of supplies that greedy contractors amassed fortunes by selling shoddy goods at inflated prices. The plight of soldiers began to improve after Edwin M. Stanton became secretary of war early in 1862. Competitive bids were required for contracts. Federal inspectors were sent into workshops to make sure that contractors met specifications. Supplies of foodstuffs were subject to army scrutiny. Improved weapons came from government arsenals or private firms.

Apart from death, the soldiers most feared illness, wounding, and capture. Illness was common. Dysentery, malaria, and fevers were among the diseases that carried off 224,000 Union soldiers—a toll significantly higher than the 140,000 killed in action.

The wounded often fared worse than the sick. Care was primitive. Until 1863 there was no effective ambulance corps to recover wounded from the battlefield. Once rescued, the wounded were jammed into makeshift field hospitals, made up of tents and available buildings, including chicken coops. Such hospitals were hardly models of cleanliness and order, and the doctors who worked in them were all too often something other than paragons of medical competence. Many volunteers were doctors of repute, but too large a number were quacks and incompetents. And even the best of doctors were frustrated by shortages of instruments, medicines, drugs, and bandaging. Soldiers dreaded the hospitals because surgeons often treated wounds by amputating the damaged limb.

From field hospitals the wounded went to general hospitals behind the lines. These facilities, too, were hastily organized and little better than the field hospitals. Located in warehouses, schools, and other large buildings, the general hospitals often lacked even such necessities as bedding and medicines. In some, the staffs cheated patients out of their rations and stole medicinal whiskey and drugs for sale on the civilian market. The standard of care was low. Nursing was done by escaped slaves, convalescent soldiers barely able to take care of themselves, and army misfits. Civilian male nurses were also hired. Many of these turned out to be petty thieves and drug pushers.

Gradually, care of the sick and wounded improved, largely because of the work of the United States Sanitary Commission. A quasi-official body dominated by private citizens, the commission mobilized public opinion for changes and itself carried on a ceaseless program to aid the sick and injured. Incompetent doctors were weeded out. Corrupt staff members were dismissed. New general hospitals were built, some of which were models of enlightened medical care. The commission, over bitter opposition within the army, brought about the introduction of female nurses. Carefully selected and trained, these women carried into service new standards of care and honesty that earned them the respect and affection of their patients.

Soldiers captured in battle fared even worse than the wounded. The Confederacy, like the Union, had made no long-range plans for prison camps. In consequence, prisoners were herded together in makeshift centers characterized by shoddy housing, poor food, inadequate clothing, and disease. Of 195,000 Union prisoners, 30,000 died in Confederate camps, the most notorious of which was Andersonville.

Soldiers' grievances, accentuated by the prolonged war and the periodic expressions of war weariness among civilians, contributed to low morale among some troops. Men sought refuge from their hard life in alcohol and sexual promiscuity, creating a major problem of venereal disease. More ominous, small-scale mutinies broke out as early as the fall of 1861. In February 1863, officers of an Illinois regiment led their men in cheering Jefferson Davis! The mutinies were easily put down. Desertion, though, was harder to handle. By the end of the war 200,000 officers and men had permanently deserted, many escaping to Canada and the far West.

Nevertheless, despite their problems, Union troops as a whole were not demoralized. They fought doggedly and faithfully, even when, as at Fredericksburg, Virginia, in 1862, they lost nearly 10,000 casualties in one day. A year later, at Chattanooga, Union soldiers ordered to occupy rifle pits at the base of Missionary Ridge instead went through them, stormed up the hill under heavy fire, and routed the Confederates at the crest. Politically, Union soldiers voted for candidates committed to all-out war, whether Republican or Democrat. In the elections of 1864, the soldier vote helped elect Lincoln.

SOLDIERS IN GRAY

Confederate soldiers had much the same grievances as Union troops—but magnified many times. As the war went on, the plight of the Union soldier improved. That of the Confederate worsened.

Pay of the common soldier, for example, was $11 a month until 1864, when it was raised to $18. But inflation was much worse in the Confederacy than in the Union—in Richmond in 1864 a pair of shoes cost $125! Even so, by 1864 there were many instances of troops having received no pay for a year. Troops in Mississippi and South Carolina refused to obey orders until they were paid. The supply of clothing and shoes became so pitiful that men fought barefoot in rags. The food supply became increasingly inadequate, and all too often it was of wretched quality. Poor diet, poor personal hygiene, and poor camp discipline led to diseases that killed about 190,000 men, twice as many as combat.

Medical care in the Confederate army also declined. Quacks and incompetents flourished among the doctors, almost impossible to weed out because of the acute shortage of qualified physicians. Medicines and drugs became so hard to get that the army appealed to civilians to grow medicinal plants and herbs. Dressings and bandaging were in such short supply that wounds were often wrapped in any available rags, helping spread gangrene that killed off many patients. Field hospitals were as crude and unsanitary as those of the Union army and just as dreaded by the soldiers because of the surgeons' readiness to amputate. General hospitals were eventually organized behind the lines, but besides lacking medicine and food, they also had to do without such essentials as kitchen utensils, spoons, and dishes. As in the Union, nursing was mostly done by untrained men, with the same unfortunate results.

Captured Confederates fared somewhat better than their Union counterparts. The Union was better able to furnish needed supplies, but the camps were poorly organized and the prisoners often ill-nourished and in rags, little prepared to withstand the rigors of northern winters. The death rate was high, more than 12 percent of the 215,000 prisoners—but not as high as the death rate of 15 percent in Confederate camps. It indicates a crack in Confederate army morale that in the last year of the war increasing numbers of deserters, despite the horror stories of Union prison camps, surrendered to Union troops.

Confederate conscription laws contributed to the low morale that led to desertion. Supervisors of twenty or more slaves—a figure later reduced to fifteen—were automatically exempt from military service. Rich men could hire substitutes. Numerous other exemptions provided a field day for lawyers who could obtain them for well-heeled clients. The use of substitutes was forbidden after December 1863, but there were so many other ways for men of wealth to evade service that bitterness grew among poor civilians and soldiers alike.

Two other elements also destroyed the morale of common soldiers. One was family distress. Many soldiers were married yeoman farmers. During their absence, farms ran down, women and children could not produce the necessary food, and families sank into abject poverty. Like the Union government, the Confederate government assumed no responsibility for soldiers' families. As a result, wives wrote soldiers imploring them to return home to help their families. Faced with a choice between cause and family, many family men chose to go home.

The other element in lowered morale was a growing conviction after 1863 that the war was lost. Increasingly, men questioned whether it was worth risking their lives for a cause that had no future. The records show that at least 100,000 officers and men deserted, but the figure is doubtless too low. In February 1865, Lee reported he was losing "hundreds of men" nightly through desertion. Even more significant, soldiers organized secret peace societies within the army. One such movement in Alabama planned to rebel on Christmas Day 1864 by laying down their arms and calling for peace. Such societies were quickly suppressed, but their very existence indicated a rising tide of disaffection.

Yet, despite their problems and grievances, most Confederate soldiers fought doggedly to the end. They gave ground reluctantly, sustaining heavy losses themselves while inflicting heavy tolls on Union troops. As late as June 1864, Lee's half-starved troops in northern Virginia battled Grant's legions to such effect that the Union army suffered 60,000 casualties in one month. The Confederacy lost at least 25,000 men. Cold military logic, however, was against Lee. Grant could replace his losses; Lee could not.

HEROES AT A DISCOUNT

Soldiers were heroes during the war, but with peace heroes were at a discount. The rapidly demobilized Union veterans returned to a collapsing economy. Jobs were hard to come by, and falling farm prices greeted returning farmers. Unemployed veterans in the cities did not accept their fate passively. Feeling they had claims on the country, they petitioned public authorities for relief. When the petitions brought little action, veterans took to the streets in demonstrations and riots, which sometimes resulted in temporary aid. They also formed veterans' associations, which eventually united to form the Grand Army of the Republic. The new organization rapidly became a powerful force within the Republican party and won increasing benefits for Union veterans.

For Confederate veterans the future was bleak indeed. A defeated and impoverished South had no way of caring for its own, whether well or disabled. Hungry, angry, and embittered, veterans formed terrorist organizations, such as the Ku Klux Klan, that preyed upon the vulnerable symbol of all their frustrations: the now free blacks. Guiding them were the remnants of the planting aristocracy and the tough new men of business who emerged from the war, such as John B. Gordon of Georgia.

"A WHITE MAN'S WAR"

When the war came, both governments made it plain that it was going to be "a white man's war." Black people expected nothing more of the Confederacy, but they were dismayed by the actions of the Lincoln administration.

The Union government promptly informed the American public and foreign governments that slavery was not an issue of the war, that its sole aim was to restore the Union. No blacks were permitted to enlist in the army. Escaping slaves were returned to their masters by Union troops. Lincoln himself countermanded orders of two generals freeing slaves within their commands. Within the army, avowed enemies of black freedom were promoted, including George B. McClellan, who became general-in-chief in November 1861. In contrast, John C. Fremont, who had tried to free slaves in Missouri, was relieved of his command.

In the face of such developments, black sentiment divided. Some said from the beginning that the war was simply another white man's quarrel. With the backing of folk wisdom they predicted that no good could come from black involvement in such squabbles. Some who had looked on the war as a means to liberation became disillusioned with Lincoln. A prominent black clergyman said the president "is not now, and never was . . . an anti-slavery man."

There were also those who perceived that the war was indeed a black people's war. Their most notable spokesman was Frederick Douglass, who had a keen sense of the contradictory processes of history. Although he often expressed anger and despair, Douglass held firm to a basic understanding: no matter what white politicians might say, slavery was the root issue of the war, and the Union could not win without getting rid of it. Since the war involved black freedom, blacks must fight, even if whites tried to keep them out. Fighting for freedom and the Union would establish the black claim to equality.

Lincoln's policy was pragmatic. He was a cautious man, influenced by such conservative advisers as William H. Seward, the secretary of state. To win the war, Lincoln felt, he must not antagonize the border states, provoke the white racism rampant in northern states, or alienate those elements in the Union army, symbolized by McClellan, that were opposed to emancipation. Yet, still as a pragmatist, Lincoln could not disregard the growing strength of white abolitionism. This was not simply an abolitionism of sentiment, but an abolitionism of political power, personified in Senator Benjamin Wade of Ohio, Senator Charles Sumner of Massachusetts, and Representative Thaddeus Stevens of Pennsylvania.

On such men prowar blacks pinned their hopes. The mounting strength of the abolitionists in Congress actually began the transformation of the black role long before formal emancipation. In December 1861, the House of Representatives refused to reaffirm its earlier resolution that slavery was not an issue of the war. In March 1862, Congress called upon Union commanders to cease returning escaped slaves to their masters. Also in 1862, it held that all slaves of "rebel owners" were free, and it authorized the enlistment of black troops in the Union army. In other actions, Congress freed all slaves in the territories without compensation, ordered compensated emancipation in the District of Columbia, and approved Lincoln's similar offer to the border states—a proposal the states did not accept.

Lincoln's failure to interfere with the trend in Congress reflected his own movement in the same direction. Increasingly he was impressed with the arguments pressed on him by white and black abolitionists. The president, it should be noted, also took frequent counsel with black leaders, including Frederick Douglass—the first president to do so.

White and black abolitionists felt that abolition was right as a matter of principle, but they pressed on the administration arguments of expediency. Emancipation would disrupt the Confederate economy by encouraging slaves to desert the plantations. It would further injure the Confederacy by giving heart to the pro-Union forces in the South. It would release the enthusiasm of white abolitionists in the North and rally black people to the war. Declining white enlistments would be compensated by enlistment of free blacks and slaves. Making the war into a struggle for liberation would frustrate foreign intervention.

Lincoln, too, believed that emancipation was right, but he waited for events to prove the wisdom of the arguments of expediency—not only to himself, but also to the northern white public. Lincoln was ready to act in the summer of 1862, but he was dissuaded by cabinet members who argued that emancipation would be construed at home and abroad as a desperate measure designed to stave off defeat by inciting slave insurrection. In September came Union victory at the bloody battle of Antietam, destroying Lee's projected invasion of the North. A few days later Lincoln issued his preliminary Proclamation of Emancipation, granting freedom to all slaves in rebel territory as of January 1, 1863.

Blacks hailed the proclamation, although they noted that it freed no slaves in the border states or in areas occupied by the Union army. Despite its limitations it was a major step toward freedom—but would Lincoln take the next step? Would he indeed issue a final proclamation? They were well aware of the political pressures applied to the president to modify or withdraw the document. Their fears mounted when many Republicans were defeated in the fall elections. Lincoln, however, held firm. The final proclamation was issued and became effective January 1, 1863. The first major step toward abolition had been taken.

Most blacks shared the exultation of Frederick Douglass, who hailed the proclamation as "the greatest event of our nation's history, if not the greatest event of the century." While northern blacks exulted, slaves began deserting plantations by the thousands, seeking refuge in the Union army. They were unwelcome guests, except for the young women preyed upon by white soldiers. They received scanty food, clothing, or medical care. The death toll from hunger and disease rose so high that General Grant wondered whether the race would survive. The desire for freedom was so strong, however, that slaves continued to stream into Union lines.

Once initial enthusiasm over the Emancipation Proclamation cooled, blacks came to share Lincoln's view that the proclamation was not enough to abolish slavery. It had been issued by Lincoln in his capacity as commander-in-chief and justified on grounds of "military necessity." When the war ended, it would no longer be valid. Blacks held as slaves at that time would still be slaves. At the nadir of Lincoln's political fortunes, in August 1864, he told Frederick Douglass that he wished there were some way of getting more slaves within Union lines, for only such slaves would be free after the war was over.

Black discouragement—and Lincoln's—sprang in part from the Congress's reluctance to approve the proposed constitutional amendment abolishing slavery without compensation. In Lincoln's view, an amendment provided the only lawful way of general emancipation. Many members of Congress, including some Republicans, questioned the legality of such a move. At issue were the rights of private property. The Fifth Amendment specifically forbade the taking of private property "for public use, without just compensation." To be sure, the amendment did not involve the "public use" of freed slaves, but it did involve what was in effect the confiscation of property worth about $4 billion. Could the Constitution be amended to take away traditional property rights? A number of Republicans doubted it. Together with those who were opposed to abolition on principle, they were able to stop the administration short of the two-thirds vote in both houses necessary for approval of an amendment. The Senate approved, but the House refused.

The picture changed abruptly in the fall of 1864. In September, Sherman captured Atlanta, the arsenal of the Confederacy, and opened the way for his March to the Sea. Shortly afterwards, Sheridan devastated the Shenandoah Valley in Virginia and deprived Lee of his food supply. The North now tasted victory. The movement within the Republican party to replace Lincoln as presidential candidate collapsed. The Republican party swept the fall elections. Taking advantage of the situation, Lincoln used every means at his command to bring recalcitrant congressmen into line. In January 1865, Congress approved the Thirteenth Amendment, and by the end of the year it was part of the Constitution. At long last, slavery had been abolished forever in the United States.

THE PROMISE OF LAND REFORM

Winning their freedom was a necessary first step for black people on the way to their rightful place in American society—but it was only the first step. To make that freedom secure, the former slaves must have economic independence. How could they get it? By working their own land, said black leaders and some white sympathizers, such as Thaddeus Stevens. How was the land to be obtained? By taking over the plantations of Confederate leaders and distributing the land among former slaves.

For a time it appeared that such a policy would be implemented by the federal government. Abandoned plantations were taken over in the Sea Islands of South Carolina and in Mississippi. In both places former slaves not only worked the land but also managed their own affairs with a high degree of success. Early in 1865 General W. T. Sherman and Secretary of War Stanton, after meeting with black leaders in Georgia, set aside several hundred square miles of coastal lands to be distributed among freed families in forty-acre lots, with provisional title to the land until Congress established the necessary regulations. More than 40,000 families settled in the area by June 1865, setting in motion what James M. McPherson calls "the possibility of a truly revolutionary land reform program."

Congress also appeared to favor land reform. In March 1865 it passed a bill setting up a Freedmen's Bureau to provide emergency relief for war refugees. The new bureau was also empowered to take over confiscated and abandoned estates and distribute the land to former slaves and "loyal" white refugees. The new occupants were given three years to purchase their land and "receive such title thereto as the United States can convey." That clause indicated the administration's doubts about the legality of the measure.

Many blacks looked forward to owning land. Indeed, the belief spread, encouraged by some ardent agents of the Freedmen's Bureau, that on January 1, 1866, there was to be a general land distribution to former slaves. The blacks were speedily disillusioned. The land of the Sea Islands, on which blacks had lavished so much labor and care, were sold off at auction, with Yankee speculators getting 72,000 of the 77,000 acres involved. President Andrew Johnson returned the Davis Bend plantations of Mississippi to their owners, one of whom was Jefferson Davis himself. The lands covered by Sherman's order were also restored to their original owners. The former slaves were thrust downward to the status of propertyless laborers.

THE STRUGGLE FOR EQUALITY

In the North, the status of free blacks improved during the war. The federal government issued passports to blacks, declaring them citizens despite the Dred Scott decision. In 1862 the attorney general of the United States declared that all persons born in the United States were citizens, regardless of color. State action came more slowly, and then only under pressure from black organizations and their white allies. Laws barring black testimony against whites in court actions were repealed. Some segregated schools were integrated, although courts continued to uphold the principle of segregation. Illinois repealed its notoriously discriminatory "black laws" in 1865, and Indiana soon followed.

Such gains were important for blacks because white racism in the North continued to be strong. Mobs in Detroit and Cincinnati attacked the black residential sections, burning and looting buildings and beating the residents. For four days in July 1863, what had started out as a protest against unfair application of the draft law in New York City turned into a bloody rampage against blacks. A black orphanage was burned to the ground, and many blacks were savagely beaten and lynched. Order was restored only when Union troops were sent to the city. Less dramatic, but affecting more blacks in their everyday lives, was continued discrimination in restaurants, hotels, theaters, and public transportation.

Discrimination was also the rule in the Union army. When it became apparent that black manpower was needed to win the war, the government did not merely welcome blacks—it drafted them. By the end of the war more than 186,000 blacks, half of them from southern states, had served in the Union army.

The army wanted blacks, but not on terms of equality. Black soldiers were paid less than white, and they were denied the clothing allowance granted white soldiers. Blacks were also excluded from the federal bounties paid for enlistment. Their rations were inferior to those of whites, as was their medical care. Some commanders believed blacks were poor fighters and insisted on using them only as laborers. Others employed them as shock troops who bore the brunt of Confederate assaults. Some racist officers picked up only white wounded from battlefields. Fewer than 100 blacks received officers' commissions. The federal government itself for long took no action to protest the enslavement of blacks captured in battle or the massacre of surrendering black troops by Confederates.

Despite such conditions, blacks fought with courage and heroism. In July 1863, the 54th Massachusetts Regiment set an example of bravery by leading an assault on Fort Wagner in Charleston harbor. Under heavy fire they stormed the defenses until they were repulsed, with a loss of nearly one-third of their men. As the evidence of black courage mounted, generals used blacks increasingly in combat. In the last eighteen months of the war blacks fought in nearly every major campaign. As General George H. Thomas said after the battle of Nashville in 1864, "Gentlemen, the question is settled; Negroes will fight."

They also fought against discrimination. Some South Carolina volunteers mutinied in protest of their treatment. The men of the 54th Massachusetts Regiment refused for eighteen months to accept their pay until they were treated as equals. Finally, in 1864 Congress approved equal pay for blacks who had been free when they enlisted. Soldiers who had been slaves had to wait until 1865 for their pay to be raised to white levels. Congress also granted a federal enlistment bonus of $100 to blacks and voted pensions to widows and orphans of black soldiers.

The government also acted to protect captured blacks. The war department held that former slaves in the Union army were legally free and not subject to reenslavement. Lincoln threatened reprisals against Confederate prisoners for killing or enslaving black prisoners. Actually, however, Union authorities did little to enfore the policy.

SOUTHERN BLACK PEOPLE

In the South, many free blacks, especially among the well-to-do, rallied to the Confederate cause. After all, the South was their country, and many were linked by blood to the leading white families and shared the white outlook. Free blacks also hoped that by identifying themselves with the Confederacy they might obtain relaxation of the restrictions on black freedom. Thus, they raised funds for the war effort, helped recruit blacks for work on fortifications, and organized military units that volunteered for active service. Some of these organizations were accepted for service, but none saw combat.

Actually, the war made whites more wary than ever of free blacks—or at least of poor free blacks. Long regarded as a source of disaffection among slaves, they were now seen as potential dangers to internal security, and their freedom was restricted even more stringently. Nevertheless, since free blacks were exempt from military service and labor was in short supply, they were able to get jobs at better wages than ever before. This gave them a new confidence in themselves, expressed in behavior whites called "impudent." But the galloping Confederate inflation took its toll among the blacks as among the whites. Also the manpower needs of the army brought about the drafting of free blacks for service as laborers and teamsters in 1864. The improved lot of free blacks proved temporary indeed!

Slaves were also subjected to greater control. Most slaves found it expedient to continue toiling in the fields, mines, and factories until conditions were such that they could break away. But whites took no chances. The night patrols were enlarged, and "home guard" troops were organized to deal with possible slave insurrections. Planters and overseers were excused from military duty to maintain order in the countryside. Punishment of real or imagined conspiracies became harsher. Scores of slaves and some free blacks were hanged for allegedly participating in plots for armed insurrection.

White fears had some basis in fact, for slaves did indeed subvert the Confederacy. They harbored escaping Union war prisoners and sped them on their way to safety. Slaves passed on vital military information to Union scouts. Often they acted as guides to advancing Union troops. In a number of states, ranging from Arkansas to Virginia, they escaped into swamps and mountains. There they formed armed bands, sometimes in collaboration with Confederate deserters, and lived by stealing food from loyal Confederate farmers. In 1863 slaves in Lafayette County, Mississippi, drove out white overseers and took over the land and property of their masters. A year later, about 1,200 slaves impressed for war work in Mobile, Alabama, escaped, and many joined the Union army.

Slavery was also breaking down from within. The sharp decline in the cotton economy in many places made slaves liabilities rather than assets. They were then encouraged to support themselves by growing foodstuffs to sell on the civilian market or to find employers who would maintain them. In extreme cases slaves were turned off plantations to fend for themselves.

Finally, the mounting crisis of the Confederacy compelled it to face the issue of slavery. General Patrick R. Cleburne argued for the enlistment of blacks in the army early in 1864. Slaves must be given arms, he said, and slavery abolished: "As between the loss of independence and the loss of slavery, we assume that every patriot will freely give up the latter."

President Davis and other Confederate leaders balked, forbidding the discussion of such proposals in the army. The disintegration of the Confederate war effort finally prompted General Lee in January 1865 to recommend immediate use of black troops regardless of the effect on slavery. The Confederate government waited for two months to approve the use of blacks with limited emancipation. By then it was too late. In the meantime, the Confederacy, in a desperate move to win foreign support, promised abolition if Britain would grant diplomatic recognition. Again, it was too late.

THE WAR AND THE NORTHERN POOR

The war confronted civilians with two major problems: unemployment and runaway inflation.

The first year of the war was difficult for poor people. The belief that the war would be short, the disruption of the national market, the loss of $200 million owed by southern debtors, and uncertainties about the future combined to produce business retrenchment. As a result, unemployment was widespread, and hunger common in northern cities.

In 1862 the scene changed. Business geared up for a long war, and from Washington poured a steady stream of orders together with paper currency to pay for them. Jobs were plentiful. The employment of women and children expanded. Overtime was common. Wages went up—but not as much as prices. Between 1860 and 1864, when inflation reached its peak, consumer prices rose 76 percent, but daily wages rose only 42 percent. The living standards of many workers' families declined. Coffee, butter, and sugar became luxuries working people could not afford. They cut back on purchases of shoes and clothing. In 1864, a Republican newspaper in Springfield, Massachusetts, presumably prosperous because it was the home of the famed United States arsenal, reported "absolute want in many families."

To protect their living standards—and to maintain their craft status in face of the mechanization that went on apace during the war years—skilled workers turned once again to organizing unions. This time, however, they were not content to rely on local effort, as in the prewar era. Development of the northern railroad network made national organization essential, for strikebreakers could easily be obtained from distant cities to counter local strikes. Besides, it was now clear that labor must be able to influence national policy in Washington. It must also have power to deal with the antiunion legislation won by employer interests in many northern states. The few national craft unions already existing vastly expanded their memberships, and thirteen new national unions, including locomotive engineers, coal miners, cigar makers, and tailors, emerged.

A major factor in labor's success was the wartime labor shortage. Employers were anxious to keep their workers and to avoid strikes. They preferred to make the necessary concessions to keep their workers relatively content. The success of workers in such cases stimulated organization in other establishments, and the union movement spread. The achievements of their unions, combined with the recognition that labor's support was necessary to win the war, gave workers a sense of confidence in themselves, a "feeling of manly independence," as the leader of the iron molders, William H. Sylvis, put it.

The employers granted concessions with no thought of accepting unions as permanent bargaining agents. As the war went on, employer resistance stiffened, indicated by the increased number of strikes. There were only 38 strikes in 1863, but in 1864 the number rose to 108. Although strikes against mechanization usually failed, those called for wage increases usually succeeded—a fact that did not favorably impress employers.

Employers then organized various associations dedicated to halting the spread of labor unionism. Their workers were happy, they said, but were subject to corruption by outside agitators. Employers then acted to protect their "happy" workers. Through their organizations they checked the union practice of playing off one employer against another. They collaborated in maintaining blacklists of active union people and in enforcing the "yellow dog" contracts requiring workers not to join unions as a condition of employment. They encouraged individual employers not to deal with unions. When such refusals brought strikes, strikebreakers were recruited from among recent immigrants, blacks, women, and prison inmates, who were rented out to employers for nominal fees. In addition, employers sought to use the powers of government against unions. Several state legislatures voted penalties for those who promoted strikes.

Workers also discovered that employers had powerful friends in the Union army. When munitions workers at a plant near West Point, New York, went on strike for wages of $1.50 a day, federal troops moved in and arrested the leaders, breaking the strike. Strikes of coal miners, longshoremen, and locomotive engineers also failed through military intervention. In Missouri, General Rosecrans not only broke strikes but also prohibited all organizations of workers. A similar order was issued in Kentucky.

Such developments placed responsible labor leaders in a quandary. They admired Lincoln and were ardent in the cause of the Union, but they could not ignore the trampling under of the rights of workers by Union commanders. Nor could they ignore the increasing bitterness of workers who had come to feel that their only role in the war was to "bear its burdens and shed their blood," as the Chicago Trades'

Assembly said in 1864. Labor leaders responded by denouncing the military commanders and by urging unions to take their grievances directly to the White House. Lincoln, they said, would prove friendly to labor. In the meantime, unions reaffirmed their support of the Union and of the war.

Faring worse than the men and women in the shops and factories were those who worked on the docks and in the coal mines. They were poorly paid, their work dangerous, and their attempts to form unions crushed.

The grievances of poor white working folk found expression in resistance to the federal draft law. They resented it as a demonstration of class privilege. The wealthy could hire substitutes, for fees ranging up to $1,500, or secure commutation for $300. (Those who could afford it made full use of their privilege. They paid for 118,000 substitutes and 86,000 commutations.) Another source of resentment was the way the draft boards operated. Somehow, they tended to overlook eligible native-born men and to call disproportionate numbers of Irish and other foreign-born men. Antidraft riots, stimulated by Democratic politicians opposed to the war, erupted in several cities, most notably in New York City.

Less dramatic than riots, but perhaps more significant of the mood of many poor people, was the prolonged resistance to the draft itself. Such resistance was especially marked in the isolated coal-mining regions of Illinois, Indiana, and Pennsylvania. Long the scenes of violent class warfare between operators and miners, the mining camps were seething with resentment over destruction of their unions, frequent accidents that killed and maimed, and living standards—already low—declining under the pressures of inflation. Miners resented the class inequities in the draft law, but they had a special grievance in that company officials were often chosen to enforce it. The company men used the draft to get rid of active union men. With the approval of their families and communities, many men refused to go. They formed armed bands, often including deserters and discharged Union war veterans, and they disrupted the operation of the draft. Only the use of federal troops in overwhelming numbers brought about an end to armed resistance. Many of those defeated joined other draftees who chose to evade rather than fight the draft. More than 160,000 drafted men never reported for induction. They had gone off to Canada, the far west, and the South.

Although employers were quick to brand miners' resistance to the draft as disloyalty to the Union, the miners were actually protesting the employers' longstanding refusal to settle grievances and their abuse of the draft to cripple union organization. Where such factors were not important, working people loyally cooperated in the war effort.

WAR RESISTANCE IN THE CONFEDERACY

Inflation was even more disastrous for the poor people of the South than for the northern poor. The fall in living standards was limited to some degree by the practice of some employers in paying wages in kind—that is, food and clothing—and by some workers raising food on small plots of land. Nevertheless, destitution and hunger were prevalent by early 1863. Rumblings of discontent prompted attempts at relief. Some cities provided food for the poor at "fair prices" for a while. State and

Confederate governments experimented unsuccessfully with price controls. Private charities doled out meager supplies of food.

Passive discontent turned into active protest early in 1863—protests that were led by women. In Atlanta, Mobile, and other cities, groups of poor women raided stores and took food and other supplies. Richmond, the Confederate capital, was rocked by a major riot in April 1863, when a mob of women, joined later by men, sacked the business district and carried off clothing, shoes, and food. Only a personal plea by Jefferson Davis persuaded the mob to disband. Another women's demonstration for food was broken up by the city guard, and Confederate troops were sent to the capital to prevent further demonstrations. Throughout the countryside, small bands of armed women raided mills and country stores and seized food, cloth, and thread.

Workers who organized unions and went on strike had little success. Slaves were always available as strikebreakers, and as the war went on, the Confederate government became increasingly hostile to strikes. After passage of the draft law in 1862 it sent strikers off to the army by canceling their industrial draft deferments. In February 1864, a new draft law ended all such exemptions and workers were under almost as much government control as if they had been in the army.

Riots and strikes could not keep hunger from spreading as the Confederate economy broke down. In 1864 Governor Joseph E. Brown of Georgia said the situation in his state was "alarming." The governor of Virginia said many citizens faced "absolute starvation." In the cities the poor were embittered by the opulence flaunted by the wealthy. In the countryside, farms were pillaged by Confederate and Union troops alike. Farmers also suffered from the Confederate policy calling for impressment of foodstuffs for the army. Often such food turned up in the civilian markets, sold by corrupt officers.

The grievances of the poor prompted resistance to the draft, which, as in the Union, favored the wealthy. Many draft evaders and even army deserters simply returned home and worked their farms, secure in community approval and in the sympathy of local officials. Others formed armed bands that took refuge in isolated areas and preyed upon farmers for necessary supplies. When draft officials sought to enforce the law, they met armed resistance. So successful and so widespread was the resistance that eventually Confederate army units were used against the resisters. The military action succeeded, in part because some commanders terrorized women and children into inducing the men to surrender.

Such policies antagonized poor folk still further. The alienation resulted in the spread of peace societies throughout the Confederacy. Of necessity, the societies were secret, but they grew rapidly in number and strength as it became apparent that the war was lost. The societies enjoyed the tacit support of a growing number of Confederate politicians who hoped for a negotiated peace and thought to use the peace movement for that end. The movement's program was more drastic. It called for immediate peace through restoration of the Union and acceptance of emancipation.

The peace societies were not content with propaganda. They also collaborated with peace societies within the army, obstructed the draft, supplied intelligence to Union forces, and entered politics. The strength of the movement was shown in

Alabama in 1863, when several peace candidates were elected to the state legislature and the Confederate congress. In North Carolina in 1864, a peace-society member, William Holden, narrowly failed at being elected governor.

The Confederate government responded with repression, but its tactics failed. By late 1864 disillusionment with the war and with the planting aristocracy was too widespread among the mass of poor whites to be stamped out by such methods. Besides, the white working poor were already looking beyond the war to a new day. With planter power destroyed, they thought, poor people would come into their own.

"A RICH MAN'S WAR"

After the initial dislocations caused by the war, which brought disaster to many merchants and bankers, businessmen on the whole did well in the North. Debt-ridden railroads settled their obligations and began paying dividends for the first time. Prosperous railroads, such as the Pennsylvania, substantially increased their dividends. The woolen industry, straining to meet war demands, tripled its prewar dividends. One company, on an investment of $2.5 million, paid out $3 million to its stockholders during the war. Western Union, the telegraph company, made record profits, as did major iron and coal companies. Infant industries, such as oil, food canning, and ready-made clothing, expanded vigorously.

Not all businesses fared equally well, of course. Because of shortages of raw materials, cotton manufacturing declined and many small mills went out of business. Shoe production also declined, as did railroad building and residential construction.

Businessmen did not confine their attention to production of goods. The combination of wartime needs and inflation enabled them to speculate profitably in such essentials as foodstuffs, cotton, wool, oil, and gold. On Wall Street, stock market activity was so feverish that, as one financier observed, only "a natural idiot" could fail to make a fortune.

Government policy also aided business, especially big business. Tariffs were raised, enabling domestic producers to charge higher prices without fear of foreign competition. Investors in the new national banking system were given a monopoly on bank-note currency. Taking advantage of the Homestead Act of 1862 and an earlier preemption act, speculators amassed millions of acres of good land at bargain prices. Later, of course, they sold the land to bona-fide farmers at many times its original cost. Speculators also benefited from the federal program to aid higher education. States were given public lands to help finance agricultural and mechanical colleges. The states, hard pressed to meet their immediate obligations, often sold off their claims to speculators, sometimes for as little as 50¢ an acre. Transcontinental railroad promoters did better. The federal government gave them more than 130 million acres, while western states donated 49 million acres.

Big business also tended to benefit from wartime innovations in technology, largely because of the great capital investment required to finance them. This was particularly true of the new process of producing good steel at low cost, developed in England by Henry Bessemer and in the United States by William Kelly and put to use in this country in 1864. The improved shoe-making machinery patented by Gordon McKay in 1862 also called for considerable capital. Improvements in iron making and marine engineering made during the war also required large initial capital outlay, although ultimately the costs were more than met through government contracts. The effect of this technological change was to strengthen a trend: more and more of the economy came under the control of big business.

FARMERS AND THE WAR

Northern farmers who escaped military service also benefited economically from the war. After an initial drop in markets in 1861, the needs of war and expanded foreign buying brought about an astronomical rise in the prices of farm products. Indeed, in terms of its purchasing power, farm income during the war reached its highest point in the nineteenth century.

For many farmers, the boom was a godsend. They were able to pay off their debts in depreciated paper money while selling all they could produce in highly profitable markets. But not all farmers shared. To expand output in a time of manpower shortage required increased use of machinery, which called for great investment. The machines themselves were expensive, and they could be employed profitably only on farms of considerable size. Farmers with little capital or credit were often squeezed out. Farmers who went to war were in especially dire straits when the war ended. All too often they possessed inadequate funds to compete with neighbors who had prospered while they were away, and they returned to farming at a time when prices began to fall.

Some southern planters and farmers prospered during the war, but most did not. With cotton markets sharply curtailed, many planters became food producers. Like farmers, they stood to profit from mounting prices. Their gains, however, were offset by a heavy tax in kind on foodstuffs and by impressment of much of their output by army agents at prices far below market levels. As the war went on, planters and farmers suffered because they could not replace worn out equipment.

The farmers also suffered from hungry Confederate troops who preyed on farms and from the policies of some commanders who in retreat destroyed all property that might help the Yankees. The Yankees, in their turn, lived off the land when possible and plundered and destroyed anything that might be of value to Confederates. So great was the destruction that in 1870 the value of southern farms had fallen to only 53 percent its 1860 level.

"NEW MEN" OF THE POSTWAR SOUTH

The traditional picture of the South as a region devastated by war and reduced to destitution, while true in many respects, has obscured the fact that some white southerners did well during the war. Profits in running goods through the Union naval blockade were so great that syndicates of wealthy investors, often in collaboration with English interests, took over the business. Returns were also high for those planters and merchants engaged in the illegal overland traffic in which cotton was traded for weapons, ammunition, salt, and medical supplies. Speculators also profited from hoarding food, clothing, and other necessities until they could be sold at high prices.

Manufacturers and railroad operators also did well, despite Confederate government attempts to regulate rates, prices, and profits.

Much of this war-time wealth was illusory, expressed in Confederate dollars that were falling sharply in value. White southerners who were in position to profit from the war sought to protect themselves by getting rid of Confederate dollars as quickly as possible. They invested in urban real estate, gold, and jewelry. They exchanged Confederate money for United States currency and English pounds. They sent funds to English banks and invested in English concerns. Such white southerners emerged as the "new men" of the postwar South—men of wealth with little concern, except for symbolic purposes, for the old ideal of "gentleman."

WOMEN AND THE WAR

The war did not shatter, but it weakened, the stereotypes that had dictated the place and role of women in northern white society. The needs of war were so pressing that women were not simply permitted to leave home for outside activities—they were actually called on to do so as a patriotic service. They responded positively. Women were particularly active in two important organizations: the United States Sanitary Commission and the Women's Loyal National League.

Under the leadership of the wealthy, like Mary Livermore of Chicago and Louisa Lee Schuyler of New York, women were often the moving spirits in the 7,000 local societies that gave the sanitary commission its needed clout in Washington. These local groups staged "sanitary fairs" to raise funds to aid soldiers and their families, and they involved women in other wartime activities. They were also important in maintaining morale on the home front, especially at times when war weariness seemed to threaten the war effort. The commission also supported the drive for employing women nurses in the army initiated by Dr. Elizabeth Blackwell, the pioneer woman physician. Directing the new nursing service was the indefatigable activist Dorothea Dix.

The Loyal League grew out of Lincoln's campaign for the thirteenth Amendment. Many leading women abolitionists had long been distrustful of the president's cautious policies, but when he called on them for aid they responded with enthusiasm. Under the leadership of Elizabeth Cady Stanton, Susan B. Anthony, and Lucretia Mott the league was formed, a network of local societies organized, and a grassroots campaign for the amendment initiated. As a result, 400,000 signatures were obtained on petitions to Congress to pass the antislavery measure.

In contributing significantly to the Union war effort, women gained organizational experience. Thousands of women learned how to keep records, handle finances, resolve disputes, conduct meetings, and decide policy. When one recalls that in 1848 none of the women at the opening meeting of the Seneca Falls convention felt competent enough to chair, the war's organizational contribution to the liberation of white women becomes one of its least appreciated consequences.

Such activities mostly involved women with some leisure, but the war also brought great numbers of women into the work place. So many male teachers went into the army or got better paying jobs that the teaching field became dominated by women and remained so afterwards. Office work, too, which had been a male domain, became largely a woman's occupation, as did clerking in department stores. More women than ever before labored in factories.

Wages paid women in some fields were so low as to arouse public outcry when they were made known. A. T. Stewart, the millionaire department store magnate of New York, was publicly criticized for the wages paid his clerks. In the New York needle trades conditions were even worse. Shirt makers, for example, received 24¢ pay for a twelve-hour day in 1863. Umbrella sewers worked an eighteen-hour day for a salary of $3 a week.

There were sporadic revolts among women workers, particularly in the needle trades, but they usually got nowhere. The women's organizations were too weak, and the women too isolated—much of the work was done in homes—to cope with determined resistance by employers. More successful was the Working Women's Protective Union. Led by middle-class women who felt that such low wages forced young women into prostitution, the union trained women for better-paying jobs and saw to it that they were placed. It also won passage of a law penalizing fraudulent employers who did not pay their women workers—a fairly common practice. Similar associations were formed in other northern cities. The Philadelphia society won wage increases for women working on war orders and encouraged women workers to organize unions.

The discontent of many working-class women led them to join men in resisting the unfair application of the draft law. Hundreds were arrested for participating in the New York riots of July 1863, during which several women were killed and many injured. In the coal-mining regions women misled draft officials with false information, sheltered deserters and draft evaders, and provided support for the armed bands who defied enforcement of the draft.

Although to a lesser degree than in the North, the war did afford southern women opportunity for more active roles. With husbands and sons in service, upper-class women took over management of plantations and poorer women struggled with the problems of running farms. There was nothing comparable to the network of sanitary societies in the North, but local groups of women made bandages, socks, and shirts for soldiers and roamed the fields and woods in search of medicinal plants. Wealthy women contributed funds for private hospitals, and many also served as nurses and hospital managers. Perhaps the most notable of these was Sallie Tompkins, whose pioneer private hospital in Richmond was a model of care and cleanliness. When reform of the army medical service required that all hospital directors be under direct army control, President Davis appointed Tompkins a captain of cavalry so that she could continue her work.

The war also brought women into occupations hitherto closed to them: teaching and office work. Thousands more went to work in war industries. As in the North, the hours were long and wages low. When the purchasing power of the Confederate dollar declined, the plight of working women became woeful indeed. As the war went on, with misery mounting and hopes dimming, many white southern women rebelled. Poor women in several cities formed mobs demanding "Bread or Peace."

Women were also active in the peace movements that spread throughout the Confederacy. They put their beliefs into practice by sheltering deserters and draft evaders. Such women became a prime objective in the army's campaign to end desertion and draft evasion. In the isolated areas where deserters and evaders tended to settle, army officials made dire threats against the women and children if the offenders did not give themselves up. In Florida, villages of antiwar people were destroyed and women and children locked up in concentration camps. Elsewhere, women and children were deported into "no man's land" between contending armies. Resistance to the war was not confined to poor women. The wife of a prominent Confederate officer, Mrs. Roger Pryor, confided, "I am for a tidal wave of peace—and I am not alone."

THE BEGINNING OF A NEW ORDER

The war affected the lives of nearly every American. Not only were lives altered personally, but also relations were changed between whites and blacks, men and women, workers and employers, and northerners and southerners. Some accepted the changes eagerly, some reluctantly. Many, worn out by the long war, wanted nothing more than a speedy return to what now seemed the calm and simple ways of the past—a return they quickly found impossible. They were caught up in a new era of dynamic economic growth, social turbulence, and public and private perplexities.

FOR FURTHER READING

The most comprehensive history of the war is Allan Nevins, *Ordeal of the Union,* Vols. 1–8, (1947–71). The standard one-volume history is J. G. Randall and David Donald, *The Civil War and Reconstruction* (1969). For fuller treatment of issues discussed in this chapter see Robert Cruden, *The War That Never Ended* (1973).

Problems of soldiers are the subjects of Henry S. Commager, *The Blue and the Gray* (1950); Dudley T. Cornish, *The Sable Arm* (1966), which deals with black troops; and Bell I. Wiley, *The Life of Johnny Reb* (1943) and *The Life of Billy Yank* (1952).

Roles of blacks are discussed in James M. McPherson, *The Negro's Civil War* (1965). See also Willie Lee Rose, *Rehearsal for Reconstruction* (1967), for an account of an experiment in which former slaves showed they could work productively and manage their own affairs as free people.

Economic problems are covered in Ralph Andreano, ed., *The Economic Impact of the American Civil War* (1967). There is material of importance in E. D. Fite, *Social and Industrial Conditions in the North During the Civil War* (1910).

Two views of the Confederacy by southern historians are presented in E. M. Coulter, *The Confederate States of America* (1950), and Clement Eaton, *A History of the Southern Confederacy* (1954).

The age of John D. Rockefeller, Booker T. Washington, Sitting Bull, Eugene V. Debs, and Jane Addams

phase three INDUSTRIAL AMERICA

1865 to 1918

1877 End of congressional Reconstruction halts trend toward racial equality.
1879 Formation of Standard Oil trust symbolizes concentration of power in industry.
1883 Supreme Court upholds racial discrimination by individuals.
1886 American Federation of Labor organized.
1887 Dawes Act endangers Indian cultures.
1888 Photography popularized by production of cheap Kodak cameras.
1890 Use of electrical power in industry begins.
1893 Beginning of most severe economic depression until that time.
1894 Massive federal intervention breaks Pullman labor boycott.
1896 Election of McKinley symbolizes triumph of urban, industrial America over rural America.
1896 Supreme Court approves state-ordered racial segregation.
1901 President McKinley assassinated. Succeeded by Theodore Roosevelt who symbolizes "Progressive Era."
1901 Organization of United States Steel Corporation, biggest holding company in American history to that time.
1905 Formation of Industrial Workers of the World indicates labor militancy.
1908 Supreme Court decision in Danbury Hatters case jeopardizes labor unions.
1909 Henry Ford begins production of cheap automobiles.
1910 National Association for the Advancement of Colored People organized.
1912 Woodrow Wilson elected president.
1914 Clayton antitrust law provides some protection for labor unions.
1917 United States enters World War I.
1918 End of World War I.

By industrial America we mean the period between 1865 and 1918, between the end of the American Civil War and the end of World War I. It was an era of great economic expansion, marked by the dominance of industry in national life. Expansion derived from the development of a national market, made possible through a nationwide network of railroads and telegraphs—and later, telephones—that bound the countryside and the rapidly growing cities together. Industry itself matured, expanding from the production of consumer goods, such as shoes, cloth, and flour, to the production of capital goods, such as machines and machines to make machines. So rapid was progress that by 1900 the United States was the world's leading industrial power.

The national market developed under conditions of free enterprise inherited from Jacksonian America. Unrestricted competition meant jungle warfare among businessmen. Out of that struggle emerged as victors a small group of men who dominated entire industries, such as Andrew Carnegie in steel and John D. Rockefeller in oil. The process of concentration of control was not yet ended, however. Increasingly, major corporations fell under control of great investment banking houses.

Business dominated political life as it did economic life. As earlier, business relied heavily on professional politicians, contributing lavishly to the campaign funds of both major parties and paying off individual politicians for services rendered. The Senate came to be known as the "Millionaires' Club." The Supreme Court was dominated by men imbued with a business point of view.

Thus, while businessmen quarreled among themselves over specific issues such as the tariff or currency, they shaped basic national policy in a way that served the general business interest. Those outside the prevailing concept of business interest—organized labor, small farmers, blacks, Indian peoples, and the poor—fared ill at the hands of government.

Another major aspect of industrial America was urbanization. The decline of the countryside is mirrored in population movement. Although rural Americans increased in absolute numbers, they declined in relative terms. In 1860 only 20 percent of Americans lived in towns and cities with more than 2,500 inhabitants. In 1900 the figure was 40 percent and the trend was continuing. In terms of wealth, the shift was even more impressive. In 1880, the value of rural and urban estate was estimated at about $10 billion each. Within ten years, however, the value of urban real estate jumped to $26 billion, while rural land value rose to only $13 billion. That trend also continued.

The huge increase in wealth that accompanied economic expansion contributed to still another aspect of industrial America: the increasingly unequal distribution of wealth. In 1890 it was estimated that the wealthiest 1 percent owned more than 50 percent of the nation's wealth. In 1825 the top 1 percent owned about 25 percent of the wealth.

Paradoxically, that very inequality may help explain another major characteristic of industrial America: the overwhelming acceptance of the gospel of success. Inequality provided a powerful incentive for aspiring Americans to work toward the day when they, too, could enjoy the fruits of success. Nowhere was the triumph of business values more apparent than in the South. The "gray ghosts of the Confederacy" lingered on in southern mythology, but the gentlemanly ideal they represented had little place in the new southern society. The ideal now was the successful businessman, whom the South produced in large numbers.

16 business in power

Probably at no time in American history has business enjoyed the prestige that it had in the post–Civil War era. The cult of business and the gospel of success, which were budding before the war, now dominated opinion. Businessmen were credited with having helped save the Union. They were regarded as the men who spanned the continent with railroads, forged the country into the mightiest industrial giant in the world, and provided jobs for millions. The image was reinforced by the great business leaders of the day, such as Andrew Carnegie and John D. Rockefeller, who proclaimed that men of great wealth were public benefactors.

INDIVIDUALISM, EVOLUTION, AND SUCCESS

With such conspicuous examples of self-made men in the public eye, the gospel of success attained new vigor. Russell Conwell, a Baptist preacher, made a success of himself with a lecture he delivered 6,000 times. Entitled "Acres of Diamonds," it urged Americans to "get rich, get rich" so that they might do good. The Episcopalian bishop of Massachusetts, William Lawrence, averred that "godliness is in league with riches" and identified success with superior morality. These preachments were not confined to Protestants. Many Catholics and Jews agreed.

As in prewar days, another strand was woven into the religious and moral elements of the gospel: nationalism. Only in America, it was said, were there so many opportunities for poor folk to succeed, providing they possessed the necessary "character"—a favorite word of the exponents of the gospel. Andrew Carnegie, a Scottish immigrant, never ceased extolling the virtues of American institutions as the means through which poor young men, like himself, could rise to riches.

In addition to these familiar themes, individualism now had a new "scientific" rationale supplied by the English social philosopher Herbert Spencer. Later called Social Darwinism, although Darwin had nothing to do with it, this view held that human society, like nature, was in process of evolution. Like evolution in nature, evolution in society was rooted in a struggle for existence. Out of that struggle came "survival of the fittest," under whose aegis would come a harmonious society providing maximum happiness for its members. This was a "natural law," and any attempt to impede its operation was socially dangerous. Government, in particular, was to take no action on behalf of the "unfit." Spencer's dicta were avidly seized upon by American businessmen. His visit to the United States in 1882 turned into a triumphal tour, and his works sold sensationally well. Few bothered to read his long, opaque discourses, however. Actually there was no need of it. A host of popularizers broadcast Spencer's message loud and clear. Among the most notable were E. L. Youmans, editor of *Popular Science Monthly,* and Professor William Graham Sumner of Yale University.

The minds of the young were also indoctrinated with the virtues of individualism. *McGuffey's Readers,* begun in 1836, became a staple of American schools, selling 122 million copies through several generations. The novels of Horatio Alger sold over 20 million copies, bringing him a fortune he spent on good works. McGuffey and Alger extolled the self-made man, offering popular heroes like Abraham Lincoln as examples. They also emphasized the personal qualities necessary for success: honesty, hard work, thrift, sobriety, and devotion to the interests of one's employer. These were hardly the attributes of the tycoons of the day, who were notorious for dishonesty and ruthlessness in fighting their rivals and labor unions and showed no sobriety in displaying their wealth. The traits in which children were indoctrinated, however, were admirably suited to providing the kind of employees the tycoons wanted. As has been pointed out by students of their work, McGuffey and Alger expounded not the values of big business, but the values of the middle class—a doctrine of "limited success."

In this lay the mass appeal of the gospel of success. Aspiring Americans yearned to become Carnegies and Rockefellers, but they knew their chances were slim. They perceived, through the blurring vision of the self-made man, what William Miller and others later demonstrated empirically: namely, that most business leaders came from the rich, the well born, and the educated. It was possible, said Russell Sage, the multimillionaire, for any young man to become a millionaire—but the goals of most ambitious Americans were more modest. They hoped to rise in the world somewhat and believed that their children could do even better.

In the expanding economy of industrial America such hopes could well be realized. But not by all—unskilled workers in factories and sharecroppers and tenant farmers in the South had little chance to move upward. For those who were white, male, native-born, and somewhat schooled, the opportunities were present—and many took full advantage of the openings. Carpenters and bricklayers became contractors. Clerks moved upward to office managers and confidential secretaries. Locomotive engineers became division superintendents. The development of indoor plumbing and of electric power provided well-paying jobs for young men handy with

A jibe at the unreliability of the newfangled contraption, the automobile, in the early twentieth century.

Scientific American, 1891

their hands and their heads. The growth of big business, with its consequent bureaucracy and dependence on technology, provided high-status jobs for thousands of managers and technicians.

The opportunities were not limited to older-stock Protestant Americans. People of the "old immigration"—Irish, British, Germans—also moved up. Two religious groups that had faced discrimination, Catholics and Jews, not only shared in the benefits of an expanding economy but also produced their own success symbols. Archbishop Ireland, son of an Irish carpenter, hobnobbed with railroad magnates and was the confidant of presidents. Thomas Fortune Ryan, said to have been left a penniless orphan at age fourteen, made a fortune in New York City street railways and donated generously to Catholic causes. In that same city, the Straus brothers, sons of a German Jewish immigrant who began his American career as a peddler in the southern countryside, dominated retail merchandizing through such department stores as Macy's. In Chicago, Julius Rosenwald was by 1900 a power in Sears, Roebuck, the leading mail-order house in the country.

Upward mobility depended, of course, on conforming to the patterns of behavior expected by business. As McGuffey and Alger showed, Americans had to be good employees rather than independent individuals. In attaining some measure of success through such behavior, achieving Americans identified themselves with the great symbols of success, the men of big business.

Successful folk also gave business credit for the many new inventions and products that made middle-class life more comfortable and convenient than ever be-

The Sears Roebuck catalog of 1908 said these were "Strictly New Styles of Waists and Skirts."

fore. By 1914 great numbers of middle-class Americans enjoyed telephones, electric lighting, and bathrooms in their homes. Men liked the new safety razors, and women welcomed mechanical clothes washers and carpet cleaners. People of all ages and sexes were delighted with the cheap cameras produced by George B. Eastman. Some were already buying the new and inexpensive automobiles coming from the factory of Henry Ford. Looking at America through the eyes of successful people, James Bryce, the British author of the immensely popular *American Commonwealth,* had written in the 1880s that "life in America is in most ways pleasanter, easier, simpler than in Europe; it floats in a sense of happiness like that of a radiant summer morning." Successful Americans then and later found little reason to disagree with Bryce's judgment.

Cheap, mass-produced automobiles revolutionized American life. Here is the primitive assembly line at the Ford plant in Highland Park, Michigan, in 1912.

The Archives of Labor and Urban Affairs, Wayne State University

WHAT SELF-MADE MAN?

Legend still has it that the great men of business in industrial America rose from rags to riches. Not so. William Miller's analysis of the backgrounds of major business leaders of the early twentieth century—that is, of men who got their start in the nineteenth century—shows that only 5 percent came from lower-class families. Fifty percent came from upper-class backgrounds, and 45 percent from the middle class. This is understandable, for such folk had the necessary education, personal associations, family connections, and capital and credit to take advantage of the opportunities afforded by an expanding economy. The legend of rags to riches takes as typical what was in fact exceptional.

The legend also obscures the role of the milieu in which the tycoons flourished. The vast expansion of the railroad network after the Civil War stimulated activity throughout the entire economy, providing orders for all types of business, ranging from food to steel rails. When the boom in railroad building declined, the developing cities themselves offered lucrative markets as they paved streets, built bridges, installed street railways, laid sewer lines, and lit homes and streets with gas and electricity.

In addition to these markets, business benefited from generous governmental policies. Protective tariffs assured American manufacturers freedom from foreign competition that might have cut into their profits. Railroad promoters obtained from federal, state, and local governments grants of land that included not only farms but also vast forests and areas rich in mineral deposits. Lumber and mining operators profited from legislation that disposed of public forest and mining land for $2.50 an acre.

Big business received yet another stimulus from government. In 1883 Congress authorized building of an up-to-date navy. Secretary of the Navy Whitney insisted that the new "steel navy" be of United States manufacture. Only major steel producers, such as Carnegie, could meet the requirements. The extent of this governmental aid to business may be seen in the fact that by 1900 the United States was the world's third greatest naval power, outranked only by Britain and Germany.

Government came to the aid of businessmen in still other ways. The use of federal authority to break strikes, begun during the Jackson administration, increased in the post-Civil War era. It culminated in the massive federal intervention that broke the Pullman strike in 1894 and set back the cause of industrial unionism for two generations. Federal courts issued injunctions against strike activities almost as a matter of course. The Supreme Court, in a series of decisions in the early twentieth century, curbed labor unions by making them subject to the Sherman antitrust law of 1890. However, the Clayton antitrust law of 1914 exempted unions from antitrust provisions and banned the use of federal injunctions against unions. The law's protection of labor was not as strong as it appeared. Federal courts so interpreted the law as to permit injunctions against unions.

Indeed, the Supreme Court interpreted the Sherman law to favor business consolidation. In 1895 it held that the law applied to commerce rather than to manufacturing, thus placing most combinations beyond the reach of the law. In the early twentieth century the court did apply the law to some combinations. The most notable example was its decision in 1911 upholding dissolution of the Standard Oil Company of New Jersey, a holding company that represented the Rockefeller interests. The court, however, held that the Sherman law applied only to combinations that exercised an "unreasonable" restraint of trade—leaving the door open to "reasonable" consolidation of business. As for Standard Oil, it found an easy way around the order to dissolve. On paper the holding company disappeared, but management practices had become so sophisticated that the various individual Standard Oil companies worked together in a "community of interest" in essence little different from the old Standard Oil.

The Supreme Court was helpful to business in other ways. It struck down state laws designed to regulate railroad rates. It outlawed state attempts to limit the hours of labor, although it made an exception for women workers in 1908. In 1895 it held a federal income tax unconstitutional.

Business also profited from a huge reservoir of cheap labor. In the South, so many people lived in poverty that cotton mills, mines, and foundries got an ample supply of labor at bare subsistence wages. State governments aided businessmen by leasing out convicts, usually black, to private employers. This revived form of slave labor helped depress wages for free labor throughout the South.

In the Far West, competition between Irish and Chinese workers made it possible to hold down wages. In the Southwest, farmers and ranchers benefited from low wages paid Mexican-Americans. In the industrial North the influx of millions of immigrants after 1880 made it possible to pay subsistence wages to the unskilled. Immigration was a boon to employers in still another way. Together with peasants from rural Europe came highly skilled men from industrial Europe and Britain. American employers benefited from such men's skills without bearing the cost of training them.

Benefits of another kind accrued to those who could profit from depressions, such as those of 1873 and 1893. During these financial storms, great and small businesses alike went under—and men with sufficient capital and credit picked up the properties at bargain-basement prices. Such periodic contractions of the economy contributed to the increasing control of major industries in fewer and fewer hands.

CONCENTRATION OF CONTROL

By 1900, free enterprise had produced oligopoly, that is, control of an industry by a handful of big corporations. Steel was dominated by Carnegie. Rockefeller's Standard Oil Company controlled oil refining. Sugar refining was in hands of a trust led by Henry O. Havemeyer. Trusts existed in other industries ranging from whiskey to lead. Meat packing was the preserve of five big Chicago companies.

The process was not confined to the North. In the South, tobacco manufacturing came to be dominated by the Duke family of Durham, North Carolina. Through the American Tobacco Company the Dukes expanded into the North, won effective control of the national market, and became so powerful that they could impose on rival British interests an agreement providing for allocation of world markets. Another southern white, Henry De Bardeleben, amassed vast holdings in coal and iron mines, blast furnaces, and railroads. These in turn were absorbed into the Tennessee Coal, Iron and Railroad Company, which for a time was the largest single owner of coal and iron lands in the United States.

Events followed the same course in the Far West. The vital shipping, railroad, and banking interests of the region were controlled by a handful of men, typified by Collis P. Huntington and Leland Stanford. The romantic figure of the prospector receded as mining became big business, symbolized by the Guggenheim interests and the Anaconda Copper Company. The vast forests of the West were largely in the hands of railroad corporations or of such emerging giants in lumbering as the Weyerhaeuser company.

Oligopoly was the result of a generation of unrestrained economic and political warfare. The story of this struggle has been told many times, and its drama has tended to obscure two important historical developments. First was the emergence of the holding company as the preeminent device through which small elites gained control of myriads of operating companies and thus shaped the economic destinies of millions of Americans. Second was the development of a new form of internal corporate government dedicated to efficiency above all else.

A holding company engages in no productive enterprise. As its name implies, it is a legal entity that "holds" strategic blocks of stock in operating companies to assure control of their policies. Basic to the rise of the holding company was the individual corporation, a legal "person" that had its beginnings in pre-Civil War America and became the typical form of industrial enterprise in the postwar era. The corporation was chartered by a state and limited to specified activities. The competition between corporations often proved disastrous, and businessmen sought ways to limit it. The first attempt took the form of "pools" in railroads and similar organizations in such industries as rubber footwear. These were gentlemen's agreements allocating markets, fixing rates and prices, and regulating competition. The pools were short-lived. Businessmen proved to be no gentlemen when it came to making money, and eventually the courts held pools unlawful.

The next step was formation of "trusts." Under this form, stockholders in several corporations in a given industry turned over their voting rights to a board of trustees, who then directed a uniform policy for all member corporations. The prime mover in this field was John D. Rockefeller, who in 1879 set up the Standard Oil Trust. Others rapidly followed suit in other industries. Public outcries against the resulting monopolies, passage of the Sherman antitrust law, and state court decisions against trusts caused businessmen to seek more effective and more discreet measures to continue consolidation.

The means was at hand: the lax incorporation law passed by New Jersey in 1889, which permitted corporations chartered by the state to do much as they pleased. The instrument was the holding company. Although the device had already been used by a few companies, such as American Bell Telephone, the trend toward the holding company did not become decisive until Standard Oil took advantage of the New Jersey law in 1899.

Integration of productive enterprises through holding companies marked yet another phase of industrial evolution: control of industries by a small group of in-

YOUR MONEY WILL BE IMMEDIATELY RETURNED TO YOU FOR ANY GOODS NOT PERFECTLY SATISFACTORY. 673

THE 4x5 CONLEY SENIOR BOX CAMERA

$1.95

WITH GENUINE CONLEY FLEXIBLE VALVE PLATE HOLDER

MADE AT OUR OWN FACTORY AT ROCHESTER

BETTER THAN BOX CAMERAS SOLD BY OTHER DEALERS AT FROM $4.00 TO $5.00.

WE ARE FIGHTING THE CAMERA TRUST

WITH BETTER CAMERAS AT LOWER PRICES THAN THEY CAN OFFER.

PRACTICALLY ALL CAMERAS except ours are sold by the Trust or marketed by the Trust through their dealers, and these cameras are sold at prices from two to four times the prices which we ask for Conley cameras of corresponding styles and better quality. We have been threatened with all sorts of trouble by the Trust if we refuse to join this combination of camera manufacturers in an effort to compel you to pay two or three prices for your camera, but we refuse to be intimidated, and will continue to manufacture our own cameras, in our own factory and sell them at our own prices, prices which represent but the mere cost of materials and labor, with our one small percentage of profit added.

Sears Roebuck & Co. catalog, 1908

This mail order house joined in the "trust busting" crusade during the era of President "Teddy" Roosevelt.

vestment bankers. Mergers and acquisitions, as well as expansion in itself, called for vast amounts of capital—much more than American savings could provide. Businessmen then turned to the private bankers who could tap resources abroad. These included August Belmont, agent of the powerful Rothschilds; Kuhn, Loeb and Company, with ties to a major German bank; and J. P. Morgan, the colossus of Anglo-American banking. In return for their aid, the bankers insisted on representation on corporate boards of directors.

Since the banks were the prime source of corporate credit, their representatives soon came to dominate corporate policy. They shaped that policy toward still further consolidation, which was made easier by the bank representatives sitting on the boards of scores of corporations. Through these interlocking directorates the great bankers guided American industry into bigger combinations that controlled key sectors of the industrial economy. Thus, by 1900 what had been more than 1,000 independent rail lines had been merged into 6 great systems, all under banker control.

The passing of power from the captains of industry to the generals of the banking houses was dramatically demonstrated in 1901. Andrew Carnegie surrendered (at great profit) his steel empire to J. P. Morgan, who merged it with steel companies already under his control into a holding company of unprecedented size—the United States Steel Corporation. Six years later, in another demonstration of power, Morgan persuaded the "trust-busting" President Theodore Roosevelt to approve Morgan's takeover of the financially ailing Tennessee Coal, Iron and Railroad Company as part of U. S. Steel.

There were some variations in the trend. Edward H. Harriman, the railroad magnate, was a financial power in himself. The Rockefellers were so powerful that they moved into banking themselves, through the National City Bank of New York. In Pittsburgh the relatively small family bank of the Mellons was in no position to finance giant takeovers, but it was shrewd enough to gamble on the research of

Charles M. Hall, the chemist whose work made possible the Aluminum Corporation of America, a monopoly that made the Mellons one of the richest families in the country.

Not all bankers were as shrewd. Morgan, for example, in 1910 turned down an opportunity to finance a new company seeking funds. The company went elsewhere. Its name was General Motors.

BUSINESS GOVERNMENT: THE MILITARY MODEL

The emergence of large-scale enterprise required a formal and disciplined type of corporate governance. The relatively loose and informal style of earlier business organization was not possible in corporations with factories and offices scattered throughout the land. Nor was it congenial with the new breed of business managers who were bent on promoting efficiency, cutting costs, and eliminating waste. Corporate organization now became formalized in a business bureaucracy modeled after an army command structure.

At the apex was a board of directors, which set policy and made major decisions. A president was assigned responsibility for carrying out board orders and supervising the work of vice-presidents. The vice-presidents had full authority over departments under their control: supply, production, sales, and finance. Beneath the vice-presidents were various layers of bureaucracy—factory managers, branch managers, superintendents, foremen—to execute orders from above. At the bottom were the masses of workers in offices, factories, railroads, mines and mills—the industrial soldiers, whose duty was to obey orders. Such management was possible because business now had at its command new devices of communication and control that enabled headquarters to monitor and direct performance of units in the field: telephones, telegraphs, typewriters, comptometers, adding machines, and a shorthand system especially devised for American business by John R. Gregg.

Of the headquarters staff, perhaps the two most significant posts were those of sales and finance. By 1900 the problems of supply and production were regarded as largely solved, but competition and the drive toward consolidation made the others of increasing importance. The sales department was held responsible not only for meet-

In the 1870s the typewriter revolutionized communications.

Scientific American, *1891*

These scenes from the Chicago stockyards show an early application of conveyor belt production. Workers had to keep up with the "line," or else.

ing the needs of the existing markets but also for creating markets where none existed. Thus, J. B. Duke made his cigarettes an American staple through unprecedented use of advertising. Duke's success inspired other businessmen to follow suit. As a consequence, there emerged a new specialized type of business, the advertising agency, whose sole purpose was to develop demand for the products of its clients.

A major function of the finance department was to cut expenses. Top officials of Standard Oil, for example, required daily reports on operating costs, kept firm rein on them, and made corporate decisions on the basis of such findings. Thus flowered a new profession, the cost accountant. The cost accountant wielded influence in all other departments, for they were strictly responsible for their expenses. Thus, all departments were prompted to reduce their costs. The people at the bottom bore the brunt of cost-cutting, but executives who faltered in meeting corporate goals were weeded out ruthlessly.

"Cost," however, was a relative term. Men at the top, such as Rockefeller, Carnegie, and Duke, were bent on spending money on new and expensive processes and machines that promised to cut costs in the long run. It was up to the finance departments to see to it that the promises were kept.

Business organization, then, was akin to military organization. Orders were issued from the top and were to be executed speedily and without question. Argument and disagreement among top managers might be tolerated, even encouraged, as in the case of Standard Oil, but once decisions were agreed on, underlings were expected to carry them out. Thus, military virtues were incorporated into business on a large scale: obedience, punctuality, loyalty, devotion to duty. In such a milieu, most Americans found little opportunity to express their individuality. There was no place for a Walt Whitman to loaf and invite his soul.

FOR FURTHER READING

A good brief treatment of business developments appears in Thomas C. Cochran, *Business in American Life: A History* (1972). For a somewhat different emphasis, see *The Age of Enterprise* (1961) by Cochran and William Miller. The role of business in the New South is well described in C. Vann Woodward, *Origins of the New South* (1951). Business leadership is discussed in William Miller, ed., *Men in Business* (1952).

For the ideas involved in the gospel of success the best introduction is Richard Hofstadter's classic *Social Darwinism in American Thought* (1959). For a handy collection of arguments for and against Social Darwinism see Gail Kennedy, *Democracy and the Gospel of Wealth* (1949). The influence of *McGuffey's Readers* in shaping attitudes is analyzed in Richard D. Mosier, *Making the American Mind* (1947).

For comprehensive studies of economic expansion, see Edward C. Kirkland, *Industry Comes of Age* (1967), and Robert Higgs, *The Transformation of the American Economy* (1971).

17 business as urbanizer

Business was primarily an urban enterprise. Indeed, urban civilization as we know it is largely the product of industrial America. That is, cities were not merely great aggregates of population but were also functional units shaped to meet the needs and promote the interests of business. As business located its offices and factories in cities, foreign immigrants and country folk flocked into them. So powerful was the attraction of cities to native-born whites that many rural counties in the East and Middle West suffered sharp drops in population in the late nineteenth century.

THE RISE OF BUSINESS AND THE RISE OF THE CITY

Older cities grew in size, most dramatically demonstrated by Chicago, which expanded from fewer than 110,000 residents in 1860 to more than 1 million in 1890. New cities sprang up in the developing West and South, typified by Tacoma, Washington, and Birmingham, Alabama. The urban centers were linked together by rapid means of communication: railroads, telegraphs, and later, telephones. The geographic pattern thus established remained a basic element in economic activities until the rise of new urban centers after World War II.

The rhythms of city life were attuned to the needs of business. Railroad schedules were arranged primarily with the requirements of businessmen in mind. Street railways were laid out with an eye to linking offices, factories, and residential districts. "Rush hours" in early morning and early evening, with the crush of people hurrying to and from work and the consequent traffic congestion, were a constant feature of city life, a testament to the regimentation the needs of business imposed. Working hours and the intensity of labor shaped eating, sleeping, and recreational habits.

Regimentation brought tension. One cause was sheer overcrowding. By 1900 the eight largest cities in the country accounted for one-tenth of the entire population. In some areas of downtown New York the density of population exceeded that of the most crowded cities in Europe. Most of these residents, of course, were poor folk jammed together in suffocating tenements. In other cities the overcrowding was not so intense, but landlords reaped the profits from crowding as many people as possible into each acre of land.

Residential overcrowding was complemented with work overcrowding. Development of the elevator and improved structural steel made possible the skyscraper, which could house thousands of office workers. As such buildings proliferated, business areas of cities were congested with masses of people. The same was true of factories. Workers and machines were so placed that not an inch of space was lost.

Another factor adding to urban tensions was the fast pace of life. Improvements in transportation and communication may have made business more efficient, but they added to the strains of living. More than ever, time meant money. So, businessmen hustled—and their employees had to hustle, too. In a time when the economy was both expansive and unstable and businessmen were fighting each other for dominance, businessmen had to be alert—all the time—and make their decisions promptly. In the jungle warfare of the day, no businessman could afford to let down his guard or let the other guy get ahead.

Working people were subjected to the same strains. The drives for efficiency and cost-cutting required faster and faster work from office and factory workers. Those who could not keep up the pace were weeded out. Business had discovered that for routine tasks people were as interchangeable as machines and parts.

City dwellers tended to be tense, alert, nervous. There was so much psychosomatic illness in the cities that what had been a small patent medicine business in 1865 became a huge industry by 1890. Its wares, usually liberally laced with alcohol or opium derivatives, certainly soothed the tensions arising from city living even if they had little effect on the ailments they claimed to cure. The same may be said of alcoholic beverages, which were consumed in larger quantities than ever before.

City life was impersonal as well as tense. The rapid growth of cities, their sheer size, and their intensely competitive climate left little room for the development of a sense of community. In contrast to village and small-town life, city dwellers lived in anonymity, with little concern for others. Some migrants from the countryside reveled in the personal freedom such living afforded, but for many others it meant the isolation and loneliness Theodore Dreiser depicted in *Sister Carrie* and *Jennie Gerhardt*.

Families and schools did little to develop a sense of community among children, for they themselves were prime factors in conditioning children to internalize the business virtues. Each family was a competitive unit, struggling with other families for jobs or status, depending on class. Parents expected children to be industrious, punctual, and obedient. Corporal punishment for offending youngsters was accepted as a matter of course.

Schools carried on the lessons begun at home. Inculcation of the business virtues was a standard feature of education. Disobedience was discouraged with physical punishment. Punctuality was such an obsession with administrators that children often turned back from school to avoid the stigma of tardiness. Even in remote Portland, Oregon, hardly the most bustling of cities, the superintendent of schools reported in 1878 that "the vast importance" of training in punctuality could "scarcely be estimated." He explained, "Punctuality is a virtue which must be cultivated by all who would succeed in any calling, whether lofty or humble." The same official revealed unconsciously how the bleak impersonality of the business world was reflected in the classroom: "Too little is done and said in our school rooms to cultivate the affections of our children. Cold, exacting programs are followed with a zeal and precision almost tiresome to contemplate."

These programs were on the way out of urban schools by 1910. Influenced by such European educational theorists as H. H. Pestalozzi and Johan Herbart and the American John Dewey, schools gradually abandoned their traditional approach based on rote memory and paid more attention to the needs and interests of youngsters. Part of the change involved training children to meet problems of the world in which they lived. Dewey had in mind developing habits of critical thinking and the appreciation of ideas.

Businessmen—and parents—interpreted that purpose differently. For them, helping children, especially those in the rapidly growing high-school systems, meant providing students with job skills. School curricula were modified to provide for vocational education according to sexual roles. Boys learned bookkeeping, printing, woodworking, metalworking, painting, and carpentry. Some boys took such commercial courses as shorthand and typing, but these were increasingly the domain of girls. For girls there were courses in dressmaking, cooking, baking, and household management.

Businessmen were thus assured of a constant supply of workers trained at public expense. Parents were no less enthusiastic, believing that such schooling assured employment for their children. As businessmen perceived the importance of mass education, they began to take active roles on school boards, shaping policy to serve their immediate interests and their philosophy that what was good for business was good for America.

There was some sense of community in the ethnic enclaves in the cities. Germans continued to hold themselves aloof from general American society. People in the ghettos of the "new immigration"—Eastern European Jews, Poles, Russians, Hungarians, Greeks—were simply overwhelmed and dismayed by this strange new world of industry, so utterly alien from their peasant backgrounds. They clung to each other and their traditions for psychological survival in a society for which they were not prepared.

Nevertheless, they could not escape the pressures and tensions of American society. The sense of community was weakened as young children, impressed by the attitudes they met in the schools and on playgrounds, felt ashamed of their Old World parents. Many adolescents, taken by the gaudiest and shoddiest aspects of American life, turned to ways of making money quickly that made parents ashamed of them. "Americanization" programs, designed to make immigrants abandon their cultural heritage and replace it with American white middle-class values, helped to imbue immigrants with feelings of inferiority. Ethnic community consciousness was undermined as immigrants tried desperately to fit themselves into individualistic white American society. The generational and cultural conflicts this produced within immigrant communities added to the tensions of urban living.

"THIEVING AND BOODLING"

Business made its imprint on cities in other ways. Urban expansion was largely uncontrolled and unplanned, providing a rich harvest for real estate speculators and developers, men more interested in profits than in orderly planning with human needs in mind. Expansion also called for great outlays for public works. Businessmen vied with each other for these lucrative contracts, while the political machines that dominated many city governments extracted every possible dollar in "kickbacks."

Businessmen fought each other also for the franchises that gave them monopolies in providing gas, electricity, and street railway service to city dwellers. The franchises went, as did public works contracts, to the businessmen with the closest ties to the political bosses.

Like their counterparts in other industries, the men in public utilities consolidated their holdings. One group of six men controlled more than 100 street railway systems in the East and Middle West, including those of Chicago, New York City, Pittsburgh, and Philadelphia. The same men controlled gas and electricity franchises in more than eighty towns and cities throughout the country. From such operations men like Thomas Fortune Ryan amassed their fortunes. These "monopolistic corporations," said Hazen Pingree, reform mayor of Detroit in the 1890s, were "responsible for nearly all the thieving and boodling" plaguing municipal government.

Corruption was not confined to top-level dealings between political bosses and businessmen. It was spread through the entire system of many major city governments. Political machines saw to it that their men were elected judges—and judges were expected to look after the interests of their patrons and their business allies. Municipal employees had to kick back part of their salaries to politicians. Policemen afforded protection to saloon keepers, brothel keepers, gamblers, and streetwalkers in return for payoffs.

The organized gangs that dominated big-city crime were linked to the political machines and thus enjoyed considerable immunity. They also lived in a symbiotic relationship with the police. They provided payoffs and inside information on rival gangs, especially arrivals from out of town, that enabled local police to round up criminals and project an image of protectors of public order. The police, in return, let the gangs run their own affairs.

Businessmen also found the gangs useful. The "robber barons" Jim Fisk and Jay Gould used thugs against rivals, who responded in kind. Newspaper owners employed hoodlums in the "circulation wars" of the early twentieth century. Antiunion employers hired gunmen to break strikes.

Corruption was so outrageous that time and again reformers, including businessmen who suffered from the corruption, rallied to oust the machines. Sometimes they won, but their successes were short-lived. The reformers were business-oriented middle-class folk, and their very prejudices against the working poor and immigrants kept them from developing a mass base of political support. The machines, on the other hand, never neglected such people. With the aid of their business allies and the support of the poor, the machines soon resumed power. Indeed, the reforms put into effect usually involved centralizing power in municipal government, a move that made political bossism more effective than before. It is significant that "Boss" Tweed, the most notorious of the Tammany Hall breed in New York City, endorsed such reforms.

Machine politics was, in essence, the application of free enterprise to government. As such, it was wasteful and inefficient. Public payrolls were notoriously padded. Public works contractors did shoddy work. Police, no matter how much their ranks were increased, seemed unable to cope with mounting crime. Unless one had the right political connections, doing business with government was slow, cumbersome, and—owing to all the graft—expensive. To the new breed of businessmen who came to power in the late nineteenth century, all this was anathema. They wanted government to be as efficient as their offices and factories. Working with reformers, they were able to obtain the beginnings of a nonpolitical federal civil service in 1883. The movement gradually spread within state governments.

Businessmen and reformers helped to change the form of government in many cities prior to 1914. Arguing that politics had no place in municipal affairs and that cities were not so much small states as large corporations and should be run the way a corporation would be, the business and reform alliance persuaded voters to abandon or modify the traditional system of government by mayors and councilmen elected from individual wards. In its place were offered two substitutes: the commission and the city-manager plans. The former, touted successfully as "businessman's government," provided for the complete administration of city affairs by a small group of nonpolitical commissioners elected on a citywide basis. The latter provided for appointment of a professional administrator with sweeping powers by elected officials.

The civic rejoicing that such innovations meant the end of political bosses and machine politics was premature. Later in the twentieth century these very reforms furnished the basis for some of the most powerful local and state machines in American history, as in New Jersey and Missouri.

The reforms, however, had another aspect that has received less comment: they drastically reduced the political power of blacks and ethnic minorities. The wards, mainstays of traditional local politics, were simply urban neighborhoods. Blacks and immigrants were isolated in slum neighborhoods, which because of their votes, were important to machine politicians. Thus, the blacks and newcomers could exert some political influence and gain some attention to their needs, even if only in the form of municipal jobs, free fuel and food, and friendly intercession with police and judges when the need arose.

Eliminating the ward system and replacing it with citywide voting weakened black and immigrant political strength in relation to the mass of native white voters. In short, the reforms meant white middle-class domination of local government. It was no coincidence that the reforms were carried through in the early years of the twentieth century, when blacks nationally were being relegated to second-class citizenship and when there was mounting nativist clamor about the role of immigrants in political life.

"YELLOW JOURNALISM"

The growth of business hastened urbanization, while, in its turn, urbanization stimulated further business growth. In the process there emerged a major new urban industry: cheap, mass-circulation, daily newspapers. Some were designed primarily to serve the business interests of their owners. Public-utilities magnates, such as Charles T. Yerkes in Chicago, routinely acquired newspapers to influence politicians and public opinion. A few others used newspapers to promote the larger cause of civic betterment. Henry Villard, the financial genius of the Northern Pacific railroad and founder of what came to be the General Electric Company, gave his editors on the *New York Evening Post* free rein to campaign for reform.

Newspapers attracted businessmen because, in addition to furnishing a means of influencing public opinion, they were lucrative. Before the Civil War, James Gordon Bennett had demonstrated in New York City that there was money to be made in providing cheap newspapers that, in simplified language, emphasized the dramatic: violence, crime, sex, money, sentimentality. After the war, Joseph Pulitzer exploited the formula successfully in St. Louis and New York City, as did the brothers James and E. W. Scripps in Detroit and Cleveland. These men added a new element: they gained readers by crusades against big business and its political henchmen. It should be noted, however, that these men were not merely newspaper owners. They were experienced editors who had learned the business from the inside.

Their financial success attracted the attention of businessmen who knew nothing of newspaper work and had no use for crusades. Urban newspapers, however, were expensive operations. Their success lay in volume, and volume was possible only through heavy investment in new technology, such as linotypes (1886) and huge rotary presses (1875) eventually capable of turning out 1 million copies a day. Besides, payrolls had to be met and money spent on such new sources of reader appeal as comic strips, colored Sunday supplements, photographs, and news furnished by such organizations as the Associated Press. Nevertheless, businessmen found the prospect alluring. Between 1880 and 1900 the number of daily newspapers rose from fewer than 1,000 to more than 2,200. Many employed the "yellow journalism" techniques of a newcomer in the field, William Randolph Hearst, heir to the fortune of Senator George Hearst of California, who exploited the public's interest in the sensational.

These men perceived that winning readers was not in itself the way to success. Indeed, given the investment in publishing, no mass newspaper could support itself through mere sales. Rather, profits lay in getting advertising. The bigger the circulation, the easier it was to attract advertisers. And the bigger the circulation, the higher the advertising rates.

Publishers were able to turn newspapers into gold mines largely because of the revolution in retail merchandising then under way. National firms, such as the American Tobacco Company, spent lavishly to promote retail sales of their products. In every city there were new local department stores, symbolized by Macy's in New York and Marshall Field in Chicago, which competed with each other for the consumer dollar. To reach consumers, the cheapest and most efficient way was through the mass-circulation daily newspapers. As the golden flow of advertising revenue mounted, publishers used every gimmick to increase circulation. The most notorious were the lurid and often false accounts of Spanish ''atrocities'' in Cuba published by Pulitzer and Hearst in New York, producing an inflamed public opinion that helped bring on the Spanish-American war.

Some publishers were not content to build up their own circulations. They tried to damage the circulations of rivals. In some cities, most notoriously Chicago, publishers hired gangsters to terrorize news dealers, newsboys, and distributors and to destroy stocks of rival newspapers ready for sale.

The dependence of newspapers on advertisers reflected itself in news and editorial policy. No major advertiser was to be offended. No significant section of the advertiser's buying public was to be alienated. Nearly every newsroom in the country had its list of ''sacred cows,'' about whom no adverse report or comment was permitted. The lists, of course, were not confined to advertisers. Political and business friends of the owners also enjoyed immunity. Some publishers, such as Pulitzer, Hearst, E. W. Scripps, and Adolph Ochs of the *New York Times,* felt strong enough to resist business pressures. Most newspaper owners felt no such urge.

While this made for a certain blandness in treating issues and people connected to newspaper owners, it did not mean dullness in news and editorial columns. On the contrary. Newspapers preached the gospel of success incessantly. They directed a strident nationalism against Britain, Spain, and Germany. Editorials thundered against anarchists, socialists, and communists. Front pages reported the Pullman strike of 1894 as if the streets of Chicago were awash with blood. Governor Altgeld of Illinois was crucified because he pardoned the anarchist survivors of the Haymarket case of 1886. Militant labor unions, such as the Industrial Workers of the World, popularly called the ''Wobblies,'' found themselves portrayed as the enemies of society. The women's suffrage movement was always good for ridicule, or if taken seriously, it was denounced as an enemy of the family. Blacks were almost uniformly pictured as irresponsible, shiftless, and criminal. Lynching of blacks was often reported with levity. Immigrants were associated with crime, violence, and vice. Comic strips, cartoons, and joke columns helped condition children to absorb adult prejudices.

In short, while newspapers reflected the beliefs of their owners, they gained readers by reinforcing the attitudes and the stereotypes of minorities already prevalent among large masses of native-born white Americans. The immediate aim, of course, was profit, but such treatment of minorities paid another dividend: it helped maintain the status quo. So long as the ranks of its potential challengers remained divided, the power of business was secure.

THE STATUS SEEKERS

''Polite society'' before the Civil War was preoccupied with questions of rank and status, but in postwar society the preoccupation expanded into an obsession. Many more people were eligible for elite membership in terms of wealth, but it was more difficult to establish oneself at the top. Owning $1 million was no longer of much moment when there were many multimillionaires about. Indeed, a few notables, such as John D. Rockefeller, Andrew Carnegie, Leland Stanford, and Andrew Mellon, counted their wealth in the hundreds of millions of dollars. In short, a new class of wealthy emerged, which in the course of a generation rose from relative obscurity to manifest riches. Like their business activities, the social life of the newly rich was centered in the cities.

Successful though they might be in business, the newly rich found that the "polite society" of the old elites, especially in the East, had little room for them. The newcomers were regarded as ostentatious, uncouth, and ignorant. Charles Francis Adams, Jr., scion of the great Adams family and himself a successful businessman, had only contempt for them. They were, he said, "mere money-getters and traders," without "humor, thought or refinement." And, he added, "Not one that I have ever known would I care to meet again, either in this world or the next."

The new men—and their wives—bitterly resented such attitudes. Yet they were all too conscious of their lack of the poise, the sureness, and the ingrained sense of superiority that went with inherited wealth. The frustrations generated by such feelings prompted an obsession with status, which found expression in the "conspicuous consumption" that Thorstein Veblen, the famous social philosopher, analyzed in *The Theory of the Leisure Class* (1889).

The old elites had demonstrated their status by public display of their affluence. The newly rich set out, not only to imitate them, but also to outdo them. Along such fashionable thoroughfares as Fifth Avenue in New York, Euclid Avenue in Cleveland, and Lake Shore Drive in Chicago, and on Nob Hill in San Francisco, millionaires erected great mansions, with dozens of rooms. Collis P. Huntington's home on Fifth Avenue took five years to build and cost $2.5 million. Andrew Carnegie wrote that it was the "duty" of rich men "to set an example of modest, unostentatious living," but he himself maintained a magnificent mansion on Fifth Avenue.

The interior decorations of the mansions were designed to impress visitors. Massive chandeliers, ornate mirrors, imported furniture, luxurious rugs and carpets, and paintings and sculptures by old masters testified to the opulence, if not to the taste, of the owners. Such palatial homes testified in still another way to the wealth of their owners. They required retinues of servants to do the work that made life in "society" so easy.

The desire to impress others was reflected also in the social life of the newly rich. They entertained at home in a fashion copied from the English nobility. Dinner guests were waited on by liveried footmen directed by a lordly butler. The food, prepared by skilled chefs, was served on silver or gold plates. An orchestra played

Elite and middle-class Americans enjoyed private baths in post-Civil War America. This bathtub model offered both "sitz" and "plunge" baths (1876).

soft music while the guests made conversation. Publicly, the newly rich frequented such restaurants as that of Lorenzo Delmonico in New York. Delmonico, a Swiss immigrant and himself a parvenu with keen insight into the psychology of the newly rich, taught Americans that appreciation of fine cuisine was a mark not only of good taste but also of status. He drove his point home with his prices: it was not uncommon for a dinner party at Delmonico's to cost more than $100 per person. The shrewd Swiss made himself a fortune, and his success inspired imitators in other cities.

Since patronage of the arts had long been associated with aristocracy, the newly rich became art patrons. They subsidized opera companies and symphony orchestras. Since more prestige was to be gained by importing European talent, American musicians, even the well-reputed New England Conservatory of Music, were neglected. The same discrimination held true for painting and sculpture. There was an emerging school of vigorous American painters and sculptors, but the newly rich preferred works with already established reputations. With business acumen, they hired expert art dealers to scour Europe for the old masters—and some not so old—that graced their baronial mansions.

Indeed, patronage of the arts involved both "old" and "new" money in a great symbolic battle in New York City in the 1880s. Private boxes at the opera were a sure sign of high status, and competition for the seats was keen. When New York's leading opera house barred the newly rich from its "golden horseshoe," the parvenus raised $2 million to build the Metropolitan Opera House, which boasted not of a "golden horseshoe" but of a "diamond horseshoe." The Metropolitan was soon the leading opera house in the country, foreshadowing other victories of the newly rich.

Those who could afford it enjoyed the palatial comfort of the new railroad sleeping cars of the 1870s.

THE BUSINESS OF PHILANTHROPY

Philanthropy was another sign of high status, and the newly rich threw themselves into it with the same zeal that marked their building of mansions. Like old elites, the new gave aid to churches, hospitals, and museums, but they had little interest in helping the poor or in such causes as prison reform. Imbued with the teachings of Herbert Spencer, they preferred to help those who could help themselves. Thus, they gave generously to institutions that would aid poor young men of talent and ambition to rise in the world and thus indirectly benefit society as a whole.

Another, and not entirely disinterested, motive prompted the generosity of the newly rich. It was apparent to a growing number of business leaders that the old, informal, "on the job" training in business was no longer adequate for the needs of an economy steadily becoming more sophisticated and complex. These leaders saw that ways had to be found to train young people in science, technology, and business management.

They subsidized libraries and such self-help organizations as the Young Men's Christian Association, but the principal beneficiary of this philanthropy was higher education. It has been estimated that between 1878 and 1898 at least $140 million were donated to colleges and universities by individuals. John D. Rockefeller and associates in the Chicago business world financed a new University of Chicago, while Rockefeller himself donated $100,000 to Wellesley College, a private school for women. Johns Hopkins in Baltimore and Jonas Clark in Worcester, Massachusetts, endowed the new universities that bore their names. In the Far West, Leland Stanford made possible a new school to provide college work for "poor" young people.

Science, technology, and management were specific areas of training in such new centers as the Case Institute of Technology in Cleveland, Ohio; the Armour Institute of Technology in Chicago; and the Wharton School of Finance and Economics at the University of Pennsylvania. The trend toward highly specialized training in management was symbolized in 1908 when Harvard organized its graduate school of business administration.

Just as bankers took seats on boards of directors, so the benefactors of higher education took seats on the boards of trustees of colleges and universities. Trustees set policy and depended on hired administrators to carry out their wishes. With a tradition of academic freedom not yet established, trustees felt free to fire professors whose opinions were unorthodox. E. W. Bemis, for example, was forced to resign from the University of Chicago in 1895 because of his utterances about local public utilities. Perhaps the most glaring example of business control was at Cornell University, where for years Henry W. Sage, who had made a fortune in lumbering, so dominated affairs that President Andrew White referred to him as "our millionaire master." Indeed, trustees and many middle-class Americans looked upon colleges and universities as merely business operations, with presidents and professors to be hired and fired like other employees.

Business influence extended also to public colleges and universities. Businessmen directly or through surrogate politicians and lawyers served on the governing boards and sought to shape policy in line with business outlook and interests. They were not always successful. In 1894 some business interests in Wisconsin sought the dismissal of Professor Richard T. Ely, an economist at the University of Wisconsin who advocated social reform. The board of regents established a precedent by supporting Ely's claim "to follow the indications of the truth wherever they may lead." Other governing boards, however, were slow to follow Wisconsin's lead.

The philanthropists were many, but towering above them all were Rockefeller and Carnegie. These men were signicant not simply because of the sheer size of their gifts, but also because they introduced into philanthropy the same principles of scientific management they employed in business. In fact, they assigned the distribution of funds to professional managers. Thus, the Carnegie Corporation (1911) and the Rockefeller Foundation (1913) were in themselves major operations, with assets of several hundred million dollars. Since the foundations were intended to continue after the deaths of the donors, the funds were invested as well as distributed. By 1965 the assets of the Carnegie Corporation had reached nearly $334 million and those of the Rockefeller Foundation $862 million.

The positive contributions of the new philanthropies cannot be gainsaid. The Rockefeller-financed General Education Board helped upgrade black and white colleges in the South and later stimulated innovative programs in colleges throughout the nation. Carnegie funds made possible Abraham Flexner's report in 1910 that revolutionized medical education. Rockefeller money sparked the campaign that led to eradication in the South of the hookworm, the parasite that had afflicted the region for generations. In 1909, scientists at the Rockefeller Institute pioneered research in poliomyelitis; twenty-five years later that research resulted in identification of the virus that causes the disease.

Good works, however, added up to control. With colleges and universities clamoring for grants, the foundations were in a position to shape general policy for higher education. Programs that seemed worthy were funded; the others languished without money. More, the very generosity of the givers inhibited free inquiry. William E. Dodd, the noted southern historian, wrote in 1908 with special reference to Rockefeller philanthropies in the South, that "many subjects which come every day into the mind of the historian may not with safety even so much as be discussed." Blacks who did not share Booker T. Washington's views of vocational training for blacks protested that foundation funds went to Washington and his followers, while liberal arts colleges that upheld the ideal of racial equality were neglected.

"TITLE HUNTING"

While the newly rich resented the exclusiveness of the old elites, they asserted their status by being exclusive themselves. They wanted no association with those beneath them. Since they were unfamiliar with the intricacies of "polite society," they relied upon such men as Ward McAllister, the wealthy arbiter of New York society, to tell them who was, and who was not, socially acceptable. Once assured, they kept themselves within the charmed circle.

They also saw to it that their children met only the right kinds of people. The wealthy sent their youngsters to schools and colleges where the children of the old and the new elites mingled and were prepared to take their places as members of a class in which the differences between "new" and "old" money were diminishing.

Intermarriage with the old elites was avidly sought by the newly rich. Even more, they sought to establish their status by alliances with English and European nobility. Of the numerous trans-Atlantic marriages, perhaps the most notable for present-day Americans was that in 1874 of Jennie Jerome, a Brooklyn heiress, to Lord Randolph Churchill. Their son Winston became the famous British prime minister of World War II.

Through all these means—display of wealth, patronage of the arts, philanthropy, common educational experiences of the young, and intermarriage with older American elites and European nobility—the newly rich eventually gained entrance into the most exclusive circles of American society. Besides, both old and new elites were bound together by a common interest in meeting the challenges to elite rule that arose from many sources. Frederick Townsend Martin, a scion of inherited wealth, stated the elite view bluntly in 1911: "We are not politicians or public thinkers; we are the rich; we own America; we got it, God knows how, but we intend to keep it if we can."

THE IDLE RICH

Another bond linked old and new elites together: the men in both believed in work, and they expected their sons to be equally dedicated to the pursuit of business affairs. The tradition was weakening, however, by the end of the nineteenth century. Thanks to inherited wealth, often in the form of lifetime trusts, there were increasing numbers of men and women who enjoyed generous independent incomes and had no need to work. Such wealth, together with inherited high social status, produced a new leisure class with little interest in either business or public affairs.

Rather, they spent their time in cultivated uselessness, aping the ways of the English aristocracy. They engaged in an endless round of dances, dinner parties, concerts, opera parties, and attendance at fashionable theaters. Some played the new upper-class games: tennis, polo, and golf. Others bred pedigreed dogs and horses. Hunt clubs were organized in the English fox-hunting tradition, replete with horns, hounds, and red-coated riders. An early, if ironic, example of the new leisure class was Elliott Roosevelt, father of Eleanor Roosevelt, the most public-spirited and independent woman ever to grace the White House.

FOR FURTHER READING

A good introduction to urban development is Charles N. Glaab and A. Theodore Brown, *A History of Urban America* (1967). More thorough is the notable study by Blake McKelvey, *The Urbanization of America* (1963). See also John W. Reps, *The Making of Urban America* (1965), for a history of city planning. One of the first historians to note the importance of the city was Arthur M. Schlesinger, Sr., whose *Rise of the City* first appeared in 1933.

Various aspects of urban living are discussed in Lewis Mumford, *The Brown Decades* (1955); David M. Potter, *People of Plenty* (19654); and Ray Ginger, *Altgeld's America* (1958). Problems of social status are analyzed in Robert Wiebe, *The Search for Order* (1967). Urban housing reform is the subject of R. Lubove's *Progressives and the Slums* (1962). A pioneer study in the linking of improved transportation and suburban growth is Sam B. Warner, *Streetcar Suburbs* (1962), which centers on Boston. See also Stephan Thernstrom and Richard Sennett, eds., *Nineteenth Century Cities: Essays in the New Urban History* (1969).

Changes related to urban development are discussed in Bernard Wishy, *The Child and the Republic* (1967); Lawrence A. Cremin, *The Transformation of the School* (1961); and David J. Pivar, *Purity Crusade: Sexual Morality and Social Control* (1973).

The link between municipal political bosses and businessmen was first laid bare in 1904 by Lincoln Steffens, *The Shame of the Cities*. More recent works include Harold Zink, *City Bosses in the United States* (1930); Walton Bean, *Boss Ruef's San Francisco* (1952); Seymour Mandelbaum, *Boss Tweed's New York* (1965); and Alexander Callow, Jr., *The Tweed Ring* (1966).

18

the "new woman": middle class and white

The ''new woman,'' about whom there was much ado at the turn of the twentieth century, was a far cry from the ''lady'' of preindustrial America. The lady was cold, passive, and submissive. She had no public role; she was restricted to home, church, charities, and fashionable social life. She had little, if any, higher education, and she did not talk about such subjects as sex, venereal disease, prostitution, and divorce.

The new woman was quite different. She had been to college. She played sports, such as golf and tennis. She took an active part in public life. She was represented increasingly in the professions. Outspoken, she demanded the right to vote and discussed ''tabooed'' subjects. In her private life, the new woman also defied tradition. In the face of all pressures to the contrary, she might remain single—and indeed extol the virtues of the single life. If she married, she bore fewer children than her mother and grandmothers. If her marriage failed, she was prepared to sue for divorce.

Obviously, the new woman represented only a small, privileged sector of the female population, but she was significant because she became the role model for millions of American girls and women who did not share her background or affluence. The journalistic genius of Edward W. Bok lay in linking the new woman with the unvoiced yearnings of ordinary middle-class women. After he became editor of the *Ladies' Home Journal* in 1889, his cautious acceptance of many ideas associated with the new woman won him a mass of readers. By the time he retired in 1919, his magazine had reached a monthly circulation of 2 million copies. The new woman was a popular figure indeed.

ORIGINS OF THE NEW WOMAN

Generally, the new woman was the product of economic expansion, industrialization, urbanization, and a ferment that marked American thought at the turn of the century. Other, specific factors were also at work.

Girls and women made up an increasing proportion of the labor force. By 1910 they represented 20 percent of the working population. The largest single group in that year were white-collar workers—nearly 2 million of them. Of these, 726,000 were counted as technical and professional workers, representing the successful invasion of traditional male occupations that began after the Civil War. Women were now secretaries, bookkeepers, typists, telephone operators, and department-store clerks. Women also had worked their way into such professions as journalism, law, and medicine, and they dominated schoolteaching, nursing, and librarianship. Almost as many girls and women were employed in manual labor as in white-collar occupations, and nearly 1,784,000 worked in domestic service. More than 1 million women also served on farms as laborers, according to the census.

The employment of so many women outside the home indicated a weakening of the old sanctions against such labor. Indeed, the proportion of married women in the female labor force was rising. In 1910 it stood at nearly 14 percent, and it increased steadily thereafter. Employment provided these workers a larger measure of economic independence and personal freedom than their mothers had known, but it was a limited freedom. At least a substantial portion of the wages paid young blue- and white-collar workers went to help support their families. Indeed, for many of the working poor, even the children had to work for the family to make enough to survive.

The independence of working women was also limited because, even though the sanctions against working outside the home were weakening, the tradition of paying women less than men was as strong as ever. Indeed, the two processes went hand in hand: hiring women meant hiring cheap labor. Thus, in 1914 men employed in manufacturing worked a fifty-two-hour week for an average wage of $13.65. Women in similar employment worked fifty hours for a weekly wage of $7.75. The men made more partly because more of them held skilled jobs, but that fact emphasizes still another factor keeping women in the low-wage category. It was almost impossible for a woman to move beyond unskilled and semiskilled jobs. The discrimination was not confined to business. It extended also to the professions. Teachers, mostly women, in 1914 received an average annual salary of $564. Ministers, mostly men, were paid $938.

The emergence and influence of the "new woman" may also be traced to the growing importance of higher education among women of the elites and middle class. By 1901 there were 128 private women's colleges in existence, while publicly supported normal schools, colleges, and universities attracted thousands of young women. In 1910 women students received 22 percent of all undergraduate degrees granted. In short, women's battle for higher education was won.

But the fruits of victory were bittersweet. While some schools did little to stimulate intellectual activity, others encouraged young women to find self-fulfillment by developing their minds, talents, and independence. Indeed, some educators, such as M. Carey Thomas at Bryn Mawr, encouraged independent careers for women. When the students graduated, however, they found that society, while tolerating career women, still expected women to settle into the traditional pattern of wife and mother.

The heightened expectations of college women thus clashed with the established expectations of society. The now familiar dilemma was posed starkly: marriage or career. Those young women who had looked upon college as simply an essential step toward suitable marriage saw no basic problem. But for those who took college work as serious in itself, the dilemma brought great anguish. It involved a basic decision about what one was going to do with one's life: whether to pursue an independent life as an autonomous person or to submerge one's personality in the roles of wife and mother. It also involved the issue of sex, in itself a source of anxiety since so few young women knew anything about it.

Likewise, the decision affected the religious values many of these young women cherished. They questioned traditional dogmas, but they wanted to cling to the "truths" of their religious backgrounds. As idealistic young people, they were dismayed by the contradictions between the avowed principles of church and nation and the realities of American life. It is small wonder that the tensions were reflected in the "restlessness" of college women that so dismayed adult contemporaries, in psychosomatic illness, and in nervous breakdowns.

Some women solved the problem by combining marriage and career, such as the eminent Mary Putnam Jacobi, M.D. Others gave themselves up to marriage and family, while striving to find additional personal fulfillment in clubs and reform movements. About half of the college graduates never married, seeking realization of their ideals in the professions and in what was called "social service."

Tensions over sexual roles were not confined to college graduates. Charlotte Perkins Gilman, author of the influential *Women and Economics,* never went to college, but the strain between trying to conform to traditional marriage and expressing her own needs brought on a nervous collapse and wrecked her first marriage. Margaret Sanger, the birth control crusader, attended college only briefly, but she too found the roles of wife and independent person imcompatible in her first marriage. It was a problem, indeed, for all married women who valued their individual identities.

Some new women were new women because they had to be. Single women and widows tried to maintain themselves—and their families—even if it meant invading men's traditional domains. Belva Lockwood and Ellen Mussey were widowed lawyers who found their means of livelihood curtailed by professional custom. Lockwood won the right for women to plead before the United States Supreme Court in 1879. Mussey in 1898 established the first law school in the District of Columbia to admit women as well as men. In other fields, also, women with no great commitment to women's rights as such found themselves compelled to assert women's rights in order to make a living.

This situation was particularly true in the South. As Anne Firor Scott points out in *The Southern Lady,* the collapse of the Confederacy brought distress to many genteel, conventional women. Many were widows. Many had husbands whose wounds or sickness made them incapable of earning an adequate living. Still others, single and married, suffered from loss of property. They had no recourse except to break with tradition and go to work. They became teachers, editors, printers, dressmakers, office workers, and librarians. Some also went to work in mills and factories. Opinion had so changed in the South that work outside the home involved no loss of status. A report in 1893 stated that only in the South could "so many well-bred women" pursue "without loss of caste vocations which elsewhere would involve social ostracism." Family and background still counted in the industrializing South. As the number of genteel women in factories declined, working women felt keenly the disdain of southern middle class society.

If gainful employment and higher education contributed to the rise of the new woman, so also did the improving legal status of women as a whole. For a variety of reasons, including the increasing political influence of women, many states removed the legal disabilities previously imposed upon women. In 1914 most states recognized a married woman's right to her own wages. Likewise, she was entitled to own property, to enter into contracts, and to carry on business in her own right. In that same year women could vote freely in eleven states, and in many others they could vote in school and local elections. Mothers were given more control over their children. And, significantly, judges tended increasingly to grant divorced women custody of their children.

Divorce became easier with the liberalization of divorce laws in many states after 1870. The result was a sharp increase in the divorce rate—by 1916 for every nine marriages registered one divorce was granted. Overwhelmingly, most seekers for divorce were women. These unhappily married women had to cope with more than legal problems, however. Respectable society for long held them at arm's length, imbued with the tradition that associated divorced women with sexual immorality. They were also, in the words of President Theodore Roosevelt, "anarchists," since in winning divorce they were destroying the family, the veritable foundation of society.

Even as Roosevelt thundered, however, opinion was changing. By 1914 the leading sociologists in the country upheld divorce as a means toward better family life: some Protestant churches eased their opposition; and conventional women's magazines, such as *Good Housekeeping,* published articles favorable to divorce. Divorced women became socially accepted. It illustrates American attitudes on sex in marriage at the time that a potent element in the change of opinion in support of divorce was the argument that divorce freed married women from the unwelcome sexual demands of husbands.

Divorce, however, was an option available only to those who could afford the expense. Few poor women could divorce. Indeed, for many poor women the shoe was on the other foot. So many fathers deserted their families that desertion came to be known as "the poor man's divorce." Very little was done to bring such men to account.

Improvement in women's status was due in part to the unceasing work of older feminists. Elizabeth Cady Stanton and Susan B. Anthony in the East and Abigail Scott Duniway in the Far West carried on their campaigns unceasingly, not only for the suffrage, but for equality. They reached women everywhere: in the colleges, in the cities, in remote rural hamlets.

Foreign influences also played a significant role in shaping the outlooks and careers of new women. Jane Addams was influenced by her personal contacts with the settlement-house movement in England. Margaret Sanger was inspired by her association in England with Havelock Ellis, author of the famous *Psychology of Sex,* and her involvement with birth control clinics in the Netherlands. Alice Paul, most militant of American suffragists, learned her lessons from English suffragists. M. Carey Thomas's insistence on a rigorous curriculum at Bryn Mawr derived largely from her graduate work in Germany.

If American women found inspiration abroad for their work, some European women found in America opportunities denied them at home. Russian-born Rachelle Yarros and German-born Marie Zakrzewska, for example, won medical degrees in the United States and later gained national reputations for their work. Two Russian immigrants, Mary Antin and Anzia Yezierska, became writers of some note. Emma Goldman, another Russian immigrant, was the living symbol of anarchism in America. Rose Pastor, a poor radical cigar maker from Poland, enthralled the American public in 1905 with her marriage to the wealthy socialist G. Phelps Stokes. Later she helped found the American Communist party.

THE CLUB MOVEMENT

By the end of the nineteenth century increasing numbers of women, including married women, were involved in organizations working for a wide variety of causes. In terms of sheer numbers, the club movement was the most impressive of these organizations. It grew out of the spontaneous efforts of women in the post-Civil War years to improve their education by reading the "great books" of the time and discussing them with friends and neighbors. The clubs offered a way for women to get together outside traditional church groups, thus helping break down the barriers that had kept women apart. In addition to widening the intellectual horizons of many women, the clubs served as training grounds for public speakers and organizational managers. The clubs, respectable and noncontroversial, attracted many conventional women.

Many clubs were not as innocuous as they appeared. Great books, after all, are notorious as disseminators of ideas—and ideas let loose on people prepared to receive them can have untold consequences. Discussion of Ibsen's plays in a North Carolina literary club, for example, led to conversions to feminism. Women's clubs later broadened their cultural interests to campaign for better schools and libraries, for parks and art museums, for good music at prices ordinary people could afford. Others became involved with social issues: prostitution, women's hours and wages, and child labor, among others. Such cultural and social involvement inevitably led clubwomen into politics. Respectable middle-class women found themselves lobbying and campaigning for their objectives, even if they did not have the vote.

Local clubs soon banded together in state organizations, followed in 1889 by the establishment of the General Federation of Women's Clubs as a national body. In 1914 the membership of its affiliates exceeded 1 million. While the club movement did much to improve the quality of American life, it reflected the prejudices of its members. Clubs of black women were denied membership in the GFWC.

WOMEN AND THE CHURCHES

Some middle-class women found in church work an opportunity to use their talents. Protestant women, especially in the South, were active in female-missionary societies, an experience that led many into later work for suffrage and reform. Many Protestant young women, caught up in the vision that the twentieth century was going to be "the Christian century," went abroad as missionaries. Among them was Sarah L. Miner, an Oberlin graduate who in 1905 founded the first college for women in China.

There was also a reverse "missionary" influence at work. Catholic nuns came from Ireland and Europe to serve as teachers, nurses, and social workers. Perhaps the most notable of these was Irish-born Mary Baptist Russell, who made the work of the Sisters of Mercy a vital part of community life in San Francisco. She also encouraged passive Catholic women to take an active role in church affairs. By the time of her death in 1898 she was the most famous Catholic woman on the Pacific Coast and enjoyed the support of Protestants as well as Catholics. Such women inspired many young American Catholic women to find meaning for their lives in various religious orders.

The most significant female religious figure of the era, however, was Mary Baker Eddy, who in 1879 founded the Church of Christ (Scientist). Her teaching that illness came from psychic rather than physical causes brought her many followers in an age when it was believed that mind, or will, could do as it wished—a point held in common by the gospel of success and Christian Science. The association helps explain the success of the church not only in the United States but also in Britain, Germany, Australia, and New Zealand, where various forms of the gospel of success were also strong. Eddy's zeal also resulted in the founding in 1908 of the only successful daily newspaper published in America under religious auspices, the *Christian Science Monitor*.

Eddy was the first woman to establish a permanent and significant religious body in the United States. Ann Lee's Shakers were never of major significance, and they were dying out. But the Lee feminist tradition found expression in Christian Science. Eddy conceived of God as "Our Father-Mother God." The feminist tradition was muted after Eddy's death in 1910. Men dominated that church as they dominated the Shakers after Lee's death.

SOCIAL REFORM

Educated women shared the mounting concern of many middle-class Americans over the consequences of unrestrained free enterprise. By 1890 it was clear to them that the nation was endangered by the economic, political, and social evils that multiplied as big business triumphed. Their resentment found expression in the "Populist revolt" of the 1890s and in the ensuing "age of reform." Some of the more radical joined the Socialist party, which attracted large numbers of followers prior to World War I.

Such movements provided means through which new women could use their talents in ways consistent with their ideas. Mary E. Lease and Annie L. Diggs contributed significantly to the work of the Populist party in the 1890s. Diggs, in fact, was elected to the national committee of the party, one of the few women ever to serve on the policy-making body of a significant political party. Another was Kate Richards O'Hare, who served on the national executive committee of the Socialist party.

Most women reformers had little interest in radical politics. Pragmatically minded, they sought solutions for pressing problems within the traditional structure, an approach that won them public support. Thus, Jane Addams attained the stature of selfless sainthood for her work among the slum dwellers of Chicago. Hull House, the settlement over which she presided, was a center of reform activism that influenced reformers throughout the nation.

In New York, Lillian Wald, a graduate nurse who came from a wealthy family, concentrated on providing health care for the poor. By 1913 her Henry Street Settlement had a staff of ninety-two nurses making 200,000 house calls a year. The program spread to other cities, often under public auspices, and gave rise to another profession for women: public-health nursing.

The plight of exploited working women was the concern of such reformers as Florence Kelley. As secretary of the National Consumers League, she organized middle-class women to purchase goods only from stores that treated women employees fairly. On a broader front, she campaigned for state laws setting minimum wages and limiting working hours of women. She played an important role in the proceedings that led up to the Supreme Court decision in *Muller* v. *Oregon* (1908), upholding the right of states to regulate the working hours of women.

Mary E. Lease, Populist leader of the 1890s, told farmers to "raise less corn and more hell."

Kansas State Historical Society, Topeka

Concern for working women also led to formation of the Women's Trade Union League in 1903, which sought to promote the cause of unionism among women workers and to overcome the indifference of many labor-union leaders to organizing women.

Women reformers were also concerned with children. Growing opposition to the evil of child labor led in 1904 to organization of the National Child Labor Committee, in which the moving spirits were Florence Kelley and Lillian Wald. In Chicago, Julia Lathrop was so revolted by treatment of children who ran afoul of the law that she led a campaign to end the abuses. Her efforts resulted in the establishment in 1899 of the first juvenile court in the United States. The institution was copied in cities throughout the country. Similar concern for children and women prompted the crusade of Rebecca Felton to end the convict-leasing system in Georgia, a crusade that was crowned with success in 1908.

Perhaps the single most important women's reform organization was the Women's Christian Temperance Union (WCTU). Under the aggressive leadership of Frances Willard, the organization made war against the liquor traffic in the name of "home protection" and "moral purity." Since these causes could not be won through prohibition alone, Willard led the WCTU into alliances with organized labor, campaigns against exploitation of working women, crusades against prostitution, demands for prison reform, and work for women's suffrage. She also actively recruited black members. However after Willard's death in 1898, the organization reverted to its purely prohibitionist origins.

The WCTU, with its mass following in rural and small-town America, involved otherwise conventional women in public activities. Also, as a purely women's organization it testified to the ability of women to manage their own organizational affairs.

Women reformers did not confine their efforts to organizational work. As individuals they also contributed to the wave of reform. Ida M. Tarbell, an influential writer, contributed to public demand for control of big business with her *History of the Standard Oil Company,* which appeared in 1904. Mary Clare De Graffenried, a daughter of the southern aristocracy, won national attention—and the hostility of southern businessmen—with her reports of the exploitation of women and children in southern cotton mills. Charlotte Perkins Gilman was a feminist who believed that the subjection of women was rooted in economic dependence on men. In *Women and Economics,* published in 1898, she proposed to end such dependence by professionalizing housework and thus freeing housewives to make their own livings. With women economically independent, marriage would become what it should be—a partnership of equals. The book received a warm welcome in the United States.

VOTES FOR WOMEN

Women involved in reform were likely to be active in the woman's suffrage movement. After the Civil War, northern women who had played an active role in the war effort believed they would receive the vote in recognition of their services. That hope went glimmering in 1869 when Congress adopted the Fifteenth Amendment, outlawing voting discrimination based on race but making no mention of sex. The debate

Library of Congress

In this parade in Washington, D.C., in 1913, women demanded the right to vote.

over the amendment divided the women's movement. One wing, organized as the National Woman Suffrage Association, led by Susan B. Anthony and Elizabeth Cady Stanton, opposed the Fifteenth Amendment and campaigned for another federal amendment assuring votes for women. A more conservative wing, the American Woman Suffrage Association, led by Lucy Stone and Julia Ward Howe, accepted the Fifteenth Amendment, since this was "the Negro's hour." Further, instead of working for a new federal amendment, the American Association favored action at the local and state level.

Having failed to get women included in the Fifteenth Amendment, some suffragists sought a judicial interpretation of the Fourteenth Amendment that would make suffrage a right of citizenship. Susan B. Anthony, for example, sought to test the thesis by voting in the presidential election of 1872. She was fined $100 and refused to pay. Federal authorities made no effort to enforce the decision, thus frustrating her design to get a Supreme Court ruling.

Virginia Minor was more successful. A resident of St. Louis, she sued the registrar of voters for refusing to register her. Her case, *Minor* v. *Happersett,* resulted in a U. S. Supreme Court decision in 1875 that had sweeping implications. Certainly women are citizens, said the court, but citizenship does not confer the suffrage. Said the unanimous court, "The Constitution of the United States does not confer the right of suffrage upon any one." Authority for the granting of such right lay, not with the federal government, but with the states.

The law stood and the movement stalled until 1890 when the divided suffragists united in the National American Woman Suffrage Association (NAWSA). The new movement proved to be quite different from its predecessors, although old-timers like

Elizabeth Cady Stanton and Susan B. Anthony continued to be powerful influences. The older associations based their case on principle: women, as human beings, had the right to vote equally with men. NAWSA, dominated by younger women, such as Carrie Chapman Catt, sought to sway public opinion by emphasizing that woman suffrage would be good for society.

The argument took various forms. Since municipal government was simply housekeeping on a grand scale, one form of the argument ran, women in their role of housekeeper could help govern efficiently. Further, since women wanted to protect their homes, they would root out the saloons, brothels, and political corruption these nourished. At other levels of government, the purifying influence of women would make politics more honest and responsible. Indeed, since the motherly instincts of women caused them to value life more than men did, the advent of women into political power would help bring about world peace.

The arguments of expediency also reached to nonpolitical issues. Mothers, it was said, would benefit society by passing on to their children a sense of civic responsibility created by participation in public life. Enjoyment of equal political rights with their husbands would make women better wives. Suffrage would also contribute to ending the exploitation of women and children in factories. Finally, women voters would put an end to prostitution and to light sentences imposed on convicted white rapists.

The desire of NAWSA to project a desirable public image also took more sinister turns. The years from 1890 to 1914 were a period of nativist hysteria in the North over immigrants and of strident assertion of white supremacy in the South. NAWSA went along with both. In the process many suffragists abandoned the old movement's claim for the suffrage as the right of all citizens and endorsed qualifications on the right. America, said Carrie Chapman Catt in 1894, was faced with the "great danger" of the "ignorant foreign vote." She proposed: "Cut off the vote of the slums and give to [native white] woman . . . the ballot." Even the militant Stanton wrote that "this ignorant, worthless class of voters should be speedily diminished."

While such appeals made converts in rural and small-town America, they won little response from such suffragists as Jane Addams and others in urban centers, who realized that use of the immigrant vote was merely a symptom, not the cause, of political corruption. Indeed, by 1914 it had dawned upon leading suffragists, including Carrie Chapman Catt, that antagonizing the foreign-born blocked success in the major industrial states. Then began a campaign to woo the "worthless" on grounds that votes for women would improve the living and working conditions of the slum dwellers.

The South's suffrage movement lagged behind the North's. Hostility to women's rights derived not only from traditional male supremacy—which most women accepted without question—but also from the association of feminism with pre-Civil War abolitionism. To advocate the vote for women was treason to the "lost cause" of the Confederacy. Only strong-minded women, such as Laura Clay in Kentucky, Elizabeth Meriwether in Tennessee, and Kate Gordon in Louisiana, could make any impression on public opinion—ever careful that their image was always "feminine."

The cultivation of femininity naturally suggested associations with the traditional ideal of "pure white womanhood" and gave added point to the suffragists' claim that votes for women would ensure white supremacy. In all southern states except Louisiana and Mississippi, they argued, the combined votes of white men and women would outnumber those of blacks. In those two states, black voting could be drastically reduced by imposing rigorous educational qualifications. The argument seems to have had little effect on southern politicians. Only four southern states—Texas, Kentucky, Arkansas, and Tennessee—ratified the Nineteenth Amendment, which legalized women's right to vote.

Nevertheless, so eager was NAWSA for southern support that it acquiesced in the southern program. Laura Clay, an official of NAWSA, explained in 1906 that the organization looked upon woman's suffrage as "a counterbalance to the foreign vote, and as a means of legally preserving white supremacy in the South." The policy of NAWSA reflected southern influence in many ways. Southern white women were elected to its governing board, but no black woman ever served. Despite the protests of black suffragists and their white allies, the organization refused to condemn segregation and the degradation of black women in the South. On the contrary, in 1899 NAWSA held that its struggle was in no way connected with the struggle for black rights. Thus, in the name of pragmatism, the abolitionist heritage was denied—ironically with the aid of Susan B. Anthony, the old abolitionist firebrand.

The new mood of the suffrage movement showed itself in still other ways. It dissociated itself from ideas and movements that might discredit the cause. In 1896 it repudiated any connection with *The Woman's Bible,* written by Elizabeth Cady Stanton, first president of NAWSA, after the book was condemned by preachers, pundits, and the press. Later, it held the birth control movement, led by Margaret Sanger, at arm's length. It also disavowed the Congressional Union for Woman Suffrage, founded in 1914 by Alice Paul and other militants dissatisfied with the conservative policies of NAWSA.

The young women who dominated NAWSA felt that the long years of arousing public consciousness on the issue were over. Their goal was to put that consciousness to work in carefully planned and organized campaigns within states to amend state constitutions, and later, to win a federal amendment. Influenced by Carrie Chapman Catt, an organizational genius, the younger suffragists carried on campaign after campaign. They were repeatedly defeated. In 1910 there were still only four states, all in the West, that allowed women full voting rights—the same number as in 1896. The woman's suffrage movement seemed to have gotten exactly nowhere.

Then, beginning 1910, the years of organizing and campaigning within the states began to pay off. Within four years seven states enfranchised women—bringing the total to eleven. The success brought a shift in strategy. Major emphasis was now placed on winning a federal amendment. Leading the new and eventually successful campaign was Catt, who in 1915 returned to the presidency of NAWSA she had left thirteen years earlier.

Suffragists' activities helped win the franchise, but there were other forces at work that aided their cause. The men of Wyoming Territory granted women voting rights in 1869 largely because they wanted a measure of law and order in a disorderly frontier society. Utah, both as territory and state, enfranchised women to protect Mormon power from the growing numbers of non-Mormons. Mormon influence also played a role in Idaho's grant of the suffrage. California women won the vote as part of a larger revolt against domination of the state by what Frank Norris, a popular novelist of the day, called "the octopus" of big business. Populist and Socialist sentiment in Kansas helped carry the day for suffrage in that state. Prohibitionists generally supported women's suffrage, for women who could vote tended to vote "dry." The prohibition cause in turn brought endorsement of the suffrage by otherwise conservative Protestant clergymen—men who enjoyed great authority in rural and small-town America.

If the suffrage movement had strong allies, it also had powerful foes. Perhaps hardest to deal with was what Thorstein Veblen called "social inertia"—the reluctance of people to make necessary social changes, especially when the changes affected their personal relationships. Masses of women were either indifferent to suffrage or hostile to it. Some women were quite content with things as they were. Others, especially among farming and urban working-class women, saw little relevance between their problems and the ballot.

Suffrage also encountered hostility in urban slums, partly because of the anti-foreign orientation of NAWSA. It also arose from the severe psychological strains set up by transplanting folk from European peasant communities to the highly industrialized society of America. Confused and frightened by an often hostile society, these immigrants clung tenaciously to familiar institutions as a means of survival. Most important was the patriarchal family. Jane Addams and others who worked in the slums reported some interest in the suffrage among foreign-born women. For the most part, men were adamantly opposed.

Powerful interests actively fought the suffrage movement. The liquor industry, fearful of prohibition, fought every suffragist move tooth and nail. Many employers were in the same camp, believing that suffrage would raise wages for women and end child labor. Machine politicians were allied with the employers, fearing an end to their rule if women voted. Prominent clergymen, such as William C. Doane, Episcopalian bishop of Albany, New York, opposed suffrage as a challenge to the divine order of things and a danger to the family. Similar sentiments were expressed by such outstanding figures as Francis Parkman, the historian, and former President Grover Cleveland.

Such virulent opposition, which in the years before 1900 often took the form of mobbing suffrage advocates, may help explain the conservative orientation of NAWSA. Only by making suffrage "respectable" could the cause triumph, its leaders believed.

BIRTH CONTROL

One cause too radical for conservative suffragists was birth control. Its prophet was Margaret Sanger, a socialist who advocated resistance to laws against birth control. Her associate was Mary Ware Dennett, also a socialist. Sanger also was a friend of Emma Goldman, the flamboyant anarchist, who advocated birth control and the sexual liberty of women. Respectable reformers wanted nothing to do with such people.

The new birth-control movement was under heavy attack. President Theodore Roosevelt said in 1906 that birth control meant "race death: a sin for which there is no atonement." The Roman Catholic archbishop of New York said that while abortion was "a horrible crime," birth control was "satanic." Protestant and Jewish religious leaders were either hostile or unwilling to discuss the issue publicly. With a few exceptions, such as Doctor Robert L. Dickinson and Doctor Abraham Jacobi, the medical profession was in opposition. Federal, state, and local governments harassed birth control advocates.

Perhaps the most shocking aspect of the new movement was that it compelled public discussion of a subject long taboo: sex. The very idea of birth control suggested there was something more to marriage than procreation, a point Sanger and her associates made quite clear. While Sanger originally intended to improve the lot of slum women condemned to endless childbearing or victimization by quack abortionists, she later won badly needed middle class support by justifying birth control on other grounds. Birth control, she said, gave women control over their own bodies—surely a basic human right. Further, birth control gave women the opportunity to enjoy sex, and such enjoyment benefited women both physically and psychologically. In addition, mutual sexual enjoyment made marriage more meaningful to both men and women. Finally, birth control benefited society by producing only children who were really wanted. Such beliefs offended many people, among them feminists who looked upon equality as a means of escape from sex.

Sanger's ideas are significant because they represented a change in outlook that began in the 1890s. The change grew out of the growing perception that the assertion of traditional individualism conflicted with the claims of people as individual persons. That is, individualism trampled down individuality. In revolt against "economic man," with his rigorous repression of the emotions, thinkers in many fields asserted that the great aim of society must be to promote the development of personal individuality, including full emotional expression. Such thinkers as John Dewey in education and William James in psychology represented the new trend. They believed in liberating, not repressing, the potentialities of human beings.

That new trend had specific meaning for women. It helped produce among them a more positive self-image and stimulated them to strike out on their own. Men and women were encouraged to look upon each other primarily as human beings, with emotions, including sex, that required expression. Marriage should provide sexual satisfaction for the wife as well as the husband—an idea that challenged traditional beliefs. In short, the curtain of conventional wisdom that closed off even private discussion of a major aspect of personal living had begun to part.

As these ideas spread, the well-to-do used contraception more and more. Despite federal and state laws, such Americans obtained birth control devices either through their own doctors or in Europe. This association of wealth and birth control angered Sanger. The poor needed the information more than the rich, but it was forbidden to them. From her experience as a nurse in the slums, she knew that such ignorance caused needless suffering and death among poor women. More, it perpetuated poverty. Big families meant children stunted in mind and body, who grew up to reproduce their own kind in an endless cycle of misery. Sanger decided to do something about it.

Her target was the "Comstock law," passed by Congress in 1873 under pressure from Anthony Comstock and other zealots in the cause of "moral purity." The law not only barred ''obscene'' matter from the mails but also outlawed the mailing of anything related to ''preventing conception.'' Although there were ways to get around the Comstock law, it was enforced sufficiently to deny birth control information to the great mass of married people.

Through her newspaper, *The Woman Rebel,* Sanger waged war against the Comstock law. Anxious to avoid confrontation with the federal government, she never provided actual birth control information, although that was the kind of information her readers wanted. Nevertheless, federal authorities indicted her in 1914. Rather than face trial on issues other than disseminating practical contraceptive information, she went to England. There she authorized distribution of 100,000 copies of *Family Limitation,* a pamphlet she had written describing in simple language various methods of birth control. Distributed by the Industrial Workers of the World, a radical labor organization with which Sanger sympathized, the pamphlet was a huge success. Indeed, so great was the demand that commercial printers with an eye to profit pirated the contents—often inaccurately.

In *Family Limitation* Sanger provided for the first time in American history up-to-date contraceptive information in a form designed to reach the masses. In so doing she initiated a revolution that has attained success and thus become respectable.

FOR FURTHER READING

Excellent general coverage of women at the turn of the century is provided in Eleanor Flexner's now classic *Century of Struggle* (1959). A concise survey of the changing roles of women in the twentieth century is in Lois Banner, *Women in Modern America* (1974). Anne F. Scott breaks new ground in *The Southern Lady* (1970). Several collections of documents are now available. Among them are Aileen Kraditor, ed., *Up From the Pedestal* (1969), and June Sochen, *The New Feminism in Twentieth Century America* (1971). Less sympathetic is Page Smith, *Daughters of the Promised Land* (1970). See also Andrew Sinclair, *The Better Half* (1965).

The feminist movement itself is discussed in William L. O'Neill, *Everyone Was Brave* (1969). Essential to understanding changes within the woman's suffrage movement is Aileen Kraditor's *The Ideas of the Woman Suffrage Movement* (1965). One of the great works of American feminism, Charlotte Perkins Gilman's *Women and Economics,* was reprinted with a perceptive introduction by Carl Degler in 1966.

Trends in sexual attitudes and family structure are covered in William L. O'Neill, *Divorce in the Progressive Era* (1967); Nelson Blake, *The Road to Reno* (1962); and Sidney Ditzion, *Marriage, Morals and Sex in America* (1953). An original and provocative study of some American attitudes toward sex is G. J. Barker-Benfield, *The Horrors of the Half-Known Life* (1976).

19 outcasts in their own land

Economic expansion brought with it increased freedom and independence for middle-class white women, but it meant disaster for the original Americans. It has been estimated that when the Spanish first set foot on this continent, there were about 2 million native Americans in what is now the United States. In 1900, there were only 236,000. For the most part, they lived in the West in abject poverty. They had few rights that whites needed to respect. Most white Americans knew little about them, except as exotic characters in Wild West shows or in western novels. In the West, white people treated these once proud and independent Americans with utter contempt.

THE THEFT OF THE LAND

The dispossession of Indian peoples began, as we have seen, in colonial times. It proceeded apace after white America achieved independence, reaching a climax with the removal policy of the Jacksonian era. Under that policy, entire peoples were deported from their eastern homelands to supposedly worthless lands beyond the limits of white settlement in the trans-Mississippi West. The policy, however, was carried through with due observance of legality. It was done under the cover of treaties entered into with Indian leaders susceptible to white pressures. Despite the coercion, the treaties did exist, recognized as valid by the United States. Among other things, they bound the United States to prevent white incursions on Indian lands. They also provided that the new lands would be held by Indian peoples "as long as waters run and the grass shall grow."

Transplanted Indian peoples, and indigenous western Indians with whom similar treaties were later made, discovered that the treaties were little more than scraps of paper. They were useful for a time in quieting Indian resistance, but when white pressures mounted, the Great Father in Washington ignored white invasions of Indian lands and then, on the basis of such invasion, demanded the yielding of the lands.

The removal of eastern peoples had been barely completed when indigenous western peoples began to feel white pressure. In 1842, when the last Seminole captives were hustled off from Florida to Indian Territory (Oklahoma), Indians of the northern Great Plains saw the first wagon train cross their country bound for Oregon. With each passing year the number of whites increased on the Oregon Trail, swelled by Mormons following the Mormon Trail to Utah. Army posts were established to protect the migrants.

In the Southwest, peoples accustomed to a weak and inefficient Mexican government in 1848 found themselves wards of a strong and efficient American government. It was also, as they found, a government responsive to the demands of white men who looked with envy on the rich farm lands and orchards of the Navahos and western Apaches and on the grazing lands where buffalo supplied the needs of hunting peoples. The white man's war with Mexico was barely over when gold was discovered in California. Hordes of whites made their way across Indian country to the new El Dorado. Many who did not prosper in the diggings nevertheless stayed on, with an eye on Indian lands as well as those of the Mexican *ricos*. Indicative of white attitudes was the constitution of the new state of California, which stripped Indians of the voting rights they had enjoyed under Mexican rule.

With United States sovereignty extending from coast to coast, white Americans changed their view of Indian country. It was no longer perceived as a dumping ground for unwanted Indians. Rather, it was seen as a region vital to linking East and West together. As such it must be organized and brought under white control. The first major step in this direction was taken in 1849 when a new Department of the Interior was set up in the federal government to assume control of Indian affairs from the War Department. The transfer was ominous for Indian peoples. It signified that the United States was no longer content to leave Indian country to the Indians. On the contrary, it was an asset to be developed for the benefit of whites.

The second major step was the establishment of territorial governments over lands in which Indian peoples lived—without consulting the Indians, of course. Utah and New Mexico territories were organized in 1850. More significant historically was the action of Congress four years later, when it created the territories of Kansas and Nebraska. Known for the part it played in the mounting controversy over slavery, the Kansas-Nebraska Act had a more immediate and dangerous significance for Indian peoples. It opened up 485,000 square miles of Indian farming and hunting grounds in the northern plains to white settlement. Some senators objected that the act was a breach of faith with Indian peoples who had signed treaties assuring them of their land. Their protests were of no avail.

The third step in controlling western Indian peoples was the reservation policy, already in effect among the remnants of some eastern tribes. Through various means, Indian peoples were induced or compelled to yield their traditional farming and hunting grounds in exchange for land reserves remote from white trade routes or settlements—that is, land the whites thought worthless. Reservation Indians would be treated as "friendly." Those outside the reservation assigned to them would be regarded as "hostiles," or outlaws, subject to death or punishment by federal troops. In return, the United States pledged that the reservation lands would remain in Indian hands forever. It also agreed to provide reservation inhabitants with necessary food and supplies supplemented by annual cash payments. These payments—annuities—represented acquisition of Indian land for a few cents an acre. To make sure that all went well, the federal government appointed white agents to manage the reservations, allowed trade only by licensed white merchants, and provided support for white missionaries to Christianize the Indians and otherwise train them in the ways of white Americans.

The Indians did not give up their lands without a struggle. For them, their lands were not only a means of sustenance but also part of that mystical link of God, nature, and humanity that was at the center of Indian religion. The earth was their "mother," not to be given over to strangers. Besides, their lands held their holy places, outward and visible signs of the inward and spiritual ties that bound Indian communities together. So, they argued, the land could not be given up—and no one had authority to do so. In any case, Indians asked, why did whites want their land? Did not whites have enough to live on? Why were they not content with what God had given them?

Federal agents pointed to the benefits of reservation life—the free food and supplies, the annuities, the freedom to live as one wished—but the most potent argument of all was that Indians had no choice. They could either get the benefits of reservation living or lose their lands and their lives to white settlers and miners whom the federal government could not control. Further, if Indians would not bargain about the conditions of removal to reservations, the United States would compel them to move under its own conditions.

These arguments were compelling to some Indian leaders, but federal agents were not content with argument. They subverted Indian leadership, exploiting rivalries among leaders. Leaders who advocated appeasement were showered with gifts. Others were bribed. Those who held out were marked for destruction. On some occasions federal agents themselves chose the leaders with whom they would deal—handpicking the "chiefs" who would sign the treaties and give their people's lands to the whites.

THE LONG DEATH BEGINS

White policy, then, was to subjugate the Indians. Other factors hastened the process.

British cession of the Oregon country and forcible annexation of Mexican lands in 1848 followed by the California gold rush brought thousands of whites into territory still legally regarded as Indian country. Regular freight and mail routes were established across the plains, and by 1861 a transcontinental telegraph line was in operation. The white incursion trampled down the grass and drove off the game on which hunting Indians depended for a livelihood.

Whites also brought with them diseases: measles, smallpox, cholera. At the time, these sicknesses were bad enough for whites, but they were disastrous for peoples who had developed no biological defenses. Entire peoples were decimated. Thus, when white power asserted itself in Indian country, it confronted many Indian peoples sharply reduced in numbers and weakened physically.

Disease took its toll of Indians in still another way. In the 1870s and 1880s some dissident peoples were transported to Indian Territory (Oklahoma), where many perished from malaria. Others were exiled to Florida, where they died from tuberculosis.

The Civil War provided a convenient pretext for seizing Indian lands: loyal whites needed the land in order to keep Confederates out. In the Southwest, Union forces rounded up Mescalero Apaches, took them from their rich farm lands, and penned them in an arid reservation that a federal official later found unfit for human habitation. When the Navahos resisted similar treatment, their livestock were seized, their crops destroyed, and their orchards cut down. The broken Navahos were then cooped up in the same reservation with the Apaches. The death rate was high, running to an estimated 25 percent.

After the war was over, the Indian prisoners were released—but only to be settled on new reservations. Most of the good land that had belonged to Apaches and Navahos passed into white control.

The sounds of Civil War were muted in the Pacific Northwest, but that did not save the Nez Perces, a people who had been friendly with whites ever since the Lewis and Clark expedition of 1805. In 1855 they had yielded about half their lands in return for pledges against white invasion of their territory. The whites came anyhow. Indian protests finally produced action in the year of Gettysburg and Vicksburg—1863. The federal government imposed a treaty stripping the Nez Perces

Geronimo, famed leader of the Apache people in Arizona. He was held prisoner by the federal government for twenty-three years after his surrender, dying in prison in 1909.
Smithsonian Institution, National Anthropological Archives

of their lands in Washington and Oregon and confining them to a reservation in Idaho. For the moment, however, no effort was made to expel the Indians.

More directly involved in the Civil War were the Five Civilized Nations of the Indian Territory—the Cherokees, Choctaws, Chickasaws, Creeks, and Seminoles transplanted from the southeastern United States. Using the devious methods characteristic of white dealings with Indian peoples, Confederate agents won treaties of alliance with leaders of these nations. When the Cherokee leader, John Ross, resisted, the Confederates recognized a more compliant rival government. Ross was not alone. Within each nation there were substantial elements that did not accept alliances with the Confederacy and fought for the Union.

In return for the treaties, the Confederacy assumed all the obligations of the United States toward the nations. Also, for the first and only time in American history, Indian nations as such were given voice in government. They sent delegates to the Confederate Congress. They were also authorized to form their own state within the Confederacy—a step that was never taken.

Actually, Indian aid to the Confederacy was minimal. Confederate Indians fought a civil war of their own against Indians loyal to the Union. When the national war was over, federal authorities failed to recognize the civil war among Indians. Friend and foe were treated alike. Since the Five Nations had formally allied themselves with the Confederacy, the United States abrogated its treaties with them. It imposed new treaties that stripped the Five Nations of much of their land. Poor stretches of the expropriated lands were used as dumping grounds for dissident Indians from other regions. The good land found its way into white hands.

Whites were still not satisfied, however, and in 1889 the Indian Territory, except for the shrunken reservations, was opened to white settlement. Shortly thereafter the Territory of Oklahoma was created with control over white areas. Four years later, under the Dawes Act (which is discussed later), the federal government began breaking up the reservations, and most Indian land passed into white hands. Finally, in 1906 the Indian Territory ceased to exist when it was incorporated into the new state of Oklahoma and Indians made subject to white law. Thus, the autonomy of the Five Civilized Nations, guaranteed to them in innumerable treaties, came to an end.

In the meantime, plains Indians, already disturbed by white incursions into their country, were menaced by forces let loose by white economic expansion and technology: most notably the railroad and a new method of tanning buffalo hides.

The first transcontinental railroad, completed in 1869, cut through Indian country. Its construction brought thousands of white workers into the Great Plains as well as federal troops to protect them. Fresh meat was supplied by hunters, who preyed on the buffalo and antelope herds. The hunting, together with the construction, drove animals away from their usual grazing grounds, finally dividing the buffalo into northern and southern herds.

Completion of the railroad—and of later railroads—brought thousands of whites into the plains country: prospectors, farmers, merchants, professional men, speculators. To their clamor for Indian land was added the powerful influence of the railroads, beneficiaries of the generous land grants given by the federal government.

Back in Vermont, an obscure businessman unwittingly dealt yet another blow to Indian freedom. A tanner, he developed in 1871 a process for making buffalo hides into fine leather. The consequent demand for hides resulted in an orgy of killing on the plains, in which millions of buffalos were slain, stripped of their hides, and their carcasses left to rot. By 1878 both the northern and southern buffalo herds were all but wiped out—and the hunting Indians deprived of their food supply.

Federal authorities looked on the slaughter with equanimity, understanding full well what it portended for the plains Indians. As General Philip Sheridan said, extermination of the buffalo was "the only way to bring lasting peace and allow civilization to advance." And indeed, destruction of their food supply compelled hunting peoples to enter reservations. The slaughter meant yet another loss to hunting Indians. Their treaties often assured them their hunting grounds so long as there were sufficient buffalo "to justify the chase." With the buffalo gone, the lands were forfeit to the United States.

INDIAN RESISTANCE

When Sheridan talked about "lasting peace," he was referring to the fact that Indians of the plains actively resisted white occupation of their homelands. That resistance was not blind. Rather, it arose from the realization that whites did not simply want to enter Indian country—they meant to take it over. In a meeting with federal commissioners in 1867 relating to Kansas, the Cheyennes pledged that they would not interfere with railroad construction, provided that Indian rights were respected. "Let us own the country together," they urged, "the Cheyennes should still hunt there." The white officials rejected the proposal. Cochise, leader of the Chiricahua Apaches in the Southwest, and Kintpuash (called by whites Captain Jack), the Modoc leader in California, voiced similar sentiments of live and let live. Whites wanted none of it. They had to have the land—or at least the good land—for themselves alone.

The white solution, of course, was putting Indians on reservations, but that in itself was a major factor in producing warfare on the plains. The Indians did not want to go. A perceptive leader of the Santee Sioux, Wamditanka, called by whites Big Eagle, noted that reservation life implied giving up Indian identity. "The whites were always trying to make the Indians give up their life and live like white men. . . . The Indians did not know how to do that, and did not want to anyway." Satanta, a leader of the Kiowas, a people of the southern plains, emphasized another aspect of Indian opposition: "I don't want to settle. I love to roam over the prairies. There I feel free and happy, but when we settle down we grow pale and die."

But even if they yielded and went to the reservation, the Indian peoples discovered once again that whites' promises were not to be taken seriously. All were assured that adequate supplies would be provided for them. A few peoples, such as the Modocs, received none at all—Congress forgot to appropriate the money. Those peoples who did receive supplies found them insufficient. Worse, the food was often unfit to eat, and the other supplies were inferior in quality. Federal investigators confirmed Indian complaints. They found flour and meat swarming with vermin, shoes that had paper soles, and blankets of glued woolen scraps that came apart in the first rain.

Apart from some temporary reforms during the Grant administration, little was done to improve the situation. The supply of shoddy goods was part of an entire system of corruption in the Bureau of Indian Affairs that stretched from Washington to the agents on the reservations. Indeed, an agency appointment was one of the most lucrative plums that politicos in Washington could hand out.

Allied with the agents were the licensed traders, who enjoyed monopoly rights in supplying Indian wants not taken care of by the government. They also sold the Indians goods intended for the Indians by the government but diverted to them by the agents—to their mutual profit. Enjoying a monopoly position, the traders did well for themselves. They charged high prices, and since Indians had little money, the traders extended them credit at high rates of interest. There was no risk involved, for traders had first claim on the cash payments made each year to reservation Indians. The agents, in return for a share of the profits, routinely approved the bills presented by traders, however inflated.

In consequence, most of the annuities destined for Indians went into the pockets of agents and traders. Protests by Indians carried little weight. Untrained in the ways of business, they kept no written records themselves. Knowing nothing of bookkeeping, they were in no position to challenge the traders' accounts. While reservation whites prospered, Indians lived in perpetual debt and poverty.

Plundering of the Indians had become scandalous by the time President U. S. Grant took office. In 1869, as part of his general "peace policy" toward Indians, Grant sought to root out corruption by appointing as agents men chosen by various religious bodies. During the five years the so-called "Quaker policy" was in effect, corruption at the agency level did decline, but that did not make the lot of Indians easier. The earlier agents, interested in money, were largely indifferent to Indian customs and beliefs. The new men, inspired by missionary zeal, were bent on Christianizing the Indians by destroying their religions and traditional customs, such as polygamy. They used all the resources at the agent's command to attain their ends, including the distribution of food and supplies.

For Indians, the honest zeal of such whites was perhaps worse than the greed of their predecessors. One group menaced the physical well-being of Indians. The other attacked Indian spirit itself. The Indians resisted, as they had done earlier and continued to do later.

Of course, as among all subject peoples, there were some Indians willing to serve the conqueror in return for favors and privileges. From their ranks were recruited the Indian police, who enforced the white man's law and order on the reservations and served as the eyes and ears of white men. From them also came the men willing to serve on the Indian courts set up by white men to discipline reservation Indians. The courts, dominated by the agents, not only punished such offenses as drunkenness but also helped to put down "old heathen and barbarous customs" and to curb the power of Indian priests—the men whom whites called "medicine men." In short, Indians were used to help suppress Indian freedom.

The treaties that recognized Indian title to the reservation lands proved to have as little substance as the promises that lured the tribes to the reservation in the first place. So long as no whites wanted their lands, the reservation Indians were safe. When whites did want Indian lands, all the power of the federal government was invoked to compel Indian peoples to give up territory guaranteed to them by that same government. Few peoples escaped such pressures. Probably the Sioux suffered more from the perfidy of the federal government than any other people.

In 1868, after a humiliating defeat at the hands of western Sioux headed by Red Cloud, the United States made the Treaty of Fort Laramie with the Sioux peoples. The Sioux pledged themselves not to make war on the United States and to take up residence in the Great Sioux Reservation, a vast area covering what is now South Dakota west of the Missouri river. The reservation included the Black Hills, regarded by Sioux as a holy place. The United States in turn guaranteed the reservation lands to the Sioux, recognized the right of the Sioux to hunting grounds in the still game-rich Powder River country of Wyoming Territory, and agreed that no white persons could enter Sioux lands without the permission of the Sioux.

Not all Sioux—or their allies among the northern Cheyennes and Arapahos—accepted the treaty. Such Indians—called the "nontreaty" Indians—remained in the Powder River country. Among them was a young leader, Tatanka Yotanka, destined to make his own place in white man's history as Sitting Bull.

The treaty had barely gone into force when two events changed the future of the Sioux. The Northern Pacific Railroad, designed to link the Great Lakes region with Puget Sound, charted a route carrying it through the Sioux hunting grounds of the Powder River country. And, in 1874, the presence of gold in the Black Hills was confirmed. Without Sioux permission, white prospectors poured into the forbidden territory.

The Sioux offered no armed resistance, but they protested to Washington. In response, the army ordered the prospectors out. By that time, however, officers had learned that interpreting orders in favor of Indians was no way to further one's military career, so enforcement was minimal. More to the point, Washington sent a

The Oglala Sioux Red Cloud. In 1868 he led the only successful "war" of the Great Plains Indians against the United States government.

Smithsonian Institution, National Anthropological Archives

Sitting Bull, the notable Sioux leader. He told whites, "You have taken away our land and made us outcasts."

Smithsonian Institution, National Anthropological Archives

commission in 1875 to buy the holy place of the Sioux. With sardonic humor, Red Cloud set the price at $600 million. The enraged commissioners reported to Washington that punitive action was called for to bring the Sioux to heel.

Thus, the Black Hills issue merged into that of the railroad project. Fortified with the report of the Black Hills commissioners, the Bureau of Indian Affairs moved against the "nontreaty Indians." Ostensibly to protect the railroad route, all such peoples were ordered to report to the Great Sioux Reservation without delay. The order violated the treaty of 1868, and it could not be obeyed. It was issued as the deadly winter of the northern plains began, making travel almost impossible, and many bands received no word of the order. When the Indians failed to report, the bureau called upon the army for enforcement.

When federal troops invaded the Powder River country, the Sioux and their allies defended the lands assigned them. In July 1876, at the Little Big Horn river in Montana, they annihilated the force led by General George A. Custer. Within a year, however, a massive military campaign crushed Indian resistance. Claiming that Indian actions had invalidated the treaty of 1868, the United States treated treaty and nontreaty Indians alike—although the reservation Sioux had been little involved. Indian rights in the Powder River country were abolished, and the Sioux were compelled to give up one-third of their reservation lands, including the sacred Black Hills. Sitting Bull, a leader in the Indian resistance, took refuge in Canada along with his followers.

The Sioux did not long enjoy even their shrunken reservation. Whites who had settled in the Black Hills region wanted free access to white settlements in eastern Dakota Territory without travel through Indian country. In 1889 the federal government responded. It stripped the Sioux of half of their remaining reservation lands to provide a sixty-mile-wide swath across the reservation through which whites could move freely without Indian contact. Having split the Great Reservation in two, the government then ordered the Sioux into five smaller reservations set up in what was left of their land. Small wonder that Sitting Bull concluded that whites were "thieves and liars. You have taken away our land and made us outcasts."

INDIAN "WARS"?

This was the background for the so-called "Indian wars": white invasion of Indian homelands, broken white promises, treaties that proved worthless to Indians, and a reservation system that reduced Indian peoples to destitution and, all too often, to disease and hunger. Yet, it must be remembered, the "wars" were not initiated by the Indian peoples. White people, backed by the might of the federal government, set off the supposed wars—which were little more than campaigns against individual bands of Indians. The Indian peoples wanted no white land, but they were determined to protect their own. Such determination on the part of white men would have been hailed as patriotism of a high order. On the part of Indians, it was regarded as a relic of barbarism.

There was another kind of Indian war—campaigns waged against Indians desperately trying to avoid conflict. These were Indians resisting confinement on reservations or refugees from reservation life. In either case, they were all too aware of white power. They wanted nothing more than to find a secure place, remote from white people, where they could live peacefully. They wanted no confrontation with federal troops, but that did not save them. Such people were classified as "hostiles," and the army was sent to hunt them down and bring the survivors to reservations. Thus, the operations against the Nez Perces in 1877, against the Cheyennes in 1878, and against the Apaches in the 1880s.

The Indian peoples never had a chance, militarily speaking. Widely dispersed over a huge territory, they could not present a common front to the white invaders. The whites, in contrast, operated under a unified command that picked off individual peoples one by one. The Indians were vastly outnumbered. They fought with obsolete firearms and with bows and arrows against an enemy equipped with up-to-date weapons. Their means of communication and transportation were primitive, while federal troops enjoyed the telegraph and railroads. When attacked in camp, the warriors were hampered by their need to protect women and children.

That need was great, because soldiers on numerous occasions gunned down young and old, men and women, mothers and infants. One of the most notorious incidents took place at Sand Creek, Colorado, in 1864. Colonel John Chivington led an attack on a camp of friendly Cheyennes after advising his troops: "Kill and scalp all, big and little; nits make lice." The resulting butchery made the colonel a hero in Denver. It caused dismay in Washington because it wrecked plans for peaceful removal of Indians. Four years later General Custer led a similar surprise attack on southern Cheyennes on the Washita River in Indian Territory. Of the 103 dead, only 11 were warriors. There were other incidents, climaxed by the massacre of the Sioux at Wounded Knee, South Dakota, in 1890. It has been estimated that only about 50 of the 350 Indians in the camp survived the slaughter. Again, women and children were shown no mercy.

In late December 1890, federal troops gunned down 350 Sioux at Wounded Knee, South Dakota. Men, women, and children were among the 153 killed immediately. The army picked up 51 wounded. Other wounded fled, only to die in the frozen countryside. Here soldiers pile up the bodies.

Smithsonian Institution, National Anthropological Archives

Also devastating to Indian morale were two other methods of white warfare. One was winter campaigning. Indian peoples never fought in winter. When whites found they could not overcome Indian resistance otherwise, they resorted to tracking down "hostiles" through the snow. Unsuspecting Indians, snugly encamped for the long dark months, were easy prey to surprise attack. Linked to this was another method, tried out long before with the Navahos: utter destruction of Indian property and means of subsistence. Even if Indians escaped oncoming soldiers, they did not escape subjection. The troops destroyed their ponies, their major means of transportation, and burned their villages. Food, tepees, clothing, blankets—all went up in flames. The despoiled Indians had little choice except to surrender.

The use of force was accompanied by other means designed to break the Indians' will to resist and to keep Indian peoples divided. Long-standing animosities between peoples were invoked to obtain the services of some, such as the Pawnees and the Utes, in campaigns against their enemies. New animosities were created when hungry warriors on reservations agreed to serve as Scouts for the army in return for regular meals and pay. Thus, Sioux were used against the Nez Perces.

On the reservations, agents subverted Indian morale by encouraging the dissension that plagues every people after defeat. Indians tried to present a common front in dealing with whites, but among themselves Indians blamed this or that leader for their misfortunes and the leaders quarreled among themselves. The whites, kept well posted by their Indian informers, fanned the flames of discord. Families of militants were denied their full rations, while advocates of submission were favored with more than their share.

Whites also sought to shift responsibility for severe punishment to Indian leaders. For example, Kicking Bird, a Kiowa, was persuaded to choose twenty-six of his compatriots to suffer exile at Fort Marion, Florida, for resistance to the federal reservation policy in 1875. His submission cost him credibility among the Indians. Indians suspected, too, that whites instigated the assassination of Indian leaders they wanted out of the way, as when Spotted Tail, a Sioux, was slain by a rival in 1881. The suspicions of the Sioux were not lessened when the killer was shown great favor by whites and became an ardent collaborationist.

Whites also sought to undermine Indian unity by suppressing Indian religions. Religion was a moving force in daily life, binding the community together in common beliefs that related people, land, and God in a harmonious trinity. Religion also imbued Indians with a sense of family and tribal continuity, linking together ancestors, adults, children, and their children's children in a meaningful pattern. Religion provided every Indian with a sense of belonging.

Each people celebrated its beliefs in its own way at great annual gatherings, which brought together scattered bands with a common heritage. The participants, under the guidance of their priests, chanted, danced, and paid tribute to the spirits that fashioned their lives. Young men and women were initiated into the mysteries of their people and came forth, no longer children, but full members of their people. Such a ceremony was the famous Sun Dance of the Sioux. From such gatherings Indians went forth with a renewed sense of community, dignity, and purpose.

Clearly, the whites could not subject Indian peoples without destroying the source of Indian spiritual strength. One way was to persuade Indians to convert to Christianity by offering more food, clothing, and supplies to those who converted. Another way was force. The army tried to suppress religious celebrations among the Puget Sound peoples and among the Nez Perces. Among the plains Indians, wrote John Collier, the white advocate of Indian rights who later served as Indian commissioner, the religious persecution was "implacable." The Sun Dance, for example, was absolutely forbidden. When a new form of religion centered on the Ghost Dance gained influence among the Sioux, the army set out to crush it in a campaign that ended with the massacre at Wounded Knee.

THE ULTIMATE SANCTIONS

Indian peoples who tried to protect their homelands and their religions suffered exile and death. The Modocs of California, for example, angry over the broken promises that had led them to a reservation, retreated to the lava-bed country around Tule Lake and successfully battled the United States Army until their leadership was betrayed by Modocs bought off by whites. Captain Jack and his associates were hanged in 1873. The rest of the Modoc resisters were deported to the hot, arid, malarial wastes of the Indian Territory. More than 150 people were deported. By 1909 only 51 Modocs were alive.

The Nez Perces suffered a similar fate. Evicted in 1877 from their homeland in the Wallowa country of northeastern Oregon, they were on their way to a reservation in Montana when whites plundered their livestock. The incident sparked the anger the young men felt over the loss of their land, earlier and unpunished killings of Indians by whites, and the arrogant contempt of the whites for Indian people. Without waiting to consult their leader, Chief Joseph, who was temporarily absent from camp, the young men raided nearby settlements, killing nearly twenty whites. Joseph, knowing that white vengeance would be swift and fearful, hurried his people toward refuge in Canada, fighting off army units along the way. Just thirty miles short of safety, Joseph and his badly depleted force, now made up mostly of old men, women, and children, were compelled to surrender.

Chief Joseph of the Nez Perces in the Pacific Northwest. Joseph and his people were trapped while trying to flee to Canada and were deported to Indian Territory, where many died.

Smithsonian Institution, National Anthropological Archives

The Nez Perces were promised refuge on the Montana reservation. Instead, they were shipped off to Indian Territory. Within a year, more than 25 percent of them were dead. Years later Joseph and other survivors were shipped to reservations in Montana and the state of Washington.

Another place of Indian exile was Fort Marion, Florida. Among other peoples deported there were the Apaches, who had carried on guerrilla warfare in the Southwest for more than twenty years before their final surrender in 1886. Indian peoples accustomed to the high plains country languished and died in the hot, humid Florida climate. Among the survivors was Geronimo, the brilliant Apache tactician who for so long had outfought and outwitted his white opponents. He was held a prisoner at Fort Marion, then at Fort Sill, Oklahoma, until his death in 1909.

Many Indian leaders were killed while they were unarmed and under white control. Big Snake, a Ponca who had challenged the deportation of his people, was killed while allegedly resisting arrest. Crazy Horse, an outstanding Sioux who advocated resistance, was slain when he refused to be locked up. Sitting Bull, the last great spokesman for Indian tradition, was under arrest when he was shot to death in 1890 by Indian police in a fight that erupted after his arrest. Mangas Colorado, a famous Apache leader, was treacherously seized after he had gone alone to parley with army officers who had hoisted a white flag of truce. That night he was killed by his guards.

A more subtle and more cruel punishment of Indians was taking their children away from them. Indian children were valued not only for themselves but also for their role as the perpetuators of the people. In them was bound up the future, the carrying on of all the sacred traditions of the people, all that gave meaning to life. When whites transported children to boarding schools, the most famous of which was located at an army post at Carlisle, Pennsylvania, they inflicted a lasting wound on Indian spirit. More, the schools tried to eliminate that very spirit. The children were taught to repudiate their heritage, to look upon their parents and grandparents as inferior, to take up the superior ways of white people. Richard H. Pratt, the army officer who founded the Carlisle school in 1879, stated the philosophy of the boarding schools bluntly: "Kill the Indian and save the man."

"THE ONLY GOOD INDIAN . . ."

Whites justified the extinction of the Indians on many grounds. For westerners, the case was simple. The Indians stood in the way of civilization. The land and its mineral riches belonged to those who could make best use of them, as God had intended. Congressman James Belford of Colorado said that "an idle and thriftless race of savages cannot be permitted to guard the treasure vaults of the nation which hold our gold and silver." The Indians must be thrust aside, so that the miner "by enriching himself [will] enrich the nation and bless the world." In Cheyenne, Wyoming, businessmen asserted that the region was "destined for the occupancy and sustenance of the Anglo-Saxon race. . . . The same inscrutable Arbiter that decreed the downfall of Rome has pronounced the doom of extinction upon the red men of America." The sentiment was not confined to westerners, however. In 1867, President Andrew Johnson told Congress: "If the savage resists, civilization, with the ten commandments in one hand and the sword in the other, demands his immediate extermination."

Extermination was also justified because Indians—often bands of young warriors operating without permission of their leaders—raided white settlements, took livestock, and killed white men. Often the raids on white farms arose from sheer hunger. The more bloody actions against whites usually were in retaliation for brutal massacres of Indian peoples, as after the Sand Creek incident. Moreover, it was not uncommon for whites to raid Indian farms and camps to steal cattle and ponies. Nor was it uncommon for white men to rape Indian women. White settlers paid little attention to such considerations. They agreed with the view expressed by General Philip Sheridan in 1869: "The only good Indians I ever saw were dead."

Indians, too, were accused of fighting in an uncivilized way—especially when their tactics were successful. Whites were revolted by reports of the scalping of fallen whites, although they themselves were also guilty of the same mutilation. In 1863, for example, after an uprising of the Sioux, the state of Minnesota offered a $25 bounty for each Sioux scalp. The legend of Indian savagery became established in the white mind, and it justified savage white reprisal. As Francis A. Walker, commissioner of Indian affairs, reported in 1873; "There is no question of national dignity . . . involved in the treatment of savages by a civilized power."

Such beliefs were related to the generally accepted notion that Indians were by nature inferior, a notion upheld by the leading scholars of the day. Doctor Oliver Wendell Holmes, the eminent medical man and essayist, thought the Indian represented only a "rudimentary" type of humanity, to be supplanted by whites who were "a little more like God's own image." The historian Francis Parkman declared that the Indian "will not learn the arts of civilization, and he and his forest must perish together."

Such attitudes were given a scientific rationale by the doctrine of social evolution that was so powerful in the latter nineteenth century. As interpreted by the followers of Herbert Spencer, the struggle for existence involved races as well as individuals. In both cases, the weak would go under and the fittest would survive. To Americans, it was clear that the fittest were American Anglo-Saxons and that Indian peoples were among the weak. In 1885 Josiah Strong, a Protestant clergyman and social evolutionist, noted in *Our Country* that in North America, Australia, and New Zealand the native peoples were "disappearing before the all-conquering Anglo-Saxons." And, he commented, "It would seem as if these inferior tribes were only precursors of a superior race" to take over not only North America but also "the earth." The book was so popular that it made Strong a national figure.

An integral part of white belief in Indian inferiority was the view that Indian peoples were immoral. Regarding their own moral code as the only right one, whites simply would not grant that Indian societies had their own moral codes. Sexual and marital customs such as polygamy whites found especially outrageous. Theodore Roosevelt opined that "the most vicious cowboy has more moral principle than the average Indian." Even in the early twentieth century a commissioner of Indian affairs declared that most Indians had no notion of "morality or chastity, according to an enlightened standard."

"FRIENDS" OF THE INDIANS

Whites might believe in the cultural inferiority of Indians, but that did not necessarily mean that they accepted the extermination of Indians. In fact, a growing body of opinion, especially in the East, was repelled by the genocidal policies followed by some westerners and some army officers. Spurred by the publication in 1881 of Helen Hunt Jackson's *A Century of Dishonor,* a documented history of white perfidy in dealing with Indians, the dissidents organized reform associations to protect the Indian by bringing about a change in federal policy.

Believing that Indian culture was inferior to white, the reformers proposed to save Indians by remaking them in the image of whites. The great obstacle to this, in their view, was the traditional concept of communal land ownership, still recognized, however imperfectly, in the reservation system. On this concept were based the laws, customs, and traditions that prevented Indian assimilation into white society. To white reformers the solution was obvious: break up the reservations; distribute the land among families and individuals under conditions that would assure federal protection of their landholdings; destroy tribal authority and organization by making Indians citizens of the United States subject to federal law and state law. In this way, the reformers thought, there would emerge among Indians a class of independent yeoman farmers, industrious, thrifty, self-respecting, and proud of their individual property. In short, Indians who could survive.

The reformers found strange allies. White westerners wanted still more reservation land, but their designs had been frustrated by eastern opposition. Now they could march shoulder to shoulder with their former opponents under the banner of humanitarian reform. Thus came about the Dawes Act of 1887.

The Dawes Act wiped out communal land ownership among many peoples. It provided that the president, at his own discretion, could order reservation lands distributed among their inhabitants. Each family head received 160 acres, single adults 80 acres, and minor children 40 acres. To protect the Indians from white designs, the land was held in trust by the United States for twenty-five years; that is, Indians could not sell their land. After the land was allotted to the Indians, the surplus was sold to whites by the federal government, the proceeds to be used to provide schools for Indian children.

The law also broke down traditional internal Indian authority, which was based in part on the United States' recognition that such authority represented Indian "nations." A major legal step toward weakening Indian national authority came in 1871, when Congress banned future treaties, although existing treaties would be respected. Later in that decade, Congress annulled existing treaties with peoples who resisted invasion of their homelands by federal troops. Now, in 1887, with Indian resistance broken, Congress decreed that henceforth those Indians covered by the act would be citizens of the United States, subject only to the laws of white men as enacted by Congress and state or territorial legislatures. Indian law was no longer recognized.

The Dawes Act proved disastrous for Indian peoples. After allotments to Indians had been made, 60 million acres out of 138 million were declared surplus and sold to whites. Somehow, the lands sold to whites proved to be better than those allotted to Indians. Further, the acreage allotted to Indians was much too small for successful farming in the plains country, a fact pointed out by President Grover Cleveland in 1894. Given the climatic conditions of the region, only big farms worked with machinery could prosper. But the law provided no credit for Indians to acquire the necessary machinery, nor did it provide funds for training Indians in the intricacies of mechanized farming.

The poverty-stricken Indians, then, were turned loose on their inadequate plots of ground with no financial support. They had little alternative except to lease their lands to white neighbors—a legal stratagem that allowed whites to evade the federal prohibition of sale of Indian land. The lease terms, of course, favored whites. The Indian "owners" of the land had to eke out a living as best they could, seeking employment from whites for such wages as whites were willing to pay. Thus developed the wretched poverty that came to characterize the settlements of dispossessed Indians. When the "trust period" expired, whites were able to buy the land for a pittance.

Another factor helped bring about dispossession of Indians. As the older generation died, the holdings of those Indians who still held their land were distributed among their children. In a generation or two these holdings were so small that nothing could be done with them except sell them to whites after it became legal to do so.

The full consequences of the Dawes Act and its successors were set forth in 1934 by John Collier, commissioner of Indian affairs. Of the 138 million acres originally held by Indians, only 48 million acres remained in Indian hands in 1933, and of these 20 million acres were classifed as unfit for cultivation.

The allotment policy also had profound psychological consequences for Indian peoples. They no longer lived in large communities, sharing common traditions and customs, bound together by a sense of belonging. They were now individuals in small segregated settlements surrounded by whites. They were stripped of their own culture, of their sense of identity. They could not identify with white culture—and a hostile white society made sure that they would not.

Physical poverty drained the body, and psychic deprivation corroded the spirit. Unable to express their frustration and anger against whites, Indians turned against themselves in self-hatred, expressed in despair, alcoholism, and violence against each other. The despair was voiced by Black Elk, a survivor of Wounded Knee, years after the massacre: "There is no center any longer, and the sacred tree is dead." But he did allow himself some hope: "It may be that some little root of the sacred tree still lives."

As recent events have demonstrated, some little root did survive. The sacred tree may have withered, but it did not die.

FOR FURTHER READING

For a general picture, the following books are valuable: John Collier, *The Indians of the Americas* (1947); William T. Hagan, *American Indians* (1961); Alvin M. Josephy, Jr., *The Indian Heritage of America* (1968); Edward H. Spicer, *A Short History of the Indians of the United States* (1969), and Ruth Underhill, *Red Man's America* (1953).

Two topics of special interest are dealt with in Ruth Underhill, *Red Man's Religion* (1965), and Wilcomb E. Washburn, *Red Man's Land—White Man's Law* (1971).

There is a growing literature dealing with different aspects of Indian history. Two such works have been popular: Ralph K. Andrist, *The Long Death* (1964), and Dee Brown, *Bury My Heart at Wounded Knee* (1971). Although concentrating on peoples of the plains, they also cover such other peoples as the Modocs and the Nez Perces. Edward H. Spicer, *Cycles of Conquest* (1962), deals with peoples of the Southwest.

White attitudes toward Indians are discussed in Thomas F. Gossett, *Race: The History of an Idea in America* (1963), and Roy H. Pearce, *The Savages of America* (1953).

A wide range of reprinted articles will be found in Roger L. Nichols and George R. Adams, eds., *The American Indian: Past and Present* (1971). A valuable collection of Indian source materials is Wayne Moquin and Charles Van Doren, eds., *Great Documents in American Indian History* (1973).

20 the nadir of free blacks

While Indian peoples struggled to save their way of life, black Americans strove to preserve themselves against a resurgent white supremacy that threatened their spiritual—and sometimes their physical—survival. The black experience was all the more traumatic in that for a brief period during Reconstruction blacks played a dynamic role in American society.

RECONSTRUCTION

That role was made possible by national policy in the immediate post–Civil War period. The Thirteenth Amendment abolished slavery. The Fourteenth Amendment made blacks citizens and provided constitutional protection for their civil and political rights. Federal civil rights legislation aimed to end discrimination by private business. States were forbidden by the Fifteenth Amendment to deny blacks the right to vote on grounds of race.

Blacks responded with enthusiasm to the new opportunities. They played active roles in the conventions that provided southern states with their first really democratic constitutions. As voters and legislators, they helped move southern states toward meeting long-neglected social responsibilities, such as setting up viable public school systems. Their votes helped pass legislation to protect the homesteads of poor farmers from siezure for debt.

Blacks dominated no southern state government—even where they were a majority of the population—but they occupied public offices, ranging from the lowly justice of the peace to lieutenant governor. For the first time in American history, blacks sat in the House of Representatives and two served in the Senate. In an era when corruption was rife in Washington, the black men earned a reputation for honesty. Blacks were the mainstay of the Republican party in the South and thus helped make possible a genuine two-party political system in the region for the first time in more than a generation.

There was also an outpouring of black spirit in fields other than public life. Challenging white claims that they could not be educated, blacks swarmed into the schools now open to them. Booker T. Washington, recalling his own experience, said, "It was a whole race trying to go to school." Blacks also went to college, to be taught not only by whites but also by such qualified blacks as Richard T. Greener, the first black to graduate from Harvard. Some new black institutions, such as Howard, Fisk, and Atlanta universities, went on to attain national as well as regional prestige.

The black church, the one institution blacks could truly call their own, expanded dramatically. Hundreds of thousands joined Methodist churches while even more became Baptists, impressed with that denomination's local autonomy and the opportunities it offered for attaining posts of leadership. Through the church blacks learned how to manage corporate affairs, and talented men rose to leadership. From the church came such Reconstruction leaders as Congressman Richard H. Cain of South Carolina; United States Senator Hiram R. Revels of Mississippi; J. Sella Martin, an official of the National Colored Labor Union; and Jonathan C. Gibbs, superintendent of education in Florida. The church itself became increasingly the focus of black community life.

Blacks also sought to improve themselves economically. Through local mutual-aid societies and such national secret fraternal orders as the Odd Fellows and the Prince Hall Masons, they pooled their funds to protect their families in case of illness or death. Black men successfully operated their own ship-repair yard in Baltimore until overtaken by the collapse of the economy in 1873. The Freedmen's Savings and Trust Company, chartered by Congress in 1865, had accumulated nearly $20 million in deposits from thrifty blacks until in 1871 it was raided by the white railroad speculator Jay Cooke and brought to disaster. When white labor unions denied membership to blacks, workers formed their own National Colored Labor Union, led by Isaac Myers, a ship's caulker from Baltimore. Throughout the South blacks sought to own land, and in some measure they succeeded, especially in Arkansas, South Carolina, Florida, Virginia, and Georgia.

Active black participation in public affairs divided southern white society. Some of the old planting aristocracy and many poor whites collaborated with blacks in the Republican Party. A few, typified by Edward A. Pollard, former defender of slavery and ardent Confederate, acknowledged that their previous ideas about blacks had been proved wrong.

Most whites were not so persuaded. They saw in black progress not an attempt to attain equality but the menace of black domination. They felt the threat the more keenly because the heavy load of their debt, falling prices for farm products, and rising taxes portended the loss of their land. As they felt themselves slipping down the social scale, their anger and fear came out in violence. Unable to overthrow the Reconstruction governments directly, they vented their frustrations on the symbol of the new order—blacks and their white allies. Secret terrorist organizations, such as the Ku Klux Klan, drove black farmers off their land, burned churches and schools, and flogged, maimed, and killed local black leaders and whites who worked with them, such as schoolteachers. Finally, in 1871 the federal government intervened. Some terrorists were sent to prison, and the violence declined sharply.

Blacks also faced danger from another source. After the Civil War there had emerged from the old southern order "new men" more attuned to the ascendancy of business than to the old planter tradition. Needing capital, they entered into alliances with Yankee businessmen to exploit the coal, iron, and timber resources of the South and to promote railroad expansion. Some of them became Republicans, but most continued to be Democrats, although they preferred to call themselves "Redeemers" or "Conservatives." Their political objective was to overthrow Republican governments in the South, partly because they themselves resented black participation in government, partly because the program won them support among the mass of whites, and partly because controlling state governments would enhance their bargaining power in dealing with the Yankees. A major element in Conservative influence among southern whites was the identification of the Conservatives with white supremacy.

The limits of black political strength now revealed themselves. Blacks controlled no state governments. Within the state Republican parties they were junior partners, in little position to shape policy. When white Republicans fell out among themselves, they sought to use blacks against their opponents. Many black leaders rebelled against the tokenism that confined black Republicans to positions lacking real authority.

Conservatives took full advantage of these divisions. They encouraged white factionalism. They fed the flames of black resentment. They exploited the personal rivalries of black political leaders, winning over a number of black Republicans, including United States Senator Hiram R. Revels of Mississippi. All the while, Conservatives mobilized the mass of southern whites, counseling against the violence that might bring federal intervention. Through such means Conservatives gained control of most southern states before the formal ending of Reconstruction in 1877.

Conservatives wooed opinion in the North. Businessmen were won over by demonstrating that Conservatives were no threat to Yankees, neither in the South nor in terms of national economic policy. Republicans outraged at corruption in Washington, such as Horace Greeley, editor of the powerful *New York Tribune,* were persuaded by highly exaggerated accounts of corruption and waste in Reconstruction governments. Conservatives pleaded with northern whites to save them from domination by "ignorant and barbarous" blacks, who, they hastened to add, were not in themselves to blame. Rather, the blacks were manipulated by dishonest northern adventurers ("carpetbaggers") and by unscrupulous white southerners ("scalawags"). They ignored, of course, their own role in corruption and their collaboration with "carpetbaggers" and "scalawags." The terms themselves, although used later by historians, were derogatory labels applied by Conservative propagandists that did less than justice to many northerners and southerners who cooperated with Republican governments.

The Conservative ploy succeeded. The message reached large sections of the northern public. The Liberal Republican party of 1872 embodied the Conservative outlook on Reconstruction. The regular Republicans won, but they too were persuaded. This was demonstrated when Conservatives, frustrated at their failure to topple Republican governments in Mississippi and South Carolina by peaceful means, resorted to terrorism, and the plea of Governor Adelbert Ames of Mississippi for federal intervention was denied in 1875. Conservatives then swept elections in which blacks voted Republican at the risk of their lives—if indeed they were allowed to vote at all. In 1876, white terrorism in South Carolina culminated in the Hamburg Massacre, in which black militiamen were slaughtered in cold blood. Only a token federal force was sent in to restore order. The Republican government lasted but another year.

In the meantime, the long depression that began in 1873 turned the attention of northerners to their own economic problems. The public, explained Attorney General Pierrepont to President Grant, was "tired" of hearing about the plight of southern blacks.

Thus was set the stage for what T. Thomas Fortune, a noted black editor, called the betrayal of 1877. The resolution of the disputed election of 1876 had one major significance for blacks. In return for agreeing to let Republican Rutherford B. Hayes occupy the White House, Conservatives were allowed to rule the South, free from federal intervention. In response to black and white protests, Conservative leaders gave solemn assurances that under their rule the rights of blacks would be fully protected.

RETREAT FROM EQUALITY

Under Conservative rule blacks paid for the mistakes of Reconstruction. Foremost of these was the failure to provide land for former slaves and thus afford them a base of economic independence. Former slaves then had little alternative except to work for whites. Some became tenant farmers, paying rent to landowners, but most became sharecroppers, working the land in exchange for a share, usually one-third, of the income at the end of the year. Given the low prices of cotton, the income of the sharecropper would have been low in any case, but it was reduced still further by his poverty. Lacking cash, he had to buy necessary goods on credit provided by his employer or a local "country merchant." Prices on the goods were inflated to begin with, and interest rates were high. Some unscrupulous whites padded black accounts. As a result, many sharecroppers discovered at the end of the year that they had little or no income—and indeed that they were in debt. Illiterate blacks, knowing nothing of record keeping, were in no position to challenge the white men.

For a time, sharecroppers sought to improve their lot by moving from place to place. Legislatures then made it a crime for a person to move away owing money to his employer. Since employers kept the records, it was virtually impossible for blacks to break out legally from this new form of bondage. When they did escape, employers often sent armed gangs after them and added the cost of their capture to their alleged debt.

Some whites found the laws useful in another way. They paid the fines of blacks convicted of petty offenses and compelled the blacks to work for them to pay them back. In some cases blacks worked for years to pay off $20 fines. Thus peonage, a legalized form of slavery, became part of the black American experience. Not until the 1940s did the United States Supreme Court completely outlaw the practice.

The failure of Reconstruction governments to end the convict-leasing system condemned thousands of black men and women to early death. Poor whites as well as blacks suffered, but most of the victims were black.

The established practice of renting out prisoners to private employers spread rapidly under Conservative rule, prompting an increase in the supply of prisoners. Legislatures rewrote criminal codes so that what had been misdemeanors became felonies, punishable by long prison terms. Prisoners were then leased for years to politicians and businessmen.

It was a highly profitable business. Counties and states reported huge revenues from the traffic in human flesh. Taxpayers were saved the cost of maintaining expensive prison systems. Politicians waxed wealthy by obtaining leases they sublet to businessmen. Businessmen were delighted to get for a few cents a day workers who dared not organize and could not quit. As outraged blacks proclaimed later, the fortunes of many outstanding white southern families derived from the blood and sweat of prisoners.

The prisoners, who for the most part labored in mines and in logging, turpentine, and construction camps, were treated in a manner compared by the southern historian Fletcher M. Green to the Nazi concentration-camp horror. Unlike slaveowners, who had an economic interest in keeping slaves alive and well, businessmen had no such interest. Prisoners were poorly fed and clothed, denied adequate medical attention, and compelled to produce their quotas of work under penalty of severe flogging. Investigating bodies of several southern states confirmed the finding of a Mississippi grand jury that prisoners were subjected to "the most inhuman and brutal treatment." Death rates were high—16 percent in Mississippi, 25 percent in Arkansas. Most of the dead were black. Perhaps more revolting to public opinion was the revelation of a Georgia legislative committee that men and women prisoners were shackled together at night in the same bunks—with consequent pregnancies.

Black and white organizations strove to abolish the system, but they made slow going. Arrayed against them were the Conservative party machines and powerful business interests, such as the Tennessee Coal, Iron and Railroad Company, which had a monopoly on all the prisoners of that state. Nevertheless, by 1913 reformers won an end to the system in six states, and it disappeared in other states in succeeding years. Penologists reported that its replacement, the chain-gang system—the use of shackled prisoners on public works projects—was as brutal and inhuman as its predecessor.

THE TRIUMPH OF WHITE SUPREMACY

Peonage and convict leasing were part of a larger degradation of black people that took place between 1890 and 1918. For years after Reconstruction, southern blacks continued to vote and hold office, although in diminishing numbers, and some blacks voted as their white employers or bankers ordered. Blacks continued, too, to enjoy some measure of civil rights. In the 1880s there began a slow slippage in black rights that became a landslide over the next twenty years.

Its source was in the inequities of white society. Entrenched after a generation in power, corrupt Conservative governments blocked all efforts at substantial reform. Politicians and businessmen waxed wealthy, while great numbers of farmers and workers lived in poverty. Indifferent to the plight of their fellow whites, Conservatives frustrated the efforts of the poor to redress grievances by controlling what was in effect a one-party system. Finally, in 1892 the anger of the poor led to the creation of an independent political movement, the Populist party, which demanded sweeping political and economic reform threatening the very foundations of Conservative power. When other means, including bribery and terrorism, failed to stem the tide of Populist success, Conservatives fell back on their last resort: the issue of race.

They pointed out that blacks in large numbers belonged to the new party and that some had been elected to high office in party organizations—proof in itself that some white men were willing to betray their own race and, particularly, pure white womanhood. The Conservative propaganda had its effect. Thousands of whites deserted the Populists, and the party was badly crippled.

White populist leaders decided to seek the white vote only. They argued that Conservatives could always use the black votes they controlled against Populists, while the black presence in Populism made the party vulnerable on the issue of white supremacy. To these leaders, the solution was clear: purge the party of blacks, identify Populism with white supremacy, and center on a demand for black disfranchisement. Once blacks were removed from the political scene, they argued, white voters would sweep Populists into power and their reform program could be attained.

Conservatives offered no opposition. They were willing to trade off the black votes they controlled for the white votes Populists depended on. Conservatives had learned from the new Mississippi constitution of 1890 that standards used to keep out blacks could also keep out poor whites, the mainstay of Populist strength. Promoted vigorously by both parties, disfranchisement was an established part of southern life by 1910. Its impact on black political power may be illustrated by the case of Louisiana. Under the state's old constitution, more than 130,000 blacks voted. In 1904, new requirements permitted fewer than 1,400 to vote. These, of course, were prestigious blacks with close ties to the white establishment. Poor whites suffered too. Educational and property qualifications in Louisiana reduced the white vote from 164,000 in 1897 to 92,000 in 1904.

So went glimmering the white Populist illusion that black disfranchisement meant success for their program. The party faded and its leaders drifted back to the Conservatives, who once again called themselves Democrats. The Populist rhetoric was still useful, however, and a generation of demagogues emerged who attained power by using it, with special emphasis on racism. Once in power, they made their own terms with the establishment, and the problems of the southern poor received little practical attention. Symbolically, Populist Tom Watson of Georgia, who had once advocated unity of black and white poor, went to the United States Senate as a virulent exponent of white racism.

The passions aroused by Conservative and Populist racist demagoguery brought not only disfranchisement but also a body of other laws emphasizing white supremacy. Schools, housing, hospitals, prisons, transportation, public accommodations—even drinking fountains—were segregated. The laws required that the separate facilities be equal, but in practice those assigned blacks were inferior. In some places no provision at all was made for the schooling of black children. Interracial marriage was, of course, forbidden.

Segregation, however, did not mean rigid separation of the races. Blacks were wanted in white residential areas—as servants. Whites ran stores and saloons in urban black ghettos, in competition with black businessmen. In small towns, white merchants were glad to get black trade. In line with a long tradition, illicit interracial sex—between white men and black women—continued.

The courts reflected the spirit of the laws. White judges and all-white juries generally took a lenient view of white offenses, including murder, even when whites were victims. Blacks, however, felt the full weight of the law. In 1906, for example, a Georgia black convicted of stealing a potato worth 5¢ received a sentence of six months on the chain gang. Even children were suitably taught to respect white supremacy. In Atlanta, a six-year-old black boy was whipped for allegedly insulting a young white girl. The punishment, a newspaper reported, would "make him remember to be good." Rape of white women was punishable by death, but black victims of white men found scant sympathy from white officials.

THE RULE OF VIOLENCE

White supremacy also produced violence. In 1901, the former Confederate army officer and Alabama governor William C. Oates was alarmed by the sentiments of his fellow whites. "The Negro is doing no harm," he protested, but "the people want to kill him and wipe him from the face of the earth." He referred, among other things, to the lynchings that claimed nearly 200 lives a year in the 1890s. Most of the victims were southern blacks. In the early twentieth century the number of lynchings declined to two a week. As before, most victims were southern blacks.

Southerners who justified lynching explained that it was due to the large number of blacks raping white women and the fear that white courts would not punish the offenders properly. The view in turn derived from the universal belief that black men had such a sexual compulsion for white women that only the strongest sanctions could keep it in check. The belief was not confined to the South. Among those who shared it in the North was Lester F. Ward, the eminent sociologist. Studies of lynching pioneered by the black journalist Ida Wells-Barnett showed, however, that in only a minority of the incidents were the victims accused of rape or attempted rape. Nevertheless, the idea that lynchings arose from attacks on white women was so firmly implanted in the white mind that it helps explain the generally tolerant white attitude toward lynching.

White mobs did not confine themselves to hanging, shooting, and burning alive individual blacks suspected of crime. Sometimes they attacked entire black communities. A particularly bloody riot took place in Wilmington, North Carolina, in 1898, during which whites killed eleven blacks, wounded at least twenty-five, and drove hundreds out of the city. Another major riot erupted in Atlanta in 1906, following sensational—and sometimes fabricated—news accounts of blacks allegedly raping white women. Whites, including the police, raided black residential areas, shooting, killing, looting, and destroying property. Ten black people were slain and at least sixty wounded. Among the whites, two were killed and ten wounded. The Atlanta riot, however, is noteworthy in another respect. Some of the blacks took up arms to defend themselves and their families.

Upper-class whites sought to dissociate themselves from such violence, blaming it on poor whites. A leader in the Wilmington riot, however, was a former congressman, and the editors of Atlanta newspapers could hardly be classified as riffraff. More to the point, upper-class whites controlled the machinery of government, but lynchers routinely escaped punishment and white rioters were rarely brought to book. Indeed, the obvious immunity enjoyed by such whites encouraged further white violence and spread fear among blacks. Thus, violence served a purpose not unwelcome to the white upper-class: it kept blacks "in their place" and precluded renewal of the Populist unity of black and white poor that had been so threatening.

WHITE SUPREMACY: NORTHERN STYLE

Antiblack feeling had been strong in the North since before the Civil War, but at the turn of the century it was intensified by the spread of racist doctrines, popularization by the media of the stereotype of the black man as killer and rapist, the use of blacks as strikebreakers, and black migration from the South to northern towns.

The mounting tensions first snapped in New York City in 1900. Aroused by the killing of a white policeman in a fight with a black man, white mobs took to the streets and, with the active assistance of police, clubbed and maimed all blacks they could find. The failure of public authorities to punish either civilian or police rioters doubtless encouraged whites elsewhere. Riots occurred later in Ohio, Indiana, and Illinois in which blacks were lynched and black businesses and houses burned.

The most notorious incident took place at Springfield, Illinois, in 1908. Angered by a white woman's false testimony that she had been raped by a black man, whites clubbed, shot, and killed blacks and burned their houses and churches. Hundreds of blacks fled the city that called itself "Abe Lincoln's Home Town." So great was the violence that it took 5,000 militia to restore order. The leaders of the riot went unpunished.

As in the South, northerners blamed blacks for white violence. In the South, whites explained that if black men were not rapists there would be no need of lynchings. A leading Springfield newspaper attributed the riot, not to "the whites' hatred toward the Negroes, but of the Negroes' own misconduct, general inferiority or unfitness for free institutions."

Patterns of segregation that had taken shape prior to the Civil War became fixed in the postwar period. There were no separate school systems as in the South, but schools were segregated nevertheless by residential segregation that confined blacks to certain neighborhoods. The neighborhood school thus became an instrument of racial separation. The quality of education in white schools was, of course, much superior to that of black schools. In many small towns, which could afford only one school, hostility toward black children was often marked.

In response to black pressures, many states banned discrimination by private businessmen catering to the public. The laws were poorly enforced, however, and in many areas white feeling ran so strong that blacks deemed it imprudent to invoke the law. Few hotels, restaurants, and saloons with a white clientele admitted blacks—except as employees. Symbolically, when the Republican party convention met in Philadelphia in 1900, white delegates stayed in the best hotels while black delegates were sent to private black homes. Many small towns in the North and Far West permitted no black residents at all.

Private organizations of great power also discriminated against blacks. The American Bar Association and the American Medical Association excluded black professionals. Northern club women joined with white southerners to ban admission of black women's clubs to the General Federation of Women's Clubs. When Josephine Ruffin, a black delegate from Massachusetts, objected, Rebecca Lowe of Georgia, national president, retorted: "Mrs. Ruffin belongs among her own people." The Grand Army of the Republic, the potent organization of Union army veterans, for years followed a nondiscriminatory policy. By 1900, however, under pressure from members who had settled in the South, the GAR permitted discrimination in its southern units—discrimination that often meant black exclusion.

Even more injurious to black wage-earners was the pervasive hostility of labor unions. The independent railroad brotherhoods and, with a few exceptions, the unions affiliated with the American Federation of Labor excluded blacks. Where they were too numerous to be ignored, blacks were relegated to "Jim Crow" local unions, where they paid their dues but were denied a voice in union policy. The aim of the unions, however, was to eliminate black employment. Many devices were used: refusal to work with blacks, manipulation of apprenticeship regulations, strikes to force blacks off the job, and violence. Unions, especially on the southern railroads, entered into agreements with employers that looked toward phasing out black workers. By 1910 there were fewer opportunities for skilled black workers than in 1865.

White labor leaders argued that blacks themselves were responsible for exclusion. Blacks, it was said, simply did not make good union members. In the words of Samuel Gompers, president of the American Federation of Labor (AFL), they did not understand "the philosophy of human rights." Besides, blacks were willing to work for lower wages than whites and were "naturally" strikebreakers—which again showed them unfit for union membership. One solution for the "black problem" was suggested in 1898 by a leading AFL organizer in the AFL's official publication: deportation of blacks from the United States. The article received warm commendation from Gompers.

Within the AFL itself, however, were unions that demonstrated the fallacy of Gompers's position. Blacks were strong in the International Longshoremen's Association. The United Mine Workers, representing coal miners, actively recruited thousands of black members, promoted integration in its local unions, and counted among its local officials many black miners.

Not all national labor federations between the Civil War and World War I were racist. Two were of major significance: the Knights of Labor, which enjoyed great influence in the 1880s, and the Industrial Workers of the World (IWW), a militant organization that attracted a considerable following between 1905 and 1914 among workers neglected by the AFL.

In its heyday, the Knights welcomed blacks as equals and successfully organized about 60,000 black workers in both North and South. A black worker from

New York, Frank J. Ferrell, served as a member of the union's general executive board. The IWW, believing that class solidarity transcended racial divisions, allowed no segregation within its affiliates and made a special point of organizing blacks. It had marked success among southern timber workers and Atlantic and Gulf Coast longshoremen. Part of its success lay in its outspoken denunciation of white supremacy. Blacks served as officials of affiliates, and Ben Fletcher, a Philadelphia longshoreman, emerged as a national leader of the organization.

"LILY WHITE" GOVERNMENT

Even before Reconstruction formally ended in 1876, the Supreme Court had seriously weakened federal protection of black rights as set forth in the Fourteenth and Fifteenth amendments and in various Reconstruction laws. The trend continued well into the twentieth century. Of the many cases reaching the court some were of sweeping significance.

In 1883, for example, the court nullified the federal Civil Rights Act of 1875. States, said the court, could not discriminate on racial grounds, but private individuals could. The court subsequently qualified that stand. In *Plessy* v. *Ferguson* thirteen years later, the court upheld state-ordered segregation, arguing it was not discriminatory if the segregated facilities were "substantially equal." The court's hostility to blacks was reflected in the decision. Blacks, it said, felt that segregation "stamps the colored race with a badge of inferiority. If this be so, it is solely because the colored race chooses to put that construction upon it." The court added that, "If one race be inferior to the other socially, the Constitution of the United States cannot put them on the same plane."

The sole dissent came from Justice John M. Harlan, a white southerner. In upholding the black case, he issued a warning that time vindicated. The decision, he said, would "prove to be quite as pernicious as the decision . . . in the Dred Scott Case." Nevertheless, the decision remained law until 1954.

The "separate but equal" doctrine did not require that separate facilities must be provided under all circumstances. A Georgia county, claiming inadequate funds, shut down its black high-school so that the white school could remain open. In *Cumming* v. *County Board of Education* (1899) the Supreme Court approved the action, holding that the alternative of closing both schools would have been of no benefit to blacks. The case involved no "clear and unmistakable disregard" of black rights, said the court.

So far, the Supreme Court had passed only on cases in which whites wanted segregation. But what if whites did not wish segregation? The issue arose in Kentucky in 1904, when the legislature ordered an end to racial integration in private schools. The law was directed at Berea College, which since 1869 had welcomed poor white and black students to a program that enabled them to work their way through college. The college appealed, arguing that since it was a private institution its students came together on a purely voluntary basis and so were beyond the reach of the legislature. In 1908 the Supreme Court held otherwise, thus empowering states to impose segregation on private institutions that did not desire it.

Three years later the Supreme Court had an opportunity to strike down the growing evil of peonage. At issue in *Bailey* v. *Alabama* was a state statute saying that leaving one's employer while owing him money was in itself evidence of intent to defraud. The same law barred such workers from giving evidence on their own behalf. The court struck down the Alabama law, but on such narrow legal grounds that peonage continued to flourish. One of the two dissenters who upheld the Alabama law was Oliver Wendell Holmes, Jr., later hailed as a champion of civil liberties.

So far as blacks were concerned, Congress posted a record as dismal as the court's. Senator Henry Blair's proposals for federal aid to education in order to reduce illiteracy among blacks and whites were thwarted by southern Democrats. In 1890 a measure to provide federal protection for black voting rights was voted down. Attempts to outlaw lynching met with no success. Some southern Senators, most notably Tom Watson of Georgia, Ben Tillman of South Carolina, and James K. Vardaman of Mississippi, stimulated white hysteria with the kind of virulent racist rhetoric that Hitler later found so useful. In 1907, for example, Vardaman said that if white supremacy were threatened in Mississippi, "every Negro in the state will be lynched." A year later a Georgia congressman told the House that "utter extermination of a race" was regrettable, but if "its existence endangers the welfare of mankind it is fitting that it should be swept away."

Nor was the record of the White House reassuring. For long, presidents ignored mounting racist violence. In 1898, however, the issue was brought home when the black postmaster at Lake City, South Carolina, was lynched. President McKinley told protesting blacks that appropriate action would be taken. Nothing was ever done. McKinley's successor, Theodore Roosevelt, won over many blacks with what seemed genuine sympathy, symbolized by his playing host to Booker T. Washington at the White House. Southern white outrage over the affair turned to praise in 1905 when in the course of a southern tour the president identified himself with white supremacy.

Black dismay over Roosevelt's change of heart turned to anger in 1906 after a riot in Brownsville, Texas involving black soldiers encamped nearby. Without waiting for a full-scale inquiry, the president ordered the dishonorable discharge of three companies—an injustice that was not fully rectified until 1972.

While President Taft appointed more blacks to federal jobs than did Roosevelt, he continued Roosevelt's policy of purging blacks from the Republican party in the South. He also tried to win over southern whites by espousing their views on disfranchisement and segregation. He told blacks that the best education for them was strictly vocational. Woodrow Wilson's outlook became apparent shortly after he took office in 1913. He initiated racial segregation in federal government offices!

THE "SCIENCE" OF RACISM

The racism of government policy reflected the almost universal racism of white society. It was sanctioned not only by white folk myth but also by the respectable scholarly and scientific opinion of the day.

On the basis of the Darwinian theory of evolution, scientists held that there was a hierarchy of races. White Anglo-Saxons were said to represent the highest stage of biological evolution. Blacks represented the lowest order of humanity, barely separated from the animals. In terms of psychology, blacks developed mentally only until puberty, at which time they came to be dominated by the senses (meaning sex, primarily). Historically, it was argued, blacks had been unable to develop any form of civilization until they came in contact with whites. With specific reference to the United States, historians interpreted Reconstruction as an era in which blacks had been given power to prove themselves fit for equal citizenship and had failed miserably.

Among the intellectuals who contributed to racist "science" were G. Stanley Hall, the famous psychologist who brought Sigmund Freud to the United States in 1909; Nathaniel S. Shaler, dean of the Lawrence Scientific School at Harvard; Lester F. Ward, the distinguished sociologist who believed in social reform; William Graham Sumner, professor of political and social science at Yale, who opposed social reform; and Lewis Terman, whose intelligence tests "proved" that nonwhite people were intellectually inferior.

Later white scholars discredited the theory of a racial hierarchy, but white historians were slow to question the racist histories of Reconstruction written by James Ford Rhodes (1905) and William A. Dunning (1907), both of whom were widely acclaimed. Believers in black inferiority, they portrayed Reconstruction, in Rhodes's words, as "a sickening tale of extravagance, waste, corruption, and fraud." Further, they thought it represented the subjection of proud Anglo-Saxons to what Dunning called "an alien and barbarous race." Both historians deprecated white terrorism, but they felt that the restoration of white supremacy justified the means. As Rhodes said, overthrow of the Reconstruction governments in the South was "a victory of righteousness." This interpretation, which was in effect a scholarly presentation of southern Conservative propaganda, became the standard view in school and college textbooks for at least sixty years and thus helped fix racial stereotypes in the minds of the young.

In addition to the work of scholars there was a veritable spate of racist literature designed for the general public. Typical of the genre was *The Negro, A Menace to American Civilization,* which appeared in 1907. Written by Robert W. Shufeldt, a popular biologist, it recommended emasculation of black men. Reaching an even wider public were racist works of fiction, ranging from the "Sambo" stereotypes of Thomas Nelson Page to the stereotype of the black as rapist in Thomas Dixon's best-selling novel *The Clansman.* Dixon's novel, in turn, served as the scenario for D. W. Griffith's famous movie *The Birth of a Nation,* which appeared in 1915. Despite black protests against its incitement to racial hatred, the movie played to packed houses throughout the country—including the White House.

ESCAPE AND MIGRATION

Black responses to overweening white supremacy were varied—as one might expect of a people who numbered 10 million by 1910—but all the responses were conditioned by white supremacy's greatest triumph: the corrosion of black self-respect. No conquest is complete until the conqueror has made the conquered internalize the values of the conqueror. In this respect white America was largely successful. The incessant insistence on black inferiority, backed as it was by white power, eventually brought about in many blacks acceptance of their "natural" inferiority and caused in them a deep shame of being black. So widespread was the feeling that in 1897 the young rebel W. E. B. DuBois angrily called upon blacks to stop being a people "that ridicules itself, and wishes to God it was anything but itself."

Nowhere was this psychological destructiveness more apparent than among a large number of poor blacks. They were double victims. Whites oppressed them as blacks, and the black middle class regarded them as obstacles to white acceptance. Such blacks took refuge in the segregated poor-black community, where they lived out their real lives and played "Sambo" for whites. They fashioned their own culture—which found musical expression in jazz—a culture little understood by either whites or middle-class blacks. Significantly, jazz was hardly the music of social protest.

At the center of the poor-black community was the impoverished church, no longer a center of black activism as in Reconstruction days. Now its highly emotional appeals to personal piety, while affording an outlet for black frustration, emphasized the element of personal guilt, and so contributed to the negative self-image of many poor blacks.

While some blacks found escape in religion, others resorted to alcohol and more potent drugs. The "drug scene" in the poor-black community was largely a white innovation. Some employers of black workers found that cocaine increased productivity and made workers indifferent to poor food, housing, and working conditions. The use of cocaine spread, and some druggists and doctors of both races were happy to supply the demand.

Some black leaders urged another form of escape—a return to Africa. Henry M. Turner, a militant leader in Reconstruction and later a Methodist bishop, urged that blacks "return to the land of our ancestors, and establish our own nation." Edward M. Blyden, an advocate of migration to Liberia, said that blacks needed their own center of power, from which "such an influence may go forth in behalf of the race as shall be felt by all nations." Few blacks responded. As with earlier exponents of African colonization, blacks listened appreciatively to criticisms of white society but preferred to stay in the United States.

A large number of southern blacks sought relief through internal migration. While most simply moved from one part of the South to another, a great many headed west. The most dramatic exodus took place in 1879 under the leadership of Henry Adams, a Union army veteran, and Benjamin Singleton, a Tennesseean who had been working on migration schemes since 1869. Perhaps as many as 40,000 blacks, mostly from Louisiana, went to Kansas. The first arrivals were welcome, but as more destitute folk arrived, the attitude of white Kansas turned sour. Private charity, largely from the East, alleviated the suffering of the newcomers. While some blacks were able to get land, most went to work for whites as laborers, coal miners, and domestic servants.

Since Kansas had not proved the utopia that Singleton had said it was, some blacks thought the solution lay in creating a black state. Their attention fixed on

Oklahoma, then in transition from Indian Territory to a white-ruled state. In 1891 Edwin P. McCabe, a former state auditor in Kansas, led blacks into the area. Welcomed by neither Indians nor whites, the blacks nevertheless established more than a score of small settlements. The idea of a black state, however, proved an illusion.

Some blacks went farther away. Between 1890 and 1910 nearly 35,000 migrated to the Southwest and to the Pacific Coast. Earlier, about 4,000 black men found jobs on cattle ranches as cooks, cowboys, and ranch hands.

Army service represented another kind of migration. Young men unable to find jobs and unable to bear daily degradation enlisted in the army as a way out. To be sure, the army was segregated and no blacks could expect to be officers, but blacks could rise to sergeant. The army, which found white recruits hard to come by, welcomed blacks. They were used in the campaigns against the Indian peoples, who called them "buffalo soldiers" for their color and hair. They made a distinguished military record in the Spanish-American war and were then used to help suppress the ensuing Filipino war of independence—a role that gave rise to the wry saying that blacks had shouldered "the white man's burden."

The most significant migration was from the countryside to cities, first in the South and then in the North. Between 1900 and 1910, blacks in Birmingham, Alabama, the new coal and iron town, increased their numbers 215 percent. Fort Worth, Texas, reported an increase of more than 200 percent. Other southern cities showed marked black population increases, including Richmond, Atlanta, and Houston. Many migrants to southern cities eventually found their way to northern cities. Between 1900 and 1910 the number of New York's blacks increased by 51 percent to a total of more than 90,000. Philadelphia's black population in 1910 was 80,000, an increase of nearly 34 percent in ten years. Chicago reported a similar increase, while the number of blacks in Pittsburgh increased substantially. In all, about 200,000 southern blacks moved to the North between 1890 and 1910. The move from countryside to city became the central feature of the American black experience in the twentieth century.

The migration set the pattern for ghetto living. The poor migrants lived in conditions recalling those of Irish immigrants of the 1840s: overcrowded, poor housing with primitive sanitary facilities. Since rents were high and wages low, black income did not allow an adequate diet—and many migrants had no notion of a proper diet, in any case. Malnutrition was common, and malnutrition plus overcrowding and ignorance of personal hygiene produced a high incidence of disease.

The frequency of tuberculosis, pneumonia, and venereal disease helps explain a black death rate 50 percent higher than that of whites. Of black children born, 25 percent died in their first year. For many rural blacks, the sudden transition from the easy-going rhythms of the countryside to the high tensions of ghetto living proved too much. Mental illness took its toll among the migrants.

Another long-lasting aspect of ghetto life soon appeared: collusion between corrupt white police departments and black criminal elements. In return for payoffs, police allowed lawbreakers a fairly free hand so long as they confined their activities to the ghettos. Brothels flourished, the most prestigious houses catering only to the white trade. Drug peddlers and professional gamblers operated with impunity. From the ranks of such elements came a "new rich" of the ghettos—blacks who wore flashy clothes, sported diamonds, and gave every evidence that crime paid handsomely indeed.

The lesson was not lost on many black youngsters. The zeal for education that had so marked blacks during the Reconstruction era was waning by 1910. Several factors contributed to this development. In most places black schooling was so inferior that it poorly prepared students to take their place in a harshly competitive society. Even in good schools, texts and teaching were based on white experience and thus were largely irrelevant to the black situation. And there was a growing feeling among blacks that no matter how well schooled they might be, they were for the most part condemned to lives in low-paid, menial jobs. The result was little incentive for formal education.

Parents with aspirations for their children were frustrated by the realities of ghetto life. To survive, both fathers and mothers had to work long hours (nearly one-third of all black women were in the labor force, compared to little more than one-tenth of white women), and youngsters often lacked adequate parental guidance. Their homes, too, were often crowded with boarders whose income was necessary to pay the exorbitant rents. Children, like their elders, took to the streets. Truancy and more serious forms of juvenile delinquency grew with the ghettos.

The city offered no easy way out for blacks—but it was still better than the southern countryside. Even southern blacks who returned home from the North after experiencing the savage competition for jobs and the chilly reception of northern blacks did not go back to farms. They gravitated toward southern cities. Like Polish and Russian Jews fleeing pogroms, they found even in the wretched conditions of American ghettos a measure of security—and within themselves, the ability to survive.

RESISTANCE OF THE POOR

Although many black poor sought escape, thousands actively resisted their exploitation and degradation. In the 1880s small black farmers in the South formed the powerful Colored Farmers' Alliance, which worked together with the white Southern Farmers Alliance in a fruitless effort to win economic and social reforms. Then, as we have seen, such blacks contributed significantly to Populist strength in the 1890s until whites turned against them, thus dooming a promising effort at cooperation between black and white poor.

Black workers, too, resisted. Coal miners by the thousands joined the United Mine Workers in both North and South. They took an active role in coal strikes, even when, as in Alabama in 1894 and again in 1908, they were the special victims of official and unofficial violence. A black union leader served on the steering committee that guided the New Orleans general strike of 1892 to a partially successful conclusion. One element in labor's success was the staunch support given by black union members. When logging-camp workers in the South formed the Brotherhood of Timber Workers in 1910, blacks joined in such numbers that they eventually formed half of the membership of 35,000. Blacks endorsed the union's affiliation with the militant Industrial Workers of the World in 1912 and played a prominent role in a long and unsuccessful strike, during which black members were singled out as targets for racist hysteria and violence, including murder. In fields where blacks were strong, they formed their own unions, as did dock workers in New Orleans and locomotive firemen throughout the South.

In view of the blacks' record as loyal union members, how does one explain their role as strikebreakers—a role that poisoned the relationship between blacks and organized labor for decades. In fact, that role was exaggerated. Most strikebreakers were white. Many, indeed, were recent immigrants who had as little an idea of what they were getting into as did rural blacks. Exaggerating the black role served the purposes of both employers and white labor leaders. Employers used it to weaken strike morale and inflame racial animosity. Labor leaders found it convenient to explain away their failures.

The practices of most unions placed black workers in a cruel dilemma. On the one hand, they wanted to protect their wages and status through union membership. On the other, unions not only excluded them but also were determined to drive them out of jobs they already held. In consequence, if they were to get work at all, blacks had to accept wages substantially below those paid white labor.

For many jobless blacks, strikebreaking offered a way out. They were assured of high wages and permanent employment. In practice, they were often fired when they had served their purpose, as happened after they had been used to break the Chicago stockyards strike of 1904. Even so, the prospect of bettering their lot continued to lure blacks into this uncertain enterprise.

Strikebreaking bore no stigma inside the black community except when blacks were used to scab on other blacks, as happened in strikes of miners and loggers. Generally, blacks felt that if it was legitimate for whites to take the jobs of blacks, the reverse was equally true. Indeed, strikebreaking received the approval of many black leaders, including Booker T. Washington, who counseled that the black worker's best friend was the white employer, not the union. W. E. B. DuBois, as a friend of organized labor, condemned strikebreaking but expressed his sympathetic understanding of the forces that drove black workers to such a course.

Blacks also felt there was racist hypocrisy in white union indignation over "nigger scabs." Union exclusionist policies made black strikebreaking possible—and then leaders of the American Federation of Labor did little to organize black workers on the ground that blacks were "naturally" strikebreakers. Besides, blacks noted, white union men scabbed on each other with no great outcry except from class-conscious radicals. Craft unions were so obsessed with jurisdictional rights that they often kept their members at work while other craft unions were on strike at the same shop.

THE AGE OF ACCOMMODATION

Black middle-class response to white supremacy found its major expression in the accommodationist philosophy of Booker T. Washington, the most influential black American for the generation prior to his death in 1915. Washington himself was the black incarnation of the rags-to-riches myth. Born into slavery, reared in poverty, sent into the coal mines as a child, he had gone on to graduate from Hampton Institute. Then, in 1881, he founded Tuskegee Institute, dedicated to the vocational training of young black men and women. Under his leadership Tuskegee won international fame, and Washington became the confidant of presidents and business tycoons.

Washington's message, outlined in his famous speech at the Atlanta Exposition in 1895, was in part pure middle-class homily: learn a useful trade; work hard; live soberly; save your money; acquire property. The white acclaim for the speech, however, resulted from Washington's advice that for the time being, blacks should accommodate themselves to the ways of white supremacy. Blacks should stay in the South and learn to get along with their white neighbors, remembering that "it is at the bottom of life we must start, and not at the top." Discrimination had to be accepted, for "the opportunity to earn a dollar in a factory just now is worth infinitely more than the opportunity to spend a dollar in an opera house."

Agitation for equality, said Washington, was not only "the extremest folly" but also unnecessary. Whites would concede black rights once blacks had shown themselves able to exercise their rights intelligently. To earn white respect, let blacks show that they possessed skills necessary for economic development: "No race that has anything to contribute to the markets of the world is long in any degree ostracized."

Recent research by Louis Harlan and others reveals that Washington was not a simple-minded "Uncle Tom," as he was often portrayed. For example, while publicly deprecating black resistance to white supremacy, secretly he helped finance court actions against peonage and disfranchisement. At the time, however, it was the public message that counted—and it was a message aspiring blacks wanted to hear. To be sure, Washington was lavishly financed by northern white philanthropists, which made it possible for him to influence black editors, preachers, and politicians. In itself that does not explain Washington's success within the black community. Rather, his success lay in articulating the feelings of a middle class that was growing rapidly because of urbanization and because of segregation.

This middle class was a new kind of middle class. In 1900, the apex of black society was occupied, as it long had been, by the families of inherited wealth in such cities as Philadelphia, Charleston, and New Orleans. They were relatively insulated from the changes taking place, since the white power structure treated them with special consideration. Not so the members of the older middle class, such as barbers, waiters, hotel keepers, building contractors, and other small businessmen with a white clientele. Mounting white racism drove their white customers away and stripped many such blacks of their status and economic independence.

As they declined, an infusion of new elements added to middle-class numbers. In addition to such former groups as leading clergymen and businessmen catering to blacks, there were by 1910 growing numbers of government workers, especially in the post office, and of relatively well-rewarded Pullman and dining-car employees. There were also increases in the ranks of teachers, lawyers, and doctors, whose opportunities increased as segregation mounted.

White racism also generated new types of black business. The refusal of reputable white insurance companies to cover blacks led to the formation of mutual-benefit societies and fraternal orders to provide financial protection. This experience gave enterprising blacks the experience to organize their own life insurance companies and banks. The men heading such ventures became highly prosperous members of the middle class. Racism in white newspapers also opened up markets for new black newspapers such as the highly successful *Chicago Defender,* founded in 1905 by Robert S. Abbott. Not only the papers' owners and publishers counted themselves among the middle class, so also did their editors, reporters, and office workers.

Black business also found a lucrative market among blacks ashamed of their color. For them, business proprietors supplied skin bleaches, hair straighteners, and other beauty aids designed to make them look as white as possible. Most successful was Sarah B. (Madame C. J.) Walker. In only nine years the former washerwoman built a cosmetics empire that employed 3,000 persons in 1914 and had its own manufacturing plant in Indianapolis. Although shunned by polite black society, Walker contributed generously to black causes, including the National Association for the Advancement of Colored People.

This new class of business and professional people furnished the base of Washington's power within the black community. Like him, they saw no progress except through accommodation to white supremacy. Indeed, they perceived that their own success lay in avoiding conflict with whites. Like the white newly rich, they were psychologically insecure—but even more so, since the ladder they were climbing was shaky and the rungs treacherous. These sentiments were particularly strong in the South. In the North, middle-class people were more apt to speak out against lynching and segregation.

The black middle class was torn by conflicting feelings. On the one hand, its members resented the slights, the indignities, and the violence that, as with all blacks, were part of their lives. On the other, they understood that their economic well-being derived largely from segregation. To promote that well-being, they fostered racial solidarity so that blacks would patronize black business rather than white. Pleas for racial solidarity, however, conflicted with middle-class social exclusiveness. People on the way up wanted as little association as possible with poor folk, as W. E. B. DuBois pointed out in 1899 in his study *The Philadelphia Negro.* Thus widened the gulf between well-to-do and poor blacks that had emerged before the Civil War.

The gulf was not so wide, however, that middle-class folk could ignore ghetto conditions. Prompted by the exposure of their children to pernicious influences, women's clubs and church groups sought to close down brothels and saloons and campaigned for parks, playgrounds, and other means of recreation for youngsters. The clubs were especially active in trying to protect young women newly arrived in the city. In 1906 a group of New Yorkers headed by William L. Bulkley, a school principal, tackled some to the problems of poverty. They worked, with some success, to get jobs for skilled workers. They also pressured unions to admit black members, and they fought for better housing.

The work of all such organizations emphasized the need for concerted action to deal with ghetto conditions. At the same time, Washington and his white philanthropist friends became worried lest this practical social work fall under radical control—and indeed many of the activists reflected the rising militancy of the period. Under the aegis of Ruth Bowles Baldwin, widow of a railroad executive who had been closely associated with Washington, the various groups were brought together in 1910 in what later came to be called the Urban League, with branches in every major city.

The league's governing body was made up of wealthy whites and middle-class blacks. Its first director, Dr. George E. Haynes, a black sociologist, stimulated entry of black college graduates into the expanding profession of social work. The league did find jobs for some blacks, sometimes through recruiting blacks as strikebreakers, and it strove to alleviate some of the worst conditions in the ghettos. The problems of poverty, however, were too deep and too pervasive for any voluntary organization to cope with. In any case, the league was dedicated to relieving the symptoms of poverty, not to eliminating its causes.

A NEW MILITANCY

Ironically, growth of the middle class led eventually to a new mood of militancy in the early twentieth century. Parents sent children to college, and while many black schools were mediocre and accommodating in outlook, others such as Fisk, Howard, and Atlanta encouraged critical thinking. Blacks also attended northern schools, including Oberlin, Cornell, and Harvard. The graduates were little disposed to accept the dicta of white supremacy.

Contributing also to the new mood was a growing realization that Washington's philosophy did not work. The more blacks accommodated, the more was demanded of them. Lynchings and race riots continued. Courts and legislatures kept chipping away at what little black freedom remained. The Republican party, for so long the only political refuge of blacks, turned against them and opted for a "lily white" party in the South.

Accommodation, too, encouraged white encroachment on the black community. The most glaring example was in relation to prostitution. When white reformers fought "the social evil," police "solved" the problem by permitting red-light districts in black residential areas. Protests of black parents and black women's clubs were brushed aside.

Black business proprietors, too, suffered from white encroachment in the ghettos. So long as their enterprises offered no threat to whites, they were let alone. But when blacks did provide serious competition, or when, as sometimes happened, they opened up markets whites had never dreamed of, blacks were in trouble. Licensing, taxing, and a host of other local regulations were invoked to drive them out of business.

Growing middle-class discontent made itself known even in the heyday of accommodation. Black organizations fought disfranchisement in the South. Various national bodies, such as the National Afro-American Council and the National Association of Colored Women's Clubs, besides endorsing such coventional principles as black self-help and racial solidarity, denounced discrimination, lynching, unjust courts, and unpunished white rape of black women. An increasing number of blacks questioned the continued validity of Frederick Douglass's dictum, "The Republican party is the ship, all else is the sea." Was it not wise, they asked, for blacks to vote independently? If neither major party could be sure of the black vote, especially in the North, might not each party pay more attention to black needs?

A few blacks disillusioned with Democrats and Republicans joined the Socialist party, which was in the early 1900s a growing influence among white workers and middle-class reformers. For the most part, however, blacks found little appeal in the party.

The most significant expression of new militancy was the Niagara Movement, founded in 1905 by a group of professional people and intellectuals including John Hope, president of Morehouse College in Atlanta; William M. Trotter, Harvard graduate and editor of the *Boston Guardian;* J. M. Waldron, a prominent Baptist clergyman in Washington, D.C.; and F. L. McGhee, a lawyer in Minneapolis. Its leading spirit, however, was W. E. B. DuBois, the first black to earn a Ph.D. at Harvard. His dissertation on the African slave trade was so outstanding that it was quickly published. Despite his brilliance, DuBois could find no white college or university that wanted him as teacher. He spent most of his academic career at Atlanta University, where he pioneered the field we today call "black studies."

The program of the Niagara Movement demanded nothing less than complete civil and political equality. "This is a large program," said DuBois. "It cannot be realized in a short time. But something can be done and we are going to do something." To this end, the new movement sought to win over college students, and it welcomed the support of sympathetic whites. The movement pulsed with a fresh element in black feeling: pride in being black. DuBois offered a new "Credo": "I believe in the Negro Race; in the beauty of its genius, the sweetness of its soul, and its strength in that meekness which shall inherit this turbulent earth."

It followed, then, that while DuBois shared Washington's belief in hard work, thrift, sobriety, and plain living, he rejected the "accommodationist's" emphasis on purely vocational training for blacks. "The object of all true education," said DuBois, "is not to make men carpenters, it is to make carpenters *men.*" Certainly, he conceded, most blacks would have to work, and they should learn useful skills. However, if it was true that "all men cannot go to college," it was equally true that "some men must." Why? Because only liberal arts colleges could produce the leadership blacks so badly needed. In DuBois's view, this leadership, this "talented tenth," would be devoted, not to its own narrow interest, but to the cause of guiding blacks toward their destiny as a separate people. Whatever the exact nature of that destiny might turn out to be, it was "*not* absorption by the white Americans." Realizing that destiny required blacks to struggle unceasingly for full freedom and equality.

In terms of numbers, the Niagara Movement remained small—and it was under constant attack from Washington's supporters in press and pulpit. Yet its message struck a responsive chord among blacks disillusioned with Washington and among liberal whites dismayed by increasing white racism. The mood of militancy it reflected was shown in 1906, when 500 Georgia blacks revived a defunct Equal Rights Convention and called for an end to peonage, disfranchisement, and discrimination. Two years later, the bishops of the three black Methodist churches (African Methodist Episcopal, African Methodist Episcopal Zion, and Colored Methodist Episcopal) took a similar stand—albeit stated more conservatively.

Perhaps the most significant aspect of the Niagara Movement was that it provided a basis for unity between militant black leadership and white neoabolitionists outraged by white racist violence. Aroused by the Springfield, Illinois, riot of 1908, such whites sought common ground with blacks to reverse the trend. Among them were many distinguished men, including John Dewey, the famous educational philosopher, and Oswald Garrison Villard, grandson of abolitionist William Lloyd Garrison and editor of the *New York Evening Post*. Less distinguished, but more active, were Mary W. Ovington, a social worker long concerned with black problems, and William E. Walling, whose report of the Springfield riot had shaken white liberal opinion.

Meetings between whites and blacks produced the National Association for the Advancement of Colored People in 1910. Whites dominated the governing board, but DuBois was named editor of its publication, *The Crisis*. Under his leadership it came to be regarded as the voice of progressive black America, both at home and abroad. Not all blacks welcomed the new organization. Booker T. Washington made it plain he wanted no part of it. Some of Washington's archcritics, such as William M. Trotter and Ida Wells-Barnett, objected because of white control of the organization. The black poor were indifferent, for the NAACP seemingly had little to offer them.

Nevertheless, the organization of the NAACP marked a turning point in black history. Now black people, in cooperation with whites, had a center from which to wage a struggle to regain the ground lost since Reconstruction.

FOR FURTHER READING

Readers interested in references dealing with the black experience should consult James M. McPherson and others, *Blacks in America: Bibliographical Essays* (1971). Several good compilations of documents are now available, but unique in their fields are Howard Brotz, ed., *Negro Social and Political Thought, 1850–1920* (1966); Richard Bardolph, ed., *The Civil Rights Record: Black Americans and the Law, 1849–1970* (1970); and Gerda Lerner, ed., *Black Women in White America: A Documentary History* (1972).

Trends in black thinking are examined in August Meier's now classic study, *Negro Thought in America, 1880–1915* (1963). Trends in white racist thought are traced in I. A. Newby, *Jim Crow's Defense: Anti-Negro Thought in America, 1900–1930* (1965). See also C. Vann Woodward, *The Strange Career of Jim Crow* (1974). How "Jim Crow" thinking was reflected in both North and South is reported in detail in Rayford W. Logan, *The Betrayal of the Negro: From Rutherford B. Hayes to Woodrow Wilson* (1965). See also Louis R. Harlan, *Booker T. Washington* (1972). The "rape syndrome" in white racism is dealt with in W. J. Cash, *The Southern Mind* (1941).

On Reconstruction see W. E. B. DuBois's ground-breaking work, *Black Reconstruction* (1935); John H. Franklin, *Reconstruction after the Civil War* (1961); Lerone Bennett, *Black Power, U.S.A.: The Human Side of Reconstruction* (1967); and Robert Cruden, *The Negro in Reconstruction* (1969).

On urbanization: Florette Henri, *Black Migration: Movement North, 1900–1920* (1976); Gilbert Osofsky, *Harlem: The Making of a Ghetto* (1966); Seth M. Scheiner, *Negro Mecca: A His-*

tory of the Negro in New York (1965); and Allan H. Spear, *Black Chicago* (1967).

For other topics see the following: Philip S. Foner, *The Negro and Organized Labor* (1974); Pete Daniel, *The Shadow of Slavery: Peonage in the South, 1901–1969* (1973); E. Franklin Frazier, *Black Bourgeoisie* (1957); Philip Durham and Everett L. Jones, *The Negro Cowboys* (1965); E. Franklin Frazier, *The Negro Church in America* (1964); and Henry A. Bullock, *A History of Negro Education in the South* (1967).

21 they who built america

The gospel of success that so enthralled white America in the post-Reconstruction era attributed the rapid economic progress of the country to successful men. Carnegie "built" the steel industry, as Rockefeller was said to have "built" the oil industry and Duke the tobacco industry. The national railroad network, it seemed, was the creation of the Leland Stanfords, the Jay Cookes, and Henry Villards. Bemused by such legendary figures, many Americans failed to realize that not a foot of railroad could have been built without the labor of Irish, Chinese, Mexican, and native American workers. They did not see that the output of factories, mines, and mills came from the work of millions, and they took for granted the work of farmers who put bread on their tables.

How did they fare—the people who really built America?

PROGRESS AND POVERTY

Some, mainly skilled workers, did very well indeed. The great majority of the unskilled fared poorly, though.

As early as 1879 Henry George, the printer turned political economist, noted in his work *Progress and Poverty* that instead of reducing poverty, economic progress increased it. Years later, in 1904, the sociologist Robert Hunter estimated that of a total population of 80 million at least 10 million people lived in poverty. In fact, he suspected that the actual figure might well reach twice that number. But, he said, he was "largely guessing," because there were no comprehensive statistics on the subject. "Ought we not to know?" he asked. The lack of data in itself testified to the indifference of government and the middle class to the plight of the working poor.

Scientific American, *1868*

Construction provided jobs for many unskilled workers, such as these men draining and diking the swamps of the New Jersey Meadows.

The indifference stemmed from the long-held belief that poverty was the fault of the poor, an indication of some moral flaw that prevented them from attaining success. But there was a difference in attitude between elites of the ''robber baron'' era and their predecessors before the Civil War. The early elites had felt a moral obligation to help the poor. Among their later counterparts that sense of obligation was much weakened.

The dominance of economic individualism, with its philosophy of ''dog eat dog,'' militated against much concern for the poor. Poverty, the new argument ran, was a testing ground from which those of sound character would emerge to take their proper place in society. Elimination of the others was the price exacted by the impersonal forces of social evolution for the benefits of progress. Many successful Americans doubtless found it easier to accept the rationale because many of the poor after 1890 were people of the ''new immigration''—Russians, Italians, Hungarians, Slovaks, Poles, and eastern European Jews. These were people whom native white Americans, including those of old-immigrant descent, regarded with aversion. The wealthy were, ironically, reluctant to expose their descendants to the testing ground of poverty they expected the poor to survive. Through trust funds and other devices they provided their children and grandchildren with ample annual incomes.

In the early twentieth century the older view of poverty as the fault of the poor was increasingly questioned. Men like Hunter attributed poverty not to personal but

Scientific American, 1879

Women workers in this New Jersey tobacco factory earned less than $5 a week.

to social flaws. Chief among these was the low income of wage earners. In 1906 Father John A. Ryan, a Roman Catholic social activist, concluded on the basis of his studies that the minimum living wage for American families was $600 a year. At least 60 percent of adult workers received less. Other studies at the same time found Ryan's figures conservative. In some of the larger cities it was reported that only an annual income of $800 a year could keep a family from poverty. Another student of wages at the time noted that the average annual wage for men was $540 and for women $289. In short, most working people lived in poverty.

Many workers had an income that was unsteady as well as too small. In some occupations, such as construction, seasonal unemployment was standard, and all workers suffered from the periodic depressions that caused mass unemployment and stripped the thrifty of their savings.

Workers faced still another hazard. Railroads, mines, and factories were dangerous places to work. The carnage on the railroads was so great that President Benjamin Harrison in 1889 compared it to war. Mine explosions killed hundreds of miners each year. In factories unprotected machinery presented constant dangers. Even in 1913, after legislation had compelled introduction of safety measures, it was estimated that 25,000 people died in industrial accidents and another million were injured, many so seriously that their chances of earning a decent livelihood were badly diminished.

Accidents meant loss of income and suffering for the families of the victims. They had little legal recourse. Under the legal doctrines of the time, the employer was not responsible unless it could be proved that he was entirely responsible for an accident—a manifest impossibility in complex industrial operations. Few working-class families had the means to employ lawyers, and few lawyers were interested in such cases.

In 1902 Maryland initiated a new trend in meeting the problem with a workmen's compensation law that provided benefits for accident victims. Other states followed suit. Unfortunately, the benefits were grossly inadequate, and not all states granted them. Not until 1948 did Mississippi finally enact a workmen's compensation law. Thus, industrial accidents continued to contribute to poverty despite the new laws.

Disease also helped keep the poor impoverished. Until the pioneer work of Doctor Alice Hamilton in the early twentieth century, little was understood of occupational disease. Quite unwittingly, workers in scores of occupations dealt with materials recognized today as carcinogens. Miners inhaling fine dust contracted silicosis, which eventually disabled and killed them. Textile workers suffered from pulmonary illness occasioned by working in a hot, humid atmosphere and inhaling tiny particles of flying lint. Prolonged illness of any kind on the part of a breadwinner spelled disaster for the family.

Contributing to both accidents and illness were long hours of labor. Most factories operated on a fifty-six-hour week—ten hours a day on weekdays and six hours on Saturdays. In urban sweatshops people toiled from 6 A.M. to 9 P.M. Steel workers labored twelve hours a day seven days a week. Every second Sunday they had time off, but since no swing shift was employed, the workers put in a twenty-four-hour

A machine shop before the advent of electric motors. Unshielded belts contributed to a high industrial accident rate.

Oregon Historical Society

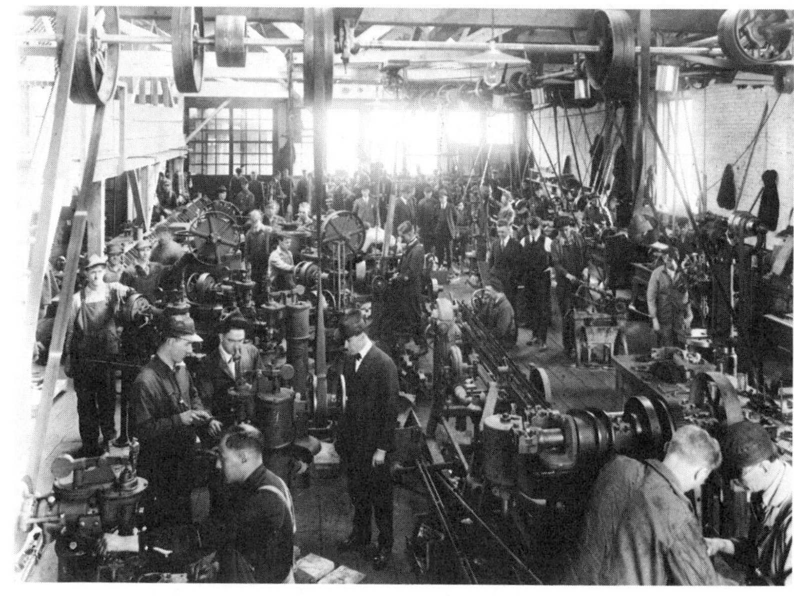

day on the Sundays they worked. The worst was yet to come. The spread of the "scientific management" of labor, initiated by Frederick W. Taylor, meant more intensive exploitation of labor. Taylor may have hoped to lighten the worker's burden, but in practice his ideas resulted in what later came to be called the "speed-up" system. The combination of long hours and intensive work produced fatigue that resulted in accidents. The wear and tear on human beings made them susceptible to illness and rendered them old before their time. Increasingly, employers of unskilled labor came to look upon workers in their forties as "too old" to keep up the pace of production.

The economy had little use for people over forty, but its need for children was insatiable. Between 1870 and 1900 the total population rose 90 percent, but the number of children employed increased nearly 130 percent to 1,750,000. Child-labor laws brought about some decline in the next decade, but in 1910 there were still 1,622,000 children working. Indeed, not until the Fair Labor Standards Act of 1935 was child labor formally ended in industry.

Child labor was both a result and a cause of poverty. Hard-pressed parents were glad to get the income of their youngsters, little realizing that children in the labor market depressed the wages of adults. Besides, there was the old American tradition and the European peasant tradition that children of the poor should earn their keep as soon as they were able. The children themselves grew up to become barely literate—sometimes illiterate—adults, apt to be sickly and ill prepared to win a better place in a harshly competitive society. Some did—and were suitably glamorized by the media of the day. Most child workers, however, were condemned to become the most menial and worst paid adult workers. Their children, in turn, as Margaret Sanger pointed out, were likely to repeat the pattern of poverty.

Child labor in industrial America was common. Here young boys separate coal from slate at a Pennsylvania coal mine.

Scientific American, *1895*

POVERTY IN THE COUNTRYSIDE

Poverty was not confined to urban areas. In the rural South, white sharecroppers, like their black counterparts, led miserable lives, enmeshed in perpetual debt. Small white farmowners were trapped in the crop-lien system, which enabled merchants to exact high prices and high interest rates for the goods farmers needed and to pay below-market prices for the cotton that farmers produced. In 1887 Congressman William D. Kelley of Pennsylvania, a friend of the New South of business, found that rural southerners lived in "the same wretched poverty" as immediately after the Civil War, a judgment in which many southerners concurred. The plight of the poor improved little in later years. In 1938 a federal commission reported that the South's "people as a whole are the poorest in the country."

Poverty also made its appearance on the "virgin lands" of the Golden West. After 1870 so many white people—native born and foreign born—swarmed into the lands taken from Indian peoples that in 1890 the superintendent of the census said there was no longer a frontier line in the continental United States. Most of the new arrivals lacked adequate capital to buy good land and the machinery necessary to work it. The Homestead Act, so often hailed as a boon to small farmers, actually benefited them little. The allotments of 160 acres were too small for profitable farming in the semiarid Great Plains. Besides, the good lands had been taken over by railroads under their land grants. Through various devices, land speculators circumvented the Homestead Act and acquired great areas of good farm land at low prices. The settlers, then, bought land on credit and went further into debt for machinery.

Farmers were not too worried about the debt; they saw only the mounting domestic and foreign demand for wheat. Until 1882 wheat rarely sold for less than $1 a bushel—a highly profitable figure. So many folk wanted a share in the bonanza that in the 1880s land prices skyrocketed and many early arrivals became minor land speculators. The boom began to collapse in 1886, and many farmers lost their property.

Even before then, increasing numbers of aspiring westerners faced impoverishment from natural causes. The Great Plains country was a hard taskmaster. Springtime often brought floods. Periodically there were droughts, and hordes of grasshoppers and other insects consumed the labor of months in a few days. In the fall, prairie fires threatened crops, and winter brought blizzards that killed livestock. Water was hard to find. Often it was contaminated and settlers were laid low with fever. Fuel for winter was scarce.

The long, cold winters, which often isolated families from each other for months at a time, took their toll in physical and mental illness. Women suffered perhaps more than the men. Like all pioneer women they had to make the food, clothing, and other necessities for their households. In addition, of course, they had to bear children under the most primitive conditions. Like their predecessors, they aged rapidly. Many families found such conditions intolerable, and others simply could not earn a living. They abandoned their farms and sought new beginnings elsewhere.

The mechanical reaper transformed farming in the 1870s.

Farmers able to stay on their land had to cope with a catastrophic fall in farm prices. The wheat selling for $1 a bushel in 1880 fetched only 63¢ in 1896. Farmers who had mortgaged themselves to the hilt faced disaster. As their income fell, their costs mounted. Mortgage rates remained constant despite falling prices. Interest rates rose sharply on the short-term loans farmers required to carry them over from one harvest to another. In addition, the rapid settlement of the West entailed increased public expenditures for schools, roads, and other services. Property taxes went up substantially.

Farmers' net incomes suffered in still other ways. The grain-elevator companies through which farmers had to market their crops misgraded wheat to avoid paying the price for top-quality products. Small merchants, who enjoyed similar monopolistic positions until the advent of the mail-order house in the 1870s, marked up their prices substantially and then charged high interest on the goods the farmers had to buy on credit. Railroads maintained artificially high freight rates.

Thousands of farmers could not keep up the struggle. The countryside was dotted with the abandoned shacks of homesteaders in the wake of a mass exodus from the Dakotas, Nebraska, and western Kansas. Men and women who had dreamed of independence went to work in cities or became laborers for successful farmers. Some found work in the growing mining industry of the West. Others went farther west, taking up new homesteads, often suffering the same fate as before. Many who did not wish or could not afford to move remained as tenants. In 1890 the rate of farm tenancy ranged from 5 percent in North Dakota to 25 percent in Kansas. Poverty and dependency had come to the prairies.

A POOR WAY OF LIFE

Poverty condemned its victims to a poor way of life. In major cities they lived in squalid tenements not much better than those that had housed Irish immigrants in the 1840s. Entire families lived in one or two rooms, an overcrowding made worse by the practice of taking in boarders to help pay the exorbitant rents. The poorest of the

Kansas State Historical Society, Topeka

At the end of the "long drive" of cattle from Texas to railheads in Kansas, cowboys relaxed in dance halls and saloons. This picture shows a dance hall in Dodge City about 1878. The festivities had obviously not yet begun.

poor lived in attics and cellars. For thousands of urban poor, their homes were also their workplaces, cluttered up with sewing machines, work materials, and the other equipment needed by "sweated" labor. In short, privacy was not for the poor.

The buildings themselves were firetraps. They lacked running water and inside toilets. Adequate lighting and ventilation did not exist. The buildings were infested with fleas, bedbugs, lice, and rats. Under these circumstances, cleanliness was almost impossible—and the poor had little money to spare for soap, hot water, or several changes of underclothing. But some slum mothers waged an unending battle against vermin and dirt, tribute to a spirit that poverty could not quench.

Poor housing for poor people was as true of the countryside as of cities. Loggers lived jammed together in vermin-infested bunkhouses. Many farm families who could afford nothing better lived in flimsy one-room shacks that offered little protection against the weather. Hamlin Garland, the chronicler of the poor northern farmer, described the typical home as "a grim and horrible shed."

Such conditions, combined with malnutrition and overwork, bred illness on a large scale. Pneumonia, tuberculosis, and various fevers carried off thousands of the poor every year. Many suffered from pellagra and other diet-deficiency diseases. Infant mortality was especially high. In some states in 1900 it reached 16 percent. Experts of the time attributed most of the infant deaths to poverty.

For those who survived, the prospect was bleak. They were likely to go to work at any early age, remain functionally illiterate, and repeat the patterns of their parents. For them, America was no land of opportunity.

For many such workers, America was no land of freedom either. Southern textile workers, coal miners in both North and South, and some other workers, such

Oregon Historical Society

Bunkhouse scene in Washington state logging camp in 1894.

as those employed by the Pullman Company, lived in company towns owned and controlled completely by their employers. Workers had no voice at all in local affairs—or even in larger affairs, for employers ordered them how to vote. Employers also chose the teachers for the schools and the preachers for the churches. They used informers to root out dissident employes and to keep out union and socialist organizers.

Workers in company towns could not even spend their money as they wished. They had to rent their houses from the company, for no other housing was available. They had to buy their food, clothing, and other necessities from the company store. Indeed, many companies paid workers in scrip redeemable only at the company store. Prices were far above those charged by merchants elsewhere. Miners, for example, had to supply their own dynamite, which the company stores sold at a price three times the going free-market rate. Prices of other necessities were marked up in like degree. Since earnings were often inadequate to meet the costs of rent and living, workers bought on credit. Thus, like sharecroppers, many miners and mill workers found themselves in perpetual debt.

Restrictions on the freedom of workers was not a monopoly of company towns. No matter where workers lived they dared not voice open dissatisfaction about their jobs if they wanted to keep them. Men and women seeking to form labor unions in nonunion industries were ruthlessly weeded out and blacklisted. Many employers required prospective employees to sign "yellow dog" contracts by which workers bound themselves to join no union during their period of employment. Workers' political freedom was also limited. During elections, employers brought pressure to bear on workers to support the candidates they favored. In the crucial election of

1896, many employers in the North threatened to close down if William Jennings Bryan were elected.

Perhaps most galling to the working poor was the contempt displayed toward them by the rest of society. They were regarded as stupid, irresponsible, dirty, drunken, immoral. The contempt made its way into the language. Southern mill workers were "lint heads," the rural poor "red necks" and "peckerheads". In the West, migratory workers were "bums" and "bindlestiffs." Other pejorative terms reflected on the immigrant background of the working poor. Mexicans were "greasers," and Chinese and Japanese "yellow bellies." European immigrants found themselves labeled as "Hunkies," "Dagos," "Polacks," "Scowegians", and "Sheenies."

The contempt of middle-class America corroded relationships within immigrant communities. For long, German Jews avoided association with Jews from eastern Europe. Among other European groups, those who had adjusted themselves to American ways ridiculed the newly arrived "greenhorns." Established Mexican-American communities often provided a chilly welcome to newcomers from Mexico. Native white middle-class Americans shunned social contact with them all, of course.

But there was some contact, of a sort the middle class did not admit. Just as white men sought out black women for sex, so did men with money use women of the poor. Domestic servants were vulnerable to the inducements offered by men of the household. Poorly paid factory girls, department store clerks, and office workers,

European immigrants getting some fresh air on deck on their way to America. They slept in overcrowded "steerage" compartments far below decks.

Library of Congress

Like many other immigrants in 1891, these Italian women were bound for the industrial centers of the Midwest.
Michigan Historical Collections

bored with their drab lives, were victimized by men who showed them the excitement of "high life." When such young women became pregnant, often their only recourse was to professional prostitution. Attractive young women of the poor were also the prey of procurers for the brothels that flourished in every city. Some were highly exclusive, admitting only wealthy men. Among these were establishments in the various racial ghettos, which specialized in selling the services of black, Mexican, and Asian women to white men only.

LABOR'S PECKING ORDER

Contempt for the poor combined with anxiety lest they too slip down into the abyss help explain the intense effort of the upper strata of the working class to maintain their social distance from the poor. By no means were all working people below the poverty level. Highly skilled men (few women workers had opportunity to become highly skilled) fared very well indeed. Their purchasing power increased substantially in the 1880s and 1890s, and the inflationary surge of the early 1900s did not significantly reduce their standard of living. Railway conductors, locomotive engineers, printers, machinists, and sheet rollers in steel were among the "aristocracy of labor," with incomes to match. They enjoyed high status in local communities, identified with middle-class values, and looked to the day when their children would enter business or the professions.

Nevertheless, they had grounds for anxiety. They might be the aristocrats of labor, but they were still wage-earners. Economic depressions, sudden unemployment, illness, accident, and death affected them as well as the unskilled. Insurance companies denied coverage to skilled as well as unskilled workers in hazardous occupations, such as railroading. More insidious, and more menacing in the long run, was the advance of technology. Increasingly, skilled workers found themselves displaced by machines. With their skills obsolete, such workers faced a future of much lower income and social status, a future of doubt and uncertainty.

Together these factors—economic, social, and psychological—combined to

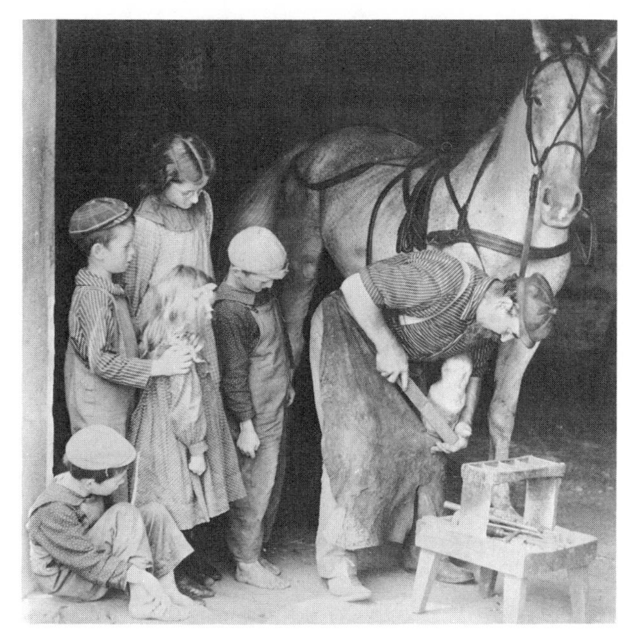

In 1901 the blacksmith still performed a necessary service. The advent of the cheap automobile a few years later doomed the smith and his craft.

Library of Congress

produce in the working class a pecking order that helped frustrate the efforts of such leaders as Eugene V. Debs and William D. (''Big Bill'') Haywood to unite the working class. Nowhere was this better illustrated than on the railroads, the major industry of the time. Each occupation had its own craft union with its own place in a hierarchy of status. At the top were the locomotive engineers, a highly paid fraternity that shunned cooperation with other unions and enjoyed close relations with management. Close to them in pay and prestige were the conductors. Beneath them were the firemen and brakemen. The operating brotherhoods as a whole looked down on shop workers, among whom machinists claimed preeminence. Shop workers, in turn, disdained clerks and freight handlers. All these groups despised the wretchedly paid ''gandy dancers'' who maintained the roadbeds.

The pecking order was not based entirely on skill and income. It embodied also American ethnic values. The highest strata were the preserves of native-born whites. The middle strata included both native whites and northern European immigrants. Far below them economically and socially were the ''new'' immigrants from southern, central, and eastern Europe. At the bottom were the blacks, Mexicans, and Asians.

ASIAN IMMIGRANTS

Although there had been Chinese on the West Coast since the gold rush of 1849, the mass influx of Chinese took place in the 1860s, when thousands of unmarried young men were brought in to build the Central Pacific Railroad, a hazardous undertaking in which many lost their lives and thousands more were injured. After completion of that project in 1869, the unskilled immigrants took poorly paid jobs as miners, seamen, cannery workers, farm laborers, and construction laborers. Their entry into the general labor market, allowing employers to drive down wages, aroused virulent anti-Chinese sentiment among West Coast white workers. The virulence spread when Chinese were brought into eastern towns to break strikes.

The Chinese who lived in cities were segregated in Chinatowns, in which the dwellings of the poor were as overcrowded, verminous, and wretched as those of the "new" European immigrants in the East. The Chinatowns were dominanted by wealthy merchants who lived in private homes on a scale consistent with their status. With white collaborators they did well in the China trade, part of which was supplying their less fortunate countrymen with the staples they yearned for. The merchants also engaged in the traffic in drugs and young Chinese women, imported to provide sexual services for an overwhelmingly male society. They also served as labor contractors, providing Chinese labor for white employers—a field that was highly profitable. The hostility of white society made it virtually impossible for Chinese to break out of the Chinatowns and thus tightened the grip of the merchants on Chinese communities.

White hostility eventually brought a federal law in 1882 prohibiting further entry of Chinese workers. The same law provided that no Chinese could be admitted to citizenship. Later additions to the law barred the entry of Chinese from Hawaii, the Philippines, Canada, and Mexico. Enforcement of law, together with the immigration of few Chinese women, made it difficult for Chinese men to form families. As a result, the Chinese population in the United States declined from 107,000 in 1890 to 62,000 in 1920. Needing new workers to take up the slack, employers in the West turned to Japanese and Mexican labor.

The Japanese, like the Chinese, performed the most menial and poorly paid labor. From California to Alaska they worked in mines, canneries, logging camps, and sawmills. They labored on railroads and farms. When the most thrifty and abstemious had accumulated a stake, they acquired land—often land whites could not

A Chinese-American migratory worker. Picture probably dates from the 1890s.

Oregon Historical Society

Fish cannery workers at Astoria, Oregon, in the early twentieth century.

Oregon Historical Society

farm profitably but on which the Japanese prospered. Others opened up small business enterprises—restaurants, grocery stores dealing in Japanese staples, and hotels that were little better than flophouses. These men then established families by bringing to America brides they obtained through family connections or marriage brokers—the so-called "picture brides." The Japanese, who had numbered only 2,000 in 1890, increased to 110,000 by 1920.

The work of the men was hard, but that of the women was even harder. Many of them had been deceived about their husbands' economic circumstances. Promised snug, comfortable farm homes, they found themselves housed instead in poorly furnished shacks that hardly kept out the rain. They were expected to work in the fields as well as to cook the meals, wash the clothing, and make the family's garments. In the cities, they lived in tiny one-room hotel apartments. They helped in their husbands' businesses besides performing all the family chores expected of women. Many such women recalled a working day that began at six in the morning and lasted until midnight. Unable to afford or unwilling to accept medical aid in an alien land, women bore their children by themselves or with the help only of their husbands.

These immigrants, who called themselves Issei, cherished their memories of Japan but wanted to identify with America. They adopted American customs, wore American clothing, learned the language, and sent their children (termed Nisei) to American schools. Some adopted Christianity and were particularly active in Methodist churches. White society, however, still nurturing its anti-Chinese prejudices, was as hostile to the Japanese. Rebuffed, the Issei took refuge in their own traditions and withdrew into their own communities, which became as tightly controlled by prosperous businessmen as the Chinatowns were by wealthy merchants.

For the Nisei, the experience was psychologically disturbing. Within the Japanese community they were expected to accept Japanese traditions and to conform to Japanese customs, including filial obedience. At school, they were exposed to

American ideas and customs, which prompted them to question the values of their parents. Thus children grew to adulthood torn by conflicting loyalties.

Anti-Japanese sentiment took many forms. The American Federation of Labor denied membership to Japanese as well as Chinese and in 1904 called for Japanese exclusion as a national policy. Throughout the West farmers and small business proprietors joined in the cry. In 1906 the San Francisco school board required young Nisei to attend a segregated school for Asians. When Japan protested, President Theodore Roosevelt obtained withdrawal of the order. To cool off white anger, however, he won from Japan the ''Gentleman's Agreement'' of 1907, which effectively halted the immigration of Japanese workers.

White feeling was also expressed in statutes that barred Issei from citizenship. California in 1913 made it unlawful for such aliens to own land. Other western states followed suit. The laws were evaded, but Japanese farmers realized full well that their property depended on the good faith of the white citizens who collaborated with them. Humiliating, too, were the laws that forbade intermarriage between Asians and whites. The proud Japanese resented being classed with the Chinese and American blacks.

NORTH FROM MEXICO

As the Chinese and Japanese sources of cheap labor dried up, employers turned to Mexicans. There was a growing number of Mexican-Americans available—small farmers unable to make a living in competition with large-scale commercial agriculture, young people who could not survive on the small plots of ground they inherited, and others who were victims of new federal land policies. Their numbers, however, were inadequate to meet the needs of mining companies, railroads, and big farmers who dominated the expanding economy of the Southwest.

These interests welcomed the Mexican peasants who, driven off their lands by the policies of the dictator Porfirio Diaz, fled to the United States. Every year thousands of poor Mexicans came across the border, often without observing the legal formalities of entry. Their ranks swelled astronomically after the collapse of the Diaz government in 1910. The consequent civil wars caused countless Mexicans to seek safety—and employment—in the United States. They concentrated in California and Texas, but many found their way to Colorado. Together with Mexican-Americans they became a major source of labor for the sugar beet industry of that state.

Wherever they lived, whether native-born or Mexican-born, such workers faced lives of poverty, living in wretched shacks in the countryside or in overcrowded *barrios* in such cities as Los Angeles, El Paso, and Denver. Their children had little schooling and went to work at an early age. For newcomers, the experience was traumatic. In the peasant culture of Mexico they had enjoyed some status, however low, and the culture was supportive of the individual. In the United States, they were nobodies and the culture was hostile. Anglos disdained them. Mexican-Americans, whose traditional culture had been diluted by Anglo influences except in some parts of New Mexico, tended to look askance at the primitive ways of the newcomers. Mexican parents, like those of other immigrant groups, were anguished as their children forsook their customs and tried to adopt Anglo ways. All too often this meant emulating the worst features of American life.

Not all Mexican-Americans remained poor. Apart from the *ricos,* who were now almost entirely Anglo in culture and associations, there emerged in the *barrios* a class of small-business and professional people who provided necessary services. Prominent among them were the labor contractors, who supplied workers to Anglo employers and profited handsomely in the process. Such leaders, who wielded great power among their people, were courted by the politicians in those areas where the Mexican-American vote was important. The poor were granted such minor favors as were necessary to secure their votes, but the real beneficiaries of the political alliances were the business proprietors. Little was done to improve the lot of the poor or to break down the walls of segregation.

THE NATIVE-WHITE RATIONALES

Native whites justified their attitudes toward the foreign-born poor by arguing that the newcomers were racially inferior to peoples of Nordic descent. Further, the superior race in America was in danger of being engulfed by the "Yellow Peril" of the West Coast and by the "new immigration" of the East. Such beliefs and fears help explain the virulent propaganda attacks on immigrants by native-born Americans of all classes and the drives to curb the entry of unwelcome immigrants. Employers, eager to get cheap labor, fought such drives and found allies among such academics as President Charles W. Eliot of Harvard.

Foremost in the crusade against Chinese and Japanese workers was organized labor. In 1901, as part of a campaign to plug loopholes in the Chinese Exclusion Act of 1882, President Samuel Gompers of the American Federation of Labor helped write a pamphlet that said Chinese "found it natural to lie, cheat and murder." They also found it natural, he said, to "prey among American girls," debauch whites through drugs and gambling, and work for wages on which no white man could live. His attitude toward Japanese was similar.

Hostility toward the people of the European new immigration was little less marked. Some labor leaders branded the newcomers as "servile and degraded hordes," characterized by "poverty, filth, and slavish willingness to work for almost nothing and to live on less." With the inconsistency typical of racist rhetoric, the "servile" folk were also held to be "radicals" and "troublemakers," unwilling to accept the leadership of responsible American-born union officials. Years later Gompers revealed yet another count against the new immigrants: they were racially inferior. The AFL, he wrote, sought to maintain "racial purity and strength."

Gompers's words reflected the fears of many scholars and other middle-class Americans that their country was about to be overrun by inferior peoples. Francis A. Walker, a distinguished economist and president of the Massachusetts Institute of Technology, held that the newcomers from southern and eastern Europe were "beaten men from beaten races, representing the worst failures in the struggle for existence." In America, they could not cope with the problems of "self-care and self-government." His views were shared by such eminent scholars as Edward A. Ross, the sociologist, and John R. Commons, the pioneer of labor history. Frederick

Jackson Turner, the famous historian, saw special danger in eastern European Jews, whom he described as biologically adapted to the harsh conditions of slum life. Their ability to survive on sweatshop wages, he said, threatened the well-being of American labor.

Another count against the new immigrants was their alleged radicalism. Beginning with the nationwide railroad strike of 1877, a wave of strikes swept the country over the next twenty-five years. Employers found it useful to blame the strikes on "foreign agitators." The media took up the cry, picturing all immigrants as anarchists, socialists, and communists. Even so astute a man as Edwin L. Godkin, editor of *The Nation,* was convinced. Himself an Irish immigrant and formerly an advocate of unrestricted immigration, he concluded in 1887 that the new immigrants were responsible for labor unrest, which he stigmatized as "un-American." The epithet proved useful for years to come. It transformed economic disputes into cultural conflicts, in which employers and other conservatives preempted the symbols of patriotism.

The Chinese, too, were seen as threats to white civilization. Such views were not confined to the Pacific Coast, where the Chinese were concentrated. As early as 1865 the *New York Times* said they were "befouled with all the social vices, with no knowledge or appreciation of free institutions or constitutional liberty." If they were permitted unlimited entry, "we should be prepared to bid farewell to republicanism and democracy." Such views were common currency throughout the country in the 1870s despite the arguments of employers, some editors, and Protestant clergymen that the benefits of Chinese immigration outweighed the disadvantages.

Scientists of the day added their own mite. Anthropologists said that the brain capacity of Chinese was so small as to make them unfit for self-government. Doctor J. Marion Sims, the eminent gynecologist, told the American Medical Association in 1876 that Chinese prostitutes were "syphilizing" the youth of America. Other medical doctors expressed fears that Chinese exposed Americans to leprosy and cholera.

In their turn the Japanese were held even more dangerous than Chinese. White believers in the gospel of success were outraged when Japanese farmers and businessmen bested them in competition. Issei success was seen as a threat to white civilization. Issei seeking to form families through the "picture bride" process were viewed as immoral. Scholars asserted that the "emperor worship" they attributed to Japanese made the immigrants unfit for a democratic society. The protection extended to its citizens in the United States by the Japanese government—as when its protests brought an end to school segregation in San Francisco—aroused whites accustomed to pushing around Chinese with impunity. Such resentment mounted after Japan's defeat of Russia in 1905. Thereafter West Coast newspapers and anti-Japanese associations stirred up white fears of Japanese invasion of Hawaii and the Pacific coast.

Mexicans were regarded, not as dangerous, but as undesirable. In 1912 a writer for *The Survey,* a journal of liberal thought, summarized prevailing views: "Their low standards of living and of morals, their illiteracy, their utter lack of proper political interest, the retarding effect of their employment upon the wage scale of the more progressive races, and finally their tendency to colonize in urban centers, with evil results, combine to stamp them as a rather undesirable class of residents." The famous sociologist Franklin H. Giddings thought the entire "Latin race" was "decadent."

HYSTERIA AND VIOLENCE

The tensions of an unstable society confronted with masses of newcomers prompted a revival of anti-Catholicism, a new anti-Semitism, and widespread violence.

The crusade against the Catholics was embodied in the American Protective Association, which in the 1890s included not only native white Americans but also German, Scandinavian, British, and Canadian Protestant immigrants. In addition to reviving old anti-Catholic legends, the APA "revealed" through fabricated documents that the pope had absolved Catholics of their allegiance to the United States and that Catholics were secretly preparing to massacre Protestants. Panic-stricken Protestants rallied to the APA—more than 1 million, said its leaders—and armed themselves to save their families, their country, and their religion.

When it became evident that no massacre was in the offing, interest in the APA waned. With the return of prosperity after the Panic of 1893, tensions eased, and by 1900 the APA ceased to have influence. Its ideas remained alive, however, in the white South. In 1911 a rabid anti-Catholic journal, *The Menace,* appeared and soon won a large circulation among southerners. Thus was prepared the soil for emergence of the new Ku Klux Klan during World War I.

Anti-Catholicism, of course, was not new. The large-scale anti-Semitism that made its appearance in the 1870s, however, was quite different from the isolated expressions of hostility to Jews earlier in American history.

By 1900 anti-Semitism was respectable. Patricians of the old school, typified by Henry Adams, believed that Jews embodied the crass materialism of a business society that had forsaken traditional American values—by which they meant patrician values. The newly rich resented both the competition of successful German Jews and their superior cultural attainments. Lacking a culture of their own and obsessed with status, the parvenus sought to affirm their status by excluding Jews from polite society, thus identifying themselves with old-money patricians.

These feelings first emerged publicly in 1877 when a fashionable summer resort hotel in New York State refused admission to the family of a leading Jewish banker. Thereafter so many resort hotels and private clubs barred Jews that Jews were compelled to develop their own. The trend was also indicated in an emerging pattern of discrimination in higher education. Beginning in the East, professional schools and many prestigious undergraduate colleges set quotas for Jewish applicants.

Paralleling this development among elites was the emergence of popular anti-Semitism fed by a body of literature akin to that of the propaganda directed against blacks, Asians, and Catholics. The anti-Jewish propaganda did not attain the influence of that directed against other groups, largely because the mass of poor Jews were engaged in the sweated garment trades and offered no immediate threat to native white American workers or business proprietors. When the children of such immigrants later sought jobs outside the ghettos, they found Jews were not wanted. Employers often specified, "Gentiles only."

Catholics and Jews suffered relatively little from violence, although it should be noted that in 1915 a Jew, Leo Frank, who had been convicted on flimsy evidence of the murder of a Gentile girl, was taken from a Georgia prison and lynched by a mob. Some immigrant groups, however, were special targets of native white violence. In

New Orleans eleven Italians accused of complicity in the murder of a police chief were taken from jail in 1891 and lynched. Japanese were frequently attacked on the streets of western cities. On occasion their homes and business places were burned down. Police were so indifferent or hostile that many victims did not even file complaints. Besides, some were in the country illegally and did not wish to draw attention to themselves. In California and Texas, Mexicans were often prey to Anglo violence, for Anglos counted killing a "greaser" no great crime. In Texas, Mexican people were especially fearful of the Texas Rangers, the state police who had a reputation for gunning down Mexicans, whether immigrants or American-born. Again, those immigrants who had entered illegally thought it prudent not to complain.

Chinese suffered most from white violence. Assaults on individual Chinese were almost daily occurrences in cities with large Chinese populations, and police showed little interest in pursuing the few complaints made. Entire Chinese communities were also attacked. In 1871 the Chinese ghetto in Los Angeles was ravaged by a white mob and seventeen residents killed. Minor outbreaks took place elsewhere, but the year 1885 witnessed three major riots. Whites in Tacoma, Washington, forcibly deported all Chinese residents. Federal troops were dispatched to end anti-Chinese rioting in Seattle. In Rock Springs, Wyoming, members of the Knights of Labor burned down the local Chinatown, killing twenty-eight of its residents and wounding fifteen.

OTHER ANNALS OF THE POOR

So far we have discussed the "working poor"—the people who were usually able to sustain themselves and their families by their labor. But there were others—the folk who never earned enough to sustain themselves, the disabled, the physically sick and the mentally ill, those who ran afoul of the law.

The public and private welfare agencies of the day gave short shrift to hungry but able-bodied men and women. They were told to find jobs—even when few jobs were available—or go to the workhouse, an institution designed to make a stay there as unpleasant as possible. Some remained in cities, earning precarious livings as professional beggars. Others wandered back and forth across the country, performing odd jobs to get enough to eat or joining the crews of migratory workers who followed the harvests in the West.

To the "deserving poor"—fathers temporarily destitute from prolonged unemployment, deserted mothers and widows with small children, the disabled—private and public charities doled out small pittances after investigating applicants with humiliating thoroughness. In large cities, political machines came to the rescue of many such people, and local governments or private charities provided hospitals for the poor. Patients often dreaded these hospitals because of inadequate care and a high death rate—a rate due in part to the reluctance of poor people to enter the hospitals except as a last resort. By 1900 there were throughout the land "asylums" for the mentally ill, but they were largely centers of confinement for "insane" people deemed too dangerous to be at large. The mentally ill of wealthy families were cared for in private institutions, where the level of medical attention and treatment were markedly superior to those of public institutions.

The poor who ran afoul of the law, especially if they were blacks, Mexicans, or new immigrants, felt its heavy hand. They were more apt to be found guilty and to receive harsher sentences than accused people from more favored backgrounds. Despite all the work of prison reformers, most prisons were in effect overcrowded human warehouses where order was maintained by sheer brutality. Conditions in local jails were even worse. If little was accomplished in the way of rehabilitation, much was done to turn first-termers into professional criminals. Released prisoners who wanted to "go straight" were frustrated by laws that forbade them entry to many occupations, businesses, and professions.

FOR FURTHER READING

A good introduction to the problem of poverty in America in the early twentieth century is Robert H. Bremner, *From the Depths: The Discovery of Poverty in the United States* (1956). The grievances of western farmers are discussed in John D. Hicks's notable work, *The Populist Revolt* (1931). C. Vann Woodward covers the plight of the southern rural poor in *Origins of the New South* (1951).

A valuable introduction to immigration history is Maldwyn A. Jones, *American Immigration* (1960). Still valuable despite its age is Carl F. Wittke, *We Who Built America* (1939). The responses of native-born Americans to new immigrants are analyzed in John Higham, *Strangers in the Land: Patterns of American Nativism, 1860–1925* (1963).

Students interested in the histories of their ethnic groups in the United States will find a growing body of reputable historical work available. Among them are Rowland Berthoff, *British Immigrants in Industrial America, 1790–1950* (1953): Theodore Saloutos, *The Greeks in the United States* (1964); Eric Ampithreatof, *The Children of Columbus* (1973); and Theodore Blegen, *Norwegian Migration to America* (1940).

Nathan Glazer, *American Judaism* (1972) is a survey of the American Jewish experience. A highly readable introduction to the problems of Mexican immigrants is Carey McWilliams, *North from Mexico* (1968). A recent brief survey is Matt S. Meier and Feliciano Rivera, *The Chicanos* (1972). A valuable collection of documents is in Wayne Moquin and Charles Van Doren, eds., *A Documentary History of the Mexican Americans* (1971).

White American images of Chinese are described in Stuart C. Miller, *The Unwelcome Immigrant* (1969). Stanford M. Lyman's *Chinese Americans* (1974) provides a general survey. Bill Hosokawa's journalistic account of the Japanese community, *Nisei: The Quiet Americans* (1969) should be supplemented with Roger Daniels's *Politics of Prejudice* (1968). A work that has not received the attention it deserves is Kazuo Ito, *Issei: A History of Japanese Immigration in North America,* translated by S. Nakamura and J. S. Gerard (1973); it is an invaluable collection of firsthand accounts by Japanese immigrants of their experiences in the United States.

protest and rebellion

22

Poor people responded in different ways to the problems confronting them. Many were passive or sought to break out of poverty by individual effort. Others sought to improve their lot by collective action in such organizations as the Knights of Labor, the American Federation of Labor, or the Populist party—all concerned with improving conditions without fundamentally changing the social order. These people enjoyed the active support of the many middle-class reformers disturbed by the ugly and threatening aspects of an industrialism without social conscience. Growing minorities who believed that social justice could not be attained under capitalism turned to the Socialist party and to the radical unionism of the Industrial Workers of the World.

POVERTY AND ORDER

To understand the people who tried to bring about reform or revolution, we must first understand those who had little concern with either. Such people played no significant positive historical role, but they did play an important negative role. They served as brakes on movements for social change. They provided no support for causes that aimed at their own betterment. Their apathy in turn encouraged opponents of social reform. The feelings of such people are not to be confused with those of successful folk, who had an obvious stake in maintaining the status quo. The feelings of the apathetic poor had quite other roots.

The northern urban poor were largely immigrants from southern and eastern Europe, and many of them had no intention of staying in the United States. Young single men for the most part, they were bent on saving enough to buy a farm or start a small business in the old country. Their ambition realized, these men left the United States by the thousands. Obviously, they had little interest in protest movements.

Along with them went those who could no longer endure poverty in America. Together such people contributed to an annual outflow that in the early twentieth century reached as high as 40 percent of the inflow of immigrants.

Those who remained wanted nothing more than to be let alone. They took refuge from the tensions of a society they little understood in the customs and traditions of the peasant societies from which they came. Far from being radical, they were fearful of authority, as Margaret Sanger discovered when she was first arrested for dispensing birth control information. Expecting support from poor women, she was shocked when they deserted her, terrified by the police. Such women brought from Europe an awe of police that was intensified in the United States. Police brutality toward immigrants was notorious, and expressions of discontent were suppressed ruthlessly. As a youthful immigrant, Samuel Gompers was so intimidated by police violence against unemployed demonstrators in New York City in 1874 that thereafter he avoided clashes with authority. Gompers was not the only immigrant who learned that lesson.

The lesson was reinforced by influential sources within the immigrant communities. Roman Catholic and Orthodox churches, as well as Orthodox Jewish rabbis, generally counseled acceptance of the social order. So also did the small business and professional class that emerged in the ghettos and dominated the ethnic fraternal groups that served as mutual-aid societies among the immigrant poor. So too did the ethnic political bosses who grew in power as immigrants became citizens. These men, prime contacts between the ghettos and the larger American society, were in a position to do favors—provide food and fuel during hard times, get jobs on the public payroll for deserving folk, and intervene with the authorities when people ran afoul of the law—and many immigrants found it prudent to collaborate with them. In short, the immigrant elites for a long time were a positive force against protest.

Practical difficulties also helped prevent collective protest in the ghettos. The immigrants' command of English was restricted, and language differences among the ethnic groups made it difficult for them to communicate with each other. Their separation was reinforced by housing patterns: each nationality had its own little ghetto, and there was little contact between them. Besides, many immigrant groups brought with them traditional ethnic hostilities. Poles and Lithuanians, for example, had little use for each other, and Magyars wanted nothing to do with Slovaks. Such animosities were fostered by many employers, who deliberately hired members of hostile nationalities together with a judicious mixture of native rural Americans—called "buckwheats"—to frustrate possible union organization.

There were other reasons, of course, for the immigrants' reluctance to become involved with labor unions. Not only were most unions indifferent to the newcomers, but also many labor leaders were openly contemptuous of them. Besides, in the immigrant experience, strikes of unskilled workers rarely succeeded, and strikes involved confrontations with the very public authority immigrants feared so much.

More subtle psychological factors also played a role in making many newcomers conservative. The men, conditioned to the male dominance implicit in the patriarchal family structure inherited from Europe, felt threatened by the talk of women's rights that seeped into the ghettos from settlement houses and other centers of liberal influence. They asserted their authority by identifying themselves with accepted authority figures. Mothers and fathers felt disturbed also by American behavior patterns adopted by their children, especially the courtship customs that to the elders smacked of immorality. They were particularly upset when such courtship led to marriage outside their own religious and ethnic groups. The parents naturally sought to enforce their own authority, turning to such authority figures as priests and rabbis for aid and guidance.

Perhaps most influential of all in damping collective protest among immigrants was the simple fact that in contrast to the Europe they had known, America was an open society where one could get ahead. One might not go far, but it was possible for a thrifty worker with an industrious family to get a little plot of ground and a small house. This goal was realized by many, especially in the Midwest, though periods of long unemployment made it difficult to keep the property. Even so, the goal was seen as possible, and it inspired workers to put up with exploitation and to avoid antagonizing the boss.

Besides, in every ghetto there were examples of poor folk who had graduated from the working class—saloon keepers, small storekeepers, landlords, petty politicians, small-time bankers and employers, among whom were to be found the worst of the sweatshop operators. For the unsuccessful, the lesson was plain: the fault was not in the social order but in themselves. The tensions generated by such self-doubt—and even self-hatred—partly explain the alcoholism rampant in the slums.

These did not operate only among European immigrants. Asians and Mexicans were also subject to them. In fact, pressures were worse for the non-Europeans because of the racist hostility of white society. Like the immigrants, native whites who lived in the mill villages of the South were disinclined to rebel. For long they were grateful to the paternalistic mill owners who provided them with jobs. Since only whites got the jobs, white supremacy linked the workers in a common cause with their employers. At the same time, they were regarded as inferior by the dominant groups of white society—and like other subject people, mill workers internalized the values of their oppressors. When, eventually, the "lint heads" did rebel in the 1890s, their strikes were crushed relentlessly. Their failures reinforced their feelings of inferiority and weakness and discouraged further immediate protest.

Another significant factor inhibiting protest among native- and foreign-born, among workers and farmers, was concern for respectability. At home, in schools, in churches, in the mass media, people were conditioned to observe the conventions. To rebel collectively was highly unconventional—indeed, it was to lay oneself open to the charge of social, political, and moral subversion. Even among those who did rebel there were many who, after the first enthusiasm wore off, felt that their behavior was not quite right. Employers skillfully exploited such feelings to divide workers during strikes. In short, protests occurred only when grievances were so deeply felt that people were willing to challenge convention and had the fortitude to dare public disapproval.

Despite all the factors working against it, protest did take place. The excesses of freebooting industrialism riding roughshod over time-honored practices and values provoked the rise of popular movements that brought about significant changes in American society.

PROTEST ON THE PRAIRIES

The first major expression of mass discontent came in the 1870s from midwestern and Great Plains farmers. Trapped between falling grain prices and high costs, farmers transformed the weak and innocuous Patrons of Husbandry into the Granger Movement, which in 1874 had a membership of 1.5 million men and women. By direct mass purchases from manufacturers not yet absorbed by the farm-machinery trust, the Grange was able to sell reapers, wagons, and other goods to its members well under prevailing market prices. The movement also went into manufacturing on its own, producing plows and mechanical reapers, which sold at 50 percent of standard price. The big corporations then slashed their prices to below cost. Such competition, together with poor management and inadequate capital, drove the Grange enterprises out of business and contributed to the decline of the movement by the end of the decade. Also, some Grange leaders felt the movement had been so successful in arousing public opinion that aggressive action was no longer required.

Grangers felt particularly successful in politics. They won legislation in midwestern states regulating the rates charged by railroads and grain elevators. Most of these laws did not long endure, but a challenged Illinois statute was upheld by the United States Supreme Court. In *Munn* v. *Illinois* (1876) the court stated that any private business "affected with a public interest" was properly subject to public regulation. This principle by implication opened the way to widespread economic and social reform. Later, however, as new justices more in harmony with the outlook of big business than their predecessors were appointed, the principle was eroded. In 1890 it was virtually abandoned when the Supreme Court ruled that a Minnesota law regulating railroad rates violated the Fourteenth Amendment.

This legal setback came at the very moment when angry farmers throughout the West and the South were mobilizing for a new campaign to win redress of their grievances. The new Farmers' Alliance movement was a product of the agricultural crisis of the 1880s. As thousands of farmers were driven off the land, those who stayed organized to protect themselves. By 1891 the three major alliances—northern, southern white, and southern black—claimed 3 million members. Their major demand was for federal aid to farmers, in the form of expansion of the money supply and low-interest loans on farm products. Through such measures farmers hoped to pay off their debts and save their property.

Failing to make headway through the major parties, alliance members promoted in 1892 a new People's Party, usually called the Populist party, which they hoped would speak not only for farmers but also for all Americans resentful of the spread of big business. While the party emphasized expansion of the money supply through the free coinage of silver, it also called for a graduated income tax directed at concentrated wealth and for government ownership of railroads, telegraphs, and telephones to assure fair treatment for all users and to provide protection for workers through recognition of labor unions and improved wages and working conditions. The party also committed itself to a greater, long-range goal: "poverty should eventually cease in the land." The Populists became the first significant political party to assert that eliminating poverty was a legitimate function of government.

Populism was more than a political movement. It was also a crusade of rural

Kansas State Historical Society, Topeka

Populists gathering for a meeting in Kansas.

and small-town Americans against the evils they saw all about them. Monopolies threatened the small business proprietor. Government was cynically used by men of wealth. Sensational newspapers and magazines from the cities corrupted the young. The cities themselves were centers of sin, luring young people to moral destruction. Populism was the stand of fearful and perplexed people in defense of an America that was passing. Americans who treasured the values of an older day—farmers, small business owners, editors, preachers, politicians—rallied to the Populist banner.

They had able and eloquent advocates in Mary E. Lease of Kansas, who spoke from experience of the harsh realities of farm life; Ignatius Donnelly of Minnesota, politician, editor, and author of a novel, *Caesar's Column,* which predicted the coming of an American fascism; Tom Watson of Georgia, a lawyer who was the idol of the despised "rednecks"; and James B. Weaver of Iowa, a Civil War hero and Republican politician so incorruptible that party bosses blocked his advancement.

Some Populist advocates, such as Henry D. Lloyd, the millionaire reformer from Chicago, did not share the backward outlook of their small-town associates. Rather, they accepted urban civilization and industrialism but rejected capitalism in favor of a new order based on social justice and cooperation. They saw in the Populist party a vehicle for mass political action that would include socialists and organized labor. They were speedily disillusioned. The major leaders of the socialists and of organized labor were openly antagonistic.

The new party made a remarkable showing in the 1892 elections. Its presidential candidate, James B. Weaver, received more than 1 million popular votes and twenty-two electoral votes. This showing, together with election of Populists to Congress and to state offices, thoroughly alarmed eastern business interests—except for silver-mine owners, who were happy to promote any party that promised relief from depressed silver prices. The party was attacked as a breeder of anarchy and socialism. Some conservatives were so distressed that they advocated a foreign war as a means of unifying the nation against the "evil" of Populism. In the South, the party was portrayed as a threat to white supremacy, and terrorism was employed against local leaders.

The pressure squeezed the strength out of Populism. The party declined further with the onset of a long depression in 1893. The 1894 elections showed that many erstwhile Populists had voted for major-party candidates in the hope that these parties could somehow cope with the immediate crisis. Besides, many western Democrats and Republicans had taken over the most popular, if not the most significant, Populist plank: free coinage of silver.

With the country plunged in deepening depression, Democrats in 1896 scented victory in the air with the silver issue. Unabashedly they stole the Populist plank and nominated as their candidate a spokesman of the western farmers, William Jennings Bryan of Nebraska. The Democratic strategy split the Populists. Over the protests of a minority that wanted to keep the party independent, the majority adopted Bryan as the party nominee and chose as his running mate the southern Populist leader Tom Watson of Georgia. The decision marked the end of Populism as an organized national political force.

Populism might have revived had the large-scale farm depression continued. But in 1897 farm prices began going up, and the inflow of gold from the Klondike a few years later brought about the inflation so many farmers and small business proprietors desired. As the economic pressures on rural America relaxed, unrest declined.

The Populists may have lost their battle against big business and urbanization, but many of their ideas influenced American development later. Thanks in part to their efforts, poverty came to be viewed as a social, rather than a moral, problem. Father John A. Ryan, for example, the famous exponent of a living wage, was deeply influenced by Populist teachings in his native Minnesota. The Populist proposal for a graduated income tax was later adopted, and the opposition to federal injunctions in labor disputes was written into the Clayton antitrust law of 1914. The Populists' belief in an activist federal government was put into practice by the New Deal and their exposure of the evils of concentrated wealth prepared many westerners for the doctrines of the Socialist party and the Industrial Workers of the World. Indeed, it is one of the ironies of American history that the Socialist party, presumably the party of the urban working class, enjoyed relatively greater voting strength in the formerly Populist western states than in the heavily industrialized East.

REBELLION IN LABOR

Workers, like farmers and small-town people, tried to cope with an encroaching industrialism. And, as the depression of 1873 produced the first farm protest, it also brought forth worker protest.

Most workers were reluctant to rebel during hard times. Any job, at any wage, was preferable to unemployment and hunger. Many unions collapsed. In 1873 there had been thirty national labor organizations; in 1877 there were only nine, and their membership was minimal. Nevertheless, despite unfavorable circumstances, workers were sometimes goaded to such desperation that they did rebel. Of these occasions, two are historically important: the anthracite miners' strike of 1875 and the great railroad strike of 1877.

The miners' strike was important not so much in itself as in its bloody aftermath, embodied in the persecution of the alleged "Molly Maguires." The strike, like many others, was defeated, but this time the operators decided to put an end to unionism once and for all. Their plan was to crush the spirit of the Irish miners, regarded as the hard core of union resistance. The guiding genius of the campaign was Franklin B. Gowen, president of a company that dominated the Pennsylvania anthracite fields, a man as ruthless in fighting unions as he was in crushing rival operators. His strategy took advantage of the violence, involving both employers and miners, that had characterized labor relations for a generation. Shootings and killings by company gunmen and by miners were frequent. Gowen planned to focus public attention on violence by the miners, arouse public opinion against them, and use public authority to destroy resistance under the guise of maintaining law and order.

Even before the strike, Gowen hired the Pinkerton detective agency to infiltrate the Ancient Order of Hibernians, a secret fraternal order to which most Irish miners belonged and which helped keep the spirit of unionism alive. Perhaps Gowen simply wanted information. Perhaps, as was later charged by the Hibernians, he wanted the agents to instigate large-scale violence, both to discredit unions and to drive small operators out of business—a tactic not unknown in those days. At any rate, the Pinkertons' activities gave birth to the myth of the "Molly Maguires," an alleged secret society of Irish terrorists who kept citizens of the anthracite regions in fear by killing or wounding all who opposed them. Apart from the dubious testimony of the Pinkertons, no firm testimony has ever been produced to prove that there was such an organization.

Nevertheless, thanks largely to Gowen's astute public relations campaign, people were convinced that the society did indeed exist. Active Irish unionists were rounded up. Public hysteria mounted. The arrested men were tried at the height of the uproar. The star witness was James McParlan, an Irish immigrant turned Pinkerton agent. Gowen himself contributed to the emotional climate of the courtroom in his capacity as special prosecutor. Of the men found guilty, ten were hanged and fourteen sent to prison. For the time being, unionism in the anthracite fields was discredited, middle-class opinion was once again conditioned to associate unionism with violence, the Pinkertons attained a national reputation among employers as an effective auxiliary in fighting unions, and the usefulness of "law and order" campaigns against labor had been demonstrated.

The railroad strike of 1877 revealed not only nationwide discontent among workers but also widespread hostility to the railroads among other people who resented the arrogant behavior of the corporations. The strike also revealed the shape of things to come in the massive use of federal power to break the strike.

The strike, spontaneous and unorganized, resulted from long accumulating grievances: unsafe working conditions, short workweeks, increased work loads, successive wage reductions. It began in July 1877 when firemen of the Baltimore & Ohio Railroad walked off the job. Soon workers of the Pennsylvania Railroad joined. Then the strike spread westward—to Chicago, St. Louis, and finally to the Pacific Coast. The strikers enjoyed much support from farmers, small businessmen, and public officials. Local police often proved unwilling or unable to act against the workers. In many places militia units fraternized with strikers or refused to take action against them. In consequence, the strike for a time was relatively peaceful and highly effective.

To conservatives, the strike was not a labor dispute but a revolution, instigated by foreign communists, and it had to be crushed. Since local militia often proved unreliable, the governors of the affected states dispatched units from distant cities to strike centers—units led by upper-class officers who had no sympathy with labor rebellion. More significantly, President Hayes sent federal troops to five states. These actions precipitated large-scale violence and bloodshed.

In Pittsburgh, Pennsylvania, militiamen from Philadelphia fired into a crowd of strikers and sympathizers, killing twenty and wounding many more, including three children. Enraged strikers and townspeople then besieged the militia in the Pennsylvania Railroad shops. In the ensuing battle, another eleven strikers or sympathizers and five Philadelphia soldiers were killed. During the fighting, someone—still unknown—set fire to the shops and rolling stock. Millions of dollars in property went up in flames. Railroad officials blamed the strikers. Union leaders charged that the arson was ordered by railroad executives who hoped to recover from insurance companies full replacement value of dilapidated buildings and rolling stock.

Federal troops helped break the strike in other cities, such as Chicago, where workers had joined in a general strike to support the railroaders and win redress of their own grievances. More than 100 people lost their lives in battles the strikers fought against federal troops, state militia, local police, and vigilante groups.

The overwhelming force was sufficient to crush the strike, but the very character of the strike made it vulnerable. Far from being the planned communist conspiracy the press painted it, the strike lacked national leadership and organization. The local committees that tried to assert control were too inexperienced to cope with their problems. Lacking organization, strikers were unable to maintain unity in their ranks. When individual companies made concessions, their workers returned to their jobs, leaving the others to fend for themselves. Further, all during the strike the brotherhoods of engineers and conductors cooperated with the employers.

The strike left its mark on the thinking of people who tried to build a viable labor movement. Some concluded that since strikes could not be won, labor must attain its goals through persuading employers to deal with unions, through arbitration of disputes, and if necessary, through boycotts. Others believed that while strikes were undesirable, they were inevitable. If strikes were to be won, unions must be tightly organized, highly disciplined, and backed with treasuries big enough to provide relief for workers' families. Besides, only through financial strength could unions hope to survive long depressions. Both groups agreed that confrontation with public authority must be avoided.

Two forms of labor organization emerged as workers strove to promote their interests: craft and industrial unions. Craft unions were made up of highly skilled workers in specialized occupations, such as carpenters, machinists, and cigar makers. Each craft union was a separate organization, with its own officers, its own agreements with employers, its own job regulations, and its own claims to job jurisdiction. While some craft unions adapted to changing technology, others fought a losing battle against mechanization. Industrial unions, in contrast, were a product of advancing technology. They included workers in all occupations in a given industry, skilled and unskilled alike. Typical of such unions were the United Brewery Workers; the United Mine Workers, representing coal miners; and the Western Federation of Miners, the organization of hard-rock miners in the West.

THE KNIGHTS OF LABOR

In the years immediately after 1877 the organization that gave promise of providing labor with a new sense of direction was the Knights of Labor, which included elements of both craft and industrial unionism. The organization was founded in 1869 as a secret order by Uriah S. Stephens and other Philadelphia garment workers. Its spread to other occupations was slow, partly because its secrecy incurred the hostility of the Roman Catholic hierarchy when the order organized such Catholic workers as coal miners. In 1881 the order abandoned secrecy and grew in numbers and significance.

The Knights nurtured the growth of craft unionism in its ranks, and at the same time it encouraged "mixed" unions that were in effect industrial unions. Unlike most labor organizations it organized black workers—although its western affiliates fought the employment of Chinese and were active in anti-Chinese violence. The order also organized women; one of its most noted leaders was Leonora Barry, a former factory worker. Like earlier unions, the Knights was not confined to workers. Employers and other "producers" were welcomed to its ranks. Only such "non-producers" as doctors, lawyers, bankers, and people engaged in the liquor traffic were ineligible. In short, the Knights harked back to Jacksonian Democracy, emphasizing the common interests of "producers" as against those of monopoly and privilege.

The policy of the Knights also reflected the experience of labor during the 1870s. Since both employers and workers were "producers," they had common interests. Since they had common interests, workers must avoid strikes. Instead, they must win their objectives through persuasion, arbitration, and if need be, boycotts. It also followed that labor should not confine itself to bargaining with employers. Rather, workers should seek to improve their condition through legislation and organization of producers' and consumers' cooperatives. According to the Knights, social reform and self-help were as important for labor as union activity.

Field organizers of the Knights, however, paid scant attention to official policy. They won members by promising immediate action on grievances, including strikes if necessary. Slowly the order gained members in the North and West. It also grew in the South, organizing coal miners, mill workers, and sugar and timber workers and welcoming both whites and blacks. By 1886 the Knights had more than 30,000 members in the South, indicative of a rising rebelliousness among working people who were said to be indifferent to unionism.

Rebelliousness was especially strong among shopmen of three southwestern railroads controlled by "robber baron" Jay Gould. When wages were reduced in 1885, the Knights led a strike so effective that Gould capitulated. The sensational victory brought such an influx of workers that in 1886 membership in the Knights exceeded 600,000.

Gould, as his business rivals well knew, never accepted defeat. Reneging on his promises, he provoked a strike in 1886, led by Martin Irons, a militant Knight. Bypassing Irons, Gould "bargained" with Terence V. Powderly, national leader of the Knights, who believed that strikes were a "relic of barbarism." While Gould "negotiated" with Powderly, he used all other means at his command and broke the strike. Powderly and the Knights were discredited. Membership declined rapidly.

The Knights also suffered from the antilabor hysteria that swept the nation after the Chicago Haymarket affair. On the evening of May 4, 1886, a meeting was held to protest the killing of pickets at the McCormick reaper works by police officers. All was peaceful until police arrived. Suddenly a bomb was thrown into their ranks. Eight were killed and sixty-seven wounded. The police went berserk, killing or wounding more than 200 of the protestors.

To this day, no one knows who threw the bomb, but that lack of information presented no problem to Chicago authorities or to the news media. To them it was clear that the bombing was the work of local anarchist labor leaders, who at the moment were leading a successful general strike for the eight-hour day. Eight such leaders were tried, not for murder—there was no evidence at all of their complicity—but for "conspiracy" to murder, a charge based on their speeches and writings, which could be construed as incitement to murder. Still the case was so flimsy that authorities took no chances. The judge was prejudiced against the defendants, and the jury was packed. All defendants were found guilty. Four were hanged, one committed suicide, and the others went to prison.

The Knights were not involved in the Haymarket affair, except that they were active in the Chicago union movement. Nevertheless, their offices were raided and leaders arrested, not only in Chicago but also in other cities. Despite Powderly's explanations that the order was conservative and law-abiding, the press linked the Knights with violence and anarchism. Members dropped out. By 1890 the Knights were no longer a major representative of American workers.

The Haymarket affair was not yet over, however. In 1893, after careful review of the trial records, Illinois governor John P. Altgeld pardoned the anarchists still in prison. The governor then was the victim of a savage campaign of character assassination so successful that it ended what had been a promising political career. To militants in the labor movement the anarchists became the "Haymarket martyrs," symbols of capitalist injustice. Of these, the most outstanding was Albert R. Parsons, born in Alabama, former Confederate soldier, a defender of black rights in postwar Texas, and finally an aggressive union leader in Chicago. After he was hanged, his widow, Lucy Gonzales Parsons, a Mexican-American, became in her own right a significant figure in radical movements.

THE AMERICAN FEDERATION OF LABOR

Even as the Knights of Labor faded away, there had already emerged an organization that has endured—the American Federation of Labor (AFL). It began in 1881 when craft unionists in and out of the Knights formed an organization to promote craft-union interests. These union leaders were soon embroiled in quarrels with leaders of the Knights, and in 1886 the craft-union leaders formed the AFL in direct challenge

Oregon Historical Society

Custom tailors of Portland, Oregon, gathering for Labor Day parade in 1902.

to the Knights. Its dominant figure was an English Jewish immigrant, Samuel Gompers, of the cigar-makers' union. Except for one year, he served as AFL president until his death in 1924. Sympathetic to socialism in his youth, Gompers became increasingly conservative in office.

Gompers was not alone; most federation leaders were conservative. Concerned with building strong unions of skilled workers, they had little interest in organizing the unskilled. Having lived through the strikes of the 1870s, the debacle of the Knights, and the Haymarket affair, they concluded that unions could be built only by accommodating to the existing social order. They felt they must avoid confrontation with powerful employers and public authority. They also had to woo middle-class opinion by demonstrating conservatism, responsibility, and respectability. The authority of responsible leaders had to be enforced against sometimes rebellious memberships.

Radicalism was to be fought whenever it appeared. Thus, AFL leaders battled Populism, socialism, and the radical unionism of the Industrial Workers of the World. Such actions won them the plaudits of leading churchmen, editors, and such businessmen as Mark Hanna and August Belmont. Gompers enjoyed being pictured as "Socialism's Ablest Foe."

Desire for respectability helps explain the enthusiastic participation of conservative labor leaders in the National Civic Federation, an important element in labor-management relationships in the first decade of this century. Founded in 1900, it was led by Ralph M. Easley, a former crusading Chicago newspaperman, who believed that America must be spared the class warfare of Europe. To this end, he brought together in a relaxed social atmosphere the leaders of business, conservative labor, and conservative public opinion. The informal relationships these meetings established would help leaders deal in a cooperative manner with crises. Labor, capital, and public would all benefit.

The businessmen active in the Civic Federation came from big business. In addition to Hanna and Belmont, they included Cyrus McCormick of the farm equipment company; Charles M. Schwab of United States Steel; and J. Ogden Armour, the packinghouse mogul. They represented new thinking about unionism in the business community. They were not enthusiastic about unions, but they accepted their inevitability. In their view, old fashioned union-busting was counterproductive. It stimulated class consciousness and made workers susceptible to socialist appeals. It was better, then, to deal with unions of skilled workers under conservative control that would not disturb management's authority over the masses of the unskilled. Further, organized labor's political influence was growing. At a time when public clamor was mounting against big business, it was wise to have friends like Gompers who not only accepted the concentration of corporate control but also looked on it as contributing to the betterment of labor and American society generally. Finally, conservative unions were highly useful in combating socialism and radical unionism.

The bargain between business and labor was spelled out in 1906 in a memo from Easley to Gompers. Easley declared that employers should recognize any union "guided by proper rules and governed by judicious and conservative leaders. In return, the union agrees that there shall be no interference with the employment of nonunion unskilled labor." Gompers agreed.

Gains made by workers through Civic Federation relationships were minimal. To be sure, Civic Federation influence contributed to settling the anthracite strike of 1902 in which miners won a 10 percent wage increase but were denied recognition of their union. Otherwise, the record of the organization was such that many union leaders, conservatives as well as radicals, come to regard it as a pernicious influence in the labor movement. In their view, labor leaders active in the federation were so anxious to demonstrate responsibility, especially by observing contracts strictly, that they were willing to help break strikes. Thus, in 1901 Gompers held aloof while U. S. Steel crushed what remained of the AFL steel-workers' union in its mills. Later, union leaders active in the Civic Federation assisted in breaking strikes on the New York subways, at a Buffalo iron works owned by Mark Hanna, and elsewhere.

UNIONISM AT BAY

Gompers and his associates believed that such behavior would win over employers. They were mistaken. Even within the Civic Federation there were many employers skeptical of cooperation with organized labor, and outside it were thousands of antagonistic employers. Their attitude was stated by an executive of U. S. Steel: "I have always had one rule. If a workman sticks up his head, hit it." In more refined language the employer position was explained by George F. Baer, a successor to Gowen as the ruler of the anthracite region of Pennsylvania. During the miners' strike of 1902 he wrote; "The rights and interests of the laboring man will be protected and cared for—not by the labor agitators—but by the Christian men to whom God has given control of the property rights of the country."

Such men felt that only evil, by which they meant socialism, could come from the growth of union membership—from 447,000 in 1897 to more than 2 million in 1904. Further, they looked with alarm at the spread of labor sympathies among middle-class reformers and at the influence of men and women who openly questioned the virtues of the profit system. These were not people given to the inflamed rhetoric of anarchists but sober, responsible folk who commanded a respectful hearing among the public. Among the most prominent were Richard T. Ely, an outstanding economist; Edward A. Ross, a noted sociologist; Edward Bellamy, whose utopian-socialist novel, *Looking Backward,* was a best seller; and the Protestant Walter Rauschenbusch and the Catholic John A. Ryan, who both advocated reconstruction of society on the basis of Christian ethics.

Employers distressed by these developments responded enthusiastically in 1903 to a call from the National Association of Manufacturers (NAM), headed by David M. Parry, for a concerted campaign to change the trends in American society. As it developed, the campaign took four major forms: a massive public relations effort; the beginnings of what came to be called "welfare capitalism"; expanded use of public authority, especially the courts, to attack unions; and old-fashioned union busting.

The public relations campaign was successful. Under the general theme "Shall Americanism or Unionism Rule?" the NAM popularized the "open shop." The "open shop," it was said, was truly American, for it was allegedly open to unionists and nonunionists alike, both being treated according to their merits. In contrast, the "closed shop" demanded by unions required that all workers be union members. Further, union control of employment meant that union members were at the mercy of corrupt and tyrannical union bosses.

As in all good propaganda, there was a measure of truth in the charges—there were corrupt and tyrannical union leaders. Two vital elements were omitted from the picture, however. One was that employers, when they dealt with unions at all, preferred to deal with corrupt and dictatorial union officials. The other was that active union members were summarily discharged from open shops. In fact, many open-shop employers required workers to sign "yellow dog" contracts that made union membership just cause for dismissal.

But to people unfamiliar with the realities of industry the NAM message was persuasive, especially since it was propagated by many presumably disinterested Americans. Among these were Cardinal James Gibbons of the Roman Catholic church; Charles W. Eliot, president of Harvard University, who extolled the strikebreaker as a type of "American hero"; and Nicholas Murray Butler, president of Columbia University.

The NAM disavowed any intention of prejudicing people against unions. It was opposed only to "bad" unions, it said. The NAM's concept of "good" unions was summed up by satirist Finley Peter Dunne. Good unions, he said, had "no strikes, no rules, no contracts, no scales, hardly any wages an' dam' few members."

"Welfare capitalism" did not flourish until after World War I, but it originated during the open-shop crusade. To head off unions, some employers made workplaces more safe and sanitary, provided meals at low prices, subsidized recreational facilities, and otherwise tried to build good will among their workers. Some employers sponsored "employee representation" plans, also known as "company unions," to take care of workers' grievances. Because of their inherent limitations, such "unions" did little to further the long-range interests of workers, but their very presence did inhibit the growth of genuine labor organizations. Further, the plans helped persuade many of the public that at least some employers were willing to deal with workers on an organized basis.

Employers also relied heavily on the courts. Their key legal weapon was the injunction. As used in labor disputes, an injunction was a judicial order, obtained without a hearing, that restricted or outlawed boycotts, strikes, and other forms of labor activity. The injunction had the force of law. If a union obeyed the order, its strike or boycott was a failure. If a union disobeyed, it was subject to all the penalties of law. Public authority, embodied in local police, state militia, and if necessary, federal troops, compelled compliance with the order and labor leaders involved were imprisoned. The use of injunctions became so widespread that labor leaders, including Gompers, bitterly denounced "government by injunction."

Indeed, Gompers himself was a victim in an injunction case. In 1908 he and two associates were found guilty of contempt of court for allegedly violating an injunction forbidding the boycott of an antiunion firm. Branded by the judge as "public enemies," Gompers was sentenced to a year in prison and his associates to lesser terms. The unusually severe sentence made Gompers a hero in the labor movement. In 1914 the United States Supreme Court dismissed the case on technical grounds.

The Supreme Court, however, was hardly sympathetic to labor. It upheld the legality of "yellow dog" contracts. It also held, in the famous Danbury Hatters case of 1908, that unions were subject to the Sherman antitrust law. The decision, involving a union boycott, meant that employers were entitled to triple damages from both unions as organizations and all individual members. Since the Danbury workers faced the loss of their homes and savings, union members throughout the country realized that they had come up against a deadly menace. The case against the Danbury workers was financed by organizations in the open-shop campaign.

Those organizations also embarked on old-fashioned union busting, destroying unions in many small cities and damaging even strong unions in major centers. Thus, the powerful Teamsters Union of Chicago was almost wiped out in a strike in 1905. Unions of Midwest packinghouse workers and of Great Lakes seamen were eliminated. New industries, such as automobiles, business machines, and electrical appliances were thoroughly open-shop. In the South, textile manufacturers and the Southern Manufacturers Association combined to keep the region free from unions, continuing an earlier program that had defeated strikes of textile workers in 1901 and 1902.

The open-shop victories were not attained without violence and bloodshed. Clashes were most frequent and bloody in the nonunion coal fields. In 1912 and 1913 virtual civil war raged in the mining areas of West Virginia as operators defeated organizing efforts of the United Mine Workers. The attempts of Colorado coal miners to form a union led to the notorious Ludlow Massacre of 1914. In that incident eleven children, two women, and six men perished when militiamen burned down a strikers' tent colony after a soldier had been killed in a fight with strikers. Angry miners retaliated, and President Wilson sent in federal troops to restore order. Under their rule, the mines resumed operations on an open-shop basis. The operators, dominated by Rockefeller interests, rejected Wilson's proposal that they mediate their disputes with their workers.

The open-shop drive did not succeed in destroying all unions, but it did play a part, together with an economic slump, in slowing their growth. After 1904, membership in the AFL declined and did not resume an upward trend until 1911. More significantly, the open shop became so entrenched in the new and expanding industries, such as automobiles and electrical goods, that their workers were not able to organize until the 1930s. Further, the open-shop public relations campaign reinforced in the public mind the identification of business with Americanism and law and order and gave unions a lawless, un-American image.

"BUSINESS UNIONISM"

The open-shop campaign influenced the course of organized labor itself. The already strong tendencies within the craft unions toward "pure and simple," or "business," unionism became permanently dominant. In 1896 Gompers defined unions as "the business organizations of the wage earners." This definition reflected the thinking of many labor leaders that previous labor organizations had failed because of financial weakness, unstable membership, lack of effective centralized control, and inefficient management. If unions were to survive strikes and long depressions, they had to operate on business lines—and above all they had to be financially strong.

Accordingly, craft unions levied high dues and initiation fees, to provide both financial strength and a stable membership. Power was concentrated in national officers, elected at conventions. The officers had authority to enforce contracts, and only they could sanction strikes. At the local level members elected their own officials, but actual power was wielded by business agents, full-time officers who could represent workers with no fear of job reprisal by employers.

Like leaders in business and politics, union leaders sought to keep themselves in power. They created effective political machines that manipulated conventions, rigged elections, and kept the membership in line with the union equivalent of the ward boss—the business agent. Through such devices many union leaders stayed in office for decades, some for as long as forty years. A few unions dispensed with even the formality of conventions. The hod carriers, for example, did not meet for thirty years prior to 1941, and the tobacco workers union held no conventions between 1900 and 1939. Members who challenged such practices were either bought off by appointment to union jobs or felt the heavy hand of authority. On occasion, entire local unions were expelled.

Some union leaders came to identify themselves with businessmen, aping business life-styles and using union office for their personal enrichment. They acquired stock in companies they bargained with—a conflict of interest that did not bother them. Some, for their private profit, sold union labels—certifying that the labeled products were made under union conditions—to companies where unionization was purely nominal. Others benefited from inside information passed on to them by friendly businessmen. Thus, John Mitchell, president of the United Mine Workers and a pillar of the National Civic Federation, accumulated an estate of $250,000 before his death in 1919.

At the local level, corruption was rife in the building-trades unions, where powerful business agents were in position to do favors for both employers and workers. Sometimes the corruption went further. In 1913 a former lobbyist for the National Association of Manufacturers reported he had bribed several hundred union officials to oppose candidates and measures favored by the AFL.

There were protests against such conditions, of course, but they were limited. Protest invited reprisal. Appeals to AFL headquarters received scant consideration. More important, most union members were like middle-class citizens who tolerated political corruption. So long as they received benefits, they were not too critical of how their representatives enriched themselves.

Although business-union leaders publicly decried violence, some used it secretly. "Goon squads" first arose when certain unions employed young thugs to battle the gunmen hired by employers. Later, they were found useful in intimidating small employers and union dissidents. Sabotage was almost routine in disputes in the building trades. The most notorious example of such violence was the dynamiting of the *Los Angeles Times* building in 1910, in which twenty people were killed and seventeen injured. Leaders of the union involved were sent to prison for long terms.

Nevertheless, despite internal problems and the opposition of many employers, business unions grew in strength. In 1916 the AFL reported a record membership exeeding 2 million, and unions outside the AFL showed similar growth. By then, the eight-hour day, long since won by building-trades unions, had spread to other industries where unions were powerful. The United Mine Workers had established itself in the anthracite fields and in the soft-coal regions of Pennsylvania, Ohio, and Illinois. In fields where small employers predominated, as in printing, hauling, and building, unions were now strong.

Business unions also demonstrated a growing political influence. They supported the successful campaign of middle-class reformers to win state restrictions on employment of children, regulation of the hours of work of women, and less enthusiastically, limits on the hours of work of men. Working hours of men, said union leaders, could be regulated only through union contract. This belief seemed vindicated in 1905 when the United States Supreme Court held in *Lochner* v. *New York* that the state could not limit the workday of bakers to ten hours. In 1908, however, the court upheld the right of Oregon to limit the working hours of women.

Organized labor hailed as its greatest political achievement the Clayton antitrust law of 1914. Unions were exempted from antitrust laws, and drastic limitations were placed on federal injunctions in labor disputes. Both parts of the law were greatly weakened by later judicial interpretation.

MILITANCY IN LABOR

While business unionism developed, the heritage of labor militancy remained alive. In July 1892, the unorganized unskilled workers at the Carnegie steel works at Homestead, Pennsylvania helped the AFL union of skilled workers to fight against Pinkertons brought in to break a strike. In a day-long battle nine workers and three Pinkertons died, and many more were wounded on both sides. The strike was broken several days later with the arrival of 8,000 militiamen. Public interest in the issues of the strike was diverted shortly when Alexander Berkman, a young anarchist who was not involved in the strike at all, shot Henry Frick, head of the Homestead works.

While the Homestead workers challenged the nation's leading steel baron, hard-rock miners in the Far West battled the giant corporations that had taken over the copper, lead, silver, and gold mines. When union miners in the isolated region of Coeur d'Alene, Idaho, rejected a wage reduction in 1892, they were locked out and replacements brought in under armed guard. Battles between miners and company gunmen followed. The entire state militia was sent in, supplemented by federal troops. Although defeated for the time being, union members held their ranks firm. From their experience a new and militant organization, the Western Federation of Miners, emerged in 1893.

That year also saw the beginning of what was until then the nation's worst economic depression. Millions of wage-earners were out of work, and their meager savings were lost as banks collapsed. Thrifty homeowners lost their property. Private charities and municipal relief agencies could not cope with the crisis. Among the unemployed rose a demand for federal action to put people back to work.

Since Washington was unresponsive, "armies" of unemployed began "marches on Washington." In the West, thousands of jobless workers—among them Jack London, later a famous novelist—commandeered freight trains for transportation. So great were their numbers that railroad companies acquiesced. Most notable of the armies was that of Jacob Coxey, a small businessman of Massillon, Ohio. Unlike many others, Coxey's army did reach Washington, but when its leaders were arrested, the army disintegrated. Other groups fell apart likewise. The federal government remained indifferent to the unemployed, but the marches indicated that many workers did not accept hunger as part of the American way of life.

At the same time, railroad workers, as in 1877, took action against wage reductions and other grievances. This time they turned to the American Railway Union (ARU), a new organization headed by Eugene V. Debs, who had been a popular official of the Brotherhood of Locomotive Firemen. Believing that craft divisions weakened railroad workers, Debs and his associates had formed an industrial union, embracing all railroad workers—white workers, that is. The new organization grew rapidly after it won a short and peaceful strike against Jim Hill's Great Northern Railroad in the spring of 1894.

Another test of strength came quickly. At the ARU convention in 1894, striking members at the Pullman works called for a boycott of Pullman sleeping cars because management would not even discuss their grievances. Debs and other leaders were opposed, believing that the union was unprepared for such an undertaking. Only when Pullman refused to make even small concessions did Debs and his associates agree to a boycott. The ARU then confronted the power of twenty-four railroads operating from Chicago, their efforts coordinated by a bitterly hostile General Managers Association. Such efforts were all the more effective because they received the blessings of leaders of the railroad brotherhoods.

The boycott was not a strike. Men went to work as usual, handling all trains except those containing Pullman cars, and special pains were taken to assure free movement of the mails. The boycott was effective and remarkably peaceful for a movement involving 100,000 workers from Chicago to San Francisco. When the railway managers failed to disrupt the boycott, they turned to Washington for aid. A special federal prosecutor—in private life, a lawyer for the railway managers—was appointed, and a federal injunction against the boycott was issued. When the workers ignored the injunction, President Cleveland sent in United States Army units over the bitter objections of Governor Altgeld. Supplementing the troops were several hundred special United States marshals, recruited in part from Chicago's underworld.

Troops, marshals, and police ruthlessly beat down the workers and trains containing Pullman cars moved again. Angered by the bloodshed and the use of federal power against labor, Chicago unions called for a general strike, and 25,000 workers responded. The unions also called upon the AFL leadership to reconsider its policy of neutrality. Instead, the leaders urged AFL members to return to work. The decision was hailed as a "death-blow" to the "Debs rebellion" by newspapers in Chicago.

The federal government then arrested Debs and other ARU leaders for violating the antiboycott injunction. With the leaders jailed, the boycott collapsed. Debs served six months in jail; his associates, three. From jail Debs, the former Democrat and Populist, emerged to become the charismatic leader of American socialism in the early twentieth century.

WESTERN MINERS ORGANIZE

While the collapse of the ARU spelled an end to industrial unionism on the railroads, the Western Federation of Miners (WFM) took firm root among the hard-rock miners of the West as a way of standing up to eastern capital and its allies among public officials. Its leaders—William D. ("Big Bill") Haywood, Ed Boyce, Vincent St. John, and Charles Moyer—reflected its membership. They were the unsuccessful folk of the West—former farmers, prospectors, cowboys, railroaders—reduced to the regimented labor of the mines. The union was firmly committed to socialism.

The miners enjoyed an advantage known to few workers elsewhere: considerable support from public opinion and from many public officials. Populism was strong in the West, and the revolt of western workers against eastern capital met with approval. Despite the bitter opposition of mining interests and often bloody strikes, especially in Colorado, the WFM spread throughout the hard-rock mining areas of the West.

So successful was the WFM that workers in other occupations clamored for its help in forming their own unions. The many unions that resulted encouraged WFM leaders to sponsor in 1898 the American Labor Union, a national organization dedicated to organizing the unorganized. After a brief period of influence, the new body declined, partly because hitherto indifferent AFL unions suddenly mounted organizing drives in the West. Nevertheless, so many workers had shown an interest in militant unionism that many radicals—Populists, socialists, anarchists, and nonideological unionists disgusted with traditional union policies—believed the time had come to present an alternative to business unionism. This belief led to the founding in 1905 of the Industrial Workers of the World (IWW), known popularly as the "Wobblies."

THE "WOBBLIES"

To the Chicago meeting that launched the IWW came most of the leaders of militant labor. In addition to Debs and Haywood, there were Lucy Gonzales Parsons, the anarchist; "Mother" Mary Jones, the veteran organizer of coal miners; Daniel De-

Leon, still a force to be reckoned with although his Socialist Labor party was dwindling; and William Trautman, an official of the AFL brewery workers' union.

The IWW, in calling for a program of industrial unionism, rejected collaboration with employers. "The working class and the employing class have nothing in common," it asserted. Further, organization of unions was viewed, not as an end in itself, but as a step toward ending capitalism and bringing about a new social order in which toilers would "take and hold that which they produce by their labor." This vague statement papered over the ideological differences between socialists and anarchists. Socialists held that labor must be organized politically as well as economically. Anarchists disdained political action, believing that workers could attain a new order through revolutionary industrial unionism.

The early days of the IWW were hardly auspicious. Two of its top leaders, Haywood and Moyer of the Western Federation of Miners, were arrested for the murder of former Idaho governor Frank Steunenberg. In 1907 Haywood was acquitted and the case against Moyer was dropped.

In the meantime, the organization was plagued with dissension. Anarchists quarreled with socialists. Socialists, divided between the Socialist party and the Socialist Labor party, feuded among themselves. Nonideological unionists complained that these disputes interfered with organizing. A split in 1906 was followed by withdrawal of the Western Federation of Miners, the IWW's most powerful affiliate. Two years later the anarchists captured the organization and the socialists left in a mass exodus. Enemies of the IWW confidently predicted its early demise.

Employment agencies in the Pacific Northwest were special targets of the radical labor union Industrial Workers of the World. This advertisement for an agency is dated 1913.

Oregon Historical Society

PACIFIC EMPLOYMENT CO.

222 AND 224 COUCH ST., PORTLAND, OREGON

LARGEST AND BUSIEST LABOR OFFICE IN OREGON

An IWW campaign among lumber workers is illustrated in this cartoon in *The Industrial Worker* in 1912.

They were wrong. The IWW was just entering its "glory days." The anarchist appeal, with its rejection of political action and of long-term collective bargaining agreements with employers, made sense to the western migratory workers who had come to dominate the organization. These young, single, rootless men worked the harvests north from Mexico through the prairie provinces of Canada, and they labored in logging camps and mines. Since they moved from place to place, they were never eligible to vote and thus politics meant little to them. Since their work was temporary, they had little interest in long-term contracts.

Everywhere these transient workers were shunned by respectable citizens. The IWW gave them a sense of their own worth and dignity as creators of the nation's wealth. It also provided a feeling of comradeship of the poor in place of the dog-eat-dog competition that had enabled employers to exploit them. In the IWW these workers were made to feel wanted. Indeed, they were expected to participate fully in all decisions and struggles, struggles that did pay off. In many places where Wobblies were active, improvements were won in housing, food, wages, and hours.

The IWW did not confine itself to the West. It also demonstrated its ability to organize the immigrant industrial workers of the East and longshoremen and timber workers in the South. In 1909 it won a bloody strike at a U. S. Steel subsidiary in McKees Rocks, Pennsylvania. Later it won another strike at another U. S. Steel subsidiary at Hammond, Indiana. Its most sensational victory came in 1912 at the textile town of Lawrence, Massachusetts. After a bitterly fought strike lasting three months and involving 23,000 workers, the IWW union won substantial wage increases and other concessions from hostile employers. In an effort to ward off further IWW unionism, other New England textile manufacturers granted similar concessions to 250,000 workers.

Lawrence marked the apex of IWW influence outside the West. In 1913 the organization suffered a crushing defeat in a strike of silk workers at Patterson, New Jersey. That same year an IWW strike of rubber workers at Akron, Ohio, failed, as did IWW organizing efforts among automobile workers in Detroit. In the South, the timber workers' union was destroyed by terrorism and racism.

IWW success in the East and South was due basically to the same appeal as it had for western migratory workers: it provided the working poor, white and black, a sense of worth and a message of hope. The unions in the IWW were thoroughly democratic, prohibiting any discrimination because of sex, race, or ethnic background, and members were expected to participate actively in union affairs.

The policy was exemplified during strikes. In Lawrence, for example, members not only walked picket lines but also helped make policy decisions. More than twenty ethnic groups participated equally, including such disparate nationalities as French Canadians, Italians, Portuguese, Poles, and Russians. Women, too, played an active role, proving to be among the most resolute of the strikers. Indeed, one of the slogans of Lawrence women caught the popular imagination: "We want bread—and roses, too." Further, there was complete identity between strikers and leaders. Joe Ettor, "Big Bill" Haywood, and Elizabeth Gurley Flynn were obviously leaders dedicated to the cause of the workers.

The IWW's spirit was fresh and exuberant, and its techniques were imaginative. In 1906 it staged the first sit-down strike in the United States at the General Electric plant in Schenectady, New York. The strike was lost, but it provided an example of a way workers could tie up production without the dangers of walking a picket line. Forbidden to picket individual mills in Lawrence, the IWW organized mass chain-picketing in which thousands of strikers marched endlessly around the mill district, singing as they went—another IWW innovation. Incredulous newspapermen reported that here was a strike "that sang." When relief funds ran so low at Lawrence that the strike was endangered, hundreds of children were sent to homes of sympathizers in eastern cities in a carefully planned operation that made sure the youngsters were well cared for. With an eye to public opinion, the exodus was well publicized. As the IWW leaders hoped, the sight of the emaciated, poorly clad children stirred a public outcry against the mill owners—an outcry that was intensified when Lawrence police attacked mothers and children waiting to leave the city. The resulting public pressure helped bring the strike to a successful conclusion.

Why then, in view of its many successes, did the IWW fail to root itself in the industrial working class? The answer lies partly in forces outside the IWW. Employers, public officials, and middle-class opinion were, of course, opposed. Also, socialists who hoped to reform the AFL stood against a "dual union" movement. Although many AFL members were sympathetic, national AFL leaders fought the IWW, looking on it as an agent of revolution that discredited "legitimate" unions. Thus, AFL leaders actually helped defeat the strikes at Paterson and Akron. Significantly, the AFL made no effort to organize these workers, who had proved themselves ready for unionism.

There were also weaknesses within the IWW structure itself. Its belief in democratic unionism free from bureaucracy led to dues too small to carry on long-range activities and to a lack of administrative authority to guide the organization's work. Its eager welcome to all applicants made it easy for informers to penetrate its unions. Most of the IWW leaders in Akron, for example, turned out to be private detectives. Perhaps most serious, the philosophy of the IWW prevented it from building unions that would carry on day-to-day operations based on written collective-bargaining agreements. When strikes were won, IWW organizers departed to carry on their work elsewhere, leaving inexperienced workers to cope with the manifold problems of maintaining unions in the face of employer hostility. As a result, with some exceptions in the West, the IWW unions were short-lived. Even in Lawrence, IWW membership dwindled to 700 within a year after the great strike. Finally, its failure to build permanent unions led to internal disputes that further weakened the IWW.

CLOTHING WORKERS ORGANIZE

Labor militancy found other expressions than the IWW. In eastern cities immigrant workers in the garment trades seethed with unrest. In New York City in 1909, more than 20,000 hitherto unorganized women workers, mostly Jews and Italians, rallied to the strike call of a weak AFL union, the International Ladies Garment Workers Union. The following year, another successful strike of 50,000 workers helped to make the union a powerful and permanent force in the industry.

A similar revolt took place among workers in the men's clothing industry in Chicago in 1910. More than 40,000 immigrant workers went on strike under the reluctant sponsorship of a notoriously corrupt AFL union, the United Garment Workers. The consequent struggle against employers and the union leadership led in 1914 to the formation of the Amalgamated Clothing Workers of America. The new union was headed by immigrant workers, of whom the most notable was Sidney Hillman, a young Russian Jewish leader of the 1910 strike. Despite the hostility of the AFL leadership, the new union became dominant in the men's clothing industry and the United Garment Workers faded into insignificance.

RADICAL POLITICS

For a brief period in the 1880s and again in the heyday of the IWW, anarchism enjoyed some support among elements of the working class—largely because its adherents were so clearly devoted to the interests of working people. The Haymarket Affair doomed anarchism in the 1880s, and the shooting of Henry Frick in 1892 and the assassination of President McKinley in 1901 inflamed public opinion against the movement. Perhaps of more lasting significance, the failure of anarchists in the IWW to form stable unions demonstrated that their philosophy was poorly adapted to the needs of workers in industrial America.

Socialism, on the contrary, seemed well designed to meet working-class aspirations. A product of the Industrial Revolution, socialism looked to creating a classless society through political action and economic power centered on strong labor unions. Its major exponent in the United States was the Socialist party, formed in 1901 through a merger of several socialist organizations. It was wide-based, including in its membership Marxists, Populists, Christian Socialists, Utopian Socialists, middle-class reformers, Wobblies, and AFL craft unionists. The electoral strength of the party lay in small-town and rural America west of the Mississippi until World War I.

For a time it appeared that socialism would become as significant a political force in America as it was already in Britain and Europe. From a few thousand members in 1901 the Socialist party grew to nearly 120,000 in 1912. Its influence was spread by a lively press, which numbered more than 300 periodicals. Socialists won office in labor unions, and by 1912 voters had elected 1,200 Socialists to public office. Among them was Victor Berger of Milwaukee, Wisconsin, who became the nation's first Socialist Congressman. In 1912 Socialist presidential candidate Eugene

"I gorry, I'm tired!"

"There you go! YOU'RE tired! Here I be a-standin' over a hot stove all day, an' you wurkin' in a nice cool sewer!"

This famous cartoon by Art Young appeared in the lively radical magazine *The Masses* in 1913. The magazine was edited by Max Eastman, and its contributors included such writers and artists as George Bellows, Stuart Davis, Jack London, Upton Sinclair, Sherwood Anderson, and Carl Sandburg.

V. Debs received nearly 900,000 votes, about 6 percent of the total—the highest proportion of votes ever given a candidate dedicated to radical social change.

As the party's influence grew, its internal divisions widened. In 1912 some reformers and intellectuals, including the famous black leader W. E. B. DuBois, resigned to support Woodrow Wilson. That same year "Big Bill" Haywood, the Wobbly leader, was ousted for defending sabotage. Thousands of his followers resigned or were expelled.

An even more serious crisis arose in 1917 when the party officially opposed American entry into World War I. Many labor-union officials and middle-class reformers, such as the novelist Upton Sinclair, quit the party. However, so many antiwar Americans were attracted to the party that its membership actually grew, and quarreling conservative and radical factions came together in defense of the antiwar policy.

Such a center of resistance could not be tolerated by the federal government. In cooperation with local and state governments and vigilante groups, it embarked on a policy of repression that wiped out nearly all party organizations in small-town America and drastically restricted the operations of urban groups. Denial of mailing privileges effectively curbed the influence of Socialist publications. Hundreds of party leaders, including Eugene V. Debs and Kate Richards O'Hare, were jailed. Nevertheless, the weakened party held its ranks together, for the time being.

WOMEN AND LABOR

Union leaders held that working women were not interested in joining unions. The figures on union membership seemed to validate the belief. In 1910, of the 8 million women in the labor force, only 74,000 belonged to unions—less than 1 percent—and these were concentrated in a few consumers' goods industries, such as clothing, textiles, and shoemaking.

It was true, of course, that women workers presented special problems. Although they worked from economic necessity, they were socially conditioned not to look upon themselves as breadwinners. As young unmarried women they tended to see their employment as a temporary necessity before marriage. While many women turned over their earnings to their families, others spent their wages on beauty aids, clothing, and other prerequisites for winning a suitable husband. When they married, they expected to confine themselves to the home, either from acceptance of middle-class values or from patriarchal family traditions inherited from Europe. Even Leonora Barry, the notable woman official of the Knights of Labor, believed that no married woman should work outside the home except from dire necessity.

Many women, too, were timid about joining unions, feeling that somehow they were not quite "nice." Such a feeling rose partly as a response to prevalent middle-class opinion that factory women were sexually promiscuous. Respectable working-class women had no desire to challenge conventions that might expose them to the charge they were little better than prostitutes. And above all, union activity would brand them as unconventional. Naturally, they shied away from it.

On the whole, unions did little to counteract such feelings among women. The AFL conducted a few sporadic, half-hearted organizing campaigns, but when these did not produce immediate results, women were written off as impossible—or at least, unprofitable—to organize. As one union official explained, the wages of women were so low that they could not afford high dues and therefore were not worth the bother. He ridiculed women seeking membership in his union as wanting "bargain counter" unionism. "We can well do without such members," he added.

While some unions did admit women to the lower-paid jobs within their control, several unions excluded them altogether. Some went further, seeking to drive women out of jobs they already held. The Molders Union, for example, in 1907 adopted a policy looking toward phasing out the employment of women. The justification for such policies was that women, since they were paid less than men, threatened union standards.

Reinforcing the union rationale against women workers was the strong feeling in the working class that woman's place was in the home. Men might accept their daughters' and their wives' work in factories as necessary, but they did not accept it as right. That view was shared by AFL leaders. In 1905, at a moment when many middle-class women were challenging the traditional view of woman's place, Gompers bluntly asserted that married women need not and should not work outside the home. An AFL publication restated the old nineteenth-century argument that when a woman left home for the workshop she destroyed her "refinement and elevating influence," with dire social consequences.

Actually, women could be organized, as the IWW demonstrated again and again. So, too, did the International Ladies Garment Workers Union after the great strike of 1909. The AFL glove workers' union was made up largely of women, and one of its founders, Agnes Nestor, became president in 1913.

In many cities, women formed their own unions under stimulus of the National Women's Trade Union League. Founded in 1903 to combat the exploitation of women workers and to promote unionism among them, the league was made up of socially conscious women of wealth, professional social workers, and active union women. It was one of the rare feminist ventures of the day that transcended class lines. Among the union women represented were Leonora O'Reilly, who helped organize New York garment workers; Mary Donovan, secretary of the Lynn Central

Labor Union; and Mary Kenney O'Sullivan, who had served briefly as an AFL general organizer. More significant, from the viewpoint of winning public opinion and influencing timid workers, were the wealthy women who led the league for many years: Mary K. Kehew, a prestigious social reformer from Boston; Ellen M. Henrotin of Chicago, former president of the General Federation of Women's Clubs; and Margaret Dreier Robins, who was such a good friend of organized labor that she served on the executive board of the Chicago Federation of Labor for several years. Associated with them were social workers of established national reputation: Jane Addams of Hull House and Lillian D. Wald of the Henry Street Settlement.

During major strikes these middle-class women had an influence denied to union women. They helped raise relief funds, persuaded newspapers to publish the grievances of the strikers, obtained legal counsel for arrested strikers, and aroused public opinion against police brutality on picket lines. The great garment workers' strikes in New York and Chicago owed much of their success to the work of the league.

In less dramatic times, the league fostered the growth of unions, not by organizing them itself but by stimulating unorganized women to establish their own organizations. The presence of women of social standing in the league's leadership helped assure doubtful women that unions were eminently respectable. Thus encouraged, women in cities where the league was active formed unions in many different occupations. Then they, and the league, encountered difficulties. Many AFL unions, while claiming jurisdiction over their occupations, denied them admission, and the AFL refused to charter their unions directly. As a result, many promising ventures in women's unionism died out.

Radical movements, unlike unions, welcomed women eagerly. For millions of Americans anarchism was symbolized by Emma Goldman, a charismatic orator whose influence was so feared by federal authorities that in 1908 they stripped her of her citizenship on legal technicalities. The leading woman in the IWW was Elizabeth Gurley Flynn. She was so active in the Lawrence strike that a commentator called her "the spirit of that strike." Kate Richards O'Hare was an effective crusader for the Socialist party among western farmers. She served on the party's national executive committee. Other notable socialists included Margaret Sanger, Crystal Eastman, Charlotte Perkins Gilman, and Rose Pastor Stokes.

THE PROSPECT IN 1914

The economic expansion that began after the Civil War changed American society. The center of social as well as of economic gravity shifted from the country to the city. Millions of European immigrants were brought in to do the nation's dirty work, as were much lesser numbers of Asians and Mexicans. The ranks of white-collar workers increased as well. The proportion of women in the labor force expanded as more and more married women became wage-earners outside the home. The same trends were apparent in the South, except that native-born whites and blacks performed the low-paid unskilled labor that immigrants did elsewhere.

While industrial America spelled the doom of such artisans as the makers of handrolled cigars, it opened up new fields for such highly skilled workers as electricians, locomotive engineers, and tool and die makers. Such workers lived relatively well. Among skilled workers the eight-hour day was the rule, and working conditions were safer and better than they had been. The overall view of such workers tended to be optimistic, especially as their children entered business, the professions, and "refined" white-collar occupations.

For the millions of unskilled workers the prospect was more dismal. Their wages continued to be so low that only the labor of all members of a family enabled them to survive as self-respecting people. Industry's adoption of the Taylor efficiency system meant more intense labor. The trend among employers to provide safe working conditions was not universal. In New York City in 1911, a fire at the Triangle Shirtwaist Company claimed the lives of 143 young women. In the coal fields explosions killed hundreds of miners every year. As for housing, most working poor continued to live in urban slums, the wretched mill villages of the South, or the shacks of company towns.

Yet some of the unskilled were improving their lot. The new unions in the clothing industry were forcing out sweatshops and gaining safer work places. Unskilled as well as skilled workers benefited from the advances won by the unions of coal and hard-rock miners. The threat of the IWW brought concessions from employers. And even among the unskilled, American-born children in increasing numbers graduated into white-collar ranks. Such upward mobility, however, was barred to most blacks, Asians, and Mexicans. It was also rare among the youngsters of southern mill villages. Poorly schooled and poorly nourished, such children had little prospect except repeating their parents' pattern of poverty.

By 1914, however, the working poor had won allies in the middle class. It was no longer universally accepted that poverty was a sign of personal moral deficiency. However reluctantly, many affluent Americans came to believe that at least in part poverty was a social product. From such considerations, among others, came the spate of legislation in the early twentieth century that earned it the title of "era of reform." The employment of children was restricted. The hours of work for women were regulated. Minimum-wage laws were enacted. Workmen's compensation laws spread, and other laws imposed safety standards in workshops. Slum housing was outlawed in many states. To be sure, the laws were often poorly drafted, poorly enforced, easy to evade, and often struck down by the courts, but the principle was gradually established that government had a responsibility to act for those who were unable to act for themselves. Unfortunately, the principle was applied only to urban folk. The rural poor, whether white, black, Mexican, or Asian, remained largely outside the law's protection.

Improvement in the condition of the working poor—and of skilled workers, too—came from an unexpected source: war. The demands of World War I produced a labor shortage in America. Women, married and single, were encouraged to go into the factories. Rural southerners, white and black, found themselves at work in northern cities. Wages went up. Prices did too, but there was so much overtime available and so many well-paying jobs open to all family members that thrifty people found it possible to break out of poverty, at least for the time being.

FOR FURTHER READING

For general labor history see Selig Perlman and Philip Taft, *History of Labor in the United States, 1896–1932* (1935), and Philip S. Foner, *History of the Labor Movement in the United States,* (4 vols. 1947–65). A very readable account of major labor conflicts is Sidney Lens, *The Labor Wars* (1973). The Knights of Labor and the Haymarket affair receive special attention in Norman J. Ware, *The Labor Movement in the United States, 1860–1890* (1929), and in Henry David, *The History of the Haymarket Affair* (1936).

Major strikes of the 1890s are discussed in David Brody, *Steelworkers in America: the Non-Union Era* (1960), and Stanley Buder, *Pullman* (1967).

Samuel Gompers's own account of the rise of the American Federation of Labor, *Seventy Years of Life and Labor* (1925), is revealing. Bernard Mandel's *Samuel Gompers* (1963) is critical of the labor leader.

The Industrial Workers of the World continues to fascinate writers and readers. Two recent works are outstanding. One is Melvyn Dubofsky, *We Shall be All* (1969), a historical study. The other is Joyce L. Kornbluh, *Rebel Voices: An IWW Anthology* (1964), a collection of cartoons, poems, stories, and articles that conveys the spirit of the IWW.

American anarchism's most noted advocate, Emma Goldman, tells her story in *Living My Life* (1931). Richard Drinnon has written her biography, *Rebel in Paradise* (1961).

On socialism, see David Shannon, *The Socialist Party of America: A History* (1955); Ira Kipnis, *The American Socialist Movement, 1897–1912* (1952); and James Weinstein, *The Decline of Socialism in America* (1967). Ray Ginger's *The Bending Cross* (1949) is a biography of Debs.

The work of Stephan Thernstrom is hardly designed for the general reader, but his conclusions on social mobility are provocative. They may be found in *Poverty and Progress: Social Mobility in a 19th Century City* (1964) and *The Other Bostonians* (1973).

More directed to the general reader is Charles A. Madison, *Critics and Crusaders* (1948), which introduces a number of Americans who refused to accept the "gospel of success." Harvey Goldberg, ed., *American Radicals* (1957), treats the same theme at a more sophisticated level.

The age of Margaret Sanger,
John L. Lewis, Eleanor Roosevelt,
Martin Luther King,
and Cesar Chavez

phase four POST-INDUSTRIAL AMERICA

1918 TO THE PRESENT

1919 Seattle general strike. Major race riots.
1920 Nineteenth Amendment provides for woman suffrage.
1928 Full-length movies with sound first shown. Hoover elected president.
1929 Beginning of Great Depression.
1932 Franklin D. Roosevelt elected President. End of New Deal.
1935 Passage of Social Security and National Labor Relations acts.
1935 CIO undertakes organization of mass-production workers.
1937 Birth control legalized.
1941 Pearl Harbor attack brings United States directly into World War II.
1945 Atomic bombing of Japan signalizes end of World War II.
1948 President Truman reelected.
1950 Korean war begins. Ended in 1953.
1950 Senator Joseph McCarthy symbolizes era of repression of dissent.
1954 Supreme Court outlaws racial segregation in public schools.
1959 Xerox automatic copying machine appears on market.
1963 President John F. Kennedy assassinated. Lyndon B. Johnson succeeds him.
1963 Emergence of new militant feminism.
1964 Passage of major federal civil rights legislation.
1968 Martin Luther King assassinated.
1969 United States lands man on moon.
1970 Students killed at Kent State and Jackson State in Vietnam War protests.
1974 Richard Nixon resigns as president.
1975 United States withdraws from Southeast Asia; end of Vietnam War.
1978 Supreme Court outlaws racial quotas as a means to end racial discrimination (Bakke case).
1979 Supreme Court upholds some antidiscrimination plans in industry (Weber case.)

Postindustrial America—roughly the period from 1918 to the present—differed from its industrial predecessor in many ways. The earlier era emphasized production of goods; the later era, consumption. The earlier economy depended relatively little on the federal government as a major market; after 1939 its successor relied heavily on government contracts, especially in armaments. Industrial America prized abstinence, frugality, thrift. Postindustrial America encouraged spending, acquisition, pleasure.

In the America of 1900 most white industrial workers were part of the immigrant working poor and lived in cities. Seventy years later nearly all were native-born, and many, no longer poor, lived in suburbs. The era of bloody labor wars came to an end in the 1930s, when a massive labor revolt led to unionization of the mass-production industries. By 1970 unions were an integral part of American society, and relations between labor and industry were generally peaceful. Farm workers, however, continued to meet with violence and repression when they tried to organize.

With the exception of the depression years of the 1930s, the era was marked by economic expansion. Even so, poverty continued to be the lot of millions of unsuccessful Americans, a disproportionate number of whom were blacks or people of other minorities. Here, too, there was a difference between the eras. In 1900 government accepted little responsibility for the poor. In 1970 the welfare state was a part of American life.

The coming of the welfare state vastly increased the power of the federal government, but it was only one element contributing to its growth. World War II, the Cold War with the Soviet Union, and the hot wars in Korea and Southeast Asia also enhanced federal power. While millions of Americans benefited from welfare-state programs, other millions enjoyed full employment in war-related industries.

There were aspects of federal power that alarmed friends of civil liberties. During World War I opposition to the war was ruthlessly crushed. After the war federal authorities sought to stamp out the political heresies associated with what they called "Bolshevism." In 1940 Congress passed the Smith Act, with the same repressive end in view. In the 1950s, under the influence of McCarthyism, Congress enacted legislation further restricting the political freedom of citizens. Some of the legislation was later struck down by the Supreme Court, but much of it remained on the statute books. Later it was revealed that undercover surveillance and harassment by federal agencies, hitherto confined to traditional radical organizations, had been extended to include civil rights groups, student movements, and the women's liberation movement.

If government became big, big business became bigger. After World War II a new form of business organization emerged: the conglomerate corporation. This was a holding company that controlled leading companies, not in one industry but in many. Accompanying this trend was the growth of great multinational corporations, which set up their own operations abroad or acquired foreign enterprises. Such developments made for increased concentration of control, and they were difficult for governments to regulate.

Concentration was also visible in the countryside, where the small family farm was disappearing. By 1970 fewer than 5 percent of America's people lived on farms, and the number of farms had declined from nearly 6 million in 1950 to fewer than 3 million in 1970. The size of farm holdings increased, operations became more specialized, and corporate farming became more and more significant. By 1969, sales of nearly 1,600 big farm operations each exceeded $1 million a year. The factory had come to the fields.

Concentration of economic control indicated that governing elites were as powerful as ever. Through interlocking directorships and other means they controlled major corporations. In addition, elites directly owned great wealth—a careful study revealed that in 1956 the top 0.5 percent of the population owned 25 percent of the nation's wealth.

Elites continued to shape government policy, not only through campaign contributions but also directly through occupation of key government posts. No matter which party won an election, elite members and their legal and academic advisors took over key cabinet positions and headed such important agencies as the Federal Reserve Board and the Central Intelligence Agency. To be sure, there were policy differences among elite groups, but these were settled through traditional political and legal channels.

Postindustrial elites proved flexible in adjusting to a changing society. They accepted mass labor unionism and the welfare state and made concessions to racial minorities and women—partly from personal conviction, partly from enlightened self-interest, and partly from a larger concern for social peace. They were not so flexible in dealing with a changing international order, as their policies toward Communist China, the Soviet Union, Vietnam, and Cuba indicated.

Elites continued to be flexible about membership in their circle. Most, as in earlier times, came from families already enjoying elite status or from families close to such status. It was still possible, however, for people of humbler origins to gain entry. After World War II elites of "new money" emerged in the Southwest, giving rise to friction with what the newcomers called "the Eastern Establishment" based on "old money." Another significant addition to elite ranks after the war was that of the leaders of the professional military.

Relatively few blacks shared in the benefits that came to many whites in postindustrial America. Nevertheless, there was a significant improvement in black status, thanks largely to the great civil rights crusade of the 1960s, which brought about new laws designed to end racial inequality.

The black struggle stimulated similar activity among Hispanic Americans and American Indian peoples. It also contributed to the rise of a new feminism among white women and helped spark the student revolt of the 1960s. The revolt reached a tragic climax in May 1970, with the killing of four white students at Kent State in Ohio and two black students at Jackson State in Mississippi during protests against the war in Southeast Asia.

In the 1970s there was a perceptible change in the American mood. Traditional optimism and self-confidence seemed overshadowed by doubt and uncertainty. Several converging developments help explain the change—the Watergate scandals, the debacle in Southeast Asia, the onset of a depression in which high unemployment was for the first time accompanied by inflation.

Some legacies of the 1960s also contributed to the mood. The assassinations of John F. Kennedy, Robert F. Kennedy, Malcolm X, and Martin Luther King shook the complacency of many Americans about their society. Also, the failure of the great reform programs of the 1960s to make appreciable progress against poverty, urban blight, and related problems bred a sense of disillusionment. So, too, did the collapse of the student revolt of the 1960s. Feminists and civil rights advocates were further disturbed by United States Supreme Court decisions that seemed to indicate a retreat from the commitments of the 1960s to racial and sexual equality. In the 1970s it was clear that Americans of all backgrounds confronted new challenges in domestic and international contexts quite different from those they were used to.

23 blue-collar militancy and conservatism

Postindustrial America brought unprecedented prosperity to blue-collar workers. The process, begun in the 1920s, reversed during the depression of the 1930s, but it reached a high point in the post–World War II era. Contributing to blue-collar affluence were the powerful unions in basic industry that emerged from the great labor rebellions of the 1930s. Such unions, militant in their origins, became increasingly conservative as they were accepted and as their members moved upward from the working poor. Also contributing to a sense of blue-collar well-being was the increasing number of two-income families as millions of married women entered the labor force.

The working poor did not disappear, of course. There were few in basic industries, but millions remained in farming, service occupations, and low-wage industries. Disproportionate numbers of working poor came from racial minorities.

LABOR IN THE DOLDRUMS

During World War I the benevolent policy of the federal government toward unionism provided workers an opportunity to join unions freely. In consequence, membership rose from 2.8 million in 1916 to a high of more than 5 million in 1920. Thereafter membership fell off. Although the labor force rose 20 percent between 1919 and 1929, the number of union members declined to 3.4 million in 1929. Usually unionism thrived in times of prosperity. How is the change to be explained?

One factor in the decline was the defeat of postwar labor militancy. The return of peace was marked by large-scale unemployment and short workweeks. Also, consumer prices rose sharply while wages lagged behind. During the war the real income of many workers had risen substantially, raising their expectations as well. Workers were in no mood to accept reduced prospects. At the same time, workers in public service and on railroads, who had shared little in wartime prosperity, felt themselves menaced by the rise in living costs. The result was a wave of strikes in 1919 involving a record number of workers—nearly one in five. These included not only industrial workers but also stage actors in New York and policemen in Boston. In Seattle, a peaceful general strike closed down business for several days while unions maintained essential services.

The middle-class public was deeply shaken by such developments, especially by the Boston police strike and the Seattle general strike. Unfamiliar with the conditions that produced the strikes, they were ready to believe that labor unrest was due to agitators, usually foreign-born, who were bent on promoting violent revolution on the model of the November Revolution in Russia. Thus, strikes were equated with attempts to overthrow the American government. Employers, who had found pinning the "red" label on militant labor so useful in earlier eras, helped promote the new "Red Scare."

Although some strikes were won, many were lost, most significantly the strike in steel. The strike began in September 1919 when more than 300,000 workers responded to a strike call from an organizing committee of leaders of twenty-four AFL unions. In addition to union recognition, the strikers wanted wage increases, the eight-hour day, and abolition of the notorious twenty-four-hour shift on weekends. Guiding the strike were two veterans of the labor wars: John Fitzpatrick, president of the Chicago Federation of Labor, and William Z. Foster, former Wobbly, supporter of the war effort, and leader of a successful campaign to organize Chicago stockyard workers during the war.

The familiar script of repression was acted out on a massive scale. Private armies were mobilized and public authority invoked, including federal troops. Eighteen strikers lost their lives, hundreds were injured, and many jailed. The companies also undermined the unity of the strikers. Smoldering ethnic animosities among immigrant workers were stirred up. Native-born American skilled workers were urged to break ranks with foreign-born radicals. Blacks were reminded of the unions' racism. Strike morale was further damaged by the recruiting of masses of strikebreakers, of whom at least 30,000 were black. At the same time employers and the media won over public opinion by portraying the strike as part of a sinister plot for "Bolshevizing American industry." Foster's radical past was raked up to prove the point.

Such factors by themselves might well have defeated the strike, but there were also factors on the union side that contributed to the loss. Some craft union leaders, lukewarm at best, were easily discouraged when problems arose. The officials generally were dedicated to promoting the interests of their own individual unions and quarreled over jurisdictions. One such official, representing a small union of skilled workers, not only made separate agreements with employers but also ordered union members back to work in plants where his union had contracts. The funds subscribed by participating unions fell far short of those required for a great strike. The identification of the strike with Bolshevism dampened the enthusiasm of conservative union leaders. The unions' failure to pledge an end to racist discrimination made it easy for the companies to enlist support among blacks. In January 1920 the strike officially ended, and the unions left the strikers to fend for themselves. The defeat discouraged attempts at organization in steel and other basic industries until the 1930s.

Another factor in the decline of organized labor in the 1920s was a renewed drive for the open shop, now called the American Plan. Well organized campaigns pictured unions as "un-American." Welfare capitalism, typified by company-sponsored recreation, stock-purchase schemes, low-cost life insurance, and the like, flourished. Capitalism in America, it was said, was not only tremendously efficient but also increasingly benevolent. Company unions grew in number.

The American Plan campaign sought to destroy labor militancy. Throughout the country employers banded together in local antiunion campaigns and were particularly successful in western states.

Nationally, unions fared little better. Strikes of seamen and railroad switchmen in 1920 were defeated. Two years later a strike of railroad shopmen was lost. Also in 1922 the unions that had established themselves in the packinghouse industry were wiped out after a disastrous strike. During the decade the coal miners' union lost ground, and even the entrenched building-trades unions suffered losses. In rapidly expanding industries, such as auto, rubber, aluminum, and glass, the open shop was standard.

GOVERNMENT AIDS BUSINESS

The decline in labor power could in part be attributed to the antiunion attitudes of public authorities. Courts routinely issued injunctions against unions in labor disputes. Local police, state police, National Guardsmen, and federal troops suppressed union resistance, often with great bloodshed. The coal fields in particular were the centers of conflict. In West Virginia, Illinois, and Colorado widespread violence raged in the mining regions. Most of the victims were union workers.

In the meantime, working people fared ill in decisions by the United States Supreme Court. Two attempts by Congress to outlaw child labor were nullified by the court. In 1923 the court invalidated a Congressional minimum-wage law for the District of Columbia in such sweeping terms as to render inoperative similar state laws and to inhibit the spread of labor-reform measures. The court also whittled away the protections organized labor thought it had gained through the Clayton antitrust law of 1914. The law, said the court, protected only "lawful" labor union activities. The court upheld injunctions against picketing, and in 1922 it declared that unions could be sued for damages incurred in labor disputes. Once again, as after the Danbury Hatters case, it appeared that unions faced the danger of forfeiting their funds to antiunion employers.

Public authorities also moved against the labor Left. During the war the Wobblies had been virtually annihilated as a movement. Because of their antiwar policy they were victimized by vigilante groups, and federal and state governments jailed at least 2,000 local and national Wobbly leaders. The Socialists, too, suffered from repression, as we have seen.

The attacks on the Left were part of a more general suppression of wartime dissent. Antiwar newspapers and magazines, whatever their political stance, were suppressed. Pacifists were jailed. German Americans found themselves so much the targets of popular hostility and government espionage that many changed their names and fervently asserted their patriotism.

The wartime hysteria gave way to an equally virulent "Red Scare" after the war. The Communist Revolution in Russia inspired fears on Wall Street and in Washington that a similar revolution might happen here. The news media contributed to popular apprehension with highly inflammatory accounts of what was happening in Russia. At home, the great wave of strikes in 1919 and the rising militancy in black ghettos were attributed to "Bolshevist influence." The result was repression.

States passed sweeping criminal syndicalism laws that outlawed teaching of revolutionary doctrines and in effect nearly all forms of labor militancy. In New York, Illinois, and California radical activists, mostly Communists, were sentenced to long prison terms under laws held valid by the United States Supreme Court. The federal government also acted. In 1920, thousands of anarchists, Wobblies, and Communists were rounded up in nationwide dragnet raids. More than 500 aliens were deported without trial, including Emma Goldman and Alexander Berkman, who were shipped off to Russia. The hysteria also took its toll in respect for representative government. The New York state legislature expelled its five Socialist members, and Congress denied a seat to Victor Berger, the conservative but antiwar Socialist.

Growing out of the Red Scare was a case that fastened international attention on America's treatment of radical dissidents. In 1920, Nicola Sacco and Bartolomeo Vanzetti, Italian anarchists who had opposed the war, were arrested in Massachusetts for murdering a company official during a robbery. The case aroused the suspicions of radicals and liberals, for they were still protesting the imprisonment of Tom Mooney, a militant labor leader of San Francisco, for alleged complicity in the bombing of a Preparedness Day parade in 1916. Although a key witness confessed perjury and federal investigators found that Mooney's trial was unfair, Mooney remained in

Posters like this one helped foment hysteria against German Americans during World War I.

The case of Sacco and Vanzetti stirred deep passions during the 1920s. Here the two anarchists are led into a Massachusetts courthouse in 1921. They were found guilty of murder and later executed. Many Americans felt the men were innocent victims of anti-Italian and antiradical prejudices.

The Bettman Archive, Inc.

prison. Labor militants and their middle-class allies suspected another frame-up in the Sacco-Vanzetti case.

The trial of the two men was so biased that the famous Harvard legal scholar Felix Frankfurter, later a Supreme Court justice, protested. Many intellectuals took up the Sacco-Vanzetti cause, believing that the men were innocent and were being persecuted for their beliefs. The AFL felt the men were "victims of race and national prejudice and class hatred." Some leading Italian-Americans, typified by Judge Michael Musmanno, came to the men's defense, feeling that they were being prosecuted on flimsy evidence because they were Italians. Such views were widespread in Europe, where students, workers and intellectuals called for release of the anarchists. The protests were of no avail. In 1927, after appeals had been exhausted, Sacco and Vanzetti were executed. The experience embittered many intellectuals and reinforced the conviction of radicals that American justice was class justice.

WEAKNESS ON THE LEFT

The labor Left, however, was in no position to influence public opinion. It had been seriously weakened by the Red Scare of 1920. Its time, funds, and energy were largely devoted to getting people out of jail.

The Left, ravaged from without, contributed to its own weakness. The Socialist party, already split over World War I, split again over the Russian Revolution. Radicals within the party saw in the Communist success the beginning of world revolution and in the postwar strike wave a sign that American workers were ready for revolt. Reformist Socialists, believing that success would be attained by gradual reform, rejected this view. As the internal quarrel intensified, conservatives used their control of party machinery to expel their opponents, who made up a majority of the membership. Thereafter the party tended to become a middle-class reform group. Eugene Debs, who died in 1926, was succeeded by Norman Thomas, a patrician idealist who lacked Debs's identification with the working class. The party ceased to be the significant political force that it had been in 1912.

The new Workers' Party, made up of a merger of rival groups of expelled revolutionary Socialists, now called Communists, had little political significance. As prospects of world revolution lessened and as the party made little headway, Communists quarreled among themselves. Internal dissension was climaxed with expulsion of the "leftist" followers of Leon Trotsky and of the "rightist" followers of Jay Lovestone during the 1920s. The undisputed leader of American Communism was now William Z. Foster, the organizer who guided the steel strike of 1919. Despite his proletarian background he lacked Debs's charisma and won little mass following.

In the meantime, many radicals dropped out of organized movements, weary of internecine warfare. The 1928 election demonstrated the decline of the Left. Socialists and Communists between them polled 337,000 votes, a substantial fall-off from Debs's vote of nearly 920,000 in 1920.

SIREN SONG OF PROSPERITY

While such factors help explain the decline of organized labor and of the Left, an even more persuasive influence thwarted both conservative unionists and radicals. It was an unprecedented era of prosperity in which millions of working people shared. After the initial surge of postwar inflation, prices fell while wages rose. The consequent rise in living standards was enhanced by the new emphasis on consumption, reflected in the easy credit that made it possible for many of the working poor to acquire low-priced homes, electric refrigerators, automobiles, and radios. Such possessions contributed to a sense of well-being—especially ownership of an automobile, which provided working people with the luxury of private transportation.

Evidence of working-class prosperity was most obvious in the centers of the relatively new and rapidly expanding industries, such as auto, rubber, radio, and electrical goods. Jobs were available and wages relatively high. To them flocked recent European immigrants, impoverished rural southerners, unemployed coal miners, midwestern farm folk driven off the land, and members of the northern urban working poor. Most of them were young and able to stand the gaff of high-pressure

A woman automobile worker in Detroit in 1929. For safety reasons women in this factory were required to wear coveralls and caps.

production. While their level of affluence was far below that enjoyed by middle-class Americans, it was much superior to what they had known before. There was little overt mass discontent. To be sure, sporadic, spontaneous strikes broke out when working conditions became intolerable, but they lacked leadership and organization. If strikers did not return to work, they were easily replaced. Union men who tried to start organizations were identified by labor spies and weeded out.

Besides, the workers were divided. Skilled workers looked down on the masses of the unskilled. White unskilled workers wanted no association with blacks and Mexican-Americans. Protestant workers, influenced by the current anti-Catholic campaign of the new Ku Klux Klan, viewed their Catholic fellows with dire suspicion. Catholics themselves were split among ethnic lines, with Poles, Slovaks, Italians, and others having little in common save their faith. Workers who belonged to Orthodox churches, such as Russians and Greeks, held aloof from the Catholics. Northern workers ridiculed the ways of southern newcomers. In the 1920s there was little sense of labor solidarity among working people.

THE UNIONS ACCOMMODATE

As unions lost ground, they sought to woo employer goodwill and public favor through joint labor-management schemes to promote higher efficiency, profits, and wages. Such plans did benefit workers to some degree, but they also resulted in job losses and more intense labor. Workers in the unions involved grew discontented. The leaders, however, were happy to maintain union ground in an antiunion era, to identify themselves as partners rather than opponents of employers, and to win public plaudits for pioneering a new concept in labor-management relations.

Dependence on employer goodwill had an even further-reaching consequence. Confronted with the success of the American plan, AFL leaders in 1926 declared that auto workers could not be organized without the consent of the auto companies. Since this view applied not only to auto workers but also to workers in other basic industries, it signified that any concerted effort to organize the unorganized had been abandoned.

Business unionism even entered business on its own. The Brotherhood of Locomotive Engineers, for example, invested heavily in Florida real estate and in coal mines, which it operated on a nonunion basis. Some unions established banks. In 1926 there were thirty-six such banks, with deposits of $109 million. Such developments were hailed at the time as presaging labor capitalism, a designation the captains of labor found flattering. The flattery ceased with the depression of 1929. By 1932 there were only seven labor banks with deposits of $26 million, and various other union ventures had gone bankrupt, with great losses to the members involved.

Accommodation was also reflected in labor's political stance. Outraged by antiunion Supreme Court decisions and by the use of public authority to support the American Plan crusade, the AFL in 1924 endorsed the candidacy on the Progressive ticket of Senator Robert M. LaFollette of Wisconsin. The party had condemned injunctions and endorsed labor's right to organize. LaFollette's defeat occasioned retreat to the traditional policy of nonpartisanship, based on rewarding labor's political friends and punishing its adversaries. Such a tactic might have proved productive had labor been united. In fact, unions divided on their endorsements and many members paid little heed to the advice of their leaders, voting as they saw fit.

Organized labor's political weakness, however, also reflected its insensitivity to major social issues. Not until 1929 did the AFL favor public old-age pensions, and then only after middle-class reformers and a fraternal order, the Eagles, had shown the cause to be eminently respectable. Likewise, the AFL did not abandon its hostility to unemployment insurance until 1932.

DESCENT INTO POVERTY

The euphoria in which many Americans lived ended in 1929 with the onset of the nation's worst economic depression. Despite the prosperity of the 1920s, many Americans lived in poverty—coal miners, textile workers, subsistence farmers, farm laborers, cannery workers. Now they were joined by millions of others. By 1933 there were nearly 13 million unemployed, meaning that one worker in four had no job. Millions of others eked out an existence on part-time employment. The annual income of factory workers fell from $15 billion to $6 billion.

The thrifty as well as the thriftless suffered. Small investors in the stock market, usually middle-class people engaging in their first speculations, faced disaster. Before the stock market finally stabilized in July 1933, stock prices fell about 80 percent, representing a loss of $74 billion. Equally tragic was the plight of working people and others who had entrusted their life savings to banks. Before the New Deal restored order, 5,500 banks collapsed, carrying with them $3.4 billion in deposits. Millions of sober, industrious folk now had to swallow their pride and apply for relief.

The aid given was inadequate. Since the federal government refused to accept responsibility, the burden fell on cities and states. Their resources proved insufficient,

This picture was designed to spur sales of Hudson automobiles in 1934, during the depression. Such appeals failed, however; automobile sales declined, and thousands of automobile workers were jobless.

Michigan Historical Collections

Kansas State Historical Society, Topeka

Fertile topsoil was blown away in this "dust storm" caused by a drought in western Kansas in 1934. Thousands of farm families moved west to improve their lot. They often became migrant farm laborers.

and relief allowances were reduced even below the previous low levels. Some cities ran out of funds altogether. Single men and women could get no relief at all. All major cities had their "Hoovervilles," miserable shantytowns in which formerly self-supporting folk struggled for survival, often by scrounging food from garbage cans. Unnumbered thousands of teenagers, boys and girls alike, hitchhiked or rode freight cars back and forth across the country, searching in vain for jobs, living as best they could in the meantime.

For people on farms, the depression was the final debacle after a decade of troubles. During the 1920s farm prices fell while farmers' costs remained high. Tenancy increased as thousands of families were squeezed off the land. The process was accelerated after 1929, when farm prices dropped catastrophically. Between 1929 and 1932 gross farm income declined 57 percent. Farm property worth $78 billion in 1920 was valued at $39 billion in 1935. By then, great numbers of farm families had lost their land and were reduced to tenancy. Many had an additional burden in relatives who returned from cities to which they had gone with such high hopes.

As if man-made problems were not enough, nature took a hand. Prolonged drought turned vast areas of Kansas and Oklahoma into "dust bowls" in which nothing could grow. A veritable exodus of "Okies" to California and elsewhere resulted.

REVIVAL ON THE LEFT

The unrest generated by the depression revived the hopes of the Left. Communists took the lead in organizing Unemployed Councils, and Socialists sponsored Workers' Alliances. Both sought to mobilize the urban jobless behind demands for jobs and relief. Many working people, without accepting the ideologies involved, rallied to the organizations as they battled evictions of renters, fought foreclosures on workers' homes, and demonstrated for jobs and government aid to the jobless. The most tragic event of the struggle happened in March 1932, when several thousand jobless, led by Unemployed Councils, marched on the Ford auto plant in Dearborn, Michigan, just across the line from Detroit. Their attempts to present to Henry Ford demands for jobs and other concessions were blocked by Dearborn police. In the clash that followed, 4 of the marchers were shot and killed and 100 wounded. A dozen police were injured by thrown rocks, but none were shot. Later, a grand jury blamed the Dearborn police for the bloodshed.

The Left was also active in the rural South. Communists inspired a Sharecroppers Union, and Socialists backed a Southern Tenant Farmers Union. Both were designed to end the poverty and oppression of the rural poor, black and white alike. Their belief in racial equality and their challenge to the traditional power structure brought persecution. Both organizations suffered from private terrorism and repression by public authority.

Unrest was too widespread to be controlled by a few thousand radicals. In July 1932, nearly 20,000 World War I veterans trekked across the country to Washington, demanding that Congress approve immediate payment of a bonus due them in 1945. When the Senate balked, most of the marchers left. Those who remained were forcibly driven out of the city by federal troops commanded by General Douglas MacArthur. Although the "Bonus Army" failed, it did call public attention to the wretchedness of many who had been hailed as heroes in 1917.

The traditionally conservative farm belt also let its discontent be known. In 1932 midwestern farmers, members of the Farmers Holiday Association, organized "strikes" to hold farm products off city markets until prices rose. Armed men dumped the contents of milk trucks and otherwise interfered with the flow of foodstuffs. Mobs of angry farmers threatened judges who signed foreclosure orders. They packed the forced sales of property of farmers who could not pay their debts. With outside bidders intimidated, the organized militants legally acquired the properties for small sums and then turned them back to their original owners.

There was unrest, too, among academics, intellectuals, and professional people. Partly it arose from dismay at the failure of the nation's leaders to cope with the problems of depression. There must be something basically wrong with a system that created so much human havoc and could do nothing about it, they felt. There was also a more immediate cause. Many upwardly aspiring people, especially among the young, found their aspirations thwarted. Graduates of colleges and professional schools found few openings available. Many employed engineers, scientists, accountants, and managers lost their jobs. Many lawyers and doctors found themselves hard pressed, and some had to go on relief.

It is not surprising, then, that there was a drift toward the Left. Some became Socialists or Trotskyites or joined other radical groups. Others supported the Communists impressed by the party's aggressive campaign on behalf of the unemployed and by the planned economy of the Soviet Union, which seemed to offer a pattern for America to follow. Among the outstanding literary men who publicly supported the party were John Dos Passos, Sherwood Anderson, Erskine Caldwell, and Theodore Dreiser.

People at both ends of the political spectrum misread the meaning of the temper of the times. Conservatives saw in urban and rural protests evidence of a grand

"Red" design to overthrow the traditional social and economic system. Spokesmen for the Left saw in such protests evidence of "radicalization" of the masses foretelling the doom of capitalism. Both were wrong. The protesters generally wanted nothing more than to get jobs and to save what property they possessed. To be sure, such limited objectives might have proved revolutionary had American capitalism proved as rigid as Russian tsarism. But, under the New Deal, American capitalism adapted itself to the new conditions brought on by the collapse of the old economy.

THE NEW DEAL

For the millions of poverty-stricken farmers and workers, the New Deal was a godsend. Massive federal emergency relief programs provided food and jobs for the hungry. Farm income was protected, family farming promoted, and the trend toward tenancy reversed. Federal insurance of bank deposits spared thrifty people the fear of bank failure. Federal loans for small homeowners made it possible for working-class families to keep their homes. Small investors were protected by strict federal regulation of stock markets. A new Social Security system provided unemployment compensation and old-age pensions, although the benefits were generally inadequate. Besides, the law excluded farm workers and domestics, thus continuing the patterns of poverty familiar to blacks and Mexican-Americans—and to the white "Okies" who had become migrant farm workers in the West.

Factory workers also benefited from legislation establishing federal minimum-wage standards and the basic forty-hour week. At long last, child labor in industry was outlawed. Once again, however, farm and domestic workers were excluded, and children continued to work in the fields. The laws were bitterly contested by business interests but were later upheld by the United States Supreme Court.

From the viewpoint of the urban wage-earner, perhaps the single most important New Deal law was the National Labor Relations Act of 1935, popularly known as the Wagner Act. The law guaranteed workers the right to join unions of their own choice, forbade employers to interfere, and set up a National Labor Relations Board with sweeping power to enforce the law. The public was ready to accept the law because the Senate Civil Liberties Committee, headed by Senator Robert M. LaFollette, Jr., had been steadily exposing the antiunion activities of many employers. These included the widespread use of professional union-busting agencies, violence against strikers, labor espionage, and the collaboration of local authorities. Employers did not accept the Wagner Act, however. Holding it to be unconstitutional, they defied the law until the Supreme Court upheld it in 1937. Even then some major companies continued to battle unionism, most notably the Ford Motor Company, which did not recognize the auto workers' union until 1941.

RISE OF THE CIO

The Wagner Act was in part a response to working-class pressures. During the short-lived National Industrial Recovery Act of 1933 masses of workers flocked into unions, and in 1934 there were major strikes in San Francisco, Minneapolis, and Toledo. Some established unions, such as the coal miners and garment workers,

John L. Lewis, leader of the CIO, addressing auto workers in a union-organizing campaign.

The Archives of Labor and Urban Affairs, Wayne State University

welcomed the newcomers. Many craft-union leaders, however, were hardly enthusiastic about accepting the rebellious young workers from the open-shop industries. Dan Tobin, head of the Teamsters, spoke for many of his colleagues when he referred to such workers as "rubbish." The AFL chartered unions in rubber, auto, and other industries, preliminary to dividing their membership among craft unions. It also tried to dampen the militancy of the new members.

In the meantime, open-shop employers used old and new antiunion techniques to thwart the surge toward unionism. Thousands of active union workers lost their jobs. When the AFL did little to protect the victims, members dropped out by the thousands, fearing that they too might find themselves out on the streets.

Failure of the AFL to provide effective leadership led in 1935 to formation of the Committee for Industrial Organization (CIO), made up of eight rebellious union leaders committed to organizing the unorganized on an industrial, rather than craft, basis. Led by John L. Lewis, the hitherto conservative president of the United Mine Workers, the CIO embarked on an aggressive campaign in the open-shop industries. To the surprise of those familiar with his antiradical past, Lewis employed not only conventional organizers but also Socialists, Communists, former Wobblies, and men whom he had expelled from the mine union for opposing his dictatorial rule. So long as he controlled them, he felt, the fervor of such people would prove invaluable in unionizing the masses of labor.

The CIO touched a responsive chord. It seemed that everyone wanted unions—waitresses, longshoremen, oil workers, fishermen, newspapermen, technicians, loggers, store clerks, and office workers as well as factory workers. The extent of the movement and the intensity of feeling indicated that this was more than another union organizing campaign. It was, in fact, an expression of the accumulated resentments against the humiliation and degradation of the depression years. In demanding a voice in their working conditions, workers were seeking to assert their human dignity against what they perceived to be an impersonal and inhuman economic system. It was, above all, a revival of the sense of working-class community that had expressed itself in the great strikes of the nineteenth century and in the campaigns of the Wobblies in the twentieth century.

The climate of opinion of the time was favorable to the CIO. Numerous middle-class people—clergymen, professors, journalists, intellectuals—actively supported the new unions. The tone of the White House, too, was sympathetic to labor. Workers believed that Franklin D. Roosevelt wanted them to organize, and they venerated Eleanor Roosevelt, who voiced her compassion for the poor and oppressed. Thus, filled with a sense of their own grievances and buoyed up by the feeling that they had many friends outside their own ranks, workers joined unions in such numbers that by 1938 the CIO claimed 4 million members. Membership in AFL unions also showed a significant rise—from 2.5 million in 1932 to 3.6 million in 1938.

In the meantime, conflict between traditional craft unions and CIO unions, which were still technically members of the AFL, resulted in the expulsion of CIO unions from the AFL in 1938. Thereafter the CIO constituted itself as a separate body, called the Congress of Industrial Organizations, with John L. Lewis as president.

Success of the CIO was due in part to its mobilization of worker militancy. Nowhere was this more evident than the CIO's acceptance of the sit-down strikes that swept the country—at least 900 between 1935 and 1937. Although antilabor interests charged the technique was another "Red" import, it was in fact in line with an

Sit-down strikers in a General Motors plant in Flint, Michigan, in 1937.

The Archives of Labor and Urban Affairs, Wayne State University

Detroit News, *from Michigan Historical Collections*

National Guardsmen on duty at a Flint, Michigan, plant of General Motors during the famous sit-down strike of 1937. The strikers' victory touched off a wave of labor organization.

American tradition, dating back to the Wobblies' occupation of the General Electric plant at Schenectady, New York, in 1906. It was revived by rubber workers in Akron, Ohio, in January 1936 and spread rapidly.

The sit-down was labor's pragmatic response to the hazards of outside picket lines. Pickets were confronted with shooting, clubbing, tear-gassing, and death. Workers reasoned that it was better to remain in the factory, halt production, and be safe from attacks by gunmen and police. They reckoned also that employers would be so concerned with protecting expensive machinery and equipment from damage that they would not use violence. While occupying plants, sit-downers enforced their own discipline, keeping the factory clean, servicing machines, ejecting drunks and troublemakers. Wives and women union members supplied the strikers with food and clothing.

The most crucial sit-down occurred early in 1937 at General Motors plants in Flint, Michigan. Both sides recognized that Flint was the key to the labor future. If the company won, the CIO campaign was all but finished. If the CIO won, then open-shop employers would have to accept unions. Both sides threw all the resources they could muster into the struggle. There was, however, one resource denied the company that employers previously had always counted on—the unlimited use of public authority, including armed forces. Local authorities cooperated with the company, but their efforts proved futile. The National Guard was sent in, but Governor (and later Supreme Court Justice) Frank Murphy banned their use as strikebreakers. It was clear that the White House would not sanction the use of federal troops against the strike.

In the meantime, the Flint sit-downers held firm against all efforts to dislodge them, and Lewis used his contacts in Wall Street and his influence in the White House to bring pressure to bear on General Motors. Finally, in February 1937, the sit-downers triumphantly ended their forty-four-day occupation of the plants when General Motors granted union recognition in all of the seventeen striking plants. The union victory established the United Automobile Workers as a permanent and powerful union. It also resulted in a new wave of worker revolt and some major CIO successes.

One such success came without even a threat of direct confrontation. In March 1937, U. S. Steel, long a leader of open-shop forces, signed an agreement with the CIO. The pact recognized the union and made numerous concessions on wages and working conditions. While a perplexed public asked questions and open-shop employers fumed, delighted steel workers signed union cards by the thousands.

Middle-class liberals and workers alike rejoiced at the change in U. S. Steel's policy, for it indicated that at least some elements in big business were prepared to accept mass unionism as permanent. What was not so apparent at the time was that in making peace with labor these elements were seeking to influence the course of union development. Alarmed by the spread of militancy, by the sit-down strikes, and by the rise of radicals to power in situations of confrontation, some business elements felt it wise to avoid confrontation. They also sought to encourage conservative leadership, which would control the membership firmly and check the spread of radical sentiment. Myron Taylor and Ben Fairless of U. S. Steel knew from experience that Lewis and Philip Murray, Lewis's trusted lieutenant and head of the steel drive, were just such men. Thus the secret negotiations between them resulted in the momentous announcement of union recognition.

While many employers followed the lead of U. S. Steel, the five big companies that made up "Little Steel" adhered to traditional open-shop policies. A strike resulted in May 1937, and companies responded with standard strikebreaking methods. The antiunion campaign reached a bloody climax in the so-called Memorial Day Massacre, when South Chicago police attacked peaceful, unarmed strikers. Ten workers were killed and scores wounded and maimed. The strike collapsed. The CIO turned to the National Labor Relations Board for redress, but the case dragged on for years.

Defeat in Little Steel, together with failure of CIO campaigns to organize southern textile workers, contributed to a drastic slowdown in the CIO's growth. The unions took a hard blow when the United States Supreme Court took away one of labor's most effective methods by outlawing sit-down strikes. Further, there was increasing friction between Lewis and other CIO founders. David Dubinsky, leader of the women's garment union, rejoined the AFL. Sidney Hillman of the men's garment union stayed in the CIO, although critical of some Lewis policies. Relations between Lewis and the White House became strained after Lewis publicly denounced Roosevelt for failing to condemn the Memorial Day Massacre. In 1940 Lewis opposed Roosevelt's reelection. When CIO members refused to follow his lead, he resigned as CIO president, to be succeeded by Philip Murray.

Meanwhile, employers who could not maintain the open shop but wanted no dealings with CIO unions turned to the AFL. Since the Wagner Act made it illegal for employers to interfere in the workers' choice of unions, they covertly assured AFL union leaders of at least their benevolent neutrality in organizing campaigns. At the same time, some unions, such as the machinists and teamsters, quietly transformed themselves into industrial unions on the CIO model and embarked on vigorous membership drives. After 1939 preparations for war and the war itself provided another boon for AFL unions, since the federal government provided a virtual monopoly on construction jobs to AFL building-trades unions. In 1940 the AFL's membership exceeded the CIO's—4.2 million to 3.6 million. The AFL kept the lead in later years.

Workers generally fared well during World War II. In return for a no-strike pledge that was faithfully respected by nearly all unions (except coal miners in 1943), the federal government pursued a benevolent policy toward unions. Decisions of the War Labor Board and other agencies helped unions in their efforts to recruit and keep members. Even Little Steel felt the pressures and accepted the CIO steel union in 1942. Thus, in 1945 union membership amounted to more than 35 percent of the nonfarm labor force, compared to 27 percent in 1940.

Union workers were better off financially than ever before. Wages and prices were controlled by government, and wage rates tended to lag behind price raises; nevertheless, workers prospered. Two factors were at work. One was the large amount of overtime work paid for at premium rates. In terms of purchasing power, the average weekly wage was 50 percent higher in 1944 than in the late 1930s. The other factor was the emergence of large numbers of two-income families as wives joined the labor force. Since consumer goods were in short supply, workers invested in war bonds and otherwise saved their money. Their savings made them affluent to a degree they had not thought possible just a few years before.

Not all workers benefited. Farm workers, mostly black and Mexican American, shared little of the new prosperity. Nor did families where fathers had been drafted. The government allotments for such families were so inadequate that mothers were compelled to work. Even then they were hard pressed to make ends meet, for they tended to concentrate in low-wage occupations.

EBB OF MILITANCY

Given the upward mobility of many union members out of the working poor, labor militancy probably would have declined in any case, but its decline was hastened by developments after 1945.

One was the Cold War and its domestic expression in McCarthyism, which equated dissent with disloyalty. Unions eager to prove their patriotism purged their ranks of Communists and others identified with Left militant groups. The purged workers lost their jobs as well as their union cards. The CIO expelled ten national unions on charges they were dominated by Communists. Most of these unions found their way back into organized labor, minus their radical leadership. Some, such as the United Electrical Workers and the Longshoremen's Union of the West Coast, survived as independent organizations. Ironically, by 1970 the longshore union, headed by Harry Bridges, who had long been attacked as a "Communist," was hailed as a model of labor statesmanship. A major casualty of the Cold War was the American Labor party of New York, headed by Congressman Vito Marcantonio. Intended as the forerunner of a national party of the Left, it showed potential as a major force in

New York state politics. Attacked from without and torn by dissension within, the party disappeared.

The labor Left also felt pressure from government. The Taft-Hartley law denied the benefits of the Wagner Act to any union whose officers refused to sign affidavits affirming they were not Communists. Its terms were so sweeping that even some conservatives like Philip Murray refused to sign. Eventually, like the radical Harry Bridges of the West Coast longshoremen, they were forced to sign to protect their unions. Among rank-and-file workers employed in defense industries, loyalty tests were so stringent as to discourage any expression of dissent lest it be interpreted as sympathy with Communism.

Meanwhile, leaders of the Communist party were sent to prison for violation of the Smith Act of 1940, a law designed to stamp out revolutionary doctrines. The Communists were not the first to experience the law's repression. At the outbreak of World War II the Trotskyite leaders of the Teamsters Union in Minneapolis were imprisoned under the act.

Also contributing to decline of labor militancy was the emergence of the welfare state, in which government assumed a major role in regulating the economy. In this new era federal policy fostered nonradical unionism as contributing to both economic stability and social peace. Disputes that might have flared into strikes were now referred to such government agencies as the National Labor Relations Board, upon which unions became increasingly dependent. Further, the importance of government as a source of jobs in public works and defense industries encouraged union members to approve the policies that provided the jobs.

With some exceptions, such as the southern cotton textile industry, management accepted the new era of labor relations. Recognizing the imperatives of the welfare state and the changed climate of opinion, industrialists abandoned old-fashioned union busting and strikebreaking. When major strikes did occur, employers simply closed down their plants and settled down to a test of wills. In the meantime, both sides sought to influence the federal government and public opinion. There was little of the violence and bloodshed that had so long marked American labor history.

Other considerations also entered into the changed attitudes of business. During wartime collaboration, many executives found that their CIO counterparts were not the irresponsible fanatics they had pictured. Also, the war industries had found it easier to get approval of increased prices on contracts if they could attribute them to higher labor costs. The practice carried over into peacetime. Each round of wage increases was accompanied by price increases that were blamed on labor. In fact, industry found wage increases a way to raise prices and increase profits. Thus, in 1946, a settlement in steel costing $185 million was used to justify a price increase amounting to $435 million.

Union leaders did little to challenge the practice and the poor public image of labor it projected. Walter Reuther of the United Automobile Workers, however, posed such a challenge in 1946 when he insisted that General Motors could raise wages without increasing prices and demanded that the company open its books for inspection. He received little support from other union leaders. Most of them, like Philip Murray, president of the CIO and of the United Steelworkers, adhered to the traditional view that corporate pricing policies were not a proper subject for collective bargaining. After a prolonged strike Reuther had to settle for a standard agreement providing wage increases but no concessions on pricing policy.

Also contributing to management's new attitudes was the realization that in the welfare state labor's political influence was important. Business policies that might encounter skepticism in the White House and in Congress received more favorable attention when they were backed by union leaders and members. Thus, employers confronted by foreign competition and by environmentalist groups found valuable allies in the unions. Likewise, industries involved in defense contracts could count on union support for expanded Pentagon budgets. Labor unions thus became an integral part of the industrial-military complex against which President Eisenhower warned the nation in 1961.

Perhaps the single most important factor making for labor peace, however, was the long era of prosperity that began after World War II and continued into the 1970s. Although there were several minor recessions, the economy expanded rapidly. There was work for more people. Between 1940 and 1970 the labor force increased from 56 million people to 86 million. Millions of the newcomers were married women, contributing a second income to their families. Such incomes often meant affluence for working-class families, for the real earnings of wage earners increased in the 1950s and 1960s.

Workers also won a larger measure of protection against the hazards of life than ever before. Many union contracts provided for free hospitalization and medical care, as well as old-age pensions to supplement social security. Some major unions also won employer-financed unemployment benefits to supplement the low unemployment insurance payments provided by government. Millions of workers, too, were protected against inflation by contracts that awarded them automatic wage increases as the cost of living rose. Such gains contributed to a growing mood of conservatism among blue-collar workers.

More indirect in its influence toward social peace was the GI Bill of Rights of 1944, which among other things subsidized higher education for veterans. The several billion dollars spent by the federal government helps explain the jump from 157,000 college degrees granted in 1946 to nearly 500,000 in 1950. All veterans benefited, of course, but for tens of thousands of talented working-class young it meant entry into business and the professions. Upwardly mobile, they identified with the middle class, and their parents were proud of their children's achievements. Indeed, the parents themselves took on a distinctly middle-class look as they moved in increasing numbers from their old ethnic urban neighborhoods into suburbia.

Despite its gains, organized labor lost ground among workers and the general public after World War II. Merger of the AFL and CIO into the AFL-CIO in 1955 led to widespread expectations of a new era of labor activism that proved groundless. Despite successful organizing efforts among public employees and other white-collar workers, union membership did not keep pace with the expanding labor force. In 1945 more than 35 percent of nonfarm workers were union members; in 1970, only 27 percent. In terms of numbers, organized labor was relatively no stronger in 1970 than it had been in 1940.

There was a difference, however. In 1940 unions enjoyed a large measure of public support. By 1970 that support had largely dissipated. In the absence of a sustained and concerted union effort to state labor's case, most Americans came to believe industry claims that inflation was due primarily to increased labor costs. Further, organized labor seemed barren of ideas to deal with the problems raised by automation, the emergence of conglomerate corporate forms, the spread of multinational companies, and urban blight. The coalition of labor, liberals, and blacks that had played an active role in the civil rights struggles of the 1960s began to disintegrate when unions resisted efforts to end union racist practices.

Other developments, too, helped lower labor's public reputation. Officials of the United Mine Workers were convicted of murdering Joseph Yablonski, a candidate for the union's presidency. James R. Hoffa, former president of the Teamsters who served a term in federal prison, mysteriously disappeared in 1975 after he indicated his ambition to regain union leadership. Corruption was revealed in the administration of union welfare and pension funds, most notably in the Teamsters. The AFL-CIO as such had little connection with these events. Indeed, in 1975 it had expelled the Teamsters and some other unions for racketeering. Nevertheless, the public made little distinction between the misdeeds of individual unions and organized labor as a whole.

Some policies of organized labor alienated potential friends. Collaboration with the Central Intelligence Agency in secret operations abroad, fervent support of the war in Indochina, antagonism to the candidacy of Senator George McGovern in 1972, and hostility to environmental reforms that might cost jobs—all these combined to isolate labor from middle-class reformers and student activists.

Organized labor's conservative policies did not enhance its political influence. On the contrary. The Taft-Hartley Law of 1947 was followed by the Landrum-Griffith Act of 1959, which further restricted union activity. Attempts to remove the restrictions applying to construction unions were decisively defeated in Congress in 1977. More ominous was the Senate's blocking in 1978 of amendments to the original Wagner Act designed to prevent antiunion employers from using loopholes in the law to thwart organization of their workers. In the meantime, at least twenty states, mostly in the South and Southwest, passed "right to work" laws that outlawed union shops and otherwise hindered union organization. Numerous employers opened plants in such states, taking advantage not only of the antiunion climate of opinion but also of wage scales lower than those of the North.

PERSISTENCE OF POVERTY

Not all working people shared in the affluence of the postwar era. High wages and other benefits gained through union contracts were enjoyed largely by workers in highly unionized major industries. Others did not fare so well, and many still lived in poverty. Despite the federal programs directed against poverty during the administration of President Lyndon B. Johnson, there were still in 1970 more than 10 million families whose income was less than $5,000 a year. Several million more lived just above the poverty line. Such people were extremely vulnerable to the ongoing inflation, for they usually lacked the protection of union contracts that assured them automatic wage raises to compensate for increased living costs.

Poor people, then, were still a substantial part of the American population in 1970, just as they had been in 1900. There were differences, however, between the poor of the two eras. The working poor of 1900 included most white workers in industry. In 1970 that was no longer true, although there was still a minority of white working people who lived in poverty. The working poor of the 1970s were largely blacks and people of other minorities. They worked at low-wage jobs in farming, hospitals and like institutions, and in the garment and similar industries. In addition to low wages, they were plagued with unemployment, illness, poor housing, and the prospect of dead-end lives. Their children received inadequate schooling, which in effect also condemned them to dead-end lives in a society geared to technological advance. There were, of course, outlets for individuals, just as there had been earlier. Sports heroes, entertainment stars, and overlords of crime made it out of poverty into the big time.

There were also in 1970 several million people who might be called the non-working poor. They included the elderly who had to live on Social Security or on other inadequate retirement plans. In 1970, 2.5 million aged couples received Social Security benefits averaging less than $2,400 a year, and 3 million aged widows each received slightly more than $1,200 annually. Not all Social Security recipients were in need, of course, but many who had been part of the working poor were in dire straits. They had worked at low-wage jobs that permitted little saving, and they received the smallest Social Security benefits. Such folk had to supplement their income through public assistance.

Also among the nonworking poor were people who wanted work but could not find it—and indeed despaired of finding it. They were the poverty-ridden residents of Appalachia, whose plight was publicized again and again. They were the rural migrants to cities, black and white alike, possessing none of the skills called for by an urban labor market, doomed to marginal employment at best. They were the men and women over forty who possessed such skills but lost their jobs through automation, plant closures, and competition from abroad. For such folk the chances of reemployment were slim. For the nonworking poor, as for many of the working poor, welfare provided the means of survival.

FOR FURTHER READING

A highly readable survey is Thomas R. Brooks, *Toil and Trouble: A History of American Labor* (1971). The drama of the union struggle is told in Sidney Lens, *The Labor Wars* (1973). More scholarly works include Irving Bernstein's two works, *The Lean Years* (1960) and *The Turbulent Years* (1970), which cover developments from 1920 to 1941.

For the impact of the depression of the 1930s, see Dixon Wecter, *The Age of the Great Depression, 1929–1941* (1948); Caroline Bird, *The Invisible Scar* (1966); and Studs Terkel, *Hard Times* (1970).

On the steel strike of 1919, see William Z. Foster, *The Great Steel Strike and Its Lessons* (1920), and David Brody, *Labor in Crisis* (1965). The sit-down strikes of the 1930s are described from different viewpoints by Sidney Fine, *Sit Down: the General Motors Strikes of 1936–1937* (1969), and Henry Kraus, *The Many and the Few* (1947).

Biographies and autobiographies provide their

own insights. See, for example, Len DeCaux, *Labor Radical: From the Wobblies to the CIO* (1970); Wyndham Mortimer, *Organize: My Life as a Union Man* (1971); David J. McDonald, *Union Man* (1969); Saul Alinsky, *John L. Lewis: An Unauthorized Biography* (1949); Matthew Josephson, *Sidney Hillman: Statesman of American Labor* (1952); and Frank Cormier and William J. Eaton, *Reuther* (1970). A valuable interpretive study of labor leaders of the industrial and postindustrial eras is Charles Madison, *American Labor Leaders* (1950).

Affluent middle-class America "rediscovered" poverty in Michael Harrington's now classic work, *The Other America* (1962).

24

sexism, feminism, and the changing roles of women

In 1920, after ratification of the Nineteenth Amendment, Carrie Chapman Catt assured her suffragist followers that women were now "free and equal citizens." In 1975 a "new feminist," Jo Freeman, decried the "sexism" that she said embodies "the particular kind of oppression" women continued to experience. These two perceptions indicate the contradictory history of women in postindustrial America.

SUFFRAGISTS AND FLAPPERS

The belief of many suffragists that, given the vote, women would vote as a cohesive bloc to improve the quality of American life soon proved baseless. It was rooted in a naive notion that women as such were more devoted than men to the nurturing and improving of life. It followed, then, that voting women would unite to end social evils and make America a more humane society. In the process, politics would be purified and America would point the way toward a new world order without war.

In fact, of course, women as well as men were products of their society and culture. Considerations of class, race, and party proved more potent than appeals to women's unity, even among those few who took part in public life. In practice, many women proved indifferent to voting and others followed the advice of family males. By 1925 politicians who had accepted social-reform measures because they feared a united bloc of women voters realized that their fears were unfounded. They reverted to form, promising women's organizations much and giving little.

The politicians were also reacting to the temper of the prosperous 1920s. The prevalent indifference to social reform was shared by many women, especially young women. It was the era of the "flapper"—the young woman with short hair, short skirts, and boyish figure who smoked, drank, swore, and horrified her elders by unconventional sexual behavior. In short, she was more concerned with personal affairs than with social issues. The young college woman of 1900 had looked toward personal independence and a career, preferably in "social service." Her successor of the 1920s looked toward marriage, home, and children. The feminist movement had lost its recruits.

The flapper reflected changes in society. The college woman was no longer a symbol of feminist revolt. Indeed, so many young middle-class women went to college that it was now normal rather than exceptional. Social service was no longer a challenge because it was now accepted and professionalized. The high hopes engendered by the war to "save the world for democracy" had turned into disillusionment. The need of the postindustrial economy for a mass market produced an emphasis on immediate gratification of wants, ranging from cosmetics to automobiles.

In sexual terms, the emphasis on gratification was reinforced by Freud, whose teachings, as popularly understood, became quite the vogue. His ideas provided medical and scientific sanction for rejecting traditional inhibitions. Freud's recognition of women's sexual needs represented a step toward women's sexual liberation, but his teaching that "anatomy is destiny" actually reinforced the traditional view that woman's place was in the home. At the time, this nuance was little understood. Young women looked upon Freud as a liberator.

The revolt of the "flaming youth," as they were known, dismayed not only conservative elders but also stalwart feminists of another day. Jane Addams reacted unfavorably to what she saw as the "astounding emphasis upon sex." Charlotte Perkins Gilman was offended by Freud, by what she thought was declining respect for chastity among young women, and by their indifference to social responsibility.

At the time, most observers failed to realize that the so-called sexual revolution was partly illusory so far as women were concerned. It often meant the substitution of one set of inhibitions for another.

In an earlier day, young women had a relatively simple code to follow in their relations with men: no demonstration of emotion, no close physical contact. In the 1920s, however, girls were expected to "pet" or "neck," without permiting actual intercourse. This imposed on young women the responsibility for inhibiting their own responses and for controlling those of men in highly charged emotional situations.

Such burdens had consequences in marriage. Young women accustomed to inhibiting themselves found it difficult to adjust to a role in which they were supposed to discard inhibitions, for free expression of sex in marriage was also part of the "revolution." Such conflicts, together with increased reluctance to accept unhappy marriages, help explain the rapid rise in divorces during the 1920s. To meet the problem, Judge Ben Lindsey of the Denver Juvenile Court recommended "companionate marriage," a relationship during which a couple would learn to live together before undertaking permanent marriage and producing children. His book, which appeared in 1927, aroused a storm of protest, but its popularity showed how much American opinion on family matters had changed in little more than a generation.

Young women were not the only ones to turn away from social concerns. The General Federation of Women's Clubs, which had finally endorsed women's suffrage in 1914, now emphasized the domestic roles of women. Likewise, the League of

Women Voters, the successor to the suffrage movement, undertook noncontroversial educational activities designed to produce a well-informed electorate. Even so, it attracted only a fraction of the 2 million women who had been active at the height of the suffrage campaign. The National Federation of Business and Professional Women's Clubs, founded in 1919, dedicated itself to improving the standing of women in business and the professions while ignoring the basic social and cultural factors that relegated women to inferior status.

Not all women, of course, abandoned public concerns. Jane Addams and Emily Balch continued to devote themselves to pacifism. Florence Kelley was a leader in the struggle for a constitutional amendment outlawing child labor. Doctor Alice Hamilton, at Harvard Medical School, carried on her pioneering work in occupational diseases. Grace Abbott, head of the federal Children's Bureau, and Mary Anderson, chief of the Women's Bureau, strove to protect the interests of children and working women. Frances Perkins, a former worker at Hull House, became chief of the New York State Department of Labor. Such women, however, were all products of an earlier generation, out of tune with the prevailing sentiments of the 1920s.

Women reformers were targets of a new kind of attack during the Red Scare of the 1920s. They were accustomed to being assailed as enemies of the home and family, but they were quite unprepared for accusations that they were enemies of their country. A committee of the New York legislature, an army general, and numerous patriotic organizations charged that women's reform organizations were part of a "Bolshevist plot" to make America communist. Jane Addams was called the "most dangerous woman in America" and "the reddest of the red." Florence Kelley was labeled a Communist because she crusaded against child labor. Hull House and the federal Children's Bureau were singled out as centers of "the most radical movements." The media of the day gave wide currency to such charges. The hysteria doubtless caused many women to avoid associating with movements for social reform.

Although women's interest in public concerns declined, more women than ever were moving out of the home into the labor force; the rate of such movement was, however, less than that of earlier decades. In 1920 women made up 20 percent of the labor force; in 1930 they represented 22 percent. More significant was the sharp rise in the employment of married women—in 1930 nearly 12 percent of married women worked outside the home. This change was less a sign of emancipation than of economic necessity. The highest proportion of working wives was in the poverty-stricken South.

Nor was the nature of female employment indicative of emancipation. As before, most women were in traditional, low-wage, dead-end jobs in domestic service, factories, offices, and stores. Unions generally continued to be indifferent to them. Professional and business women were also concentrated in such traditional women's fields as schoolteaching, library work, nursing, social work, and high-level secretarial work. During the decade the number of women doctors and dentists actually declined, and women lawyers made up only 2 percent of the profession in 1930.

Such declines were in part attributable to changing attitudes of college women, but they were also due to the policies of professional schools. Some did not admit women at all, and others imposed rigid admission quotas on women. Even when admitted, women were made to feel unwelcome. Journalism afforded an expanding field for women, but here too they were usually given assignments relating to women. In all fields women were paid considerably less than men doing similar work, and their chances of promotion were slight. These policies were followed not only by private business but also by educational institutions and government.

DEPRESSION AND THE NEW DEAL

That the "economic emancipation" of women was more apparent than real was demonstrated during the depression of the 1930s. As unemployment and distress mounted, old beliefs that women should not compete in the labor market took on new vitality. Despite all the evidence to the contrary, the notion still persisted that single women worked only for "pin money" and that married women did not need to work. Many local governments fired married women, as did many school boards. For a time the federal government banned employment of married couples, causing many wives to lose their jobs.

At the same time, men began invading traditional women's fields of teaching, librarianship, and social work. When the depression began, men felt the impact of unemployment more than women in low-wage jobs, but as the years went by, women began to suffer from joblessness more than men. Women who kept their jobs saw their wages reduced and their working conditions worsen. Teachers experienced still another problem. As school boards went bankrupt, they either closed the schools or kept them open by not paying the teachers. In Chicago, for example, teachers received no salaries for over a year.

The depression altered family relationships. Many men lost meaning in their lives along with their jobs. They also lost their traditional status as breadwinners for their families. The psychological trauma deepened when wives became breadwinners and assumed the authority that accompanied such status. While many men accommodated themselves to the reversal in sex roles, others could not and deserted their families.

Not all of the many desertions can be ascribed to this frustration, however. Many fathers of hungry families deserted in the hope that their families would receive more consideration from welfare authorities. The same consideration for family—"There will be one less mouth to feed"—prompted thousands of adolescents to take to the highways and railroads in search of handouts or jobs. Among them were about 200,000 girls.

The depression era also saw the liberation of many women from the burden of unwanted children. The birth rate fell drastically. In 1938 there were 1.6 million fewer children under age ten than in 1933. The decline was due in part to postponing marriage. But that is not the whole story, for during the decade premarital sex increased. Such sex was not the flamboyant "sexual revolution" of the 1920s but an attempt to find some measure of meaning and security in an uncertain world. The participants hoped to marry each other and raise families.

The explanation for the declining birth rate lies largely in the availability of birth control. Even in the 1920s there had been a vast black market in contraceptives. In the 1930s the market was legalized. Courts held that doctors could lawfully pre-

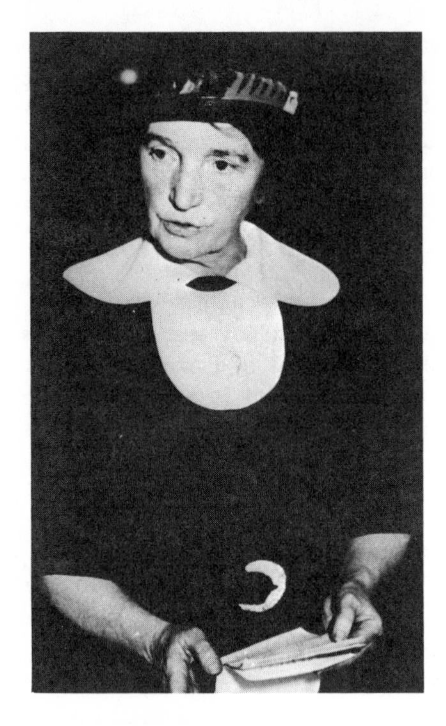

Margaret Sanger, pioneer of the birth control movement, appealed to a United States Senate committee in the 1930s to legalize birth control information.

The Bettman Archive, Inc.

scribe contraceptive devices and that such devices and related information could be shipped legally. By 1940 only two states—Connecticut and Massachusetts—prohibited dissemination of birth control information and there the laws were evaded routinely. In the new era of legality, the birth control cause flourished. In 1930 there had been only twenty-eight birth control clinics in the country; in 1941 there were 746. Birth control had become respectable, as attested by its overwhelming support in public opinion polls. Margaret Sanger, who had been reviled in 1914, was hailed in 1941 as a public benefactor.

Women reformers had been in bad repute in the 1920s, but they came into their own in the New Deal. Hundreds of such women were appointed to high office in the Roosevelt administration, some setting precedents of attainment. Frances Perkins, the new secretary of labor, was the first woman cabinet member. Justice Florence Allen of the Ohio Supreme Court became the first woman to serve on a federal circuit court of appeals. Ruth Bryan Owen and Florence J. Harriman were the first woman ambassadors to foreign countries. Mary Dawson was the first woman to wield real power within the Democratic party.

This recognition of women was largely the work of Eleanor Roosevelt, the first presidential wife since Abigail Adams to promote actively the cause of women. Her concerns, however, went far beyond governmental posts for women. She publicly identified herself with the working poor, and especially with the needs of women and children. In consequence, she won a huge and devoted following, a fact of political importance that did not escape the attention of her husband and of Jim Farley, the national boss of the Democratic party. As a figure of compassion she was a vote-getter—and because she got votes, her influence was accepted.

Women benefited not only from New Deal emergency relief measures but also from long-range reforms. The National Labor Relations Act assured them the right to join unions. The Fair Labor Standards Act provided a standard forty-hour week, overtime pay, and national minimum wages, and it outlawed child labor in industry. The Social Security Act provided for unemployment insurance, aid to dependent children, and old-age pensions.

Since the laws were based on traditional sex roles, however, they were structurally biased against women. The labor relations law left the application of the principle of equal pay for equal work to unions, and unions tended to accept inferior pay scales for women. Since the labor standards law applied only to those employed in business in interstate commerce, it excluded farm workers, domestic servants, waitresses, and women in similar low-wage occupations. Many such workers were not eligible for Social Security. The law also tied pensions to wages, with the result that even those women covered by the law tended to receive minimum and inadequate pensions. Even so, the measures represented significant steps toward protecting working women, and later amendments removed some of the inequities.

WOMEN AND WAR

World War II brought a drastic change in women's roles. During the 1930s women were told to stay out of the labor market. Now they were told it was their patriotic duty to leave the home for the factory. Women responded. Between 1940 and 1945 the number of women workers rose from 13 million to 19 million, accounting for nearly 30 percent of the total labor force. Of these workers, nearly half were married, many of them mothers. While the federal government encouraged mothers to work, it made no provision for care of their children. Only reluctantly, and only after child neglect had become a national scandal, did the government in 1943 provide child care centers. The program was inadequate, however, reaching only 100,000 of the 1 million youngsters who needed such care.

Lack of provision for care of children pointed up the double burden borne by working mothers: they worked long hours in factories yet were still expected to do housework and take care of their children. In addition, many suffered from discrimination in pay. Early in the war the War Labor Board established the principle of equal pay for equal work and enforced it in some instances. Later, however, a wage-stabilization program was applied in such a way as to lock countless women into inferior wage scales.

The working women of World War II were not as timid about unions as their predecessors. The CIO campaigns of the 1930s had brought many women into the labor movement, but during the war the number of women union members increased 400 percent. Despite their numbers, few women won posts of national leadership, although many did gain valuable experience as shop stewards and local union leaders. The failure was not altogether due to male hostility. Many women were indifferent. Others who were interested lacked experience in union affairs. Overworked mothers had little time or energy for union work. Finally, the prevailing sentiment that women were in the shops only for the duration of the war discouraged their participation in union affairs.

Perhaps the most dramatic example of the changing roles of women was their admission to the armed services for the first time in American history. Pressure from women's organizations and the urgent need for personnel overcame the objections of traditionally minded military leaders and of civilians fearful for the morals of women in uniform. In 1942 the Army accepted women for noncombatant service, and the other services followed suit. By the end of the war 250,000 women had enlisted. They posted such a good record that the various women's services were made permanent after the war. This development opened up new careers for women, especially for college graduates who constituted the officers' corps of the new services.

Whatever problems they encountered, most women workers enjoyed economic independence for the first time in their lives. Various polls indicated that these women wanted to continue working after the war. When peace came, however, women lost their jobs in large numbers. Some such unemployment was inevitable when war plants closed down entirely. But in plants that converted to peacetime production, layoffs among women were disproportionately large. Demobilized soldiers and sailors did reclaim their old jobs—a right set forth in law and approved by public opinion. In other cases, however, women with more seniority than men were laid off while the men kept their jobs.

Most unions proved indifferent to the protests of their women members. Women who were still employed found themselves victims of job and pay discrimination. Employers now avoided sexual classification of jobs, but the new terminology could not alter the fact that women were restricted to the lowest wage categories. Few unions challenged the practice.

THE FEMININE MYSTIQUE

Not all women were unhappy about the transition from factory to home. Many wives and mothers, burdened by feelings of guilt about neglecting their children and tired of their double load of housework and factory labor, were glad to go back to the traditional role of homemaker. Soldiers' wives who had been forced into war work by necessity welcomed their husbands and their own return to the home. Single women looked to the return of their soldier-lovers to establish their own homes.

The tensions of years of war, hard work, and separation found release among both men and women in seeking emotional security in the forms of home, family, and return to traditional sex roles. Public opinion polls showed that young couples now wanted four children—in contrast with the two thought desirable in the 1930s. Such a climate of feeling produced what Betty Friedan, pioneer of the new feminism, later called "the feminine mystique."

The mystique combined old and new themes. The old stressed the true role of woman as homemaker and mother. The new emphasized woman's role in providing sexual satisfaction for her husband and herself—indeed, the wife was assigned primary responsibility for meeting the husband's sexual needs. So, in addition to being homemaker and mother, the wife had to be sexually alluring and active. The message was carried by the media, especially by mass-circulation women's magazines. Educators took up the cry. College women were advised to abandon intellectual pursuits and learn the arts of cooking and housekeeping. High-school girls were told to avoid academic competition with boys if they expected to marry. These influences took their power from a public mood that sought in home and family some measure of security after a generation of depression and war.

That mood affected behavior. The marriage rate rose. Couples married earlier. The rising birth rate turned into a "baby boom" in the 1950s. Although more and more women entered college in the 1950s, the number of graduates remained fairly stable, indicating that many were dropping out of school to get married. Relatively few young women showed interest in entering the professions, except for teaching. Many worked as secretaries and teachers to help husbands get through college and professional schools.

There was a more sinister aspect of the mystique—the scapegoating of women for the presumed ills of American men. Philip Wylie, a popular novelist, blamed "momism," or overprotective motherhood, for what he saw as young men's undue dependence on women. Psychologists solemnly asserted that American women were bent on "castrating" American men. In 1947 Ferdinand Lundberg and Maryiana Farnham attributed the problems of men and women to feminism. Feminism, they said, made women neurotic and provoked them to vent their spleen on men. To such people the solution was simple: get women out of the job market, return them to the home, and teach them the value of motherhood—backed up with cash bonuses for each child born.

The popularity of the feminine mystique did not prevent married women from leaving home for office, store, and factory in record numbers. By 1952 more women were at work than during World War II, and the trend continued. In 1972 more than 33 million women worked outside the home, making up 37 percent of the labor force and nearly 44 percent of women of working age. The old stereotype of the working woman as young and single was no longer valid, for most of the women were older and married, many of them with teenage children.

This change pointed to a change in motives for working. In earlier eras, white and black women had worked from sheer economic necessity. In the new era most black women and some white women continued to work to survive, but increasing numbers of white women worked for a second income to provide their families with relative affluence. For the women themselves, such employment provided them with a sense of personal independence and with more voice in family councils. Further, working mothers gave their daughters role models of women active outside the home.

There was little outcry against the advent of mothers in the labor market. They contributed to family upward mobility. They were not perceived as threats to traditional sex roles and values. Since unemployment was low, there was no clamor that women kept married men out of jobs. At work, women offered no danger to men because they were confined to traditional women's occupations, which for the most part paid poorly and offered little chance of promotion. Also, public opinion had changed so that it no longer reflected on the father's status as breadwinner if the mother worked. On the contrary, the additional income and its visibility in consumption enhanced the social status of the family as a whole. Nor did working wives present a threat at home. While they had more voice in the family than before, they still tended to fill traditional sex roles. Nevertheless, the acceptance of working wives and mothers eventually weakened old traditions and contributed to the rise of a new militant feminism in the 1960s.

THE NEW FEMINISM

The emergence of a new feminism was signaled with the acclaim that greeted Betty Friedan's *The Feminine Mystique* in 1963. A slashing attack on Freudian theory as it related to women and on the stereotypes of women, the book articulated the hidden resentments and frustrations of many middle-class white women in an age of affluence. That same year women's grievances were set forth more conservatively in a report of a Committee on the Status of Women headed by Eleanor Roosevelt. The report supported traditional views of marriage and motherhood and opposed the Equal Rights Amendment, long sought by Alice Paul, the veteran militant suffragist. However, it also called for an end to all legal and customary discrimination against women and advocated such reforms as government sponsorship of day-care centers for children of working mothers.

Women's responses to these appeals grew out of a sense of grievance, disillusionment with the feminine mystique, and a trend toward viewing themselves primarily as human beings rather than as sexual creatures. Such changes were accelerated by the active participation of many women, especially young women, in the movements of the 1960s. They took part in the "black revolution." They were active in the protests against the war in Southeast Asia. In large numbers women students joined the student revolts on campus, calling for changes in many fields, ranging from curriculum reform to protection of the environment. Many joined Students for a Democratic Society and other organizations of the New Left, which rejected capitalism and called for a more just, humane, and peaceful social order. Even those who did not join radical organizations rejected the values of their parents in favor of simple life-styles.

The crusading spirit of the 1960s was reminiscent of that of the 1840s, when abolitionism enlisted the active support of many northern women. And, just as women abolitionists had been compelled to fight for their rights as women, the women of the 1960s were forced to examine their own role in the protest movements. Those roles were hardly appropriate to movements supposedly dedicated to equality. Women were expected to perform the chores men found distasteful. Few women helped set policies. Some male leaders were crudely sexist even in their public pronouncements about women. The sexism of the male militants inspired rebellious women to turn to feminism.

The rebellion went through two phases. The earlier phase reflected the prevailing youthful distrust of authority and structured organizations. Small groups of women met in informal "rap sessions" dedicated to "consciousness raising." Since such groups were by their nature local and ephemeral, they exercised little influence in attaining practical goals such as day-care centers for children of working women and students. It became clear that some organization was necessary to translate heightened feminist consciousness into action. Such an organization appeared in 1966 under the leadership of Betty Friedan—the National Organization of Women (NOW).

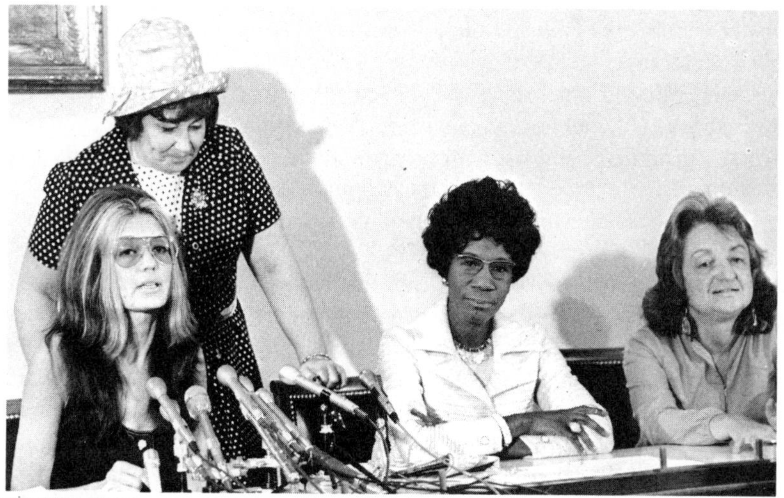

Wide World Photos

One aspect of the militant feminism of the 1970s was the National Women's Political Caucus. Among its leaders were *(left to right)* Gloria Steinem, editor of the magazine *MS*; Bella Abzug and Shirley Chisholm, representatives from New York; and Betty Friedan, whose book *The Feminine Mystique* sparked the rise of the new feminism.

Too many women were involved in what was called the "women's liberation movement" for them all to be of one mind. Some organizations wanted no help from men. Others, such as NOW, welcomed men's aid. Some new feminists looked upon the movement as a way to social revolution. Most preferred reform.

Nevertheless, despite these and other differences, all the feminists of the 1960s had some elements in common. They were much more aware than their predecessors of the pervasive nature of sexism in society, ranging all the way from subtle indoctrination of boys and girls to institutionalized sexism in law, business, labor, churches, and education. While earlier feminists had avoided discussion of sex, the new generation spoke up frankly, even on such issues as lesbianism and abortion. Feminists of 1900 fought for special protective laws for working women. Those of the 1960s, feeling that such laws were oppressive, supported the Equal Rights Amendment, which would annul them. Earlier feminists had stressed the rights of women as women. Those of the 1960s emphasized the rights of women as human beings. And, harking back to the arguments of Mary Wollstonecraft and John Stuart Mill, they pointed out that liberation of women meant also liberation of men from the traditional sex roles that limited their freedom as human beings.

The reformist mood of the era made possible many feminist gains. The civil rights law of 1964 banned not only racial but also sexual discrimination in many areas of American life. The law resulted in "affirmative action" programs designed to implement the goal of equality. Such programs provided an opportunity for women to gain employment and promotion in private business. They also made it possible for more women to enter professional schools, and they enhanced the employment of women as faculty members in colleges and universities. The number of women in the professions rose rapidly.

Women made gains in other areas. Many states legalized abortion in laws upheld by the United States Supreme Court in 1973. That same year Congress approved the Equal Rights Amendment, and within four years it had been ratified by thirty-five states—three short of the number required for adoption. So many women held high public office, including cabinet posts, that the appointments were no longer newsworthy.

In the 1970s, however, the women's movement faced new and serious challenges. Organized religious groups embarked on campaigns to make abortion once again illegal. These merged with other organizations opposing the Equal Rights Amendment. The antifeminist movement met with notable success. The United States Supreme Court ruled that states were not required to use public funds for abortions for women on welfare. Congress followed by outlawing the use of federal funds for such abortions. President Carter took a public stand against abortion, provoking a public protest by many women in his administration. The drive for ratification of the Equal Rights Amendment faltered, and some states "rescinded" previous ratifications. Before he resigned, President Nixon vetoed a measure providing federal assistance to day-care centers, explaining that they would damage the family! FBI Director J. Edgar Hoover, believing that the women's movement was potentially subversive, ordered local groups placed under surveillance.

Perhaps most ominous of all were some United States Supreme Court decisions of 1977. Although based on racial issues, the findings applied equally to women. The court held that while patterns of discrimination might result from actions of public or private bodies, those actions were lawful so long as there was no "intent" to discriminate. The implications of these decisions stirred forebodings among feminists who well knew how difficult it was to prove intent.

Women also suffered from the business recession that began in 1972. As unemployment reached the highest levels since the depression of the 1930s—exceeding 7 percent in 1976—hundreds of thousands of women lost their jobs. Cutbacks in public schools and in some colleges and universities cost many teachers their jobs. Recent college graduates found it difficult to get work, especially if they had been trained as teachers. The growing number of unemployed women and the problems of jobless college women received little attention from public authorities.

These developments underscored some problems of the women's movement. It had no program to deal with such massive social problems as unemployment except to insist on implementation of affirmative-action programs. In the highly competitive job market such insistence embittered men who claimed they were victims of "reverse discrimination." Antifeminist sentiment took on new vitality, especially among unemployed male college graduates. Feminism was attacked by some women, most notably Midge Decter and Phyllis Schafly. At still another level, many women joined new groups that glamorized the housewife and urged her to be "sexy." Many housewives resented what they felt to be the contempt feminists had for "mere" homemakers.

Perhaps of greater significance, the women's movement was still largely white and middle class. While many black and Hispanic women were in sympathy with its goals, they felt it more important at the moment to promote male and female racial solidarity in order to attain liberation of their peoples. Likewise, women active in labor unions felt ill at ease with college graduates and distrusted the abolition of protective legislation for women. The feminist organizations that did emerge in these groups tended to be weak and ineffective.

Women of postindustrial America could record many gains. In view of the conservative trend of the 1970s it appeared questionable to some feminists whether they could make further immediate progress. For women as for men, the future seemed troubled and uncertain.

FOR FURTHER READING

Two good short surveys of women in postindustrial America are Lois W. Banner, *Women in Modern America* (1974), and William Chafe, *The American Woman . . . 1920–1970* (1972). See also William O'Neill, *Everyone was Brave: The Rise and Fall of Feminism in America* (1967), and Andrew Sinclair, *The Better Half: The Emancipation of the American Woman* (1965). For the new feminism, see Judith Holes and Ellen Levine, *Rebirth of Feminism* (1971).

There are now numerous good anthologies of new feminist writings. The following are cited under names of the editors: Leslie B. Tanner, *Voices from Women's Liberation* (1970); Mary C. Lynn, *Women's Liberation in the Twentieth Century* (1975); Wendy Martin, *The American Sisterhood*(1972); and June Sochen, *The New Feminism in Twentieth Century America* (1971). Attitudes of black women are set forth in Toni Cade, ed., *The Black Woman: An Anthology* (1970).

The manifesto of the new feminism is Betty Friedan, *The Feminine Mystique* (1963). Other important works include Caroline Bird, *Born Female: The High Cost of Keeping Women Down* (1968); Kate Millett, *Sexual Politics* (1969); Shulamith Firestone, *The Dialectics of Sex* (1970); Robin Morgan, *Sisterhood is Powerful* (1970); Germaine Greer, *The Female Eunuch* (1971); and Kristen Amundsen, *The Silenced Majority* (1971).

On specific topics see Leo Kanowitz, *Women and the Law* (1969); Robert Smuts, *Women and Work in America* (1959); William J. Goode, *The Family* (1964); Mirra Komarovsky, *Blue Collar Marriage* (1964); and Jessie Bernard, *Academic Women* (1964), and *Women and the Public Interest* (1971).

The successes of the birth control movement are told in Margaret Sanger, *Margaret Sanger* (1938), and more completely in David Kennedy, *Birth Control in America* (1970). The persecution of Jane Addams for her pacifism during World War I is recounted in Allen F. Davis, *American Heroine* (1973).

the new black americans

25

The black experience in postindustrial America was marked by four major developments. One was massive migration from the rural South, so that by 1970 the typical black American lived in a city rather than in the countryside. Another was the migrants' discovery that white racism was national in scope. Third was emergence in the 1920s of the "New Negro," prototype of the proud, militant black of a later generation. Fourth was the civil rights crusade of the 1950s and 1960s, symbolized by Martin Luther King, Jr.

THE BLACK EXODUS

Black urbanization was under way by 1910, but World War I accelerated the process. When northern employers encountered growing labor shortages, they turned to the rural South. Whites and blacks alike were ready to leave, for the recent devastation of the cotton crop by the boll weevil had further impoverished the region. Blacks, too, were glad to escape an oppressive South, especially since they were offered steady jobs at high wages. No one really knows how many went north. Estimates range between 300,000 and 1 million. It is definite, though, that the black population of northern cities increased sharply between 1910 and 1920. Chicago's black citizens increased by 65,000—a rise of nearly 150 percent. Detroit in 1920 reported an additional 36,000 blacks, an increase of more than 600 percent in ten years. Other northern cities showed substantial but less dramatic increases.

The second major wave of urbanization took place in the 1940s, when the needs of war again called for black labor. During the decade the northern black population grew from 2.8 million to more than 4.2 million. In the Far West, the shift was phenomenal; the black population of 571,000 in 1950 was more than three times what it had been in 1940. For the first time, Pacific Coast cities had significant black populations.

A third major wave occurred in the 1950s when technological advances in southern agriculture made thousands of sharecroppers superfluous. Private and public agencies sped them on their way north. By 1964 nearly half of American blacks lived in northern and western cities, and the trend was continuing. In the South, the number of urban blacks continued to increase and that of rural blacks declined. By 1970 the American black was no longer rural but urban—and urban in the setting of the black ghetto. Most of the migrants were poor. Since many could not find employment, they depended on welfare.

Southern migrants during World War I—and some even later—looked upon the North as the promised land. They were eventually disillusioned, for white racism, they found, was not confined to the South. Indeed, in the 1920s the Ku Klux Klan, which had been revived in Georgia in 1915, was a powerful force throughout the country. Its 3 million members waged incessant campaigns against blacks, Catholics, and Jews. Further, migrants often received a chilly welcome from northern blacks who looked upon the newcomers as uncouth and embarrassing. Residential segregation meant that migrants had to live in overcrowded slum quarters for which they paid exorbitant rents. Segregation in housing resulted in segregated schools, which, while better than southern schools, were inferior to those of northern whites.

Blacks suffered in still other ways. Northern police and courts proved hostile. White merchants in the ghettos overcharged for inferior goods and refused to employ black help. Whites, too, resorted to physical violence. In July 1917, while America was at war, whites in East St. Louis, Illinois, killed at least forty blacks in a riot during which the black section of town was burned down. In 1919 there were twenty-five race riots. With the war's end, depression came and blacks were the first to lose their jobs. Even so, few blacks chose to return to the South.

The poor of the ghettos developed a culture of their own, distinct from that of middle-class blacks and from white society. Like the culture of the slave community, it nurtured the black personality and maintained a sense of worth, dignity, and racial community in a hostile and oppressive society. It found expression in many ways—in the social clubs that banded together blacks from the same southern localities, in storefront churches, in dance halls, and in the jazz music that expressed the joy and pathos, the hope and tragedy, of American black experience.

Blacks also confronted a new wave of "scientific racism" after World War I. Eminent scholars such as Henry Pratt Fairchild, a sociologist, and Henry Fairfield Osborn, a paleontologist, for example, attributed racial inferiority to innate deficiencies in intelligence. Fairchild called advocates of racial equality "unscientific" and "dangerous." America's future, he said, depended upon its being "a white man's country for an indefinite period." Even more strident were Madison Grant and Lothrop Stoddard, who reached great audiences of middle-class whites offended by the crude appeals of the Klan. Drawing heavily on the "scientific" evidence of the day, they preached that survival of civilization depended on maintaining "Nordic" supremacy.

THE "NEW NEGRO"

Part of the new ghetto culture was a mood of militancy. Many southern migrants were little disposed to accept the frustration of their expectations, which had been heightened by their brief experience of relative prosperity in wartime. Black soldiers returned embittered by discrimination in the American army and unwilling to accept segregation after living among the racially tolerant French. Some middle-class blacks, such as W. E. B. DuBois, who had supported the war in belief that it would help win equality for blacks, now felt betrayed as white racism reasserted itself and the federal government sided with the racists. Out of such feelings emerged what Alain Locke, black scholar and writer, called the "New Negro"—the real black person, proud of race and demanding equality, as opposed to the mythical "Sambo" and "Uncle Tom."

The new spirit showed itself most dramatically in armed resistance to white rioting in 1919. In Chicago and Washington, D.C., blacks battled whites for days. The toll was greater in Chicago, where fifteen whites and twenty-three blacks died and 178 whites and 342 blacks were injured. Even in the rural South, blacks resisted traditional white supremacy. An attack on a tenant farmers' meeting in Elaine, Arkansas, by sheriff's deputies set off armed warfare in which many whites and blacks lost their lives.

Another sign of new black spirit of the 1920s was the popularity of the black nationalist Garvey movement. The Universal Negro Improvement Association (UNIA), brought to the United States in 1916 by Marcus Garvey, a native of Jamaica, flourished in the ghettos. Garvey attacked light-skinned middle-class blacks, and he praised poor blacks who were racially "pure." "Up, you mighty race," he exhorted such blacks. "You can accomplish what you will." Not in the United States, however. America, he said, was and would remain a white man's country. The only hope for blacks was return to the "land of our fathers"—Africa.

To promote African emigration, Garvey organized the Black Star steamship line, financed by an army of small investors at $5 a share. He proposed to send out black Americans to provide leadership and know-how to Africans and to bring back raw materials. In the meantime, to promote black enterprise and foster black pride, the UNIA established a variety of business projects, including one that was ahead of its time in producing black dolls. Additionally, it sponsored an African Orthodox Church, an African Legion attired in resplendent uniforms, and a Black Cross nurses' corps, and carried on numerous other activities appealing to a wide variety of ghetto interests.

Garveyism as a mass movement claimed 500,000 members at its height, but it proved short-lived. The poorly managed and inadequately financed business ventures collapsed, including the Black Star Line. Garvey's visit to Ku Klux Klan headquarters in 1922, during which he agreed that America would remain a white man's country, endorsed the Klan's stand on "racial purity," and solicited Klan aid for his emigration program, damaged his standing in the black community. His virulent attacks on black middle-class leaders aroused the hostility of the National Association for the Advancement of Colored People (NAACP), W. E. B. DuBois, and Robert S. Abbott, editor of the influential *Chicago Defender*. Garvey blamed these enemies for his conviction on charges of mail fraud. He served two years in prison before his sentence was commuted in 1927 and he was deported to Jamaica. His movement dwindled, but his ideas, especially that of race pride, lived on even after his death in 1940.

The black middle class, disillusioned by postwar events, also reflected the new mood. The NAACP was in the vanguard of numerous organizations that campaigned against white supremacy. In 1922 its crusade against lynching won partial success when the House of Representatives passed a federal antilynching law, but a white southern filibuster blocked its passage in the Senate. The NAACP failed to get the legislation, but its appeal to public opinion did focus national attention on the issue and helped bring about a sharp decline in lynchings during the 1920s.

While the NAACP won some decisions involving racial descrimination before the Supreme Court, its most dramatic case occurred in Detroit in 1925. It undertook the defense of Henry Sweet, accused of murder in connection with a white mob attack on the home of his brother, Doctor O. H. Sweet, in a white section of the city. Clarence Darrow, arguing for the defense, won acquittal—a verdict the more remarkable because of the influence of the Ku Klux Klan among Detroit whites.

The New Negro was also exemplified by the so-called Harlem Renaissance of the 1920s. For the first time black culture was appreciated as important in itself, and large numbers of talented blacks stressed black themes and expressed pride in their own people. Black cultural expression was not new. Earlier there had been such figures as the poet Paul Laurence Dunbar, the novelist Charles W. Chesnutt, and the painter Henry O. Tanner, who was more appreciated in France than in his native land. But they were isolated figures with limited publics, cut off from the larger white cultural community. Not so with the men and women of the 1920s. They were numerous, and in Harlem they came together, stimulating one another to creativity. They had a wide audience, not only among blacks but also among sympathetic middle-class whites.

In consequence, there was an outpouring of black creative expression. Among the most notable of the new talents were Jean Toomer and Jessie Fausset, novelists; Langston Hughes, called the "Shakespeare of Harlem"; Claude McKay, the poet; Paul Robeson, singer and actor; and Aaron Douglas, painter. Jazz, the great American black contribution to music, came into its own in the 1920s. Great musicians such as "Jelly Roll" Morton, Duke Ellington, and Louis Armstrong won national and international reputations. The renaissance declined in the depression of the 1930s, but the seeds of a permanent black cultural community had been planted.

THE BLACK WORKER

There was another New Negro who figured little in black literature or art—the black industrial worker. For the first time, thousands of blacks were firmly established in such major industries as steel, auto, rubber, and meatpacking. They suffered discrimination in wages and working conditions, but they valued their jobs and had no intention of endangering them. Suspicious of white unions, they tended to identify with their employers rather than with white workers—attitudes reinforced by most black preachers, newspapers, and social-service organizations. Failure of blacks to cooperate in the great steel strike of 1919 helps explain defeat of that strike. As in the industrial era, the AFL made little effort to organize black workers, and those who were organized were confined to Jim Crow local unions.

There did emerge in the 1920s an all-black union that, it was hoped, would pioneer mass black unionism. This was the Brotherhood of Sleeping Car Porters and Maids, founded in 1925 and headed by A. Philip Randolph, one of the few black socialists of the day. The union grew rapidly among the employees of the paternalistic Pullman Company, reaching 7,000 by 1928. In that year a strike threat against the company was abandoned, and the union lost more than half its membership. Dissension in the leadership further weakened the organization. In 1936 the union finally was admitted to the AFL, and the following year it won recognition from the Pullman Company. While Randolph went on to become a major figure in the black community, the union itself played only a minor role in the labor movement.

Not until the rise of the CIO did black workers join the mainstream of American labor. Realizing that their goals could not be won without black cooperation and conscious of the black distrust of unions, CIO unions pledged equality for all members and employed black organizers to recruit blacks. Three other factors help explain the black turn to unionism. One was that blacks suffered even more than whites from the wage reductions, speed-up, and unemployment that had come with the depression. The CIO, with its avowed commitment to racial equality, appeared to be a practical step toward wage and job protection. Second, by 1936 black workers believed, as did many whites, that Franklin and Eleanor Roosevelt wanted them to join unions—and the Roosevelts enjoyed the overwhelming confidence of the black community. Third was the unexpected recognition of the CIO steel union in 1937 by the U.S. Steel Corporation. This brought not only immediate gains for thousands of black steel workers but also helped make CIO unionism respectable among many elements of the black community.

Even so, black suspicions remained strong in some places. The most notable example was among the 14,000 black workers at the Ford Motor Company, who feared that a union triumph would mean the loss of their jobs to white workers. The CIO auto union, in fact, had an outstanding record in protecting its black members, but the fears persisted, fanned by the company and its numerous allies among Detroit's middle-class blacks. Eventually, with the help of the NAACP, liberal black preachers, and a staff of black organizers, Ford's black workers were won over. They loyally supported the strike of 1941, which resulted in union recognition. Blacks not only kept their jobs but also shared equally in the gains won by the union.

BLACKS AND THE NEW DEAL

The popularity of the Roosevelts among poor blacks stemmed from a feeling that they had friends in the White House who were deeply concerned with them. Various New Deal programs provided relief and jobs, and while many were applied in discriminatory fashion, millions of blacks no longer faced the daily prospect of hunger. Also, many urban blacks enjoyed good housing for the first time, as new federal housing projects replaced festering slums.

Discrimination still persisted, however. The new Social Security law excluded domestic servants and farm laborers, thus denying millions of blacks its benefits. Likewise, southern sharecroppers and tenant farmers gained little from farm-relief legislation. Many landlords simply appropriated the checks sent sharecroppers and tenants. When that practice was halted, the landlords drove the sharecroppers and tenants off the land and received the benefits themselves. Many of the dispossessed moved north.

Some southern rural blacks fought back, sometimes in collaboration with poor whites. Through unions of sharecroppers and tenant farmers they sought to gain their share of farm-relief benefits and otherwise improve their incomes. They gained concessions from Washington and made some local gains, but on the whole they could not cope with the terrorists and public authorities bent on destroying their organizations.

In the cities, blacks also asserted themselves. They took part in organizations of the unemployed. In addition to helping block evictions of tenants and similar activities they also campaigned to get jobs for blacks in ghetto stores, a campaign that met with resistance from white storeowners. Resentment over the practices of such merchants flared up in a riot in 1935 in Harlem, in which three blacks were killed and property damage exceeded $2 million.

Communism, too, made an appeal to some blacks during the 1930s. The party's militant stand on racial equality attracted such men as James W. Ford and Angelo Herndon, who rose to positions of leadership within the party. The organization's biggest impact came, however, through the famous Scottsboro case. In 1931 nine young blacks, ranging in age from thirteen to twenty, were taken off a freight train in Scottsboro, Alabama, and accused of the rape of two white women traveling on the same train. They were speedily sentenced to death. Communists made the case a national and international issue, including special appeals to American black communities.

Many blacks responded, seeing in Scottsboro a symbol of traditional Southern "justice" that had to be challenged, however reluctant they might be to cooperate with Communists. Eventually, the NAACP, which had held aloof from the case, joined in. There ensued quarrels between rival sets of lawyers, while the accused remained in prison. Nevertheless, as a result of numerous court actions, the death sentences were set aside, and by 1950 the last surviving prisoner was released. Blacks noted that while the accused were not executed, they spent years in prison on the testimony of two women, one of whom repudiated her original testimony, asserting that no rape ever took place, and the other proved evasive and contradictory in later trials.

The Scottsboro case resulted in two major United States Supreme Court decisions. In *Powell* v. *Alabama* (1932) the court declared that defendants accused of capital crimes had to be furnished with adequate counsel at public expense if the accused could not afford such counsel themselves. In 1935, in *Norris* v. *Alabama,* the court held that systematic exclusion of blacks from juries was unlawful, thus striking down a mainstay of white supremacy.

For all their efforts, however, Communists made less of an impression in the ghettos than did a new religious group, the Lost-Found Nation of Islam, popularly known as the Black Muslims. Founded in Detroit by W. D. Fard, a shadowy figure who mysteriously disappeared in the early 1930s, the movement grew steadily under the direction of his successor, Elijah Muhammad. The group's teachings reflected the anger and bitterness of ghetto dwellers. Whites were held to be the incarnation of evil. Christianity was seen as a white man's religion designed to keep blacks in subjection. Allah was allowing whites to destroy themselves, and then the blacks would inherit the earth. The influence of the Nation of Islam went far beyond its numerous converts. The austere, puritanical life style of believers favorably impressed many blacks who did not accept the sect's teachings.

Middle-class blacks generally shunned radical and separatist movements, holding to belief in integration within the existing social order. Their faith was strengthened by New Deal policies that not only brought benefits to blacks but also sharply increased black employment within the federal government, from 50,000 in 1933 to 200,000 in 1946. Most of these were low-level, low-wage jobs, but an unprecedented number of blacks served at high levels. Robert L. Vann, a prominent newspaper editor, was special assistant to the attorney general; William H. Hastie, later a federal judge, was a legal officer in the Department of the Interior; and Mary McLeod Bethune, former college president, directed black affairs in the National Youth Administration. President Roosevelt also consulted frequently with his "black brain trust," an informal body of editors, scholars, social workers, clergymen, and other leaders in the black community. At the same time, black representation in state and local governments in the North increased substantially.

THE INFLUENCES OF WAR

Unemployment remained a basic problem for ghetto dwellers, even after 1939, when the United States undertook a massive rearmament program. As time passed without marked increases in black employment, A. Philip Randolph won enthusiastic response in the black community with his recommendation in 1941 that blacks stage a march on Washington to demand jobs in war plants. President Roosevelt, anxious to preserve national unity as the country drifted toward war, finally headed off the march with an executive order designed to end discrimination in plants holding government contracts.

The Fair Employment Practices Committee (FEPC) set up to implement the order was never adequately financed, and it had no powers of enforcement. In addition, the original order permitted so much evasion that in 1943 it was amended to close off loopholes. Even so, the FEPC spotlighted discrimination through its hearings and publicity, and after Pearl Harbor few employers wanted a public image as enemies of national unity. Partly because of FEPC and partly because of the wartime labor shortage, masses of black men and women were able to get high-wage jobs for the first time in their lives. Blacks from the rural South flocked into northern and western cities to share in the benefits.

The newcomers were not particularly welcome. Established black families looked askance at the life style of the arrivals from the countryside. In the Watts area of Los Angeles there was a veritable exodus of old black families as southern blacks came in to work in war plants. More important was the hostility of whites, many of them southerners influenced by the Klan and similar groups dedicated to white supremacy even in wartime. Such organizations instigated wildcat strikes against the employment and promotion of blacks, in defiance of the no-strike policy of the unions. The most notable of these occurred in Detroit in 1943 when a plant employing 20,000 workers was shut down for a week. Only the combined efforts of the union, the employer, and the federal government brought an end to the stoppage.

That same year, the mounting racial tensions in Detroit exploded in a major race riot. In two days of battle nine whites and twenty-five blacks were killed. Seventeen of the blacks were killed by white police, whom Detroit blacks accused of aiding the white rioters. Order was restored only after 6,000 federal troops were sent to the city.

While black people supplied needed labor for the war effort, nearly another million of them served in the armed forces. Of these, 500,000 went overseas, many in combat units that made distinguished records. Discrimination, while not as flagrant as in World War I, persisted. Racial segregation was standard in all the services. Black soldiers suffered from discrimination not only in nearby towns but also in the camps themselves. When blacks challenged these practices, they were met with repression. In some camps major riots resulted. In 1944 the army ordered an end to discrimination in its camps, but many commanders enforced the order poorly.

The war helped foster changes in black attitudes. To a greater degree than in World War I, large numbers of poor black men and women shared in the good things of American life. They wanted to continue to share in them after the war was over. Black women formerly condemned to domestic service found new independence in war work. Southern blacks who had migrated to northern and western urban centers stayed on after the war, helping to swell the concentration of black population in cities. Returning servicemen felt they had demonstrated not only courage and endurance in combat but also competence in handling the machines and other equipment of a technological society. They were in no mood to accept the traditional roles assigned blacks.

WHITE ATTITUDES CHANGE

White society also changed in the postwar era. White racism was on the defensive. There were none of the massive antiblack riots that had marred the year 1919. The ''scientific'' rationale for white supremacy, which had been widely popularized in the 1920s by such writers as Lothrop Stoddard and Madison Grant, was now discredited. The work of Franz Boas and his students, Ruth Benedict and Margaret Mead, demonstrated that there were no inferior or superior races. There were, of course, different peoples, whose nonphysical differences were cultural, not biological, in origin. Psychologists such as Otto Klineberg repudiated the findings of the psychologists of the 1920s who held that intelligence was a racial characteristic, and they also questioned the validity of the standard IQ tests. The change in white attitudes was reflected in a poll reported by *Scientific American* in 1956. It showed that only about 15 percent of white northerners and 40 percent of white Southerners believed that blacks were by nature less intelligent than whites.

Further, large numbers of white Americans realized that racism had found its extreme and logical expression in the gas chambers of Nazi Germany. Many felt, too, that white supremacy was incompatible with American ideals and with their religious beliefs, whether Christian or Jewish. In addition to moral considerations, more mundane factors were at work. Economists and sociologists argued that racism imposed a major burden on American society in both economic and social costs. Finally, the need to project a favorable image of America during the Cold War prompted public officials to move against institutionalized racism.

The changing black mood and the new white attitudes converged to produce dramatic changes in the postwar years. President Truman abolished segregation in the armed forces, ordered an end to discrimination in federal employment, and set up a committee to prevent job discrimination in private industries. Since Congress was dominated by white southerners who occupied key committee chairmanships, the legislative branch was slow to respond to changes in national opinion. In 1957 it passed the first civil rights law since 1875, providing federal protection for black voting rights and setting up the Civil Rights Commission to monitor violations of the law.

The Supreme Court proved more responsive to the changed climate of opinion. In 1948 it outlawed the restrictive covenants that had long been used to deny good housing to blacks and other minority groups. It went on to ban discrimination in interstate travel and higher education. Its most historic decision was in *Brown* v. *Board of Education of Topeka, Kansas* (1954). In this case the issue of segregation was squarely posed, for both sides agreed that the local black schools were treated equally with white schools. In its decision, the court overturned the "separate but equal" doctrine asserted back in 1896. The court of 1954 held that "separate educational facilities are inherently unequal," and by implication it ordered the integration of all public schools. In other cases, the court, under the leadership of Chief Justice Earl Warren, extended the principle of desegregation to private business as well as public institutions.

If national opinion was receptive to such changes, dominant elements in southern white society were hostile. White Citizens' Councils spread throughout the region, pledged to uphold segregation. Eight states vowed to ignore the Brown decision. Every southern state adopted legislation making it possible for school systems to evade integration. Private schools began to proliferate. Some states intensified and extended their segregation laws. Civil rights organizations, especially the NAACP, were the targets of special laws designed to destroy their effectiveness.

Some whites, not content with legal measures, resorted to violence. Blacks active in civil rights movements were murdered in Mississippi, South Carolina, and Georgia. When Autherine Lucy, a young black woman, was ordered admitted to the University of Alabama in 1956, the white students and residents of Tuscaloosa rioted. Next year President Eisenhower sent federal troops to Little Rock, Arkansas, to maintain order while black children attended a local school pursuant to a federal court order. Through legal and illegal means the white South delayed school integration for years.

White resistance to integration, combined with heightened expectations and the feeling among blacks that gains could be won, produced an upsurge of militancy. Southern blacks took the lead, beginning with the successful boycott of buses in Montgomery, Alabama, in 1956. The boycott technique spread, aimed at merchants active in the White Citizens' Councils. Such actions, however, were localized and confined to specific issues, and thus had little impact on the national consciousness. After 1 February 1960, however, national consciousness focused on black efforts to end white supremacy in the South.

THE BLACK REVOLUTION

On that day black college students initiated what was later called "the black revolution" by staging a sit-in at a segregated lunch counter in Greensboro, North Carolina. This symbolic challenge to traditional white supremacy set off a dramatic campaign throughout the South for civil rights. Black Americans and their white allies—most of them young people—occupied places of public accommodation, organized public demonstrations, and mounted drives to register black voters. They were guided by organizations such as the Southern Christian Leadership Conference, an organization of black churchmen; the Student Non-Violent Coordinating Committee, an interracial group of young militants; and the Congress of Racial Equality, a pacifist interracial group of northern origins. The charismatic leader of the movement was Martin Luther King, Jr., who preached a message of nonviolent resistance to evil, with love, rather than hatred, for the evildoer. His idealism struck a responsive chord among white Americans troubled by racism. Church people and others rallied enthusiastically to the civil rights cause.

Their response was all the stronger because of the sheer violence that met the movement. Peaceful civil rights workers, white and black alike, were clubbed, beaten, and killed. One notorious case that received international attention involved the killing and secret disposal of the bodies of three young people in Mississippi. The bombing of a black church in Birmingham, Alabama, killed four black children. Police of that city used electric goads, whips, and dogs against demonstrators. King himself was jailed in Montgomery and Birmingham, but widespread protests brought about his release. In 1962 whites rioted against the admission of James Meredith, a black student, to the University of Mississippi. Federal marshals restored order.

The violence proved self-defeating. It received so much exposure in the media, especially on television, that there was widespread revulsion against it. Millions of white Americans who otherwise might have remained indifferent to the civil rights crusade now became sympathetic. The wide support for the movement was dramatized in August 1963, when 200,000 black and white Americans gathered in Washington, D.C., in a gigantic demonstration to call for "complete equality in citizenship." The following year, in response to pressures from the White House and public opinion, Congress passed a sweeping civil rights law, committing the federal government to positive action on behalf of minorities. White southerners, in an effort to defeat the measure, offered an amendment extending the bill's protection to women. Congress accepted both the amendment and the bill. In 1965 Congress enacted another law giving the federal government more authority to assure black voting rights. Many states passed similar laws.

The very success of the civil rights movement caused some militant young activists, symbolized by Stokely Carmichael, to doubt its methods and goals. In their view, the laws and court decisions won did not really change the racist character of

American society. Further, the struggle for civil rights was largely irrelevant to the problems of the poor in the ghettos. And, the militants felt, the philosophy of nonviolence was degrading to blacks, depriving them of the sense of worth that came with willingness to defend themselves and their homes against white violence.

They expounded a revived form of black nationalism, based on race pride and exaltation of the African heritage. Under the slogan "black power," they called for a new movement composed of and led by blacks only. When the movement attained broad popular support, it was to take over control of those institutions that blacks thought vitally important to them. Then it would be possible to bargain with whites on the future of American society. Some saw in this the prospect of a separate black nation in the United States.

The militants applied their doctrine of separatism to organizations they controlled, such as the Student Non-violent Coordinating Committee. Whites were eliminated from posts of authority and advised to work in white communities to change white attitudes. Emphasis shifted from nonviolent resistance to self-defense against white violence. The inflammatory rhetoric of some militant spokesmen made it easy for their opponents to picture them as advocates of violence.

SIGNS OF UNREST

Such doctrines were rejected by King, whose goal remained a humanized and integrated American society. They were denounced by the NAACP, which felt that they played into the hands of white supremacists and that they alienated sympathetic whites. Nevertheless, the militant message found a response in the ghettos, which were themselves becoming more militant. Mounting anger over unemployment, poverty, poor housing, poor schooling, and police harassment burst out in a massive riot in the Watts area of Los Angeles in 1965. Before it ended, 34 people lost their lives, more than 1,000 were injured, and property damage exceeded $40 million. Later riots in such cities as Detroit and Newark, New Jersey, resulted in the physical destruction of entire sections of the cities. In April 1968, the assassination of King provoked riots in more than 100 cities. To many blacks, militant and otherwise, it seemed clear that believers in white supremacy would not tolerate the emergence of a black leader who served as a unifying influence, no matter how moderate he might be.

The riots produced contradictory results. On the one hand, numerous federal programs were introduced to alleviate some of the worst conditions in the ghettos. Employers in some cities, most notably Detroit, initiated special training for jobless young blacks to fit them for permanent jobs. In major cities steps were taken to improve relations between police and the black community. On the other hand, the riots proved damaging. They accelerated the flight of white population and business from the cities. In many places the ravaged areas were not rebuilt, with consequent loss of business, jobs, and housing. Tax money was also lost, leaving local governments less able than before to bear the burdens of schools, welfare, and other social services. The black poor suffered most from such retrenchment.

Unrest in the ghettos produced its own unique political expression in the Black Panther party. Organized in Oakland, California, in 1966 by Huey P. Newton and

Bobby G. Seale, it combined black nationalism with social revolution. Drawing on the teachings of Franz Fanon, the ideologist of colonial revolt in Africa, Newton and Seale asserted that American blacks were victims of an internal colonial oppression that could be ended only with the overthrow of capitalism. In this context, white police in the ghettos were viewed as an army of occupation that would be resisted by force of arms if necessary. Further, like other colonial peoples, blacks had to be willing to work with antiimperialist elements among whites—but only on condition that the whites be prepared to let the Panthers set policy on issues relating directly to blacks.

The party attained a national following after it staged an armed demonstration in 1967 on the steps of the California statehouse to protest a gun-control law designed to limit Panther activity. The party also attracted Eldridge Cleaver, a paroled prisoner who became the Panthers' most eloquent spokesman. His *Soul on Ice* had great influence among blacks and white liberals.

Panther influence in the ghettos, however, derived not so much from the party's ideas as from its practical work. It shielded ghetto dwellers from police harassment. It provided free breakfasts for children and free medical clinics for the ill. It won concessions long denied by public authorities, such as traffic lights at busy intersections. It warred against drug pushers. The prestige of the Panthers rose in the black community, despite the hostility shown toward them by public authorities, the media, and moderate civil rights advocates. In 1970 a poll of black opinion by the Louis Harris organization showed that while 75 percent of blacks expressed the highest regard for the NAACP, 25 percent accorded their highest respect to the Panthers—a remarkable showing in view of the massive efforts to discredit the Panthers.

In the meantime, an older expression of ghetto discontent continued to grow. The Nation of Islam increased its membership to at least 100,000 by 1960 and sponsored, in addition to its own schools and self-defense corps, a variety of business enterprises, including groceries, bakeries, dress shops, and dairy farms. As it prospered, its teachings became more restrained and the antiwhite rhetoric of earlier days was toned down. The movement's growth, though, prompted dissension, and several dissident leaders founded their own sects. Malcolm X was such a dissident, but he differed from the others. He had been converted while in prison and since then had so distinguished himself in the cause as to become the heir apparent to Elijah Muhammad. In 1964 Malcolm X repudiated what he called the "racist" teachings of Muhammad and condemned Muslim indifference to the struggles of ghetto blacks. He called for militant black action to obtain, not only relatively narrow civil rights, but also broad human rights. He advocated black self-defense against white violence. Blacks must control their own organizations, he said, but should be willing to cooperate with whites who fought against white racism. To promote this program Malcolm X formed the Organization of Afro-American Unity, but it was barely started when he was assassinated in February 1965.

The feelings Malcolm X stirred within the black community were intense. On his death, Carl Rowan, black chief of the United States Information Agency, branded him "an ex-convict, ex-dope peddler who became a racial fanatic." Ossie Davis, black actor and playwright, hailed the slain man as "our own black shining

Prince—who didn't hesitate to die because he loved us so.'' The Black Panthers said they carried on Malcolm's legacy.

PROBLEMS WITH UNIONS

In the 1960s, as earlier, the stable, thrifty black working class in the ghettos tended to be ignored. The men generally worked in basic industries, belonged to unions, and shared—sometimes unequally—in the benefits of union contracts. The women, for the most part, worked in low-wage industry, restaurants, hotels, and hospitals. For these working people union policy was of major importance. By 1960 the prospects for blacks were not as bright as they had seemed earlier.

Although the CIO remained formally committed to racial equality, an indirect consequence of the expulsion of Left unions from the CIO was to reduce emphasis on that goal. In some major CIO unions, such as steel and rubber, racism reasserted itself in contracts that discriminated against blacks. Even so, the merger of the CIO and AFL in 1955 was hailed by many blacks, including leaders of the NAACP, as ushering in a new day in the history of blacks and unions. The constitution of the new body provided stiff penalties, including expulsion, for unions that engaged in racial discrimination. In practice, however, there was little change.

Disillusioned blacks protested. In 1960 a group of black union officials, led by A. Philip Randolph, organized the Negro American Labor Council to bring about an end to union racism. The following year the NAACP reported that the AFL–CIO still adhered to ''anti-Negro employment practices.'' The federal Civil Rights Commission, after documenting widespread discrimination within unions, called for federal legislation to cope with the problem. The civil rights law of 1964 incorporated such a provision. Union leaders refused to concede that they were at fault. They condemned the NAACP and censured Randolph for promoting a gap ''between organized labor and the Negro community.''

Faced with such obduracy, the NAACP, which previously had few ties with black wage-earners, resorted to legal action. For their part, black workers, traditionally skeptical of white courts, found them useful for promoting black interests. Faced with legal action and attendant publicity, some unions modified their traditional practices. Even building-trades unions, the most obstinate upholders of white supremacy, admitted token blacks as members. The most notable NAACP victory came in 1973 when the United Steelworkers and the Bethlehem Steel Corporation were ordered to abolish separate seniority lists that had barred blacks from promotion.

Meanwhile, black workers began to take more active roles within their unions. Black caucuses appeared, organized to assure equality in contracts and in processing grievances. They also sought to win staff positions for blacks and election of blacks to policy-making posts. While a few relatively small unions with substantial black membership had long included blacks in their leadership, most major unions resisted the black claim for representation. A major breakthrough came in 1962, when the United Automobile Workers elected a black to its executive board. Some other unions slowly followed suit.

Blacks in unorganized fields responded enthusiastically to campaigns by unions that showed concern for black workers. By 1968 a union of drug and hospital workers had 34,000 members in the New York metropolitan area and had won substantial gains for its members, mostly black and Puerto Rican women. After a bitterly fought strike in 1969 the union established itself in Charleston, South Carolina, and later in Baltimore, Maryland. A union of government workers led a successful strike of garbage collectors in Memphis in 1968 and later organized black sanitation workers in other southern cities, winning substantial improvements for its members.

These campaigns received support from some national unions, such as steel and auto, as well as from some local white labor leaders. They also received strong support within the black community, especially among civil rights activists. Martin Luther King, Jr. was so helpful to the Drug and Hospital Workers Union that he was made an honorary member, and he had come to Memphis to aid the garbage collectors when he was assassinated. Indeed, King had long felt that the gains of the civil rights crusade had little effect on black poverty. While he supported various programs to aid ghetto dwellers, he concluded that the "key to battling poverty is winning jobs for workers with decent pay through unionism."

ECONOMIC GAINS

The turbulence of the 1960s was accompanied by improvement in the economic plight of many blacks. The proportion of black families with annual incomes above $8,000 more than doubled—from 13 percent in 1960 to 27 percent in 1967. In the same period, the number of black families living below the poverty line declined from 55 percent to 35 percent. The wide gap between white and black incomes narrowed as the median income of blacks rose one-third and that of whites rose one-fifth. Even so, the black median income was still only 58 percent of the white.

The ranks of the black middle class grew as more young people entered the professions, obtained middle-and high-level jobs in government, and were employed at managerial levels by private business. Some such appointments were made merely to meet the requirements of state or federal law, but at least they provided the first opportunity for qualified blacks to demonstrate their abilities.

Another significant new development was the mass entry of blacks into colleges and universities. In 1970 there were about a half million black students, 378,000 of whom attended integrated institutions. They played an active role in the student revolt of the 1960s. Their pressure helped bring about black-studies programs on many campuses. The black presence was also indicated by the growing number of black faculty members, who for the first time in American history found themselves in demand by white institutions.

Blacks also became more visible in public life during the 1960s. In 1967 Thurgood Marshall became the first black Supreme Court justice. Robert Weaver became the first black cabinet member, and Andrew Brimmer broke new ground with his appointment to the Federal Reserve Board. In 1972, fifteen blacks were elected to Congress, four of them women. For the first time blacks served as mayors of such major cities as Cleveland, Detroit, Atlanta, Los Angeles, Newark, and Gary, Indiana. By 1970 more than 1,200 blacks held elected offices. Meanwhile, black voting increased sharply, partly because of federal voting rights legislation.

FEARS OF SUBVERSION

The struggle for black rights aroused apprehension among conservative elements in government. In 1919, for example, Attorney General Mitchell A. Palmer attributed the black militancy of that year to ''Bolshevist'' influence. Thereafter fear of subversion influenced the attitudes of many federal and local police agencies. Although they were far apart in their policies, both the Nation of Islam and the Black Panthers were harassed and sometimes violently attacked. The most notorious example took place in Chicago in 1969, when police raided Panther headquarters and killed two leaders while they slept. A federal grand jury rejected a police claim that they had been fired upon.

Outstanding black leaders were also subject to harassment. Although he had loyally supported World War I, W. E. B. DuBois became suspect in the eyes of the Department of Justice when he urged militant action for racial equality after the war. Thirty years later his opposition to the Korean War led to a federal indictment. Although he was acquitted, continued harassment contributed to DuBois's decision to renounce his United States citizenship and retire to Ghana, where he died in 1963. During the heyday of McCarthyism, Paul Robeson, world-famous singer and actor, was mobbed and later driven out of professional life because of his leftist sympathies.

Martin Luther King, Jr., was the object of special surveillance by the Federal Bureau of Investigation, including the tapping of his telephone calls. While FBI Director J. Edgar Hoover publicly attacked King, he leaked alleged evidence designed to discredit King as a moral leader. After Hoover's death it was revealed that he had instructed his agents not only to gather information on black movements but also to take action to prevent emergence of what he called a ''Black Messiah.'' It also came out that some FBI agents did indeed engage in secret activities to disrupt and discredit the civil rights movement.

At another level, blacks were penalized for taking unpopular positions on public issues. Thus, Julian Bond was denied his seat in the Georgia legislature because of his opposition to the Vietnam War, although he was reinstated upon orders from the United States Supreme Court.

BLACK AND FEMALE

Black women shared in the general progress made by blacks after World War II. More of them went to college, entered the professions, and held relatively high-wage jobs in factories. They took much more active roles in life than ever before. Beginning with Mary McLeod Bethune in the Roosevelt administration, black women became increasingly visible in public life. They served as local officials, state legislators, and ambassadors. In 1966 Constance Baker Motley became the first black woman to serve as a federal judge. At the same time Shirley Chisholm was elected as the first black woman in Congress. Later, Patricia Harris was appointed by President Carter as the first black women cabinet member.

Such recognition was partly a product of the black revolution, in which women played significant roles. Symbolically, it was a woman, Rosa Parks, who set off the famous Montgomery bus boycott by refusing to yield her seat to a white passenger. Later, as the civil rights struggle mounted, Daisy Bates led the fight against school segregation in Little Rock, Arkansas. Fannie Lou Hamer not only crusaded for equality in Mississippi but also gained national attention at the Democratic convention of 1964 by her revolt against the Johnson administration and its ties with Mississippi segregationists. In New Orleans, Virginia E. Y. Collins battled for integration for years. Later, feeling that little had been accomplished, she became an official of a black nationalist group and changed her name to Dara Abubakari.

For black women, as for white, the civil rights movement posed special problems. Although its goal was equality, women activists were relegated to traditional inferior roles, with little voice in decision making. In consequence, many white women became militant feminists. While black women shared the same sense of grievance, they felt it imperative to maintain unity with black men in the larger cause of black liberation. The issue of women's rights, they believed, could be raised later when other goals had been achieved.

The issue was thrust upon them in unexpected form. In the late 1960s some black militant organizations campaigned in the ghettos against birth control and legal abortion, charging that both were part of a white program of genocide. The campaign brought critical response from such black women as Shirley Chisholm. She pointed out that poor black women were the principal victims of illegal abortionists and that lack of birth control helped perpetuate the poverty of the ghettos. Such issues, combined with a growing feminist consciousness, finally resulted in the 1970s in a black feminist movement.

As Shirley Chisholm pointed out, poverty was still the lot of many black women in 1970. Of the 3.6 million black women in the labor force, more than half were employed at low-wage jobs. The median income of black male workers was far below that of white males, but the median income of black women workers was only half that of black men. Many such women headed households, providing the major source of family income. More than 50 percent of such families lived below the official poverty level. Black women, too, found it hard to get jobs. The unemployment rate among them was even higher than that of black men, which was twice the rate of white men. Jobless young women contributed to a fairly constant unemployment rate of at least 40 percent among black youth. Thus, despite the gains of the 1960s, poverty remained the condition of millions of black Americans—and as with the earlier immigrant poor, women shouldered an undue proportion of the burden.

THE UNCERTAIN SEVENTIES

In many ways the black experience of the 1970s was different from that of the 1960s. Most noticeable was the decline in black militancy. Black nationalist groups, such as the Student National Coordinating Committee (formerly the Student Non-Violent

Coordinating Committee), virtually disappeared. The Black Panthers were largely confined to Oakland, where they engaged in social-service activities and in electoral politics, helping to elect the first black mayor of the city in 1977. After the death of Elijah Muhammad in 1975, the Nation of Islam changed its name to the World Community of Islam, abandoned its antiwhite outlook, and sought support within the white community.

Decline in militant influence was accompanied by weakness in moderate organizations. The grand coalition of churches, liberals, organized labor, and blacks of the 1960s disintegrated. Martin Luther King, Jr.'s organization, the Southern Christian Leadership Conference, lost much of its influence after he was assassinated. Even the NAACP, the largest and most stable civil rights organization, suffered severe losses in membership.

In part, the difficulties of such organizations were due to declining white support. Many white youthful activists lost interest in the civil rights cause after they were excluded from militant black organizations. Other sympathetic whites felt as did many abolitionists a century earlier: namely, that since civil rights laws had been enacted and favorable Supreme Court decisions won, active participation in the black struggle was no longer necessary. Still others who had applauded the laws when applied in the South became hostile when the laws were enforced in the North and West.

Labor unions battled in the courts to preserve discriminatory practices in employment and seniority. The teachers' union in New York City fought community control of schools in black and Hispanic neighborhoods. White suburbs resisted the integration of their school systems with those of the black inner cities. They also strove to keep out housing projects designed for low-income blacks. Poorer whites who could not escape to the suburbs resorted to violence in Boston and Louisville to block school integration. White males instituted court suits against affirmative-action programs, alleging that such programs constituted "reverse discrimination."

At the intellectual level, some white scholars revived the old notion that blacks were naturally inferior in intelligence. William B. Shockley, a Nobel prize winner in physics, and Arthur Jensen, a psychologist, argued that poor achievements of black schoolchildren could be traced to racial inheritance rather than to social and cultural factors. Other scholars, white and black, rejected the arguments.

The shift in white opinion was reflected in government. The Nixon and Ford administrations were far less interested in minority rights than the Johnson administration. Blacks expected much from the Carter administration, but in 1978 they expressed bitter disappointment that so little had been done to meet the problems of black Americans. Congress also showed declining interest in black problems. It either curtailed or eliminated programs designed to aid the black poor.

The Supreme Court, now dominated by appointees of Nixon and Ford, retreated from the vigorous civil rights position of the Warren court. It struck down some school desegregation plans that called for integration of urban and suburban school systems. In 1977 civil rights advocates were dismayed by a court ruling upholding local zoning regulations that in effect excluded housing for poor blacks. Such regulations were lawful, said the court, so long as there was no intent to discriminate. The court followed the same reasoning in approving seniority systems set up before 1965 that penalized black workers. Thus, the court abandoned the Warren court's position that regardless of intent, any demonstrated pattern of discrimination was unlawful. Indeed, the judicial temper had changed so much that in 1977 a federal court of appeals in New York condemned "overzealous enforcement" of civil rights laws in a case involving building-trades unions with a long record of racial discrimination.

In 1978 the Supreme Court further retreated from the Warren court's firm stand against racial discrimination. In the famous Bakke case, a sharply divided court upheld affirmative-action programs to remedy discrimination against minorities. At the same time, however, the court declared that such programs must not discriminate against qualified whites. It invalidated the program of the University of California Medical College at Davis, under which 16 of 100 admissions were reserved for minorities. Allan P. Bakke, a white engineer who had been denied admission, was ordered admitted. Justice Thurgood Marshall, the only black member of the court, observed that the decision marked a retreat from the goal of racial equality similar to that of the late nineteenth century. Some civil rights advocates, however, felt that the court's decision applied only to rigid programs and would not seriously weaken flexible application of affirmative action. The impact of the Bakke decision on business and industry was not clear, but many black leaders felt that it might block black employment and promotion. In 1979, however, the Court rejected the "reverse discrimination" suit of Brian Weber, a white factory worker. It approved some programs in industry that provided for upgrading black workers.

CHANGES IN THE BLACK COMMUNITY

There were also changes within the black community itself. The economic gains made by some blacks in the 1960s were cut back as automation and business recession wiped out jobs. The ending of some federal programs to ameliorate conditions in the ghettos also hurt many poor blacks. The economic recession of the 1970s enabled employers to drop special training programs for young blacks and to evade requirements of affirmative-action regulations. In consequence, the gap between white and black income, which had narrowed in the 1960s, began to widen again in the 1970s.

So also did the gap between poor and middle-class blacks. College graduates still found opportunities for well-paid work in public life, government service, the professions, and private business. There was also some growth in black business enterprises. Such prospering blacks tended to maintain their social and physical distance from poor folk. Some fled to suburbia, and others maintained enclaves in the cities, resisting efforts to build low-income housing projects near them. In short, it appeared that as the black middle class grew and prospered, class divisions within the black community became increasingly significant.

Such divisions frustrated efforts to present a unified black approach to national problems. The organization of the Congressional Black Caucus, made up of black members of Congress, was a step in the direction of political unity, but its effectiveness was limited by continuing partisanship. In 1972 another significant step was taken when a National Black Political Convention met at Gary, Indiana, with more than 6,000 delegates and observers. Such issues as school busing and integration proved too divisive for agreement. Although the convention failed to provide unity, it did demonstrate the growing political power and consciousness of the black community.

Another source of division appeared after the election of President Carter in 1976. Southern black leaders who had helped win 90 percent of the black vote for Carter received suitable recognition, most notably in the appointment of Congressman Andrew Young of Georgia as ambassador to the United Nations. Further, close working relations between the White House and southern blacks gave such blacks a new sense of power. Long resentful of what they felt was northern black paternalism, they asserted their own claims to national leadership of American blacks.

Another significant change was growing doubt within the black community about integration as a goal. In some cities, most notably Atlanta and Detroit, civil rights leaders and black public officials objected to further moves for integration in schools and housing. Such moves, they felt, would hasten the exodus of the whites remaining in cities and thus curtail public services and employment for poor blacks. Increasing numbers of black parents questioned the educational and social value of busing their children to white schools. Many preferred all-black schools, provided that they were adequately staffed and financed. In New York City the pressure of such sentiment led to the establishment of community education boards with some measure of control over schools in black, Hispanic, and other neighborhoods.

After the great riots of 1967, President Johnson appointed a commission to investigate their causes. In 1968 the commission, headed by Governor Otto Kerner of Illinois, reported that such riots occurred largely because of white racism. That report further emphasized that unless massive government efforts against such racism were undertaken, "our nation is moving toward two societies, one black, one white—separate and unequal."

In the 1970s it was uncertain whether this statement was rhetoric designed to influence public opinion or a correct appraisal of the future.

FOR FURTHER READING

The explosion of books and articles dealing with recent black experience is indicated in James M. McPherson and others, eds., *Blacks in America: Bibliographical Essays* (1971). Of the 400 pages of this work more than half are devoted to the years since 1915. For surveys see earlier citations.

There are many good collections of documents. Among them are those edited by John Hope Franklin and Isidore Starr, *The Negro in Twentieth Century America* (1967); Francis L. Broderick and August Meier, *Negro Protest Thought in the Twentieth Century* (1965); and Philip S. Foner, *The Black Panthers Speak* (1970)

Highly readable accounts of migration and urbanization are Florette Henri, *Black Migration* (1976), and Arna Bontemps and Jack Conroy, *Anyplace But Here* (1966). The classic work on the changing black self-image has been reprinted in Alain Locke, ed., *The New Negro* (1969). For the Harlem Renaissance, see Nathan I. Huggins, *Harlem Renaissance* (1971). On the Garvey movement, see E. David Cronon, *Black Moses* (1955). For jazz and other musical expressions see Eileen Southern, *The Music of Black America* (1970).

The black experience in the 1930s is discussed in Raymond Wolters, *Negroes and the Great Depression* (1970). The famous case involving basic civil rights is recounted in Dan T. Carter, *Scottsboro* (1969).

The changing relationships of blacks and labor unions are traced in Ray Marshall, *The Negro and Organized Labor* (1965); Milton Cantor, ed., *Black Labor in America* (1970); Julius Jacobson, ed., *The Negro and the American Labor Movement* (1968); and Philip S. Foner, *The Negro and Organized Labor* (1973).

The growth and problems of the Nation of Islam are studied in C. Eric Lincoln, *The Black Muslims in America* (1961). Among the numerous works dealing with the civil rights movement of the 1960s are the following: Charles E. Silberman, *Crisis in Black and White* (1964); Arthur I. Waskow, *From Race Riot to Sit-In* (1967); James W. Silver, *Mississippi: The Closed Society* (1964); and Howard Zinn, *The Southern Mystique* (1964), and *SNCC: The New Abolitionists* (1964).

Personal statements by black militants form the substance of such works as Stokely Carmichael and Charles Hamilton, *Black Power* (1967); Eldridge Cleaver, *Soul on Ice* (1968); Bobby Seale, *Seize the Time* (1970); and H. Rap Brown, *Die Nigger Die!* (1969).

Other expressions of black discontent are to be found in Whitney M. Young, Jr., *To Be Equal* (1964); James Farmer, *Freedom—When?* (1966); and Bayard Rustin, *Which Way Out? A Way Out of the Exploding Ghetto* (1967). Martin Luther King, Jr.'s views are set forth in *Stride Toward Freedom* (1958) and in *Why We Can't Wait* (1964). See his *Where Do We Go from Here?* (1967) for his critisism of "black power."

The life stories of black women are told in Rackham Holt, *Mary McLeod Bethune* (1964); Shirley Chisholm, *Unbossed and Unbought* (1970); Pauli Murray, *Proud Shoes* (1956); Coretta Scott King, *My Life with Martin Luther King, Jr.* (1970); Mahalia Jackson, *Movin' On Up* (1966); and Marian Anderson, *My Lord, What a Morning* (1956).

Among the most influential of autobiographies has been *The Autobiography of Malcolm X* (1965). The changing views of another militant black leader are reflected in *The Autobiography of W. E. B. DuBois* (1968). The story of Martin Luther King, Jr. is told in David L. Lewis, *King: A Critical Biography* (1970).

For a comprehensive study of the nature and function of the black family see Herbert Gutman, *The Black Family in Slavery and Freedom* (1977).

26

new— and not so new— americans

When Americans of the industrial era spoke of the ''new immigration,'' they referred to recent arrivals from southern and eastern Europe. In postindustrial America the term could have been applied to the mass migrations from Mexico and Puerto Rico and the less significant influx of Filipinos, Koreans, Cubans, and West Indian blacks.

By 1970 the descendants of southern and eastern Europeans had been integrated into American society and had generally improved their economic and social status. Despite race prejudice, Japanese- and Chinese-Americans had also won a place in American society. Other groups, such as poor Spanish-speaking people and American Indians, did not fare so well.

MOVING UP IN AMERICA

Most of the working poor in nineteenth-century industry were European immigrants. By 1970, some of their grandchildren had become rich, many were well-to-do, and great numbers of industrial workers—especially those with two family incomes—lived in an affluence they had hardly dreamed possible. The major avenue to upward mobility was education. In 1940 colleges and universities graduated 217,000 students; in 1970 more than 1 million degrees were granted. Education opened the doors to business, the professions, and academic life—a process in which the descendants of the once despised folk from eastern and southern Europe shared. They did not share uniformly. At one extreme, the ranks of Jewish wage-earners thinned as their children and grandchildren entered business, literature, the arts, and the professions. At the other extreme, Americans of Polish and Italian descent tended to remain in blue-collar occupations, although increasing numbers of them also moved into middle-class callings.

Such people had to make progress against traditional antiimmigrant stereotypes. Even in the 1970s Poles were the butts of Polish jokes. Italian-Americans were identified with organized crime. Jews faced more organized prejudice. In the 1920s Henry Ford sponsored a nationwide campaign against them. In the 1930s the popular "radio priest," Charles E. Coughlin, attributed America's ills to Jews. After Hitler's extermination of Jews was revealed, anti-Semitism lost respectability. It lived on underground, however, revealed on occasions such as the speech made by a high Pentagon official in 1977 charging that Jews controlled key areas of American life. To American Jews, the claim was all too reminiscent of Hitler's propaganda against German Jews.

Significantly, although white ethnic groups were generally accepted by the 1960s and much intermarriage had taken place, questions were raised among them of whether the price paid for assimilation was not too high. They felt that some values of their cultural heritage were too precious to sacrifice. Polish and Italian organizations strove to build up more positive self-images among their peoples, rooted in pride of their heritage and devoted to reviving traditions of the past. Jewish groups promoted a sense of Jewish community, based on Jewish tradition, memories of the Nazi gas chambers, and pride in the state of Israel.

That rejection of the "melting pot" idea, once so dominant in white American thinking, also became widespread among the Hispanic, Asian, and Indian peoples who lived in the United States.

MEXICAN PEOPLE NORTH OF THE BORDER

In 1970 Mexican-Americans were second only to blacks as a major minority group. There were more than 5 million of them, of whom 1.5 million were native-born American citizens. Most of them lived in California and the Southwest, providing the basic cheap labor supply for farms, industry, and private and public institutions. Formerly a rural folk, in 1970 Mexican-Americans were an urban people, heavily concentrated in such cities as Los Angeles, El Paso, and Denver. Only 15 percent lived in rural areas—but many city-dwellers commuted to and from jobs in the fields.

The Mexicans came north because of unfavorable circumstances at home and the lure of jobs in the American Southwest. Most of the immigrants found jobs in the fields, but others worked in mines, on railroads, and on construction projects. They came in three great waves, responding to shortages in American labor supply. The first, occurring in the early twentieth century, has already been discussed in chapter 21. The second, during World War I and immediately thereafter, brought record numbers of Mexican people to the Southwest and prompted many established Mexican-Americans to move north, where they found jobs in the auto factories of Detroit and the steel mills of Ohio and Indiana. The third and most significant wave came in World War II and the ensuing years. This wave furnished not only farm workers but also labor for the rapidly industrializing West Coast and for the service occupations that accompanied the spread of industry.

The movement north of the border was all the easier because there was no sharp cultural break involved. The immigrants moved into already established Mexican-American communities where Spanish was spoken, the Catholic church predominated, the patriarchal family structure was familiar, and Mexican traditions were still strong. To be sure, the Mexican-American culture had been diluted over the years by Anglo influences, but basically it remained Mexican. Partly its persistence was due to discrimination and segregation, which locked old-timers and new arrivals into *colonias* in the countryside and *barrios* in the cities. Relations between the two groups were not always harmonious, but the common experience of living in a hostile Anglo society strengthened a sense of community.

The culture was not simply a Mexican peasant culture. It was also a culture of poverty. The wages paid industrial workers were far below those paid Anglos, and farm workers received even less. Even in good times the unemployment rate among Mexican-Americans was double that of Anglos. The pathology of poverty, compounded by Anglo hostility, reflected itself in high rates of crime and juvenile delinquency. Many adolescents dropped out of schools that generally made them feel unwanted and inferior. Inadequate education in turn condemned them to dead-end jobs. Despite such problems, Mexican-Americans nourished their culture through which they could express their own sense of dignity and self-respect. Their music, dances, folk tales, and continuing ties with Mexico all attested to desire to maintain a sense of their own identity.

The Mexican-American community, however, felt the pressures of Anglo society. When labor shortages demanded, the doors were swung open for immigrants, legal and illegal alike, and the border patrol turned a blind eye to the thousands who streamed across the border without the formalities of law. When Anglo society suffered from depression, legal and illegal methods were used to ship people back to Mexico. During the depression of the 1930s an estimated 500,000 were sent to Mexico. Some left "voluntarily" at the behest of local authorities, and others were deported. Among them were native-born American citizens whose rights were simply ignored.

During World War II and the 1950s the federal government opened the border to *braceros,* workers admitted on temporary permits and expected to return to Mexico when the permits expired. They came in large numbers. In the first phase of the program, lasting from 1942 to 1947, at least 250,000 workers entered the United States. The second phase, lasting from 1948 to 1964, saw the admission of 4.5 million *braceros*. Since many of these were repeaters—people who gained readmission after their original permits expired—the actual number of persons involved was much smaller, but it was still significant. Some, having accumulated sufficient funds to buy land or set up small businesses in Mexico, returned to their homeland. Many others stayed in the United States, except for brief visits south of the border.

The response of Mexican-Americans to the *braceros* and other newcomers was ambivalent. On the one hand, they felt they must welcome the new arrivals, both as fellow poor people trying to make a living and as fellow Mexicans who must be shown hospitality. On the other hand, their presence kept wages low and frustrated efforts to organize field workers. The program finally ended in 1964 as the result of pressures from American labor unions, complaints from the Mexican-American community, and protests from the Mexican government charging that its citizens were being exploited. By that time, mechanization of some sectors of farming in the Southwest and California made the need for Mexican labor less pressing.

Another hindrance to Mexican-Americans trying to improve their lot were the *mojados*—called "wetbacks" by Anglos—who were in the United States illegally. There had always been such people—indeed, travel back and forth across the border was so frequent as to be casual—but their numbers swelled after World War II. How many there were was unknown. In 1977 estimates ranged between 2 and 7 million, a substantial number in any case.

The "wetbacks" were tolerated because commercial farmers and other employers wanted them. They worked for little, were ignorant of their legal rights, dared not complain, and could be used as strikebreakers when the need arose. They were also readily victimized. Some unscrupulous employers withheld their wages until the work was completed, then informed immigration authorities of the "wetbacks," who were speedily deported without being paid. This was only one of many abuses suffered by "wetbacks"; yet conditions in Mexico were such that they kept coming back. In fact, the illegal traffic was so great that it attracted the attention of Mexican-American labor contractors and criminal elements who made smuggling of human beings an organized and highly lucrative business.

The reputation of Mexican-American workers for docility was of long standing. It had some validity, of course, especially as it concerned folk who were illegal immigrants and thus eager to avoid contact with authorities. It ignored, however, the record of resistance to exploitation.

In the 1890s Mexican-American workers took part in the great strikes of the Western Federation of Miners. In the early years of the twentieth century field workers tried to form unions, sometimes in collaboration with Japanese, Filipino, and other groups. When the Industrial Workers of the World (IWW) appeared in the fields, 20,000 Mexican-American workers joined the new union. A major strike at Wheatlands, California, in 1913 was lost after four people were killed and more than 100 strikers jailed. Mexican and Anglo copper miners in 1917 and 1918 cooperated in strikes in Arizona that were ruthlessly suppressed. During the 1930s Mexican-American farm workers formed their own unions, joined unions sponsored by Communists, or affiliated with AFL and CIO unions. Such efforts were largely defeated. Employers, vigilante groups, and public authorities united to block Mexican-American labor organization. Many strikes were crushed by deporting leaders to Mexico.

In addition, Mexican-Americans had to contend with Anglo public opinion, which looked upon them in the same way that white segregationists looked upon blacks. A growing number of Anglos, typified by Roman Catholic Archbishop Robert Lucey of Texas and civil-rights activist Carey McWilliams of California, spoke out on behalf of the Mexican-Americans, but they were a small minority.

Anti-Mexican articles were a staple of the media, especially in Los Angeles, with its large Mexican-American population. In particular, Mexican-Americans were portrayed as naturally given to violent crime. Many public officials shared this view. Such expressions continued even after Pearl Harbor, when the needs of war called for promoting national unity. A law enforcement official of Los Angeles County reported to a grand jury in 1942 that resort to violence was an "inborn characteristic" of Mexican people. Thus, crime in the *barrios* was not due to discrimination and segregation, said the official, but to the Mexican's "desire . . . to kill, or at least let blood." Such a view justified the police harassment that was as much a feature of *barrio* life as it was of the black ghettos.

These stereotypes, together with sensational journalism, led to the notorious "Sleepy Lagoon" case in Los Angeles in 1942. After a trial marked by flagrant judicial bias, twelve young Mexican-Americans were sent to prison for the murder of another Mexican-American gang member. In 1944 an appeals court reversed the convictions and censured the judge and prosecutor. The cases were then dismissed, much to the joy of the Mexican-American community. Nevertheless, the way in which press and police had used the case to fan anti-Mexican feeling left bitter memories in the community.

In the meantime, Mexican-Americans were victims of a major riot in Los Angeles. In June 1943, while war raged in the Pacific, mobs of Anglo soldiers and sailors, aided by some civilians, terrorized *barrio* residents in what the media called the "zoot suit riots." Hundreds of young Mexican-Americans were brutally beaten and stripped of the clothing so detested by Anglos. Police cooperated, jailing the victims and allowing the mobs a free hand. The riots lasted nearly a week before protests from the Mexican government and federal intervention brought them to an end. Similar outbreaks took place in San Diego and other Southern California cities.

While mob violence died out, Anglo crimes of violence against Mexican people went largely unpunished. Likewise, discrimination continued, although large numbers of Mexican-Americans and Mexican citizens joined the army and distinguished themselves in combat. In Texas, the treatment of Mexican people was so harsh that the Mexican government halted entry of *braceros* to that state.

The responses of Mexican people to their problems varied as much as they did among people of other minorities. At one extreme were the descendants of old families who had intermarried with Anglos and were prominent in business, the professions, and public life. Suffering little from prejudice, they identified with Anglo society and shared its feelings toward poor Mexicans. At the other extreme were the "wetbacks," who endured any kind of hardship to stay in the United States. Many legal immigrants and American-born citizens were apathetic, despairing of improving their lot and afraid of public authority. The failure of their attempts to organize labor unions had not been reassuring.

As it had among blacks, segregation stimulated the growth of a middle class of storekeepers and other businessmen, professional people, academics, and politicians. Their responses to the problems of their people were ambivalent. On the one hand, they were proud of their own achievements, resentful of the slurs and indignities imposed on them because of their background, and aware of their dependence on their own people. On the other hand, their values tended to be those of Anglo society. They realized that getting ahead depended on Anglo acceptance, and they tried to keep their social distance from the poor, whom they blamed for Anglo society's failure to accept Mexican folk who had embraced the gospel of success. Psychologically insecure, they sought to win their ends by gradual reforms that would not alarm Anglos. Their perplexities were mirrored in the ways they sought to identify themselves. Few middle-class organizations used the term *Mexican*. They preferred such names as *Hispanic Americans, Spanish Americans,* and *Latin Americans*.

Such terms came to be seen as reprehensible by the growing number of militants who appeared during the 1950s and 1960s. The black revolution, Supreme Court decisions outlawing discrimination, and passage of civil rights laws all contributed to a feeling that militant struggle could bring about change for the better. This was something new in a community long accustomed to maintaining a low profile in American society. The new attitudes found expression on college campuses, where young Mexican-Americans were appearing in record numbers; in the *barrios,* where young people were no longer tolerant of Anglo oppression; and in the fields, where workers organized—this time successfully. The new mood produced a new term of identification: *Chicano* (a derivative of *Mexicano*), which connoted pride in the Mexican heritage and vigorous struggle for equality. It also involved a repudiation of the traditional leadership of the Mexican-American community.

The feeling expressed itself in many ways. Public-school students went on strike in Los Angeles, Denver, and other cities to protest discriminatory practices. Chicano organizations called for an end to voting requirements that discriminated against Mexican-Americans. Eligible voters were mobilized by the new Mexican American Political Association and the Viva Kennedy movement, which demonstrated great vitality during the campaign of 1960.

When Democratic and Republican office holders paid little attention to Chicano problems, a militant nationalist political party, *La Raza Unida*, appeared in 1970. After initial successes in Texas, it spread into nearby states. In Denver, Rudolfo Gonzales led a separatist movement that provided community services and promoted cultural nationalism. In New Mexico, Reies Tijerina won a wide following with his demand for return of lands that he charged had been taken illegally from Mexicans after the Mexican War. Brown Berets, modeled on the Black Panthers, appeared in the *barrios*.

The movement that did the most to stimulate Chicano pride and confidence, bring Chicano problems to national attention, and win widespread Anglo support was the union of the California farm workers led by Cesar Chavez, the Chicano counterpart of Martin Luther King, Jr. For more than ten years Chicano, Filipino, and other farm workers battled doggedly for recognition of their union. They confronted the great corporate farms that now dominated California farming, antagonistic public officials, and a local Anglo opinion that was hostile. Then, when the field workers' union seemed to be winning, it was opposed by the powerful Teamsters Union, with which corporate farms preferred to deal. Finally, in 1976 the United Farm Workers established itself by winning many state-conducted elections as collective bargaining agent.

The farm union was much more than a traditional labor union. While it was concerned with wages and working conditions, it was also a major center of the Chicano struggle for equality. Its social services, its theater of social protest, and its newspaper made the union a powerful influence far beyond its own ranks. In addition, the successive victories of the union helped to dispel the mood of defeatism and despair that had long enthralled the Chicano poor. Further, the union showed them that they were not alone, that they had powerful friends outside their ranks, including

Cesar Chavez, Chicano leader of the campaign to establish a permanent union of farm workers in the West.

Wide World Photos

the AFL-CIO; Coretta Scott King, widow of the black martyr; Robert Kennedy, attorney general of the United States; Edmund Brown, governor of California—and his son, later Governor "Jerry" Brown.

The growth of the union and rise of militant organizations in the *barrios* and on college campuses testified to a new spirit among Chicanos, not only among the poor but also among the middle class. Like black Americans, Mexican-Americans were on the move, seeking full and equal participation in American life—but not at the expense of their heritage. Chicanos cultivated pride of background and respect for their people's traditions. The era of the docile, passive peon was over.

THE PUERTO RICANS

The Mexican-American population grew fast, but not as fast as another Spanish-speaking minority, the Puerto Ricans. In 1940 there were fewer than 50,000 in the United States. Thirty years later they numbered nearly 1.5 million. Most lived in the urban areas of New Jersey, New York, and Connecticut, but there was a movement toward other cities, such as Chicago, where about 130,000 resided in 1970.

The Puerto Rican immigrants were unique in several ways. First, they were already by law citizens of the United States. Second, they were largely of mixed black and white descent. Third, although they had developed their own culture, they had never been free of foreign domination. From the early days of settlement to 1898, the island had been ruled by Spain. After the Spanish-American War, control passed to the United States, which imposed its own standards on a people generally regarded as backward and inferior.

Like Mexican immigrants, the Puerto Ricans came because of poverty and unemployment at home and in hope of a better life in the United States. Most arrived after World War II, when the booming economy and upward mobility of many industrial workers opened jobs at the bottom of the social scale. Their coming was made easier by introduction of low-cost air transportation between the island and the mainland. They found employment in low-wage industry jobs and in equally low-wage service occupations. Such fields were most vulnerable to fluctuations in the economy, so that in a sense Puerto Rican migration was a reflex of the changes in the American economy. In good times, Puerto Ricans came in large numbers. In bad times, they returned home. It was an unstable situation hardly conducive to permanent settlement.

Nevertheless, although travel between island and mainland continued, increasing numbers of Puerto Ricans decided that while life in the United States had fallen far short of their expectations, it was better than life in their homeland. They settled down, raised families, and like earlier immigrants tried to adapt themselves to American ways. By 1970 there were many young people, born in the United States, who knew no Spanish and had never visited Puerto Rico.

Most Puerto Ricans, segregated in urban slums, lived in poverty. In New York City, which contained the largest Puerto Rican community on the mainland, their median income in 1970 was the lowest of all minority groups. Half of the Puerto Rican families in the city were on welfare. Their unemployment rate nationally was double that of the general rate. Joblessness among the young was as bad as that of young blacks, meaning that at least 40 percent were out of work. The usual symptoms of slum life appeared: street-gang violence, drug addiction, high juvenile delinquency rates, and crime—usually directed against blacks and other Puerto Ricans. Poverty was also reflected in birth rates, disease rates, and death rates far above average.

Contributing to a high rate of school dropouts was the hostility of many teachers and school administrators toward Puerto Ricans, expressed in their denigration of Spanish culture, including bans on speaking Spanish in classrooms. The schools reflected general attitudes in American white society. Puerto Ricans were American citizens by law, but most white Americans regarded them as foreigners, and dark-skinned foreigners at that. White America stereotyped them as shiftless, violent, criminal, immoral, and a burden on taxpayers, ignoring the role of employers who paid wages so low that even a full-time worker could not support a family without public aid.

The prejudice was so intense that many aspiring Puerto Ricans sought to disguise their origins. Just as Jews had earlier sought to evade anti-Semitism by Anglicizing their names, so Puerto Ricans described themselves as "Hispanos" or "Latinos." Light-skinned people tried to "pass" as whites—just as some black people had done before them. Piri Thomas, the Puerto Rican writer, has told of his youthful anger at his father for bequeathing him a black skin.

Black Americans were often hostile to the newcomers. The immigrants competed for the same kind of low-wage jobs to which so many blacks were confined. The new supply of labor made it difficult to raise wages. The newcomers had little interest in unions or the black struggle for civil rights. Their arrival contributed to housing shortages and higher rents for blacks. The tension came out in violent street warfare between black and Puerto Rican gangs as well as in conflicts between black and Puerto Rican political organizations.

Paradoxically, the black revolution gave heart to those in the Puerto Rican slums who had struggled to maintain self-respect and ethnic pride against all the corrosive forces of ghetto life. It also stimulated middle-class Puerto Ricans to move more aggressively into the mainstream of American life. As with blacks and Chicanos, segregation produced among Puerto Ricans its own class of small merchants, lawyers, doctors, and politicians who relied on their people for their prosperity and influence—however much they might like to dissociate themselves from their poor compatriots. The gains won by blacks against the seemingly impregnable structure of white supremacy encouraged poor and middle-class Puerto Ricans to assert their own aspirations.

The Puerto Rican response took many forms, which sometimes transcended ethnic rivalries. They joined labor unions, working together with black people to win better pay and working conditions. An outstanding example was the Drug and Hospital Workers Union, in which Puerto Ricans took an active role in strikes and otherwise collaborated with black workers. People of both groups rose to positions of union leadership. Puerto Ricans supported the campaign for community control of schools in New York City, and their success provided opportunities for Puerto Ricans to exercise more authority in this significant area of community life. They fought successfully for the acceptance of literacy in Spanish as a substitute for English in voting requirements. They also helped Chicanos win extension of the federal Voting Rights Act to protect Spanish-speaking citizens.

In 1961 politically active Puerto Ricans in New York City demonstrated their strength by defeating machine candidates for Democratic party posts. Thereafter several Puerto Ricans were elected to public office, the most prominent being Congressman Herman Badillo, who was also a political power in local New York politics. Like the Irish, Italians, Jews, and blacks before them, Puerto Ricans seemed to be establishing themselves as a political force to be reckoned with.

Such gains seemed inadequate to groups of youthful militants that emerged in the slums. Perhaps the most important of these was the Young Lords, a former Chicago street gang whose members came to realize that warfare with other gangs solved no problems. They were American-born; spoke English as a first language, were street wise in the realities of political and economic power, and cherished their people's heritage. Distrustful of the Puerto Rican middle-class, they tried to promote a mass movement of the poor to bring an end to poverty and eventually usher in socialism. Local organizations of the Young Lords appeared in cities with large Puerto Rican populations, indicating a rise in militant political consciousness. Like the Black Panthers, they became prime objects of harassment by public authorities.

Such groups had little in common with terrorists whose activities cost the lives of numerous New Yorkers in the 1970s. The terrorists were nationalists demanding Puerto Rican independence and the release of prisoners held for attempts on the lives of President Truman and congressmen in 1954. While there might be some sympathy with such demands in the community, most Puerto Ricans were much more concerned with improving their lot in the United States and were fearful that such violence would reflect unfavorably on the Puerto Rican community as a whole. Likewise, the conflicts on the island between those who wished to preserve commonwealth status and those who called for statehood became less important for people on the mainland as they looked upon themselves increasingly as part of the mainland American people.

THE NATIVE AMERICANS

American Indian peoples slowly recovered from the devastation wrought on their lives by the land allotment policy of the late nineteenth century and the attempts to destroy their culture. The consequent poverty, disease, despair, and alcoholism took such a toll that by 1920 the native American population had dwindled to fewer than 250,000. Fifty years later it had increased to nearly 800,000 and was growing.

All racial minorities were subject to the constraints of white society, but native Americans were unique in that so many were under direct federal control. To be sure, in 1924 tribal Indians not yet citizens were granted citizenship, but it was a limited citizenship deriving from the continuing function of the federal government as the "trustee" for such people. The destiny of many Indians was still largely shaped by white men in Washington, D.C.

This fact was demonstrated by dramatic shifts in federal policy. The first major change came during the New Deal, when John Collier, a white admirer of Indian culture, became commissioner of Indian Affairs. Under his leadership, Congress passed in 1934 the Indian Reorganization Act, providing federal support for a revival of Indian culture and for an expanded land base to support such revival. The allotment system was ended, and Indian lands still held open for sale were restored to tribal ownership. Federal credit was extended to Indian peoples to acquire land previously held by them, with the result that by 1938 Indian land holdings totaled 51.5 million acres as compared with 49 million acres in 1934. Federal aid was also provided to stimulate economic enterprise on reservations.

In addition, the law encouraged revival of Indian self-government by recognizing popularly elected Indian authorities on reservations. Officials of the Bureau of Indian Affairs were forbidden to interfere with Indian cultural practices, especially those relating to religion. The traditional policy of educating Indian children in boarding schools was modified so that more children could attend public schools while remaining with their parents. These and other reforms indicated that the Collier policy looked toward helping Indian peoples so that they could function effectively in a truly pluralistic society. In keeping with such a view, the law applied only to those peoples who accepted it.

There was opposition, of course. Many white westerners objected to any policy that would nurture Indian pride and make Indian peoples less vulnerable to white business interests. There was Indian opposition, too. Indians who had prospered under existing conditions were hostile to any change. Others suspected white motives. The clash between friends and foes of the law caused bitter dissension within some Indian peoples. Several, notably the Navahos, rejected the law.

The Collier policy was disrupted by World War II, when thousands of Indian people left reservations to work in war plants. Then in 1953 the policy was reversed. With little consultation with the Indians, Congress adopted a "termination" policy under which the federal government would end its special relationship with Indian peoples and henceforth treat them as individuals like all other citizens. The rhetoric about equality that accompanied the new policy served to disguise the fact that it was an updated version of the Dawes Act designed to help whites get Indian assets.

Through persuasion, pressure, and trickery, many Indian peoples agreed to dispose of their tribal lands and their rich resources in timber and minerals. Some peoples under strong and shrewd leadership formed corporations to retain their holdings. Others, lured by the prospect of easy wealth, liquidated tribal assets on an individual basis. Their lands passed into the hands of whites.

Some few individuals who had learned the ways of white business put their funds to good use. Most, however, knew only poverty and the yearning of the poor to acquire the status symbols of wealth. White businessmen gladly sold them luxury automobiles, flashy clothes, jewelry, and the like. Gamblers and saloonkeepers separated the Indians from what was left of their money. Entire peoples, such as the Menominee of Wisconsin and the Klamaths of Oregon, were soon back to the familiar patterns of poverty—but this time there was no place for them to go. Their lands were gone, and with them went the base for their institutions and culture.

The policy of termination was accompanied by "relocation," a federal policy designed to train dispossessed Indian folk for urban living. Those few with marketable skills were able to benefit from the program, economically if not psychologically. But most Indian people lacked such skills. Besides, they were rural people, shaken by the hustle and bustle of the city. They were communal folk, frightened by the anonymity and individualism of urban life. They were shy and noncompetitive in a highly competitive setting. On all sides they felt hemmed in by a white society that was at best indifferent and at worst hostile. In earlier times, such people could always escape to their reservations. For many, such escape had been cut off by termination.

Federal policy changed a third time in 1970 when forced termination was abandoned in favor of "self-determination without termination". Indian peoples were left free to choose termination, but at the same time the authority of existing tribal governments was recognized and enhanced. If these governments so desired, they were given power to administer various federal aid programs relating to their peoples. Later, Congress enacted legislation designed to undo the termination program and to remedy some of the ills it had caused. Further, the Bureau of Indian Affairs was reorganized so as to bring in more Indians in policy-making posts and to make the agency more sensitive to Indian needs.

Even earlier there had been signs of changes in governmental policy more favorable to Indian interests. In 1946 Congress authorized an Indian Claims Commission to hear claims of Indian peoples against the federal government, many of which the commission upheld. The black revolution also had its impact. In 1964 a law setting up community action agencies to aid the poor applied also to Indian peoples. Under its provisions, many idealistic young lawyers made the mass of poor Indian folk aware of their legal rights and battled in the courts against business interests and others who had taken unlawful advantage of Indians. Such actions not only offended white interests but also some Indian tribal leaders who collaborated with them. Then in 1968 a civil rights act extended to Indian peoples the protection of the Bill of Rights of the federal constitution. The progress of native Americans toward fully enjoying their legal rights while maintaining their own identity was also enhanced by federal court decisions upholding Indian claims under treaties long since forgotten by whites.

Symbolic of the change in white attitudes—and in Indian attitudes—was the resolution of the long dispute over the holy ground of the Taos people at Blue Lake, New Mexico. The land had been taken from the Taos in 1906 and unlawfully made part of a national forest. Faced with continuing protest, federal agencies at various times sought to compensate the Taos with money. The Taos, sounding a note taken up later by other peoples, refused money and insisted on restoration of the land. In 1970 the federal government yielded. The triumph of the Taos helped stimulate the growth of Indian self-confidence and self-respect.

During the postindustrial era some Indian people prospered and some even became wealthy, especially among those whose families owned oil lands. Intermarriage between such people and whites took place, and the children tended to be proud of their Indian descent. Indicative of the growth in Indian status was the growing number of Indian students attending college, of whom there were about 15,000 in 1970. Such people were a small minority, however.

Most Indian folk remained poor, continuing victims of discrimination. In 1970 the average annual family income of people on reservations was only 25 percent of that of the general population. Income of nonreservation Indians was 50 percent below the general level. Unemployment among Indians was ten times higher than among white Americans.

Other indices of Indian life were even more appalling. Infant mortality was three times higher than that of the general population. Those who survived lived much shorter lives than did whites. Suicide among Indian youth was 100 times more frequent than among white teenagers.

Such conditions, together with a heightened sense of grievance and lessons learned from the black revolution, help explain the emergence of a militant Indian rights movement in the 1960s. Initiated by college students and young urbanized Indians, the movement spread to the reservations. The militants attacked white policies toward Indian peoples and particularly assailed the Bureau of Indian Affairs, which they accused of promoting the interests of whites and their Indian allies while neglecting the problems of ordinary Indians. The militants were also hostile to tribal leaders, whom they charged with selling their people out to federal authorities and white business interested in getting concessions on Indian land. Such antagonism was especially marked among the Navahos, who resented the mining of their land by a major coal company. Like their black and Chicano counterparts, the militants emphasized race pride, extolled their own culture, and resisted integration.

Their message was received sympathetically by many whites, whose consciousness of old wrongs had been revived by the writings of such men as Vina Deloria, Dee Brown, and Ralph Andrist. White awareness of Indian discontent was also stimulated by events such as the occupation in 1969 of Alcatraz Island, site of a former federal prison in San Francisco Bay, by Indian militants who announced their intention of turning it into an Indian cultural center. Then, in 1970 the American Indian Movement (AIM), which sought to unify various militant movements, symbolically "occupied" Wounded Knee, scene of a massacre of peaceful Sioux in South Dakota in 1890. In the violence that ensued two federal agents were killed. Attempts to convict AIM leader Russell Banks for murder ended in failure, but AIM charged that it was the target of continuing state and federal persecution.

Rising Indian militancy reflected forces that were transforming traditional Indian society and Indian self-concepts. None was more important than urbanization. By 1970 at least half of the American Indian population lived in cities, particularly Los Angeles, Chicago, Denver, and Minneapolis. Many had come during World War II. Others had come during the relocation program. Still others had left reservations on their own, hoping to find a better life. Regardless of their disappointments, many such people stayed in the cities. For many, there were no reservations to return to.

In urban life, traditional tribal distinctions ceased to be important. Increasingly, urban Indians saw themselves as an Indian minority group with common interests that transcended tribal concerns. Tecumseh's 150-year-old vision of a unified Indian power was revitalized. With it came the hope for a new era in the troubled history of native Americans.

ASIANS: THE JAPANESE

If some minority groups were despised by whites because so many of them were poor, the Japanese were resented because so many of them were successful. The Issei and the Nisei thrived on the work ethic that white Americans extolled among themselves but found detestable when practiced by Asians. Anti-Japanese feeling came out not only in segregation and discrimination but also in law. The California statute of 1913 that banned ownership of land by Japanese and others ineligible for citizenship was strengthened in the 1920s. Similar laws were passed by other western states and also by Louisiana, Delaware, and Missouri. In 1922 the United States Supreme Court finally ruled that Japanese-born immigrants were not eligible for citizenship, and many who had already been naturalized now lost their American citizenship. Two years later Congress virtually banned all immigration from Japan.

Such laws and court decisions struck at the economic well-being of immigrant Japanese-Americans since they not only banned land ownership but also closed the doors to many professions and even encouraged cities to restrict the licensing of Japanese-American enterprises. Nevertheless, the Japanese thrived. The wealthy formed corporations, with whites in ostensible control, which carried on major farming and business operations. Small businessmen prospered by catering to the needs of their own people and to whites with a taste for exotic food and entertainment. Others found employment as farm laborers, fishermen, gardeners, and flower growers.

During the depression of the 1930s Japanese-Americans may have suffered less than other people because of their willingness to work for low wages, but even so there was much hardship. Few applied for public relief, however, both for reasons of pride and distrust of public authorities. As best it could, the Japanese-American community cared for its own. It could do little for the growing number of Nisei college graduates. The job market was tight for all new college graduates during the depression, but it was closed to Japanese-Americans.

The depression years were difficult for Japanese-Americans in yet another way. The Japanese invasion of China in 1937 not only offended the traditional American friendship for China but also revived old fears on the West Coast of Japanese invasion there. Emotions were further stirred when Japanese planes bombed an American warship in Chinese waters, killing and wounding several sailors. Japanese-American business enterprises were boycotted. Oregon and Washington closed commercial

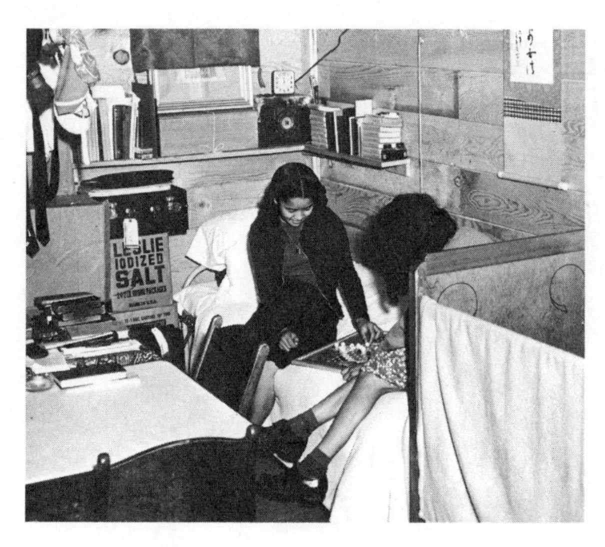

Overcrowding was typical of the camps in which Japanese-Americans were confined during World War II. A family of five lived in the "apartment" shown here.
Oregon Journal Collection, Oregon Historical Society

fishing to Japanese-Americans on the suspicion that they were naval officers in disguise. As the hysteria spread, it was widely believed on the West Coast that all Japanese-Americans, including the American-born, were potential spies and saboteurs.

To counteract white prejudice Nisei had earlier organized the Japanese-American Citizens League, pledged to support the American way of life and to defend the United States against all enemies. Their assertions of loyalty made little impact on a public opinion growing steadily more hostile.

For Issei and Nisei alike Pearl Harbor was a disaster. Federal agents raided Japanese-American communities in search of enemy agents. Adults were fired from their jobs. School children, college students, and church members were shunned by many former friends. Early Japanese successes in the Pacific stirred a clamor for removing all people of Japanese ancestry from the West Coast. In February 1942, President Roosevelt authorized such removal. About 120,000 people, citizens and noncitizens, old and young, well and sick, were rounded up. Under army contol they were confined in temporary prison camps, often located in fairgrounds and race tracks. Later they were transferred to permanent camps in isolated areas of the West and in Arkansas. The removal was justified on grounds of military necessity, but Japanese-Americans noted that few German and Italian "enemy aliens" suffered such treatment and that no one suggested locking up American citizens of German and Italian ancestry.

The permanent camps were hastily built and were too small for the number of people confined in them. The overcrowding resulted in a lack of privacy, which families bitterly resented. For the first year food supplies were inadequate and meals often unpalatable. There were too few doctors and nurses. Residents worked hard at making their quarters habitable, producing food in adjacent fields, and performing essential camp jobs. They did not mind the work but they objected to the wages they received, ranging from $12 a month for unskilled labor to $19 a month for such professionals as doctors. Such wages did not permit them to buy necessities or amenities not furnished by camp officials.

Oregon Journal Collection, Oregon Historical Society

Uprooted Japanese-Americans were confined at a livestock exposition center in Portland in 1942. They were later sent to a "relocation center" in Wyoming.

There was bitterness toward some of these officials. The War Relocation Agency (WRA), which managed the camps, was headed by men like Dillon Myer, who sympathized with the prisoners and tried to make their detention as tolerable as possible. His view was not shared by all camp administrators. Some were openly hostile to their charges. Some camp officials and employees were also corrupt, selling on the black market food and other supplies intended for residents. These officials were weeded out as the agency learned of them.

The deepest source of discontent, of course, was detention itself. Nisei in particular were angered by the assumption that they were disloyal. Educated in American schools, they were dismayed to find that constitutional guarantees did not apply to them in wartime. They were held as prisoners without formal charges and without trials. And in the process of removal many Japanese-Americans lost their property. Their feeling of injustice was compounded by the knowledge that no such action was taken in Hawaii, in the heart of the Pacific war zone, despite its very large Japanese population.

While there were strikes and violent rebellions in some camps against administrators, the tensions generated by confinement, overcrowding, and unsettled grievances also prompted bitter quarrels among the prisoners themselves. There was bound to be friction when people of different generations, occupations, status, and background were locked up together, but eventually such internal feuding took political form.

On the one hand were those, mostly Nisei followers of the Japanese American Citizens League, who called for full cooperation with the WRA, arguing that demonstrated loyalty would contribute to ending detention early. On the other hand were those—including many Issei, Kibei (American-born but educated in Japan), and disillusioned Nisei—who called for resistance to WRA, avowed their loyalty to Japan, and looked forward to Japanese victory. Since the advocates of cooperation enjoyed the support of agency officials, their enemies resorted to terrorism, hoping by violence to obtain control of the camps. The violence ended when federal authorities sent pro-Japanese leaders to isolation centers and segregated their followers. Loyal residents of the camps then settled down to make the best of their condition.

That condition was changing. As early as 1942 about 10,000 people were released temporarily for work on farms, and later others were "paroled" for work in war industry. In 1944 the federal government decided to phase out the camps entirely and by the end of 1945 all were closed. The change was not welcomed by all detainees. Many of the elderly, shaken by the hatred shown them after Pearl Harbor, were afraid to leave the relative security of life in the camps for life in a hostile society. Often, too, they had lost their property and had little heart to begin over again. The transition was made easier by the establishment of government hostels for the freed Japanese-Americans in major cities and by aid given them by friendly white people.

The belated decision by authorities that Japanese-Americans as a whole were no danger to national security was reflected earlier in changed army policies. After Pearl Harbor the army rejected Nisei volunteers and then excluded them from the draft. In 1943 the army reversed its policy and began active recruitment of Nisei in the camps. They were organized in a segregated unit, the 442nd Combat Team. Together with the 100th Infantry Battalion, made up of Hawaiian Japanese-Americans, they posted an outstanding combat record in Europe and suffered heavy casualties. None were accepted for combat service in the Pacific, although some were used in intelligence and interpreting work.

In the meantime lawyers for Japanese-Americans had been fighting the legality of removal and detention. Finally, in December 1944, the United States Supreme Court passed on some of the constitutional issues. In a case involving Fred J. Korematsu, a Nisei, removal was upheld on grounds of the military necessity prevailing when the orders were issued in 1942. The court also decided in the Mitsui Endo case that detention of loyal American citizens was unlawful. In neither case did the court clarify the basic issue of the conflict between alleged military necessity and the rights of citizens in wartime. The immediate impact of the decisions was slight. A day before the Korematsu decision the army rescinded its removal orders, and the WRA was already phasing out its camps.

While there was much hostility, including violence, directed against evacuees who returned to the West Coast, feelings died down relatively quickly. The acceptance by defeated Japan of an American-made constitution, the onset of the Cold War, and the emergence of Japan as ally and center of American influence in the Far East all contributed to damping anti-Japanese fervor. Besides, many white Americans now regretted their part in the hysteria that had led to the prison camps.

It should be noted that even during the height of the hysteria a minority of white Americans had spoken out on behalf of the victims. Among the more notable were Robert Millikan, the famous physicist and Nobel Prize winner; Harry Bridges, leader of the West Coast longshoremen's union; and Carey McWilliams, long-time friend of minorities. For their efforts they had been virulently attacked by the media and were maligned by various committees of Congress and the California legislature. After the war their stance became respectable. As detainees returned to their West Coast homes, the pleas of such people for fair treatment of Japanese-Americans were taken up by numerous religious bodies, leading newspapers, and formerly anti-Japanese politicians.

Changing sentiment was reflected in many ways. After some initial difficulties, Japanese-Americans found homes and jobs, while their children experienced comparatively little prejudice in schools and colleges. Encouraged by such reports, detainees who had gone to other parts of the country came back to the West Coast. Court decisions also mirrored changed attitudes. In 1948 the Oregon Supreme Court nullified that state's alien land law. Four years later the California Supreme Court followed suit. Washington did not repeal its law until 1966, but by that time the law was largely irrelevant.

National policy also showed change. In 1952 Congress permitted Issei to become citizens and allowed limited immigration from Japan. Also, beginning in 1948 Congress passed laws authorizing payment for property losses incurred by Japanese-Americans during their internment. Since many claimants lacked the necessary documents, however, they fared poorly. Others had to settle for 10¢ on the dollar of the value of their property, far less than the awards to Italian and German enemy aliens whose property had been seized at the same time.

In the new climate of opinion, Japanese-Americans made rapid recovery from their losses. They thrived in farming and business and so valued education that their children attained higher levels of schooling than the general population. In large numbers they entered business, the professions, the arts, and academic life. They also did well in politics. Hawaiians sent Japanese-Americans to the House and Senate, and California elected S. I. Hayakawa to the Senate. The Japanese-American community itself grew in numbers. In 1970 there were 591,000 people of Japanese ancestry living in the United States.

The new atmosphere tended to disintegrate the old tightly knit Japanese community, leading to new generational conflict, this time between Nisei and their children, the Sonsei. The youth were so Americanized that they broke the tradition of accommodation to white ways, as well as that of respect for their parents. Some experimented with drugs, like their white counterparts, and otherwise identified with the "counterculture" emerging among the young. Some were active in the student revolts of the 1960s, and a few participated in the struggle for black rights. They also abandoned the low profile of the traditional Japanese-American community to battle for other Japanese-Americans. Together with some Nisei they took part in the successful campaign for the pardon of "Tokyo Rose," Mrs. I. Togoni D'Aquino, imprisoned for allegedly broadcasting Japanese propaganda during World War II. Even so, there were sources of unease. Memories of the camps were so bitter that detainees were reluctant to talk about them. They realized all too well that the atomic bomb had been used only against Japan. Many Japanese-Americans were disturbed by the law of 1950 that authorized prison camps for people suspected of political subversion. Although the law was later repealed, there was always the fear that what happened once could happen again.

Chinese-Americans shared in the growing white acceptance of racial diversity in American society and in the process came to develop a new view of themselves and their role. As with Japanese-Americans, it has been a comparatively recent development.

In 1920 their immigration was still illegal, and in 1924 Congress intensified the prohibition by making it unlawful for Chinese-American citizens visiting China to bring back Chinese-born wives. The laws, together with a scarcity of Chinese-American women, had resulted in a dwindling community that numbered fewer than 70,000 in 1920. That census figure is an understatement, however, for there were many illegal immigrants in the United States who were reluctant to call attention to themselves. There were also "legal" immigrants—alleged sons of Chinese-American citizens—who had entered the country on fraudulent papers supplied by Chinese-American businessmen. None of these people wanted to call themselves to the attention of authorities. The eagerness of so many Chinese to pass unnoticed accentuated the isolation of the Chinatowns.

Continuing white hostility also contributed to isolation. In many states intermarriage with whites was forbidden. In some western states it was virtually impossible for Chinese to engage in business outside the Chinatowns. Alien land laws likewise made it impossible for Chinese to own land legally. Workers found it difficult to get jobs in the white community. Chinatowns were frequently raided by local police and federal agents in search of illegal immigrants.

White hostility was not without its benefits for Chinese-American businessmen. Employers found it provided a source of cheap labor that would neither complain nor rebel. Isolated Chinatowns, especially in San Francisco and New York, attracted thousands of tourists who spent freely with merchants and other businessmen. Further, white antagonism drove the Chinese community in upon itself and compelled its residents to accept the leadership of organized "big business," such as the famous Six Companies, which had its ties with the white power structure.

Nevertheless, the Chinese-American community was changing. As the number of American-born Chinese rose, many entered the professions as well as business. Unlike their parents, the aim in life of the Chinese was not to return to China but to make their way in the United States. The change was symbolized in the 1920s by organization of the Chinese-American Citizens Alliance, which cautiously moved toward protection of the legal rights of Chinese-Americans. They were also concerned with the Chinese image in white society and supported the Six Companies in the campaign to end the violent tong, or gang wars that furnished much sensational copy for the white media. Suppression of the last tong war in 1931 contributed eventually to emergence of a new image of Chinese-Americans as a law-abiding folk with strong family ties whose children rarely figured as juvenile delinquents.

Chinese-Americans also benefited from the growing anti-Japanese sentiment of the 1930s. White Americans generally sympathized with China as a victim of Japanese aggression and such feeling tended to be reflected in attitudes toward Chinese-Americans. Pro-Chinese feeling rose during World War II when China was

Oregon Historical Society

Chinese-Americans picketing shipments of war supplies to Japan in 1939.

an American ally and affected public policy. In 1943 the Chinese-exclusion law was repealed, Chinese were made eligible for citizenship, and Chinese-Americans were allowed to bring in Chinese wives on a nonquota basis. The quota for Chinese immigrants, however, reflected lingering prejudice. It provided for only 105 immigrants a year, a limit increased in later legislation. Further, some states modified their laws to permit white and Chinese intermarriage, and eventually in 1967 the United States Supreme Court struck down all laws prohibiting interracial marriage.

Growing white acceptance of Chinese-Americans together with the frugality practiced by many parents enabled large numbers of young people to enter colleges and universities. They went on to business, the professions, and academic life in growing numbers. By 1960 there were 1,300 people of Chinese-American ancestry on college and university faculties, and 18 per cent of the population was engaged in professional and technical pursuits. Nearly another 13 percent were business proprietors or managers. Some became famous. Among them were I. M. Pei, the architect; Chen Ning Yang and Tsung Dao Lee, Nobel Prize winners in physics; M. C. Chang, one of the three scientists who devised the first effective oral contraceptive; and Gerald Tsai, Jr., a power on Wall Street.

Such upward mobility helps explain why the median family income of Chinese-Americans exceeded that of the general population by 1959—$6,200 a year compared to $5,660. The pressure of such people, as well as relaxed white attitudes and civil rights laws, contributed to break down housing segregation. Chinese-Americans who could afford it found it possible to move into white middle-class suburbs and win acceptance from their neighbors. The Chinatowns remained, of course, as places of business and the residences of the poor and the old.

If Chinese-Americans benefited from changing international relationships during the 1930s and 1940s, they learned that such changes could turn to disadvantage during the 1950s and 1960s. The coming of the Cold War and the Communist victory in China changed attitudes in the federal government. Chinese students, mainly those in engineering and the sciences, who wished to return to mainland China were barred from leaving the United States. Government officials hinted that the loyalty of many Chinese-Americans was questionable. As late as 1969 J. Edgar Hoover testified that "there are over 300,000 Chinese in the United States, some of whom could be susceptible to recruitment" by Chinese Communists. He conjured up visions of Communist sympathizers ready "to aid in operations against the United States."

Mindful of the earlier propaganda campaign against Japanese-Americans, leaders of the Chinese-American community feared that in event of war their own people might end up in prison camps. Partly in response to such fear and partly from conviction, they wholeheartedly endorsed American hostility toward the Communist regime, supported the Nationalist government in Taiwan, and tried to repress within their own ranks any expression of sympathy for the new Chinese government. Such sympathy grew as the People's Republic of China demonstrated its ability to maintain itself. The young especially took pride in the fact that for the first time in more than a century there was a Chinese government Western powers treated with respect. These feelings became more reputable after President Nixon's visit to Peking in 1972, and even more so after the United States recognized the People's Republic in 1979.

The political conflict was only one of the forces of disintegration at work within the Chinese-American community. As middle-class folk dispersed to suburbs, parental authority broke down. Children yielded to the teachings of American schools and to the pressures of their white peer groups. The adoption of white youth values by children alarmed their parents, even when the parents themselves were American-born. Young people's involvement with drugs and juvenile delinquency, hitherto almost unknown among aspiring Chinese-Americans, proved especially upsetting. In short, white acceptance of Chinese-Americans proved corrosive of the traditional family values to which American-born Chinese adhered.

At the other extreme, grandparents left behind in Chinatowns when prosperous parents moved out felt neglected. They also resented among their children and grandchildren that lack of reverence for the old that had been so marked an attribute of traditional Chinese society.

Also contributing to tensions within the Chinese-American community was the great influx of Taiwan and Hong Kong Chinese after the immigration laws were liberalized in the 1950s and 1960s. While a considerable number were professional people, many others were young, few had marketable skills, and even fewer had any notion of the realities of American life. Expecting to become rich quickly, they were shocked to discover that if they were lucky they could get jobs only in low-wage factories or service occupations. Others could find no jobs at all. The Chinatowns were overcrowded with immigrant poor living in slums. Poverty took its usual toll in crime, juvenile delinquency, and higher than average disease and death rates. Street gangs, often preying on Chinese-American merchants, appeared for the first time in Chinatowns.

The bitterness of the newcomers was compounded by two other factors. One was realization that many of their low-wage employers were themselves Chinese-Americans. Another was social rejection of immigrants by established Chinese-American families. Prosperous folk wanted no part of the poor and uncouth who, in their view, all too often showed criminal propensities. Such activities, it was feared, might injure the reputation of all Chinese-Americans. For their part, newcomers accused Chinese-Americans of having sacrificed Chinese traditions to appease white people.

Chinese Americans in the 1970s, then, faced problems, but problems quite different from those that plagued their predecessors. Their community, which at one time had seemed to be dying out, now numbered more than 435,000. Made up once almost entirely of immigrants, the community was now mostly American-born. The lopsided sexual ratio that had made family formation so difficult was approaching normal. Once divided between a small group of rich merchants and a mass of poor folk, the community now ran the gamut from extreme wealth to poverty, with a strong middle class of business and professional people. A hundred years earlier they all had been pariahs of American society; now many were established folk highly respected by whites.

Recent newcomers were not numerous enough to alter the trend toward integration of Chinese-Americans into the larger American society. Like European immigrants, they might strive to keep certain customs and traditions alive in a formal sense, but in outlook and practice they had adopted the values of American society.

FOR FURTHER READING

Recent changes in ethnic communities are discussed in Nathan Glazer and Daniel P. Moynihan, *Beyond the Melting Pot* (1963); Perry Wood, *The White Ethnic Movement and Ethnic Politics* (1973); Leonard Dinnerstein and Frederic C. Jaher, *The Aliens* (1970); and Michael Novak, *The Rise of the Unmeltable Ethnics* (1972). Upward mobility is studied in Stephan Thernstrom, *The Other Bostonians* (1973).

Recent developments among Mexican-Americans are covered in the survey of Matt S. Meier and Feliciano Rivera, *The Chicanos* (1972). Carey McWilliams, *North from Mexico* (1968), vividly reports Chicano history to the end of World War II. See also Joan W. Moore and Alfredo Cuellar, *Mexican Americans* (1970). Another work, Leo Grebler, Joan W. Moore, and Ralph C. Guzman, *The Mexican American People* (1970), has a wealth of statistical and other data not available elsewhere.

The role of César Chávez is described in Mark Day, *Forty Acres* (1971) and in Peter Matthiessen, *Sal Si Puedes* (1969). The campaign of Reies Tijerina is discussed in Richard Gardner, *Grito* (1970).

Problems of Puerto Ricans are discussed in Oscar Handlin, *The Newcomers* (1962), and Joseph P. Fitzpatrick, *Puerto Rican Americans* (1971). For the response of a Puerto Rican writer to his experience see Piri Thomas, *Down These Mean Streets* (1967).

The more positive role of native Americans is indicated in Stuart Levine and Nancy O. Lurie, eds., *The American Indian Today* (1970); Stan Steiner, *The New Indians* (1968); and Robert Burnette, *The Tortured Americans* (1971). Still valuable is an earlier work, Oliver LaFarge, ed., *The Changing Indian* (1942). Valuable documentary material is in Alvin M. Josephy, Jr., ed., *Red Power* (1971), and Wayne Moquin and Charles Van Doren, eds., *Great Documents in American Indian History* (1973). A statement of the new militancy is Vine Deloria, *Custer Died for Your Sins* (1969). A good summary of recent federal policy changes is Wilcomb E. Washburn, *Red Man's Land: White Man's Law* (1971). Two books that strongly influenced white opinion are Dee Brown, *Bury My Heart at Wounded Knee* (1970), and Ralph K. Andrist, *The Long Death* (1971).

Japanese-Americans are discussed in Henry H. L. Kitano, *Japanese Americans* (1969); Bill Hosokawa, *Nisei: The Quiet Americans* (1969); and Roger Daniels, *The Politics of*

Prejudice (1968). Two works deal with the prison camp experience of World War II: Edward H. Spicer and others, *Impounded People* (1969), and Dorothy S. Thomas and R. S. Nishimoto, *The Spoilage* (1969).

On Chinese-Americans, see Stanford M. Lyman, *Chinese Americans* (1974); Betty Lee Sung, *Mountain of Gold* (1967); and Francis L. K. Hsu, *The Challenge of the American Dream* (1971).

27 where do we go from here?

One of the most significant developments in postindustrial America was improvement in the living standards of masses of lower-class Americans. The rich did become richer and the gap widened between rich and poor, but it was also true that millions of blue-collar and white-collar workers moved upward and their children often attained middle-class status. In the 1960s, also, the federal government undertook to ameliorate the condition of the poor through the massive War on Poverty program.

Women and racial minorities also made gains, reflected in laws designed to assure equality in civil rights and to provide equality of opportunity. Women gained further in the widespread acceptance of their right to control over their own bodies.

Such gains did not come without struggle and pain. American society might be open, but its benefits were available largely to those able and willing to fight for them. Working people made progress because they sacrificed to form and maintain unions. Black Americans and people of other racial minorities had to face persecution, violence, and bloodshed. Women of these minorities were not immune to such hazards. White feminists confronted ridicule and ostracism, not only from men but also from many women.

If militant class consciousness diminished because of the upward mobility of workers, the struggles of racial minorities heightened race consciousness. This found expression in positive self-images as peoples, in race pride, and in increased self-respect and self-confidence. Many women, too, were able to shake off the old stereotypes to which they had been subject and to assert their rights as human beings. Psychological changes on such a scale became in themselves historical forces that seemed to assure that a new era of cultural diversity and equality was at hand.

It is significant that the changes were made without basic disruption of American society. The dominant elements in the nation proved flexible enough to accommodate many of the demands of the discontented. Such flexibility was partly due to the strength shown by rebellious groups. It was also partly due to the allies among respectable middle-class folk the discontented won through appeal to the nation's conscience, especially to the moral principles enshrined in the Declaration of Independence. Often denounced as revolutionaries, the masses of the discontented actually sought to conserve basic American values by making them applicable to increasing numbers of people, regardless of class, race, or sex. Far from wanting to destroy the American dream, they wanted more people to share it.

Questions were raised, however, about the relationship of the dream to the quality of life. Some youthful white middle-class rebels decried the traditional American way of life as too regimented and materialistic. They extolled individualistic life styles, asserted the virtues of the simple life, and often embarked on communal living. Young industrial workers were troubled by the same questions, although their responses were different. Their rate of absenteeism was high, they refused to work overtime, and in other ways they asserted their own values against traditional practice. The issue was dramatized at Lordstown, Ohio, in 1972 when 8,000 young workers closed down a General Motors plant for three weeks because, they said, the pace of work was too intense for them to enjoy their personal lives. Emphasis on the quality of life was not confined to the young. Increasingly, older workers, including those who were well paid, expressed discontent over the monotony and meaninglessness of their jobs. Further, after publication of Rachel Carson's *Silent Spring* in 1962, concern for the environment and its relationship to humans became widespread. Great numbers of middle-class citizens enlisted in a crusade that brought them into conflict with giant business interests and their political allies. The environmentalists won some gains in legislation ranging from protection of wilderness areas to regulation of automobile emissions.

It should be noted, however, that these changes took place within the context of an expanding economy and of a reformist public mood. Contributing to the changes also were certain general bodies of belief: that America was a land of unlimited resources; that economic growth would continue forever; and that an enlightened public opinion would lead to the easing and perhaps the solution of such vexing social problems as poverty and race while providing an environment that would make America a healthful and pleasant place to live.

Such beliefs came a cropper in the late 1970s. Economic growth slackened, unemployment rates mounted, inflation worsened, and the zeal for reform waned. The War on Poverty was virtually abandoned. The gains of minority peoples were jeopardized by an increasing hostility among whites to the goal of equality because of what that goal would cost them. Public officials, including the courts, showed a tendency to retreat from the commitments to racial equality made in the 1960s. The women's liberation movement faltered in the face of well-organized opposition. The affirmative-action programs designed to end sexual and racial discrimination came under heavy attack as reverse discrimination. Environmentalists found themselves on the defensive as unions and employers joined forces to weaken the new protective legislation.

Related to these developments was growing realization that America was not a land of limitless resources. Economists had long pointed out the growing dependence of the United States on foreign raw materials, but not until the Arab oil embargo of 1973 was the point brought home to ordinary Americans. Millions of American remained skeptical of the energy crisis the nation's leaders proclaimed, but there was no gainsaying the fact that America depended on foreign sources not only for oil but also for a wide variety of products ranging from iron ore to coffee.

Here, too, there was change. In earlier days exporting countries, usually colonies of imperial powers, had provided such goods at bargain prices. Now, as independent countries and as members of the newly self-conscious Third World, they adopted the standard practice of European and American big business—they banded together to maximize profit by controlling prices. The era of low prices that colonialism had provided was over. Americans found it difficult to adjust to the new era.

Such considerations prompted American leaders, in and out of government, to warn of an impending age of austerity. If their predictions were correct, they raised questions about the future. How would white Americans, accustomed to rising living standards, respond to static or lower standards? Would they seek to invigorate the democratic process or would they resort to some form of authoritarianism? How would racial minorities fare in an age of scarcity? What would their responses be? Could women maintain their gains in an era of austerity? These, and other questions of equal importance, preoccupied thoughtful Americans of the 1970s.

There are, of course, no ready answers. The future remains as much a clouded crystal ball to us as it did to our ancestors. But we might help clarify the future if we try to shape it now. Fannie Lou Hamer, the black civil rights activist of Mississippi, made the point well in a parable she told of a wise old man whose authority two young men sought to undermine by making him look ridiculous. They brought him a concealed bird and asked whether it was alive or dead. The old man saw the trap. If he answered that the bird was dead, they would release it, showing it to be alive. If he said that it was alive, they would kill it and display the corpse. The old man chose neither alternative. He said, "It's in your hands."

indexes

NAME INDEX

SUBJECT INDEX